THE OXFORD HANDBOOK OF

GLOBAL
RELIGIONS

THE OXFORD HANDBOOK OF

GLOBAL RELIGIONS

Edited by

MARK JUERGENSMEYER

OXFORD
UNIVERSITY PRESS

2006

OXFORD
UNIVERSITY PRESS

Oxford University Press, Inc., publishes works that further
Oxford University's objective of excellence
in research, scholarship, and education.

Oxford   New York
Auckland   Cape Town   Dar es Salaam   Hong Kong   Karachi
Kuala Lumpur   Madrid   Melbourne   Mexico City   Nairobi
New Delhi   Shanghai   Taipei   Toronto

With offices in
Argentina   Austria   Brazil   Chile   Czech Republic   France   Greece
Guatemala   Hungary   Italy   Japan   Poland   Portugal   Singapore
South Korea   Switzerland   Thailand   Turkey   Ukraine   Vietnam

Published by Oxford University Press, Inc.
198 Madison Avenue, New York, New York 10016

www.oup.com

Library of Congress Cataloging-in-Publication Data
The Oxford handbook of global religions / edited by Mark Juergensmeyer.
p. cm.
Includes bibliographical references and index.
ISBN-13 978-0-19-513798-9
ISBN 0-19-513798-1
1. Religions. I. Juergensmeyer, Mark.
BL74.O94 2006
200.9—dc22   2006004402

1 3 5 7 9 8 6 4 2
Printed in the United States of America
on acid-free paper

Dedicated to the memory of

Ninian Smart and Wilfred Cantwell Smith,

pioneers in the exploration of global religion

ACKNOWLEDGMENTS

Oxford University Press is to be admired for their conviction that a book such as this is timely, useful, and possible. I thank Cynthia Read for accepting the idea and Theo Calderara for persisting with it. Alison Mudditt helped to conceive the original project. Jochin Banash helped translate one of the articles from German, and Ben Schonthal made certain that the whole volume was completed. My colleagues at the University of California, Santa Barbara, were helpful at several critical moments. It is also common to thank one's spouse or partner for his or her support, and I gladly acknowledge the implicit encouragement of Sucheng Chan in this project, who would politely inquire from time to time about whether it would ever be finished. This volume has indeed been a significant venture, and I would like to thank the authors for their patience and perseverance, and for sharing with me the idea that the terrain of global religion is a landscape worthy of being surveyed. This volume is dedicated to two great pioneers in the study of global religion—Wilfred Cantwell Smith and Ninian Smart—with gratitude for their insights and admiration for their vision. They have shown us the way.

Contents

PART III: JEWISH CULTURAL REGION

PART VIII: UNDERSTANDING GLOBAL RELIGION

CONTRIBUTORS

REUBEN AHRONI is professor of biblical and Yemenite Studies at The Ohio State University, Columbus, Ohio. He is the author and editor of several books, including *Yemenite Jewry: Origins, Culture and Literature.*

FRITZ ERICH ANHELM is the director of the Protestant Academy Loccum, the Conference Centre of the Lutheran Church of Hanover in Germany. He is author of several books and articles relating to religion in society, ecumenism, and civil society.

SAID AMIR ARJOMAND is distinguished service professor of sociology at the State University of New York at Stony Brook, and the inaugural Crane Fellow in law and public affairs at the Woodrow Wilson School of Princeton University. His most recent edited book is *Rethinking Civilizational Analysis.*

ALI S. ASANI is professor of the practice of Indo-Muslim languages and cultures at Harvard University. He is author of *Ecstasy and Enlightenment: The Ismaili Devotional Literatures of South Asia* and other publications on the devotional and mystical literatures of Muslim communities in South Asia.

LAWRENCE A. BABB is professor of anthropology and Asian studies at Amherst College. He is the author of several books including *Alchemies of Violence: Myths of Identity* and the *Life of Trade in Western India.*

RANDALL BALMER teaches American religious history at Barnard College, Columbia University. He is the author of ten books, including *Mine Eyes Have Seen the Glory: A Journey into the Evangelical Subculture in America*, which was made into a three-part series of television programs for PBS.

KAREN MCCARTHY BROWN is professor of anthropology of religion in the Graduate and Theological Schools of Drew University. She is the author of *Mama Lola, a Vodou Priestess in Brooklyn* and leader of The Newark Project, ten years of research on urban religion outside the institutions.

AMILA BUTUROVIC is associate professor of humanities and Noor Fellow of Islamic studies at York University, Toronto. She is the author of *Stone Speaker: Medieval Tombstones, Landscape, and Bosnian Identity in the Poetry of Mak Dizdar* and other works on cultures and religions in the Balkans.

JOSÉ IGNACIO CABEZÓN is XIVth Dalai Lama professor of Tibetan Buddhist and cultural studies at the University of California, Santa Barbara. He is the author of *Buddhism and Language* and other publications on Tibet, Buddhism, and the study of religion.

JUAN E. CAMPO is associate professor of Islamic studies, Arabic, and the history of religions at the University of California in Santa Barbara. His book *The Other Sides of Paradise: Explorations into the Religious Meanings of Domestic Space in Islam*, received the American Academy of Religion's Award for Excellence. His other publications are in the areas of Islamic studies, pilgrimage, and culinary cultures of the Middle East.

DAVID CHIDESTER is professor of comparative religion and director of the Institute for Comparative Religion in Southern Africa at the University of Cape Town. He is the author of *Authentic Fakes: Religion and American Popular Culture* and other books on religion in North America and South Africa.

HARVEY COX is Hollis professor of divinity at Harvard University. He is currently at work on the history of Christian interpretations of Islam. His most recent book is *When Jesus Came to Harvard: Making Moral Choices Today*.

SERGIO DELLAPERGOLA is professor at the A. Harman Institute of Contemporary Jewry of the Hebrew University of Jerusalem and senior fellow at the Jewish People Policy Planning Institute. He is a specialist in Jewish demography and has published many books and articles on Jewish population in Israel and the Diaspora.

KAREL DOBBELAERE is emeritus professor of sociology and sociology of religion at the Katholieke Universiteit Leuven and secretary general of the International Society for the Sociology of Religion. He is the author of *Secularization: An Analysis at Three Levels* and other publications on secularization and religious life.

JOSEPH W. ELDER is professor of sociology, languages, and cultures of Asia, and integrated liberal studies at the University of Wisconsin, Madison. He is the main co-editor of *India's Worlds and U.S. Scholars: 1947–1997*.

AINSLIE T. EMBREE, professor emeritus of history, Columbia University, was chairman of the history department and associate dean of the School of International and Public Affairs. He was counselor for cultural affairs at the American embassy in Delhi in 1978–1980, and in 1994–1995 he was special consultant to the U.S. Ambassador to India. His books include *India's Search for National Identity*, *Imagining India: Essays on Indian History* and *Utopias in Conflict: Religion and Nationalism in India*.

RICHARD C. FOLTZ is associate professor of religion at Concordia University in Montreal, Canada. His most recent book is *Animals in Islamic Tradition and Muslim Cultures*.

ROGER FRIEDLAND is professor of religious studies and sociology at the University of California, Santa Barbara. He is the co-author of *To Rule Jerusalem* and *Matters of Culture: Cultural Sociology in Practice*.

DRU C. GLADNEY is professor of Asian studies and anthropology at the University of Hawai'i at Manoa. His books include *Muslim Chinese: Ethnic Nationalism in the People's Republic*; *Making Majorities: Composing the Nation in Japan, China, Korea, Malaysia, Fiji, Turkey, and the U.S*; *Ethnic Identity in China: The Making of a Muslim Minority Nationality*; and *Dislocating China: Muslims, Minorities, and Other Sub-Altern Subjects*.

HARVEY E. GOLDBERG is professor in the department of sociology and anthropology at the Hebrew University of Jerusalem. He was a visiting professor at the University of California, Berkeley, and Boğaziçi University, Istanbul; visiting lecturer at the Ecole des Hautes Etudes en Science Sociale, Paris; and fellow at the Oxford Centre for Hebrew and Jewish Studies. His books include *Jewish Life in Muslim Libya: Rivals and Relatives* and *Being Jewish: Cycles of Jewish Life*.

RICHARD D. HECHT is professor of religious studies at the University of California, Santa Barbara. He is the coauthor of *To Rule Jerusalem*.

NIMACHIA HERNANDEZ is assistant professor of Native American studies at the University of California, Berkeley. She is author of *Mokakssini: Blackfoot Knowledge* and other publications on Native American philosophy, religion, and lifeways.

SAAD IBRAHIM is a professor of sociology at the American University in Cairo, and is coeditor with Nicholas S. Hopkins of *Arab Society: Class, Gender, Power, and Development*.

JOHN ISKANDER is an assistant professor of Religious Studies at Georgia State University in Atlanta. His research includes Islamic and Coptic topics and the making of saints and heretics in modern Egypt.

CHRISTIAN JOCHIM is professor of comparative religious studies and director of the Center for Asian Studies at San Jose State University. He is the author of *Chinese Religions: A Cultural Perspective* and has published articles on Chinese religion and philosophy in *Journal of Chinese Religions, Modern China, Philosophy East and West*, and other journals and compilations.

MARK JUERGENSMEYER is professor of sociology and global studies and director of the Orfalea Center for Global and International Studies at the University of California, Santa Barbara. He is author or editor of twenty books, including *Terror in the Mind of God: The Global Rise of Religious Violence* and *Religion in Global Civil Society*.

NATHAN KATZ is professor of religious studies at Florida International University. His most recent book is *Who Are the Jews of India?*, which was a finalist for the

2000 National Jewish Book Award in Sephardic Studies and winner of the 2004 Vak Devi Saraswati Saman Award.

ALEXEY D. KRINDATCH is a research associate at Patriarch Athenagoras Orthodox Institute. During 1988–2004 he was a member of the staff of the Center of Geopolitical Studies of the Russian Academy of Sciences in Moscow, Russia. He is an expert on religion in the former USSR and on Eastern Christianity in the United States. He is an author of the monograph *Geography of Religions in Russia.*

SCOTT KUGLE is assistant professor in the department of religion at Swarthmore College. His research focuses on Islamic law and ethics, especially within Sufi communities of South Asia. He is the author of "Islam in South Asia" in the *Encyclopedia of Islam and the Muslim World.*

LEWIS LANCASTER is professor emeritus of the department of East Asian languages and culture at the University of California, Berkeley. His research and publications have centered on Buddhist studies. He currently serves as the president of the University of the West in Los Angeles.

J. SHAWN LANDRES is director of Research at Synagogue 3000. He has taught at the University of California, Santa Barbara; the University of Judaism in Los Angeles; and Matej Bel University Banská Bystrica, Slovak Republic. He coedited *Religion, Violence, Memory, and Place* and *After The Passion Is Gone: American Religious Consequences.*

DAVID N. LORENZEN is a professor of South Asian history at El Colegio de Mexico in Mexico City. He is the author of *Praises to a Formless God* and other publications on Hindu religion and Indian history.

T. N. MADAN is emeritus professor of sociology at the Institute of Economic Growth and chairman of the Centre for the Study of Developing Societies in Delhi, India. His most recent publication is an edited volume: *India's Religions: Perspectives from Sociology and History.*

RICHARD MADSEN is professor of sociology and director of the Council on East Asian Studies at the University of California, San Diego. He is the author of *China's Catholics: Tragedy and Hope in an Emerging Civil Society.*

GURINDER SINGH MANN is Kundan Kaur Kapany professor of Sikh studies and director of the Center for Sikh and Punjab Studies at the University of California, Santa Barbara. His latest books include *Sikhism* and *The Making of Sikh Scripture.*

JOHN HILARY MARTIN is professor emeritus of philosophy and theology at the Graduate Theological Union and the Dominican School of Theology and Philosophy at Berkeley. He is author of *People from the Dawn* and other writings dealing with Aboriginal people and land in sacred traditions.

RICHARD C. MARTIN is professor of Islamic studies and history of religions at Emory University. He is author of many works on Islam and Islamic society and is editor in chief of *The Macmillan Encyclopedia of Islam and the Muslim World*.

MANSOOR MOADDEL is professor of sociology at Eastern Michigan University. Among his publications is *Islamic Modernism, Nationalism, and Fundamentalism: Episode and Discourse*. He has recently been involved in a project on values surveys in Egypt, Iran, Iraq, Jordan, Morocco, and Saudi Arabia.

EBRAHIM MOOSA is associate research professor at Duke University and director, Center for the Study of Muslim Networks. He is author of *Ghazali and the Poetics of Imagination* and other publications related to Muslim law and ethics.

TARA VILLALBA MUNSON is a graduate student in religious studies at the University of California, Santa Barbara. She is a Filipino citizen whose research focuses on religion and politics in Southeast Asia. She has published articles on the historical relationship of religion and colonialism in the region and on contemporary issues of nationalism and the transnational impact of political Islam in the Philippines.

VASUDHA NARAYANAN is professor of religion at the University of Florida and past president of the American Academy of Religion. She is the author or editor of six books, including *Hinduism* and *The Vernacular Veda*, and has written more than ninety articles, chapters in books, and reference entries on Hindu texts, temples, and contemporary practices.

VIVIAN-LEE NYITRAY is an associate professor of religious studies and chair of Asian studies at the University of California, Riverside. She is the author of *Mirrors of Virtue* and numerous publications on popular Chinese religion and women in the Confucian tradition.

GANANATH OBEYESEKERE is professor emeritus of anthropology at Princeton University, and his most recent book is *Imagining Karma: Ethical Transformation in Amerindian, Buddhist and Greek Rebirth*.

JACOB K. OLUPONA is professor of African American and African studies at the University of California, Davis. He is author of *Kingship, Religion and Rituals in a Nigerian Community*. He has edited and authored many publications on African religions.

KOFI ASARE OPOKU is professor of religious studies at Lafayette College, Easton Pennsylvania. He is the author of *West African Traditional Religion* and other publications on African culture and African proverbs.

JUHA PENTIKÄINEN is the founding professor of the department of comparative religion at the University of Helsinki, Finland. He initiated the discipline of religious studies at the Institute of Social Science at the University of Tromsö; chaired the Centre for Advanced Study, Norwegian Academy research team on Shamanism; and has been a visiting professor at the Universities of Minnesota, California, Indiana, and Texas. His books include: *Oral Repertoire and World View*, *Kalevala Mythology*, *Shamanism and Northern Ecology*, *Shamanism and Culture*, and *Shamanhood Symbolism and Epic*.

SABRINA P. RAMET is professor of political science at the Norwegian University of Science and Technology in Trondheim, Norway. She is the author of nine books, among them *Nihil Obstat: Religion, Politics and Social Change in East-Central Europe and Russia*.

IAN READER is professor of religious studies at Lancaster University, England. He is author of *Making Pilgrimages: Meaning and Practice in Shikoku*; *Religious Violence in Contemporary Japan: The Case of Aum Shinrikyo*; and, co-authored with George J. Tanabe, *Practically Religious: Worldly Benefits and the Common Religion of Japan* as well as numerous articles and chapters on new religions in Japan, pilgrimage, religion and conflict, and other topics.

MARTIN RIESEBRODT is professor of sociology at the University of Chicago. He is author of *Pious Passion: The Emergence of Modern Fundamentalism in the United States and Iran* and other publications on fundamentalism and sociological theory, including the works of Max Weber.

JOEL ROBBINS is associate professor of anthropology at the University of California, San Diego. He is the author of *Becoming Sinners: Christianity and Moral Torment in a Papua New Guinea Society* and a number of articles on the globalization of Pentecostal and charismatic Christianity.

WADE CLARK ROOF is the J. F. Rowny professor of religion and society at the University of California at Santa Barbara. He is the author, most recently, of *Spiritual Marketplace: Baby Boomers and the Remaking of American Religion* and other publications on American religion.

ROLAND ROBERTSON is professor of sociology and global society and director of the Centre for the Study of Globalization at the University of Aberdeen, UK. He is also distinguished service professor emeritus of sociology at the University of Pittsburgh, USA. He has recently coedited the six-volume *Globalization: Critical Concepts in Sociology*.

SUSUMU SHIMAZONO is professor in the department of religion of Tokyo University. He is author of *From Salvation to Spirituality: Popular Religious Movements in Modern Japan* and other works on contemporary religious movements and modern Japanese religions.

JAN SHIPPS is professor emeritus of religious studies and history at Indiana University–Purdue University, Indianapolis. She is the author of *Sojourner in the Promised Land: Forty Years among the Mormons*.

PAUL E. SIGMUND is professor of politics at Princeton University. He has written *Liberation Theology at the Crossroads*, edited *Religious Freedom and Evangelization in Latin America*, and published twenty books and more than two hundred articles on political theory and Latin American politics.

NINIAN SMART was J. F. Rowny professor of religious studies at the University of California, Santa Barbara. For many years he also held a joint appointment at the University of Lancaster, England, where he founded the department of religious studies. Among his many books are *Dimensions of the Sacred*, *The Religious Experience*, *The World's Religions*, *World Philosophies*, and *The Science of Religion and the Sociology of Knowledge*.

JANE I. SMITH is professor of Islamic studies at Hartford Seminary and codirector of the Macdonald Center for the Study of Islam and Christian-Muslim Relations. She is author of *Islam in America* and other works on Muslims in the West.

DONALD K. SWEARER is the director of the Center for the Study of World Religion and visiting distinguished professor of Buddhism at Harvard Divinity School. He is the author of *Becoming the Buddha: The Ritual of Image Consecration in Thailand* and other publications on Buddhism and comparative religion.

ABDULKADER TAYOB is professor of the International Institute for the Study of Islam in the Modern World at Radboud University, Netherlands. He has written on Islam and public life in frica, and on contemporary Islamic thought. He is author of "Islam in South Africa, Islam: A Short Introduction," and numerous other essays and articles.

THOMAS A. TWEED is Zachary Smith professor of religious studies at the University of North Carolina at Chapel Hill. He is the author of *Crossing and Dwelling: A Theory of Religion* as well as historical and ethnographic studies of the religious practices of transnational migrants in the United States.

PHILIP WALTERS is head of research at Keston Institute, the Oxford-based center for research and information on religion in Communist and post-Communist countries. He is editor of the scholarly journal *Religion, State & Society* and the author of many chapters and articles on aspects of religious life and church-state relations in Russia, the former Soviet Union, and Central and Eastern Europe.

JAYNE S. WERNER is professor of political science at Long Island University and associate research scholar at Columbia University. She is the author of *Gender,*

Household, Stare: Doi Moi in Vietnam and other publications about Vietnamese history, religion, and society.

MARK WOODWARD is associate professor of religious studies at Arizona State University. He is the author of *Islam in Java: Normative Piety and Mysticism in the Sultanate of Yogyakarta* and other works on religion in Southeast Asia.

THE OXFORD HANDBOOK OF

GLOBAL
RELIGIONS

CHAPTER 1

THINKING GLOBALLY ABOUT RELIGION

MARK JUERGENSMEYER

Maps can deceive. Several decades ago cartographers were fond of providing maps that allegedly demarcated the spatial locations of world religions. A great wash of red would stretch from Tibet to Japan, engulfing China, to show where Buddhism was. The Middle East would be tinted green for the terrain of Islam, a yellow India for Hinduism, an orange for African religion, while Christianity's color—often blue, I recall—was brightly emblazoned on Europe and the Western Hemisphere. Some of the more sophisticated maps would make a distinction between the light blue of Protestant Canada and the United States, and the dark blue of Catholic Latin America, but there was no question as to clarity of the demarcation. I imagined slipping across the border from a Buddhist red zone to an Islamic green one and suddenly encountering mosques where previously there had been only stupas, temples, and chanting monks.

It has never really been like that, of course. Although there are regions of the world that serve as dense centers of gravity for certain religious traditions, much of the world is less certain as to its religious identity, and always has been. Even Hindu India was a quarter Muslim before Pakistan was created, and even today 15 percent of the Indian population reveres Islam. Indonesia—the largest Muslim country on the planet—is the home of a rich Hindu culture in Bali and contains at Borabadur one of the world's most important ancient Buddhist shrines. China has such diverse religious strata, with most of its population simultaneously accepting Confucian values, Taoist beliefs, and Buddhist worship practices, that most scholars prefer to speak of a multicultural "Chinese religion," rather than any of those three strands by itself. Much the same can be said about the religions of Korea and Japan. In the Western Hemisphere, Haitians are said to be 90 percent Roman Catholic and 90 percent followers of Vodou; needless to say, it is the same 90 percent. Jews, of course, are everywhere, and have been since biblical times.

Today it seems that almost everyone is everywhere. The city of Los Angeles, for instance, is the second largest Filipino city in the world. It is also the second largest Iranian city and the second largest Mexican one. In Southern California, Tibetan Buddhists do not hide in the mountains in monasteries. They drive Lexus SUVs to the studio lot for a photo shoot: some are rich, some are Caucasian, and some are among Hollywood's celebrities. In Beijing the Chinese government has to contend not only with new forms of Chinese religion, such as the Falun-Gong, but with dissident Chinese Muslims and Christians.

Scarcely any region in the globe today consists solely of members of a single strand of traditional religion. In an era of globalization the pace of cultural interaction and change has increased by seemingly exponential expansions of degrees. So an accurate coloration of the religious world, even fifty years ago, would have to show dense areas of color here and there with enormous mixes and shadings of hues everywhere else. Moreover the map would have to be changed from time to time, perhaps even from decade to decade, and re-tinted as religions move and intertwine.

This fluid process of cultural interaction, expansion, synthesis, borrowing, and change has been going on from the earliest moments of recorded history. In fact, the most ancient epic to which we have access—the *Gilgamesh Epic* of ancient Sumeria some two thousand years before the time of Christ—tells the story of a great flood brought on by divine wrath, and a human who built an ark to escape it. It is a story retold within the context of the biblical book of Genesis and now respected by the great religious traditions of Judaism, Christianity, and Islam. The historian of religion, Wilfred Cantwell Smith, was fond of pointing out that even as ordinary an artifact as a string of prayer beads illustrates the interaction of religions: Smith speculated that the Roman Catholic idea of the rosary was borrowed from Muslims in Spain who were inspired by the prayerbeads of Buddhists in Central Asia, who in turn appropriated the idea from Brahmans in Hindu India. The expansion of Christianity from the Mediterranean world into Europe was a gradual one, involving "archipelagos of centrality in a sea of insouciance," as the historian Peter Brown described it. Along the way Christianity picked up many pre-Christian indigenous European cultural practices, including the idea of saints and the festival seasons of Christmas and Easter—the latter named for Eostre, the pagan goddess of spring.

Religion therefore has always been global, in the sense that religious communities and traditions have always maintained permeable boundaries. They have moved, shifted, and interacted with one another around the globe. If one thinks of religion as the cultural expression of a people's sense of ultimate significance, it is understandable that these cultural elements would move as people have moved, and that they would interact and change over time just as people have. Though most religious traditions claim some ultimate anchors of truth that are unchangeable, it is indisputable that every tradition contains within it an enormous diversity of characteristics and myriad cultural elements gleaned from its neighbors.

All this is part of the globalization of religion. Religion is global in that it is related to the global transportation of peoples, and of ideas. There is also a third way that religion is global, which might be called the religion of globalization—in which forms of new religion emerge as expressions of new interactive cultures. In this volume we will consider all three kinds of religious globalization: diasporas, transnational religion, and the religion of plural societies.

GLOBAL DIASPORAS

The term *diaspora* comes from a Greek word meaning "to scatter," and it referred originally to the dispersion of the Jewish people and their culture. The first diaspora was in biblical times, when Israeli kingdoms were conquered and the Jewish people taken into Babylonian captivity. The second occurred after the fall of the Jerusalem Temple in 70 CE, with Jews scattered around the Mediterranean world—and later dispersed to Europe and much of the rest of the world. Perhaps no religious tradition has had such a long sustained existence without a geographic homeland as Judaism. It is the very paradigm of a transnational, diasporic culture.

Judaism is not, however, the only religious tradition in which its members have been scattered far and wide and taken their customs and loyalties with them. Increasingly every religious tradition is a religion in diaspora. There are Pakistani Muslims in New Jersey, Tibetan Buddhists in Germany, and European Catholics in Hong Kong. The rapid and easy mobility of people has produced expatriate communities of dispersed cultures around the globe. Almost half of the world's twelve million Sikhs, for instance, live outside their native area of Punjab in northern India. There are large concentrations of Sikhs in Houston, Washington, D.C., and Northern California; others are to be found in London, Africa, and Singapore. Though one thinks of Hinduism as the religion of the people of India, Hindus have traveled abroad and settled in such diverse places as Trinidad and Fiji, where they make up almost half the population.

In these cases we are talking about people moving from place to place and taking their old religion with them. Yet even in these cases beliefs and customs are affected. When people settle in a locale as an expatriate community, some curious things begin happen to their old religious beliefs and practices—they adapt and change as they interact with the cultures around them. Sometimes this interaction produces hostility, as Sikhs discovered when they had to confront the prejudices of European-Americans in California in the early part of the twentieth century, or as Hindus found when they tried to exert their political muscle among the indigenous population of the South Pacific island nation of Fiji. But regardless of the social tensions that cultural interaction creates, in time a certain amount of acceptance and assimilation occurs.

Some of this social tension is experienced within the diasporic community itself. In the Sikh community in the United States, for instance, the older generation has been deeply suspicious of attempts to "Americanize" Sikh culture. Disputes have arisen over such matters as whether young Sikh women should go on dates with non-Sikhs, whether Sikh men should shave their beards, and whether those attending a Sikh function should be allowed to sit at a table to eat rather than sitting on the floor. The more conservative members think—correctly—that their culture is changing. At the same time, Sikhs in the Punjab fear that the sheer size of the diaspora Sikh community, the diffusion of the religion's authority around the world, and the steady erosion of traditional cultural practices in these expatriate societies are changing the nature of Sikhism as a whole. And they too are right.

The global diasporas of peoples and cultures can transform traditions. Though it is likely that Sikhs will retain certain fundamental elements of their tradition— just as Jews and Chinese have in expatriate communities that they have established abroad—it is also likely that there will be changes. They will face some of the issues of acculturation and transformation that Judaism has encountered and raise questions that go the core of their religion—such as whether outsiders can convert to the faith. They will be forced to question whether the Sikhs are a community, as some Orthodox Jews claim about Judaism, that is defined solely by ethnicity and demarcated only by kinship. The way a community deals with questions such as these will shape the way that Sikhism and other religions in diaspora become global religions.

TRANSNATIONAL RELIGION

In other religious traditions, such as Islam, Christianity, and Buddhism, there is no doubt about whether outsiders can covert to the faith. In these traditions, at the very core of their faith is the notion that their religion is greater than any local group and cannot be confined to the cultural boundaries of any particular

region. These are religious traditions with universal pretensions and global ambitions. It is a hallmark of Muslims, Christians, and Buddhists that they believe
that their religious ideas are universally applicable. The followers of each of these
competitive global ideologies often regard their faith as intellectually superior to
the others; some adherents feel that their own traditions alone have a birthright
to inherit the earth.

These are transnational religions, religions of expansion. But they also have
geographic and cultural roots. Buddhists revere Sarnath, where the Buddha first
preached, and study the Sanskrit and Pali of early Buddhist texts. Muslims go on
pilgrimage to Mecca, where the message of Allah was revealed to the Prophet
Muhummad, and respect the Arabic language in which that revelation was made.
Christians have a certain appreciation for Jerusalem; Roman Catholic Christians
look to Rome and learn the Latin, Hebrew, and Greek of their textual tradition.

Yet despite these emblems of cultural homogeneity, each of these traditions
are remarkably diverse. What holds transnational traditions together are their
cores of central ideas, images, and customs. Because these are thought to be
universal they must be available to everyone. And as the many everyones join the
faiths and adopt these central teachings and practices to their own contexts, the
religions take on a rich diversity. Yet despite the cultural differences between
the celebrity Buddhists of Los Angeles and the chanting monks in Chinese villages,
constants remain. Although there are many kinds of Buddhists, and thus many
Buddhisms—and for that matter, many Christianities and Islams—the interesting
feature of transnational religion is its ability to transcend any particular region's
claims.

Perhaps for that reason there has been a persistent tension between transnational religions and the state. Political leaders have employed Buddhism, Islam,
and Christianity as ideologies of conquest in their attempts to subdue regions
over which they have triumphed militarily. When the Spanish conquistadors
marched into South America during the seventeenth century, for instance, they
were accompanied by priests. The idea was not only to spread the religion and
win more souls for Christ; the Spanish also hoped to domesticize the native
population and make it more susceptible to rule through what they regarded as
the civilizing process of religious conversion. The goals of Buddhist military leaders in Central Asia and Muslim generals in the Middle East were much the same.

Yet although religion and politics have been linked through the ages, transnational religions have not been very reliable allies for state power. The same
Christianity, Buddhism, and Islam that provide for some rulers a supportive ideology have been for others a basis for rebellion. By latching onto their ideologies
some rulers may think they are harnessing religion's vision of global expansion
for their own political fortunes. But it is just as likely that these same religions
could be the resource for anti-national or transnational forces that would undermine the legitimacy and support of state power. Such is the tension in Islam at

the dawn of the twenty-first century between new religious nationalisms in such states as Iran, Afghanistan, and the Sudan, and the transnational guerrilla forces of Islamic activists such as Osama bin Laden's al Qaida warriors whose activities and organizations are beyond any national borders. Although these rogue transnational activists find safe harbor in some Muslim states the contradiction between their purposes may ultimately lead them to be at odds.

THE RELIGION OF GLOBAL SOCIETIES

This contradiction between transnational religion and the religion of nations is overcome in instances where religion is itself the expression of a transnational culture and society. The early Christian church is an interesting example. Although Christianity had its roots in Jewish messianism, the apostle Paul brought the transnational elements of Jesus' teachings to the Mediterranean world. This was a region studded with dense population centers much like today's cosmopolitan global cities. In Paul's day, the urban communities of Rome, Antioch, and Corinth consisted of multiple ethnic groups—displaced persons uprooted from their traditional cultures and religions, thrown together in urban melting pots. In such simmering contexts, new religions were concocted; many of them thrived. The worship of Roman gods, Gnostic ideas from Greek culture, the deity cults from Egypt, astrological sects from Persia—all of these competed with the radical Jewish group of Christians for the multicultural population's attention and support.

Ultimately Christianity won. It did so for a variety of reasons—one was sheer luck, as the Emperor Constantine decided to honor a vision he had during a dream and in 325 CE and made Christianity the state religion of the Roman empire. But Christianity had more than Constantine's imprimatur: it had an appeal of its own. Part of this attraction came from the universal character of its central messages of love, salvation, and redemption. Another part of its appeal was multicultural. Christianity had within a hundred years or so of its existence in the Mediterranean world become a religion of a diverse population. It had absorbed into its beliefs the idea of the Logos from Gnosticism, the devil and the promise of heaven from Zoroastrianism, messianic prophecy from Judaism, and civic responsibility from Roman emperor worship. Its ideas were therefore eclectic, touching many of the traditional beliefs of its potential adherents. Its practices were also portable—relying on prayer and worship that could be performed virtually anywhere. And its ability to create its own community and lines of authority was a powerful appeal to people who came from fragmented backgrounds and felt displaced and alienated from the cultures in which they found themselves.

The people of the Mediterranean world were much like the urban populations of global centers today. But official forms of Christianity became over time institutionalized and defensive, and hence unable to respond readily to pluralistic cultural settings in the same way that the early church did in the formative years of the Christian tradition. Much the same can be said of every institutionalized religion. In some cases, however, radical forms of traditional religion—such as the Islamic Ahmaddiya movement and Japan's Soka Gakkai—provide a religious expression for modern cultures. In other cases it is relatively new branches of old traditions, such as Hindu guru movements and the Mormon Church, that appeal. In yet other cases, this need is filled by new religious movements such as the African syncretic religions and America's Scientology. Still other movements incorporate elements of nature worship and indigenous practices into a kind of religion of global ecology.

Thus religion evolves as the world changes. The various forms of economic, social, technological, and cultural globalization at the dawn of the twenty-first century are the channels for new expressions of religion. New opportunities for the global transmission of religion are created through social mobility and the establishment of diaspora communities and through the ability to communicate easily the universal ideas of transnational religions to their expanding communities worldwide. As populations merge in plural societies, religions of globalization emerge as well. In an era of shared communication, culture and ideas, it may be possible to imagine the evolution of a global civilization with its own global religion. Widely revered figures such as Mohandas Gandhi, Desmond Tutu, the Dalai Lama, and Mother Theresa may be the forebears of such a religion's pantheon of saints. As in the past, religion in the future is certain to adapt as it responds to changes in the world around it.

THINKING ABOUT RELIGION GLOBALLY

This volume is intended to help expand our thinking about the way that religion is evolving in the emerging era of globalization and to provide a reliable handbook of its global diversity. Most studies of religion focus on single traditions, and even these studies often present the traditions as if they were discrete immutable entities that seldom change or interact with the cultures around them. Religions' own philosophical and theological understanding, however, has often been more sensitive to the existence of other religions. The writings of the early communities of both Islam and Sikhism contain appreciative comments about the various religious cultures around them, and attempt to appropriate elements of these religions within their own theologies. Christian theologians in recent centuries have become increasingly aware of the necessity of positioning their own understandings of God within a multicultural context. The early nineteenth-century theologian, Friedrich Schleiermacher, posited true religion as transcending the dogmatic limitations of confessional faith. The nineteenth-century Danish theologian, Soren Kierkekaard, thought that a natural religiosity lay beneath the apparent diversity of religious traditions. Early in the twentieth century, F. S. C. Northrup wrote about the "meeting of East and West"; William Ernest Hocking imagined an evolved form of Christianity in a transforming interaction with other faiths in what he imagined to be the "coming world civilization"; and Arend van Leeuwen understood Christianity's role in world history as one of leading all religions into a global secularism that would transcend the cultural limitations of particular religious creeds. One of the last writings of the twentieth-century Protestant theologian, Paul Tillich, was devoted to Christianity's encounter with other faiths and the necessity of moving beyond a religious exclusivism. In the twenty-first century, the Roman Catholic theologian, Hans Kung, proposed a global interfaith ethic to be endorsed by all the world's religious communities.

The field of comparative religion that developed in the twentieth century also contributed to the idea that a universal form of religion could link all faiths together. Although most comparative studies limited themselves to the objective analysis of the similarities and differences among religious traditions, some ventured into subjective speculation about the universal elements of religiosity. One of the mid-twentieth-century's best-known comparative religionists, Mircea Eliade, who studied the myths and rituals of ancient and arcane cultures, was sometimes accused of advocating the idea of an essential religion to be found at the heart of all mythic imagination. Joseph Campbell, relying on the psychological insights of Carl Jung, made explicit what he thought were religion's common archetypes. Huston Smith mined the ideas of the great religious traditions to discern a "perennial philosophy" found within them all. And the Harvard scholar of comparative religion, Wilfred Cantwell Smith, proposed that a "world theology" could be fashioned that would eventually surmount the cultural limitations of particularistic faiths.

At the end of the twentieth century and in the first decade of the twenty-first, this somewhat cheery optimism faded, and the role of religion in global society was seen as not necessarily leading to harmony and spiritual union. The eruption of religious violence and strident forms of religious nationalism seemed to counter the unifying trend toward a global religion. The civilizing role that Arnold Toynbee, writing in the first part of the twentieth century, imagined that religion would contribute to world society, was in stark contrast to the image of religion in world society portrayed by Samuel Huntington, writing at the end of the century, when he envisaged religion's role in a clash of civilizations. At the beginning of the twenty-first century, however, Huntington seemed more optimistic. In an essay cowritten with sociologist Peter Berger introducing essays in a project on "many globalizations," Huntington observed that despite the variety of cultural perceptions of globalization, religion and other forms of culture need not always be hostile to globalization and can play a positive role in it. Other sociologists of religion, including Martin Riesebrodt and Roland Robertson, have also observed that despite the role that religion has played in endorsing parochial movements in the last decades of the twentieth century it can also be a useful resource in creating a global civil society. I agree. On the one hand religion has often been a part of the ideology of antiglobal movements. But on the other hand, the absolutism of religious language and images can help people reach beyond the limitations of their narrow creedal affirmations to a wider sense of tolerance and global understanding.

One of the founders of the modern field of religious studies, Ninian Smart, presented a positive vision of religion's role in an increasingly global world. In an essay on the global future of religion written for this project and completed shortly before his death, Smart observed that religion was sometimes linked with violence in protests against global modernity. Writing eight months before the September 11 terrorist attacks, Smart prophesized that "weapons of mass destruction" might be used "for religious purposes" to destroy New York or other cities in what Smart said would be considered "the first major crime of the twenty-first century." But Smart also speculated on the emergence of a spiritual and ethical dimension of global civil society—a "global higher order" of civility—that would provide the cultural basis for international order and transnational regulations. This new form of religiosity Smart predicted would be "the coming global civilization."

What will become the global religion—and the religion of globalization—in the twenty-first century? This is one of the questions that lie behind the essays in this handbook. Their authors, some of this generation's most thoughtful social analysts of religion, have attempted to understand how religion has been altered by, and in turn is helping to shape, a globalized world. This handbook explores the variations of Christianities, Islams, Judaisms, Buddhisms, Hinduisms, and other religious traditions, and helps us understand how these traditions are shaped by their changing cultural contexts in various parts of the world. In each case a lead essay introduces the subject in a globalized context. Specific essays follow that explore the ways in which religious traditions are configured in specific geographical and cultural milieus.

In this volume we have asked scholars who are close to the religious communities they study to describe how these communities have changed over time, how they have responded to the plural cultural contexts around them, and how they are shaped by the current forces of globalization and social change. The result is a series of essays that not only gives an up-to-date insight into the diversity contained within the world's great religions but also provides a broad view of global religion in a new millennium. These essays show that, if the history of religion is a guide, we can expect religion's global future to be much like its global past. The religious imagination in a global era reaches out to encompass images and ideas that stretch beyond the limitations of particular and parochial affiliations to animate all levels of spiritual sensibility—its social vision and intimate individuality, its arresting particulars and expansive universals, its disturbing depths and soaring heights.

BIBLIOGRAPHY

Brown, Peter. 1981. *Cult of the Saints: Its Rise and Function in Latin Christianity.* Chicago: University of Chicago Press.

Campbell, Joseph. 1974. *The Mythic Image.* Princeton, N.J.: Princeton University Press.

Eliade, Mircea. 2005. *Myth of the Eternal Return: Cosmos and History.* Princeton, N.J.: Princeton University Press.

Hocking, William Ernest. 1928. *The Meaning of God in Human Experience.* New Haven: Yale University Press.

Huntington, Samuel. 1996. *The Clash of Civilizations and the Remaking of World Order.* New York: Simon and Schuster.

Huntington, Samuel, and Peter Berger, eds. 2002. *Many Globalizations: Cultural Diversity in the Contemporary World.* New York: Oxford University Press.

Juergensmeyer, Mark, ed. 2005. *Religion in Global Civil Society.* New York: Oxford University Press.

Kierkekaard, Soren. 1997. *Christian Discourses.* Eds. and trans. Howard V. Hong and Edna H. Hong. Princeton, N.J.: Princeton University Press.

Kung, Hans. 1998. *A Global Ethics and Global Responsibilities.* London: SCM Press.

Schleiermacher, Friedrich. 1999. *The Christian Faith.* Eds. H. R. MacKintosh and J. S. Stewart. Edinburgh: T and T Clark.

Smith, Huston. 1958. *The Religions of Man.* New York: Harper Press.

Smith, Wilfred Cantwell. 1991. *The Meaning and End of Religion.* Minneapolis, Minn.: Fortress Press.

Toynbee, Arnold Joseph. 1947. *Christianity and Civilization.* Wallingford, Pa.: Pendle Hill.

Tillich, Paul. 1963. *Christianity and the Encounter with the World's Religions.* New York: Columbia University Press.

Van Leeuwen, Arend. 1964. *Christianity in World History: The Meeting of the Faiths of East and West.* Trans. H. H. Hoskins. London: Edinburgh House Press.

PART I

INDIC CULTURAL REGION

CHAPTER 2

THINKING GLOBALLY ABOUT HINDUISM

T. N. MADAN

ALTHOUGH Hinduism is associated with one region of the world—South Asia—it is a global religion in two senses of the term. It has provided a religious complement to the diaspora of Hindus around the world and thus contributed to pluralist cultures in such disparate places as contemporary Fiji and England. Moreover, throughout its history Hinduism has embodied the spirit of pluralism. It has been open to a diversity of religious ideas and communities. In that sense it has supplied an early prototype of global religion.

Because of its diversity, the very definition of Hinduism has been contested. At its most basic, Hinduism may be defined as the religion of Hindus—the way they affirm their inner faith and order their everyday life. India is, of course, where most of the Hindus of the world live and where they have the status of the dominant religious community. There they constitute 82 percent of India's over one billion person population. This figure includes the lowest castes, the "Scheduled Castes" formerly known as Untouchables, many of whom prefer to be called Dalits ("down-trodden") and who often deny that they are Hindus. If such exclusion finds general acceptance, the proportion of the Hindus in the total population declines from four-fifths to two-thirds—approximately six hundred and sixty million adherents. Throughout the country, Hindus outnumber other religious communities everywhere except in the State of Jammu and Kashmir and the Union Territory of Lakshadweep, which have Muslim majorities.

The only predominantly Hindu country elsewhere in the world is Nepal, where Hinduism is the religion of nearly 90 percent of Nepal's twenty million residents. Hindus are the largest religious minority in Sri Lanka (17 percent) and Bangladesh (12 percent), which adds an additional three million and thirteen million, respectively. Beyond South Asia, a form of Hinduism combined with Buddhism is found among the four million residents of the island of Bali in Indonesia, recalling an eastward cultural expansion from India that occurred two thousand years ago. The wide distribution that makes Hinduism a world religion is relatively recent, beginning with the migrations of indentured laborers in the nineteenth century, under the auspices of British colonialism, which gave countries as far apart as Fiji, Malaysia, South Africa, and Trinidad their Indian (predominantly Hindu) populations. The outflow of migrants has increased considerably in the second half of the twentieth century: they have gone everywhere, but particularly to the United Kingdom, the United States, and West Asia in search of economic opportunities. There are well over a million Indians each in the United Kingdom and Malaysia and about a million in the United States.

THE PLURALISTIC CHARACTER OF HINDUISM

Hinduism as we know it today is fairly recent, but its roots go back in time to the Vedic religion that prevailed in north India three thousand years ago. Hinduism evolved over the millennia as the earlier Vedic and Brahmanical traditions spread spatially. It absorbed elements from folk religions (a "universalization" of the local traditions) and it also contributed to them (a "parochialization" of the great literary tradition). Hinduism is also a product of the encounter of Indian with Semitic religious faiths, Islam and Christianity.

Although for most centuries India had no single name for its religious tradition, the term *Hinduism* emerged and became popularized by Christian missionaries, Indologists, and colonial administrators during the late eighteenth and early nineteenth centuries. While some Indian intellectuals initially questioned its use, it gradually gained acceptance. The projection of a pan-Indian identity, cutting across regional linguistic and cultural boundaries had an obvious appeal in the context of the emergent nationalism of the late nineteenth century. The internal religious heterogeneity was thus covered over: what was a family of religions came to be seen as one religion.

Max Weber (1864–1920), one of the founders of the sociology of religion, warned against misleading assumptions about Hinduism as a uniform religion. Drawing attention to its internal variations and the concomitant religious tolerance, he concluded that Hinduism was not a religion in the Western sense of term (Weber 1958: 23). In common speech as well as scholarly discourses (including sociology), the characteristics of religion are largely derived from the Semitic religions of the West such as church, creed, and founder. Hinduism lacks most of these and other features. Although Weber did not put forward a precise definition of religion, another major contributor to the sociology of religion, Emile Durkheim (1881–1918) emphasized the importance of fundamental beliefs (such as the notion of the sacred as opposed to the profane) and related rites and practices in the constitution of religious faiths and of church-like organizations in the making of religious communities (Durkheim 1995: 44). Hinduism lacks both of these and other features, along with characteristics from other religions, such as the historic memory of a founder (like the Buddha) and the availability of a revealed text (like the Qur'an).

Although the Vedas are indeed regarded as revealed texts by some Hindus, the manner of revelation is not external. It rather consists of the recovery of the perennial wisdom of the sages. Modern Indological scholarship has tended to emphasize belief in the Vedas as scripture—and also the authority of the Brahmans as its interpreters—as essential features of Hinduism. Sociologists hesitate in concurring, for the great majority of Hindus today have no or only rudimentary ideas about the contents of the Vedas. They do not worship Vedic gods nor do they perform Vedic rituals. Their gods and goddesses come from the post-Vedic textual tradition of the Puranas and the Epics, their mode of worship is eclectic, and their rituals are primarily domestic. What is more, there is considerable variation from region to region.

The regional congregations (sampraday) may have a particular god or goddess at their religious center (as in the case of the worshippers of the Puranic gods Vishnu and Shiva and the goddess Shakti), or a particular ritualistic style (as in the case of devotional Smarta worship or the assertive Tantricism). Sociological studies of religion focus on the regional and local levels, for that is the level of observable socio-cultural reality. This does not of course mean that there are no common elements of belief and practice across regional and community boundaries and that the reality of pan-Indian Hinduism is wholly illusory. For example, if the Brahman priest is completely excluded from the religious ceremonies of a householder, a critical boundary beyond the socio-cultural world of Hinduism is crossed. Similarly, the taboo on the consumption of beef has gained wide acceptance among all Hindus since the late nineteenth century. Moreover, the Bhagavad Gita (a late subtext of the epic Mahabharata) has acquired in modern times the status of a central scripture, comparable to the Bible and the Qur'an. It is believed by many Hindus to be the word of God.

The teachings of the Gita are, however, far removed from the Vedas. The Gita adumbrates the notions of moral orientation and obligation through the key Sanskrit term *dharma*, which is found not only in all Indian languages (with minor lexical variations) but also in all Indic religions, and is widely used as the Indian equivalent of the word *religion*. Dharma is thought to govern all legitimate worldly ends (*purushartha*) including the pursuit of economic and political goals (*artha*) and aesthetic and sexual enjoyments (*kama*). The relationship of dharma or moral righteousness to the other objectives is hierarchical: it includes in itself the others even though they may seem opposed to it.

Dharmic guidance to action (*karma*) is highly context sensitive and varies with place and time and with the age, gender, and essential nature (*svabhava*) of the moral agent. One's essential nature is usually determined by the fact of birth into a particular varna, or endogamous hereditary social grouping. There are four such groupings, namely Brahmans (specialists of scriptural knowledge and priestcraft), Kshatriyas (warriors, kings), Vaishyas (merchants), and Shudras (tillers of the soil, artisans, providers of menial services). The Gita virtually reduces dharma and karma to appropriate varna duties (like dharma, karma is also found in all Indian languages and the Indic religions). The Gita also attributes the proliferation of castes (*jati*) within each category to cross-varna marriages and the dereliction of duties.

Moreover, karmic action has consequences of reward or punishment that the actor must bear. From this premise are derived the notions of transmigration of souls and bodily reincarnation—the cycle of birth, death, and rebirth (*samsara*). Weber considers the doctrine of karma-samsara "the most consistent theodicy ever produced by history." For the devout Hindu there is no escape from caste, for, as Weber puts it, "the inescapable on-rolling karma causality is in harmony with the eternity of the world, of life, and, above all, the caste order" (1958:121). In other words, Hinduism is the religion of caste—an equation that has found wide support in sociological literature.

Caste, Sect, and the Family

Indologists have long described Hinduism as varna-ashrama dharma—the morally grounded way of life appropriate to one's varna and one's ashrama. The latter is one's stage of life, of which four are recognized in the textual tradition: the preparatory stage of studentship, householdership, retirement, and finally renunciation of all worldly engagements. From the sociological side, the most rigorous attempt to argue a critical relationship between Hinduism and caste is Louis Dumont's *Homo Hierarchicus*. Rejecting the characterization of the caste system in terms of Eurocentric categories such as race, occupation, and class, and echoing M. N. Srinivas's earlier assertion that "ideas regarding pollution and purity are cardinal to Hinduism" (Srinivas 1962: 151), Dumont maintains that status positions within the caste system represent more than a simple ranking of strata. Being superior or inferior in a hierarchical pattern of relationships is an expression of the overriding values of ritual purity and pollution. Consequently, status is independent of economic and political power or powerlessness. Srinivas (1959) defined dominance in terms of the convergence of high ritual status, numerical strength, and economic power.

Secular values can at best pretend to be of the same importance as religious values, counters Dumont. The complexity of real life situations may mask this crucial distinction, he adds, but it holds good at the ideological level. Dumont's critics have accused him of looking at the caste system from the perspective of the highest-ranked Brahmans to the grievous neglect of the view from below. The latter perspective lends credence to the portrayal of caste as a system of power relations.

Dumont's structuralist analysis leads him to discover anti-structure too in the domain of religious values in the form of sects that break away from the world of caste and its underlying exclusivist values, but often end up becoming new castes. One may even opt for a truly radical alternative, namely renunciation (*sannyasa*), and obtain total release from caste rules. The renouncers follow their own dharma, however, and often become the founders of new sects.

The renouncers turn their back not only on caste rules but also on family values and obligations. Dumont has suggested that "the secret of Hinduism may be found in the dialogue between the renouncer and the man-in-the-world" (Dumont 1960: 37). I have myself argued that the preoccupation with caste and renunciation has led to the grievous neglect of the empirical presence and ideological vigor of the householder as the bearer of the values of Hinduism. Through life-cycle rites, rituals of feeding of ancestors, domestic worship of one's favorite gods and goddesses, propitiation of malignant forces of nature, pilgrimages, and so forth, the householder sustains the way of life that is Hinduism. He affirms the values of domesticity and auspiciousness, plenitude and moral equipoise, and promotes a rich and sensible philosophy of life in this world (Madan 1987: 17 passim).

MODERN HINDUISM:
REVIVAL AND REINTERPRETATION

The renouncer's return to the society in the role of a reformer or innovator is an abiding theme in the history of religions in India. The last quarter of the nineteenth century was witness to the seminal contributions of two unusually gifted renouncers.

Dayananda Sarasvati (1824–1883) was distressed by the ascendence of the Hinduism of the later Puranas at the cost of the religion of the Vedas. Ritualism, idolatry, supremacy of the priests, ill treatment of women, and subjugation of the lower castes were some of the many curses that had invaded Hinduism and Hindu society. Internal decay, Dayananda maintained, was complemented by the external threat posed by the proselytizing religions of Islam and Christianity. India's alternative religious paths—the sectarian secessions that Buddhism, Jainism, and Sikhism offered, before maturing into independent non-Vedic religions—seemed to him worse than the malady of decadent Hinduism. He thought that the only correct course was to excoriate the excrescences and return to the Vedas for inspiration. For this purpose he established the Arya Samaj (association of the Aryas) at Bombay in 1874. Aryas were the people who had produced the Vedas, which he considered the only truly revealed scriptures of humanity.

Dayananda's attitude to Islam and Christianity was hostile. Breaking with tradition, he advocated readmission of those people into the Arya Dharma—he did not use the word Hinduism—who had converted to Islam or Christianity, but regretted having done so. The Arya Samaj was not so successful in western India as it later became in Punjab, where Christian missionaries had been active. Although the Arya Samaj had no explicit political objectives, resentment against the government's patronage of the church was readily translated into support for the Indian National Congress when this organization was established in 1885.

In the early nineteenth century, many Bengali intellectuals were attracted to some of the theological and ethical ideas of Christianity. Evangelical activities had only begun in Bengal and were not yet seen as threatening there. The most notable of these intellectuals was Rammohan Roy (1772–1833), who founded the Brahmo Sabha at Calcutta in 1828—later renamed the Brahmo Samaj ("the society of God")—to promote a new syncretistic religion incorporating late Vedic speculative ideas and the ethical precepts of Jesus. The Samaj gathered a considerable following, but its success (unlike that of the Arya Samaj) turned out to be short lived. Partly in reaction to this development, and partly owing to certain fortuitous circumstances (including the overwhelming impact of a devout Brahman mystic, Ramakrishna, on the urban middle classes), Bengal witnessed, in the closing decades of the century, a movement of religious reform and revival among the Hindus.

The central figure in this movement was Vivekananda (1863–1902), who maintained that Vedanta ("the culmination of Vedic thought") was the "mother" of all religions, each of which was, however, a legitimate way of arriving at the eternal truths. Vivekananda is generally regarded as the prophet of religious pluralism. He was also a modernizer of Hinduism, for he did more than most others to awaken the social conscience of taboo-ridden, caste-minded, inward-looking, Hindus. Moreover, he had a dream of Vedantic Hinduism as a world religion. Although Dayananda and Vivekananda were unlike each other in most respects, one of the critical similarities between them was their lack of interest in formal politics. Indeed, the latter considered politics an enemy of the true spiritual quest that he considered the characteristic genius of India.

Modern Hinduism found its most eloquent expression in the politics of Mahatma Gandhi (1869–1948). His Hinduism was grounded not in any profound knowledge of the scriptures—although he did write a commentary on the Bhagavad Gita—but in his deep involvement in politics, which he described as the characteristic mode of moral action in the modern age (*yuga dharma*). Gandhi did not subscribe to the notion of secular politics divorced from religion or morality. To him these were synonymous.

Unlike the elitist emphasis of Dayananda and Vivekananda on the Vedas and Vedanta respectively, the twin pillars of Gandhi's Hinduism were, on the one hand, devotion to a personal deity (*bhakti*) and prayer for divine blessing (*anugraha*) and, on the other, introspection and moral reason. Since the ancient ideas of devotion, prayer, and grace are readily accessible even to unlettered people, this helped Gandhi to communicate with them as well as to the more intellectually inclined. His appeal to moral reason, which he placed above the authority of the Vedas, recalled the post-Vedic tradition of Brahmanical teaching in which "personal satisfaction" (*atmatushti*) is considered one of the sources of dharma (alongside the Vedas, the Smritis and the actions of moral exemplars). Gandhi thus bridged the gap between Sanskritic (textual) and popular Hinduism.

Gandhi combined a critical awareness of tradition with a finely tuned sensitivity to the challenges and opportunities of his own time. This was exemplified by his deeply felt moral repugnance for caste discrimination. He attached equal importance to the eradication of the evil practice of untouchability and the ending of colonial subjugation. He also had an intense yearning for interreligious communication and concord. He went beyond Vivekananda's hierarchical pluralism by acknowledging his spiritual indebtedness to Christianity and Islam. He considered the Sermon on the Mount in the New Testament crucial to the evolution of his own moral sensibility and preferred mode of political action (*satyagraha*, insistence on truth) based on nonviolence (*ahimsa*).

CONTEMPORARY TRENDS: RELIGIOUS EFFLORESCENCE AND COMMUNALISM

In the second half of the twentieth century, following India's independence in 1947, an interesting mixture of apparently contradictory trends has emerged. While the familiar processes of secularization has proceeded apace, and the caste system has become more a political than a ritual structure of intergroup relations, the concept of secularism has been redefined to connote a religiously plural society and a nondiscriminatory state that shows equal respect for all religions. The continuing importance of religion in public life has thus been formally recognized.

During this period, Hinduism has evidenced considerable vitality at home and abroad. Alone among the world religions, popular Hinduism has added new divinities to its traditional pantheon. The goddesses Santoshi Ma and Vaishno Devi have gained a prominence they did not enjoy earlier. The shrine dedicated to the latter is now attracting pilgrims from many parts of the country, including Bengal, long known for goddess worship. Worship of the Puranic god Krishna, prevalent virtually all over the country, has curiously received a fillip from the activities of the International Society for Krishna Consciousness (ISCON), founded by the Indian guru Shrila Prabhupada in the United States in 1967. A publisher of religious literature, ISCON also builds temples and hospices and holds religious processions and pilgrimages to holy places associated with the Krishna legend. Similarly, the well-organized activities of Mahesh Yogi to promote transcendental meditation (TM), Vedic sciences, and physical culture (yoga) have attracted worldwide attention. From his communities in India and Oregon, Acharya Rajneesh preached a culture of esoteric knowledge through personal experience that was in some ways a modern echo of the traditional path of spiritual quest through enjoyment (*bhoga*) as opposed to austerity.

These movements peaked in the West in the 1970s and '80s in the ambience of counterculture movements and were more a commentary on the socio-cultural situation of Europe and America there than on Hinduism. Moreover, following the death of the charismatic gurus Prabhupada and Rajneesh, the cults that grew out of their teachings have weakened. Still, god-persons—both men and women— are a notable component of contemporary Hinduism. One of the most prominent among them is Satya Sai Baba who has acquired a countrywide following among the urban middle classes though his alleged ability to perform miracles, and his role in providing spiritual guidance and material succor to his faithful. He has also successfully persuaded his followers to contribute to educational, healthcare, and other social goals.

Among other manifestations of the contemporary vigor of Hinduism is the salience of pilgrimage as religious activity. Pilgrimage (*yatra*) to holy places (*tirtha*) such as the meeting places of rivers, or other places associated with events in the two epics, Mahabharata and Ramayana, or with Puranic legends, are part of the Hindu religious tradition. They have provided collective religious experience somewhat removed from domestic and caste-governed settings. A gradual shrinkage of regular religious performances at home or in temples has occurred as a result of the pressures of urban life. At the same time the middle classes have been expanding in size, and salaried people among them receive employment benefits that include partly paid holidays (travel by train in India and Nepal for the employee and his or her dependents is covered). A very large number of people combine religious devotion with sight-seeing and choose a holy place as their destination.

Expressions of religiosity have in recent time been utilized by right-wing political organizations, notably the Vishwa Hindu Parishad (VHP) and the Bharatiya Janata Party (BJP), to mobilize support for their own agendas. These have included, first, a general call for the promotion of Hindu culture as the national culture of India, equating Hindu identity (*hindutva*) with national identity, and, second, the demolition of several Muslim mosques of north India. These places of worship are either known or believed to have been constructed at sites where Hindu temples had been pulled down earlier in celebration of Muslim supremacy.

One of them in the city of Ayodhya, at a place known among religious-minded Hindus as the "birth place" of the god Rama, was actually demolished by frenzied Hindu mobs in December 1992, allegedly under the guidance of VHP and BJP. The destruction of the mosque was followed by widespread killings of Muslims by Hindus and, later, by a Muslim reaction that took the form of bombing of public buildings in Bombay.

These were the worst incidents of communal violence in India after the riots that accompanied the partition of the subcontinent in 1947. The Indian Parliament enacted legislation in 1993 requiring the union and state governments to protect the status of all religious buildings. The question whether the destroyed mosque in Ayodhya is to be rebuilt at its original site, or a Rama temple is to be erected there, was passed on to the judiciary for decision. What the VHP and BJP has achieved is a transformation of the personality of Rama, emphasizing his role as a warrior at the cost of the more traditional beatific image of amoral exemplar.

The regrettable chain of events that resulted in the vandalism at Ayodhya underscores the communal politics into which Hinduism has been dragged in the present century. Hinduism in the twenty-first century is not only the religious faith of millions but also a political ideology shaped for the capture of power. The spirit of tolerance of Hinduism that sociologists such as Weber and Srinivas have written about, and modern-day Hindus like Vivekananda and Gandhi have extolled, faces its severest test. Nevertheless, Hinduism as global religious faith is not about to disappear "from the home and the world of most of India's Hindus" (Fuller 1992: 261).

BIBLIOGRAPHY

Babb, Lawrence A. 1986. *Redemptive Encounters: Three Modern Styles in the Hindu Tradition*. Berkeley: University of California Press.

Chatterji, Margaret. 1983. *Gandhi's Religious Thought*. London: Macmillan.

Dumont, Louis. 1960 "World Renunciation in Indian Religions." *Contributions to Indian Sociology* 4: 33–62.

———. 1970. *Homo Hierarchicus: The Caste System and Its Implications*. Chicago: University of Chicago Press.

Durkheim, Emile. 1995. *The Elementary Forms of Religious Life*. Trans. Karen E. Fields. New York: Free Press.

Eck, Diana. 1982. *Banaras: The City of Light*. New York: A. Knopf.

Fuller, C. J. 1992. *The Camphor Flame: Popular Hinduism and Society in India*. Princeton, N.J.: Princeton University Press

Jordens, J. T. F. 1978. *Dayananda Sarasvati: His Life and Ideas*. Delhi: Oxford University Press.

Kopf, David. 1979. *The Brahmo Samaj and the Shaping of the Modern Indian Mind*. Princeton, N.J.: Princeton University Press.

Madan, T. N. 1987. *Non-Renunciation: Themes and Interpretations of Hindu Culture*. Delhi: Oxford University Press.

———. 1998. *Modern Myths, Locked Minds: Secularism and Fundamentalism in India*. Delhi: Oxford University Press.

Madan, T. N., et al. 1971. "Review Symposium on Louis Dumont's Homo Hierarchicus." *Contributions to Indian Sociology* 5: 1–81.

Nandy, Ashish, Shikha Trivedy, Shail Mayaram, and Achyot Yagnik. 1995. *Creating a Nationality: The Ramjanambhumi Movement and the Fear of Self*. Delhi: Oxford University Press.

Srinivas, M. N. 1959. "The Dominant Caste in Rampura." *American Anthropologist* 61: 1–16.

———. 1962. "Hinduism." In M. N. Srinivas, ed., *Caste in Modern India and Other Essays*. Bombay: Asia.

Weber, Max. 1958. *The Religion of India: The Sociology of Hinduism and Buddhism*. Translated and edited by Hans H. Gerth and Don Matindale. Glencoe, Ill.: Free Press.

CHAPTER 3

TRADITIONAL BRAHMANICAL SOCIETY

JOSEPH W. ELDER

WHEN one uses the term *Hinduism* for the religious culture of India that has influenced much of Asia, one thinks of the brahmanical tradition. Yet it is difficult to say precisely what a Hindu is. The term *Hindu* is derived from the ancient Indo-European word *Sindhu*, referring to the Indus River. Persians during the days of their great empire (sixth to forth centuries BCE) labeled as *Hindhu* both the Indus River and those people on the subcontinent east of it. Centuries later, Europeans labeled as *Hindus* those people on the Indian subcontinent who were not Buddhists, Jains, Jews, Christians, Muslims, or Zoroastrians. Europeans adopted the generic term, *Hinduism,* for all of these people's widely varying religious observances, beliefs, and practices.

One common feature among all of these Hindus throughout much of the Indian subcontinent was their labeling of certain priests as brahmans. This brahman label provided a suggested link between currently active brahman priests and the creation of brahman priests at the beginning of time. The brahman label also suggested a link between currently active priests and an elaborate corpus of oral texts (primarily in the Vedic language that eventually evolved into the Sanskrit language) transmitted and/or composed centuries ago by brahmans.

This corpus of texts, beginning with the revealed Vedic hymns or Vedas (many of which were composed prior to the first millennium BCE) and supplemented during later centuries by remembered teachings and commentaries, provided the basis for a worldview that could be shared by those throughout India who wanted to be called brahmans and were willing to learn Sanskrit and familiarize themselves with the texts. Even brahman lineages whose marriage practices violated marriage rules outlined in the Sanskrit texts (e.g., south Indian brahman lineages who practiced cross-cousin marriage despite the prohibition of such marriages in the remembered Sanskrit texts) could share the brahmanical worldview outlined in the revealed and remembered texts.

Today, well-established centers of instruction where brahman boys can learn the Vedic and Sanskrit texts exist throughout India, from Rishikesh and Varanasi (Kashi, Banaras) in northern India to Sringeri and Kanchi (Conjeeveram, Kanchipuram) in southern India. Supplementing these well-established centers of instruction are numerous monasteries, ashrams (intentional communities), and traditional *guru-kulas* (where boys receive training in the homes of their gurus).

It is probably true that at no time in India's recorded history did traditional brahmanical society actually exist in its full form. However, it is probably equally true that at no time in India's recorded history has the traditional brahmanical society not been viewed by some Hindus and their brahman priests as an ideal society the current world would do well to emulate. Brahmans have probably never made up much more than their current 6 percent of the total population of India. But brahmans' widely scattered presence throughout India and Nepal, their authoritative position in local cultural and religious matters, and the incorporation of elements of the traditional brahmanical society into popular epics and folklore have meant that the majority of Hindus today share significant features of the traditional brahmanical society.

Key elements of traditional brahmanical society go back to the Rig-Veda, Hinduism's earliest revealed, authorless text considered true from the beginning of time. The tenth Rig-Vedic hymn describes the creation of the universe from different parts of Purusha, the Primeval Man, when he sacrificed himself on the funeral pyre. The ninetieth verse describes the creation of four categories of humans: the brahman from Purusha's mouth, the *rajanya* (ruler) from Purusha's shoulders, the *vaishya* from Purusha's thighs, and the *shudra* from Purusha's feet.

Subsequent revealed texts (including later Vedic hymns, the Brahmanas and Aryanakas) reflect the increasing specialization of brahmans in the memorization and preservation of the Vedic hymns and the performance of increasingly elaborate sacrifices. These revealed texts also state that shudras (the once-born) are unfit to sponsor sacrifices and are barred from being present at the sacrifices of others. The Upanishads (also considered revealed texts) introduce the concepts of the transmigration (*samsara*) of one's spirit from one body to another, the law of karma (deed, action) whereby every virtuous act is inevitably rewarded and every evil act punished in some subsequent life if not in this life, and the view that the goal of life is the release (*moksha*) of one's spirit from transmigration and the blending of one's spirit with the spirit of the universe.

The post-sixth century BCE cryptic Sutras and versified Shastras (considered to be human-authored remembered texts rather than authorless revealed texts) provide instructions for human conduct and domestic rituals. Preeminent among the Shastras is one on correct behavior (*dharma*) attributed to Manu, believed to be a progenitor of the human race. Manu's Dharma Shastra refers to the four original categories of humans as the four *varnas* (ranks, colors) and distinguishes between the twice-born and once-born varnas. Sons of the twice-born varnas may undergo a sacred-thread initiation rite and then study the Vedas. Sons of the once-born varnas may not; nor may the daughters of any varna.

According to Manu's Dharma Shastra, the twice-born varnas include: brahmans (whose duties are to study, teach, sacrifice, and give and receive gifts); kshatriyas (modified Vedic rajanyas, whose duties are to rule, protect people, sacrifice, and give and receive gifts); and vaishyas (whose duties are to sacrifice, study, breed cattle, till the earth, pursue trades, and lend money). The duties of the shudras (the once-born varna) are to serve the three higher varnas. In times of distress, Manu's Dharma Shastra allows the twice-born varnas to follow the occupations of lower varnas and the shudras to maintain themselves by handicrafts.

Manu's Dharma Shastra enjoins men to marry women from their own varna or from one lower varna (thereby prohibiting shudra men from marrying any but shudra women). It bars shudras from using brahmans to perform their ceremonies, and it bars brahmans from giving religious instructions to shudras. Manu's Dharma Shastra also explains how the world came to contain more than the four original varnas: outsiders (e.g., Greeks, Persians, Chinese, southerners, etc.) exist who were never part of the original four-varna system, and categories of mixed-varna offspring exist as products of sexual improprieties.

Most despised of the mixed-varna offspring were the *chandalas*, the products of shudra men impregnating brahman women. Manu's Dharma Shastra instructs chandalas to live outside cities and villages, carry out the corpses of those with no relatives, execute those condemned to die, wear the clothes of the dead, and eat from discarded or broken bowls. Manu's Dharma Shastra states that the varna into which one is born results from one's conduct in previous lives. Being born a brahman rewards virtuous actions in previous lives. Being born a chandala punishes evil actions in previous lives. In the Buddhist Jataka Tales (compiled from extant folk stories around the fifth century BCE) chandalas are described as so ritually contaminating that a kshatriya princess who sees a chandala washes her eyes with perfumed water, and brahmans who discover that chandalas posing as brahmans have eaten with them beat the chandalas and drive them away. The Jataka Tales also include criticisms of the four-varna view of society. In one Jataka Tale the Buddha (in a previous incarnation) who is living and teaching in a chandala village, punishes one of his brahman students who learns truths from the Buddha and later, because of brahman pride, tries to conceal that he has learned truths from a chandala.

The later Upanishads and Manu's Dharma Shastra present the view that humans are born into each life owing three debts: to seers, to their own forefathers, and to the gods. Before one can attain release (moksha) from transmigration (samsara), one must repay all three debts. Men of the twice-born varnas can do this by passing through four stages (*ashramas*) of life: the student stage (repaying debts to the seers by remaining unmarried and studying the sacred texts); the householder stage (repaying debts to one's ancestors by marrying, having progeny, earning wealth, and performing ceremonies for the dead); the forest-dweller stage (repaying debts to the gods by turning over one's affairs to one's sons, living in the wilderness with or without one's wife, and sacrificing to the gods); and finally the homeless, wandering-ascetic stage, living by begging, harming no living creatures, and meditating on the presence of the ultimate spirit in all beings. A man who dies having lived appropriately in this fourth stage can attain release (moksha) from transmigration (samsara), and his spirit can blend into the ultimate spirit of the universe and cease to exist as a separate entity.

Supplementing the idealized four-varna view of society were the four ages (*yugas*) of human existence. According to Manu's Dharma Shastra, in the first age truth and correct behavior stood "on all four feet," and nothing was gained by incorrect behavior. People lived four hundred years, were free from sickness, and achieved their goals. In each subsequent age, truth and correct behavior stood on one less foot, people lived shorter lives, suffered more sickness, and achieved fewer of their goals. In the fourth (current) age truth and correct behavior stand on only one foot. Humans' lives are unsuccessful, brief, and marred by poor health. And people do not perform their correct behavior as defined in the Sutras and Shastras.

The idealized four-varna view of society was supported by such other human-authored remembered texts as the Shastras on correct conduct (dharma) attributed to such brahman sages as Yajnavalkya, and the Sutra on sexual behavior/erotics (*kama*) attributed to the sage Vatsyayana. The Shastra on power-wealth (*artha*) attributed to the sage Kautilya listed varying levels of punishment according to a criminal's varna and declared that the most severe punishment a brahman should receive would be branding and exile—never execution.

Hinduism's two great epics, the Mahabharata (with its insert, the Bhagavad Gita) and the Ramayana, and Hinduism's Puranas (ancient stories), in their Sanskrit-language forms, reflect the idealized brahmanical four-varna pattern of society. Brahmans preserve the Vedas and sacred rituals, kshatriyas rule and listen to their brahman advisors, vaishyas produce wealth, and shudras serve the three higher varnas. According to the Bhagavad Gita, it is better to perform one's varna's duties badly than to perform the duties of another varna well. Those who deviate from their varna's prescribed duties inevitably suffer. Harmony fills a land in which each varna performs its duties. The Ramayana's description of Lord Ram's rule (Ram-raj) in the Kingdom of Ayodhya following Ram's return from exile epitomizes such a harmonious land.

Sanskrit dramas that flowered between 500 and 800 CE presented the brahmanical idealized four-varna view of society. On stage, educated brahmans and kshatriyas spoke in Sanskrit; the uneducated brahman buffoon, women, children, and the lower varnas spoke in colloquial languages. It was forbidden to show on stage a murder or the revolt of a province or kingdom. The Shastra on drama/ dance/music (*natya*) attributed to the sage Bharata states that those who listen to brahman Shastras and perform and witness appropriate dramatic performances will attain release from transmigration.

The idealized four-varna view of society with brahman supremacy did not go unchallenged. Beginning in the sixth century BCE, Buddhism and Jainism (both founded by kshatriyas in northern India) challenged the authority of the brahmans and Vedas, criticized the four-varna view of society and the notion of an original creator, supplemented Sanskrit with vernacular languages, and endorsed widespread release from the cycle of transmigration through insight, asceticism, and/or joining monastic orders. Buddhism remained a dominant religious force on the Indian subcontinent for the next fifteen-hundred years and continues to be a dominant force in neighboring Tibet and Sri Lanka. Jains remain a small but vital religious community in contemporary India.

In southern India the idealized four-varna view of society was challenged by Tamil poet-singers from even the lowest levels of society. Beginning in the fourth century CE, such poet-singers criticized reliance on high birth and learning as the path to release from transmigration. They sang, instead, that people from all social backgrounds—even the lowest—could achieve release. In time the belief that people from all walks of life could attain release through sufficient devotion (*bhakti*) to the Divine spread throughout the Indian subcontinent, enabling people from all classes, if they so desired, to bypass brahman priests and Sanskrit rituals. Pilgrimage sites arose in many parts of India where worshippers from all social backgrounds could express their devotion and receive a blessed vision (*darshan*) of holy rivers (e.g., the Ganges), cities (e.g., Banaras), mountains (e.g., Mt. Kailash), images of deities, and auspicious humans. Lineages with functional roles at pilgrimage sites could (and sometimes presumably did) negotiate brahman status for themselves, as could low-caste lineages performing priestly functions for other low-caste lineages when migration or good fortune enabled them to negotiate brahman status for themselves.

Eyewitness accounts of Indian society suggest that for centuries any efforts to implement the idealized four-varna view of society were restricted to the small, elite members of society who understood Sanskrit. Megasthenes, the Greek ambassador to the north Indian capital c. 300 BCE, described seven endogamous and craft-exclusive classes that differ significantly from the idealized four-varna society: philosophers (small in number but highest in dignity), farmers (the most numerous), herdsmen who also hunted and trapped, artisans/tradesmen/day-laborers, soldiers (the second most-numerous group whom Megasthenes demeaned for their idleness and drinking bouts), government inspectors, and councilors (smallest in number). According to Megasthenes, there were no slaves in India.

A Chinese Buddhist pilgrim traveling through the Indian subcontinent in the fifth century CE wrote about brahmans' ritual and intellectual activities and described the stigmatized chandalas who lived apart from others and who, when they entered public places, struck a piece of wood so that people could avoid them. Another Chinese Buddhist pilgrim traveling though the Indian subcontinent in the seventh century CE described the four-varna system as well as tribals and the stigmatized chandalas, and added that there were many other classes of people who intermarried according to their callings, of whom it would be difficult to speak in detail. An eleventh century CE Muslim visitor to northern India described the four-varna system and the Vedic account of their creation. He also wrote of people who lived apart from the four varnas and were not reckoned with them, including eight nonvarna groups following such crafts as weaving, wool-preparing, shoemaking, and basket-making. He then described several other non-varna groups (including chandalas) who did dirty work such as cleansing the villages, and he reported that chandalas were viewed as the illegitimate offspring of shudra fathers and brahman mothers.

In 1757 the British East India Company began to acquire territories on the Indian subcontinent. The Company, assuming that the Shastras had once been the implemented law of the land, declared that the Company's courts would decide civil cases on the basis of various Shastras. In Bengal, Company law was based on Jimutavahana's twelfth-century commentary on the Shastras. In much of the rest of India, Company law was based on regional variations of Vijnanesh-vara's twelfth-century commentary on the Shastra attributed to the sage Yajna-valkya.

Between 1867 and 1872, after the British Crown had displaced the East India Company, the government of India ordered its first all-India census. From the 1881 through the 1931 decennial census, British and Indian civil servants tried, with limited success, to fit India's complex Hindu population into a government-modified version of the Shastras' four-varna framework. In Madras Presidency, for example, the census categories included brahmans, kshatriyas, vaishyas, and then introduced such categories as good shudras, shudras who habitually employ brahmans, shudras who occasionally employ brahmans, castes that pollute without touching but do not eat beef, castes that eat beef but do not pollute except by touch, castes that deny the authority of the brahmans, etc.

In 1936 the government issued an all-India list of scheduled castes—those castes denied access to certain neighborhood temples, roads, ponds, sacred sites, etc. and considered to cause "pollution" by approach or touch. Finally, in the 1941 census, the government of India stopped tabulating all-India caste data except for the scheduled castes and scheduled tribes in order to provide such castes and tribes with special protections. The government of India's 1960 list of 405 scheduled castes and 255 scheduled tribes still included a shastric element, constructing under single all-India names (as though all of India had once been shaped by the four-varna categories) scores of different unrelated and non-intermarrying lineages that sometimes did not share even a common language.

According to the 1931 census, approximately 6 percent of India's Hindu population were brahmans (with larger percentages in northern India and smaller percentages in southern India), about 21 percent were "exterior castes" (later called "scheduled castes and tribes"), and most of the remaining 73 percent were "other interior castes."

Nationalist leaders such as Mohandas Gandhi and Dr. Bheem Rao Ambedkar based some of their pronouncements on their belief that the traditional brahmanical four-varna society historically existed on the Indian subcontinent. After India's independence in 1947, a number of Hindu teachers and political parties have advocated India's return to some version of the brahmanical four-varna society. India's scheduled castes (or Dalits—the oppressed—as they call themselves) have denounced the four-varna society and Manu's Dharma Shastra for establishing ideologies they feel legitimize discrimination from which they, the Dalits, continue to suffer. For many Hindus, especially in northern India, the annual dramatic productions of the epic Ramayana reach their moral climax when the victorious Lord Ram returns to his kingdom of Ayodhya to establish his golden age in which members of each varna fulfill their prescribed duties, and all four varnas live in peace and harmony.

BIBLIOGRAPHY

Basham, Arthur L. 1959. *The Wonder That Was India: A Survey of the Culture of the Indian Sub-continent Before the Coming of the Muslims.* New York: Grove Press.

Fa-hsien. 1965. *A Record of Buddhist Kingdoms.* Trans. James Legge. New York: Dover Press.

Galanter, Marc. 1970. "Dharma Sastra and the Administration of Justice." In Joseph W. Elder, ed., *Lectures in Indian Civilization,* 74–76. Dubuque, Iowa: Kendall/Hunt.

———. 1970. "Family Law in Modern India." In Joseph W. Elder, ed., *Lectures in Indian Civilization,* 261–63. Dubuque, Iowa: Kendall/Hunt.

Hsuan-Tsang, Si-yu-ki. 1957–8. *Buddhist Records of the Western World: Chinese Accounts of India.* Trans. Samuel Beal. Vols 1–4. Calcutta: Susil Gupta (reprint).

Francis, H. T., and E. J. Thomas, trans. 1956. *Jataka Tales.* Bombay: Jaico.

Kautilya. 1960. *Kautilya's Arthasastra.* Trans. Rudrapatna Shamasastry. Sixth ed. Mysore: Mysore Printing and Publishing House.

Majumdar, Ramesh C. 1963. *The Classical Accounts of India.* Calcutta: Firma K.L. Mukhopadhyay.

Manu. 1967. *The Laws of Manu.* Georg Buhler, trans. Delhi: Motilal.
————. 1991 *The Laws of Manu.* Trans. Wendy Doniger and Brian K. Smith. New York: Penguin Books.
Vatsyayana. 1962. *The Kama Sutra: The Classical Hindu Treatise on Love and Social Conduct.* Trans. Sir Richard F. Burton. New York: Dutton Books.

CHAPTER 4

POPULAR HINDU
MOVEMENTS

DAVID N. LORENZEN

ONE way of thinking about Hindu religion and society is to distinguish between the traditional religious society led mostly by Brahmans and the large number of popular movements that have been led mostly by members of other caste groups. The term "popular" primarily refers to the fact that a large number of people belong to these movements or are influenced by them. In many cases, however, the masses who are attracted to such movements come from the less-educated and poorer social classes. In India, religious movements are associated not only with different social classes but also with different castes. Since caste and class boundaries do not always correspond, and since the influence of religious movements often extend across both, the social character of religious movements in India is varied and complex. In a pluralistic and multicultural society, figures associated with popular Hindu religious movements are often touted as harbingers of religious tolerance.

Before focusing on non-Brahman popular religious groups I should mention that there are popular groups that are led by Brahmans. In some cases, such as the Smartas, the followers are almost exclusively Brahmans themselves. The followers of most of the other Brahman-led movements come from a wide variety of castes, generally excluding only members of the Scheduled Castes (Untouchables and low Shudras). The followers of those popular Hindu movements that are led by non-Brahmans, on the other hand, are usually open to members of all castes, including Scheduled Castes (although some non-Brahman movements are restricted to one or two castes). Few of these movements that are led by non-Brahmans, however, will have any Brahmans among their followers.

The social ideologies of Brahman-led and non-Brahman Hindu movements differ most clearly over the religious status of *varna asrama dharma*, the ideology of the caste system itself. Most Brahman-led movements support this system, while most non-Brahman movements reject it. In practice, however, the nature and extent of this support and this rejection vary in important ways from movement to movement on both sides of the Brahman/non-Brahman divide. Some Brahman-led movements demand the strictest adherence to the rules of caste behavior, while others, particularly those that reflect the impact of modernity, support the system in only a vague and theoretically rationalized fashion. On the other hand, non-Brahman movements range from those that accept the practical workings of the caste system (though rejecting its divine legitimacy), to those that actively proclaim anti-Brahman sentiments and protest against the ritual deference that the system imposes on them.

In both Brahman-led and non-Brahman movements, the leaders and followers often interpret important aspects of the social and religious ideologies of the movements in quite different ways. In Brahman-led movements, for instance, non-Brahman followers may be skeptical of Brahman claims to innate social and religious purity. In the implicit and explicit dialogue between leaders and followers, the leaders generally have the advantage since they are the principal authors and "official" interpreters of the texts and practices of the movements. On the other hand, most movements are loosely organized, and the followers generally have considerable autonomy. How exactly they exercise this autonomy to rework and reinterpret the official texts and practices is a question that needs much further empirical study. In the long term, it is this dialogue of leaders and followers that determines the social and religious directions that the history of each movement takes.

Another significant difference between Brahman-led and non-Brahman Hindu movements concerns their respective attitudes to Sanskrit, the ancient language of the sacred Vedic and Hindu texts. Here again the situation is complex. Many Brahman priests know little or no Sanskrit, and many of the key texts of Brahman-led movements, such as Tulasidas's *Ramayan*, are written in vernacular languages. On the other hand, many intellectuals in non-Brahman movements do know Sanskrit. The key point is that Brahman-led movements consider Sanskrit religious texts such as the Vedas to be divinely inspired; while in non-Brahman movements, such texts may or may not be highly respected, but they are not regarded as divine creations beyond rational and moral criticism.

It is this rejection of the culture of sacred texts in Sanskrit, and a greater reliance on oral texts composed in vernacular languages, that enables us to classify non-Brahman religious movements as "popular" in the sense of being non-elite and less literate than Brahman-led movements. Nonetheless, many non-Brahman movements have, over the years, developed their own traditional intellectuals, usually monastic sadhus, and their own written religious texts, even texts written in Sanskrit.

The range and number of non-Brahman religious movements is quite large. Some are local, limited to a single city or group of villages; some extend over an entire linguistic area. Some are highly structured with at least a core of initiated members and a leadership group of sadhus or priests; some comprise only a loose group of followers associated with some charismatic personality or sacred shrine. With the important exception of the Sikhs, most identify themselves as Hindus and incorporate many elements of hegemonic Brahmanical Hinduism in their religious beliefs and practices.

Here I will limit the discussion to a few important regional non-Brahman movements whose social dynamics have been well studied. The movements chosen all embody fairly explicit elements of dissent against the religious and social ideology of Brahmanical Hinduism. Not included here are three influential regional movements whose early leadership included persons from both Brahman and non-Brahman castes: the Alvars and the Nayanmar of Tamilnadu and the Varakaris of Maharashtra. Today these movements mostly fall within the orbit of Brahmanical Hinduism.

The most influential early non-Brahman Hindu movement was that of the Naths or Kanaphata Yogis, said to have been founded by Gorakhanath in perhaps the tenth or eleventh centuries. This movement seems to have originally evolved out of Tantric Saiva tradition and has concerned itself particularly with the beliefs and practices of Hatha Yoga. Where the movement first appeared is uncertain, perhaps the Punjab or Kashmir, but it eventually spread throughout North India and even south into Tamilnadu where it was transformed into the tradition of the Tamil Siddhas. Today the Nath movement is still active in parts of North India, most notably in Rajasthan. For the most part, however, it seems to have run its course.

Much of the literature of the Naths is written in Sanskrit, and some of its authors were undoubtedly Brahmans. Other Nath works, however, were written in vernacular languages, probably mostly by non-Brahmans, and express religious and social ideas remarkably similar to those of other non-Brahman movements, including a marked hostility to Brahman pretensions. Among present-day Naths, it is these songs and verses—and longer vernacular works about the lives of early Nath saints—that are the chief medium for the transmission of Nath tradition. One important collection of Hindi songs and verses attributed to Gorakhanath and edited by P. D. Barthwal embodies ideas, sentiments, and even language remarkably similar to those found in the songs and verses attributed to the famous Hindi saint-poet Kabir, about whom more shortly.

Another important early non-Brahman Hindu movement is that of the Virasaivas or Lingayats of the Karnataka region in South India. As in the case of the Naths, the beliefs and practices of the Virasaivas seem to derive in part from those of Saiva cults, especially the Pasupatas and Kalamukhas. The chief founder of the Virasaiva movement was a Brahman named Basava, who lived in the Karnataka region in the twelfth century. Most of his early associates and successors, including several women, were non-Brahmans. He and others among them composed a large number of songs in Kannada that still serve as key texts of Virasaiva tradition. A. K. Ramanujan has translated an attractive selection of these songs in his *Speaking of Siva*. These songs express the devotion of the poets to the god Siva as well as their rejection of the caste hierarchy of Brahmanic tradition. A particularly noteworthy feature of these songs, and Virasaiva tradition in general, is a positive attitude toward the rights of women and the dignity of manual labor.

The Virasaivas are estimated to make up about 16 percent of the population of Karnataka state, for a total of perhaps eight million. This large population is divided into several hierarchically ranked endogenous castes, all of whose members belong to the Virasaiva community. One important exception, however, is the Aradhya Brahman caste whose members may be Virasaivas or non-Virasaivas. Unlike most other non-Brahman religious movements, the Virasaivas have developed their own set of life-cycle rites, usually performed by Virasaiva priests or sadhus of the Jangama caste. The autonomous caste organization and independent life-cycle rites of the Virasaiva community provide interesting parallels to the Sikh community. However, although a few Virasaiva intellectuals have claimed a non-Hindu identity, the separation of the Virasaiva community from Hinduism has not found the general consensus reached in the Sikh community.

Another striking feature of Virasaiva practice is the strong influence that the Virasaiva monasteries exercise over the lay community. The monasteries are usually responsible for performing life-cycle rites and also play an important role in the education of the children and young men and women of the community. Nowadays this educational role usually takes the form of offering room and board to students who attend government schools and universities.

In North India many non-Brahman movements are associated with the Sant or Nirguni tradition whose early leaders include the poet-saints Kabir, Ravidas, Guru Nanak, and Dadu Dayal, all of whom became the focus of important sectarian movements or *panths*. The discussion here is limited to the *panths* associated with Kabir and Ravidas.

Kabir was in many ways the creator of Nirguni tradition, but the vernacular poetry of the Naths and of the Maharashtran poet-saint Namadev had an important influence on his ideas and poetic style. Islam was also important, although its influence is less visible. What Kabir added to this mix was an ample measure of poetic genius, a carnivalesque taste for grotesque satire directed against the hypocrisy of both Hindus and Muslims, and a religious vision based on a sharp awareness of the immanence of death and the chaste inner worship of a deity without anthropomorphic form or personality. Academic scholars usually assume that Kabir himself had little to do with organizing the sect that bears his name, but he did play a key role in developing the mixed vernacular dialect that enabled his poetry to be understood and loved throughout most of North India.

Kabir was raised in a family of low-caste Muslim weavers of Varanasi. Tradition claims that he at some point became a disciple of a Brahman teacher named Ramananda, who was also the guru of Ravidas. Kabir probably died in the early sixteenth century. His followers are said to have organized themselves into several rival spiritual genealogies soon after his death. However true this may be, the Kabir Panth was early divided into several rival branches. Some branches were led by celibate sadhus who passed the leadership from guru to disciple, while others were headed by married men who passed the leadership from father to son. Most of the sadhus and the married leaders come from middle- to low-ranking castes in the government category of Other Backward Castes. Many lay followers, called *bhagats*, belong to these same castes, although many also belong to various Scheduled Castes and Tribes.

At some point early in the history of the Kabir Panth, many of Kabir's songs and verses were collected together in the *Kabir Bijak*. This text is regarded as authoritative within the Kabir Panth, but most the songs attributed to Kabir that are popular today are more recent compositions not found in the *Bijak*. Group recitations from the *Bijak* and other Kabir Panthi compositions are performed daily in the larger monasteries.

Among the branches of the Kabir Panth, two have been historically most influential. One traces its descent from Kabir's disciple Srutigopal and has its main center in a monastery established on the site of Kabir's reputed homestead in the Kabir Chaura neighborhood of Varanasi. This branch claims to be the "root" from which the others are descended. Nowadays the Kabir Chaura monastery houses a semi-floating population of some thirty or forty sadhus. Another group of ten to twenty sadhus lives on the large farm owned by this branch near Magahar, the site of Kabir's death, not far from the city of Gorakhpur. This branch also controls a large number of smaller monasteries, generally housing from one to five sadhus, located throughout northern India. Most are concentrated in eastern Uttar Pradesh and Bihar, but there are others as far afield as Rajasthan, Gujarat, and Nepal.

The other main branch claims descent from Kabir's disciple Dharamdas. Today it has two rival centers at Damakheda and Kharsiya in the Chhattisgarh region of Madhya Pradesh. The Damakheda sub-branch is headed by a married man who inherited his office from his father. This sub-branch has only a few sadhus associated with it, but it does have a large following of lay bhagats. The Kharsiya sub-branch was established in the 1930s during a dispute about the succession at Damakheda. The head of the Kharsiya monastery is a sadhu and is expected to pass on his office to one of his disciples. Other monasteries of this sub-branch are found in Chhattisgarh and in roughly the same regions as those of the Kabir

Chaura branch. The total number of Kharsiya sadhus is comparable to that of the Kabir Chaura branch. A very rough estimate of the total number of sadhus now in all the branches and sub-branches of the Kabir Panth would be anywhere from about fifteen hundred to three thousand.

The lay bhagats of the Kabir Panth are more loosely defined and even harder to count. Rough projections from figures given in the censuses of 1901 and 1911 suggest a present-day population of from two to three million. Ideally bhagats should take an initiation from a monastery abbot or from the married head of the Damakheda branch, but it is unclear how many actually take a formal initiation. The connection between the sadhus and bhagats is, for the most part, rather tenuous. Bhagats do make occasional visits to monasteries and many of them attend the celebrations at major centers held on special dates such as those of Kabir's birth and death. The only other clear marks of being a Kabir Panthi bhagat are devotion to Kabir, regular or occasional recitation of his songs and verses, the wearing of a simple string necklace, and a vegetarian diet. Life-cycle rites such as marriages and funerals are performed by the priests, not usually Kabir Panthis, normally employed by the different castes to which the bhagats belong.

The movement associated with Ramananda's untouchable Chamar disciple Ravidas, also known as Raidas, makes an interesting contrast with the Kabir Panth. The religious foundation of the movement is provided by the songs attributed to Ravidas. These songs have a content and style similar to Kabir's. The older songs are fewer in number, however, and mostly lack the poetic brilliance and sharp satire found in Kabir's compositions. A distinctive feature of many Ravidas songs is a cry from the heart against the indignities and hardships imposed on him for being an Untouchable.

The Ravidas Panth is more loosely organized than the Kabir Panth. There are few monasteries, few sadhus, and the initiation of lay bhagats is less common. Virtually the only important center is the temple located in the village of Seer Govardhanpur on the reputed site of Ravidas's homestead near Banaras Hindu University. A larger temple is now being constructed, with government help, on the bank of the Ganges in Varanasi, but the extent of community support for it is uncertain. The traditional strength, and limitation, of the Ravidas movement has been its close association with the Chamar cluster of castes to which Ravidas himself belonged. Particularly in North India, to be a Chamar is also to be a Ravidasi. Some followers are found in other low castes, but their numbers are small.

One consequence of the close association between Chamar and Ravidasi identities has been that the modern struggle of the Chamars for better economic conditions and greater political influence has become linked to devotion to Ravidas. In 1925, Mangoo Ram, a Chamar intellectual from the Punjab, organized the Ad Dharm movement. This Ad Dharm movement fostered secular Chamar aims together with a social and religious ideology based on the life and songs of Ravidas. Although the original organization no longer exists, it has been succeeded by the All-India Adi Dharm Mission with a headquarters in New Delhi. In Varanasi, this organization is the principal organizer of an annual parade on Ravidas's birthday that has become a major expression of Chamar unity.

Another sort of non-Brahman religious movement developed around the person and songs of the woman poet-saint Mirabai, a younger contemporary of Kabir and Ravidas. According to the legends of her life, she belonged to a high, but non-Brahman, royal Rajput caste of Rajasthan. She felt a strong religious calling before her marriage and dedicated her life to Krishna as her divine husband. After being forced to marry a neighboring prince, her continued devotion to Krishna came into conflict with her social and religious obligations to her husband and his family. Eventually she left them and wandered about as a religious mendicant singing songs of devotion to Krishna. Today the songs attributed to Mirabai remain favorites throughout North India. They are particularly appreciated by women, who identify with her trials and tribulations in the house of her in-laws, evoked in many of the songs, and with her idealized love of Krishna.

Mirabai's followers, then, are mostly women and come from a wide range of castes. This sharply limits the ability of the movement to organize itself. Parita Mukta has written about how many of Mirabai's women followers in present-day Rajasthan and Gujarat have organized small independent groups of women who periodically meet to sing Mirabai's songs. Through these songs, mutual friendships, and conversation, these women are able to express their discontent about harsh demands of traditional Hindu patriarchy and about the inequalities of the economic and political system as well.

The religious movements we have discussed here originated in the early and later medieval period. New movements similar to, and partly derived from, those of Kabir and Ravidas continued to appear in North India in the nineteenth and early twentieth centuries. Three that have been well studied are the Radhasoamis, a highly literate and mostly middle-class movement strongest in western Uttar Pradesh and the Punjab; the Satnamis of Chhattisgarh, a movement limited mostly to a section of the Chamar community; and the Mahima Dharma movement of Orissa, whose followers have traditionally come mostly from Scheduled Castes and Tribes.

Since Indian Independence in 1947, the number of followers of non-Brahman religious movements such as these has, in most cases, suffered a dramatic decline. The social protests of low-caste groups have mostly been channeled into political movements whose explicitly religious content is limited but rarely completely absent. The resurgence of Scheduled Caste militancy under the general heading of the Dalit movement is a good case in point. On the other hand, more apolitical religious sentiments have increasingly found an outlet in mass media spectacles such as filmed "mythologicals" and televised series such as those of the *Ramayana* and *Mahabharata* that generally foster a moderately liberal version of traditional

Brahmanical norms and values. A more ominous development has been the increasing popular appeal of religious communalism founded on mutual distrust and hatred among the Hindu, Muslim, Sikh, and Christian communities. At the same time, figures such as Kabir and Mirabai persist in popular culture—including films and comic books—as symbols of intercaste and interfaith harmony in multicultural social settings.

BIBLIOGRAPHY

Banerjee Dube, Ishita. Forthcoming. "Taming Traditions: Legalities and Histories in Twentieth Century Orissa." In Gyan Prakash and Susie Tharu, eds., *Subaltern Studies X: Writings on South Asian History and Society*. Delhi: Oxford University Press.

Barthwal (Barathvala) P. D. 1960. *Gorakh-bani*. Allahabad: Hindi Sahitya-sammelan.

Caturvedi, Parasurama. 1964. *Uttari Bharat ki samta-parampara*. 2nd ed. Allahabad: Bharati Bhandar.

Dube, Saurabh. 1998. *Untouchable Pasts: Religion, Identity, and Power among a Central Indian Community, 1780–1950*. Albany: State University of New York Press.

Gold, Ann Grodzins. 1992. *A Carnival of Parting: The Tales of King Bharthari and King Gopi Chand as Sung and Told by Madhu Natisar Nath of Ghatiyali, Rajasthan*. Berkeley: University of California Press.

Juergensmeyer, Mark. 1982. *Religion as Social Vision: The Movement Against Untouchability in Twentieth-Century Punjab*. Berkeley: University of California Press.

———. 1991. *Radhasoami Reality: The Logic of a Modern Faith*. Princeton, N. J.: Princeton University Press.

Lorenzen, David, ed. 1995. *Bhakti Religion in North India: Community Identity and Political Action*. Albany: State University of New York Press.

Mukta, Parita. 1994. *Upholding the Common Life: The Community of Mirabai*. Delhi: Oxford University Press.

Ramanujan, A. K. 1973. *Speaking of Siva*. Harmondsworth: Penguin Books.

Sadasivaiah, H. M. 1967. *A Comparative Study of Two Virasaiva Monasteries: A Study in Sociology of Religion*. Mysore: Prasaranga, Manasa Gangotri.

Schomer, Karine, and W. H. McLeod, eds. 1987. *The Sants: Studies in a Devotional Tradition of India*. Delhi: Motilal Banarsidass.

CHAPTER 5

THE SIKH COMMUNITY

GURINDER SINGH MANN

SIKHS represent the youngest and least known of the world's monotheistic religious traditions. The community was founded in the early sixteenth century and has been historically situated in the Punjab, in the northwestern area of the Indian subcontinent near what is now Afghanistan. Over time this formerly regional community has increasingly become a global community and is confronting the challenges that this transition involves.

During the twentieth century there were significant demographic changes for the Sikhs. By the beginning of the twenty-first century only seventeen of the world's twenty-three million Sikhs lived in the present-day Indian state, Punjab. Four million now live in other parts of India, with large concentrations in the city of Delhi and the states of Uttar Pradesh, Rajasthan, and Harayana. Approximately two million Sikhs live in other parts of the world: 750,000 are in North America, 750,000 in England and Western Europe, and the remaining number are in former British colonies in Southeast Asia and East Africa.

HISTORICAL DEVELOPMENTS

The Sikh community regards the golden years of its history as those in the sixteenth and seventeenth centuries when a succession of ten spiritual leaders—the Sikhs' founding Gurus—shaped the original tradition. From the first, Guru Nanak, to the last, Guru Gobind Singh, these figures are remembered both for their piety and their ability to forge a common identity out of diverse followers. The modern Sikh community has been shaped by more recent events—those in the nineteenth and twentieth centuries.

The historical developments that engulfed the South Asian subcontinent during the nineteenth century left a profound impact on Sikh thinking. First, the British annexation of the Sikh kingdom in 1849 created the opportunity for Sikhs to become acquainted with Western educational, social, and political institutions. Unlike other Punjabi communities, the Sikhs developed a special sense of loyalty to the British and worked closely with them. Now familiarized with Western modes of thinking, they began to examine their Sikh heritage and generate statements pertaining to Sikh history, doctrine, and code of conduct. By the turn of the twentieth century, the first phase of this work was largely completed and these ideas began to serve as the ideological basis for the Sikh community.

During the middle decades of the twentieth century, the Sikh leadership nurtured the hope that the British would ensure the protection of Sikh interests when the British Raj ended and they departed from the subcontinent. The idea of an independent Sikh state figured prominently in the protracted negotiations, but the small size of the Sikh population (approximately 5.5 million at the time) thinly spread throughout the state became a serious impediment to these dreams. The partition of the Punjab in 1947 into a Pakistani and Indian division of the region was a traumatic experience for the community. Over 1.5 million Sikhs migrated from western to eastern Punjab and bloodshed engulfed the movement. The new political boundary vivisected Sikh sacred geography and a large number of religious sites were left behind in the newly created Pakistan.

As India developed politically after its independence in 1947, the Akalı Dal, the primary Sikh political party, forged programs and created a set of criteria for membership that had a distinctly religious character. Increasingly it found itself in conflict with the central government in Delhi. The party capitalized on a change of demographics: the movement of Sikhs to eastern Punjab at the 1947 partition created a concentration of Sikhs in the central districts of the Indian Punjab. Through a series of political agitations and negotiations, the Akali Dal's sustained efforts led to the restructuring of state boundaries and the establishment of a new state of Punjab in 1966. In the new state Sikhs are in the majority and Punjabi, their sacred language, is the official language. This is the first time in their five-centuries'-old history that the Sikhs have constituted a majority in the land of their origins.

At the same time that the Sikhs were developing politically in India the community was beginning to expand internationally. Beginning in the late nineteenth century, the Sikh association with the British resulted in the opportunity to travel outside the Punjab. The Sikhs joined the Imperial army in large numbers and were taken to different parts of the British Empire. After serving abroad in the army for a period of time, some settled permanently in those locales rather then returning to the Punjab. During the first quarter of the century, small Sikh settlements emerged in different parts of the world with Sikh houses of worship—*gurdwaras* (literally, the house of the Guru)—built in such places as Hong Kong, Southeast Asia, East Africa, London, Vancouver, and Stockton, California. This movement away from the Punjab continued even after the departure of the British from the subcontinent. By the first years of the twenty-first century, 15 percent of the world Sikh population lived and worked away from the region of the Punjab.

The contact with the British thus started a process that has resulted in the presence of Sikh communities in many parts of the world. In December 2001, Sikhs living in Hong Kong celebrated the first centennial of their gurdwara there and the first century of life in their new home. In their planning for this event, Sikhs in Hong Kong did not focus on the nostalgia they may have experienced for the "home" that they left behind in the Punjab, but on the gratitude that they felt for the mainstream community in Hong Kong and their renewed commitment to working toward a bright future for the territory.

THE COMPOSITION OF THE SIKH COMMUNITY

Like all social groups, the Sikh community is diverse. The Sikh population has been historically concentrated in three geographical areas in the Punjab: the Majha, in the north, the Doaba, in the center, and the Malwa, in the south. These divisions can be traced back to the early history of the community. The Sikh community started in the Majha and then spread out first to the Doaba and later to the Malwa. Because of a complicated set of social and economic circumstances, the Sikh leadership largely came from the Majha area. The kingdom at Lahore, which is in the Majha, under Maharaja Ranjit Singh (1789–1839), the most prominent Sikh leader after the Gurus, was seen as the manifestation of the vision created by Guru Gobind Singh (1675–1708), the tenth and the last Sikh Guru.

Until the middle of the twentieth century, the Sikhs largely married within their areas of birth, and Sikhs from each of these areas tended to make fun of the others. The general movement in the past decades and the consequent changes in demography have diluted these geographic differences. The developments in irrigation in the post-British period brought large tracts of sandy land under cultivation that changed the face of the southern Malwa area. In the meantime, the partition of Punjab, and the following population migrations, put pressure on the resources of the northern Majha Sikhs. Beginning in the mid-1960s, the Malwa Sikhs moved to the roles of leadership and for the first time in Sikh history they dominated Sikh politics.

Sikhs migrated overseas from all three areas at different moments in the past century. A large majority kept ties with their places of origin, but by the beginning of the twenty-first century, the area loyalties were no longer central to their thinking. A pilgrimage to Amritsar became the goal that inspired their visits to the Punjab, and purchasing a retirement home in Chandigarh, the territory under the central government, was regarded as more practical than owning a house in their place of origin.

Sikhs living overseas bonded together as a single community. They received special treatment while visiting the Punjab, a favor they reciprocated to Punjabi Sikhs traveling abroad. Expatriate Sikhs served as hosts for traveling Sikh religious leaders and as sources of funds for Punjabi politicians. Sikh families abroad became attractive sources of prospective brides and grooms for families in the Punjab seeking marital matches for their sons or daughters. Preference was given to Sikhs living in certain regions, usually in this order: first, the United States, and then Canada, England, Australia, Singapore, and other areas of the world. Families that had settled in the less prestigious areas of the world would encourage their children to move to the United States, and American Sikhs were often sought for leadership in sorting out issues confronting the expatriate community in other parts of the world.

Sikhs in the Punjab—and to some extent in expatriate communities—are divided along social lines. Although Sikh doctrine rejects the relevance of any caste or class divisions, the community has not been able to entirely eradicate these divisions in the five centuries of its history. The institution of the community kitchen (*langar*), where Sikhs bring food, cook it, and then eat it together, has eliminated restrictions on food sharing among different groups. Restriction on eating together is an important feature of the Hindu caste hierarchy that pervades Indian society. Yet the marriage patterns within the Sikh community generally follow along social lines.

The Jats comprise the largest social group among the Sikhs. They, along with other ancillary farming groups, constitute over 80 percent of the Sikh community. The Jats, nomads in their pre-Sikh history, emerged as the executors of the political vision of establishing Sikh political supremacy in the Punjab and have continued to take keen interest in Sikh politics. Historically they constituted the largest component in the Sikh army, which then became part of the British army. They have established themselves as accomplished farmers. They were instrumental in the Green Revolution in the 1970s, which turned the Punjab into the breadbasket of India. Other farming groups such as the Kambojs, the Arains, and ancillary groups such as the Ramgarhias (carpenters), the Lohars (blacksmiths) have worked closely with the Jats.

The Khatris, the urban trading group, constitute around 6 percent of the Sikh community. Because all the founding Gurus of the Sikh tradition came from this group, the Khatris have historically been considered the Sikh elite and the custodians of its spiritual heritage. As the best-educated group they have frequently served as the spokespersons for the community. They are the only Sikh group that has kept close ties with their counterparts in the Hindu community. Since the Khatris are a highly visible group within Sikh society, outsiders often gather the impression that Khatri customs are normative of all Sikhs and that Hindus and Sikhs maintain close social ties (*roti beti ki sanjh*), which is definitely not the case with the majority group within the Sikh community, the Jats.

Sectarian divisions within the Sikh community have historically originated from differences around the issue of religious authority. The first of these groups emerged in the early history of the Sikh community and was started by those who challenged the lineage of Sikh Gurus. The three primary groups to have emerged from these dissentions are presently based in Guru Harsahai, Kartarpur, and Dehradun. Guru Gobind Singh declared the community as the Khalsa Panth (community of the pure) and thus dissolved the office of the Guru and the personal authority that went with it. The leaders at Guru Harsahai and the Kartarpur groups joined the larger Sikh community in the late eighteenth century but continued their own lineage of leaders. They recognized the authority of the Sikh scriptures, the Adi Granth (original book), but simultaneously served as authoritative figures for their followers. The Deharadun group eventually left the Sikh community to become part of the larger Hindu fold.

Another set of sectarian groups emerged after the death of Guru Gobind Singh in 1708. The leaders of these groups did not challenge the authority of the Adi Granth but asserted their right to interpret the text. In practical terms, the personal authority of these individuals and their right to decide what it meant to be a Sikh was in conflict with the mainstream community's belief that Guru Gobind Singh assigned this role to the community as a whole (Panth). Unlike the earlier leaders who challenged the Gurus, these people challenged the community's right to decide what it meant to be a Sikh.

Baba Dayal (who died in 1853) and Baba Balak Singh (who died in 1862) represented two early attempts to eradicate Sikh beliefs and practices from Hindu accretions. Their activities resulted in the emergence of the Nirankari and the Namdhari sects within the community. The followers of these groups, which remained restricted to a few thousands, came primarily from Khatri and Ramgarhaia groups, respectively. More recently other religious leaders, often known as Sants or Babas, have developed followings and have forged some degree of autonomy from the mainstream community. These groups often fade away after the death of their leaders.

SIKH INSTITUTIONS

While these social and geographical divisions have persisted in the contemporary Sikh community, Sikh institutions have worked well in keeping it together. The Adi Granth serves as the highest religious authority within the community. The belief in it is based on two fundamental assumptions: that its text is revealed and hence immutable and that answers to all religious and moral questions are available within its pages. The language in which it is written—the Punjabi written in Gurmukhi script—has attained the status of a sacred language and script. The text constitutes the center of Sikh devotional and ritual life.

The first compilation of the Sikh sacred text can be traced back to the 1530s. This text contained the compositions of Guru Nanak. It was then expanded to include the compositions of his successors in the Sikh lineage and other religious writers of the time. These included Hindu and Muslim saints whose ideas conformed to Sikh religious and social vision and some poets at the Sikh court in the seventeenth century. The text attained its canonical status as the Adi Granth in the 1680s.

In 1708, Guru Gobind Singh dissolved the office of the personal Guru and vested the authority of Guruship in the book, the Adi Granth, and the Panth. The text was elevated to the status of the Guru Granth Sahib, "the Guru as manifested in the book," and the Sikhs literally became the people of the book. The community was assigned the authority to address issues confronting the Sikhs in the presence of the Adi Granth and reach a consensus, which was then binding on every Sikh. This twin doctrine came to constitute the core of Sikh authority and helped to create the community's identity.

Congregational prayer is central to Sikh worship. Its history goes back to the time of Guru Nanak (1469–1539), the founder of the Sikh community. In early times, the prayer sessions were held at the house of the Guru, *gurdwara*. The Sikhs living away from the Guru's place prayed at the *dharamsal* (place for temporary residence). After Guru Gobind Singh's elevation of the Adi Granth to the office of the Guru, all dharamsals turned into the gurdwaras as the sacred text representing the Guru was installed there.

By the turn of the eighteenth century, the Sikh understanding of sacred space included places associated with the ten Gurus and those where Sikh blood was spilled while fighting for the communal cause. As the gurdwaras were erected on these sites, the Sikhs began to visit these places. The Darbar Sahib (the divine court) at Amritsar emerged as the center of Sikh sacred geography and consequently became the most significant pilgrimage center. Amritsar had been established as the headquarters of Sikh authority during the closing decades of the sixteenth century during the leadership of Guru Ramdas (1574–1582) and Guru Arjan (1582–1606). It became recognized as the center of the Gurus' religio-temporal power (*halemi raj*). In the mid-eighteenth century, the Darbar Sahib served as the site of contestation between the Afghans who wanted to see it destroyed to establish their political supremacy and the Sikhs who rebuilt it in order to symbolize their independence.

The Shiromani Gurdwara Parbandhak Committee (Supreme Gurdwara Management Committee, also known by its initials, the SGPC) is perhaps the most important authority to be housed in the precincts of the Darbar Sahib, Amritsar, in modern times. Brought into existence by a legislative act in 1925, the SGPC is an elected body of the Sikhs created to oversee historical gurdwaras. The Sikh community look up to the SGPC as its central institution and in this status enjoys the authority to decide matters of Sikh religious beliefs and practice. The Akal Takhat (throne of the Immortal), built in the precincts of the Darbar Sahib, was developed as the forum to make public pronouncements deemed obligatory for all Sikhs.

The SGPC has made seminal contributions in two important areas. Working under its auspices Sikh scholars and savants have developed an authoritative statement of the Sikhs' code of conduct (Rahit Marayada). The manuals of rahit were first compiled at the turn of the eighteenth century and were built around three sources of moral authority: the Adi Granth, the activities and the sayings of the Gurus, and the communal consensus on an issue under discussion at any given time. Working within this context, the SGPC published a Sikh code of conduct in 1951, and this manual has successfully guided the community around the matters of belief and practice since then. Beginning in the 1940s the SGPC began creating an authoritative text of the Adi Granth, a task that was still in process in the first decade of the twenty-first century.

SIKH CONCERNS

With a commanding population majority in the Punjab and Sikh institutions discussed above well entrenched, the concerns of Sikhs in the Punjab tend to focus on their political aspirations. Once a Sikh majority state was established in the 1960s, the Akali Dal leadership expected to establish its religiopolitical dominance. The internal differences and the constant interference from the central government did not permit this to happen.

Two opposing positions that emerged were: (1) an acceptance of the existing relationship with the Indian government as a permanent arrangement, or (2) an effort toward the creation of an independent Sikh state. In the 1980s, a Sikh secessionist movement led by Sant Jarnail Singh Bhindranwale (1947–1984) to create Khalistan (Land of the Khalsa) paralyzed the Punjab. The Indian government under Indira Gandhi ordered an attack on the Darbar Sahib, Amritsar, the center of this movement, and the confrontation that followed left several thousand dead and initiated a ten-year period of violence that completely engulfed the state. A degree of normalcy was regained in the mid-1990s. At present, the Akalis under Parkash Singh Badal, have made a sustained effort to establish their nationalist credentials; the vision of an independent Sikh state, however, continues to fire the imagination of a segment of the community.

The community outside the Punjab has been busy creating a religious life that is essentially a replica of what it was in the Punjab. If any changes were made, they were largely cosmetic. The Sikhs abroad, however, are aware that serious decisions will have to be made on certain fundamental issues. It is amply clear that the SGPC authorities do not always understand the reality confronting the Sikhs overseas. Discussions have already started regarding the autonomy of each congregation and questions are asked about the hierarchical model, which has the SGPC at the top. Punjabi, written in Gurumukhi, is the Sikh sacred language, but Sikh children growing up away from the Punjab are often unable to read or understand it. The need to translate the Adi Granth into local languages is acutely felt and use of these translated versions in ritual service is beginning to be attempted. Finally, there is concern with the issue of social practice. For the first time in history, Sikhs have to draw lines between the religious and the cultural aspects of the Sikh heritage. The children growing up away from the Punjab and a small group of Euro-Americans who have joined the Sikh community have brought this distinction to focus. They prefer to follow the Sikh beliefs rather than incorporate cultural aspects in their day-to-day living. In some ways, the Punjabi culture has stifled the growth of Sikh belief in gender and social equality, but the adopted lands offer unique opportunities to allow these beliefs to grow. These decisions will have a lasting impact on the future face of Sikhism, not only in places away but also, owing to processes of rapid globalization and the sharing of Sikh leadership internationally, in the Punjab itself.

BIBLIOGRAPHY

Barrier, N. G., and Dusenbery, V. A., eds. 1989. *The Sikh Diaspora: Migration and the Experience beyond Punjab*. Columbia, Mo.: South Asia Books.

Cole, W. Owen, and Piara Singh Sambhi. 1995. *The Sikhs: Their Religious Beliefs and Practices*. Brighton: Sussex Academic Press.

Grewal, J. S. 1990. *The Sikhs of the Punjab*. New York: Cambridge University Press.

Juergensmeyer, Mark. 2003. *Terror in the Mind of God: The Global Rise of Religious Violence*. Berkeley: University of California Press.

Mann, Gurinder Singh. 2004. *Sikhism*. Upper Saddle River, N.J.: Prentice Hall.

McLeod, Hew. 1998. *Sikhism*. New York: Penguin Books.

Singh, Nikky-Guninder Kaur. 1993. *The Feminine Principle in the Sikh Vision of the Transcendent*. New York: Cambridge University Press.

Oberoi, Harjot. 1994. *The Construction of Religious Boundaries: Culture, Identity and Diversity in the Sikh Tradition*. New Delhi: Oxford University Press.

Tatla, Drashan Singh. 1999. *The Sikh Diaspora: The Search for Statehood*. Seattle: University of Washington Press.

CHAPTER 6

....

THE JAIN COMMUNITY

....

LAWRENCE A. BABB

FROM its inception the Jain religious community has interacted with other forms of religious faith and practice, though unlike Buddhism it did not develop globally until quite recently. Jainism is a South Asian religion that emerged into historical view in the first half of the first millennium BCE. Along with Buddhism, Jainism is the only other surviving example of ancient India's non-Vedic, heterodox traditions.

Nobody knows exactly how many Jains exist. The 1991 Indian Census gives a total of about 3.4 million, but it should be stressed that these census figures are almost certainly low, because many Jains identify themselves as "Hindu" when asked about their religion by census takers. The largest numbers of Jains are found in five Indian states: Gujarat, Karnataka, Madhya Pradesh, Maharashtra, and Rajasthan. Currently the largest overseas Jain populations are found in North America (Canada and the United States) and the United Kingdom. The number of North American Jains has been estimated at about sixty- to one-hundred thousand, and perhaps twenty-five thousand or so live in Britain and the rest of Europe. There was once a substantial immigrant Jain population in East Africa, but most African Jains (together with other groups of Indian origin) were compelled to move elsewhere, mainly to Britain and North America, during the expulsions occurring between 1960 and 1971.

The term *Jain* means one who follows a Jina. A Jina (also known as a Tirthankara) is a "conqueror," which in this context refers to one who has vanquished the desires and aversions that prevent the soul from achieving omniscience and liberation, who did so without assistance, and who teaches the means of liberation to others. Because the Jain cosmos is without beginning or end, an infinite number of these great teachers have already come and gone. However, in our small corner of the universe, and in the present cosmic era, there have been twenty-four of these figures, and of these the most recent was Mahavira, who lived and taught about 2,500 years ago. He and Parsva, the twenty-third in the series, are the only Jinas who left traces detectable by historians. All Jains revere the Jinas and consider their teachings as authoritative.

Jainism shares with other Indic religions a belief in the transmigration of souls and the goal of liberation from the cycle of rebirth, but the tradition also has certain features that, in combination, differentiate Jainism from other Indic religious traditions and endow it with its special character. The most distinctive feature of Jainism is undoubtedly its doctrine of karma as an actual physical substance that adheres to souls and prevents their liberation. Another crucial element in Jainism is its powerful commitment to *ahimsa*, or nonviolence. Other Indic traditions share this ideal, but it is part of the very foundation of Jainism and is extended beyond the animal kingdom to include all forms of life, including plants and microscopic beings. Jainism is noted, too, for the extent and severity of the ascetic practices it promotes. Asceticism is a feature of many Indic traditions, but the Jains are rightly famed for their extraordinary development and elaboration of ascetic techniques, especially fasting.

As idealized within the tradition, the Jain social order is fourfold, encompassing monks and nuns, laymen and laywomen. The monks and nuns are initiated, peripatetic ascetics and comprise a small renouncer elite, whose way of life incorporates the principles of asceticism and nonviolence to the fullest possible extent. They are the custodians and transmitters of the tradition, exemplars of its highest ideals, and are physically completely dependent on laity, on whom they confer teachings, blessings, and merit. Laymen and laywomen, in turn, perform the ordinary chores of life and support the monks and nuns with alms and in other ways. They, too, are expected to adhere to the tradition's strictures of non-violence, but to a lesser degree than initiated ascetics. The requirements of ascetic practice are also less onerous for laity; but even Jain laity, especially laywomen, engage in remarkable feats of ascetic practice.

In contemporary India, Jainism has supported a general pattern of life among its adherents, a identifiable subculture, that is recognized as Jain by Jains themselves and by Indian society at large. This is a way of life that incorporates Jain beliefs and values at various levels and with varying degrees of modification or compromise. Without question the most important element of this way of life, certainly the most conspicuous, is nonviolence, especially as it is manifested in restrictions of diet. Jains are not only strict vegetarians, but they are also forbidden to consume root vegetables (believed to contain multiple souls) and to eat at night (for fear of consuming small forms of life that might fall into the food in the darkness). Because there are other vegetarian groups in Indian society, these rules can be seen as social markers helping to distinguish Jains from other, sub-culturally similar groups.

Jains are generally stereotyped as wealthy merchants, and to some extent this is accurate. Many Jains are indeed traders and merchants, especially in northern and western India where they are extremely prominent within the regional trading and banking class. Some of India's richest merchant families are Jains. It is some-times said that Jains have taken up business because nonviolence prevents them from entering other occupations. Against this, however, it must be said that not all Jains are traders. Although quantitative data are lacking, it is clear that, even in northern India, large numbers of Jains are in the professions or service occu-pations and is likely that a majority of southern Jains are farmers.

Although Jainism possesses a strong historical identity as a religious tradition, and although Jains everywhere participate in a common culture to some degree, the notion of a Jain "community" is highly problematic. The reality of such a community is largely rhetorical, for the Jain world is in fact quite fragmented. There is no single source of religious authority within the Jain world; such au-thority, strictly speaking, is vested in initiated ascetics and nonperipatetic func-tionaries, and these operate entirely within sectarian and subsectarian compart-ments. Nor is there any generally recognized apex organization representing all Jains. Rather, the actual organization of Jainism is based on sectarian, subsectar-ian, regional, local, and caste groups, with which most Jains strongly identify, and within which Jain traditions are socially transmitted and preserved.

The most basic division in the Jain world is a sectarian split over the issue of whether monks should wear clothing. Monks and nuns belonging to the sect known as Svetambara, meaning "white clad," wear white garments. Monks (but not nuns) belonging to the Digambara sect, meaning "space clad," wear nothing. The mutual alienation between these groups is nearly absolute and in some con-texts relations are actually hostile. The separation is partly regional, with the Digambaras prominent in the south and the Svetambaras concentrated especially in western India. But even in areas where they live together, social interaction is limited by the fact that Svetambaras and Digambaras belong to different castes. This means, for example, that intermarriage is normally not possible. In any given locality, the two sects have separate temples, and with the exception of Mahavira's birthday they engage in no common religious observances. The two groups revere many of the same pilgrimage sites, but, as might be expected, this has been a source of rivalry and hostility, not unity. Both groups have evolved permanent organizations dedicated to pursuing litigation about disputed pilgrimage sites, thus guaranteeing the perpetuation of conflict. The Svetambara and Digambara branches are each further subdivided by subsects. These have emerged around such issues as religious leadership, the legitimacy of image worship, and the proper methods of image worship.

The Jain world is also partitioned by caste, but the relationship between Jainism and caste is not simple. In theory, Jain teachings are relevant only to the spiritual aspirations of individuals and thus have nothing whatsoever to do with castes or groups of any other kind. Nonetheless, the Jain tradition accepts the *varna* system (an ancient, idealized social order in which society is divided into four classes: priests, warrior-rulers, agriculturists and merchants, and menial servants). In fact, Jain tradition even insists that all Jinas must belong to the warrior-ruler class, and most Jains consider themselves to belong to the merchant (*Vaisya*) class. However, the varna and caste systems are not the same system, although they are related. The caste system—properly speaking, an order of hierarchically ranked, endogamous groups called *jati*—is not sanctioned by Jainism. But despite this, Jain society is in fact organized into castes that mirror, and in some cases overlap with, the caste divisions of the surrounding Hindu social order.

As is the case with castes generally, Jain castes differ from one region to another. In South India there are castes, poorly known to social science, that are entirely Digambara Jain; the only Svetambaras are recent immigrants. The most prominent castes among North Indian Digambaras are the Agravals and the Khandelvals, both renown trading castes. The Agravals—found in large numbers in Uttar Pradesh, Haryana, Madhya Pradesh, and parts of Rajasthan—are mostly Hindus with a Jain minority. Intermarriage between Jain and Hindu Agravals occurs freely. The Khandelval Jains—especially prevalent in M.P. and parts of Rajasthan—are apparently all Digambara Jains; currently they have no relationship at all with Khandelval Hindus, and are thus an independent, endogamous caste. There are likewise several castes among Svetambara Jains. Two of the most prominent are the Osvals and the Srimals (or Srimalis). Found mainly in Gujarat and Rajasthan, these are also famous trading castes; they include Hindus as well as Jains, and interreligious marriage is common.

The contemporary social and religious identity of Jains is an ambiguous matter that continues to evolve and to be the subject of debate among Jains themselves. The dominant religion of India is Hinduism, and a vexed question is whether or to what degree Jainism is an extension or part of Hinduism. In a strict sense, Jainism cannot be said to be a form of Hinduism. When Jainism first appeared, what is now called Hinduism did not yet exist. Furthermore, Jainism has always opposed the Vedic orthodoxy that remains a part of the Hindu mix. Nonetheless, many Jains do not sharply differentiate themselves from Hindus. It is not in the least unusual for Jains to worship Hindu deities in Hindu temples, and Jain temple liturgy has borrowed much from Hindu ritual culture. Moreover, significant numbers of Jains identify deeply with the political goals and aspirations of those who are called "Hindu nationalists."

In considering the relationship between Jainism and Hinduism, it must be remembered that Hinduism itself—and thus Hindu identity—is largely a modern concept that has yet to achieve complete clarity. To the degree that Jain and Hindu identity are mutually implicated, the clarification of Jain identity must await the full sorting out of the religious, social, and political dimensions of Hindu identity and, indeed, Indian citizenship.

Leaving aside nagging questions of identity, the vast changes that have occurred in post-Independence India have of course affected Jains deeply but for the most part in ways that have less to do with Jainism than with the social and economic classes to which Jains generally belong. Jains are generally well off by Indian standards and have therefore been able to benefit from the economic and political trends favorable to the growing Indian middle and upper-middle classes. As have all Indians, Jains have had to come to terms with various developments and issues usually attributed to modernization and/or Westernization: the erosion of caste-endogamy and other marriage rules, excessive dowry and marriage expenditures, the alleged decline in moral standards, intergenerational strains of various sorts, and so on. The limitation of marriage-related expenses has been a special concern shared by Jain and non-Jain business communities, and this has generated a recent vogue for low-expense group marriages.

A few specific issues have been pushed to the fore by twentieth-century reform movements among Jains. These include such matters as temple use by lower status Jains, the printing of Jain scriptures (favored by progressives and opposed by conservatives because of the potential for disrespectful treatment of easily available copies), child initiation (a perennial issue that regained prominence in the late 1990s), and the propagation of Jain marriage rites (as opposed to the commonly utilized Hindu rites). Although intercaste marriage is increasingly common among Jains, at the time of this writing it remains a difficult issue for some, and a nationally important Digambara organization continues formally to oppose it.

It seems likely that the greatest contemporary challenge to Jainism is not in India but in overseas Indian communities. Jains are an enterprising people, and because of the success of Jains abroad, Jainism clearly has a cosmopolitan future. Overseas Jains, however, are still in the process of discovering what the outlines of this future will be. They have had to confront the usual and predictable deviation of immigrant children from the customs and expectations of their parents. But they also face a more basic problem, which is that Jain traditions are not easily exportable from India. In dramatic contrast to Buddhism, Jainism failed, until quite recently, to sink any roots outside India. The difficulty is ascetic discipline; the commitment to nonviolence prevents Jain monks and nuns from using any means of transportation other than their own unshod feet, and for this reason they normally cannot travel outside the Indian subcontinent. Because monks and nuns are crucial to the transmission of the tradition, this has meant that Jains have faced special difficulties in maintaining their religion abroad. For example, there appears to have been significant diminution of traditional ceremonial life and lay ascetic practice outside of India. This fact is probably directly attributable to the absence of ascetics, whose exhortations are important factors in the maintenance of these patterns in India.

But Jains and Jain traditions have also adjusted and adapted. The consecration of new Jain temples outside India continues apace. There is also some evidence of doctrinal changes in Jainism abroad in the direction of more streamlined, theistic, and modernistic-seeming beliefs (such as health-based justifications for vegetarianism). Finally, sectarian, regional, and caste divisions are present, but are generally less pronounced than in India (Digambaras are, in fact, only a small minority among overseas Jains). The reduction of sectarian divisiveness may be a positive byproduct of the absence of ascetics.

Obviously the future of Jainism abroad will belong to those Jain sects that have either found ways of sending ascetic specialists to overseas Jain communities or that have managed successfully to represent and propagate the tradition in the absence of initiated ascetics. Some Svetambara ascetics or semi-ascetics have begun to travel abroad. No Digambara monk has yet left India, and it seems unlikely that this will ever occur, but other types of Digambara religious leaders have made the journey. A twentieth-century sect known as the Kanji Svami Panth—a movement that was begun by a Svetambara Jain, that calls itself Digambara, and that downplays ritual and the role of ascetics—probably has a very bright future abroad.

BIBLIOGRAPHY

Babb, Lawrence A. 1996. *Absent Lord: Ascetics and Kings in a Jain Ritual Culture.* Berkeley: University of California Press.

Banks, Marcus. 1992. *Organizing Jainism in India and England.* Oxford: Oxford University Press.

Dundas, Paul. 1992. *The Jains.* London: Routledge.

Carrithers, Michael, and Caroline Humphrey. 1991. *The Assembly of Listeners: Jains in Society.* Cambridge: Cambridge University Press.

Cort, John. 2001. *Jains in the World: Religious Values and Ideology in India.* New York: Oxford University Press.

Jaini, Padmanabh S. 1979. *The Jaina Path of Purification.* Berkeley: University of California Press.

Kumar, Bhuvanendra. 1996. *Jainism in America.* Mississauga (Ontario): Jain Humanities Press.

Laidlaw, James. 1995. *Riches and Renunciation: Religion, Economy, and Society among the Jains.* Oxford: Oxford University Press.

Sangave. Vilas A. 1980. *Jaina Community: A Social Survey.* Second Revised Edition. Bombay: Popular Prakashan.

CHAPTER 7

....

HINDU COMMUNITIES
ABROAD

....

VASUDHA NARAYANAN

For more than two thousand years Hindu communities have flourished outside the subcontinent of India. The largest and most sustained communities in the first millennium of the Common Era (CE) have been in Southeast Asia, and in the latter half of the second millennium, in Africa, the Caribbean, England, and northern America.

HISTORICAL CONTEXT

....

Despite the prohibitions against traveling across the ocean found in many Hindu texts, Indians settled in Malaysia and Singapore probably before the first millennium CE. Trading communities seem to have been set up in Cambodia by the first century CE. The kingdom of Funan, established around 200 CE, supposedly by a Brahman from India, flourished for over four hundred years. Waves of Indian immigration followed, primarily from the east coast of India and especially from the southern states. By the first millennium, the lands corresponding to Vietnam (Champa), Cambodia (Kambuja), parts of Thailand, and Indonesia were inhabited by Hindu communities. While most of the earlier settlers were traders, in time, with the arrival of some Brahman ritual specialists, the ruling classes were

"Brahmanized." Hindu and Buddhist communities existed in relative harmony and kings from both traditions are to be seen in these places.

In the nineteenth century, indentured workers arrived in Fiji and in the Caribbean. By the time indentured labor was abolished in 1919, there were more than sixty thousand Indians in Fiji. Hindus, who had come to work on plantations, settled in Uganda and other African countries in the early twentieth century and eventually became successful business entrepreneurs. The Hindu communities in these places reflect the culture and ethnic sensibilities of where they came from in India. Thus, we find a largely Tamil population in Singapore, Malaysia, Fiji, and Sri Lanka; Gujarati communities in East Africa, Punjabi, and England; and so on. In some places like Guyana, the distinctions relating to the places of origin in India linger, sometimes in an idiosyncratic way. In the United States there are "Tamil" groups and "Hindu" groups; the former refers to Tamil-speaking Hindus and the latter to the immigrants from northern India.

Hindu Communities in the United States

While Hindu and Sikh immigrants from the Punjab area settled on the west coast of North America in the beginning of the twentieth century, it was after the loosening of immigration laws in 1965 that the major waves of professional Hindus began to settle in the United States. Immigrants in the United States are from almost every state, linguistic, and religious community in India. The Asian Indian population in the United States, in the beginning of the twenty-first century, is estimated as upward of 1.2 million, with a very high percentage being Hindu.

Many kinds of Hindu communities exist in the United States. There are groups associated with temples or institutions with an explicit religious identity. There are also Indian groups that rely on other criteria like language for their cohesion but that end up having primarily Hindu constituencies. Examples of the latter include groups like TANA (Telugu Association of North America), Tamil Sangam (Tamil Society), Kannada Koota (The Kannada group), The Gujarati Samaj (The Gujarati Society), and ATA (American Telugu Association). While these groups are based on language identity, most of the people who belong to them (with the exception of the Malayali and Tamil associations, which have healthy Christian minorities) are Hindu. These communities meet regularly and have annual events, which in some cases like ATA, involve a turnover in the millions of dollars and are attended by several thousand people. These celebrations include programs with classical and semiclassical dances, popular cinema, visits by movie stars and political officials (in some cases the two categories coincide), clothing and jewelry exhibits and sales, and continuing medical education courses to attract physicians. Apart from language-based groups, there are other Indian associations that have predominantly Hindu members in America. Many of these are based on professional ties such as the American Physicians of Indian Origin, which wields considerable economic and, now, political clout.

Hindu communities in America can be divided into those that are connected with a temple and those that are based on a group with a specific theological orientation and/or social identity, like the Bochasanwasi Akshar Purushottam Sanstha (BAPS) movement of the Swaminarayan tradition in India. In discussing Hindu communities in this country, we will first focus on the centrality of temples and then attempt a taxonomy of the Hindu institutions. Finally, we will consider the creation of Hindu communities on the Internet that speak broadly to the category of transnational religion.

BUILDING TEMPLES

Perhaps the most noticeable feature of Hindu communities that settled outside of India is the tremendous time, monies, and energy expended on the building of temples. The Mi Son temple in Champa (Vietnam) was rebuilt in the early seventh century after fire had destroyed the earlier shrine. The Prambanan temples of Java (Indonesia) built around the ninth century and the Angkor Wat Temple (c. twelfth century CE) are the best-known examples of Hindu architecture overseas. These temples tell us that the Hindus who built them were devotees of the gods Siva or Vishnu. From the architecture and inscriptions on them we understand that there was regular contact with India but that local forms of art had also found their way into the building enterprises. Contact with India with regular influxes of ritual specialists, builders, and traders as well as integration with local traditions seem characteristic of the Hindu colonies in Cambodia, Vietnam, and Java.

The major royal endowments in the late ninth century in Cambodia seem to have favored the creation of many Hindu *ashramas* (monasteries and study centers). These centers were attached to a temple and headed by an abbot (*kuladhyaksa*) who, apart from following the many rules incumbent on his monastic institution and the law books of dharma, also distributed food, medicine, and other necessities to those who needed it in the community. About a hundred of these ashramas were set up in the late ninth century alone by King Yashovarman, knitting together a larger Hindu population along sectarian lines of Shaiva (wor-shipers of Shiva), Vaishnava (devotees of Vishnu) with Brahman ritual specialists, and Buddha worshippers.

The kings' patronage of large temples in Southeast Asia made them centers of piety and power, controlling large tracts of land, water storage units, and in charge of monetary and water distribution. In contrast to the temples set up in the first millennium, Hindu temples in Canada and the United States in the second millennium that attract devotees of South Asian origin have largely been built through the combined efforts of many sectarian groups and traditions. While smaller towns in the United States and Canada can only afford to build one community temple, larger cities like Chicago or Atlanta have between eight to twelve in the metropolitan area. New York, New Jersey, and the Bay area have large Hindu communities with more than a dozen temples in each place. The temples form the center for people from either (1) a particular sectarian group from India (like the Swaminarayan); (2) a larger cultural area whose people share a common idiom of worship (like the Hindu temple of Atlanta, which attracts South Indians primarily from the states of Andra Pradesh, Tamilnadu, and Kar-nataka); or (3) a linguistic group with a particular devotional focus (like the Shakti Mandir in Atlanta that is the center for devotees who speak the Gujarati language and who worship the Mother Goddess in various forms).

When a Hindu community decides to build the first temple in a city or town, tensions mount on questions of sectarian affiliation, which deity is to be en-shrined, and proposed styles and modes of worship. It is in this context that there is greatest fragmentation among the sectarian communities. Devotees of Vishnu, Shiva, the Goddess, Ganesha, or those who worship Vishnu as Rama or Krishna want the temple to be primarily dedicated to that deity. The temple which, is meant to unite the Hindu communities in diaspora, frequently becomes the cause for divisions. The reason is clear: there is no single, monolithic Hindu community and because there are many communities (*sampradaya*) and many traditions and thus a consensus is almost impossible. Lines are drawn along sectarian, caste, and regional lines, and the debates continue, as they have throughout the history of the tradition. In the larger towns the sectarian groups sometimes have a large enough population base to build a temple just for themselves.

It is clear then that in addition to being a center for individual piety, temples set up by Hindus from India serve as large community halls for the local popu-lation. These temples function as institutions that have self-consciously under-taken the role of educating the younger generation of Hindus born in the United States, through weekly language and religion classes; frequent religious discourses; teaching of classical music and dances (which have a broad religious base in India); and through summer camps. Regular newsletters and updated Web pages provide an outreach function. New temples are rising up all over the American landscape and in many cases the community hall is being built even before the shrine. This is understandable in a situation where members of the Hindu tradition are trying assert their identity in the midst of a larger society in which they feel marginalized and disenfranchised culturally and linguistically. The community hall is a place where different Hindu groups can meet and enjoy their own language, music, and dance, and celebrate the many festivals of the religious calendar.

COMMUNITY ACTIVITIES

While there are many differences in architecture and modes of worship, there are at least two common elements in the temples set up by many of these Hindu communities of Indian origin. In most cases the temples focus primarily on devotional practices, as opposed to meditational or yogic exercises. Second, many of them—whether they are located in Fiji, Mauritius, or America—sponsor either regular classes or programs involving various forms of classical Indian dance like Bharata Natyam. This dance form has become one of the main ways of transmitting Hindu culture to the younger generation of girls in the diaspora. The performing arts are, of course, central to many Hindu traditions, and both the form and content have religious significance. Learning the dance forms and performing them in public events and during festival days, therefore, becomes one main avenue for young girls to participate in the larger Hindu community.

In addition to activities of worship and performing arts, many temple communities with Indian Hindus also have service, or humanitarian, programs through which they connect with the larger Judeo-Christian American community. Many of the communities organize blood drives through the temples—an act that is unusual, given the polluting quality of blood in the Hindu tradition. The Atlanta Swaminarayan Temple and the Hindu Temple of Atlanta both participate in food drives in the city and have in successive years been the institutions to donate the most food among participating local charities. Other outreach activities may involve working with Christian organizations: members from the Hindu Temple of Atlanta work in the soup kitchens of the Atlanta Union Mission, an evangelical institution, on weekends close to Hindu festivals like Sankaranti; devotees from the Kalamazoo Temple community work with Gospel Kitchens providing food for the homeless during Thanksgiving, and so on. One way to understand Hindu communities is through their activities, whether the temples they belong to are primarily devotional, meditational, or service oriented.

OTHER COMMUNITIES

Apart from the temple communities consisting of Hindus from India (and sometimes Sri Lanka, as in the Ganesha Temple in Bayview, near Toronto), there are Hindu groups whose members are primarily of West European descent. These are sometimes devotional in nature and revere a founding teacher as well as Hindu deities. Well-known examples are the International Society for Krishna Consciousness (more popularly known as the Hare Krishnas) founded in 1966 by Sri Bhaktivedanta Prabhupada (1896–1977) and the International Society of Divine Love (ISDL). The ISDL is located in a beautiful large temple built in the center of 230 acres and is dedicated to the "divine cowherd" (Krishna). Ironically, it is right in the middle of ranch country, near Austin, Texas. Many others like the Self-Realization Fellowship, founded by Swami Yogananda (1893–1952, best known for his *Autobiography of a Yogi*), focus on yoga and meditation and attract Hindus from India as well as westerners. Movements like Transcendental Meditation, started by Maharishi Mahesh Yogi (b. 1911) have initiated millions of members, but the focus is more on individual meditation rather than community activities; there is also some ambiguity about whether the members want to be identified as being part of a Hindu community.

In sharp contrast to Hindu communities in the Americas and Western Europe that enjoy freedom of worship, minority communities in some countries either feel openly discriminated against or are prohibited from gathering for religious reasons at a public place of worship. These communities frequently gather in private homes for celebration of Hindu festivals and sometimes spend a great deal of time downloading religious music, chanting, and texts from the Internet. Others air their pain and problems through mass dissemination of e-mails and through Web pages, and some link with people of the same sectarian persuasion across the globe through e-mail listservs.

DESIGNER COMMUNITIES IN CYBERSPACE

Just as the Hindu tradition appropriated and utilized print and audiovisual technologies, the Internet revolution has also been used to help articulate traditions and create communities. The Internet and the availability of e-mail networks have had a tremendous impact on the transmission of the Hindu tradition and creation of cyber and physical communities worldwide. Tens of thousands of Hindus are in the software business in India and in America and have been enterprising in using the technology to learn more about their particular *sampradaya,* or traditional community. Hindus have also used the technology to connect with other members of their particular subcaste and community around the world. The result is that many Hindu traditions are global and transnational in a way that they have never been before. From the creation of cyber communities of Hindu subcastes to software with cyber worship of Ganesha, which clicks into place when the computer is turned on, the technology is transforming the dissemination of Hindu culture and rituals. One may say that because of this technology, more middle-class urban Hindus who may have had only a desultory and cursory understanding of their tradition now have a broader and deeper knowledge and are linked with other members of their subcaste or their subcommunity, or with people who follow a particular teacher, guru, or *acharya* (traditional teacher who is from a lineage established in the past).

The dissemination of information in a speedy and accessible manner has made Hindus pro-active in their efforts to understand theological doctrines and participate in ritual actions. The circulation of information results in Hindus getting in touch with their traditional teachers, reading about and then supporting activities in temples in their ancestral villages India as well as those in their own vicinity. The gurus, leaders of diaspora temples, and traditional teachers of the various Hindu theological lineages have all set up Web pages to create communities for their adherents. Sometimes, the adherents set up Web pages in honor of their teacher. If one considers the Sri Vaishnava community of Hinduism, for example, there is not just one Web page for the tradition as a whole but many Web pages for the various subcommunities and groups that follow a specific lineage of teachers, as well as a plethora of e-mail listservs to connect Sri Vaishnava devotees of various institutional affiliations. Thus, the trend in diaspora temples, which had been moving in the direction of creating a generic, nonsectarian Hinduism (with many deities in one place of worship), is now reversed through Web pages and listservs creating groups that are set up by and for adherents of a particular teacher belonging to a particular lineage, leading to the formation of *a designer Hindu cyber community*. Further, the proliferation of listservs for specific communities and the creation of cyber communities of sectarian denominations seems to reverse the trend toward a generic, nonsectarian Hinduism that we see in the building of temples in Canada and the United States. The rather casual and easygoing relationship that one had to these teachers or lineages in the past is being transformed into closer ties. Articulation of these relationships and the connections of traditional texts in ritual contexts further encourages others to participate in the same structures.

Web pages for gurus are the most copious, and adherents of popular teachers like Sathya Sai Baba have set up dozens of pages in their honor. There are hundreds of Web pages devoted to gurus listing their itineraries; discussing their teachings, thoughts, and sayings for the day; accounts of miracles; and participation in educational and charitable enterprises. Local chapters of devotees for popular teachers like Sathya Sai Baba or women's gurus like Ammachi are also listed by Internet services leading to the formation of small congregations that meet regularly to sing devotional songs and share stories and teachings.

E-mail listservs also create a community of people who may have the same beliefs but who are spread out geographically all over the world. Some listservs address all Hindus; others focus on specific groups like the philosophical advaita tradition, the Madhva tradition, or the Sri Vaishnava tradition. Still others are more narrow and focus, for instance, on the Vadakalai subcommunity of the Sri Vaishnava tradition, or the disciples of one particular teacher within this sectarian community. These members also participate in e-journals to circulate information like the celebration of traditional birthdays of teachers, ritual fasting days, and so forth. This knowledge seems to lead, at least from what can be gleaned from e-mail listservs, to increased participation in community institutions like temples and community gatherings in private homes in areas where there are no temples.

Although there is a veritable flood of information available through the Net, some traditional safe restraints are self-imposed and observed. Thus, in some e-mail discussion groups, members may self-consciously refrain from explaining "secret" or esoteric mantras and say that such expositions are only proper within the context of a personal teacher-spiritual aspirant relationship.

Hindu communities outside the subcontinent, therefore, can be classified broadly as those that focus *primarily* on devotion, meditation, or service. They frequently emphasize devotion to a deity or teacher and these ties frequently form a major part of the groups' cohesion. While the communities in Southeast Asia in the first millennium CE were part of a society where royal patronage was a major factor in the creation of centers for worship, since the nineteenth century, it is through combined community resources that all temples have been built and maintained in the diaspora. Many of the diaspora temples in America tend to be nonsectarian in nature; however, the creation of designer-cyber communities reverses this trend and emphasizes the formation of specific sectarian groups.

BIBLIOGRAPHY

Kurien, Prema. 1998. "Becoming American by Becoming Hindu: Indian Americans Take Their Place at the Multicultural Table." In *Gatherings in Diaspora: Religious Communities and the New Immigration*. Eds. R. Stephen Warner and Judith G. Wittner. Philadelphia: Temple University Press.

Leonard, Karen Isaksen. 1997. *The South Asian Americans*. Westport, Conn.: Greenwood Press.

Llewellyn, J. E. 1999. "The Arya Samaj in America: The Legacy of the Hindu Renaissance

Outside India." Paper presented at Annual Meeting of American Academy of Religion.

Majumdar, R. C. 1980. *Kambuja-Desa or An Ancient Hindu Colony in Cambodia*. Philadelphia: ISHI.

Narayanan, Vasudha. 1992. "Creating the South Indian 'Hindu' Experience in the United States." In *A Sacred Thread: Modern Transmissions of Hindu Traditions in India and Abroad*. Ed. Raymond Williams. Chambersburg: Anima Press. Distributed by Columbia University Press.

Sharma, J. C. 1997. *Hindu Temples in Vietnam*. India: Sankalp Publications India.

Wilson, Boyd H., and Jami Becksvoort. 1999. "Gopurams Over Georgia: Why Here? Why Now?" In *Hindu Diaspora: Global Perspectives*. Ed. T. S. Rukmani, 329–348. Montreal: Concordia University Press.

PART II

BUDDHIST/ CONFUCIAN CULTURAL REGION

CHAPTER 8

THINKING GLOBALLY
ABOUT BUDDHISM

GANANATH OBEYESEKERE

BUDDHISM, like other religions of salvation, has had two forms of global outreach. First, through its long history in South, Southeast, East, and Central Asia, Buddhism has incorporated village and perhaps even local tribal communities into its fold. In this sense it is very much in the spirit of other salvation religions with a universalistic vision, such as Christianity and Islam. This process was aided when kings became Buddhists, following the example of the model king Asoka who, at least in the self-conceptions of Buddhists, initiated a Buddhist state in India. Wherever Buddhism was established, either with royal patronage or without it, Buddhism was visibly present through its monks, monasteries, temples, and symbols of the Buddha's presence, such as the bodhi tree, stupas where relics were enshrined, and pilgrimage centers where Buddhists from different parts of the larger state or nation could congregate and give expression to a larger translocal sense of communal consciousness. When Buddhist kingdoms were established in South and Southeast Asia in particular, the idea of the *sāsana* took on a purely local meaning as the religion of the "nation," as it were. *Sāsana* can be glossed as the "dispensation of the Buddha" or the "Buddhist church" in the Durkheimian sense as the community of the faithful and the beliefs and symbols associated with an imagined sense of communal unity. Ordinary Buddhists continue to use the term *sāsana* alongside the other term *Buddhāgama* or "Buddhism" as I will also do in this chapter. The term *Buddhism* is a Western neologism that has come to stay and, like the sister term *Hinduism*, has become indigenized such that people will say today they belong to the *Buddhāgama* or the "religion of the

Buddha," (*agama*, which literally means tradition, but has become a modern rendering of the European term *religion*). Though it is impossible in contemporary discourse to do away with Buddhism (and religion) it is important to remember that the traditional rendering of that idea was *Buddhāsana*.

In addition to nation, another meaning of sāsana is in the true spirit of the founder; and is the second form of Buddhism's translocal, indeed global, outreach. This meaning of sāsana is the large Buddhist order that knows no ethnic or national bounds and represents the universal Buddhist church, if one may use that phrase. For ordinary Buddhists, the sāsana simply meant the Buddhism of their nation; but even ordinary Buddhists knew that Buddhism's home was in India and most Buddhist elites in both Mahayana and Theravada were aware of the larger meanings of sāsana that transcended the physical bounds of one's nation or speech community. Throughout Buddhist history pilgrim monks traveled to parts of the then-known Buddhist world. This double meaning of sāsana is true to the idea of a church in other universal religions also. One cannot understand globalization in relation to Buddhism without bearing in mind the interplay of the two meanings of sāsana and that both meanings, in their differing ways, have a translocal significance.

However much one might disagree with Karl Jaspers regarding the term *Axial* and his idea of periodization of Axial Age religions, he was right in seeing religions like Buddhism, Islam, and Christianity as having a transcendental and universalizing vision which then informed their missionary activity. Though they were universal religions they were not world religions in any obvious sense. Buddhism did not penetrate fully even the then-known world of Asia; and neither did Islam. It was with the discovery of the new world and European imperialism that one universal religion, Christianity, began to take root in virtually every part of the world and in this sense it becomes the first world religion, and perhaps remains the only one. Islam expanded with trade but it also constituted a colonial penetration to some degree, though it was not associated with the implantation of religion in the new worlds opened up by the European voyages of discovery and imperial expansion. But the expansion of Christianity came up with an inescapable dark side; it was inextricably tainted with colonialism and the appalling cruelties associated with imperial conquest, something it has never been able to shed to this very day. I am suggesting that globalization provides a means for Buddhism, if not Islam, to penetrate our world in somewhat limited ways but without the shadow of colonialism. But insofar as globalization is the contemporary manifestation of capitalism's world expansion, one must see the beginnings of Buddhist penetration into Europe and America (but certainly not the world) in historical terms.

BUDDHISM AND THE EUROPEAN
ENLIGHTENMENT

Buddhism was known to Europe superficially for a long time, but it was in the eighteenth and nineteenth centuries that its impact was felt on the popular level as European romanticism's Other (in a favorable sense) and (less favorably) as the philosopher's Other (notably Hegel's). What influenced Europe powerfully was *The World As Will and Representation* by Arthur Schopenhauer (1788–1860) who used Buddhism and Vedanta as a foil to what he believed was the soteriological bankruptcy of both the Judeo-Christian tradition and Enlightenment notions of rationality. Schopenhauer was interested in Vedanta and Buddhism equally, though his appropriation of Buddhism was perhaps closer to the spirit of Buddhism than his Vedanta. Halbfass puts it well in saying that Schopenhauer "showed an unprecedented readiness to integrate Indian ideas into his own, European thinking and self-understanding, and utilize them for the illustration, articulation and clarification of his own teachings and problems" (1990: 120). Halbfass goes on to say that Schopenhauer used these concepts to mount "a radical critique of some of the most fundamental propositions of the Judaeo-Christian tradition, such as the notions of a personal God and the uniqueness of the human individual and the meaning of history" while retaining "the modern Western belief in the powers of the intellect, rationality, planning and progress"(1990: 120). At times he referred to his few followers as "we Buddhists" (Kantowsky 1995: 103).

It is hard to imagine how Europe could do otherwise than appropriate Buddhism into its own scheme of things, however different such schemes might well be. The major scholarly translations of Buddhist texts and pioneer Buddhist scholars whose work influenced twentieth-century notions of Buddhism appeared after Schopenhauer in the later nineteenth century: they were figures like Herman Oldenburg, Max Muller, Sylvain Levi, La Vallee Poussin, Rhys Davids, E. J. Thomas, and more recent scholars like Etienne Lamotte. Though the early research was focused on both Mahayana and Theravada, the latter received a boost from the founding and publication of the Pali Text Society by Rhys Davids in 1881, which soon furnished reasonable translations of virtually all Buddhist texts of the Theravada canon.

There may, however, have been a hidden agenda to nineteenth-century Europeans engaged in Buddhist studies. Because the work of these great European Buddhist scholars took place in the wake of Darwinism and the death of God, Buddhism stood out as a religion that did not need a god and a doctrine of creation that went counter to the scientific rationality of that century. Buddhism became a religion without a god, a kind of "non-theistic religion," as von Glasenapp (1970) put it, and in this sense it was consonant with Europe's own Enlightenment. Much of this was true; but it did place the well-known Buddhist ideas of the miraculous birth of the Buddha, the signs of the great man that he displayed, his discourses on heaven and hell, and virtually all of the Buddhist mythos as alien to its true spirit. Thus, one of the most fascinating of Buddhist texts, the *Janavasabha Sutta*, which deals with the Buddha's shamanic-like powers were ignored, or pejoratively labeled, as Rhys Davids did, as an interesting "fairy tale." So were the great popular traditions of the Buddha's past births or *jatakas*. Most significantly the Buddha's own powerful experience under the bodhi tree was rendered as the "Enlightenment," rather than an "Awakening." In doing so this neglects awakenings that were both physical (after suffering a symbolic death owing to the ascetic starvation practices he performed) and spiritual (when he becomes the "fully Awakened One" after the discovery of Buddhist truths through his state of deep meditative trance). I believe that the conscious or unconscious choice of the term *Enlightenment* helped promote Buddhism's consonance with Europe's own Enlightenment and hastened the process where the sāsana became Buddh-*ism*, a systematic, unmetaphysical, and rational religion opposed to the unscientific burden (and even perhaps the colonialist cross) that Christianity had to bear.

For Theravada scholars the great traditions of Mahayana were tissues of irrational magical accretions comparable to the very few in the Theravada tradition already listed earlier as practices "alien to its true spirit." Theravada Buddhism as formulated by Indologists then had an appeal to a European audience—though as a foil to Christianity. The circle that Buddhism influenced was still a very restricted one, at least in the late nineteenth and early twentieth centuries. The change came with the embrace of both Theravada and Mahayana (as well as forms of Hinduism) by one of the most popular intellectual movements of the late nineteenth century, Theosophy.

THEOSOPHY: RATIONAL BUDDHISM AND MAGICAL MAHAYANA

The impact of Theosophy on the traditional worlds of Buddhism and Hinduism is only beginning to be understood, though the history of the Theosophical Society is well known. The society was formed in 1875 in New York, cofounded by H. P. Blavatsky, Colonel Henry Steel Olcott, and William Q. Judge (Prothero 1996). It was the heir to European and American Spiritualism even though formally opposed to it. Theosophy claimed to be "scientific" and it is no surprise that many scientists (one of the most eminent being Thomas Edison) were members. Early Theosophy believed in the powers of forces known as elementals. To this idea was soon added a more important one, that of Mahatmas or Masters (or Adepts) who lived in the Himalayas but could manifest themselves in their apparitional forms to specially gifted Theosophists, Olcott included. Olcott had one Mahatma known as Koot Hoomi or KH who appeared before him during crises and helped him resolve them, very much like spirit helpers in other religions. Though Olcott became a Buddhist rationalist later on, and was critical of Blavatsky's occult powers, he never gave up his belief in Mahatmas.

From our point of view the crucial event for Theosophists was the debates between Christians and Buddhists between 1865–73 in Sri Lanka which Olcott and Blavatsky heard about. They decided to join forces with Buddhists and arrived in Sri Lanka on May 17, 1880, to a spectacular welcome and formally adopted the Buddhist faith with the public recital of the Five Precepts. Elsewhere I have described at length the later development of the Theosophical Society and I shall here summarize the key events (Obeyesekere 1991: 219–39; 1995: 32–71). Though the two Theosophists decided to establish the society's headquarters in Adyar (Madras), Olcott paid several visits to Sri Lanka, taking upon himself the task of resuscitating Buddhism in that nation. He founded the Buddhist Theosophical Society; soon it established a network of schools totaling 103 in 1898, modeled on the missionary ones, some equal to the best of them.

Olcott railed against the fact that Buddhism had taken over Hindu practices, undermining Buddhism's rationality. With the aid of learned Buddhist monks he soon formulated *The Buddhist Catechism* (1881), a distillation of the essence of his rationalist doctrine and a vehicle for educating "our children" about the true Buddhism uncontaminated by "superstition." Initially, Olcott wanted to introduce Vedantic ideas of *atman* (Self) and Theosophist ideas of Mahatmas into Buddhism but the monks would have none of it. The *Catechism* was translated into twenty languages and went into forty editions in his own lifetime. It seems then that Olcott himself, in his relationship with learned monks and through his voluminous reading of Buddhist texts, came to *learn* Theravada Buddhism, but from a Eurorational viewpoint. Olcott's catechistic dictum that Buddhism was a philosophy and not a creed has been adopted virtually as axiomatic by Buddhist intellectuals. Spurred by Olcott's example, a group of prominent Buddhists developed the Buddhist flag that soon became a visible symbol of pan-Buddhist unity and ecumenicalism everywhere. Few are aware of its recent origins.

While Olcott was becoming more and more Buddhist, his colleague and friend Blavatsky was becoming more committed to her own brand of occultism, which one could label as magical Vajrayana. Blavatsky's occult powers were well known through the popular English press in India. Her powers were impressive: she could materialize objects, produce telepathic messages (much like faxes), create illusory palaces, and produce flowers from seemingly nowhere. Some of her writings, she claimed, were not products of her direct authorship but that of Mahatmas. By contrast, Olcott, in spite of Mahatmas and spirit healing, was a product of the Enlightenment, continuing the Enlightenment's self-imaginings of rationality, unable to see what Peter Gay calls its "rationalistic myopia" (Gay 1968: 83). Blavatsky was not; her's was a more eclectic vision compounded of both Eastern and Western mysticism and hermetic thought. She was a prophetess full of crazy and brilliant insights but by no means given to experimental validation or conceptual systematization, though she did believe that her powers were rooted in a deeper science ("wisdom religion," "transcendental philosophy") that had yet to await its realization. If Olcott popularized a Eurorational view of Buddhism, Blavatsky's influence was quite different. Its effect was more on the Hindu consciousness, creating a space for a certain class of modern gurus and saviors to emerge into prominence, especially those who learned to validate their charisma by materializing objects. The precedent for these public displays of occult powers is Blavatsky's because, as Olcott contemptuously pointed out, such forms of occultism were contrary to the spirit of both Vedanta and Buddhism. When Olcott and Blavatsky met Vedantic gurus and asked them to display their knowledge of "phenomena," they were told that such displays were the popular arts of the marketplace and had no relevance for salvation.

The contributions of Olcott and Blavatsky can be put in another perspective. Whether or not they directly influenced the many Buddhisms of the West, they exemplified two important strands in the exported Buddhism: one that found Buddhism consonant with the European Enlightenment and the other that stood diametrically opposed to it. Regarding the former, Martin Baumann says insightfully of Europeans, prior to the nineteen sixties: "Buddhism [in Germany and Europe in general] was praised as a scientific and analytical religion which did not contradict the findings of modern science." Rather, Baumann claimed, "it confirmed the results of modern biology or physics and thus amounted to the religion of the modern age" (Baumann 1995: 82). Parallel with this orientation is a selective return to the Pali Canon to restore the original teachings of the Buddha without resorting to cosmology and metaphysics. For much of Europe this purified Buddhism, according to Baumann, could be seen as a form of "Protestant Buddhism," a term that was invented by me to designate the absorption by Buddhists in the late nineteenth century of colonial and Protestant values. By contrast Blavatsky's teachings were fundamentally concerned with cosmology and metaphysics. As a founding figure of the later counterculture and New Age religions, her work expectably extolled the enchanted world of magic, astrology, popular notions of karma and rebirth and mysticism (defined as the production of "phenomena") (Hanegraaff, 1996).

Globalization, Diasporas, and the Institution of Meditative Disciplines

Globalization has multiple facets: not only is the world interconnected by global capitalism controlled by multinational corporations located primarily in the West, but associated with it are global communications via television and the Internet and also, as Saskia Sassen says, with cities where the global economies have their "homes," these being places like New York, London, Paris, Frankfort, Tokyo and (perhaps) an emergent Bombay (Sassen 1998). Many theorists of globalization imagine that the global might undermine the local; or the local may persist within the frame of the global or deny that these processes are occurring, or that both accommodation and resistance are taking place (e.g., Featherstone 1990; Appadurai 1997; Amin 1997; Mittelman 2000). It seems to me that these theories are premature, largely because the future of global technologies cannot be predicted except very tentatively and hence one cannot predict in any long-term fashion the world into which they exert their power, as Karl Popper noted some time back (Popper 1961). Further, and more important, as Max Weber (1949) suggested, human beings must give meaning to their existence and respond to the threat of the homogenization of the world, though the development of global economic rationality might itself pose problems of meaning that people might resolve in multiple ways. There are those like Jean Baudrillard (1975; 1997) who see modern communications occurring within globalization as part of a postmodern field. But the postmodern idealization of the fractioning of the world and the emergence of multiple cultures and the constant movement of signifiers without stable significations (signified) can be seen as a new form of romanticism for giving meaning to the seemingly meaningless world of our times.

In order to speculate how these random thoughts relate to Buddhism, let me continue my narrative of the Theosophical Society. Even in the lifetimes of Olcott and Blavatsky the movement began to be selectively indigenized in several of the societies of South and Southeast Asia. For example, Laurie Sears has convincingly shown that scholars such as Clifford Geertz might have misinterpreted the Javanese mysticism of the shadow theater, especially its purported Indic origins in texts like the Bhagavad Gita, when it probably was influenced by Dutch Theosophy via its impact on the cultural life of Javanese elites (Sears 1996). In Sri Lanka the Buddhist Theosophical Society functioned primarily in the field of education; the actual takeover of the new Buddhist renaissance was the work of Anagarika Dharmapala who was once a disciple of Olcott and later his foe. For Dharmapala, Buddhism was not only a movement of spiritual re-awakening but also a nationalist and anti-imperialist one. Since Dharmapala's work is well known I shall only sum up his achievement in both the ecumenical and the nationalist level, that is, as the two forms of *sasanization* (Obeyesekere 1972; 1976; 1995; Seneviratne 1999).

For Dharmapala, Buddhism, divested of superstitious elements, had to be restored in the land of its origin and introduced into other Buddhist nations, much in line with Olcott's thinking. Olcott, however, had no sympathy whatever for the nationalist (and sometimes horrendously jingoistic) stance of Dharmapala. Yet from Dharmapala's own perspective, his twin goals were not contradictory. Thus he continued his ecumenical work, particularly through the Mahabodhi Society he founded and its associated journal. Dharmapala also had a profound impact during the World Parliament of Religions in Chicago in 1893, as did the Vedantic reformer Vivekananda. Here Dharmapala made the point that Buddhism was consonant with evolutionary theory and the "law of cause and effect" and it "condemns the idea of a creator." Yet he placated his Western audience by saying that Buddhism did after all posit the idea of a "supreme God who is all love, all merciful, all gentle, and looks upon all beings with equanimity" and who accepts the cosmos as "a continuous process of unfolding itself in obedience to natural laws"; and he added, "to guide humanity in the right path a Tathagata (Messiah) appears from time to time" (quoted in Verhoeven 1998: 213; Prebish 1979; Williams and Queen 1999). Dharmapala also asserted a year later that "Christ is a Buddha of a later time." (Dharmapala 1894 in Verhoeven 1998: 222). If Dharmapala produced a rational Protestant Buddhism consonant with European rationality and capitalism (which he idealized) so did Vivekananda who transformed Ramakrishna's passionate and ecstatic Tantric-based religiosity and devotional worship of Kali into the Neo-Vedantic rationalized Hinduism, which has become the standard ideology of the various Ramakrishna missions that he founded and are now scattered in most European nations (Kripal 1995; Kakar 1991). Neo-Vedanta has become the orthodoxy of most Hindu immigrants and Western converts to Hinduism (though the latter do not practice the popular devotionalism and Brahmanic calendrical rituals obligatory for Hindu immigrants).

A similar situation seems to occur in the post-Dharmapala transplantation of various forms of Buddhism among immigrant communities who have come to Europe and the United States for employment in the globalizing economy. Unlike transmigrants to the Middle East who will eventually return home, the Asian Buddhists in the West are a permanent group. For them, Buddhism is a way of retaining their core cultural identity and resisting being swallowed by the homogenizing processes of globalization and the powerful presence of Christian churches in their midst. They too practice a purified or Protestant form of Buddhism in the wake of Olcott and Dharmapala but they also worship the Buddha (if not the Hindu deities assimilated into popular Buddhism) and continue to practice Buddhist rituals and offer alms to monks. As with their home bases, meditation is a rare practice, though becoming increasingly popular owing to its acceptance by EuroBuddhists (Buddhists of European descent). Thus immigrant

Buddhism is *primarily* in terms of the local meanings of sāsana as the religion of one's homeland. Indeed, this was so with Dharmapala, if not Vivekananda. The passion and commitment that drove Dharmapala's ecumenicism is not that of the early Buddhist missions. Rather, it was national pride in his religion, his passionate hostility to the Christian missions, and his anti-imperialist stance that provided the dynamo that drove his ecumenical zeal. His hostility to the ethnic Tamils and Muslims in Sri Lanka paralleled a hostility to Hinduism that had supplanted Buddhism in the land of its birth. The two meanings of sāsana I mentioned earlier coexisted in the work of Dharmapala and were on occasion fused together as it is today in a lesser degree in the many ethnic Buddhist temples in the West. To put it differently: the religion and politics of the home countries are very much alive (even more intensely so) in the adopted nations of immigrants, and the Buddhist temples constitute their base. It is therefore not surprising that when the British started their own "eurorationalized" Theravada temples they had little appeal to Asian immigrant Buddhists in Britain.

Yet, what connects indigenous Buddhists with EuroBuddhists is in fact meditation, even though few Buddhists anywhere traditionally practiced it with any seriousness. One of the striking features of the contemporary global scene is the rapid spread of meditational practices among the lay intelligentsia, not only in today's Buddhist nations but also among EuroBuddhists. Meditation is the royal road to salvation in Buddhism and it is no accident that it is this feature that has spread globally in recent times, particularly after the sixties and more spectacularly after the Tibetan diaspora to the West. Buddhist "insight meditation" is known as *vipassanā* (Pali), which attempts to diagnose the human condition, to recognize the illusory nature of the Self, and sometimes all structures of existence, nirvana included. It is intrinsically related to Buddhist existential understandings of the world, especially the Four Noble Truths and the ultimate achievement of nirvana along with the cessation of rebirth. Calming meditation known as *samatha*, found in other religious traditions also, is at best a preliminary to the more arduous path of vipassanā, which requires extraordinary difficult exercises and the help of a "spiritual guide" or "true friend" so that the meditator can overcome the terrors of the fantastic. All Buddhist systems entail some form of vipassanā with the possible exception of the two major forms of Zen. Yet virtually all forms of EuroBuddhist meditation, including those of the middle-class Asians, are a much more shortened, communally oriented retreat, in the double sense of that term, from the labors of modern society.

The earliest attempt to modernize meditation was the work of the Burmese monk Bhikkhu Sadayaw who invented a form of Buddhist meditation that dispensed with the preliminaries of calming (samatha) and produced a rationalized technology of vipassanā divested of devotional practices, Buddhist cosmological understandings, as well as many doctrinal underpinnings. In a further radical move he said that monks were not necessary for teaching vipassanā; and indeed non-Buddhists might also benefit from it—moves that touched the heart of modernity. One of Sadayaw's pupils from Sri Lanka founded a Buddhist meditation at Kanduboda which provided meditation courses in English and also formal certification (Gombrich and Obeyesekere 1988: 238–39). Another extremely influential figure was Jack Kornfield who was a major figure in training Americans as vipassanā instructors in Goenka meditation; in 1981 Kornfield founded the Spirit Rock in Calfornia where nine of the regular teachers are trained psychotherapists (Fronsdal 1998: 170). I have already mentioned Goenka who radically shortened Sadayaw's arduous three-month program to ten-day retreats (sometimes longer but not more that thirty days). Goenka came from a wealthy Indian business family, and his techniques not only gained ground among educated native Buddhists but also spread very fast among EuroBuddhists (Fronsdal 1998: 166–67; Epstein 1995; Molino 1998). Perhaps most impressively, they were introduced to the newly emergent Theravada community of Newaris in Vajrayana Nepal. Goenka meditation is available in videocassettes and presumably one can practice it without the guidance of a teacher. But it is not only Goenka who produces short-cut vipassanā sessions; all Buddhist groups do, including Tibetan and other forms of Mahayana. Zen, the most popular form of Buddhist meditation in the United States has always been short, based as it is on sudden illumination (*satori*). It seems to me that here we touch on an important feature of Buddhist meditation that can have a decided impact on the world. It is possible, and indeed may be happening this very moment, to introduce these revised meditational techniques not just through video but almost certainly via the Internet. In this sense one might say that Buddhist meditation has the prospect of becoming available globally such that one might begin to imagine Buddhism as a world religion, not a popular one, but one that might eventually have small numbers of educated aspirants in virtually every nation under the sun.

BUDDHIST MEDITATION AND RATIONALITY
IN A GLOBAL ECONOMY

Because I have concentrated on meditation I have had to ignore the impact of Buddhism on New Age religions. Buddhist meditational techniques entered Europe and America only after the 1970s and especially with the large presence of Asian refugees in Europe and America. The distinguished Weber scholar Detlef Kantowsky, himself a Buddhist, ironically comments that one does not need to go to Lhasa nowadays because "Lhasa really is everywhere today!" (Kantowsky

1995: 101). And there is the visible presence of the charismatic Dalai Lama who conducts weeklong meditative retreats in different parts of EuroAmerica. And the reasons for Buddhism's appeal? According to Kantowsky, "the optimism of the Western rational enlightenment has been so thoroughly discredited that it is no longer able to justify man's subjection of nature: the arrogant cosmology which held that we could divorce ourselves from the rest of the world, cultivate it as a resource, or subject and fight it as a rival, is now bearing fruit" (Kantowsky 1995: 102)—though not of a pleasant kind. These trends are only accelerated in global capitalism's discontents documented by Saskia Sassen (1998), fostered by the amoral accumulation of wealth and the greed of the contemporary market which in turn produces a further reification of the Self—all of which Buddhism diagnoses rather well in its idea that desire, greed, or attachment is the source of the unsatisfactoriness of the world. But to me this is merely the spur that the clear spirit might raise; it does show Buddhism as an alternative, nondestructive model for contemporary living, but it does not answer the question, why Buddhist *meditation*?

To answer this question in an admittedly speculative manner, I would like to go back to a powerful nineteenth-century thinker who questioned Enlightenment rationality, scoffed at mainline reifiers of reason from Socrates and Plato to Kant, and, like Buddhists, pointed out the falsity of the Self and the entrenched Western idea that the limit of language is the limit of thought. I am, of course, looking at Friedrich Nietzsche, but not a relativist or postmodern Nietzsche, but rather the Nietzsche who formulated very early the opposition between Dionysian and Appolonian, an idealistic distinction that he maintained to the very end of his life in *Twilight of the Angles* and *Anti-Christ* (Nietzsche [1885, 1889]). The two oppositions were reconciled in the past in the best of Greek tragedy, though most of the time they remained split.

Yet I think there is a problem here: Nietzsche and many modern and postmodern thinkers are critical of the Enlightenment project and its iron cage of rationality. Yet, can one living in the modern West escape from rationality's bondage or, to put it in early Nietzschean language, can one pierce "the veil of maya?" For Nietzsche the Dionysian in his ecstatic "entrancement" or "intoxication" can do it because his work is "an annihilation of the usual borders and limits of existence"(Nietzsche [1872] 2000: 46). "Something supernatural sounds forth from him: he feels himself a god, now he himself strides forth as enraptured and uplifted as he saw the gods stride forth in dreams. . . . Man is no longer the artist, he has become the work of art . . . in the shudder of intoxication" (Nietzsche 2000: 23). But it is one thing to sketch a lost past as Nietzsche does in *The Birth of Tragedy* or to imagine a powerful figure like Zarathustra as the Dionysian model prophet of the future who can cry out, "But I say unto you: one must have chaos in oneself to be able to give birth to a dancing star . . ." (Nietzsche [1883] 1978: 17). Yet, it is another thing to *be* Zarathustra, to incorporate him into one's own being; worse still to be able to create such things as visions and ecstatic trances in the field of modernity even for those who have intellectually rejected Cartesian rationality and the primacy of the Ego. Sure there is art and music as expressions of the sublime, "the acre of green grass" that Yeats spoke of. And one can reenchant the outside world in many ways as, for instance, the European Romantics did, but what about "inner experience," to use Georges Bataille's phrase (Bataille 1988)? How can one *become* the living artist, if indeed the living artist as the ideal of a mode of living isn't itself an illusion?

Most of us are caught up in Claude Levi-Strauss's structuralist dilemma: Levi-Strauss rejected the agency of the Ego yet his work is in the true spirit of science; it is Apollonian in the narrowest sense because it is without the benefit of living in the "magic mountain," the domain of Apollo who was also the god of the Delphic oracle (Nietzsche [1872] 2000: 28). Apollonian thought is consonant with reason and moderation but it is not consonant with Enlightenment rationality that cannot tolerate any cultivation of a magic garden or an enchanted world.

Dilemmas similar to Levi-Strauss's present themselves in many of the great figures of our time: Heidegger wanted to create, like Nietzsche himself, an authentic mode of existence or *dasein*; but it lead him tortuously into the blind alley of Fascism, a perilous land into which Nietzsche himself came close to trespassing. Wittgenstein passionately defended St. Augustine; he himself periodically lived in isolation very much like a medieval mystic but he was too much of an abstract thinker ever to be able to become someone like Augustine. Yet even those post-structuralist thinkers who protest against the rationality of the Enlightenment end up as prisoners of rationality. Foucault is the prime example of an anti-rationalist rationalist who tried to pierce the veil of maya in his own personal life—through sexuality, through the ingestion of hallucinatory drugs, through the visceral life of San Francisco's gay bars. Even the picture thinking of surreal painters is close to the visuality of hysterical patients and the pictorial thinking of dreams, rather than to Buddhist meditative trance or Nietzsche's imagined Dionysianism. Except in rare instances trance and vision continue to be relegated to psychosis in today's world. There is no way that one can be a modern or postmodern European living in the global economy and achieve a mode of being or nonbeing that one associates with visionary trance, Apollonian or Dionysian, and yet remain sane.

There is, however, at least one exception: and that is the Buddhist meditative askesis, a mode of nonbeing that can coexist with rationality though not in the same space-time. Why so? Because all forms of Buddhist meditation must eschew language and discursive reason for true understanding to develop, ideas that are hostile to rationality and science as commonly understood. Yet, a modern Buddhist meditator can hark back to the world of discursive reason after the space-time of meditation is over, better equipped, he would say, to deal critically with that world. Buddhist meditation has also a complex disciplinary technology exemplified in Buddhaghosa's *Path of Purification*; but it is a technology that can be drastically modified and adapted in varying ways to modern life, sometimes in ways disturbing to those of us familiar with the history of Buddhism.

Yet whatever the form of meditation that one adopts from among the various forms of vipassanā or Zen, it is Buddhist meditation and not Nietzschean Dionysianism, Buddhists could claim, that can "pierce the veil of Maya," that illusory world of becoming or samsara in which human beings are entangled but without the necessity for reifying the principle of individuality or sense of Self or Being which Nietzsche's Apollo exemplified. No wonder its appeal to educated middle-class intellectuals discontented with the world of increasing globalization, allowing one to combine Dionysian rejection of the Self and retain Apollo's commitment to reason and moderation and yet live in the magic mountain, for a while at least, through meditation's askeses.

BIBLIOGRAPHY

Amin, S. 1997. *Capitalism in the Age of Globalization: The Management of Contemporary Society*. London: Zed Books.

Appadurai, Arjun. 1997. *Modernity at Large: Cultural Dimensions of Globalization*. Minneapolis: University of Minnesota Press.

Bataille, Georges. 1988. *Inner Experience*. Trans. Leslie Ann Boldt. Albany: SUNY Press.

Baudrillard, Jean. 1975. *The Mirror of Production*. St Louis: Telos Press.

———. 1997. *Simulacra and Simulation*. Ann Arbor: University of Michigan Press.

Baumann, Martin. 1995. "Adapting a Religion in a Foreign Culture: Rationalist Interpretations of Buddhism in Germany." In *Buddhism and Christianity: Interactions Between East and West*. Ed. Ulrich Everding, 72–99. Colombo: Goethe-Institut.

Epstein, Mark. 1995. *Thoughts without a Thinker: Psychotherapy from a Buddhist Perspective*. New York: Basic Books.

Featherstone, M., ed. 1990. *Global Culture: Nationalism, Globalization and Modernity*. London: Sage.

Fronsdal, Gil. 1998. "Insight Meditation in the United States." In *The Faces of Buddhism in America*. Eds. Charles S. Prebish and Kenneth K Tanaka, 164–180. Berkeley: University of California Press.

Gay, Peter. 1968. *The Enlightenment: An Interpretation*. New York: Viking Books.

Gombrich, Richard F., and Gananath Obeyesekere. 1988. *Buddhism Transformed: Recent Religious Change in Sri Lanka*. Princeton, N.J.: Princeton University Press.

Hanegraaff, Wouter J. 1996. *New Age Religion and Western Culture*. Leiden: E. J. Brill.

Kakar, Sudhir. 1991. *The Analyst and the Mystic: Psychoanalytic Reflections on Religion and Mysticism*. Chicago: University of Chicago Press.

Kantowsky, Detlef. 1995. "Buddhist Modernism." In *Buddhism and Christianity: Interac-*

tions Between East and West. Ed. Ulrich Everding, 101–115. Colombo: Goethe-Institut.

Kripal, Jeffrey J. 1995. *Kali's Child: The Mystical and the Erotic in the Life and Teachings of Ramakrishna*. Chicago: University of Chicago Press.

Molino, Antony. 1998. *The Couch and the Tree: Dialogues in Psychoanalysis and Buddhism*. New York: North Point Press.

Nietzsche, Friedrich. 2000. *The Birth of Tragedy*. Trans. Douglas Smith. Oxford: World Classics.

———. 1978. *Thus Spoke Zarathustra*. Trans. Walter Kaufmann. New York: Penguin.

———. 1990. *Twilight of the Idols/The Anti-Christ*. Trans. R. D. Hollingdale. London: Penguin Classics.

Obeyesekere, Gananath. 1996. "Buddhist Identity in Sri Lanka." In *Ethnic Identity, Creation, Conflict, and Accommodation*, 3rd ed. Eds. Lola Romanucci-Ross and George deVos, 222–247. Walnut Creek, Calif.: Altamira Press.

———. 1972. "Religious Symbolism and Political Change in Ceylon." In *The Two Wheels of Dhamma*. Ed. Bardwell L. Smith, 58–78. Chambersburg, Pa.: Wilson Books.

———. 1976. "Personal Identity and Cultural Crisis: The Case of Anagarika Dharmapala of Sri Lanka." In *The Biographical Process*. Eds. Frank Reynolds and Donald Capps, 221–252. The Hague: Mouton.

———. 1995. "The Two Faces of Colonel Olcott: Buddhism and Euro-rationality in the late Nineteenth Century." In *Buddhism and Christianity: Interactions Between East and West*. Ed. Ulrich Everding, 32–71. Colombo: Goethe-Institut.

Popper, Karl. 1961. *The Poverty of Historicism*. London: Routledge and Kegan Paul.

Prebish, Charles S. 1979. *American Buddhism*. North Scituate, Mass.: Duxbury Press.

Sassen, Saskia. 1998. *Globalization and its Discontents*. New York: New Press.

Sears, Laurie. 1996. *Shadows of Empire: Colonial Discourse and Javanese Tales*. Durham, N.C.: Duke University Press.

Seneviratne, H. L. 1999. *The Work of Kings: The New Buddhism of Sri Lanka*. Chicago: University of Chicago Press.

Verhoeven, Martin J. 1998. "Carus and the Transformation of Asian Thought." In *The Faces of Buddhism in America*. Eds. Charles S. Prebish and Kenneth K Tanaka, 207–227. Berkeley: University of California Press.

Weber, Max. 1949. *The Methodology of the Social Sciences* Trans. and eds. Edward A. Shils and Henry A. Finch. New York: Free Press.

Williams, Duncan Ryuken, and Christopher S. Queen, eds. 1999. *American Buddhism: Methods and Findings in Recent Scholarship*. Richmond, Surrey: Curzon.

CHAPTER 9

THERAVADA BUDDHIST SOCIETIES

DONALD K. SWEARER

THOUGH the Theravada school of Buddhism has not had the global reach of the Mahayana branch, it has the distinction of being the earliest form of Buddhist expansion. Indeed, Theravadins consider their tradition to be the oldest and most authentic form of Buddhism.

The school of Buddhism known as Theravada (Teachings of the Elders) traces its origins to the Buddha himself whose traditional birth date is 543 BCE. Classified as one of the eighteen original sects of Indian Hinayana Buddhism, Theravadins believe the orthodoxy of their tradition was upheld by the monastic ruling council at an assembly convened at Pataliputra by the great Indian monarch, Asoka, in 247 BCE. The doctrinal roots of modern Theravada are associated with an early Indian Buddhist sect known as the Vibhajyavadins (those who teach discrimination) that flourished in the Tamil Nadu region of South India in the early centuries of the common era. The most distinctive features of Theravada doctrine and practice, however, were forged in Sri Lanka.

According to Theravada chronicle sources, Asoka's son, Mahinda, and daughter, Sanghamitta, brought Buddhism to the island during the reign of King Devanampiyatissa (who ruled from 247–207 BCE). Devanampiyatissa is credited with donating the land on which the Mahavihara monastery was built in the capital city of Anuradhapura where Mahinda and Sanghamitta founded an order of monks and nuns. This legendary story underlines the close relationship that existed between Theravada Buddhism as a monastic institution (*sangha*) and the monarchical context in which it developed.

Although Theravadins believe their canonical scriptures in the Pali language were codified at the council of Pataliputra, the definitive Theravada commentaries were written in the fifth century CE by monks associated with the Mahavihara. Of special importance was the South Indian pandit, Buddhaghosacariya. The most widely used ritual manual throughout the Theravada tradition, the *Parittapot-thaka*, was also compiled by monks of the Mahavihara in Anuradhapura. Although other schools of Buddhism flourished in Sri Lanka and much of mainland Southeast Asia, patronage by the ruling monarchs in this region often favored monasteries of the Mahavihara lineage.

From the tenth through the fifteenth centuries Theravada Buddhism gradually came to dominate the religious, social, and political landscape of mainland Southeast Asia known today as Myanmar (Burma), Thailand, Laos, and Cambodia. During the reigns of such powerful monarchs as Parakramabahu I (1153–1186) of Polonnaruva, Kyanzittha of Pagan (1084–1113), Lu'thai of Sukhothai (1347–1361), and Tilokaraja of Chiang Mai (1442–1487), the sangha flourished. Political and economic factors figured prominently in the development of the Theravada tradition. Royalty supported the construction of temples and monasteries, and the capitals of the classical city-states became centers of Theravada regional and pan-regional Buddhist scholarship. In return, by its cooperation and support, the sangha sanctified and legitimated the authority of particular kings. This symbiotic relationship between the state and the Buddhist sangha established during this formative period has continued to the present. The relationship between Theravada Buddhism and the state has never been a monolithic one, however. Historical developments and political upheavals, especially the colonial interregnum and the subsequent emergence of modern Asian nation-states has had profound consequences for the relationship between the state and the Buddhist sangha in Theravada Asia. Several events are particularly noteworthy.

Beginning with the reign of Rama V (King Chulalongkorn) in Thailand (1851–1902), the creation of a centralized, bureaucratized national Buddhist sangha was a crucial factor in integrating the diverse regions of the country into a modern nation-state. The trend toward the creation of a civil religion supported by Buddhism accelerated during the reign of Rama VI (King Warjirawut, r. 1910–1925) and continues to the present. During and subsequent to the regime of Sarit Thanarat (prime minister, 1959–1963), government-sponsored development programs involving Buddhist monks had specific political aims principally to counter communist influence in the northeastern provinces bordering Cambodia and Laos.

In Sri Lanka, Buddhist support of Sinhalese nationalist sentiment in the early twentieth century led to the 1956 election of S. W. R. D. Bandaranaike as prime minister. In this election, a chauvinistic Sinhalese Buddhist nationalism appeared in the political landscape setting the stage for the violent sectarian conflicts in the 1980s and 1990s between the Sinhalese Buddhist majority and the Hindu Tamils fighting for an independent state. Sinhalese Buddhists are divided in their attitude toward armed suppression of the Tamil Tigers' (LTTE) liberation struggle. Some advocate a course of nonviolence, although the majority support the government's decision to resolve the conflict by military victory.

Burmese nationalistic sentiment in the early twentieth century against British colonial rule also had strong Buddhist roots, culminating in the election of U Nu as prime minister of Burma (Myanmar) in 1948. His policies of promoting Buddhism as a national religion were met with resistance by Burma's sizable non-Buddhist minorities that include the Christianized Karens, and U Nu's philosophy of a democratic Buddhist socialism was attacked by the country's right-wing generals. In a 1962 coup d'etat General Ne Win overthrew the democratically elected U Nu government. The Ne Win regime created a military dictatorship that imposed a harsh, state-controlled economy to support the army and police, and has pursued a military campaign to defeat the semi-autonomous ethnic states in the country, e.g. Karens, Shans, Chins, and Kachins. Since 1980 the government has actively sought the support of the sangha through the creation of various national programs, including a more tightly controlled national sangha organization. Resistance to government policies by some elements in the sangha came to the fore when Myanmar's government, the State Law and Order Commission (SLORC), abrogated the 1989 political victory of Aung San Suu Kyi and her party in the first democratic election held in the country in over twenty-five years.

Beyond its monastic institutional structures and its political influence on classical kingship and the development of the modern nation-state, Theravada Buddhism has been thoroughly assimilated into the cultures of Sri Lanka, Myanmar, Thailand, Laos, and Cambodia. In each country, Buddhism defines the personal and social values as well as the cultural identity of the majority population. In Thailand, Laos, and Cambodia, non-Buddhist animistic tribal groups that include the Yao, Hmong, Akha, Lahu, and Lisu live on the political, economic, and social margins. For them assimilation into the dominant Thai, Lao, and Khmer culture often includes conversion to Buddhism. A government-sponsored program in Thailand, for example, is directed specifically at missionizing northern tribal groups and educating young tribal boys as novice monks.

Greater tensions exist between Buddhist and non-Buddhist populations in Myanmar and Sri Lanka principally because non-Buddhist minority groups in these countries are larger and command more political, economic, or military power. In Myanmar, where the dominant Burmese and the Tai Shans in the northeast share a common Buddhist faith, the conflict between the two groups reflect ethnic and political tensions rather than religious differences. Sri Lanka, on the other hand, offers a tragic example of opposition between Buddhist and non-Buddhist populations. The current armed conflict between Sinhalese Buddhists who constitute the majority (75 percent) and the minority Hindu Tamils (18 percent) has deep historical roots. Throughout the history of the island the relationship between the two communities has been contentious at worst and suspicious at best. Political accommodations between the Sinhalese and Tamils were reached when Sri Lanka gained its independence from Great Britain in 1948, but the rhetoric of Buddhist nationalism that inflamed the 1956 election campaign and the 1958 riots over a proposal to impose Sinhala as the official language foreshadowed the bloody fratricidal conflict of the 1980s and 1990s.

The role of Buddhism in identity formation can be analyzed in various ways. From a cultural perspective, Theravada Buddhism as a living religious system has succeeded in absorbing and transforming both exogenous and endogenous elements into a unified, essentially syncretic religiocultural system. Consequently, while Theravada Buddhism in Sri Lanka, Myanmar, Thailand, Laos, and Cambodia shares the Pali canon and a common monastic discipline (*vinaya*), differences abound. These differences can be found at virtually every level of religious thought and practice. They range from distinctive vernacular literatures and teaching lineages to forms of meditation, ritual, and communal celebrations. For instance, while many Theravada rituals have an apotropaic dimension, the practice of protecting the body with magical tattoos or wearing sacred amulets containing the ashes of cremated holy monks is more typical of Buddhist practice in Thailand than it is in Sri Lanka.

Theravada Buddhism absorbed diverse autochthonous and non-Buddhist religiocultural traditions but not in precisely the same way throughout Southeast Asia. Although often classified as "animism" (the worship of spirits) and "Brahmanism," these traditions vary considerably from country to country. For example, although Theravada Buddhism absorbed Brahmanical-Hindu deities and indigenous spirits into its religious system, the hierarchical pantheon that developed in Sri Lanka differs considerably from the cult of *nat* divinities in Burma or the propitiation of *phi* spirits in Thailand and Laos.

In addition to integrating diverse religiocultural elements into a cultural ethos identified as Buddhist, Theravada Buddhism has defined the personal and communal ideals and values of the societies where the monastic sangha became the dominant social institution outside of the family and the monarchy. Unlike Tibet or China where Buddhism competed with *Bon-po* shamans and Confucian literati for cultural, social, and political dominance, Buddhism in Sri Lanka, Myanmar, Thailand, and Laos faced no serious rival. While Hindu-Brahmanical influence from India influenced the formation of the religious culture of these countries, it was never dominant. Hinduism did not attain the supremacy that it achieved among the Khmers at Angkor from the tenth through the twelfth centuries. Even in Cambodia the strong Hindu influence on Khmer culture eventually yielded to Mahayana and finally to Theravada Buddhism.

Buddhist teachings and values are mediated to Theravada societies primarily through the sangha. These teachings include ideals of the supreme good and highest end of human life, moral sanctions and exemplary moral virtues, as well as the means to cope with suffering and achieve success. It is important to note that while colonial regimes and the forces of modernization eroded the place of the sangha in Theravada societies, until the middle of the twentieth century the monastic order continued to occupy a place of unsurpassed importance in village and town life. The monastery performed, and continues to fill, a variety of social roles essential to the education, health, and general well-being of individuals and communities.

In an ideal sense, monks symbolize the supreme goal of human life represented by the life of the Buddha and his enlightenment or nirvana. Max Weber's characterization of early Indian Buddhism as a type of world-renouncing, otherworldly mysticism, ignores the simple fact that monks are, after all, members of families and many continue to live in their natal towns and villages. Even forest monks who devote their lives to meditation are often well known in their regions, are venerated by lay people, and bear witness to the exemplary power of the Buddha. The story of the Buddha's renunciation and attainment of nirvana not only provides a model for monastic behavior but embodies spiritual ideals of emotional and mental equanimity highly prized in Theravada societies. A Thai's plea to his friend during the heat of an argument to keep a "cool heart" (jai yen) may be a distant but powerful reflection of the Buddhist ideal of overcoming anger and achieving a state of calm equanimity associated with the Buddha's life story.

The Buddhist monastery serves not only as a place for the pursuit of spiritual knowledge, but also provides many other important functions. Foremost, the monastery is a school for both monks and laity. Until the advent of modern education, monasteries in Theravada societies held a virtual monopoly on public education. Young boys were taught reading and writing primarily in vernacular languages while the Pali scriptures of Theravada Buddhism were taught mostly to monks. In the modern period, the educational role of the monastery has declined but has not been entirely replaced by government-sponsored or private educational institutions.

The monastery also continues to be the venue for moral education. Every ritual involving monks and laity begins by repeating the five moral precepts: not to kill, not to steal, not to lie, not to commit acts of sexual fornication, and not to ingest intoxicants. Each of these training rules has positive counterparts. One should not only not take the life of sentient beings, steal, or lie, one should also perform acts of compassion, be generous, and tell the truth. These moral values are not only embodied in moral action guides but are also embedded in sabbath-day sermons or more informal conversations that might include the beloved jataka tale of the young boy, Sama, who embodies the virtue of lovingkindness by caring for his aged, blind parents.

The physical presence of the sangha also provides the context for merit-making (punna), which is one of the most important ways Buddhism addresses the problem of suffering and the attainment of worldly success. Although the

Buddha taught that the ultimate resolution to the ontological problem of suffering (*dukkha*) was the achievement of nirvana, Theravada Buddhism also addresses the wide variety of injustices and inequities everyone experiences in daily life. These injustices and inequities are explained by the teachings of karma and rebirth (*samsara*). From a karmic point of view one's condition in life results from the balance between good and bad deeds and intentions in past lives as well as those in one's present life. Meritorious actions that benefit and support the sangha, ranging from morning food offerings and major financial gifts to ordination as a monk, positively affect one's karmic balance and, therefore, one's condition in present and future existences. The ideology of merit-making occupies the most prominent place in the practical understanding and daily activities of monks and laity in Theravada societies. The great majority of rituals performed by monks such as those that mark the end of the three-month monastic rains retreat (*vassa*) in October and November or ceremonies dedicating a new house or business are grounded in the ideology of merit-making.

In more general terms, however, participation in festivals and ritual events related to the Buddhist calendar or community celebrations that have been appropriated by Buddhism help to constitute members of Theravada Buddhist societies as a unified moral community. Buddha's Day (Visakha Puja) and New Year's are two such events. The lunar New Year celebration in the spring that marks the end of the dry season and the onset of the monsoon rains, has been incorporated into the Buddhist festival calendar. Many New Year celebration activities take place at Buddhist temples and monasteries. Pilgrimage to sacred sites believed to enshrine relics of the Buddha may also occur during the New Year season symbolizing a renewal of sacred physical space as well as sacred time. This month-long sacred season culminates with Visakha Puja that celebrates the birth, enlightenment, and death of the Buddha, thus linking the advent of Buddhism with the beginning of the lunar year and the renewal of the agricultural cycle.

These annual festivals of New Year and Visaka Puja provide participants with a sense of membership in a universal Theravada Buddhist community. Other rituals such as the annual dedication of a village monastery or rites of passage marking a major event in the life of a member of the community, have regional, local, or communal significance. For example, temporary ordination as a novice monk not only involves a limited period of monastic training; in Myanmar, Thailand, Laos, and Cambodia, the occasion constitutes a rite of passage into the adult male community not unlike a Jewish bar mitzvah or Christian confirmation. There is a Thai saying that before a lad spends some time as a novice monk he is "unripe" (*dip*) in the sense that he lacks the maturity to assume adult male responsibilities in the community, principally marriage.

Theravada Buddhist societies have undergone dramatic change in the twentieth century. External events have caused some of them; others have evolved as part of the worldwide process of globalization. Wars have been a major factor, especially the Vietnam War and its impact on Laos, Cambodia, and Thailand; the Sinhala-Tamil conflict in Sri Lanka; and the continuing civil war in Myanmar between the majority Burmese and the country's minorities. Certainly the most devastating example of military violence on a Theravada Buddhist society was Pol Pot's program in the 1970s to transform Khmer society that included the dismantling of the sangha. Hundreds of temples were destroyed and thousands of monks either killed or forced to enter lay life. In the 1990s Cambodian society, including the sangha, began to slowly recover from over a decade of genocidal conflict.

Numerous modernizing trends have occurred in Theravada Buddhist societies in the twentieth century. Of special significance has been the increasingly important role of the laity in relationship to the monkhood, the emergence of new sectarian movements, and the pervasive impact of globalization on the place Buddhism takes in the cultures and societies of Southeast Asia and Sri Lanka. Traditionally, the principal role of the laity in Theravada societies was one of providing material support for the sangha. Today, not only does the laity perform leadership roles once solely held by monks, lay Buddhist associations sponsoring a wide range of activities have emerged. Lay Buddhist groups independent of monasteries are active in education and social welfare and also promote meditation, an activity formerly associated primarily with the monastery. The Sarvodaya Shramadana movement in Sri Lanka, founded by a former schoolteacher, has recruited over 800,000 volunteers since its formation in the 1950s to work on rural uplift projects in over 8,500 villages on the island. In Myanmar, U Ba Khin, an accountant general, established the International Meditation Center in Yangon (Rangoon) in 1952. It has inspired thousands of Burmese and international students of insight meditation to train at the center. The laicization of Theravada societies has seen an increasingly active role for women, including a move to reestablish the order of Theravada nuns (*bhikkhuni*). Several women have gained international fame as meditation teachers as well as devoted followings in their own countries.

In the late nineteenth century new movements within the sangha promoted various reforms in Buddhist practice. They included the Dhammayuttika sect in Thailand, the Schwegyin sect in Myanmar, and the Ramanya sect in Sri Lanka. These reforms emphasized the study of the Pali scriptures, meditation, and stricter adherence to the monastic discipline (vinaya). During this period, a resurgence of the forest monk tradition in Sri Lanka, Myanmar, and Thailand also occurred. Although these trends have influenced the development of Theravada Buddhism in the twentieth century, they have been overshadowed by the gradual erosion of the central place occupied by Buddhism as the key factor in Sinhalese, Burmese, Thai, Lao, and Khmer identity. Governments have assumed many of the roles formerly performed by Buddhist monks in Theravada societies. Furthermore, the important place that Buddhist rituals and festivals once held in villages and towns in these countries is being replaced by television and other types of commercial entertainment and activity. As Theravada Buddhists in South and Southeast Asia as well as the increasingly large number of diaspora Theravadins in the West enter the twenty-first century, their response to the challenge of increasingly rapid change and globalization will severely test the traditional religiocultural ethos on which Theravada communities were built, nurtured, and sustained.

BIBLIOGRAPHY

Bond, George E. 1988. *The Buddhist Revival in Sri Lanka: Religious Tradition, Reinterpretation and Response.* Columbia: University of South Carolina Press.

Bunnag, Jane. 1973. "Buddhist Monk, Buddhist Layman: A Study of Urban Monastic Organiztion in Central Thailand." *Cambridge Studies in Social Anthropology,* no. 6. Cambridge: Cambridge University Press.

Gombrich, Richard F. 1988. *Theravada Buddhism: A Social History from Ancient Benares to Modern Colombo.* London and New York: Routledge and Kegan Paul.

Gombrich, Richard F., and Gananath Obeyesekere. 1988. *Buddhism Transformed: Religious Change in Sri Lanka.* Princeton, N.J.: Princeton University Press.

Nash, Manning. 1965. *The Golden Road to Modernity: Village Life in Contemporary Burma.* Chicago and London: University of Chicago Press.

Sam, Yang. 1987. *Khmer Buddhism and Politics, 1954–1984.* Newington, Conn.: Khmer Studies Institute, Inc.

Spiro, Melford E. 1982. *Buddhism and Society: A Great Tradition and Its Burmese Vicissitudes,* 2d ed. Berkeley: University of California Press.

Swearer, Donald K. 1995. *The Buddhist World of Southeast Asia.* Albany: State University of New York Press.

Tambiah, Stanley J. 1973. Buddhism *and Spirit Cults in North-East Thailand. Cambridge Studies in Social Anthropology,* no. 2 Cambridge: Cambridge University Press.

———. 1992. *Buddhism Betrayed? Religion, Politics, and Violence in Sri Lanka.* Chicago: University of Chicago Press.

Tannenbaum, Nicola. 1995. *Who Can Compete Against the World? Power-Protection and Buddhism in Shan Worldview.* Monograph and Occasional Paper Series, No. 51. Ann Arbor, Mich.: Association for Asian Studies.

CHAPTER 10

TIBETAN BUDDHIST SOCIETY

JOSÉ IGNACIO CABEZÓN

BEFORE the unique form of Buddhism that developed in Tibet was *ex*ported, Buddhism had first to be *im*ported to Tibet, for Buddhism is not indigenous to Tibet. Prior to the introduction of Buddhism to Tibet, it was already well established in neighboring regions—Buddhism had had a millennium of development in India, the land of its origin, and over half a millennium of growth and expansion in China, where it was introduced during the Han dynasty. Up to the seventh century CE the religion of Tibet consisted of astrological, divinatory, propitiatory, healing, exorcistic, funerary, and other rites. This amalgam of practices, especially under the pressure exercised by the introduction of Buddhism, came to be systematized into the religion known as Bon.

The traditional Tibetan religion of Bon had a unique mythology of creation, had its own hierarchical pantheon of gods and spirits (many associated with specific geographical sites in Tibet), its own founder (gShen rab mi bo) and its own religious functionaries (known originally as *bon* or *gshen*), whose main work was to identify "the causes of human ailments and misfortunes, and then to prescribe a suitable cure." (Snellgrove and Richardson 1968: 55; see also Samuel 1993a, b, 1997) Although there has always existed a tension in Tibet between the imported religion of Buddhism and the indigenous religion of Bon, it is also the case that each has influenced the other. In particular a good deal of the this-worldly, magical character of Tibetan Buddhism is a result of Bon influence. Tantra, the esoteric tradition of Buddhism, also had a strong magical element, and to that extent was compatible with Bon. Hence, tantric Buddhism most likely seemed familiar to Tibetans, and this is probably one of the reasons it made such swift inroads into Tibetan culture. This is important to note because it is the Bon/tantric derived magical character of Tibetan Buddhism that has made it appealing to many of the cultures to which it has spread.

THE TRANSMISSION OF BUDDHISM
TO TIBET

Though Tibetans may have been acquainted with Buddhism in earlier times, it appears that Buddhism made its first real incursions into Tibet during the reign of Tibet's first "dharma-king," Song brtsan sgam po, who lived in the first half of the seventh century. Song brtsan sgam po is said to have taken Nepalese and Chinese princesses (both Buddhist) as wives. He is credited in the traditional Tibetan sources with founding several temples, the most important of which is the Jo khang (Lha sa's central "cathedral"), which contains Tibet's holiest Buddha-image known as the Jo bo rin po che (The Precious Lord), brought to Lha sa by Song brtsan sgam po's Chinese wife. The king is also credited with having introduced the first Tibetan script, which, among other things permitted the translation of Buddhist texts into Tibetan. During the reign of Song brtsan sgam po and his next two successors what Buddhism existed in Tibet did so under royal patronage and was chiefly centered in the court. The monks living in the court were principally foreign invitees. It was under the reign of Tibet's second great dharma-king, Khri srong lde brtsan, who lived in the second half of the eighth century, that Buddhism began to spread widely. Khri srong lde brtsan is credited with having built Tibet's first monastery, bSam yas, where monks of Tibetan origin were for the first time systematically trained. Two important religious figures from India were also invited to Tibet during Khri srong lde brtsan's rule: Padmasambhava, a great tantric yogi, and Śāntarakṣita, an erudite scholastic monk. These two figures, whose importance to the history of Tibetan Buddhism cannot be overestimated, in many ways prefigure the very character of the later religion, which would have in most of its various developments and major schools, pronounced monastic/scholastic *and* tantric/magical foci.

One other important event in the early history of Tibetan Buddhism is the so-called bSam-yas debate. Historical sources seem to imply that during the reign of Khri srong lde brtsan there emerged a need to decide between the two strands of Buddhism that had gained a foothold in the country: the gradualist, scholastic, intellectualist approach of the Indians, and the sudden-enlightenment, ineffabilist, anti-analytical approach of the Chinese.[1] A debate was supposedly organized at the monastery of bSam yas between the Indian scholar-monk Śāntarakṣita and the Chinese (Ch'an/Zen) monk Hwa shang Mohoyen. In the standard accounts, the Indian side is said to have won the debate, causing the banishment of the Chinese doctrine, and forever sealing Tibet's fate as a land permanently aligned to the Buddhism of India. Whether or not such a debate ever took place, it is clear that as a metaphor, the bSam yas debate is indicative of a general Tibetan bias in favor of Indian Buddhism. The rhetoric of the Indian triumph notwithstanding, China has had substantial influence on different aspects of Tibetan Buddhism, from doctrine to practice to religious art.

The period from the seventh to ninth centuries was the period of the initial establishment of Buddhism in Tibet. It was also the age of the great Tibetan empire under the Yar (k)lung(s) dynasty, a time of unequalled Tibetan military expansion. The following three centuries (tenth through twelfth) are best characterized as the period of sectarian developments within Tibetan Buddhism, as Tibetans sought out different Indian teachers and established distinct institutions with unique identities. It was during this period that three of Tibet's four main schools emerged as distinct entities: the rNying ma, Sa skya, and bKa' rgyud.[2] The last major tradition, the dGe lugs pa, or dGa' ldan pa, school would be founded later in the fourteenth century.

This pattern of Buddhism's establishment in Tibet is significant, for it is variously recapitulated (or reversed) in the diffusion of Tibetan Buddhism outside of Tibet's borders in later historical periods. Especially significant to note is (1) the pattern of sponsorship of the religion by a ruling elite, the so-called priest-patron or preceptor-donor (*yon mchod*) relationship (see Seyfort Ruegg 1997); (2) the role of material culture, especially art (statues, painting) and architecture (temples, monasteries, and stūpas), ideally, as outward signs of the establishment of Buddhism; (3) the importance of translation as an activity; (4) the centrality of monasticism as an institution that is considered reflective of the vitality of the religion; (5) the perceived triumph of the Indian tradition in general, and of Indian scholasticism in particular, especially as a model for education; and (6) the role of individual and charismatic teachers, both Indian and Tibetan, in the founding of different schools of Tibetan Buddhism.

THE TRANSMISSION OF TIBETAN BUDDHISM TO MONGOLIA

Up to the thirteenth century, the energy of different Tibetan Buddhist schools was directed internally, as they sought to consolidate their respective traditions, both religiously and politically. With the rise of Mongol hegemony of Central Asia under Genghis Khan at the beginning of the thirteenth century, however, Tibetans could no longer ignore what was happening outside of their borders. They realized that their culture and religion were at risk. In 1207 Tibetan emissaries were sent to the great Khan to submit, and this peremptory action kept the Mongols at bay for over three decades. In 1240, however, Godan Khan invaded Tibet, although he did not seek to establish himself as ruler of the country. In 1244 he summoned the great scholar-monk Sa skya paṇḍita (1182–1251) and his erudite nephew 'Phags pa (1235–1280) to his court. When Sa paṇ finally arrived in 1247, Godan was suffering from an illness. Sa paṇ pan cured him and then proceeded to prove his spiritual worthiness by performing a series of miracles (Powers 1995: 387). Godan was so impressed with Sa skya paṇḍita that he converted to Buddhism, took tantric initiation from him, and began the process of making the Sa skya pa(s) the ostensive rulers of Tibet. Sa skya pandita and Godan Khan died in the same year, but the priest-patron relationship was continued between Kublai Khan and 'Phags pa, whose many accomplishments include the design of a literary script for the Mongolian language, something that made possible the translation of the Tibetan canon into Mongolian. 'Phags pa, like his uncle Sa paṇ, is said to have been not only a great scholar but also an accomplished adept of the Tantras and a skilled miracle worker. This combination of qualities that we find in figures like Sa skya paṇḍita and 'Phags pa—ethical uprightness based on monastic discipline, erudition derived from scholastic studies, and magical power based on tantric practice—is probably as close to a formula for charisma as we are likely to find. The role that this form of charisma has played in the dissemination of Tibetan Buddhism cannot be overestimated.

The pattern of priest-patron that had been established during the time of Buddhism's introduction to Tibet was thus repeated between the Sa skya pa(s) and the Mongols, but with two important twists. The patron now was not a Tibetan but a Mongolian king; and the "priest" was given not only financial support but also considerable political power over the entire country, and even over other schools of Tibetan Buddhism.

The history of the following three centuries is extremely complex. Suffice it to say that the Sa skya pa(s)' rivals quickly learned that they could exploit the factionalism of the Mongols to their advantage and so sought allegiances with different Mongol groups, a fact that led to tremendous intrigue and internecine warfare in Tibet for centuries. In the fourteenth century Tsong kha pa (1357–1419) founded the last major school of Tibetan Buddhism, the dGe lugs, and his spiritual heirs would, repeating the pattern of the Sa skya pa(s), resort to re-establishing the priest-patron relationship with the Mongols, this time with tremendous success. bSod nams rgya mtsho (1543–1588), recognized as the third incarnation of a direct disciple of Tsong kha pa, became, in 1578, the preceptor of Altan Khan (the chief of one of the surviving Mongol factions), and was given by him the title of

Ta-le (meaning "ocean"), a title which all of his subsequent incarnations would bear in the form of "Dalai," and in their personal names (*rGya mtsho* = tib. for "ocean"). The third Dalai Lama spent much of his life converting the different Mongol clans throughout eastern Tibet and Inner Mongolia, founding monasteries, and in the process consolidating power for the dGe lugs pa school. After he died in 1601, it was a Mongol boy, the great grandson of Altan Khan, who was recognized as his next incarnation (*yang srid*).

What is interesting is not so much the details of the historical evolution of the relationship of Tibetans to their Mongolian overlords, which in any case is extremely complex, but rather the role that Buddhism played in this process. Buddhism was not simply exported to the Mongols. Instead what we have here is a species of exchange. From their side, the Mongols received the Buddhist religion, an ideological/institutional system that, at least in theory, could serve as a unifying cultural force; they acquired a written language, a religious canon in their own language, the institution of monasticism that catered to the needs of the laity, and an ethic that served to temper their militarism. In return for Buddhist teachings, the Mongols granted Tibet cultural and religious autonomy; they provided financial resources for the maintenance and flourishing of Tibetan monasteries, including tax-exemption (Stein 1972: 145); and they responded positively to the Buddhist call for more compassionate treatment of enemies (by banning the torture and drowning of political opponents) and animals (by banning blood sacrifice) (Deshung Rinpoche 1995: xxx; and Stein 1972: 82). These of course were the perceived positive effects of such an exchange, but there were also arguably "negative" repercussions. For example, it can be argued that the "civilizing" influence of Buddhism also weakened the Mongol empire, leading eventually to its downfall. For Tibetans, the precedent set by accepting the Mongols as overlords would be exploited by the Ming and Ch'ing dynasties that succeeded the Yuan (Mongol) dynasty, and even by present-day Chinese Communists, in their claims of suzerainty over Tibet.[3]

Most of the six factors mentioned in relation to the introduction of Buddhism to Tibet were of course also factors in Tibetan Buddhism's introduction into Mongolia: the importance of the charismatic teacher as a force, the subsequent priest-patron relationship, the founding of monastic institutions, and subsequent translation (this time of Tibetan texts) are all found in the Mongolian context. There is, however, one crucial factor in the diffusion of Tibetan Buddhism to Mongolia that we do not find in the earlier tradition, and this is the *tulku* (*sprul sku*), or "recognized incarnation." The system whereby a child is recognized as the incarnation of a dead lama predates the spread of Buddhism to Mongolia, being the established practice of succession of, for example, the Karma pa(s) since the thirteenth century. With the identification of a Mongol child of royal lineage as the fourth Dalai Lama at the end of the sixteenth century, however, the tulku system takes on a political dimension that clearly serves the interest of the propagation of the faith into the new culture. Ideologically, the claim that lamas cross ethno-cultural lines when they take rebirth is at once an assertion of the universal character of Buddhism, and a validation of the foreign culture as fertile ground for Buddhism. Politically and economically, it serves as a force motivating the foreign culture to take a more active role in accepting and propagating the new faith, providing it with tangible (blood) ties to the new religion. This practice of finding old lamas in new cultures is of course still operative today, as Western children, Brooklyn housewives, and Hollywood movie stars are recognized as tulkus. We will have more to say about this phenomenon in the West below. For now it is sufficient to point out that this practice has played a role in the diffusion of Tibetan Buddhism from at least the sixteenth century.

The Mongol practice of taking Tibetan lamas as spiritual advisors was sometimes emulated by the Chinese emperors of the Ming and Ch'ing dynasties. For example, both the fourth and fifth Karma pa(s) served in this capacity in the Ming court, and Tsong kha pa himself was invited to the court of the third Ming emperor in 1408, though he chose to send a senior student in his stead (Snellgrove and Richardson 1968: 150, 157). Later, in the eighteenth century, the famed dGe lugs pa scholar lCang skya Rol pa'i rdo rje would also establish ties, this time with the Manchu court. His close relationship with the emperor Ch'ien-lung would go a long way to maintaining the hegemony of the dGe lugs pa school in the Chinese court. Whatever may have been the personal commitments of Chinese emperors, and despite complex political ties between Tibet and China throughout history, Tibetan Buddhism never became popular in China. There are many reasons for this, not the least of which is the fact that China already had developed its own unique form of Buddhism that by this time already had more than a millennium of history on Chinese soil.

The distinctive form of Buddhism fashioned in Tibet would spread over the centuries to other regions and kingdoms on Tibet's western and southern frontiers, notably to Ladakh, Nepal, Sikkim, and Bhutan. In fact, the Bhutaneses' own name for their country, 'Brug, is derived from the popularity in that country of the 'Brug pa branch of the bKa' brgyud school, whose lamas ruled there, much as the Dalai Lama did in Tibet, from the seventeenth to the early twentieth century.

THE TRANSMISSION OF TIBETAN BUDDHISM TO THE WEST

Tibetan Buddhism had little contact with the world outside of its cultural borders for centuries. In the late nineteenth and early twentieth centuries some Westerners, influenced by the Theosophical movement, traveled and studied with Tibetan informants on Tibet's southern and western frontiers. Even if tinged with the occultism of their day, the works of Alexandra David-Neel and Walter Evans-Wentz were some of the first to introduce Westerners to Tibetan Buddhism (see Lopez 1998: chap. 2). From their side, some rare Tibetans also initiated contact with Westerners. The great Tibetan polymath dGe 'dun chos 'phel (1903–1951), for example, traveled extensively throughout India, coming into contact with, and even serving as a consultant for, some Western scholars. In 1955, the Mongolian Geshe Wangyal founded the first "Tibetan" Buddhist monastery in the United States, but this was, at least in its early days, focused chiefly on serving an immigrant Kalmyk community that had settled in New Jersey (see Lopez 1998: 42, 163–64).

The global expansion of Tibetan Buddhism that we are witnessing today did not begin in earnestness until 1959. As is by now well known, after a decade of Chinese military expansion into Tibet, Chinese troops had reached Lha sa. In 1959, a Tibetan uprising against the Chinese authorities led to the flight of the Dalai Lama, who, together with approximately 100,000 Tibetans, sought political asylum in India. The Chinese, with their overwhelming military superiority, established control over the entire country in short order, and began to implement a colonialist policy that has had devastating consequences for Tibetan religion and culture in Tibet (see Avedon 1984).

Tibetans in exile have generally seen their work as twofold. On the one hand, they have been concerned to set up institutions in India to preserve the national culture and religion, whose existence is threatened by Chinese policies in Tibet itself. On the other, they have turned outwardly to the world to garner support for their political cause, but also in response to the rise of interest in their religion. In the early 1960s, refugee Tibetans, under the Dalai Lama, set up a government in exile, a variety of cultural and religious organizations, and the Library of Tibetan Works and Archives (LTWA), all based in Dharamsala, a hill station at the foot of the Himalayas in north India where the Dalai Lama still resides. From its founding, the LTWA has served not only as a venue for serious scholarly research into various aspects of Tibetan religion and culture, but also, after the founding of a program of study in which Tibetan teachers taught traditional texts through translators, has served as a popular study-center for Western students of Buddhism. The LTWA must therefore be seen as one of the first attempts on the part of Tibetans to reach out religiously to the outside world.

Some of the first Tibetan teachers to come to the West traveled not on religious but on scholarly missions. Hence, Deshung Rinpoche, an eminent Sa skya lama (1906–1987), was brought to the University of Washington, Seattle, as a consultant in 1960. In that same year Namkhai Norbu Rinpoche, a rDzogs chen master, was invited by Giuseppe Tucci to Rome (IsMEO) (he is now at the University of Naples); and Dagpo Rinpoche, a dGe lugs lama, went to teach at the

INLCO university in Paris. Samten Karmay, a scholar of Bon and rNying ma, went to London (SOAS) in the early 1960s (and is now at CNRS, Paris); and Geshe Lhundub Sopa, a renowned dGe lugs scholar, was invited in the late 1960s by Richard Robinson to the University of Wisconsin (where he is now emeritus).[4] That Tibetan scholars should have from the outset found themselves in Western academic settings is of course not surprising, given the rigorous academic training they received in their own traditional educational systems. The presence of these and other, Western, scholars of Tibetan Buddhism in North American and European universities made the university setting congenial to many first-wave students of Tibetan Buddhism. These in turn earned doctorates, and find themselves now teaching in various universities throughout the West.

While Tibetan Buddhism was being established in Western educational institutions, it was also attempting to found its own such institutions in the West. For example in 1970, Trungpa Rinpoche founded the Naropa Institute in Boulder, Colorado. Naropa is the first accredited Buddhist university in the Western world. After years of struggle, it has just recently begun to flourish. Its Bachelor of Arts degree program has nearly quadrupled in the past three years, its MA programs in Engaged Buddhism and Contemplative Psychotherapy are filled to capacity, and it is just now inaugurating a Master of Divinity program whose goal it is to prepare individuals for Buddhist-based ministry of various sorts. Finally, mention should be made of the Buddhist publishing houses that have been so integral to the diffusion of the Dharma in the West: especially important in this regard are Shambhala Publications (founded in 1969), Dharma Publishing (in 1971), Wisdom Publications (in 1975), and Snow Lion Publication (in 1980) (see Lopez 1998: 175–77).

Even though the rise of Tibetan Studies in the Western academy has been one factor in the spread of Tibetan Buddhism to the West, it is not the only, nor even the most significant, one. That honor, it seems to me, goes to Tibetan teachers and their students, for it is through their efforts that Tibetan Buddhism has become known and institutionalized in the West. During the 1960s and early 1970s, which of course coincided with a period of tremendous social change in the United States and Western Europe, Tibetan teachers of all lineages, now in exile in India, began to come into contact with Western students. For example, by November 1971 meditation courses directed specifically to Westerners were being held at the Kopan monastery on the outskirts of Kathmandu, Nepal—a monastery founded by two charismatic dGe lugs pa lamas, Lamas Yeshe and Lama Zopa.[5]

The pattern for the diffusion of Buddhism to the West seems to have been the same in most cases: refugee lamas living in India or Nepal would come into contact with Western students, who would then invite them to visit their respective countries. On these or subsequent visits, the lamas would set up "dharma centers" there. Even though some Tibetan Buddhist centers had already been established in the West by the 1960s,[6] it was not until the 1970s that some of Tibet's most famous lineage holders made their first trips to the West. Kalu Rinpoche, an eminent bKa' brgyud lama (see Batchelor 1994: 110–12), began traveling to the West in 1971; Dujom Rinpoche, the head of the rNying ma school in exile, in 1972 (see Batchelor 1994: 71–76); the Gyalwa Karmapa, the head of the Karma bKa' brgyud school (see Batchelor 1994: chap. 8); and Sakya Trizin Rinpoche, the head of the Sa skya school, both in 1974; and Drikung Kyabgon Rinpoche, the head of the 'Bri gung bKa' brgyud school, in 1975. Khetsun Sangpo Rinpoche, a renowned rNying ma scholar, was a visiting scholar at the University of Virginia from 1974 to 1975. H. H. the Dalai Lama made his first tour of the West in 1979.[7] These visits, as we have mentioned, led to the founding of various institutions in the West, whose number has only continued to increase over the years. By 1987, Morreale (1998: xvii) estimates that there were 180 "Vajrayana" (almost all Tibetan) Buddhist centers in North America alone. A decade later, in 1997, that number had increased to 352.[8]

Most of these centers were founded by, and are under the direction of, Tibetan teachers. The founding lamas would install one of their senior Tibetan students, or another teacher of their lineage, as the director of the center, and would continue to visit it periodically, as their travel schedule permitted. Despite the fact that Tibetan Buddhism has existed in an institutionalized form in the West for over forty years, it is really only in the last decade that Westerners have begun to emerge as religious leaders in this tradition (see Lavine 1998). In the last few years several congresses of Western dharma teachers have been convened (in Dharamsala, Boston, San Francisco, and in Colorado), and these have served as a venue for the airing of problems and concerns related to the spread of Buddhism in the West.[9]

Despite the fact that a variety of lamas from different schools of Tibetan Buddhism have been actively involved in the diffusion of Buddhism to the West for over three decades, it is the charismatic fourteenth Dalai Lama whom I believe to be the greatest single factor in the spread of Tibetan Buddhism to the West, at least in the last decade. Especially after being awarded the Nobel Peace prize in 1989, the Dalai Lama has traveled widely throughout the world. These visits have, from the outset, had religious components: he has taught traditional texts, given initiations (most notably the Kâlacakra), and given more general sermons. At the same time, given that the Dalai Lama is not only the spiritual but also the temporal leader of the Tibetan people, his travels have also been devoted to bringing greater visibility to the Tibetan political cause and to garnering greater support for Tibetan autonomy. The religious purposes and political aims of the Dalai Lama's sojourns are in many ways distinct and separate, but not completely so. For one thing, the Dalai Lama has sometimes argued for his political views and methods on religious grounds (see Cabezón 1996). More important, followers of Tibetan Buddhism in the West have been staunch supporters of the Tibetan political cause. Although not all Westerners who support and work for Tibetan autonomy are Tibetan Buddhists, I know of no Tibetan Buddhist in the West who is not pro-autonomy. Although the situation here is quite different from that of medieval Tibet, it is not difficult to see some resonance with an earlier historical era, when the introduction of Buddhism into a quite different cultural setting (namely Mongolia) also served Tibetan (or at least some Tibetans') political aspirations. The point, of course, is that religion and politics are never completely separate. Each sphere reflects, and has repercussions in, the other.

Although much attention has been given to the diffusion of Tibetan Buddhism to the West and its appropriation by Westerners, it should be pointed out that Tibetan Buddhism is increasingly found throughout the world. Tibetan Buddhism has not only come West but also gone East. Tibetan Buddhism of all lineages is popular among ethnic Chinese living in Singapore, and especially in Taiwan. It is also important to remember that Tibetan Buddhism abroad is not only a religion of Westerners but also of indigenous Tibetans who have migrated to various parts of the globe as part of the Tibetan diaspora. This latter phenomenon, what has been called "ethnic" Tibetan Buddhism, is as much a part of the diffusion of Tibetan Buddhism as is its appropriation by Westerners. It is also important to note that the two phenomena—ethnic and Western Buddhism—are not independent of each other. For one thing there are many dharma centers in the West that serve the needs of *both* ethnic Tibetans and Western Buddhists.[10] For another, sometimes a center that begins by serving one of these two communities ends up principally serving the other.[11]

Just as Tibetan Buddhism has changed the West, so too has the West changed Tibetan Buddhism. Much of the transformation of Tibetan Buddhism has been the result of the present Dalai Lama's commitment to reform and modernization. In particular, the Dalai Lama has opened up new horizons for Tibetan Buddhism and encouraged an openness to new ideas and institutions in what is an otherwise very traditionalist religious landscape. For example, the Dalai Lama has encouraged, and been an active participant in, inter-religious (and especially inter-monastic) dialogue. He has also been the impetus behind a dialogue between Tibetan Buddhism and Western science.[12] Also, in the 1980s, at the urging of the Dalai Lama, the very conservative large monastic universities of the dGe lugs pa school in exile in south India introduced for younger monks a curriculum comprising in large part Western subjects (English, math, science, etc.). Today, most of these same monasteries also have large computing centers for the digital input of Tibetan religious texts. All of this has meant that Tibetan Buddhism has become less fearful of external influence, more confident, and more open to dialogue with the world outside of its cultural borders.

One of the most important changes to have occurred as a result of Tibetan Buddhism's encounter with the West has to do with the status of women in Tibetan culture. The conspicuous and almost total absence of female religious teachers among ethnic Tibetans, and the relatively low status of Tibetan nuns in particular, from early on caught the attention of Western students of Tibetan Buddhism, and especially women and committed feminists.[13] Traditionally, nuns in Tibetan society were concerned almost exclusively with performing rituals for the laity, and this has meant that they have lacked the traditional educational opportunities available to monks. Once again with the backing of the Dalai Lama, Tibetans and Westerners have established collaborative projects to provide nuns with financial resources that make them less dependent on ritual activity, and therefore free to pursue programs of study. Moreover, although women teachers were not completely unknown in Tibet, they were rare. Those that did exist often lacked the status and prestige of their male counterparts. I believe that the prominence that has been achieved in recent years by several ethnic Tibetan women lamas—for example, Khandro Chenmo Rinpoche (see Huckenpahler 1992) and Sakya Jetsun Chimey Luding (see Coleman 1993)—is at least partially the result of Tibetan Buddhism's encounter with the West, where women lamas, both as teachers and role models, are in high demand.

FACTORS IN THE TRANSMISSION
OF TIBETAN BUDDHISM

It is interesting to compare the factors operative in the transmission of Buddhism from India to Tibet, and from Tibet to Mongolia, with the spread of Tibetan Buddhism to the West. Each of the factors display some similarities between the past and the present, and some significant differences.

The importance of patronage is still very much a factor, although today this is more financial than it is political.[14] Tibetan Buddhism has not, nor will it, spread to the West through the conversion of kings and presidents. Nonetheless, the religion's association with high-visibility personages, like Hollywood movie stars—perhaps the queens and kings of our own time and place—cannot be underestimated as a factor in its diffusion. Moreover, even though the financial patronage of the wealthy has been an important factor, the spread of Tibetan Buddhism to the West has been in large part a grass-roots phenomenon. Rather than depending on an individual large benefactor, then, it seems to me that dharma centers have been principally sustained through the small contributions of its many members. Only serious sociological analysis of these institutions, however, will allow us to make accurate generalizations of this kind.[15]

As was the case with the introduction of Buddhism into Tibet, material signs, especially artistic and architectural ones, have also accompanied the spread of

Buddhism to the West. A temple room, with a traditional Tibetan altar (*chos shom*) and a teacher's throne (*khrid*), is one of the first such signs in the founding of a dharma center. Once centers become more established, they often undertake the building of one or more "stûpas" (*mchod rten*)—pagoda-like structures that vary in size, some several stories in height, filled with portions of religious texts, small clay statues, blessed substances, etc.—that symbolize enlightened mind. Both the art and architecture of Tibetan Buddhism in the West to date is relatively conservative and traditionalist, evincing little departure from indigenous Tibetan forms. This is to be expected in this early period of its diffusion, when there are still very strong ties to Tibet as a culture and Tibetans as a people. Such aesthetic traditionalism is also bolstered by a Western romanticist ideology that sees everything Tibetan as endangered and therefore as being in need of preservation in a "pure" unaltered form.[16]

Given that few Tibetan lamas speak English, and that few Tibetan texts exist in Western languages, translation has also been extremely important in the spread of Tibetan Buddhism to the West. Trained oral translators fluent in doctrinal terminology (*chos skad*), though a rare commodity, are often not very well paid, making their work more an act of devotion than a mode of subsistence. Translations of doctrinal and scriptural literary works are, with few exceptions,[17] the purview of academics, who have both the leisure and the professional incentive to publish such texts. Liturgical texts are often translated in-house in various dharma centers as the need for these arises, and because of their tantric (and therefore esoteric) content, tend not to be widely distributed. Although not translations, periodicals have also been extremely important in the diffusion of Tibetan Buddhism, e.g., as venues for more popular writings by dharma teachers, as forums for the discussion of controversies, as clearinghouses of information, and so forth. In this regard, the *Snow Lion Newsletter*, the *Shambhala Sun*, and *Tricycle* have been especially important for Tibetan Buddhists.

The Tibetan tendency to favor Indian over Chinese Buddhism, a pattern that begins in the eighth century, is of course tied to the fact that there were powers (royal patrons especially) who had a say in such matters. In the West, the separation of church and state renders moot the question of the form of Buddhism to be practiced by the society as a whole. Rather than being a top-down decision, the demographics of the sectarian division of the religious marketplace is determined bottom-up, based on the decisions of "religious consumers," who are, *pace* sociohistorical forces, relatively free agents. Whereas Tibetan Buddhism began as a minoritarian movement within a minoritarian tradition (Buddhism) in the West, it has grown to the point where, both in Europe and in the United States, it is on a par with its closest Buddhist "competitor," Zen (see Morreale 1998: xvii; Obadia 1999: 170–72). Despite a rhetoric to the contrary, tensions (e.g., competition for adherents) do exist between different Buddhist traditions in the West, but what is even more marked is the tension that exists within Tibetan Buddhism itself, that is, between the different schools of Tibetan Buddhism. This tension, which obviously has precedent in Tibet, has in large part been muted by virtue of the present Dalai Lama's staunch anti-sectarianism (*ris med*). At times, however, it has erupted, as in the present controversy over the protector deity rDo rje shugs ldan.[18]

Finally, as opposed to the situation in Tibet and among Tibetans in exile in India, Tibetan Buddhism in the West is overwhelmingly a lay, that is, *non-monastic* tradition. Despite the fact that many Tibetan teachers in the West are monks, few of their students have taken up the monastic way of life, and of those that have, few have remained monks and nuns.[19] There are undoubtedly many reasons for this, not the least of which is the strict discipline that monks and nuns must adopt: vows that require celibacy, that prohibit evening meals (even if this was little practiced by Tibetans themselves), and that require the wearing of robes. In Tibet there were strong social-, and *less* strong financial-, support systems for monks and nuns (both within the monasteries and in the society generally), something that up to this point has been all but lacking in the West. Finally, in Tibet there were few, both religious and secular, educational opportunities outside of monasteries, whereas this is clearly not the case in the West. Despite all of this, some Western monks and nuns have succeeded in keeping the discipline, and, though there are very few Tibetan Buddhist exclusively monastic institutions in the West, Western monks and nuns live, and increasingly serve in various leadership roles, in mixed lay/monastic communities.

Let me also add a note on tulkus (recognized incarnations). As we saw, the tulku system has been an important religiopolitical institution in Tibet, especially since the time of the fourth Dalai Lama. It should not be surprising, therefore, to see its repetition in the West. Many young Western (to my knowledge, exclusively male) children have been found to be the reincarnations (*yang srid*) of various Tibetan lamas, a glamorized re-enactment of which we find in the narrative of the film *The Little Buddha*. That the tulku system will have an important role to play in the diffusion of Tibetan Buddhism to the West can hardly be denied. It would be reductionistic, however, to see only political or financial motives at work in the recognition of Western children as lamas. For the most part these children come from humble Western families, and in most cases there seems little to be gained financially by the Tibetans who consider them as the reincarnations of their teachers. Arguably more controversial is the recognition of wealthy and/or famous Western *adults* (such as the Hollywood movie star Steven Segal) as tulkus, where ulterior motives would, on the surface at least, seem to be operative. Even this, however, was not unknown in Tibet.

The diffusion of religion is a historical process. What is a factor in the spread of Tibetan Buddhism in one culture and period will often be a factor in another place and time. However, sometimes what is an important factor (e.g., monasticism) in one setting (such as Mongolia) will be less so in another (such as the

West), and in some instances we actually find actual reversals of, or strange twists in, previous historical patterns (as in patterns of patronage shifting from royalty to Hollywood). But whether history repeats or reverses itself, it is always useful to be aware of history, if for no other reason than that historical consciousness is an antidote to romanticism, which, in the case of Tibet, has been, and continues to be, a constant temptation for the West.

NOTES

1. Richardson (1998:142) shows, interestingly, how the Chinese and Indian sides were supported by different aristocratic Tibetan clans, so that the "debate" at a religious/ doctrinal level was being recapitulated in a struggle for political power.

2. For a concise history and description of these four traditions, and maps showing the distribution of their monasteries throughout Tibet and Mongolia, see Coleman (1993).

3. See Richardson's remarks in Powers (1995: 140) for a repudiation of the logic of this position.

4. For more details on some of these teachers, as well as others who founded centers in the United States, see Lavine (1998) and Prebish (1999: 40–46). Concerning the spread of Tibetan Buddhism to Europe, see Obadia (1999: chap. 7).

5. These two lamas would later go on to establish a worldwide network of "dharma centers," the most extensive of the dGe lugs pa school, under the umbrella of the Foundation for the Preservation of the Mahayana Tradition (FPMT); see Batchelor (1994: chap. 12).

6. Most notably the Lamaist Buddhist Monastery of America, founded in 1958 by the Mongolian Geshe Ngawang Wangyal; the Sakya Monastery founded by Sakya Dagchen Rinpoche in Seattle in 1960; Samye Ling meditation center in Scotland, co-founded by Trungpa and Akong Rinpoches; and the Nyingma Meditation Center in Berkeley, founded by Tarthang Tulku Rinpoche, both institutions founded in 1968.

7. Most of these dates are culled from Coleman (1993: pt. 2).

8. Morreale gives a listing and description of many of these centers in his book (1998: pt. 3), although the focus is principally on the tradition founded by Chogyam Trungpa Rinpoche. The work of Coleman (1993), and his collaborators at the Orient Foundation (Bath, England), though somewhat out of date, is also useful, and not only because its focus is Tibet. The book treats Tibetan religion worldwide, contains short biographies of major teachers, and also a useful glossary.

9. An interesting account of the Boston congress can be found in Prebish (1999: chap. 6).

10. In North America this has been increasingly the case after the immigration legislation that permitted the resettlement of a thousand Tibetans in the United States.

11. This is the case with the Lamaist Buddhist Monastery of America that began chiefly as a ministry to Kalmyk Mongolians in New Jersey, and that later became the

Tibetan Buddhist Learning Center, an organization run by and serving principally American Buddhists.

12. The resultant dialogues have been published in a series of books under the auspices of the organizing body, the Mind and Life Institute. See Cabezón (2003) for a discussion of the Dalai Lama's role in the Buddhism and Science dialogue, and the relevant bibliography for the Mind and Life conferences.

13. See, for example, Gross (1998), which is valuable not only because it raises the issue of the "female guru," but also because it confronts head-on the question of the sexual misconduct of male teachers. On another controversy, concerning the reintroduction of the full-ordination lineage for nuns into Tibetan Buddhism, see Hengching Shih (2000).

14. This is not to say that the spread of Tibetan Buddhism has not had political repercussions, e.g., on the issue of Tibetan autonomy, as mentioned above.

15. Sociological analyses of Tibetan Buddhism in the West is still in its infancy, but see Obadia's (1999) excellent study of Tibetan Buddhism in France as exemplary of how such analyses might be conducted.

16. Although see the essays in Korom (1997) for examples of moves away from aestheticist traditionalism on the part of Tibetans themselves, including the interesting anecdote (1997: 6) of the work of a Tibetan *thang ka* painter in Santa Fe that contains representations of a bodhisattva on one mountain peak and Santa Claus on another!

17. A notable exception is the Nalanda Translation Committee of the Shambhala organization founded by Trungpa Rinpoche.

18. A full understanding of the intricacies of this controversy are beyond the scope of this chapter. Those interested should consult Dreyfus (1999) the most detailed and accurate account of the issues and their historical background.

19. However, it should be pointed out that overall Western women (nuns) seem to be more successful at keeping their monastic vows (in the sense of having a lower rate of recidivism to lay life) than Western men (monks), but this is known to me only anecdotally.

BIBLIOGRAPHY

Avedon, John F. 1984. *In Exile from the Land of Snows.* New York: Vintage.

Batchelor. Stephen. 1994. *The Awakening of the West: The Encounter of Buddhism and Western Culture.* Berkeley, Calif.: Parallax Press.

Brauen, Martin. 2000. *Dreamworld Tibet: Western Illusions.* Bangkok: Orchid Press, 2004.

Cabezón, José Ignacio. Forthcoming. *Consuming Tibet: On the Commodification of Tibetan Buddhism.*

———. 2003. "Buddhism and Science: On the Nature of the Dialogue." In *Buddhism and Science: Breaking New Ground.* Ed. Alan Wallace, 35–70. Oxford: Oxford University Press.

———. 1996. "Buddhist Principles in the Tibetan Liberation Movement." In *Engaged*

Buddhism: Buddhist Liberation Movements in Asia. Eds. Christopher S. Queen and Sallie B. King, 295–320. Albany: State University of New York Press.

———. 1995. "Buddhist Studies as a Discipline and the Role of Theory." *Journal of the International Association of Buddhist Studies* 18, no. 2: 231–268.

Coleman, Graham, ed. 1993. *A Handbook of Tibetan Culture: A Guide to Tibetan Centres and Resources Throughout the World.* Boston: Shambhala.

Deshung Rinpoche, Kunga Tenpay Nyima. 1995. *The Three Levels of Spiritual Percpetion.* Boston: Wisdom Publications.

Dreyfus, Georges. 1999 "The Shugs ldan Affair: History and Nature of a Quarrel." *Journal of the International Association of Buddhist Studies* 21, no. 2: 227–270.

Fields, Rick. 1986. *How the Swans Came to the Lake: A Narrative History of Buddhism in America.* Boston: Shambhala.

Gross, Rita. 1998. "Helping the Iron Bird Fly: Western Buddhist Women and the Issues of Authority in the Late 1990's." In *The Faces of Buddhism in America.* Eds. Charles S. Prebish and Kenneth K. Tanaka, 228–52. Berkeley: University of California Press.

Heng-ching Shih. 2000. "Lineage and Transmission: Integrating the Chinese and Tibetan Orders of Buddhist Nuns." *Chung-hwa Buddhist Journal* 13: 503–48.

Huckenpahler, Victoria. 1992. "Interview with Khandro Chenmo Rinpochey." *Cho yang* 5: 61–64.

Jackson, Roger, and John Makransky. 2000. *Buddhist Theology: Critical Reflections by Contemporary Buddhist Scholars.* Surrey: Curzon.

Korom, Frank J. ed. 1997. *Tibetan Culture in the Diaspora.* Proceedings of the 7th Seminar of the International Association of Tibetan Studies, Graz, 1995, vol. 4. Wien: Verlag des Österreichischen Akademie der Wissenschaften.

Lavine, Amy. 1998. "Tibetan Buddhism in America: The Development of American Vajrayāna." In *The Faces of Buddhism in America.* Eds. Charles S. Prebish and Kenneth K. Tanaka, 99–118. Berkeley: University of California Press.

Lopez, Donald S., Jr. 1998. *Prisoners of Shangri-la: Tibetan Buddhism and the West.* Chicago: University of Chicago Press.

Morreale, Don. 1998. *The Complete Guide to Buddhist America.* Boston: Shambhala.

Obadia, Lionel. 1999. *Bouddhisme et Occident: La diffusion du bouddhisme tibétain en France.* Paris: Editions L'Harmattan.

Powers, John. 1995. *Introduction to Tibetan Buddhism.* Ithaca, N.Y.: Snow Lion.

Prebish, Charles. 1999. *Luminous Passage: The Practice and Study of Buddhism in America.* Berkeley: University of California Press.

Richardson, Hugh. 1998. *High Peaks, Pure Earth: Collected Writings on Tibetan History and Culture.* London: Serindia.

Samuel, Geoffrey. 1997. "Some Reflections on the Vajrayâna and its Shamanic Origins." In *Les habitants du toit du monde: Études recueillies en homage à Alezander W, Macdonald.* Eds. Samten Karmay and Phillippe Sagant, 325–342. Nanterre: Société d'ethnologie.

———. 1993a. *Civilized Shamans: Buddhism in Tibetan Society.* Washington, D.C.: Smithsonian Institution Press.

———. 1993b. "Shamanism, Bon and Tibetan Religion." In *Anthropology of Tibet and the Himalaya.* Eds. C. Ramble and M. Brauen, 318–38. Zurich: Ethnological Museum of the University of Zurich.

Seyfort Ruegg, David. 1997. "The Preceptor-Donor (*yon mchod*) Relation in Thirteenth

Century Tibetan Society and Polity, its Inner Asian Precursors and Indian Models." In *Tibetan Studies*, vol. 2, Proceedings of the 7th Seminar of the International Association of Tibetan Studies, Graz. Eds. Helmut Krasser, et. al, 857–872. Wien: Verlag der Osterreichischen Akademie der Wissenschaften.

Snellgrove, David, and Hugh Richardson. 1968. *A Cultural History of Tibet*. N.Y.: Frederick A. Praeger.

Stein, R. A. 1972. *Tibetan Civilization*. Trans. J. E. Stapleton Driver. Stanford: Stanford University Press.

CHAPTER 11

VIETNAMESE RELIGIOUS SOCIETY

JAYNE S. WERNER

IN some ways, Vietnam is a microcosm of global religions. Vietnamese religious society comprises a great diversity of religious traditions, practices, and beliefs, not only among the majoritarian ethnic Vietnamese population but also among to the more than fifty other ethnic groups residing in Vietnam. In addition to Buddhism (both Mahayana and Theravada), Taoism, Confucianism, Islam (among the Cham minority), and Christianity, there are the specific religious practices of the highland ethnic groups, as well as the southern religious sects such as the Cao Dai and the Hoa Hao. Among the Vietnamese, "religion" is manifested by a flexible conception of the "unity of the three religions" (Buddhism, Taoism, and Confucianism) and is anchored in the veneration of family ancestors, known as the cult of the ancestors. Almost all Vietnamese keep an altar at home with incense, fruit, and pictures of deceased family members, whom they honor at times of death anniversaries (*gio*) as well as the first and fifteenth days of the lunar month, at which time visits may also be made to a nearby pagoda.

It is virtually impossible to determine the extent of religious adherence in Vietnam. Most religious activity is unorganized and a matter of individual preference within a wide-ranging spiritual landscape. Estimates of the more definable religious communities such as Catholicism include about 10 percent of the population who are Catholics, possibly 500,000 adherents of Protestantism, 60,000 followers of Islam, with the Cao Dai representing 1.5–2million adherents and the Hoa Hao 500,000–1 million. There are about 12,000 pagodas in Vietnam of which most are in the south. The number of *Buddhist monks* and *nuns* is estimated to be around 25,000.

Those who fall outside organized religious communities embrace a wide variety of religious tenets and practices within the three-religions context. It is often said that there are three hierarchies of saints in Vietnam: first the buddhas (*phat*), then the holy saints (*thanh*), followed by the immortals (*tien*). The spirit world also includes Holy Mothers (*thanh mau*), tutelary spirits, national heroes and spiritually endowed natural phenomena, such as an old venerable banyan tree or a special rock formation. There are thousands of communal cults in Vietnam, organized around village patron saints—these are called tutelary genies (*thanh hoang*). Most of the tutelary genies are historical figures who have achieved some great distinction. There are even state-sponsored patriotic cults to venerate martyred heroes and heroines of the revolution (including Ho Chi Minh). These cults resonate deeply among the Vietnamese, where spirituality is called upon to embrace the horrific losses and traumas of long wars with both Western and Asian powers and current economic and social pressures.

Buddhism comes closest to representing the majoritarian religion. Both Theravada and Mahayana traditions are practiced with the latter the most prevalent. The two major schools are the Pure Land (Tinh Do) school and the Thien school (Zen). Buddhism was introduced to Vietnam in the second century AD, from both India and China during the period of Chinese domination (second century BC to tenth century AD). During the independent royal dynasties (tenth to fourteenth centuries), Buddhism played a predominant role in society and politics. It was the official state religion under the Ly dynasty. Even after Confucianism gained ascendancy as a state doctrine and system of governance, Buddhism continued to affect national politics and culture, including literature, such as the classical prose-poem *The Tale of Kieu* by Nguyen Du (1765–1820). Indeed, the popular saying, "the king owns the land but Buddhism owns the village," reflects the centrality of the Buddhist temple (*chua*) in the spiritual life of rural Vietnam.

Today Quan Su pagoda in Hanoi comprises the national headquarters for Buddhism in Vietnam and houses the national Buddhist Institute. It serves as a central distribution center for Buddhist materials. There are three Buddhist universities in Vietnam and forty centers for Buddhist studies. Magnificent pagodas and pilgrimage sites abound in Vietnam, in both the north and the south, of which the most famous is Perfume Pagoda in the mountains southwest of Hanoi. There have been attempts by the socialist state to unify all the schools and branches of Buddhism, without much success. Many pagodas, such as Thich Tri Quang's An Quang pagoda in Danang and Thien Mu in Hue, remain outside the official orbit.

Vietnam has the second largest Catholic following in Southeast Asia, after the Philippines. Unlike China, Vietnam has maintained ties with the Vatican and has allowed the Catholic Church to appoint a new Cardinal and to increase the number of seminaries to six throughout the country. Catholic bishops must be approved by the government but are allowed to travel to Rome. However, the government closely controls and limits the ordination of new clergy, proscribes missionary activities, and has censored a section of the Catechism on human rights. One-half million Catholics fled North Vietnam in 1954 for the south, where the Catholic Church was closely linked to the anti-communist Saigon regime.

The fastest growing religion in Vietnam may be Protestantism, estimated today to have over a half million adherents. There are an estimated five hundred churches and four hundred pastors. Protestant denominations in Vietnam include the Christian and Missionary Alliance, Seventh Day Adventists, Jehovah's Witnesses, Pentecostals, World Vision, Baptists, Methodists, Quakers, and Mennonites. The government does not allow foreign missionary activity but there are foreign Protestant leaders living in Vietnam who work for the vast nongovernmental organization network who may assist local pastors. Protestant churches are active in the urban areas and appeal to the emerging middle-class population for their emphasis on individual salvation and sense of freedom, as well as among the ethnic minorities in the central highlands. House churches in the highlands operated by evangelical Protestants were shut down in l99l but were gradually reopened in 2005, subject to state approval and registration.

The Cao Dai, founded in the south in 1926, is a "new religion" which aptly reflects the unity and diversity of Vietnamese religious society. Based on the Vietnamese conception of the amalgam of the three-religions (*tam giao*), its goal is to unify all the world's major religions into one. The term *Cao Dai* is a Taoist term meaning "high tower," or an exalted place for spiritual meditation. There are from one to two million Cao Dai adherents (*tin-do*) scattered among ten splinter groups north of Ho Chi Minh City and the Mekong delta. The largest branch has a "Holy See" (*Toa thanh*) in Tay Ninh province. The Cao Dai have a hierarchically organized priesthood; a plethora of "saints" including Victor Hugo, Ho Chi Minh, and Jesus Christ; elaborate rituals; and a strong devoted following. Cao Dai doctrine (*giao-ly*) is based on the revelations of spirit seances with deceased personalities, which have been collected and printed in bibles. Priestly mediumistic practices were forbidden by the government after 1975, although they probably exist underground. The government argues that the giao-ly has already been "received," so there is no longer a need for a continuation of mediumism. Cao Dai religious practice continues to consist of daily services at Cao Dai temples, observance of religious anniversaries, vegetarianism, and charity activities such as medical care dispensed to the poor. The government legalized the main Cao Dai branch at Tay Ninh in l997 and relations have been gradually improving since then.

The Hoa Hao, named for Hoa Hao village where this religion was founded in 1939 by Huynh Phu So, is a second new religious movement. Unlike the Cao Dai, the Hoa Hao are a kind of Buddhism and in fact are called Hoa Hao Buddhism (Phat Giao Hoa Hao). The Hoa Hao have less elaborate rituals than the Cao Dai, and their adherents practice their faith mainly at home. Relations between the Hoa Hao and the Communist government have historically been antagonistic. The government disbanded the Hoa Hao after l975, although individual practitioners were allowed to worship at home. Hoa Hao military forces fought against the Communists during the Vietnam War, and Hoa Hao founder Huynh Phu So was probably killed by Communists in the late 1940s. Nonetheless Huynh Phu So is still venerated as a religious saint, and the Hoa Hao have remained very popular in their locale of the western Mekong region of the south. The Hoa Hao reflect the popularization of Buddhism (some would call it "vulgarization") in the south, as it accommodated itself to the frontier spirit of the western Mekong and the folk beliefs of the southern peasantry.

A pervasive religious conception among the Vietnamese is the correspondence between the world of the living and the world of the dead. This unites practices as diverse as ancestor worship, Christianity, the July 27th national holiday to commemorate war martyrs of the last two wars, and pilgrimages to the highly popular Lady of the Realm shrine in southern Vietnam. It also animates spirit worship in the Cao Dai religion, mediumistic practices, soul callers, and private seances held in pagodas and temples to communicate with and seek advice from dead parents and grandparents. It is not surprising then that religious activity among the Vietnamese has increased dramatically since the end of the Vietnam War (1975). Organized religious communities have all experienced a growth in their membership. Ancestor worship has taken on new dimensions as family rituals have increased in size and scope, including the restoration of family tombs and renovation of new lineage worship houses. Buddhist pagodas, Taoist temples, Catholic churches, and communal houses where the statues of tutelary genies reside, have all been refurbished. The Cao Dai Holy See in Tay Ninh province has been totally renovated in recent years, thanks to contributions from Vietnamese residing abroad. The Vietnamese government generally encourages the refurbishing of major religious buildings and historical sites of religious significance, and pagodas receive state certificates as national historical monuments.

Indeed, religion itself has been redefined in recent years in Vietnam. Whereas organized religion played both a conservative and a revolutionary role in Vietnam in the twentieth century, the Communist Party, dating back to 1930, was always avowedly secularist. With the collapse of the Soviet Union and the decline of Marxism-Leninism in Vietnam, however, religion has started to take up the slack. It has done so by representing "national tradition" and the revalorization of "culture" as the "nation." What is now represented as authentically Vietnamese is religious faith, none more so than Vietnam's now-labeled "indigenous" religions of Caodaism and Hoa Haoism, compared to the "imported" religions of Buddhism, Taoism, and Christianity! Of course the state permits religious activity within strictly prescribed limits; top political figures visit well-known pagodas or even Cao Dai temples at Tet, but the government does not allow religious activity that is political, illegal, or compromises national security. To wit, dissident Buddhist demonstrations in Hue, Catholic disturbances in Dong Nai in the south, and recent Protestant protests in the central highlands, reported as human rights abuses in the West, have not been tolerated by the regime because they ostensibly fell within these categories.

Another reason for renewed religious activity stems from the recent introduction of market reforms called *doi moi* (starting in 1986), designed to speed up the country's economic development. These reforms have led to a general loosening of the party/state's grip on "civil society," resulting in a greater sense of religious freedom. In 1991 the government issued a decree permitting forms of religious expression which were prohibited before, such as some forms as mediumism (e.g., *len dong*). The state's more liberal attitude toward the Cao Dai, the Hoa Hao, and Catholicism which had opposed the regime in the past, also stems from this period. These religions were viewed with suspicion after the entire country became Communist in 1975. Soon after that date, the Hoa Hao leadership was virtually disbanded and the Cao Dai were reorganized. There was an attempt by Cao Dai associated with the Tay Ninh Holy See to stage an armed rebellion against the regime. This was swiftly put down. Vietnamese Catholics, tarnished with the brush of collaboration with French colonialism, escaped political opprobrium by the extraordinary leadership of Msg. Nguyen Van Binh, the archbishop of Saigon, who in 1975 adopted a conciliatory stance toward the new regime. He did much to restore the standing of Catholicism in the eyes of the regime.

The Vietnamese Communist government has had a long history of experience with religiously based counter-hegemonic movements, especially those allied with Western powers. Their approach has been to draw potentially dissident religious groups into state-sponsored networks. In 1981 the government set up the National Buddhist Church by organizing a Congress for the Unification of Buddhism held at the famous Quan Su pagoda in Hanoi. The slogan of this Congress was "Religion-Nation-Socialism." The state-sponsored unification of Buddhism, however, has not been a success. In fact many pagodas and bonzes resent the intrusion of the government into their affairs. To its credit, however, the government has allowed Buddhist schools to open in Hanoi and in the south, and there are newly founded Buddhist institutes and libraries, especially in the south. A new Catholic archbishop of Hanoi has recently been consecrated, for the first time in fifty years. There are Catholic seminaries in the north, center, and south. The social service or charity and medical functions of temples, pagodas, and churches have been given limited scope to operate once again. In the past they were feared as competition for the social welfare functions of the state, but given the decline in government social services, they are now seen as performing a useful function. Elected representatives of the National Assembly and appointed members of the Executive Committee of the Fatherland Front currently include a fair number of religious delegates from all the major groups. However, several prominent Buddhist, Catholic, and Protestant religious figures have been under house arrest in recent years for allegedly unlawful religious activities, and their cause has been taken up by human rights organizations in the United States and Europe. The government monitors religious activity through its Religious Board (Ban Ton Giao) located in Hanoi, the mass-organizations committee of the Communist Party, and the Fatherland Front.

The diversity of religious practices within Vietnam are also found within the Vietnamese diaspora overseas. Vietnamese Catholics are more numerous in France and the United States among the Vietnamese population than they are in Vietnam. Many Vietnamese refugees among the "boat people" who fled to the United States after 1975 were sponsored by churches in the United States, and some of the new arrivals can be found among their sponsoring congregations. There are Buddhist, Cao Dai, and Hoa Hao circles among the Vietnamese in both France and the United States. Possibly the most famous Vietnamese Buddhist living abroad is the erudite Zen master Thich Nhat Hanh, who resides in France at Plum Village in the Dordogne, France. Thich Nhat Hanh was in exile for thirty-eight years, unable to freely practice in Vietnam. In January 2005, however, Master Hanh and members of his Zen Buddhist community returned home to Vietnam for a state-sponsored visit. It is too soon to tell whether or not this augurs greater religious freedom in Vietnam.

BIBLIOGRAPHY

Elman, Benjamin A., John B. Duncan, and Herman Ooms, eds. 2002. *Rethinking Confucianism: Past and Present in China, Japan, Korea and Vietnam*. Los Angeles: UCLA Asian Pacific Monograph Series.

Ho Tai, Hue-Tam. 1983. *Millenarianism and Peasant Politics in Vietnam*. Cambridge, Mass.: Harvard University Press.

Marr, David. 1986. "Religion in Vietnam." In *Religion and Politics in Communist States*. Eds. R. F. Miller and T. H. Rigby, 123–133. Canberra: Australian National University Press.

Nguyen The Anh. 1995. "The Vietnamization of the Cham Deity Po Nagar." In *Essays into Vietnamese Pasts*. Eds. K. W. Taylor and John Whitmore, 42–50. Ithaca, N.Y.: Southeast Asia Program Publications, Cornell University.

Taylor, Philip. 2004. *Goddess on the Rise: Pilgrimage and Popular Religion in Vietnam*. Honolulu: University of Hawaii Press.

Thich Nhat Hanh. 1975. *The Miracle of Mindfulness*. Boston: Beacon Press.

Werner, Jayne. 1981. *Peasant Politics and Religious Sectarianism: Peasant and Priest in the Cao Dai in Vietnam*. New Haven, Conn.: Southeast Asian Monograph Series, Yale University.

CHAPTER 12

TRADITIONAL CHINESE RELIGIOUS SOCIETY

VIVIAN-LEE NYITRAY

TRADITIONAL Chinese religious society is not limited to the geographical boundaries of China and Taiwan or to the billion and a quarter people who live in those areas. For centuries traditional Chinese religious customs were spread by émigrés, first throughout East and Southeast Asia and then beyond, to Europe, Africa, and North and South America.

But it is not easy to describe the contours of religion in these communities, nor to define what is meant by "traditional Chinese religion." Most scholars regard Chinese "religion" as encompassing not only the better-known traditions of Confucianism, Daoism (also romanized as Taoism), and Buddhism, but also the equally important popular traditions ranging from shamanism and spirit writing to Feng shui (geomancy) and the cults of local deities. This characterization is complicated by long-standing cultural preferences that define certain traditions, particularly Confucianism, as "philosophy" or "family tradition" rather than as "religion." Other practices, such as divination and spirit possession, tend to be relegated to the realm of "superstition." A final complication arises insofar as people practice several traditions simultaneously, in various combinations and to varying degrees. For all these reasons, although traditional Chinese society is often characterized religiously in terms of a syncretism of the "Three Traditions," or *sanjiao*, of Confucianism, Buddhism, and Daoism, the reality has always been more complex.

CONFUCIANISM

Confucianism takes its Western name from its founder, the scholar-teacher Master Kong Fu Zi (latinized as Confucius). In Chinese, it is known as the *ru* or "scholarly" tradition. From its beginnings in the sixth century BCE, Confucianism hoped to create a stable and peaceful society led by sage individuals who maintain social harmony through the charismatic power of their virtue and their ritual interactions with others. The Confucian vision for human society takes the form of a series of concentric circles: every individual, centered in home and family, has the potential to cultivate virtue that will radiate out to village and state and thence to "all under Heaven" through ritual actions.

Beginning in the home, attention to family duties and ancestral veneration places the individual in a matrix of hierarchical responsibilities. Vertically, there are responsibilities to and for one's parents, siblings, spouse, children, extended clan relations, and forbearers. There are further relationships with one's social superiors and with friends. Age, gender, and status nuance all relationships so that truly horizontal relationships, even with friends, are rare. When responsibilities are properly fulfilled and relationships properly maintained, the harmony that results is said to "mirror Heaven."

There are no Confucian clergy or religious professionals other than temple caretakers and ceremonial officiants. Authority has always been vested in scholars, and formal education in the classics—works of history, poetry, divination, ritual, and philosophy—is the key to self-cultivation. There are no gods to be worshiped, only sages and worthies to be venerated. Confucius's birthplace in Qufu is home to the most prominent temple, but every Chinese city and major town had a temple where spring and autumn sacrifices to Confucius's spirit were conducted by local officials. Although virtually all of the temples in the People's Republic of China were destroyed or converted to other uses after 1949, the Qufu temple complex was rebuilt in the 1980s. The annual late September ceremony to honor Confucius's spirit, replete with offerings of food, incense, music, and dance, has been reinstated. The day of the memorial ceremony marks the anniversary of Confucius's birth, which is now celebrated as Teachers' Day. Temples have no membership rolls and are primarily quiet, auspicious places for study and contemplation.

It is important to note that Confucian temples are actually called *wen miao* (temple of culture). The identification of Confucianism with traditional Chinese society is deeply rooted, yet the tradition remains extremely diffuse. Few people self-identify as Confucian, yet fewer still would deny the vital importance of promoting filiality and family cohesion, of pursuing formal education, and of fulfilling one's responsibilities within the traditional pattern of five relationships (ruler-ruled, parent-child, husband-wife, elder-younger, and friend-friend). The centrality of the tradition to Chinese society is evident in the pervasiveness of its rhetoric, images, and ideals. Even at the height of Maoist-Marxism in the modern People's Republic of China, the power of familiar Confucian texts was recognized, and subtly quoted excerpts were pressed into the service of Communist ideals, even as Confucius himself was vilified. In the current era of market reforms, Confucian values and virtues—without being overtly labeled as such—are again touted as the urgently needed antidote to rampant corruption and exploitation.

DAOISM

Daoism focuses on the preservation of life and on securing optimal pleasure and success in one's affairs. These benefits are achieved through processes of discerning and then aligning oneself with the movements of the Dao, or natural laws of the cosmos. The workings of the cosmos are observable in patterns of bipolar alternation (night and day), cyclical waxing and waning (the moon), and in the linear progression of all things from birth to death. The cosmic vision of Daoism is a large and mysterious one; the present earthly realm of existence is not perceptible in its entirety, nor is it the only realm of existence. The world is inhabited not only by the living but by the dead and the divine as well: ghosts, spirits, and deities abound, and their actions and attitudes impinge directly upon human life.

The origins of Daoism as a school of thought are found in the classical texts of the *Daodejing* (often romanized as *Tao Te Ching*), the *Zhuangzi,* and the *Liezi* (fourth to first century BCE), all of which offered glimpses of a life lived free from the constraints of fate and physical form. The Daoist sage remained youthful and vital, soaring with the breeze and "breathing from the heels"—perfectly attuned to the constant changes of the Dao, as manifested in the natural world. Sectarian traditions promising longevity and personal benefit arose in the second century CE and have continued to the present. Some, for example the Celestial Masters sect (*Tianshi Zhengi Dao*), are headed by ordained priests who perform rituals of exorcism, protection, and renewal on behalf of their communities. Others, emphasizing self-cultivation in secluded places of sacred power, gave rise to monastic groups whose centers, typically located in the mountain ranges of Sichuan, Guangdong, Jiangsu, Jiangxi, and Hubei, remain popular pilgrimage destinations. Of particular repute are Tai Shan or "Mt. Tai," and Mao Shan.

Estimates of the numbers of Daoists vary wildly. There are upward of twenty-five thousand priests and nuns in the People's Republic of China alone, with thousands more in Taiwan, Hong Kong, Singapore, and in diasporic communities worldwide. As lay followers are not necessarily dedicated to a particular temple or sect, it is virtually impossible to know their numbers. Moreover, many small Daoist temples are not exclusively dedicated to Daoist divinities, such as the legendary author of the *Daodejing,* Laozi. Rather, they are multipurpose temples of popular local deities, and thus anyone worshipping there is not necessarily a Daoist. One expects to find Daoist priests and nuns in Daoist temples (*gong*), and Buddhist monks and nuns in Buddhist temples (*si*), but regardless of the primary enshrined figures, any temple may house side altars to any of a variety of devotional figures: the sea goddess Mazu, the bodhisattva Guanyin, or local worthies.

CHINESE BUDDHISM

Buddhism was founded in the sixth century BCE in India by Prince Siddhartha Gautama of the Shakya clan. The tradition posits that suffering in this life can be alleviated through moral actions and meditation, best accomplished through the monastic vocation. Buddhism envisions a society of monks and nuns, complemented by a lay community. The laity divide further into groups of dedicated, sometimes initiated practitioners and into those who are merely occasional ritual participants and petitioners. The religious goal is the elimination of suffering, itself karmically caused by ignorance of the consequences of one's actions through the processes of life, death, and rebirth. Once enlightened, the individual's ties to the world dissipate and death brings a final release, nirvana, from the cycle of rebirth.

By the turn of the first millenium, schisms had developed within the Buddhist world. One group of traditions, collectively termed Mahayana (Great Vehicle), espoused an expanded metaphysics, doctrinal and textual liberalism, and greater lay participation. By the fourth century CE, the Mahayana form of Buddhism had gained wide acceptance in China. Its monastic tradition offered an alternative to public involvement in a time of political turmoil and social disruption. Nunneries offered refuge for the unmarriageable and for the widowed and childless. Buddhism's mix of meditation for the dedicated and devotional practice for the masses readily took root. Original notions of karma, rebirth, and even the notion of nirvana altered to fit a society that did not share the Indic worldview. Rebirth was subtly transformed into the transition to an afterlife in a paradise realm such as the Western Pure Land or into any of a number of unlovely hells. Through faith and meritorious deeds, one could assure oneself of a better place in the afterlife; one could also purchase the services of monks and nuns whose reading of the sacred texts, *sutras,* could alleviate the torments of those suffering in hells. As a result, Buddhist monastic communities are closely associated with funeral practice.

Most Buddhists practice a combination of meditation and merit-making, with monks and nuns performing more of the former and the laity generally focused more on the latter. The Buddha himself is not only venerated as Shakyamuni Buddha (the Awakened One of the Shakya clan), but he is understood to manifest the cosmic principle of enlightenment itself, and thus remains active and available to dispense grace and benefit to the faithful. Devotion to the Buddha and bodhisattvas—celestial beings who possess great storehouses of merit that is transferable to supplicants—forms the third component of traditional practice.

The early monastic retreat centers established along the Silk Road, e.g., the caves at Dunhuang, Yungang, and Mogau, remain important sites of pilgrimage and tourism. The later mountain-based monastic centers gave rise to elaborate pilgrimage routes, the most famous of which focus on Wutai Shan, Emei Shan (originally a Taoist center), and Putuo Shan, the reputed home of the bodhisattva Guanyin. Despite the widespread destruction of religious architecture and artifacts in the People's Republic, especially during the Cultural Revolution (1966–1976), once restrictions on religion were eased in the 1980s, the numbers of pilgrims making their way to these traditional sites have risen steadily into the tens and hundreds of thousands annually.

INTERACTION AND SYNTHESIS

Discussing the Three Traditions of Confucianism, Daoism, and Buddhism individually enables the observer to appreciate the distinctive characteristics of each. However, this approach downplays logical inconsistencies between belief systems that belie the easy cohesion of traditional religious praxis. Religion in traditional Chinese society is dynamic and comprehensible, yet not necessarily systematic or logically coherent. The sometimes morally ambiguous tenets of Daoism cannot be made to fit comfortably within Confucian notions of human relationship and responsibility; Buddhism's underlying beliefs in karma and rebirth find little logical connection with ancient traditions of ancestral veneration. The Three Traditions approach also describes local and so-called folk traditions secondarily, thus consigning important popular traditions to an unbounded and unmanageable periphery that belies their centrality in daily life. People are commonly, whether serially or simultaneously, Confucian, Buddhist, Daoist, syncretic, and eclectic. Kinship-based Confucian social structures shape and lend support to Buddhist and Daoist monastic communities. Buddhist practices of meditation, compassionate action, and devotion provide socially acceptable outlets for spiritual impulses. The Buddhist vision of afterlife paradises complements the bureaucratic and often harsh afterlife of Confucian-Daoist tradition, and Buddho-Daoist hells validate this-worldly Confucian morality. Daoist techniques for maximizing optimal life conditions are increasingly secularlized and run the gamut from health practices such as Tai chi chuan and acupuncture to popular divination procedures such as astrology, Feng shui, and even discerning job aptitude through blood-typing.

The landscape of Chinese religious society, then, is a shifting terrain across which populations dynamically reconstitute themselves. Individuals participate in religious activities uniquely as they move across life's terrain—joining, leaving, and even creating religious communities along the way. Traditionally, people have entered or were drawn into religious communities out of shared concerns for harmonious and beneficial interactions between the individual and others, between the living and the dead, and between the mundane and the sacred. In the twentieth century, traditional concerns were enlarged and new concerns emerged.

"New Confucian" scholars such as Tu Wei-ming and Julia Ching have spearheaded public debate on issues such as the new nuclear family and the challenges of feminism and same-sex unions; the need for a new sixth relationship of "fellow citizens" in a democratic civil society; the definition of human rights; the problems of environmental degradation; and the value of inter-religious dialogue. As scholars who have made their homes outside geographic China, they form part of what Tu has called "cultural China." In so doing, they expand the reference and meaning of "Chinese society" and "Confucianism" to take on global significance.

New Forms of Chinese Religion

Chinese Buddhism has also moved in new and global directions. In the aftermath of the 1949 Communist victory on the mainland, many respected monks and abbots fled to Taiwan, where they established temples, mountain retreat centers, and re-established their lineages. By the 1970s, however, Buddhism began actively to respond to the perceived challenges of modernity, affluence, and Western ideas of social action. New schools of what is known as "engaged Buddhism" developed, of which two are notable for their focus on lay participation, the prominence of women in the organization, and for manifesting an increasingly global or transnational character.

The first of these, Fo Kuang Shan Buddhism, was founded in Taiwan by the Venerable Hsing Yun. In 1967, he established the Fo Kuang Shan (Buddha's Light Mountain) Buddhist monastery in southern Taiwan. A principal goal of the sect is to promote "the establishment of the Pure Land on earth," that is, to improve conditions in this life and in this world. As part of this plan, Fo Kuang Shan Buddhism engages lay participation in every aspect of the temple's affairs, from managing finances to staffing welcome centers and gift shops. Laypeople are encouraged to sample the monastic life for short periods of time. In a deliberate blurring of the boundaries between the monastic and lay populations, Ven. Hsing Yun established an order of laywomen celibates who reside on temple grounds. In 1991, he established a community-based lay organization, the Buddha's Light International Association (BLIA), which rapidly expanded its activities worldwide. There are now BLIA chapters in two dozen countries. Although many members are ethnic Chinese, non-Chinese members are increasingly common. BLIA worldwide is fast leaving any sense of Taiwanese provincialism behind. What it will retain of its Chinese character remains to be seen.

The second group is the Tzu Chi Buddhist Compassion Foundation, founded in 1966 by the Venerable Cheng Yen, a young woman who initially ordained herself, thus ignoring centuries of tradition of novitiate training in favor of getting her life's plan underway at once. Unlike Fo Kuang Shan Buddhism, the Tzu Chi Foundation is primarily a lay organization, having begun with a handful of housewives who sold handmade goods and donated a share of their daily profits. Tzu Chi now claims a membership of over five million followers (almost all of whom are ethnic Chinese) in more than thirty countries. Although Ven. Cheng Yen's dharma-talks (lectures on Buddhist doctrine) are sprinkled with Confucian admonitions to maintain good (traditional) families, members of her organization are altering the ways in which Taiwanese families operate. Current research indicates that men who have been drawn into Tzu Chi by their wives, mothers, and sisters gradually shed their traditional notions of sex-role stereotyping in household labor.

Tzu Chi's mission focuses on disaster relief and on the provision of medical services for the needy. The foundation has established its own hospital along with a medical school, a nursing school, and one of the first hospices in Taiwan. Contradicting deep-seated Chinese syncretic folk traditions about the necessity of keeping one's body intact (whether out of respect for one's ancestors or because it will be needed in the afterlife), Tzu Chi developed the first bone marrow registry in Asia. It also maintains a body donation program to provide cadavers for its medical school anatomy lab—an astonishing program of considerable success. Students in the lab address the cadavers as "teacher" and bow respectfully to them at each class; at the end of the term, the remains are cremated and interred in the on-site columbarium.

Tzu Chi lay volunteers mobilize quickly to assist in disaster relief worldwide, and their overseas centers extend their medical outreach efforts. The branch in southern California, for example, offers nursing scholarships to inner city students in Los Angeles, conducts mobile immunization clinics for the children of migrant workers in the farms of California's Central Valley, and crosses the border to organize short-term medical and dental clinics in rural Mexican towns. The greatest uncertainties for Tzu Chi stem from its essentially transnational rather than global character. Despite its global profile, the organization maintains an extremely close affinity with Taiwan. That is, its members are often expatriate Taiwanese corporate families or recent immigrants from Taiwan to other countries. Typically, Tzu Chi followers worldwide continue to live in "cultural China"—enclaves with significant ethnic Chinese populations, where Mandarin or Taiwanese are the languages of everyday life. In diasporic settings, perhaps the greatest challenge facing Tzu Chi will be whether the organization can attract and retain a second generation of members, for whom Chinese is not the language of choice, nor Buddhism the majority community's common tradition.

Modernity, global consciousness, and transnational experience have brought a range of intriguing religious changes to traditional Chinese societies. Tzu Chi Buddhists sing hymns in choirs, and sign while they do so. Some prominent New Confucians are professing Christians. A Daoist master announces that revelations have made clear the fact that heaven will encompass people of all faiths; he then identifies the specific level and section of hell where certain Christian televangelists will go, having been convicted of "bilking others in the name of religion." New religious groups such as Falun Gong or the cult of Ch'ing Hai (a stylish promoter of self-actualization techniques, or, to her critics, "the fashion guru") appear constantly. By every indication, the legacy of the Three Traditions remains strong, and the practical syncretic impulse of traditional Chinese society is as vital and complex as ever as the twenty-first century begins.

BIBLIOGRAPHY

Ch'en, Kenneth Kuan Sheng. 1973. *The Chinese Transformation of Buddhism*. Princeton, N.J.: Princeton University Press.

Jones, Charles Brewer. 1999. *Buddhism in Taiwan: Religion and the State 1660–1990*. Honolulu: University of Hawaii Press.

Kong Demao, and Ke Lan. 1984. *In the Mansion of Confucius' Descendants—An Oral History*. Beijing: New World Press.

Lopez, Donald S., Jr., ed. 1996. *Religions of China in Practice*. Princeton, N.J.: Princeton University Press.

Pas, Julian F., ed. 1989. *The Turning of the Tide: Religion in China Today*. Hong Kong and New York: Royal Asiatic Society, Hong Kong Branch; Oxford University Press.

Queen, Christopher S., and Sallie B. King, eds. 1996. *Engaged Buddhism: Buddhist Liberation Movements in Asia*. Albany: State University of New York Press.

Schipper, Kristofer M. 1992. *The Taoist Body*. Trans. Karen C. Duval. Berkeley: University of California Press.

Tu, Wei-ming. 1985. *Confucian Thought: Selfhood as Creative Transformation*. Albany: State University of New York Press.

Yang, C. K. 1961. *Religion in Chinese Society: A Study of Contemporary Social Functions of Religion and Some of Their Historical Factors*. Berkeley: University of California Press.

Yao, Xinzhong. 2000. *An Introduction to Confucianism*. Cambridge: Cambridge University Press.

CHAPTER 13

POPULAR RELIGION IN MAINLAND CHINA

CHRISTIAN JOCHIM

WITHIN Chinese culture wherever it exists around the world, folk religion is an important aspect of daily life. Much of Chinese religious activity has been practiced outside the institutional forms of Buddhism, Christianity, Islam, Taoism, and other major religions. This activity has been characterized as "diffused," rather than institutional, in the sense that it permeates existing social units (family, village, state) instead of having its own specifically religious forms (Yang 1961). Its leaders have been family patriarchs, members of village temple committees, mediums, astrologers, geomancers, and so forth. To these we must add those who have led syncretic lay sects in recent centuries, providing religious alternatives to the major religions.

These popular forms of religion have created tensions within mainland China where the state attempts to maintain a tight control on social order. In general, the story of folk religion in the People's Republic of China (PRC) has been one of state suppression followed by popular revival. Religion is a particularly sensitive subject for the Chinese Communist Party (CCP). Though it has sometimes been tolerant of institutional religion, it has been less permissive about popular religious activities, especially in four key areas of religious life: family rituals, divination, temple worship of deities, and syncretic lay sects.

These activities are not considered "religious" in any formal sense by CCP authorities and therefore are not protected by constitutional guarantees of religious freedom. At one time or another during the past half century, each of these activities has been attacked as "superstitious," "wasteful," "harmful to the people," and so forth. From 1949 through the death of Mao Zedong in 1976 attacks were often severe; since then there has been relatively more tolerance.

Article 36 of the revised constitution adopted in 1982 allows for freedom of religion, described as "legitimate religious activities." But it does not allow any religious practices which violate the vague proscription against "counterrevolutionary activities or activities which disrupt social order, harm people's health, or obstruct the educational system" (MacInnis 1989, Document 4). In general folk religious activities are not regarded as "legitimate religious activities" and hence do not benefit from the constitutional protections of Article 36. They have benefited, however, from the general relaxation of state control over society and the overall improvement of economic conditions in post-Mao China. This is seen with special clarity in the case of family-related activities.

FAMILY RITUALS

In traditional China, the most sacred obligations were to the family rather than to any church or sect. Among family rituals, funeral and ancestral rites were central. Funerals were elaborate affairs whose symbolism expressed key social values, such as filiality, continuity of the (patrilineal) family line, and ordered hierarchy. Elements of this symbolism were found in the status-differentiated mourning clothes worn at funerals, the order of participants in funeral processions, and the rites of supplication for ancestors. These ritual proceedings culminated in the act of burial for all but a few Chinese, who had come under the influence of the Indian custom of cremation by way of Buddhism. After the funeral, ancestral offerings were made regularly to specific ancestors on their death-day anniversaries and to family ancestors in general during seasonal festivals, such as Chinese New Year. Rites were performed at grave sites as well as at home ancestral altars.

Knowing that family rituals were the symbolic backbone of traditional "feudal" society, the CCP suppressed them as part of its campaign to create a new society. In the 1950s, the government converted ancestral halls to public uses and confiscated the lands from which they earned revenue to operate. It also advocated new forms of ritual in place of traditional funeral rites. These included cremation (instead of burial); memorial meetings featuring eulogies on the deceased's contributions to the new society (in place of family funerals); silent listening and simple bowing (instead of wailing and kowtowing); the elimination of references to spirits or ghosts; and the absence of food, incense, and other offerings (Whyte 1988). During the Cultural Revolution, further steps were taken. In some areas, authorities converted existing graveyards to farmland, and Red Guards removed household altars, genealogical scrolls, and ancestral tablets from homes to burn them publicly.

Today, nonenforcement of prohibitions against "superstitions," combined with newfound wealth, has led to a resurgence of elaborate traditional-style funerals. Especially in rural areas, burial is usually chosen over cremation, even if there are difficulties in having it approved and performed. Considering that families are smaller and relatively less important than previously, one must wonder whether or not funeral rites continue to serve the old function of supporting family and lineage solidarity. Some observers think that costly rituals, weddings as well as funerals, are now more likely to serve the function of building a network of relationships with authorities and business persons (Siu 1989). Nonetheless, one cannot help but feel that the resurgence of local family customs expresses dissatisfaction with central state rule in general and suppression of popular customs in particular.

DIVINATION: THE CASE OF FENGSHUI SHUI

A plethora of means to know one's fate and, if necessary, to change it have always been popular in China. This fits well with the pragmatic orientation and worldly goals of Chinese folk religion (health, wealth, progeny, social status); and it reflects a way of thinking according to which all parts of the social and cosmic whole are interrelated. Many popular religious specialists practiced some kind of divination. Among various types of mediums, astrologers, and other diviners, the fengshui master held a prominent position. One reason for this was the role he (almost always a man) had in family funerals as the one who chose the time, place, and directional properties of a burial. Of course, he also had to be consulted about dwellings for humans (houses) and deities (temples). He could perform his role, it was believed, due to his talent to see in the lay of the land yin and yang cosmic breaths (qi) as well as his ability to make calculations about the qualities of a location that matched the personality (astrologically defined) of a client. In light of his importance, the identity and reputation of local fengshui masters was usually well known. Of course, during the Maoist era, being well known as the practitioner of a "superstition" that one used "to cheat the people" was not advantageous. Fengshui masters had to practice in secrecy, if at all. During the Cultural Revolution, they were often persecuted; and their books and implements, such as the elaborate compasses they used to determine locational qualities, were confiscated and destroyed.

In the twenty-first century, however, fengshui masters appear to have become more important than ever. As the practitioners of a form of divination that has survived and prospered, they expanded their role to incorporate practices once performed by others. There are several explanations about how their expanded role came about. One is the state's relaxation of relevant prohibitions. Other theories cite economic factors (Bruun 2003). A boom in home building as well as a return to burial as the preferred way of dealing with deceased ancestors has created an increased need for fengshui services. This factor is related to the free market ideology, the adoption of which encourages individuals and families to pursue the kind of selfish goals that the CCP had vehemently opposed and for which fengshui services are so useful. To seek the help of a fengshui master to gain an advantage over others, and to justify one's greater fortune by reference to fengshui principles, fits well into the new market ideology.

Moreover, to the extent that the CCP still promotes a universal ethic of self-sacrifice and obedience to central authority, using fengshui asserts ones support for an alternative worldview. Interestingly, the revival of fengshui in the PRC also coincides with its growing popularity in the West, making possible an instance of the "pizza effect" (by which native traditions are re-imported to their land of origin in altered forms). Its increased acceptance abroad, for ecological as well as spiritual reasons, has helped to improve its reputation among urban Chinese and to give it new meaning. At least in rural areas, even CCP officials take advantage of fengshui services, despite their formal pronouncements. This situation reflects a more general revival of religious activities, especially in the countryside, that extends to the construction of village temples and the expansion of community festivals.

DEITY WORSHIP AND VILLAGE TEMPLES

Temples for Confucius, Buddhist monasteries, and Taoist hermitages dot the Chinese landscape, along with occasional mosques and churches. But most temples in China cannot be categorized as Confucian, Buddhist, or Taoist. They are community temples in honor of local gods and goddesses, often figures who had a role in local history and were deified after death. They are managed by local temple committees rather than by religious professionals, although Taoist priests are usually hired to perform major rituals, such as temple consecration ceremonies or the rites of purification performed each year on a deity's birthday. Community festivals center on these temples and require the support and participation of the local population. Such temples are symbols of local pride, and cooperative arrangements for conducting their major rituals provide a basis for the personal networks in local society. Individuals also go to these temples on an ad hoc basis for personal reasons, such as to consult the deity on financial, procreative, or medical matters.

After 1949, community temples often suffered the same fate as ancestral halls, being converted into schools or administrative offices. But just as often they were simply left in disrepair, as no one was willing to invest politically or financially in their support. During the Cultural Revolution, they were subject to acts of destruction. Until recently, community festivals connected with the temples were prohibited or restricted in scale. Today, especially in areas experiencing economic growth and the infusion of funds from overseas Chinese, there is a veritable boom in temple construction and repair. Observers in Fujian Province, for example, assert that people with money are now more likely to rebuild their temples than they are to buy televisions and refrigerators, with close to 30,000 temples of various kinds restored since 1979. They are willing to celebrate festivals on an unprecedented scale, although they know that large gatherings will raise the ire of authorities (Dean 1993). Of course, it is hard to measure the degree to which people still believe in the religious worldview that lies behind the worship of temple deities. However, it is certain that the use of temple activities to assert local pride and to create local networks is still a fact of life in the Chinese countryside. While this is less so in urban areas, other forms of revival have occurred there.

POPULAR LAY SECTS:
THE CASE OF FALUN GONG

Perhaps the most important development in Chinese religious life in recent centuries has been the growth of popular lay sects. They stand alongside institutional Buddhism, Taoism, and Confucianism, on the one hand, and the diffused popular religion of families and villages, on the other hand. They are syncretic in their borrowing of elements from both sides. They also tend to be evangelistic, salvationist, and millenarian; led by charismatic figures; characterized by strict moral guidelines; and to some degree esoteric. Despite their popularity, or perhaps because of it, they have been criticized and even persecuted by state authorities of both modern and pre-modern regimes. When Falun Gong (Dharma Wheel *gongfu*) rose to public attention in 1999, its popularity demonstrated the potential of syncretic lay sects for rapid growth. It also showed the ability of Chinese authorities to respond in alarmed and dramatic ways. The events of 1999, however, have a historical precedent.

During the early years of the PRC, a major target of the state's anti-religious campaigns was the Way of Unity (*Yiguan Dao*). Its leader, Zhang Tairan (1889–1947), had succeeded in spreading the sect's message from its base in Shandong Province to many other areas of China and in bringing the number of its members into the millions. The followers saw their leader as the latest in a series of patriarchs sent to earth by the Eternal Venerable Mother to save humanity. They interpreted the chaos of war and the distress of poverty in terms of Buddhist-rooted millenarian ideas. In joining the sect, members "received the Dao" (*dedao*) in an esoteric rite and, thereby, put themselves on a path of moral discipline, including vegetarianism, which distinguished them from other people and assured their salvation.

The nationalist government made the sect illegal before 1949 but had few resources to obstruct its growth. After retreating to Taiwan, this government reiterated its ban. However, Way of Unity leaders, who had also come to Taiwan from the mainland, were more successful in spreading its message than the government was in obstructing their efforts. In 1987, authorities relented and legalized the sect. Today it claims to have over one million members in Taiwan alone. Even if this number is slightly exaggerated, there is no doubt that it ranks second only to Buddhism in Taiwanese religious life. In the PRC, despite thoroughgoing efforts to eliminate it, remnants of the sect survive. This might not be newsworthy were it not for the phenomenal success of another syncretic lay movement, Falun Gong, whose followers probably number in the tens of millions.

Li Hongzhi (1952–) established Falun Gong in 1992 on the basis of his alleged personal success in using unique forms of *qigong* (the *gongfu* of cultivating one's *qi* through certain bodily movements and meditative exercises). The movement has spread above all through dissemination of books by Li, whom followers consider an enlightened being. Its basic tenets are found in his best known work, *Chinese Falun Gong*, which is available in both Chinese and English and can be found on the sect's Web site. Explaining that earth has already been destroyed many times, it has a mildly apocalyptic tone (surely enough to alarm PRC authorities). It is also partly esoteric, offering a method whereby one can "open the Celestial Eye" (*kai tianmu*), preferably with help from an initiated master, and thus begin the orthodox and effective practice of *qigong*. Falun Gong requires a disciplined moral lifestyle because, as one moves to higher and higher Celestial Eye levels, one gains powers that could be used for ill as well as for good. Through correct moral and spiritual practice, one is able to cultivate one's *xinxing* (moral mind/spiritual nature), ensuring good health and progress toward enlightenment.

The syncretic nature of these teachings is obvious. Li acknowledges that he borrows much from traditional Buddhism and Taoism. It is also clear that the sect's moral guidelines are built on traditional Confucian morality. Moreover, as with other syncretic sects in recent history, its view of the cosmos and of the human microcosm is built on Neo-Confucian conceptions of *qi*, *xinxing*, yin-yang, and so forth. However, it does differ in key ways from other sectarian movements in general and from the Way of Unity in particular. Considering the extremely public way Falun Gong spreads its message, its esoteric dimension is not strong. By the same token, it is largely dependent on publications and a Web site for increasing its membership, not on the efforts of propagation units to multiply themselves. Nonetheless, it has been able to form meeting groups with local leaders to guide practice sessions; and it has managed to assemble large groups of protesters on short notice. This means it is probably able to give members the congregational experience for which syncretic lay sects are known and by means of which they can serve as surrogate villages or families for alienated urbanites. Whether or not Falun Gong can serve this social function, it surely can provide an alternative cosmology for members who have become disenchanted with the dull materialism of CCP ideology. However, at present its problem is not lack of success but, instead, too much success. Due to its rapid growth, alarmed Chinese authorities pronounced it illegal on July 22, 1999. During the following month, they arrested dozens of leaders nationwide and confiscated millions of the group's books, audiotapes, and videotapes.

The lesson to be learned from this case is that authorities can and will selectively enforce prohibitions against using religion "to conduct counterrevolutionary activities or activities which disrupt social order." Religious freedom extends only to approved activities of the formal organizations of major religions. Authorities would first have to acknowledge the existence of popular religion, as opposed to "superstition," before its free exercise can enjoy constitutional protection.

BIBLIOGRAPHY

Bell, Catherine. 1989. "Religion and Chinese Culture: Toward an Assessment of 'Popular Religion.'" *History of Religions* 29, no. 1: 35–57.

Bruun, Ole. 2003. *Fengshui in China: Geomantic Divination between State Orthodoxy and Popular Religion.* Honolulu: University of Hawaii Press.

Dean, Kenneth. 1993. *Taoist Ritual and Popular Cults of Southeast China.* Princeton, N.J.: Princeton University Press.

Link, Perry, Richard Madsen, and Paul G. Pickowitz. 1989. *Unofficial China: Popular Culture and Thought in the People's Republic.* Boulder, Colo.: Westview Press.

MacInnis, Donald E. 1989. *Religion in China Today: Policy and Practice.* Maryknoll, N.Y.: Orbis Books.

Overmyer, Daniel L., ed. 2003. *Religion in China Today*. Cambridge and New York: Cambridge University Press.

Pas, Julian F., ed. 1989. *The Turning of the Tide: Religion in China Today*. New York: Oxford University Press.

Siu, Helen. 1989. "Recycling Rituals: Politics and Popular Culture in Contemporary Rural China." In *Unofficial China: Popular Culture and Thought in the People's Republic*. Eds. Perry Link, Richard Madsen, and Paul G. Pickowitz, 121–37. Boulder, Colo.: Westview Press.

Teiser, Stephen F. 1995. "[Chinese Religions—The State of the Field] Popular Religion." *Journal of Asian Studies* 54, no. 2: 378–95.

Watson, James, and Evelyn S. Rawski. 1988. *Death Ritual in Late Imperial and Modern China*. Berkeley: University of California Press.

Whyte, Martin K. 1988. "Death in the People's Republic of China." In *Death Ritual in Late Imperial and Modern China*. Eds. James Watson and Evelyn S. Rawski, 288–315. Berkeley: University of California Press.

Yang, C. K. 1961. *Religion in Chinese Society*. Berkeley: University of California Press.

CHAPTER 14

TRADITIONAL JAPANESE RELIGIOUS SOCIETY

SUSUMU SHIMAZONO

JAPANESE culture, whether it is practiced in Japan or in expatriate Japanese communities around the world, is built on a foundation of traditional Japanese religion. By "traditional," as opposed to "modern," one refers to aspects of Japanese culture that originate before the modern era, a line that is usually drawn at the Meiji Restoration in 1867. Shinto and Buddhism were firmly established in Japanese society before 1867, as were folk religions with deep association with the two major religions. Japanese Christianity and the New Religions that have arisen after the beginning of Japan's modernization process are categorized as non-traditional religions.

It is difficult to determine what percentage of the Japanese population currently follows traditional Japanese religions. The Religion Yearbook compiled by the government's Agency for Cultural Affairs lists the number of followers as reported by each religious organization. In 1995, for instance, the Yearbook reported the total number of Shinto followers as 101,387,654, and that of Buddhism as 63,881,859. More than 90 percent of those indicating Shinto adherence and over 80 percent of those with Buddhist leanings are followers of traditional religious organizations, the remainder being followers of New Religions. Since the total population of Japan is a little over 120 million, the number of followers of traditional religions, according to the Yearbook, is larger than the total population.

The reason for these impossibly large figures is religious organizations count their "followers" according to a very broad definition. They include many people who visit a Shinto shrine or Buddhist temple only once a year for making New

Year wishes and who contact a temple once in several years for the funeral of a family member. There are some people whose parents have some relation with a temple or shrine but they themselves have no contact with it. In many cases, these people seem to be counted as followers. One person may be counted by more than one organization as their follower. Therefore, it has little significance to infer the influence of traditional religions on the Japanese society from the figures reported in the Religion Yearbook.

More reliable are survey results. The 1994 survey by the *Yomiuri Shimbun* newspaper included the question, "Do you believe in a religion?" To this, 26.1 percent of the respondents said "Yes." This figure reflects the portion of people who consider themselves to be deeply associated with a specific religion. Though this number includes those who have a sense of belonging to New Religions and Christianity, it is reasonable to consider that at least half have a sense of belonging to traditional religions.

It is interesting to note that the same survey indicated that even though most say that they do not believe in religion, the overwhelming majority of Japanese people observe some sort of religious practices. Most notably, over 70 percent conduct religious rites for the deceased and over 60 percent worship to pray for luck (including new year wishes, fortune telling, and obtaining amulets). These two religious practices have a certain level of importance in New Religions, but they are more closely related to traditional religions. Hence regardless of whether or not Japanese people claim to be members of traditional religions, the customs associated with those religions continue to play a significant role in Japanese cultural life.

SHINTO AND SHINTO SHRINES

Although Shinto religion revolves around the religious practices at shrines, it is virtually impossible to say how many Shinto shrines exist in Japan. There are prestigious shrines such as the Grand Shrines of Ise with a huge compound, and at the same time there are small shrines on roadsides. Many companies have shrines within their premises and many of them conduct regular rites. Often a small shrine of Inari (the god of harvests) will be placed in the garden of a private house. Some 54 percent of houses are said to have a household (miniature) shrine in their houses, according to a survey by the *Asahi Shimbun* newspaper in 1995. If these household shrines are included, the number of shrines in the country could reach several tens of millions.

Shrines that are worshiped by community residents usually focus on one of the major Shinto deities. The Inarii, Ise (the supreme shrine of Japan since before the sixth century), Hachiman (the god of war), Tenjin (the deified spirit of Sugawara Michizane, a scholar in the ninth century) are the most popular deities. These deities are enshrined respectively in tens of thousands to several tens of thousands of shrines across the country. Major shrines are authorized as religious corporate bodies by the Agency for Cultural Affairs or the prefectural governments, and most shrines are affiliated with Jinja Honcho (the Association of Shinto Shrines).

The number of shrines affiliated with the Association of Shinto Shrines is a little more than seventy-nine thousand and Shinto priests conducting rituals are about twenty thousand in total. These shrines have important events including several annual festivals. At these occasions, solemn divine services are conducted, often accompanied by merry festivals. In general, tranquility prevails in shrine compounds. However, famous shrines are always crowded with tourists or worshippers making new year wishes, praying for recovery from illness, for passing entrance examinations, or winning god's favor for traffic safety. Two universities closely associated with the Association of Shinto Shrines are known as the Shinto universities and both have a faculty specializing in Shinto study.

The Emperor's family members were considered to be descendants of various Shinto gods. This belief was propagated to every member of the nation through school education and national holiday events from the Meiji Restoration until the end of World War II. The deceased soldiers in the wars in the modern times were enshrined in Yasukuni Shrine in Tokyo and Gokoku Shrines in various localities by the state, and national rituals were performed on a large scale. The constitution of Japan was promulgated in 1946 by which the government and religion were strictly separated. After the war, Shinto rituals on the national level became limited to a minimum under the law. However, the funerals of the emperor and other royal family members and coronations still continue to be celebrated by the whole nation through the media.

BUDDHISM AND TEMPLES

Whereas many Shinto shrines are not constructed in the shape of a house, Many of the Buddhist temples are built like houses and have live-in priests. Unlike Shinto, Buddhism makes a distinction between a temple with followers in a community and a small household Buddhist altar in an individual home. There are more than seventy-seven thousand Buddhist temples in the country. They are mostly grouped under the seven major sects, namely, Tendai-shu, Shingon-shu,

Jodo-shu, Jodoshin-shu, Rinzai-shu, Soto-shu, and Nichiren-shu, and the rest belong to smaller sects. Most of these major sects are further branched into subsects. The sects and subsects that have more than a hundred affiliated temples amount to nearly fifty. There are quite a number of independent temples that are authorized as religious corporate bodies without any sect affiliations. The temples of each sect are organized with the grand temple on the top. The largest sect is the Soto-shu Sect (14,702 temples); followed by the Jodoshin-shu Honganji Subsect (10,335); Judoshin-shu Otani Subsect (8,709); Jodo-shu (6,929); Nichiren-shu (4,633); Koyasan Shingon-shu (3,487); Rinzai-shu Myoshinji Subsect (3,401); Shingon-shu Chizan Subsect (2,853); Shingon-shu Buzan Subsect (2,632); and so on.

Each sect venerates the founder priest. The founders of these sects are Buddhist priests who were active in Japan around the thirteenth century. Their names are widely known and are respected by the public. Not a small number of them are venerated as the subjects of religious worship. The aforementioned large sects have their own universities (except for one which is run by a consortium of different sects) and offer programs on Buddhism and the teachings of different sects.

Almost all Buddhist sects in Japan allow priests to eat meat and to get married. Except for the Grand Temples and other large-scale temples, the majority of temples are administered by a priest and his family. In most temples, the living quarters for the priests' families are attached within the compound. Children born and brought up inside the temple generally succeed their fathers to become priests. In other words, the majority of temple priests are hereditary.

Temples have *danka* (parishioners or supporters) in the community. When someone dies in a family, it is considered desirable to ask the temple with which the family has maintained a relationship from the time of its ancestors to perform funeral rites. Customarily, the family asks the same temple to hold memorial services for the dead on the forty-ninth day, first year, third year, seventh year after the death, and so on. Danka is a family that maintains a relationship with a temple. (Such a family/person would call that temple *danna-dera*.) It is generally said that a temple is sustainable with three hundred danka. If the number of danka is less than the sustainable level, the priest family must have a side job to make a living. Some priests work as schoolteachers. In large cities, some temples use their spaces as parking lots, or construct a building on temple land to rent for supplementary income.

The first and foremost opportunity for interaction between a temple and community people is through holding rituals for the dead by a danka. Other than worship services for the dead, temples are visited by people making wishes and offering prayers. There are temples that function exclusively for these latter purposes.

Rites for the Dead and Ancestors

The main function of a Buddhist temple is to perform rites for the dead and for the ancestors for danka. In fact, the involvement of a temple and priests is indispensable for funerals and accompanying services, though some of the rites for the dead and ancestors conducted by individuals are not held in temples.

Some graveyards are located in the danna temples, and some are not. In rural areas, community cemeteries are often located somewhere other than temple compounds. In large cities, large-scale cemeteries are publicly built, or new cemeteries are being developed and sold. Families visit their graveyards to mourn for specific dead members on their death-days, or to give prayers to the entire body of ancestors during the spring and autumn equinoctial weeks or during the Festival of the Dead in summer.

Many households have a household Buddhist altar. The survey by the *Asahi Shimbun* in 1995 shows that 59 percent of households have a Buddhist altar. In an altar, the Buddha, in guises such as Sakyamuni or Amitabha, is deified together with the name tablets of the dead or ancestors. As mentioned at the beginning of this essay, a great number of people offer rice, water, and rice wine, and sit before the altar and pray as an everyday religious practice. They pray to the Buddha that the souls of the dead and ancestors may rest in peace and happiness, and they also pray to the spirits of their ancestors for their favor to protect and bless the family.

This praying to ancestors is a practice that cannot be explained from Buddhist doctrines. Hence, many explanations are found that say that although the rites for the dead and ancestors practiced in Japan appear to be Buddhism-inspired, they are in fact rooted in indigenous folk religions or in the Confucian thought and belief conveyed from China.

Making Wishes, Prayers, Fortune Telling, and Taboos

Contemporary Japanese take various religious measures to protect themselves against evil and to invite fortune into their life. They sometimes visit Shinto shrines or Buddhist temples, being aware of the difference between them; but sometimes they are not so conscious about the difference. Many may think that they should go to a Shinto shrine for New Year worship, but quite a large number of people visit large Buddhist temples for New Year worship. It is quite natural that people are little concerned about the difference between Shinto and Buddhism even today because the nation had long lived with little awareness that Shinto and Buddhism were different religions until the Meiji Restoration when Shinto and Buddhism were separated by the state.

Even so, prayer-offerings at some occasions in life are held under Shinto rites. Newborn babies are taken to a Shinto shrine, and prayers for children's healthy growth at ages of three, five, and seven are usually held at a shrine. A ground-breaking ceremony before building a house is often conducted by a Shinto priest. In contrast to rituals for the dead to be held by a Buddhist temple, people tend to choose a Shinto shrine to offer prayers at auspicious occasions related to the growth of life.

Furthermore, some rites and practices that have no close historical association either with Shinto or Buddhism are conducted with a sense of longstanding religious conscientiousness as if they were based on tradition. A majority of the wedding ceremonies, for example, have been held in Shinto rites (now Christian ceremonies are becoming more popular). In fact, this is quite a recent custom created in the twentieth century that became widespread after World War II. In selecting the date for a wedding ceremony, people avoid certain days of ill fortune according to the lunar solar calendar. This is a folk tradition which has nothing to do with a specific religion.

Contemporary Japanese like divination. Many fortunetellers receive customers at street corners or at their shops. They tell fortunes according to birthdays, onomancy, palmistry, astrology, the tarot, and many other indicators. There are some people called spiritual intermediaries and praying persons who pray to gods and the Buddha to tell fortunes, or who pray to gods and the Buddha to expel evil from customers and bring fortune to their lives. Many recognize these roles as viable modern occupations.

CULTURE AND TRADITIONAL RELIGIONS

Shinto and Buddhism are believed personally and practiced in the form of rites. In addition to the religious aspect, Shinto and Buddhism play great roles as cultural resources and legacies. For scholars and writers to speak or write on the subject of how to face death to the general public, the teachings, terminology, and the symbols of Shinto and Buddhism are very useful. For authors and artists to express the agony and love in life in accordance with the tradition of Japanese culture, the terminology of traditional religions, and the patterns related to religious leaders, are used as effective materials. Furthermore, people are often influenced, be it consciously or subconsciously, by the concepts of traditional religions in their moral value systems and their ways of thinking in everyday life. In the field of cultural sciences, cultural resources of traditional religions including Shinto and Buddhism are referred to not only in relation to death, agony, and love but also in reference to all kinds of important questions in the personal and social life of people. As mentioned above, traditional religions may not directly set the framework for the lives of individuals, but they are increasingly exercising influence on people indirectly as cultural resources through responding to various basic questions in life. This tendency has shown no sign of abating in the busy, globalized urban societies in which most Japanese live in Japan and around the world.

BIBLIOGRAPHY

Agency for Cultural Affairs, ed., 1995. *Shukyo Nenkan 1996nen-ban[Religion Yearbook for 1996].* Tokyo: Agency for Cultural Affairs.
Ishii, Kenshi. 1997. *Data Book: Gendai Nipponjin no Shukyo [Data book for Religions of Contemporary Japanese].* Tokyo: Shinyo-sha.

CHAPTER 15

....

JAPANESE NEW RELIGIOUS MOVEMENTS

....

IAN READER

FROM the first half of the nineteenth century onward a new stratum of religious affiliation has developed in Japan that is not directly related to the traditional customs, practices, and beliefs of Shinto shrines, Buddhist temples, and household gods. The emergence of a number of new religious movements (*shin shukyo*) offers alternative modes of religious faith and belonging. Many of these movements have generated a large following in Japan; some have become global in their reach, attracting a transnational membership.

Originally affiliation with these movements was a matter of personal conversion and individual faith. But this did not necessarily create conflicts of interest with the converts' commitments to traditional forms of religiosity. Adherents of new religions might also participate in family funerals under the auspices of the Buddhist temple to which the household belonged and take their offspring to Shinto shrines for baptismal blessings.

This pattern has changed in recent times, however. As the traditional emphasis on the household has eroded in modernity, there is evidence that some of the new religions have made inroads into the areas formerly dominated by the established religions, including creating their own funeral rites.

DEFINITIONS AND CHARACTERISTICS

There is no clear-cut definition of what constitutes a new religion in Japan. Legal registration of religious movements is carried out under Japan's Religious Corporations Law (Shukyo hojinho) and supervised by the Ministry of Education's Agency for Cultural Affairs (Bunkacho), which publishes an annual statistical guidebook to religion in Japan. The categories of religious organization as used in the guidebook by the Bunkacho are Buddhist, Shinto, Christian, and "other," and one finds groups registered under each of these categories that might be termed by scholars as new religions. The religious groups themselves often dispute the title new religion since they feel it conveys images of instability and a lack of historical roots. Soka Gakkai, for example, is usually regarded as the largest of all new religions, but it does not like the term and sees itself firmly located in the Buddhist tradition centered on the thirteenth-century prophet Nichiren. It thus regards itself as a Buddhist movement with a long history.

Generally, however, the term *new religion* in Japanese stands in antithesis to the established religious traditions (*kisei shukyo*) of Buddhism and Shinto, the religions that have traditionally formed the basis of social and religious belonging in Japan. These traditions operate through organized priesthoods and as such have been underpinned by a division between the laity and an ordained professional clerical hierarchy. By contrast, the new religions have centered on lay leadership and proselytism, with the ordinary members playing leading roles in spreading the faith and recruiting members. In general the term *shin shukyo*, or new religion, thus relates to lay-oriented Japanese religious movements. One should note also that movements from outside of Japan such as the various mainstream Christian churches, although not part of the traditional religious structures of Japan, are not normally categorized by scholars as new religions.

New religions generally are eclectic in nature, drawing on numerous sources and influences from within the Japanese religious traditions (using Buddhist, Shinto, and folk religious influences) and occasionally those from outside (such as Christian ideas and imagery) and presenting them in new and innovative formats. One dominating characteristic has been the focus on the charismatic nature and powers of their founding figures whose claims to religious authority are not based on their affiliation to or position in the traditional, official religious structures but on their own newly discovered truths and revelations. Such figures may thus serve as conduits between human and divine, receive revelations from previously remote deities, or claim new insights into Buddhist practices and texts, while displaying a capacity to provide their followers with spiritual healing and personal benefits, as well as with new ethical codes through which to live. However, it is a recurrent theme in their historical and structural development that such founders, even if they commence primarily as mediums or mouthpieces of deities, gradually assume a more powerful and central role, even appearing to supersede the deity as a focus of worship.

New religions of Japan have frequently originated as loosely affiliated groups gathered around a charismatic healer or medium who possessed beneficial powers, only gradually becoming more formally structured into a religious organization. A prime example of this is Tenrikyo (a name that means "teaching of heavenly wisdom"), which grew around Nakayama Miki, a woman who lived in Tenri, a small village near the former capital of Nara, in the nineteenth century. Miki originally fell into a trance and became possessed during a faith healing séance to heal her son, and in her trance she spoke as if possessed by a divine spirit, who revealed himself to be a powerful deity ignored by humanity but now returning to bring truth and a new order to the world. The deity had chosen Miki as his mouthpiece and gave her the power to dispense his blessings; she first attracted attention and support from others because of her apparent powers to communicate with the gods in séance and to bestow the benefit of safe childbirth. However, as a movement grew around her, she began to expand her activities beyond healing and safe childbirth and developed doctrines and worldviews centered on a mission of world salvation. As her circle of followers grew, an organization developed around her as the leader and she progressed from being primarily a prophet of a divine figure to being a source of teachings and religious inspiration. Eventually the religion of Tenrikyo grew around her, using her writings as its sacred scriptures and (see below) placing her at the center of its worship and structure. This type of pattern, from inspired prophet to position of veneration often as a form of deity, is a basic characteristic that occurs recurrently in the new religions.

A BASIC TYPOLOGY OF JAPANESE NEW RELIGIONS: SOURCES AND ROOTS

The eclecticism of many new religions makes it hard to categorize them succinctly. For example, many new religions draw on Shinto, Buddhist, and Christian cosmologies for their figures of worship, incorporating deities from all of these traditions within their own. Kofuku no Kagaku, a new religion of the 1980s, for example, has included the Buddha, Jesus, and the Shinto Sun Goddess Amaterasu in its pantheon. However, there are a number of basic patterns and types that are commonly seen, and here attention will be drawn to four common types of new religions.

One of the most prominent types of new religion are those that use Shinto-style ritual formats and that are centered, in origin, around the manifestations of deities (often previously unknown) to charismatic figures who become their mediums charged with missions of world salvation. Movements such as Tenrikyo, Kurozumikyo, and Omotokyo are of such a type.

They may pose a critique of the materialistic foundations and orientations of society and emphasize the importance of world renewal (*yonaoshi*), which is a prominent theme in Omotokyo, a movement begun in 1892—not so much in political or social but spiritual terms. As such they tend to look forward to the realization of an idealized state of existence on earth. They also tend to emphasize spiritual healing, often interpreting misfortunes as a product of malevolent spirits that need to be exorcised through magical rituals.

Many new religions, including several that emerged in the Tokyo region in the 1920s and 1930s, have had Buddhist orientations, looking for inspiration in the Lotus Sutra, finding this text to hold the keys to spiritual advancement in both individual and social terms. Movements of this type, such as Soka Gakkai, Reiyukai, and Rissho Koseikai, may disagree with each other over their interpretations of the sutra, but they share a faith in its efficacies, both as a ritual means of recitation and in its promises of salvation and enlightenment. While many new religions have developed political links and orientations, it has perhaps been the Lotus-based movements that have been most active in this area. Soka Gakkai, for example, formed its own political party (Komeito, with which it is now formally separate, but with which it retains close links) to help realize the aims of its form of Lotus-based Nichiren Buddhism, of creating a state based on Buddhist ideals through which the word of Nichiren could be spread to the wider world and through which the ideals of a rich civilization based on veneration of the Lotus could be achieved. Rissho Koseikai has also been active politically, emphasizing its ideals of world peace and opposition to nuclear weapons (themes prominent also in Soka Gakkai) and of protecting religious ideals from state interference.

A further source of inspiration for new religions has been esoteric Buddhism, and several new religious movements of this type have appeared in Japan, usually focused on a founder who has undergone austerities and ascetic and ritual training in one of the esoteric Buddhist sects, often as a lay member of, for example, the mountain religious orders. This type of new religion is exemplified by Shinnyoen (whose leader Ito Shinjo was ordained in the Shingon sect), Bentenshu (whose founder Omori Chiben was the wife of a Shingon Buddhist priest), and Gedat-sukai (whose founder Okano Eizo also became an ordained Shingon priest, and whose movement retains close links with Shingon temples). These retain close relations with Buddhist sects; use Buddhist-style rituals such as the *goma* or Buddhist fire ritual in their practices; and invoke the powers of esoteric Buddhism to bring about personal salvation, healing, and the attainment of happiness. The influences of esoteric Buddhism are also prominent in several of the most recent

new religions: both Agonshu (whose founder Kiriyama Seiyu claims esoteric ascetic training and knowledge) and the now infamous Aum Shinrikyo.

While using themes, techniques, and practices found in the existing religious
traditions, the Japanese new religious movements seek to extend them to the
ordinary person. This process, in which the traditional divide between the laity
and the ordained priesthood is thus set aside, is what especially marks the new
religions out from the established ones. Often this process is underpinned by
critiques of the older religions for trying to monopolize the means of salvation
and for having restricted access to spiritual techniques: Kiriyama Seiyu of Agonshu
has thus criticized the older esoteric sects for being secretive and not allowing
wider access to the means of salvation, while movements such as Mahikari, in
extending the powers of spiritual healing to their members, can be seen as examples of the "democratization of magic" through which new religions have provided the laity with the techniques and means for solving problems. In this sense,
all the new religions have roots in, and may be seen as formalized expressions of,
the folk religious traditions of Japan, with their close links to the needs of ordinary
people and their promise to make the paths of salvation and attainment of happiness realizable to all.

GENERATIONS OF NEW RELIGIOUS
MOVEMENTS IN JAPAN

The roots of many of the new religions can be traced back to ethically based
reformist movements of the eighteenth century such as Shingaku (established by
Ishida Baigan). The earliest recognized new religion is usually considered to be
Nyoraikyo (founded in Nagoya in 1802). Since then new religious movements
have come into being with regularity in Japan, testimony to the continuing vi-
brancy of the indigenous religious tradition as well as the continuing tensions and
upheavals that have typified Japanese history of the past century and a half.

The first major period of formation was in the earlier part of the nineteenth
century, prior to the Meiji Restoration, an era when the structures and authority
of the old feudal society were eroding and causing unrest especially in rural areas.
Movements of this period include Kurozumikyo (1814) and Tenrikyo (1838). The
latter part of the nineteenth century was also a time for the rise of new movements. This was a period of rapid modernization that caused unrest in rural
society and led to the emergence of a dispossessed rural peasantry and a new and
unsettled urban underclass. Movements of this era include Omotokyo founded in

1892 by the peasant woman and prophet Deguchi Nao, who preached a millennialist message of hope and salvation, in which the ills of the material world would be replaced by a new spiritual order.

The decades from the end of Meiji to the beginning of the Showa eras (c. 1910–25) were a period of reaction to the excessive pace of modernization in the Meiji period. Heightened interest in some of the "pre-modern" dimensions of Japanese folk religion led to a tremendous growth in new movements that emphasized magical healing: Omotokyo grew rapidly in this period, as did other movements of a similar bent such as Taireido.

A combination of rapid urban growth followed by economic depression characterized the late 1920s and 1930s. This was an era that saw the development of a number of urban-based new religions, many of them focused on the Lotus Sutra and appealing to the impoverished urban working classes. Reiyukai (c.1925) and Soka Gakkai (1930) are movements whose origins stem from this era, while Rissho Koseikai developed out of Reiyukai in this era, emerging as a separate movement at the end of the 1930s.

The latter years of World War II and the immediate aftermath of it was yet another period of growth for new religious movements. They provided people with a means of support in the wake of the turmoil of war and the shock of defeat. This was a critical period in which the older established religions, and especially Shinto, were discredited because of collaboration with the fascist war regime and when the overarching national ethic of the 1930s and 1940s collapsed. In this era, many new movements emerged to offer alternative voices and ways of formulating a new sense of identity attuned to the changing situation of postwar Japan. Many of these were movements that had developed in the last years of the war but that had suffered repression in that era (e.g., Tensho Kotai Jingukyo, founded in the 1940s by Kitamura Sayo) or whose leaders had spent much of the war in prison because of their refusal to go along with the ethos of wartime Japan, such as Soka Gakkai.

The postwar rebuilding of Japan, and the period of rapid economic growth of the 1950s and early 1960s, saw a huge increase in the number of new religions and in the numbers of those who joined them. The rebuilding of a fractured economy was carried out successfully but at a heavy social cost, in terms of mass migration to the cities, the fragmentation of older communities, and the heavy emphasis on self-sacrifice and hard work for the sake of rebuilding the nation. In this environment many new religious movements such as Soka Gakkai and Rissho Koseikai grew swiftly, especially in the big cities, both because of their ability to cater to the individual needs of followers with direct and clear messages of spiritual hope and practical help, and because they offered a new sense of community and belonging in an era in which older social structures appeared to break down.

The period from the late 1970s on brought a new wave of religious movements. This was a period when Japan was economically successful but torn with questions of identity, reactions to the processes of modernity, and concerns about the erosion of its cultural roots and in which widespread questioning of the materialistic mores of modern society had occurred. Because these movements appear to represent a new era of religions, and because their "newness" contrasts with the age of some of the earlier new religions (by this era, movements such as Tenrikyo had been in existence for well over a century), they have been termed "new" new religions (*shin shin shukyo*) to differentiate them from the "old" new religions. This new wave of religious movements, including Agonshu, Kofuku no Kagaku, and the infamous Aum Shinrikyo, has flourished most particularly in large cities and among the young and highly educated elites. These movements are commonly seen as reflecting a reaction against the processes of modernization and cultural erosion, while also articulating concerns about the future: they all have expressed millennialist orientations and concerns about the potential end of civilization through war or environmental disasters, while offering the hope of world salvation, normally with a Japan-centered (and nationalistic) orientation. Japanese new religions have in general had a nationalistic focus (a partial exception is Aum Shinrikyo), viewing Japan as the emergent new spiritual center of the world.

In this pattern of wave after wave of new movements there is a readily identifiable link between the emergence of new religions and social turbulence. But it should be stressed that the development of new religions, and their appeal, cannot be attributed only or even primarily to concepts of crisis on a social level. Studies of new religions have repeatedly demonstrated how such movements have spoken directly to individual needs and provided personal assistance on a spiritual level. Indeed, the importance of the democratizing aspects of individual salvation has been emphasized as a crucial theme in the development and nature of the new religions. At the same time, attention must also be paid to the social circumstances at different periods over the past century and a half, for these have been a critical element in the growth of new religious movements. The continuing circumstances that produce such movements, and the persistence of their appeal, indicates that they will continue to be a factor in Japanese society for the foreseeable future.

STRUCTURES, FAMILIAL PATTERNS, AND CONSERVATISM

A central organizing principle of most new religions has been the founder, who becomes transformed into a figure of veneration, often as a living deity (*ikigami*) or, as in the "new" new religions, a world savior, or (as with Kofuku no Kagaku) an eternal Buddha figure. Founder worship generally becomes transformed after the leader's death into an ancestral cult of veneration, with the founder becoming a sacred ancestor of the religion and the focus of worship. In this process it is common for his or her descendants, often-immediate family, to become the new leaders. Authority thus is frequently passed through the blood and descent—examples of this include Omotokyo, Reiyukai, and Shinnyoen. In the case of Shinnyoen, also, deceased members of the founder's family become incorporated into the movement's spiritual hierarchy, serving as spiritual guides in the other world.

Even Aum Shinrikyo—which with its focus on communal living and rejection of the family is arguably the most radical of all Japanese new religions—has adhered to the familial principle of charismatic inheritance. When its leader Asahara Shoko renounced the leadership for legal reasons connected with his trial for murder in the release of nerve gas in the Tokyo subways, he was initially replaced by his two sons, then aged five and three. The boys became the focuses of veneration in Aum, with followers believing that they contained within them the seeds of spiritual power and will develop into religious leaders in their own right as they mature. Subsequently Aum (now renamed Aleph) has undergone leadership crises, as senior disciples have sought to balance their devotion to Asahara, their founder who now is under sentence of death for his crimes, with the need to move on and distance itself from its violent past.

Structures too often reflect this familial pattern. In many new religions great emphasis has been placed on patterns of recruitment, with the new convert being considered as a "child" of the recruiter. A good example is Shinnyoen, in which new members are linked or connected to the movement through the agency of an existing member who becomes their teaching parent. The connected "child" thus becomes part of a teaching lineage in which the recruiter/parent has a continuing duty of teaching and instruction. Successful recruiting activities thus can lead to the development of an extended network of followers owing some allegiance to the initial "parent," whose stature in the movement rises in line with his or her successful activities. Such structures provide a stimulus to active proselytism, encouraging members to raise their own status through bringing in new members.

This hierarchical *oyabun-kobun* (parent-child) relationship typifies much of Japanese social structure, and as such the social structures of many new religions reflect a reiteration rather than a distancing from traditional social structures in Japan. Indeed, studies into the patterns of recruitment in Japanese new religions have shown that the most common path is to be converted or recruited by close family members or friends; in other words, the familial nature of the recruiter-convert relationship may mirror their existing social relationship. This is frequently underpinned by a Confucian mentality of respect for elders, seniors, and the existing social order—respect for ancestors and for those who preceded one into a movement (i.e., one's lineage "parents") are common features of the new religions which, it has been widely observed, tend to be socially conservative in nature. Many, especially movements formed prior to World War II, tend to suggest that females should be subservient to males, for example by interpretating various personal and familial problems (e.g., the infidelity of males) as necessitating self-reflection on the part of the wife and on the principle that "other people are mirrors" (i.e., that the ways others behave toward one is a product of one's own state of being). While this concept operates for both sexes, it is very often the case, as detailed studies of the interpretation of problems and the dynamics of problem solution have shown, that greater emphasis is placed on female self-reflection. It is ironic that while the new religions have provided a new means of spiritual expression and development and while many of their founders have been female, they have tended toward conservatism and reinforcing Japanese society's traditional discriminatory tendencies. The "new" new religions (which have largely had male founders) appear to be a little less inclined toward this reinforcement of existing mores and tend to place women in a more equal status relationship with men.

CENTERS OF FAITH, CENTERS OF PILGRIMAGE

A common feature in the new religions is the construction of a sacred center (or centers) that manifests or represents the worldview of the religion concerned. These centers signify that the religion stands at the hub of the universe and symbolize its mission to bring a new truth and a new spiritual dynamism to the world. This can be seen through the examples both of the older and newer new religions: Tenrikyo, for example, has built a vast complex at the site where Nakayama Miki lived and had her revelations, and that site is believed to be the place where humanity first emerged on earth, produced by God the Parent. Tenri thus is the center of the human universe, the place of human beginnings, and the center from which the new truths and spiritual salvation of the modern age have emerged. Pilgrimage to this center is emphasized as an act of faith in Tenrikyo, and visitors to its headquarters are greeted with the words *okaerinasai*, "welcome back," to signify the belief that anyone visiting there is actually returning to the place of their origins. The "new" new religion, Agonshu, also uses this greeting of okaerinasai to its visitors, to signify that they are returning to the roots of "original Buddhism" that Agonshu propounds. It has also constructed a huge sacred center near Kyoto, which is the place from which its self-perceived mission to restore an original form of Buddhism to the world, spread world peace, and help avoid a catastrophic end-time scenario that it prophesies for the end of the century, is to be accomplished.

Such sacred centers may operate also as memorials to the founder, reflecting the ancestral and familial dimensions of many of the new religions. Thus, while Tenrikyo's construction of a sacred center graphically displays Tenri concepts of the emergence of humanity and the idea that this is the sacred center of the world to which all return, the fact that it is built where its foundress Nakayama Miki lived and received her revelations, and that the foundress is memorialized in the complex, shows the extent to which Tenrikyo is a movement centered on faith in and veneration of the spirit of Nakayama Miki. This pattern of the birthplace or place of revelation of the founder becoming the sacred center of the religion, and his or her mausoleum becoming a place of pilgrimage in the movement, is found so repeatedly in the new religions that it can be discerned as a common feature of them.

CONTROL AND SECESSION

The emphasis on charismatic control has often produced an emphasis on hierarchic control and strict authority within new religions. In general terms there exists in the new religions a tension between the spiritual freedoms and "democratization" of salvation and magic proffered to lay followers and the drive toward authoritarian control that emanates from an emphasis on personal charisma and the socially conservative patterns of familial control.

Niwano Nikkyo, for example, was originally a successful local leader in Reiyukai, whose interpretations of doctrine and personal following led to a rift between him and Reiyukai's leaders and to Niwano's secession to found Rissho Koseikai. Various religious movements have developed out of Omotokyo as a result of the secessions of charismatic personalities such as Okada Mokichi, who seceded after receiving personal revelations to form Sekai Kyuseikyo. Okada took with him some of Omotokyo's healing techniques, which later were diversified into other movements that split from Sekai Kyuseikyo. One such was Mahikari, whose founder Okada Kotama, was a member of Sekai Kyuseikyo but who had a revelation of his own status as a messiah and thus left to establish his own movement, using as a prime practice the spiritual healing techniques imbibed from Omotokyo via Sekai Kyuseikyo, as well as many shared doctrinal formulations. Mahikari has produced further secessions after Okada's death, with a split between the claims of familial charismatic inheritance and the rights of leading disciples. Mahikari split into two movements, each using the word Mahikari as part of its name, one headed by Okada's (adopted) daughter, the other by a close disciple, each claiming to have received Okada's benediction on his deathbed.

Not all movements have been weakened by secession, and some such as Shinnyoen have averted these dangers by imposing a rigid control on its systems of spiritual development, in which loyalty to the family of the founder plays a crucial part. Shinnyoen has developed a system of ordained ministers, who serve as a bulwark against the potential for secession, but it has also experienced the problem that an overemphasis on such centralized control can lead to stagnation and to restrictions on its potential to proselytize. In short, then, the new religions display a continuing tension between systems of hierarchic control that hold movements together but that work against dynamism and fluidity on the one hand, and the freedom of local leaders to innovate and build followings on the other—which can greatly increase the numbers of faithful but that can also produce the possibility of secessions.

MEMBERS, NUMBERS, COMMUNITIES, AND LOCATIONS

It is difficult to say precisely who is a member of a new religion. The patterns of becoming a member or being counted as a member vary from movement to movement. In general, movements have assumed a rather loose and casual concept of belonging and of counting members. An example is Seicho no Ie, which in one set of statistics in 1985 had 3 million members, and in a different set in 1989 had 80,000 members: it appears that the discrepancy was not due to massive membership loss so much as to different ways in which membership figures were collated.

In some movements simply attending a particular set of lectures or rituals or filling in a form for such a purpose can cause one to be counted as a member. Some movements of this type have high turnovers: Mahikari, for example, runs regular teaching seminars in which prospective members are offered opportunities to acquire the ability to heal and perform miracles through acquiring Mahikari's talisman; many hundreds of thousands of these have been distributed, but the numbers of people who can be counted as faithful or long-term members of Mahikari is perhaps less than one hundred thousand.

Similar statistical problems are found in Kofuku no Kagaku, which claimed in the early 1990s to have become the largest movement in Japan, surpassing Soka Gakkai (generally assumed to be the biggest and with several million followers) and at one point in 1995 claiming 10 million followers. However, observers have noted that Kofuku no Kagaku at times had trouble filling large auditoriums for its special events and that the movement tended to count people who had acquired copies of books written by the leader (Okawa Ryuho) or who had received copies of the movement's newsletter. Since members are encouraged to take out subscriptions for four other people (normally friends or relatives) to whom the newsletter will also be sent, and since all those who received the newsletter were counted as members, this implies that for every person who joined four more are counted as members. In fact in 1991 Kofuku officials admitted that 85 to 90 percent of its members did nothing except subscribe to its monthly magazine. A more conservatively realistic estimate of the movement's strength in the mid-1990s has been put at between 100,000 and 300,000 active members.

While Kofuku no Kagaku is perhaps extreme in its claims about size, it reflects a continuing problem in determining the extent of active membership of new religious movements. These problems may gradually be resolved as stricter controls on membership data collection are sought from religious groups (due to the general tightening of laws relating to religious movements after the Aum affair of 1995) but as yet it remains difficult to determine a clear picture of the numbers of those belonging to new religions. In general terms, scholars in the field have estimated that perhaps between 20 and 30 percent of the population is affiliated with such movements, and it is clear that some of them can claim memberships in the millions. In the 1994 statistics supplied to the Agency for Cultural Affairs by the various religious movements, Rissho Koseikai claimed over 6 million members, Reiyukai 3 million, and Tenrikyo 1.8 million; Soka Gakkai is perhaps larger still. Moreover these movements have a striking public presence: Rissho Koseikai commands vast premises in Tokyo spanning several blocks; Tenrikyo dominates the town of Tenri and runs a university, hospital, and numerous overseas missions; and Soka Gakkai's immense facilities include a newspaper (the third largest selling one in Japan) and it claims close affiliation to the political party Komeito, which generally takes the third largest number of seats in Japanese parliamentary elections.

Besides the lack of coherent figures relating to membership, there is little clear data to show the geographical spread of new religions or their age structures. Here, however, some generalizations can be made. The first is that many new religions, and most particularly those that developed out of Nichiren Buddhism in the inter-war eras, along with the "new" new religions of the recent period, tend to be based around urban areas. This can be seen, perhaps, in the ways that Komeito (the political party linked closely to Soka Gakkai) fields candidates for election. It relies heavily on the block Soka Gakkai vote and only puts up candidates in the small percentage of constituencies where it has a reasonable chance of success because of the existence of blocks of Soka Gakkai members. In all, it fields around sixty to seventy candidates in an election (most of whom succeed in being elected) concentrated in the main urban areas.

Indeed, in many rural areas of Japan the older religions have maintained their traditional dominance and one can find many regions where new religions have barely attained a foothold. Where they have done so in rural areas, it has more commonly been the older (and originally more rurally based) movements such as Tenrikyo that have done so, rather than the "new" new religions.

Although it is thus reasonable to associate membership of new religions with urban Japan, there are also some caveats to be made. The first is that many of the older new religions originated in more rural areas (e.g., Tenrikyo in Nara prefecture), Konkokyo and Kurozumikyo (in Okayama), and, although they may subsequently have developed urban bases as well, they still retain strong ties of allegiance in the regions where they originated. Some new religions have a more clearly defined regional focus than others. Thus, Ennokyo, a new religion formed in the 1920s in the rural northern Hyogo prefecture, retains a strong following and a large center in that region, although it has not developed to a great degree beyond it. While to some extent the new religions have remits that cover the whole of Japan, many are more clearly regionally defined movements with little strength beyond their immediate place of development.

Membership patterns also vary from movement to movement. A standard generalization is that the membership of the older new religions tends to be slightly older than those of the "new" new religions that are largely considered as the preserve of the urban young. The average age of those who renounced the world to live in Aum communes under its monastic order was twenty-seven years old. However, such generalizations should not be allowed to blur the fact that even supposedly youth-oriented movements such as Aum also had elderly followers and that Japanese new religions in general have attracted a wide age span, at least in urban areas.

One further point on membership is that early assumptions made about the new religions suggested that their appeal was largely confined to the poor and the under-educated urban masses. This assumption dominated discussions of the new religions for much of the postwar period. However, subsequent research has shown a rather different picture: studies of Mahikari and Gedatuskai, for example, show they have a fairly representational cross-section of the populace in terms of employment, while in educational terms members' levels of achievement may be at least on a par with, or somewhat above, the national average. The "new" new religions appear to have a high proportion of highly educated graduates from elite universities; this is a distinct contrast to the prevailing images of new religions from the 1950s and before.

THE IMPORTANCE OF JAPANESE NEW RELIGIOUS MOVEMENTS IN THE STUDY OF RELIGION

As the new religions age and become old, they change. Movements such as Tenrikyo, for instance, have large numbers of third- and fourth-generation members who have been born into the movement, rather than converted into it. As a result the movement tends to lose dynamism, at least in contrast to the "new" new religions that are still first-generation individual conversion movements. There is evidence that some of those who have converted to the "new" new religions have done so from older new religions and have been attracted by the enthusiasm of these movements compared to the more institutionalized religions of their birth.

The rise of Japanese new religious movements is an example of a global phenomenon, which is the relationship between religious activism and social change. It also shows the changing processes and patterns of appeal that new religions in general offer: the types of follower who join "new" new religions today present a very different picture from those who might have joined, say, Tenrikyo in the mid-nineteenth century. Indeed, the differing patterns of appeal illustrate the need for new terminologies and terms to describe the more recent new religions. The Japanese religious world, with its capacity to continually generate new movements, provides both an example of intense religious dynamism and an arena vital to the study of religion in a global era.

BIBLIOGRAPHY

Astley, Trevor. 1995. "The Transformation of a Recent Japanese New Religion: Okawa Ryuho and Kofuku no Kagaku." *Japanese Journal of Religious Studies* 2, nos. 3–4: 343–80.
Davis, Winston B. 1980. *Dojo: Magic and Exorcism in Modern Japan.* Stanford, Calif.: Stanford University Press.
Earhart, H. Byron. 1989. *Gedatsukai and Religion in Contemporary Japan.* Bloomington: University of Indiana Press.
Hardacre, Helen. 1984. *Lay Buddhism in Contemporary Japan: Reiyukai Kyodan.* Princeton, N.J.: Princeton University Press.
———. 1986. *Kurozumikyo and the New Religions of Japan.* Princeton, N.J.: Princeton University Press.
Reader, Ian. 1991. *Religion in Contemporary Japan.* Basingstoke: Macmillans.
Tani Fumio. 1987. "Shinpi kara shukyo." In *Gendai no kokoro: Sukyo Mahikari.* Edited by Hatakenaka Sachiko. Tokyo: Bundu.

CHAPTER 16

KOREAN RELIGIOUS SOCIETY

LEWIS LANCASTER

KOREAN religious society is pluralistic in that it includes traditional shaman, Buddhist, and Christian elements. The three strands of religion interact, but Korean religiosity is built on a basis of indigenous nature-oriented beliefs. The earliest sources for studying the religion of ancient Korea indicate that there was worship of the spirits of wind, rain, and clouds.

The traditional political structure of Korea was one of clan-centered communities, loosely connected in confederations. The importance of these social groupings can be seen in the worship of certain totemic animals that were identified with specific clans, e.g., the horse and the Pak family. In this environment, it was important to seal the decisions made during the deliberations of the confederations. For major decisions, the clan chieftains would gather at one of four sacred sites. In this way at a very early date, religion was a way of enforcing the political decisions. All of these early religious practices were within the parameters of what we call shamanism, looking to the ancestors and spirits in nature and calling upon them in times of need.

As the tribal federations gave way to more centralized state governance, there were different religious needs. Buddhism became part of court life. From the fourth to the sixth centuries, Buddhism became the primary religion of the courts of the Three Kingdoms, Koguryo, Paekche, and Silla. Using the teaching of the Cakravartin (Universal King), the royal houses sought for legitimization on the basis of their karmic heritage and their moral behavior, not just on heredity. Buddhism was an excellent tool for empire builders since it had a portable sanctity, which allowed it to spread far and wide. Buddhism was in many ways the first world religion in that it transcended family, ethnicity, language, culture, geography, and social structure in its move from India through Central Asia to Korea. A religious tradition of this sort helped kings establish themselves as rulers over clan groups that were locally centered.

Geomancy offered one example of the way in which Buddhism was able to expand some aspects of society. The kings and aristocrats had first used it to determine the best spots for constructing cities and tombs and used this special knowledge of the art of divination of the terrain. This use of geomancy enhanced the authority of the king or the local officials who used it. Buddhism, by contrast, maintained that a monastery could be built anywhere because it could alter the structure of the power that existed at any physical location. The spread of the relic cult was another way in which Buddhism was able to sanctify a place by using an object that contained its own importance and did not rely on the history of the site where it was enshrined.

The Three Kingdoms were followed by the Unified Silla, which eventually fell to the Koryo dynasty. This was a time of great upheaval throughout East Asia. The Yuan dynasty of Mongols rose and fell in China, but not before opening up the Euroasian land mass to international travel and commerce. Europeans were now able to travel to China from Italy and return and the modern world was emerging. Under the Koryo, Buddhism thrived as never before. However, at the same time the Confucian approach to government and society was gaining power and influence among some of the officials. The Koryo and the other kingdoms of Korea had often followed the patterns of kingship found among the nomadic and steppe empires to the West. These were patterns still based on confederation, selection of leaders based on merit and popularity rather than heredity, levirate marriage of widows to the brother of the deceased husband, and shared role between the king and the religious holy men in governance. As the Yuan dynasty collapsed and the Han people reassumed leadership under the Ming, Korea moved rapidly toward sinification and in particular government and society ruled by the Neo-Confucian values of Chu-hsi. As part of this sinification, the Koryo was replaced by the Choson dynasty that rejected Buddhism and native religious traditions in favor of the Neo-Confucian teachings. The Confucian values led to the establishment of a highly structured patrilineal pattern of descent. Under this new pattern of government, the Confucian rituals began to replace previous ones. The worship of ancestors was no longer allowed in the Buddhist monasteries or among the shamans. All ancestral veneration was delegated to family altars, and with this came a complete focus on male descent with the role of women being subordinated. The Confucian rituals became central to the life of the elite. These rites included capping (coming of age), marriage, death ceremonies, and ancestral veneration. It was ritual behavior that dominated society and gave instruction for behavior in public and private life. This Neo-Confucian teaching came to be known as Sirhak, the Teaching of Substance.

During this time of the Choson dynasty, Buddhism was severely suppressed, monks and nuns were denied entry into the capital or major cities, women were restricted from going to monasteries for religious activities, and monasteries were required to pay tribute to the government and local officials. As a result, Buddhism shifted from being part of the urban life and eventually was supported only in the rural areas, in particular in a few monasteries that were pilgrimage centers. These monasteries were located in the mountains and in them developed the meditation schools that gave modern Korean Buddhism its distinctive character.

By the eighteenth century, Korea was facing a rapidly changing world situation and with it the spread of missionaries from Europe and the introduction of the Roman Catholic tradition to East Asia. Koreans living in China were converted by the Catholic mission and when they returned to their native land they formed the first group of believers in 1784. For a time the movement was limited to Korean laymen because no foreign missionaries were allowed to enter the country. After some years of trying to operate a church without priests or authority, the lay group was instructed to wait until a priest could come to assist them. In 1794, the first Catholic priest, a Chinese, arrived and by 1800 there were ten thousand converts. There were signs of trouble as the Catholics grew in number. In 1785 the first martyrs were killed, mainly over the issue of veneration of ancestors.

Another round of government repressions in 1801 resulted in death and the near destruction of the new church. Officials became concerned about the religion since it taught that there was an authority greater than the king. This conflict grew into a full-blown repression and in 1801 most activities among the Catholics were halted. It was not until the 1860s that Protestants came to Korea, at first with the help of Korean Catholics in China. In 1885 the first Protestant church was constructed and with the growing power of the tradition came a period of conflict with the Catholics over the old issues of the papal system, sale of indulgences, and transubstantiation. At first the Protestants were involved in teaching and social welfare such as medical services, but after 1887 they became active within the religious sphere.

A major rebellion (in 1894–95) broke out among the provinces led by a group known as the Tonghak, "Eastern Teaching," who opposed the Catholics who were called Sohak, or "Western Teaching." This was a turning point in Korean history. The Tonghak group spoke out against foreigners, especially Japanese. Borrowing from all of the religions of Korea, Tonghak taught that all men were to be treated as if they were gods. The Western approach in religion and economy was opposed by this peasant-dominated group and by the Confucian elite. On the other side, there were those who looked to Christianity as the way to modernize Korea and help to bring it into equal relationship to the rest of the world. One of the important contributions of the Christians was the use of the Korean syllabary known as *han'gul*, rather than Chinese characters. As early as 1801 the Catholics were printing books in the han'gul that allowed people to read them without having the years of training necessary to be able to read Chinese. Later the Protestants would follow the same scheme in their publications, making the Korean "alphabet" better known.

Japanese control in Korea was constantly growing. As a result of the Japanese army involvement with the Russian war, there were troops passing through and being stationed in Korea. Control of the Korean government started in 1905 when all diplomatic affairs were assumed by Japan, and by 1910 the nation was under complete domination. This brought about a crisis among the religions. Koreans needed to decide whether to cooperate with the Japanese or stand out for Korean nationalism. This became an even more crucial issue when military council required that all Koreans do some form of veneration at Shinto shrines. Some Christians complied, with the understanding that it was a national event rather than a religious one, but others opposed the practice.

By the 1920s, Communism became active in some of the farming areas, brought by Koreans living in the eastern part of the Soviet Union. At first, the religious traditions were uncertain of how to consider the movement, but later it would be a major factor in the way in which Koreans would relate to all faiths. When World War II ended and Korea was freed from Japanese control, Christians rejected the Marxist teachings about religion. Divided into two nations by the action of the Allies, the North became a Communist state and all religions were suppressed. In the South, the role of religions was a major part of the way in which society developed. The Korean War brought much more destruction to Korea than World War II, since pitched battles were fought from one end of the nation to the other. When a truce was declared, the nation remained divided and the religious situation was little changed. In the South, the presence of American troops and the reliance on the United States for support gave the Christian church more influence than ever before. From 1950 to 1980, Christian membership grew from less than a million to more than seven million. Missionary and local involvement have since been active in the creation of schools and hospitals as well as assisting in labor affairs, women's issues, and social policy. By the end of the century, at least 25 percent of the Korean population in the South were Christian.

Buddhism was challenged by all of these events. Under strict suppression from the Choson dynasty, denied access to society and education, the tradition was forced to find new ways of survival. By 1860, changes began to occur, and a revival of Buddhism began. Monasteries were refurbished, officials could no longer use monks for forced labor, and even tribute payments by the monasteries were curtailed. The monasteries had continued to exist under the most trying of circumstances and were ready to receive the growing support. Under the Japanese control of the government, Buddhism was seen as a possible ally since it was an important part of life in Japan as well as Korea. Since Japan had married priests and few celibate monastics, this pattern was encouraged and even required by the authorities in Korea. By the end of World War II, perhaps as many as 90 percent of the monks and nuns were married. After the war this issue was a major one and the cause of much unrest, since many viewed the marriage of monks as a Japanese practice and not a Korean tradition. Slowly celibate monks began to gain more power and increasing financial support was taken away from the married group. By 1990, only 8 percent of monastics were married; the old way of the precepts of "leaving homelife" had reasserted its hold over the Buddhists of Korea.

Growth among Buddhists has kept pace with the spread of Christianity and nearly 30 percent of the population is now listed as officially Buddhist. As circumstances have changed, the monasteries are returning to the urban areas, and Buddhism has entered a new era with the establishment of radio stations and one TV station. Korean society is unique in Asia in this situation of having two of the major world religions attracting sizable numbers of believers. It is interesting to note that the two exist side by side with little in the way of conflicts or active hostility. As part of the great growth of religious institutions in Korea, missionary and foreign activities have increased. There are several thousand Christian missionaries in over a hundred countries, and hundreds of Buddhist monks and nuns from Korea now have centers wherever immigrant populations exist.

By the 1960s, Korea was undergoing a rapid transformation as the agrarian society gave way to an industrial and urban one. With the growth of industry, labor issues have came to the fore. The Catholic Church became involved in union activity, led by Bishop Kim who was elevated to the status of cardinal in 1969. Still under military rule, there was a growing protest movement of students, workers, and farmers speaking out against the government, often being jailed for so doing. Anti-government activity reached its peak after the attack against protestors in Kwangju by the Korean army. Catholics, Protestants, and Buddhists were all visible in the streets of Seoul as protest marchers called for free elections and a democratic constitution.

Thus the religions of Korea have all played a role in the emergence of a civil government in South Korea. While Christianity and Buddhism have become dominant in religious life of South Korea, the shamanic tradition has continued to be practiced. Shamans are especially important to women who make use of the rituals in daily home-life as well as the public ones. Among expatriate Korean communities around the world this interaction of religions persists.

BIBLIOGRAPHY

Buswell, Robert E., Jr. 1992. *The Zen Monastic Experience: Buddhist Practice in Contemporary Korea.* Princeton, N.J.: Princeton University Press.

———, ed. 2002. *Korean Religions in Practice.* Princeton, N.J.: Princeton University Press.

Grayson, James Huntley. 1985. *Early Buddhism and Christianity in Korea: A Study in the Emplantation of Religion.* Leiden: E. J. Brill.

Keel, Hee-Sung. 1978. "Buddhism and Political Power in Korean History." *Journal of the International Association of Buddhist Studies* 1:1–24.

Lancaster, Lewis R., and Chai-shin Yu, eds. 1989. *Introduction of Buddhism to Korea: New Cultural Patterns.* Berkeley: Asian Humanities Press.

Lancaster, Lewis R., and Sung Bae Park. 1979. *The Korean Buddhist Canon: A Descriptive Catalog.* Berkeley: University of California Press.

Sorensen, Henrik H. 1999. "Buddhist Spirituality in Premodern and Modern Korea." In *Buddhist Spirituality II.* Ed. Takeuchi Yoshinori, 109–133. New York: Crossroad Publishing Company.

Yu, Chai-Shin. 2004. *The Founding of Catholic Tradition in Korea.* Berkeley: Asian Humanities Press.

———, ed. 2004. *Korea and Christianity.* Berkeley: Asian Humanities Press.

CHAPTER 17

BUDDHIST COMMUNITIES ABROAD

THOMAS A. TWEED

BUDDHISM arose during the fifth century BCE in what is today Nepal and north-eastern India to become one of the world's first transregional religions. In crossing from one region to another hybrid practices emerged as it made contact with other spiritual and cultural traditions. That sort of transculturation, in which both itinerant religious practices and shifting local cultures were transformed, has characterized the history of Buddhism as it moved throughout Asia and the rest of the world.

When Śākyamuni Buddha began to teach about suffering and its cessation, the cultures of the Indian subcontinent already had been shaped by contact and exchange. Although the Himalayas blocked the entrance to the north, and imposing seas surrounded India on three other sides, Aryan invaders managed to enter from the northwest between 1800 and 1400 BCE. By about 800 BCE the religious poetry of Aryan priests would be collected into the Vedas, the most ancient of Hindu sacred texts. Much of that Vedic worldview, a product of centuries of cultural exchange, would find its way into the new religion that the Buddha founded.

If the worldview of the Buddha already included multiple cultural influences, the transculturation of beliefs and practices continued as the religion moved beyond the Indian subcontinent during the reign of Emperor Aśoka in the third century BCE Aśoka, a Buddhist ruler, sent emissaries abroad, and Buddhist communities soon flourished in the Himalayas to the northwest and in Sri Lanka, just off the southern tip of India and across the Gulf of Mannar. In subsequent centuries, traders, travelers, and missionaries carried Buddhism north to central Asia and east to China. From there it traveled to Vietnam, Korea, and Japan. The teachings of the Buddha also crossed the Bay of Bengal into Southeast Asia and moved farther south across the Indian Ocean into Indonesia. So by the time Buddhism died out in India during the thirteenth century it had spread throughout almost all of southeastern, central, and eastern Asia. Buddhism was transnational and transcultural—with new hybrid rituals, institutions, artifacts, and beliefs emerging as it crossed borders and interacted with local cultures and vernacular religions.

BUDDHISM OUTSIDE ASIA

Buddhism continued to be diverse and hybrid as it made its way around the globe. There is evidence of Buddhist influence in the ancient Mediterranean world, and firsthand reports of Buddhism by Europeans appea in the medieval and early modern period. In the spring of 1254, for example, the great Khan arranged an interreligious debate in the Mongol capital in Karakorum. William of Rubruck, a Franciscan who had been dispatched by Louis IX to gather information, win converts, and form alliances participated in that day-long conversation among Buddhists, Christians, and Muslims. We know about that debate because Rubruck left an account of the exchange, and after centuries of this sort of intermittent contact, Western knowledge of Buddhism began to deepen during the 1840s, as European scholars translated sacred texts and chronicled Buddhist history. During the middle of the nineteenth century a few Western intellectuals expressed sympathy for the religion, and by the 1880s the first self-proclaimed Buddhist converts appeared in Western nations.

At the same time—during the late nineteenth and early twentieth century—migrants from Asia began to settle around the globe, and they brought Buddhist practices with them. For example, Japanese immigrants introduced Buddhism to Brazil when they arrived at the port of Santos in 1908 to work on the coffee, cotton, and banana plantations. The descendants of those earlier migrants continued to practice their faith in Brazil and other Western nations during the first half of the twentieth century. Buddhism's globalization intensified after the 1960s because of increased transnational migration from Asia and improved communication and transportation technologies.

In the recent past there has been a surge in the number of Western Buddhists, both cradle Buddhists, who have been born into the tradition, and converts, who have embraced it as adults. That pattern also holds in Australia, Europe, South

Africa, and the Americas. According to one scholar, Martin Baumann, the number of Buddhist organizations tripled in Great Britain between 1979 and 1991, and Germany saw a five-fold increase during the same period. By the mid-1990s there were 400 German Buddhist centers or temples as well as 130 in France and 300 in Great Britain. Other European nations also boasted increases in the number of adherents and centers. Tens of thousands of converts and cradle Buddhists now practice in Italy, Switzerland, and the Netherlands. According to some estimates, Russia, with its many followers of Asian descent, might have as many as one million Buddhists. Buddhism has a long history in South Africa, but since 1990 the number of Buddhists has swelled so that they now practice at more than forty centers or temples. The government census figures for Australia and New South Wales show the same rise. Adherents rose 42 percent between 1986 and 1996, when 199,812 Australians told the census officials they were Buddhist. Those Australian Buddhists could chant or meditate at more than 150 centers or temples. By 2000 the full range of Buddhism—Mahayana, Theravada, and Vajrayana—had taken root outside its traditional areas of influence in Asia.

Buddhist communities now also flourish in North America—from Mexico City's El Centro de Meditación Vipassanā, where converts meditate, to Toronto's Maha Dhammika Temple, where Burmese immigrants chant sutras. The 2001 Canadian Census reported 300,345 Buddhists, an 84 percent increase over the 1991 figures, and metropolitan Toronto, now one of the world's great centers of ethnic and religious diversity, includes dozens of Buddhist temples and tens of thousands of adherents.

Among nations in the Americas, and the West, the Buddhist presence is especially strong in the United States. That presence extends to those who do not claim Buddhist identity: As sociologists Robert Wuthnow and Wendy Cadge have argued, a "significant minority" of Americans have had contact with Buddhism and been influenced by it, as many as one in eight or twenty-five to thirty million Americans. That Buddhist "presence" also includes those who see themselves as Buddhists. It is not always easy to decide who is a Buddhist, however, and it is impossible to find official statistics on the number of adherents. Unlike Canada and Australia, the United States census no longer includes questions about religious affiliation. Recent estimates of the number of U.S. Buddhists range from five-hundred thousand to more than five million, with the average estimate about 2.3 million. As the Buddhist Sangha Council of Southern California has suggested, those cradle and convert Buddhists practice at approximately 1,500 temples and centers, if we count converted homes and former churches where a few dozen Buddhists gather as well as the imposing new buildings with more traditional Asian designs that boast large memberships. And as in other nations in the West, more and more immigrant temples are opening all the time. So are the sites where European American and African American converts practice. In 1997, Don Morreale found 1,062 convert meditation centers in the United States. The number of centers had doubled between 1975 and 1984, and doubled again in the twelve years between 1985 and 1997.

TRANSCULTURAL THEMES
IN U.S. BUDDHISM

The hybrid forms of Buddhism practiced at these U.S. centers and temples retain much from ancient and contemporary Asian models. An Asian Buddhist visitor might recognize much that is familiar in these American Buddhist communities—narratives, beliefs, values, rituals, institutions, and artifacts. Buddhists in the United States still tell the story of the Buddha and take the founder's life as exemplary. Most still read Buddhist sacred texts and learn about the four noble truths. To affirm their identity as Buddhists most still take refuge in the Three Treasures: the Buddha (the founder), the Dharma (his teachings), and the Sangha (the community). Following a long tradition in Asia, U.S. Buddhists dedicate themselves to living morally by following the precepts: not killing, not stealing, not misusing sexuality, not lying, and not using intoxicants. And, as in Asia, American monks and nuns—both Asian-born and Western-convert monastics—vow to follow even more demanding moral guidelines. A lay Buddhist from Bangkok who visited Wat Dhammaram in Chicago would recognize the gold statue of the seated Buddha on the main altar, and a Sōtō Zen monk from Kyoto could find the familiar image of that sect's founder, Dōgen, hanging near the altar at San Francisco Zen Center. And our hypothetical Asian visitors would find familiar rituals: the recitation of sutras, the invocation of Buddha, and the practice of meditation.

Those visitors also might notice some distinctive patterns. Western converts, some of whom sit on benches instead of cushions, seem more preoccupied with meditation than many lay followers in Asia. While many immigrant communities still use only Asian languages—Thai, Chinese, or Vietnamese—others turn to English when they gather for collective rituals on Sunday mornings. And there are other distinctive patterns and hybrid practices. Throughout its history, Buddhism has shown extraordinary malleability as it has traversed cultural boundaries, for example, in its passage from India to China, where for example Chan emerged from the encounter with indigenous values and vernacular religions, especially Daoism. A similar process is happening now in the United States as Buddhist communities construct identity, negotiate power, and find meaning amidst cultural flows that have been generated by Protestantism, democracy, global capitalism, church-state separation, ethnic and religious diversity, and longstanding commitments to individualism, pragmatism, and activism. Interpreters of U.S. Buddhism—including Rick Fields, Surya Das, Jack Kornfield, Richard Seager, and Peter Gregory—have offered insightful accounts of its distinctive features. Building on those accounts, and revising them, I suggest that we can identify seven noteworthy themes in the Buddhism now emerging in the United States. Although we should be careful to keep in mind the diversity and dynamism of the tradition in the U.S., it seems useful to note that American Buddhism seems democratic, individualistic, ecumenical, Protestant, experiential, pragmatic, and transnational.

1. U.S. Buddhist communities tend to be somewhat more egalitarian or *democratic* than their Asian counterparts. Religions, like political systems, make claims about the source of authority, and U.S. Buddhists are more likely to celebrate the spiritual authority of the people, as opposed to leaders, tradition, or texts. Lay followers play a somewhat larger role in the life of many American Buddhist communities than they traditionally have in most parts of Asia. In a related way, and on similar grounds, although female devotees have participated vigorously, even in disproportionate numbers, in Asia, women seem somewhat more prominent as leaders in the United States, especially in Zen, Tibetan, and Vipassanā convert centers. In 2000, women served as priest, abbess, or dharma teacher in dozens of groups across the nation—including San Francisco Zen Center, Insight Meditation Society in Massachusetts, and Maryland's Kunzang Palyul Chöling, a Tibetan center in the Nying-ma tradition.

2. Another way to make the same point: U.S. Buddhists, like many other Americans, tend to emphasize the value and authority of the individual. American Buddhism is *individualistic*. There are countervailing impulses, especially in the embrace of the guru's authority in some convert communities and the respect, even reverence, for monks in some immigrant groups. Yet, on the whole, there is an inclination among many American Buddhists to be somewhat suspicious of the group, the hierarchy, and the institution. This spiritual individualism, which sociologists tell us characterizes many in the contemporary United States, helps to explain why millions of Americans acknowledge some Buddhist influence and why there are so many nightstand Buddhists, those who have sympathy for the religion but fail to affiliate fully. Instead, they might place a how-to book about meditation on the nightstand—say, Philip Kapleau's *Three Pillars of Zen*—and read it before they sleep. They then rise the next morning to practice—however imperfectly or ambivalently—what they learned the night before. That practice seems to be another example of the impact of American individualism.

3. The first two themes—individualism and egalitarianism—have multiple

sources, national and transnational. They are endorsed by democracy and laissez-faire capitalism, but they also have spiritual roots that extend to the Protestant Reformation in sixteenth-century Europe. U.S. Buddhist communities negotiate meaning in conversation with others in the culture—Catholics, Jews, Muslims, Hindus, agnostics, and atheists—yet, despite the long-standing and continuing religious diversity of the nation, Protestantism has had a good deal of cultural clout in America. It's not surprising, then, that U.S. Buddhism includes some values, institutions, and practices that seem to resonate with *Protestantism*. American individualism has Protestant echoes in Martin Luther's championing of "the priesthood of all believers." The influence on American Buddhism takes other, more mundane, forms too, however. Immigrant Buddhists send their children to Buddhist summer camps, and Japanese Pure Land Buddhists meet on Sundays for "worship" in "churches" where their children attend "Sunday school." As early as the 1920s, members of the Buddhist Churches of America were sitting in pews singing hymns such as "Onward Buddhist Soldiers." Even if we should not overemphasize this point, Protestantism has had its influence.

4. U.S. Buddhism is also more *experiential*. Some traditions in American Protestantism have emphasized the personal experience of Christ's saving grace. The Puritans, the first Protestants in the new land, were preoccupied with that. Contemporary Americans' concern for direct experience has multiple sources, however, some of them secular. Whatever the sources, many seem drawn to intense and transforming experiences. Pentecostalism, with its emphasis on encountering the Holy Spirit, is only oneobvious contemporary example. Many U.S. Buddhist communities, especially convert centers, also highlight personal religious experience. Members of Sōka Gakkai International (SGI) chant *Namu—myō hō renge kyō*, (Homage to the Sūtra of the Lotus of the True Dharma), at private domestic rituals and collective public ceremonies. And, as many observers have noted, Euro-American and African American converts seem especially drawn to meditation, whether it is from Tibetan, Zen, or Vipassanā traditions. In general, these lay followers in the United States seem to spend more time and energy on meditation than most devotees in Asia.

5. American Buddhism also seems somewhat more activist and *pragmatic*. There are intellectual resources for social concern and vigorous traditions of political activism in some forms of Asian Buddhism. The image of the Vietnamese monk Thich Quang Duc might come to mind to Westerners, for example. To protest the repression of Vietnamese Buddhists, on 11 June 1963, Quang Duc sat stoically at a busy intersection in Saigon and put a match to his body, which had been doused with gasoline. Since the late nineteenth century, however, American followers of the Buddha also

have highlighted social activism, the concern to be good and do good.
For example, inspired by another Vietnamese monk, Thich Nhat Hanh,
many contemporary converts have embraced "engaged Buddhism," a
movement centered on efforts to promote world peace and social justice.
In a similar way, members of a large Taiwanese immigrant Buddhist temple have emphasized "Involved Buddhism," charitable practices that aim
to establish Amitābha Buddha's Pure Land on earth. In fact, cradle Buddhists at that Taiwanese-American temple, sociologist Carolyn Chen has
argued in a comparative study, are more socially involved than members
of a Taiwanese evangelical Christian church, which emphasizes evangelization instead of charity. Those immigrant Buddhists were propelled, in
part, by transnational forces—doctrines and practices that emerged from
a reform movement in Chinese Mahayana Buddhism that was founded
more fifty years ago in Asia. This activist theme, however, also harmo-
nizes with pragmatic impulses in American culture and American Buddhism—the inclination to evaluate religions by their ability to be effective. As in the philosophical movement, pragmatism, many Americans
have suggested that the truth and value of anything, including a religion,
should be measured pragmatically. They ask: Does it work? Does it lead
to bodily health, psychic peace, economic prosperity, political strength,
and social equality? For example, this pragmatic impulse seems to be behind the proliferation of Buddhist self-help books, which apply Buddhist
principles to aspects of everyday life. For example, in 2005, *Books in Print*
listed 319 volumes with "Zen" in the title, and more than one hundred of
them were how-to books that claim to demonstrate the usefulness of Zen,
including *Zen of Selling, Zen of Permanent Weight Loss, Zen and Horseback
Riding, Zen in Golf and Life*, and *Zen and the Art of Diabetes Maintenance*. However Buddhist adherents and scholars might assess these popular texts, which sometimes have little to do with Zen as it has been practiced in Asia or America, they point to the enduring pragmatic impulse
in American culture and U.S. Buddhism.

6. Buddhism in the United States is polysectarian or *ecumenical*. The English
   word ecumenism comes from a Greek term (*oikoumene*) meaning "the
   whole of the inhabited world." In Christian contexts, the term came to
   signify the concern to bridge differences among forms of Christianity and,
   more recently, even to seek conversation and commonalty with followers
   of other religions. I borrow the term here to point to three slightly different patterns. First, Buddhism in the United States is more diverse than
   almost anywhere in the world, with all forms of the tradition finding an
   institutional home by the 1970s. Intersectarian Buddhist councils now
   have formed in several cities with large immigrant populations, including
   Los Angeles and Chicago. Second, there also is somewhat more contact

and exchange among Buddhist sects than has been common in most regions of Asia and during most periods of Asian history. As one Vipassanā teacher, Jack Kornfield, has observed "American Buddhists have already begun to learn actively from each other's traditions." That self-conscious borrowing has created hybrid forms. Third, Buddhism, like all faiths, has been forced to be more ecumenical in the American cultural context. Transnational migration brought multiple faiths to the United States, and the First Amendment of the federal Constitution established a legal and political system that, on the whole, has preserved, even promoted, diversity. Even if all faiths don't celebrate the values and practices of other religions, in the United States all traditions must find ways to co-exist, and flourish, in the spiritual marketplace. Many Buddhist leaders now participate in interreligious dialogue and join local ministerial associations. Even those who hail from Buddhist nations have had to come to terms with the U.S. religious and political pattern: all faiths, even the culturally dominant ones, are one among many.

7. This polysectarian or ecumenical American Buddhism is also increasingly *transnational*. It is forming and reforming in a larger international network of contact and exchange. This is not new. Since the colonial period, U.S. religions emerged in interaction as peoples, artifacts, ideas, and practices circulated throughout the Atlantic World and the Pacific World. Buddhism in nineteenth-century America also formed in relation to transnational political, economic, and cultural exchanges. What seems new is the pace and scope of this global exchange. Improved communication and travel technology means that those exchanges happen more frequently and more quickly. Earlier migrants maintained links with the homeland, and their religious practice played an important role as they negotiated identity and constructed meaning in the new land. Some nineteenth-century migrants returned home. Some sent a flurry of letters back and forth. Others flew their native flag beside the American symbol, and they prayed at domestic and public altars filled with Old World symbols. In recent decades, however, the crisscrossing exchanges between and among nations have increased, both for cradle and convert Buddhists. Korean Buddhists in Seattle e-mail friends back home. Sri Lankan immigrant Buddhists in Los Angeles send for family members still on the island. Thai monks arrive in Greensboro, North Carolina, to nurture members of a recently formed temple. The Dalai Lama and other exiled Tibetan leaders lecture in New York City, and Vajrayāna monks create a traditional sand painting at an art museum in Miami. American Buddhists make pilgrimages to sacred sites in India, and some Zen followers even spend months or years in monastic training in Japan. Nightstand

Buddhists watch how-to videos about meditation by an Asian teacher and read books on mindfulness by an exiled Vietnamese monk. Devotees at Southern California's Hsi Lai Temple witness a constant flow of people and practices back and forth between the United States and Taiwan, the international center of Fo Kuang Buddhism. As at Hsi Lai Temple, the exchanges move both ways. The influence is not always from East to West. As Buddhist historian Peter Gregory has noted, with the exception of China, Buddhism "usually has been adopted as a bearer of higher civilization." It usually has entered as part of the culture of a politically and economically dominant nation. In this case, however, the receiving nation— the United States—is dominant in entertainment, science, technology, business, and the military. And, in many fields, English has become the international language. In this sort of contact zone, and in most others, individuals and groups enter and leave the site of exchange with differences in power, and America's cultural clout influences the patterns of exchange and alters the process of transculturation. Although the long-term effect of this inequality of cultural power remains unclear, it seems likely that new forms of American Buddhism will maintain strong transnational connections.

To suggest that transnationalism and the other six themes characterize contemporary U.S. Buddhist communities is not to claim that there is uniformity among American practitioners. U.S. Buddhists are divided along class and ethnic lines, as are most American congregations. The theologian and sociologist H. Richard Niebuhr had good reason to suggest that Sunday morning at eleven o'clock is the most segregated hour of the week, and most U.S. Buddhists have acculturated enough already that they do congregate on Sunday mornings. In their patterns of segregation, too, American Buddhists seem, well, American. Most Buddhists of Asian descent go to a temple with other Asian Americans; most European Americans chant or meditate together, too. Some African Americans report that they feel like outsiders in both communities. Even at temples where devotees from multiple racial and ethnic heritages meet in the same building, they often congregate at different times. They form—in Paul Numrich's insightful phrase—"parallel congregations." Like parallel lines, some American Buddhists never really meet.

To propose that these seven themes characterize contemporary U.S. Buddhism also is not to suggest that there is an essentialized and unchanging "Buddhism" that undergoes only minor transformations in its passage to the new cultural context nor to affirm that there is a fixed American character that all transplanted religions must resist or accommodate. As I have suggested in my use of the term *transculturation*, the situation is more fluid, more complicated, than that. As I understand it, collective identity and cultural power is always contested, always negotiated. It is process not a product. There is no static culture or fixed religion, only more or less prominent patterns, only more or less shared practices, only women and men continually constructing identity and negotiating power at varied social sites. There is only transculturation, reciprocally transformative exchanges between dynamic Buddhist traditions, which already had been formed through contact before their arrival on American shores, and shifting local cultures, which change further through their interaction with imported Buddhist traditions.

And I do not mean to suggest that these themes apply exclusively or fully to U.S. Buddhist communities. They characterize Buddhism in other Western nations, too. Many of these themes are found, for example, in German, Canadian, and Australian Buddhism. Further, in the United States these themes seem to be somewhat more prominent in Zen, Tibetan, and Vipassanā convert centers and at old-line Buddhist temples, whose members include the descendents of the earliest Asian immigrants such as the predominantly Japanese Buddhist Churches of America.

Some social forces might work against continued acculturation among U.S. Buddhists, but the history of religion in America and the experience of Buddhism in Asia suggest that those forces probably will not win in the end. Asian American, African American, and European American Buddhists might never practice their faith together regularly. Communication and transportation technologies might increase the Asian cultural influences, and transnational migration might continue to bring a steady flow of foreign-born Buddhists. Still, it seems likely that the process of transculturation—and hybridization—will continue and intensify in the United States, as it did as the religion moved throughout Asia. If current Asian American Buddhist temples manage to socialize their children, and if interest in the religion continues among those born into other religions, there are reasons to think that the diverse U.S. Buddhist communities might come to share more and more as the decades pass, even though divisions of ethnicity, class, and ethos probably will remain.

Whatever the future holds for Buddhism in the United States and in other places outside Asia, as I have suggested, these contemporary U.S. Buddhist communities seem egalitarian, individualistic, Protestant, experiential, pragmatic, ecumenical, and transnational. These themes do not point to immutable traits of an essentialized religious tradition or an enduring national character. They are not found exclusively in the United States, and are not equally prominent in all American Buddhist communities. Yet they help us to identify some noteworthy patterns. We can begin to get some sense—however imperfect—of what might be *American* about American Buddhism.

BIBLIOGRAPHY

Adam, Enid, and Philip J. Hughes. 1996. *The Buddhists in Australia*. Canberra: Australian Government Publishing Service.

Almond, Philip C. 1988. *The British Discovery of Buddhism*. Cambridge: Cambridge University Press.

Baumann, Martin. 1995. "Creating a European Path to Nirvana: Historical and Contemporary Developments of Buddhism in Europe." *Journal of Contemporary Religion* 1, no. 1: 5–70.

———. 1993. *Deutsche Buddhisten: Geshichte und Gemeinschaften*. Marburg: Diagonal-Verlag.

———. 1997. "The Dharma Has Come West: A Survey of Recent Studies and Sources." *Critical Review of Books in Religion* 10: 1–14.

Baumann, Martin, and Charles S. Prebish, eds. 2002. *Westward Dharma: Buddhism Beyond Asia*. Berkeley: University of California Press.

Cadge, Wendy. 2005. *Heartwood: The First Generation of Theravada Buddhism in America*. Chicago: University of Chicago Press.

Chen, Carolyn. 2002. "The Religious Varieties of Ethnic Presence: A Comparison between a Taiwanese Immigrant Buddhist Temple and an Evangelical Christian Church." *Sociology of Religion* 63 (no. 2): 215–238.

Coleman, James William. 2000. *The New Buddhism: The Western Transformation of an Ancient Tradition*. New York: Oxford University Press.

Croucher, Paul. 1989. *Buddhism in Australia*. Kensington, New South Wales: New South Wales University Press.

Gregory, Peter N. 2001. "Describing the Elephant: Buddhism in America." *Religion and American Culture* 11 (summer): 233–263.

McLellan, Janet. 1999. *Many Petals of the Lotus: Asian Buddhist Communities in Toronto*. Toronto: University of Toronto Press.

Morreale, Don, ed. 1998. *The Complete Guide to Buddhist America*. Boston: Shambhala.

Numrich, Paul David. 1996. *Old Wisdom in the New World: Americanization in Two Immigrant Theravada Buddhist Temples*. Knoxville: University of Tennessee Press.

Prebish, Charles S., and Kenneth K. Tanaka, eds. 1998. *The Faces of Buddhism in America*. Berkeley: University of California Press.

Queen, Christopher S, ed. 2000. *Engaged Buddhism in the West*. Boston: Wisdom Publication.

Seager, Richard Hughes. 1999. *Buddhism in America*. New York: Columbia University Press.

Tweed, Thomas A. 2000. *The American Encounter with Buddhism, 1844–1912: Victorian Culture and the Limits of Dissent*. Revised edition, with a new introduction by the author. Chapel Hill: University of North Carolina Press.

———. 2005. "American Occultism and Japanese Buddhism: Albert J. Edmunds, D.T. Suzuki, and Translocative History." *Japanese Journal of Religious Studies* 32 (no. 2): 249–281.

Tweed, Thomas A., and Stephen Prothero. 1999. *Asian Religions in America: A Documentary History*. New York: Oxford University Press.

Van Esterik, Penny. 1992. *Taking Refuge: Lao Buddhists in North America*. Toronto: York University, Centre for Refugee Studies, York Lane Press.

Van Loon, Louis H. 1995. "Buddhism in South Africa." In *Living Faiths in South Africa*. Eds. John W. de Gruchy and Martin Prozesky, 209–217. Cape Town: David Philip.

Williams, Duncan Ryuken, and Christopher S. Queen, eds. 1999. *American Buddhism: Methods and Findings in Recent Scholarship*. Surrey, U.K.: Curzon Press.

Wuthnow, Robert, and Wendy Cadge. 2004. "Buddhists and Buddhism in the United States: The Scope of Influence." *Journal for the Scientific Study of Religion* 43, (no. 3): 363–380.

PART III

JEWISH CULTURAL REGION

CHAPTER 18

THINKING GLOBALLY ABOUT JUDAISM

HARVEY E. GOLDBERG

JUDAISM is perhaps the most global of religious traditions, since for most of its history it has existed in myriad diaspora communities throughout the Middle East, Europe, and eventually the Americas and elsewhere. There are currently some fourteen million Jews around the world: the largest number, almost six million, are in North America; about four and a half million live in Israel, three million in Europe, a half million in Latin America, and the remainder in Asia, Australia, Africa, and elsewhere in the Middle East. The global diversity of Jewish residency has therefore created challenges for those who have attempted to study Jewish society as a whole.

THE STUDY OF JEWISH SOCIETIES THROUGHOUT THE WORLD

A broad view of Jewish life throughout the globe was implicit in the new "science of Judaism" formulated early in the nineteenth century, but the systematic and mature application of sociological thought to the historical study of Judaism around the world emerged only slowly. In his programmatic essay of 1818 outlining the nascent Science of Judaism (*Wissenschaft des Judentums*), Leopold Zunz (1794–1886) included statistical studies, but the major intellectual thrust that followed immediately thereafter, however, was heavily influenced by an idealist approach to history. It pictured the forward march of Judaism conceived of as a set of religious and philosophical ideas that had an impact on world history as Jews spread throughout the globe. This was prominent in the work of Abraham Geiger (1810–1874), who, along with other historians, sought a respectable intellectual place for the Jewish religion as Jews in West and Central Europe sought to be accepted into Gentile society in the wake of political emancipation. A modification of this approach appeared in the work of Heinrich Graetz (1817–1891), which, taking a more pluralistic view of Jewish experience, presented it as being made up of diverse histories which were all worthy of study. In his view, different periods did not move beyond earlier ones, but constituted varying expressions of Judaism envisioned as a set of religious ideas linked to a people. Peoplehood continued to be basic to Judaism after the loss of political independence, although this view did not imply Jewish nationalism such as later emerged in the Zionist movement.

A more explicit diaspora nationalism emerged in the work of Simon Dubnow (1860–1941). Dubnow showed how new centers of Jewish life emerged in different parts of the globe, enjoying autonomy from the majority polity and culture and replacing those that had declined. Babylonia succeeded the Land of Israel, which in turn was succeeded by Spain and the Rhineland, and the latter two were succeeded by Eastern Europe. Following the historical progression of these centers implied close attention to the communal institutions that comprised them. Another social perspective was supplied by Salo Baron (1895–1989) whose emphasis on social institutions was an alternative to what he called the lachrymose conception of Jewish history. His multivolume *Social and Religious History of the Jews* is probably the last attempt of a single generalist to provide an overview of Jewish history. His perspective on Jewish social life, however, is not informed by any particular theoretical orientation.

Jewish nationalism in the form of Zionism also gave rise to sociological orientations. These were often linked to practical concerns. Alfred Nossig (1864–1943) was among the founders of scientific study of Jewish statistics, and also utilized the perspective of social hygiene to argue that the laws of the Bible and the Talmud were beneficial in terms of personal and public health. His thesis was aimed against antisemitic theories of Jewish degeneration. Arthur Ruppin (1876–1943), an economist and sociologist, headed the Palestine Office of the Zionist Organization. In addition to research on current conditions in the Levant, he authored the *Soziologie der Juden* (Sociology of the Jews; Berlin 1931), a landmark in the historical demography of world Jewry. Martin Buber (1878–1965), known mainly as a philosopher, also saw himself as a comparative sociologist of the ancient Near East including biblical civilization. Arriving in Palestine in 1938, his courses laid the groundwork for the Department of Sociology at the Hebrew University of Jerusalem.

Sociological and anthropological approaches to the Bible first emerged in the nineteenth century. William Robertson Smith (1846–1894) showed that biblical religion reflected the social structure of the Ancient Israelites. He was one of the tutors of James Frazer (1854–1941), author of the multivolume *The Golden Bough* (1890), who also produced a three-volume study of *Folklore in the Old Testament* (1918). Frazer's oeuvre, in turn, influenced rabbinic scholars such as Louis Ginsberg and Jacob Lauterbach, but their research on legends and rituals did not contain a systematic sociological component. In another direction however, Smith had an impact on Emile Durkheim (1858–1917), who did not focus on Judaism but drew upon biblical and Talmudic material in formulating his general principles in the sociology of religion.

Another major figure in the history of sociology, Max Weber (1854–1920), studied ancient Israelite religion and its transformation into rabbinic Judaism. In his *Das Antike Judentum* (1920; Ancient Judaism, 1952), he sought to unravel the relationships between social structural factors and the religious history of the Jews. He sought to understand how, on the one hand, the religious orientations of Judaism led to Christianity, the emergence of Protestantism, and the development of capitalism which he saw as linked to the "Protestant ethic," while, on the other, Judaism itself did not lead to these developments but to the creation of "pariah capitalism." His comparative sociological approach to Judaism received some attention from scholars of Judaism, but much less attention than his work on Protestantism or on the religions of ancient India and China. One attempt to apply sociological thought inspired by Weber was in the work of Louis Finkelstein (1895–1991) on the formative stages of rabbinic Jewry, where the differences between the Pharisees (viewed as the forerunners of rabbinic Judaism) and the Sadducees were presented as paralleling the class conflict between plebeian Jews and the aristocracy in Roman Palestine. This thesis was oversimplified and the effort did not encourage further work in that direction. A later attempt to build upon Weber was made by Jacob Katz (1904–1998) who adopted the notion of an "ideal type" in describing Central European Jewry on the eve of the emancipation in his *Tradition and Crisis* (1961; original Hebrew, 1958). Katz's work may be seen as a turning point in the creation of modern Jewish social history. His focus on the interaction between religious developments and a variety of social-historical factors, including economic, institutional, and political trends, has proven to be more illuminating than strictly Marxist approaches to Jewish history.

Another input into the sociological study of Judaism around the world came from anthropology. The linkage between anthropology and biblical research that developed in the nineteenth century was weakened when anthropology became associated with field research in the first part of the twentieth century. By mid-century, there began to coalesce interest in the ethnographic study of contemporary Jews, with special emphasis on those immigrating to Israel from Middle Eastern countries, on memories from Eastern Europe survivors of the Holocaust, and on varieties of religious life emerging in America. Some Jewish historians found anthropological studies, both among Jews and generally, to be useful in relating to documents of earlier periods. An example is the work of S. D. Goitein (1900–1985) on the Jews in the Muslim world in the tenth to thirteenth centuries. More recently, Jewish historians have added a cultural emphasis to their work. Examples are the concern with collective memory, pioneered by Yosef Yerushalmi (b. 1932), and the utilization of anthropological insights in research on rituals within their family and communal contexts. These studies add a more experiential and intimate dimension to the understanding of earlier periods that supplements the results of institutional approaches.

There has always been some tension between the strong emphasis on textual study in Judaism and the salience of a sociological approach to history. Zunz's founding essay concerned "rabbinic literature" although his vision was to include much more than traditional rabbinic scholarship. The study of Ancient Israel could at first rely only on the biblical text, until archaeological finds began to complement that source of data with both material objects and written documents from the Ancient Near East. These, however, often leave a glaring gap between the biblical sources and the other materials. It is difficult to sort out the social formations at the base of the biblical texts, while material remains yield hints to social arrangements but rarely are sufficient to provide solid information. Similar gaps characterize periods of the Mishna and the Palestinian and Babylonian Talmuds. While much is known about these periods from Greek and Roman sources, for example, the way that external data links up with the textual traditions in rabbinic sources is often very unclear.

In the post-Talmudic period, correspondence between the centers of study in Iraq (called Babylonia by the Jews), and Jewish communities elsewhere in the Muslim world, is a source of important data on everyday life. These took the form of questions from far-flung communities to the centers, and the *responsa* of the latter are a crucial source of social history even though their primary purpose was the clarification of Jewish law. From a somewhat later period in the Islamic world, a mass of material survived in the storehouse of a synagogue known as the Cairo *Geniza*. Known to the scholarly world from the 1890s, these documents were first plumbed for the light they shed on traditional subjects such as grammar, philosophy, or the history of rabbinic law. From the 1950s, S. D. Goitein began to utilize them for the writing of socioeconomic history, as recorded in his multi-volume *A Mediterranean Society* (1967–1988).

Earlier, Louis Finkelstein had sought to provide a sociological-like portrait of Jewish life in Europe, at a corresponding period, in his *Jewish Self-Government in the Middle Ages* (1924), but the data available to him were mostly rabbinic writings with a normative perspective. Some noted historians of Judaism, such as Gershom

Scholem (1897–1982) in his studies of mysticism, expressed skepticism over the ability of sociology to illuminate religious phenomena. Similarly, there were scholars who were hesitant about the sociological approach of Jacob Katz.

DIVERSITY IN ANCIENT JUDAISM

The tension between unity and diversity in the society of Ancient Israel is manifest in the relationship between centralized monarchy and tribal structure. First emerging in the eleventh century, the monarchy reached its pinnacle of political strength under David who established Jerusalem as his capital at about 1000 BCE. After the reign of his son, Solomon, there was a split into a Northern and a Southern Kingdom. The former, with its capital in Samaria, lasted until 722 BCE when much of its leadership was led into exile by Assyria, while the latter, which came to be called Judea, survived until 586 BCE when it succumbed to Babylonian power and the Jerusalem Temple built by Solomon was destroyed. Much about the social processes paralleling these developments is still to be understood.

Some stress the encroachment of the monarchy and the urban-based aristocracy on the village-based agricultural sector of society. The Pentateuch's emphasis on protecting widows and orphans, and the cry of the prophets for social justice, is seen as reflecting growing class tensions. Another view sees rural life and its associated social structures as continuing vigorously until the Babylonian exile. This calls for a fuller understanding of mechanisms of taxation, corvee, and army service, through which kinship units supported the monarchy, while those units still maintained their own resources and institutions.

Another major issue entailing the link between various levels of society is the centralization of worship. It is clear that the Pentateuchal portrait, in which an estate of priests, descended from Moses's brother Aaron, was designated to serve at a single sanctuary is an idealized, rather than historical picture. The emergence and enforcement of the norm that sacrificial worship could take place only in Jerusalem emerged slowly, crystallizing in the seventh century. The history of the priesthood, itself, is also subject to very differing interpretations. It is similarly an open question as to what other forms of local religious organization might have arisen as the ritual hegemony of Jerusalem became established.

There was a strong linkage between the priesthood and the emerging sacred literature. At the same time, there were other sources of religious inspiration in the form of the literary prophets appearing in the eighth century. The extent to which literacy was widespread in the society is a central question, to which only tentative answers have been given. In any event, there began to develop a canon of sacred writings that had several sources that probably were in the process of being merged with one another before the Babylonian exile. Some sources may have stemmed from literary creations in David's court, others were based in the priestly culture, and yet others reflected the consciousness of exile that affected Judea even as it survived for almost a century and a half longer than its northern brother-kingdom. In the period of the Second Temple, made possible by the return of exiles to Judea in the late sixth century after the Persian Empire had displaced the Babylonians, the canonization of what we now call the Bible (the Torah) and its placement at the center of Jewish ideology and identity became even more marked. The creation of the Torah as a key symbol, and the cultivation of the value that its contents should be known to all Jews, laid the groundwork for possible diversity as well as a unified religious culture. Some speculate that the synagogue originated among the Judean exiles in Babylonia even though there is no concrete evidence of synagogue life, in Palestine or in the Diaspora, until several centuries later. Early synagogues were places in which lessons based on selections from the Torah and from the Prophetic writings were read, thereby constituting local centers for the teaching and dramatization of societal norms separate from sacrifice in the Temple. The building of the Second Temple also introduced sectarianism into Jewish life. Local Israelites from the earlier Northern Kingdom who had not gone into exile developed syncretic religious forms based on their own traditions and religious influences imported by exiles from other regions transplanted by the Assyrians into Samaria. They sought to join the returnees from Babylonia in the rebuilding of the Temple, but were rebuffed and excluded. They coalesced as a religious group called the Samaritans, with a canon made up of the Five Books of Moses and the Book of Joshua. This "sexateuch" depicted the period before Jerusalem was made the political and religious capital of the united kingdom. Samaritan scrolls of the Torah continued to be written in ancient Hebrew script, while the returnees adopted a new script influenced by their Babylonian contact. That experience also made the Aramaic language an important component of Jewish culture, as reflected in several biblical books and, later, in the Babylonian Talmud.

Further diversity was introduced by the Greek conquest of the whole area in the late fourth century, and the Hellenization of the region that continued thereafter. Within Judea, ruling Hellenic culture proved attractive to some members of the upper classes, but was simultaneously perceived as a foreign influence by many others. The attempt to forcefully Hellenize Jerusalem and the Temple stimulated the Maccabean revolt in 167 BCE leading to the brief reemergence of Judean autonomy. A century later, Judea was incorporated into the expanding Roman Empire.

Far-reaching political changes, and the exposure to many cultural crosscurrents were the background for further internal religious diversity. Josephus, writing in the first century CE, described the Sadducees, Pharisees, and the Essenes.

The first two groups are mentioned in the New Testament while the latter were probably the sect whose building remains were found near the Dead Sea and whose literature is now known from the scrolls discovered in the region. The Sadducees and Pharisees also appear in rabbinic writings. The former were linked to the priesthood, while the latter enjoyed mass support and adopted for themselves stringent ritual rules of priest-like behavior in everyday life at the same time that they claimed the authority to interpret the Torah. Within this milieu, Christianity arose and challenged the authority of the Pharisees and their stress on ritual behavior. It claimed that it was the true continuation of religious truths first revealed in the Torah. It demoted the importance of circumcision and the Torah's dietary laws, practices that became cultural markers delineating the social boundaries of the two religions.

Pharisaic Judaism fed into rabbinic Judaism represented in the authoritative code called the Mishna, compiled in its final form about 200 CE. In the first century, the Temple was destroyed and in 133 CE a major revolt against the Romans was crushed. The former event brought an end to the concrete symbolic center of Jewish life and did away with the central ruling body, the Sanhedrin. Processes that had begun before the fall of the Temple, where an "aristocracy" of Torah scholarship challenged the aristocracy of the priesthood, were given further emphasis. The synagogue developed forms of prayer worship which were interpreted as replacing, while also symbolically continuing, the sacrificial cult. Representations of Temple worship were also incorporated into domestic life, particularly with reference to food, both on a daily basis on festivals like Passover. These strengthened the groundwork enabling the further development of Judaism in diverse and separated locales.

MULTICULTURAL ASPECTS
OF DIASPORA JUDAISM

In rabbinic Judaism, the Torah and its elaborations became the practical center of Jewish life. The term *torah* came to represent not only the Pentateuch but also the other biblical books and the growing corpus of rabbinic literature. Two parallel sets of Talmudic literature evolved around the Mishna, one in Palestine (receiving final form at about 400 CE), and the other in Babylonia (final redaction in the sixth century), which became the demographic center of Jewish life. The Mishnaic code contained many laws not directly found in the Pentateuch, and one major thrust of Talmudic discussion was to demonstrate how rabbinic law ultimately depends upon the written Torah. This rhetoric concretized the notion that Jewish life, even as it adapts to new conditions, draws its authority from the sacred writings of the past. The rabbis, who were specialists in those writings, thus became a key element in emerging forms of communal organization and leadership, complementing economic and political elites.

With the establishment of Christianity in the Roman Empire (fourth century), and the spread of Islam throughout the Middle East (seventh century), Jewish life was organized under the political and ideological hegemony of these religions. Both made theoretical room for the existence of a Jewish minority (under Islam, Jews were in the same category as Christians), granting Jews internal autonomy in both religious life and many mundane spheres. The Jewish community in Babylonia emerged as the main center of rabbinic authority in the post-Talmudic era. Even as Jewish communal life coalesced and strengthened elsewhere, such as in Kairouan (in Tunisia), the Talmudic academies in Iraq and their heads—the *Geonim*—still maintained some authority as reflected in the *responsa*. Another symbolic statement of Babylonia's centrality and of Judaism's unity was the claim of the political heads there that they were scions to the royal line of David. The office of Head of the Exile depended upon appointment by the Caliph, and the extensive links between Jewish communities and the center took place on the background of the far-flung Abbasid Empire.

The waning of that empire coincided with the growing importance and religious autonomy of Jewish centers elsewhere in Cairo, North Africa, Spain, and the Rhineland. The eleventh century was a period in which some of these developments took shape. Rabbinic leaders in these areas formulated the theoretical basis of the authority of local leadership and courts, and cultivated instruments such as the ban to enforce their authority. Geographic distance, political borders, the impact of local mores, and the eminence of local authorities combined to create regional religious cultures, in particular the distinction between the Sephardi (Spanish) tradition and the Ashkenazi (emerging in the Rhineland).

The former had absorbed influence from both the Muslim environment and the Christian milieu reintroduced to Spain with the *Reconquista*, while Jews in Europe were only exposed to Christianity. One example of the difference is the creation of a permanent ban on polygamy in Ashkenaz, while the Sephardi tradition found ways of discouraging the marriage of one man to more than one woman but did not totally eliminate the practice. After the final expulsion of Jews and Moors from Spain in 1492, there were many locales in Europe in which the two traditions came in contact with one another, but they often maintained their own traditions and recognized one another as legitimate variants. Outside of Europe, Sephardi rabbinic tradition eventually became dominant in the Jewish communities of the Muslim world.

The diversity of Jewish historical experience and the continual expansion of rabbinic literature gave rise to attempts at codification. One well-known code was

that of Maimonides from twelfth century Cairo, and another was that of Joseph
Caro, an exile from Spain who moved to the Ottoman Empire in the sixteenth
century. A salient difference between them is that Maimonides included laws
relating to the ancient Jewish monarchy and Temple worship, while Caro followed
a scheme concerning the laws relevant to Jews at the present time. Sephardi
literature, including the codifications, had an impact on Ashkenazi Jewry. Caro's
famous work was the basis for the glosses of a Polish sage, Moshe Isserles, and
their printed publication in a single book in the sixteenth century has been a
major reference point for Jewish law ever since. The same period saw the growth
of Jewish population in Eastern Europe, and the challenges of autonomous Jewish
life were faced in the framework of the Council of Four Lands, involving both
religious and lay leaders, which functioned from the mid-sixteenth to the mid-
eighteenth centuries. Some Polish rabbis relating to community issues drew upon
the writings of their Spanish predecessors.

Among the former Spanish Jews migrating to other European and Middle
Eastern lands were Marranos—people who had outwardly lived as Catholics while
secretly keeping part of their Jewish traditions—who openly returned to Judaism.
In doing so, they accepted normative rabbinic Judaism, but the fact that they had
linked themselves to the Jewish community by choice, while fully familiar with
another religious way of life, may have enhanced the feeling of Jewish observance
being based on individual volition. In addition, extensive participation in commerce within Europe and around the Mediterranean in the early modern period,
engendered a sense of choice. From the seventeenth century onward, wealthy Jews
with connections to local rulers became familiar with the wider society and culture
and experienced a degree of freedom from rabbinic authority. The careers of these
"court Jews" had an impact on the expectations of the wider community. One
symptom of these trends was the weakening of the power of the communal bans.
The evolution of burial societies, ideologically fed by Kabbalistic beliefs concerning
the individual soul, may reflect the cultivation of internal motivation toward religious observance at a time when age-old communal controls were beginning to
weaken in potency.

Ideological change undermining the traditional community appeared in late
eighteenth-century Europe in the form of the haskala (Jewish enlightenment).
Jews were encouraged to be active participants in the surrounding non-Jewish
culture. A leader of the movement, Moses Mendelssohn, advocated the abolition
of the ritual ban within Jewish communal life. Jews were politically emancipated
for the first time in France in 1791 and this political process spread eastward. The
result was not a complete disestablishment of organized Jewish life, however, as
various forms of state-supported Jewish communal organization were created in
some countries. With the gradual weakening of religious observance, however,
orthodox groups in Central Europe pressed to be released from inclusion in the
general Jewish community and be allowed to organize autonomous communities

following their own norms. Their ideology, freed from concrete communal ground, could be applied to other regions wherever Jews there were so inclined. For non-orthodox Jews, the new loyalty to the states in which they were incorporated paved the way for new formulations of Judaism in which the choice of individuals played a greater role. This is the background to what became Reform and Conservative Judaism in the United States where these liberal versions of Judaism developed in a context of strict separation of religion and state.

In Eastern Europe, the demographic center of world Jewry during the nineteenth century, emancipation made slow inroads and most Jews did not develop an identification with emerging nation states. Influenced by currents in the West, however, many did seek to be free from rabbinic authority and communal control. The struggle against traditional religion yielded forms of explicitly secular Jewish identity. This left the field of religious creativity and organizational initiatives to various trends of orthodoxy. Neither the liberalizing trend nor the growth of orthodoxy had much of an impact on the Jews in Muslim countries, most of whom later migrated to Europe and Israel in the twentieth century. In that century, after religious life was suppressed by the Soviet Union and most of European Jewry was annihilated under Nazi rule, a split emerged in which the new demographic center of Jewry in North America was characterized by Jewish liberalism, while state-supported orthodoxy was established in the new and growing State of Israel. In the context of contemporary democratic regimes, different versions of Judaism have been able to develop on a voluntary basis, while the context of Israeli life has given orthodox Jews the ability to impose some norms upon Jews who are opposed to them. This is salient in the case of rituals like marriage and divorce that determine the status of children, and conversion to Judaism, both of which affect inclusion in or exclusion from the Jewish collectivity. At the same time, orthodoxy itself is now sustained by democratic culture and institutions. Orthodox Jews are free to choose to live within orthodox frameworks and to select from a range of options, all falling under the orthodox rubric. All these groups claim that their lives are shaped by the authority of the same basic collection of sacred texts, while significant differences among them are linked to their differential valuation of recent and contemporary rabbinic leaders, each of whom is seen as embodying the true expression of Torah tradition as it should be lived in present times.

BIBLIOGRAPHY

Baron, Salo. 1957–1983. *Social and Religious History of the Jews*, 2nd ed., 18 vols. New York: Columbia University Press.

Buber, Martin. 1919. *Der heilige Weg, ein Wort an die Juden und an die Völker* (The Holy Way, A Word to the Jews and the Nations). Frankfurt a Main: Rutten and Loening.

Dubnow, Simon. 1967–73. *History of the Jews*, 5 vols. Trans. from the Russian, 4th definitive rev. ed. by Moshe Spiegel. South Brunswick, N.J.: T. Yoseloff.

Durkheim, Emile. 1995 [1912]. *The Elementary Forms of Religious Life*. Translated by K. Fields. New York: Free Press.

Finkelstein, Louis. 1924. *Jewish Self-Government in the Middle Ages*. New York: Jewish Theological Seminary of America.

Frazer, James. 1890. *The Golden Bough: A Study in Comparative Religion*, 2 vols. London: Macmillan.

———. 1918. *Folklore in the Old Testament*, 3 vols. London: Macmillan.

Geiger, Abraham. 1911 [original German 1865]. *Judaism and Its History*, in two parts. New York: Bloch.

Ginsberg, Louis. 1909–38. *Legends of the Jews*, 7 vols. Philadelphia: Jewish Publication Society of America.

Goitein, S. D. 1967–1988. *A Mediterranean Society: The Jewish Communities of the Arab World as Portrayed in the Documents of the Cairo Geniza*, 5 vols. Berkeley: University of California Press.

Graetz, Henirich. 1891–98 [original German 1853–76]. *History of the Jews*, 6. vols. Philadelphia: Jewish Publication Society of America.

Katz, Jacob. 1961 [original Hebrew 1958]. *Tradition and Crisis*. New York: Free Press.

Lauterbach, Jacob Z. 1970. *Studies in Jewish Law, Custom, and Folklore*. Ed. B. J. Bamberger. New York: Ktav.

Nossig, Alfred. 1894. *Die Sozialhygiene der Juden und des altorientischen Völkerkreis*. Stuttgart: Deutsche Verlags-Anstalt.

Ruppin, Arthur. 1931. *Soziologie der Juden* (Sociology of the Jews). Berlin: Juedische Verlag.

Scholem, Gershom. 1946. *Major Trends in Jewish Mysticism*, rev. ed. New York: Schocken.

Smith, William Robertson. 1894. *Lectures on the Religion of the Semites*, rev. ed. London: A. & C. Black.

Weber, Max. 1952 [original German 1920]. *Ancient Judaism*. Translated and edited by Hans H. Gerth and Don Martindale. Glencoe, Ill.: Free Press.

Yerushalmi, Yosef H. 1982. *Zakhor, Jewish History and Jewish Memory*. Seattle: University of Washington Press.

Zunz, Leopold. 1823. "Grundlinien zu einer kunftigen Statistik der Juden." *Zeitschrift fur die Wissenschaft des Judentums* 1: 523–32.

CHAPTER 19

JEWISH COMMUNITIES
IN ISRAEL

ROGER FRIEDLAND
RICHARD D. HECHT

THE formation of the state of Israel in 1948 represents not only a historic achievement but also an extraordinary experiment in the nationalization of a global
religion. It is remarkable in part because every strand of Judaism was suddenly
condensed into one tiny country—just as many of the world's religious communities were compressed into ancient Babylon or modern Los Angeles. Curiously, Israel contained the very seeds of exilic existence that its founders sought
to overcome in the new national existence.

But it is also striking since the creation of a Jewish Israeli state represents the
re-nationalization of a global religion. With the Roman destruction of the Temple
in 70 CE, Judaism progressively became a religion more like early Christianity,
severed as it was from a sovereign and a ritual center, deprived not only of its
original territorial ambit but also its capacity to provide the legal and ethical
compass for a sovereign state. The creation of the modern state of Israel appeared
to be a reversal of that trend.

For two thousand years, Judaism evolved into a transportable, de-
territorialized, ethical, and ritual system, one that could be practiced anywhere.
Under both Christian and Muslim rule, this de-territorialization took the form
of a tolerated and eminently movable *ethnos*, a people with a history but without
political claim. The category of Jew was a politically empty category. To give Jews

a political identity would, in fact, contradict the claims of Christianity and Islam to supersede Judaism.

When Theodor Herzl, the "founder" of political Zionism, met Pope Pius X in 1903, he sought the latter's support for Zionist territorial claims in Palestine. The pope was adamant that Jerusalem not fall into Jewish hands. Herzl proposed that Jerusalem be given extraterritorial status, *res sacrae extra commercium*, to which the pope replied, "I know, it is not pleasant to see the Turks in possession of our Holy Places. We simply have to put up with that. But to support the Jews in the acquisition of the Holy Places, that we cannot do."

Herzl insisted that he wanted to avoid any religious issues. The pope, however, declared: "Yes, but we, and I as the head of the Church, cannot do this. There are two possibilities. Either the Jews will cling to their faith and continue to await the Messiah who, for us, has already appeared. In that case they will be denying the divinity of Jesus and we cannot help them. Or else they will go without any religion, and then we can be even less favorable to them . . ." (Vital 1982: 339). The pope could not countenance the Jews' restoration as a collective political actor, particularly in the Holy Land. For Islamists, the threat of collective Jewish organization over the site to which the Prophet made his miraculous "night journey" was no less threatening. Accorded the status of a *dhimmi* under Islamic regimes or a *millet* under the Ottoman empire, this was a category of control, making Judaism a de-territorialized ethnic identity.

From the Second Commonwealth of the ancient Jews in the mid-fifth century BCE to the Roman destruction of Jerusalem in 70 CE, the Jews had a polity, for some periods more limited than others. Then for the next 1,878 years Judaism was disconnected from sovereign power and from a territorial identity. The rise of the nation-state created "religion" as we know it today, by extending the logic of the de-territorialization and de-politicization of Judaism to all religions, so that religion became a faith interior to the soul and whose competence was primarily the ritual organization of birth, marriage, and death. The nation-state imposed a kind of "internal secularization."

THE HAREDIM

The early Zionist leaders were quite uncomfortable with the term *Zion*, a biblical name for Jerusalem, precisely because it was so religiously meaningful. Moreover, they disliked it because the area was filled with a pre-Zionist population of Jews who likewise were waiting for the ingathering of the exiles and the restoration of Jewish sovereignty in Israel, but who believed that only the Davidic Messiah could achieve such a fantastic outcome. This community, a kind of "missing link" of contemporary Zionism, would quickly become "the old *yishuv*," the old Jewish community of Palestine. Most of the religious Jews who got to Zion before the Zionists saw a secular, democratic nation-state for Jews as anathema. Their intent in returning to Zion was to counter the secularization of Europe and the modernization of Judaism as a de-territorialized religion (Ravitzky 1996: 145–80).

Today, the Jews of the "old yishuv" are known as the *haredim*. Their self-definition is those who are fearful of divine punishment for collective Jewish disobedience. Indeed the most brazen form of disobedience is to deny God's sovereignty, and hence to ground Jewish sovereignty in anything other than Torah—which is precisely how they understand secular Zionism (Soloveitchik 1994: 223–24)

The haredi community is multiply divided within. The most explosive cleavage is between *hasidim* and *mitnagdim*, which first emerged among Eastern European Jewry in the eighteenth century between those who intensified the immanence of God in daily life and those who restricted the divine to a transcendent realm accessed by the study and recitation of the divine word. The Hasidic movement grew during the late eighteenth and early nineteenth centuries, when Jewish communal authority was being eroded by central rulers who wanted direct control over their citizens, unmediated by ethnic, communal, and ecclesiastic authorities. For millions of Jews in Eastern Europe, this meant forced assimilation, as they came under pressure to stop speaking Yiddish and using it as the primary language of cultural production. They were forbidden to wear traditional clothing and forced to cut their ritual sidelocks (many hid them behind their ears or up in their hats), and brides were prevented from shaving their heads at marriage.

Hasidism represented one of the many "great awakenings" of Jewish life in the modern world. Drawing its original following from the poor and uneducated, it spread rapidly and eventually drew to its ranks even scholars skilled in Talmud. Eventually half of the Jews of Poland and Russia were swept into the movement. The Hasidim—*hasid* means pious, *hasidim*, the pious ones—elevated prayer over study, piety over scholarship, Yiddish over Hebrew, Kabbalah and the writings of their own spiritual leaders over Talmud. A Hasid prepared carefully for prayer, purifying his mind, emptying his bowels to prevent "vapors" that would contaminate his thoughts, girding his loins with a special girdle to divide his heart from his genitals. Swaying, gesticulating, shouting, and singing were ways for the hasid to achieve higher levels of concentration, to escape the body's constraints, so that his soul could soar to God.

In Hasidism the guiding hope for a single messiah was taken over by the many *tzaddikim*, or "righteous ones," the religious leaders of the movement, who were understood to act as intercessors with God, channels by which His blessings could reach their flock. The Hasidim used the Yiddish term *rebbe* to distinguish their spiritual leaders from the rabbis. Wherever the *tzaddik* was located thus became a center of the cosmos. These men, it is still believed, have special powers to bless and to curse, to heal and strike down, to read the mind, to make barren or undo infertility, indeed to travel to the divine realm and intervene in the trajectory of the cosmos.

Jews went to the rebbe to be cured of diseases, to learn about their future, to seek repentance for past sins, to guarantee the success of their business ventures, and to be granted children. Hasids developed elaborate theories about the tzaddik's powers. The tzaddik was no mere seer, but could anticipate and reverse decrees with which Gentile rulers were oppressing the Jews. A powerful rebbe might even alter divine will. The hasidim consider their rebbe as the pathway by which their prayers might better reach God. Naturally, they seek the rebbe's company and presence. He listens to their problems, instructs them in the mysteries of the universe, and advises them on the conduct of their most private lives. In exchange for the tzaddik's intercession, his followers accord him their absolute faith and provide for his worldly needs.

Today the Hasidim of Jerusalem are divided into the followers of different rebbes, each with his own court, some centered in Jerusalem and many not. Although most individuals are born into their Hasidic group, only one thing is absolutely required for membership: a willingness to submit to the rebbe's authority. Dissenting voices are not tolerated and those who disagree with the rebbe must leave.

Competition between different Hasidic courts can be ferocious. The Belz and Gerrer are Jerusalem's two largest Hasidic groups. Members of each can instantly recognize the other on the street, for each group's mark is inscribed upon its members' clothing, the movement of their eyes, even their gait. By the style of their hat, whether or not their eyes wander on the street, whether they let themselves pause for conversation on the corner, whether they are willing to stand next to a strange woman on the street all allow easy perception of their respective position in cultural space. The Torah, for example, obliges observant Jewish men to let their *payot*, or sidelocks, grow long. The Gerrer Hasidim leave their payot uncurled; the Belz curl their payot behind their ears.

The right to rule a Hasidic community derives from the spiritual gifts with which one has been blessed, from claims about one's being. In many communities, the Hasidic courts are hereditary dynasties, in which the claim to lead is passed from father to son. Even so when a rebbe dies or becomes too infirm, succession can be a dangerous affair to settle (Friedman 1994: 334–45).

Hasidism transformed the messianic hope of liberating the real Jerusalem into an effort to liberate the invisible city inside the Hasid's soul. It sought redemption not from exile, but in exile. It is perhaps for this reason that the Hasidim have been more hostile to Zionism than have other haredi groups who must come to terms with Zionism's material accomplishments.

Today no single rabbi or rebbe dare speaks for all *mitnagid* or Hasidic Jews.

The haredi community is fragmented among followers of rival rebbes and rabbis, whose animosities are based on differences over Zionism, personal rivalries, competition for money and living space, and doctrinal differences, large and small. Although the haredim all share an antipathy to the secular Jewish world, the tensions between their separate communities are ferocious.

Each haredi community, whether Hasid or mitnagid, is self-contained, providing its members with all their necessities, jealously guarding the resources it raises that enable it to insulate its members from the outside world. Each has its own newspaper; schools; cooperative, called a *kollel*, through which funds for housing and material support are allocated; its own residential neighborhoods; and sometimes even its own taxi or bus service. Within each, housing, jobs, places in the yeshivah, military deferments, and services of every kind are distributed at the personal discretion of the leader.

There is no overarching structure of governance to which all haredim will adhere. Certainly no haredi group fully recognizes the authority of the Israeli state. The haredim do not generally call the police when trouble arises, and they try not to use the Israeli civil courts to litigate their differences. Indeed, although the Israeli security forces have easily infiltrated the Palestinian communities, they have found it difficult to penetrate those of the haredim. Informants are rare and simulating the haredi lifestyle is difficult. As a result, the haredim host a significant number of smugglers and tax evaders. Some haredi communities have also operated largely unregulated banking operations in Jerusalem used by the PLO to launder money for their activists inside.

In this system of competing party machines, each dishing out jobs, favors and services to its constituents, power has a personal basis. Cliques develop quickly and the stakes are too high to allow much representation in the parties that claim their allegiance to reach for power by forming their own.

Once anti-Zionist, most haredi communities now depend on the Jewish state for survival, while at the same denying its theological legitimacy, the Zionist's appropriation of the biblical redemptive narrative.

SHAS

In the first years of the new state, a tidal wave of Jews from North Africa and the near East broke on Israel's shores. Between 1949 and 1951, more than a quarter million Jews from Morocco, Iran, Iraq, Yemen, Syria, Egypt, and Turkey immigrated (Dowty 1998: 143–58). These were overwhelmingly religious Jews. These *edot ha-mizrach,* the olive-skinned "peoples of the east," were bitter that their own distinctive rituals and liturgies were not respected, their songs not sung, their culture demeaned, and their institutions given short shrift in the allocation of resources. The Ashkenazi haredim regarded them as social inferiors. Intermarriage is a sensitive index. Whereas secular Ashkenazi increasingly married Jews of Moroccan or Iraqi origin, among the haredim family alliances with Jews from the Arab world were almost unheard of.

The Oriental Jews concluded that their form of Judaism, not to mention their ethnic dignity, depended on power. In Israel's municipal elections in 1983, for the first time, they formed their own party, the Sephardi Torah Guardians, or SHAS, as it is known by its acronym. Although the Oriental Jews call themselves Sephardim, the "true" Sephardim originating in Spain and Portugal do not regard them as such. These latter refer to themselves as the *samekh tet,* the Hebrew letters for *sephardi tehorah,* meaning pure Sephardi, to distinguish themselves from Oriental Jews who arrived in Palestine centuries later. If the classical Sephardim once disdained the Ashkenazi newcomers as uncouth and ill bred, both groups looked down upon the largely lower-class Jews from North Africa and the Middle East who poured into Palestine in the early 1950s, those of Morocco being the largest and most problematic group.

There had always been traffic between the Jews of Spain and North Africa, but they had never been a single people. When Spain and then Portugal exiled their entire Jewish communities in 1492 and 1495, Jews fled in waves across the channel to the Maghreb—west in Arabic, referring to the region to the "west" of Egypt. A great many exiles settled in Fez and Casablanca in Morocco, where they met Jews who were, by their standards, uncultured and desperately poor, some of whom had intermarried with members of Berber tribes. The highly cultured exiles looked with disdain upon most of the indigenous Jews, whom they called Berberiscos. The skilled Jewish administrators and merchants from Spain and Portugal quickly dominated the community, many becoming brokers between the sultans in the Muslim interior and the Portuguese who held tenaciously to their outposts along the coast.

Before 1948, Zionists had tried to persuade the Moroccan Jews to come to Palestine, but without success. The Zionists were seen as white moderns, socialists without faith, speaking about the incredible, while Jewish life in Morocco seemed to be improving steadily. By the end of the 1950s, however, almost a million Jews immigrated to Israel from Islamic lands. These Jews were both pushed by pogroms that swept through the Arab world in the wake of the 1948 war and pulled by the prospect of living in an actually existing Jewish state. Some walked hundreds of miles across the deserts; others were airlifted in emergency convoys, like the Yemenite Jews, whose very existence was at stake. In the aftermath of the 1948 war, more Jews were forcibly exiled by Arab terror and the threat of it than Arabs who had been pushed out of their lands by the conquering Israelis. Many did not come voluntarily. They simply had no place else to go. The chairman of the

Zionist executive committee said in 1949, "even Jews who don't wish to leave [their homes] must be forced to come..." (quoted in Segev 1986: 110).

Faced with a wave of immigration that would test any nation's capacities, especially an impoverished, infant state that had just won a war to secure its survival against tremendous odds, the Ashkenazi Zionist elite did not have the time or temperament to assimilate these Jews in a delicate fashion. In 1949 *Ha-Aretz* published a description of the Oriental Jews who were then being assimilated into Israel, which was destined to become one of the most controversial commentaries ever published in the nation. Its author wrote "This is a race unlike any we have seen before.... The primitiveness of these people is unsurpassable. They have almost no education at all, and what is worse is their inability to comprehend anything intellectual. As a rule, they are only slightly more advanced then the Arabs, Negroes and Berbers in their countries. It is certainly an even lower level than that of the former Palestinian Arabs.... In the [North] African corners of the camps you find filth, gambling, drunkenness and prostitution. Many of them suffer from serious eye diseases, as well as skin and venereal diseases.... The [North] Africans bring their ways with them wherever they settle. It is not surprising that the crime rate in the country is rising. In certain parts of Jerusalem it is no longer safe for a young girl or even a young man, to go out after dark.... They all say that in [North] Africa they were 'merchants.' What they really mean is they were peddlers. And they all want to settle in the city. What can be done with them? How are they to be absorbed?... Have we given sufficient thought to the question of what will happen to this state if this should be its population?—And then, in addition, [other] Oriental Jews will eventually join them, too! What will happen to the State of Israel and its standards with this type of population?" (quoted in Segev 1986: 159–61). It did not help matters that many of the more prosperous, educated North African Jewish families, those who might have better brokered their people's entry into this new land, chose not to go to Israel, but left for Paris or New York.

The Israelis considered it their job to make the new immigrants into Israelis as fast as possible and to use them to bolster the state's vulnerable defenses. Men's beards and boys' earlocks were unceremoniously sheared as they passed through the transit camps. The Labour Zionists saw no great need to co-opt the Oriental Jewish leaders; and the old Sephardi elite did not want to be identified with these tattered masses landing on Israel's shore. North African Jews were not integrated into the kibbutzim but used as unskilled labor to settle peripheral areas (Smooha 1978: 151–82). Many a skilled artisan was forced to do unskilled manual labor in order to survive. Fathers held their shame, while their sons grew up with their rage.

The religiosity of the North African Jews was and still is an embarrassment to many observant Ashkenazim. Ashkenazi tradition reveres the prophets; it does not worship them. The Moroccan Jews, in contrast, believe in and worship saints.

They obey their rabbi not simply because he understands the law but, not unlike the Hasidic rebbe, because he is an intercessor to God with powers to cure and heal. The rabbis of the edot ha-mizrach are a communion of powerful saints who may be enlisted as allies and agents in the struggle for financial success and political power.

The Sephardi Jews who immigrated to Israel right after statehood were absorbed by organizations on the Left and the Right, religious and secular, largely controlled by Ashkenazim. The Sephardim were unable to reach beyond the lowest levels of the political hierarchy. And so it was the highly observant among them who became loyal clients in the non-Zionist haredi political party, Agudat Yisrael's religious machine.

But beginning in the early 1970s, young North African Jews in Jerusalem—often unemployed, living in dilapidated state housing projects—launched a series of social movements that challenged, sometimes violently, their miserable condition. What galled them in particular was the juxtaposition of the state's apparent indifference to them to the loans and superior housing lavished on new immigrants from Russia, Poland, and Romania. Ethnic hostility against the Ashkenazim of the ruling Labour Party steadily mounted.

By the early 1980s, the most devout Sephardi Jews who had been part of Agudat Yisrael had had enough. Among North African Jews the rabbis were always real, as well as ritual, leaders. In 1983, with the blessing of the Sephardic chief rabbi, Ovadiah Yosef, and the renegade mitnagid rabbi, Eliezer Shach (who, when asked what was the closest religion to Judaism, replied, Chabad, referring to the Hasidic followers of Rabbi Menachem Mendel Schneerson), the North African Jews broke away to form the Sephardic Torah Guardians, or SHAS.

SHAS went on to become the largest religious party in the Knesset, making and breaking national coalitions, becoming part of the dominant bloc of the Israeli state. Its leaders routinely inject religious invective into political discourse. For example, speaking against the secular Supreme Court justices in 1999, Ovadia Yosef called them *ba'ale-niddot*, meaning those who have sexual intercourse with ritually unclean women, specifically women who are menstruating. And secular women, he went on, who do not pay attention to the rules of family purity give birth to "sons born of uncleanness," who would grow up to become murderers and thieves. To the Orthodox East European Jewish communities, the rising political power of SHAS portends the eventual hegemony of Sephardic forms of Judaism in Israel, which, Benjamin Lau, a kibbutz rabbi, warns, would transform the state into "occupied territory," the imposition of an alien religious law (Bar-Moha 2000: Internet version).

JEWISH RELIGIOUS NATIONALISTS

The secular Labour Zionists settled the coasts and the lowland valleys, not the highlands that had been the core of ancient Israel. That territory had been ceded by the United Nations to the Palestinians for them to establish their own independent state at the time of Partition in 1947. The Palestinians had refused and in 1948 the Jordanians had taken and absorbed the territories allocated to them. In 1967, those lands were "liberated" by the Israeli army, which pushed all the way to the River Jordan. The biblical heartland was now in Israeli hands.

The Gush Emunim, or "Bloc of the Faithful," fused religion and nationalism, Judaism and Zionism, unlike the two forms of separation found in the secular Zionist community on the one side and the haredi community on the other. Dedicated to populating the land of Israel, from 1968 onward the Gush Emunim moved outward from Jerusalem, Haifa, and Tel Aviv from 1968. The success of this settlement movement lay in its ability to recast religiously Israel's foundational myths. Gush Emunim claimed to reincarnate the heroes of Israeli history, the *halutzim,* the pioneers, and to create the vital, expansive successors to the kibbutz settlements they founded (Sternhill 1998: 74–131). For decades the religious Zionists, who had a kibbutz movement of their own, had been looked down on by the Labour Zionists as not measuring up to the ideal of the new Israeli, somehow tainted by their continued attachment to Torah their holding on to traditions of exile. As the religious nationalist movement grew and held tenaciously to one place after another, the settlers' claim that they were the true embodiment of the Zionist settlement did not go unheeded.

It was not just right-wing Revisionists who fell under the spell of the religious nationalists. There were Labour Zionists, too, who were drawn to their mission. The Gush Emunim and the largely Labour Zionist kibbutzim diverge dramatically in their cosmology. The differences have consequences for the pattern, form, and strategy of settlement. These differences help explain why Gush Emunim was so effective in moving from a marginal social movement of a few hundred people to an institutionalized structure that has vast resources at its control, access to the highest centers of power, and an ability to wreck any peace negotiations between Israel and the Palestinians (Sprinzak 1991: 107–66).

The Gush Emunim and the settlement movement it generated have often used biblical geography to choose settlement sites. The identification and building of the sacrality of each site has been a key ideological weapon by which they have gained access and legitimated their presence. Gush Emumim's first surprise strike into occupied territory was typically to a spot to which mythical and ritual connections could be made and worship organized. When the military pushed them out, the compromise was that a yeshivah be established and the original community be allowed to remain, albeit often at another proximate site, usually a military zone. Given that these interventions were often associated with violent Palestinian response, it was easy to create a permanent settlement.

Many of these sites did not make any strategic sense. The first Jewish settlement in the heart of Hebron, for example, is, of course, in the city where Abraham purchased the burial sites for his family. However their community is surrounded by tens of thousands of hostile Muslims who could easily overrun these few Jewish homes and apartments in the event of war. It was, in fact, their military vulnerability that motivated the government's opposition. Although Hebron's Jewish residents are heavily armed, they have not been able to defend their members from repeated violent attacks. Large numbers of Israeli soldiers have had to be brought in to protect them. Gush Emunim's failure to consider the strategic value of its settlements was evident in its first major penetration into Samaria, the whole region to the north of Jerusalem. In 1973, led by two yeshivah students from Kiryat Arba, a group began a long bitter struggle to settle Elon Moreh, near Nablus, the largest Palestinian city, where Abraham had built an altar to the Lord after he had promised the land of Canaan to Abraham's offspring.

Many of the settlements founded by Gush Emunim are not militarily defensible. Their male residents, who work elsewhere, are absent most of the day. Most are quite small, a dozen or so families, and must recruit reserve soldiers from outside to protect them. By the late 1980s, the security implications of diffused Jewish settlement throughout the West Bank and Gaza became clear. Violent Palestinian attacks on Israeli settlers and soldiers became increasingly frequent well before the first intifada exploded in 1987. As a result, elite troops, demobilized from the war in Lebanon, had to be deployed to protect the Jewish settlers. During the first intifada, some argued that the settlers' indiscriminate responses contributed to, rather than controlled, Palestinian violence. This was also a period of sustained Israeli mobilization made necessary by the growing Syrian and Iraqi military threats. As a result of these internal and external challenges, Israeli forces were stretched thin and Israelis were called upon to serve longer and longer stretches of reserve duty.

During the second intifada, which began in 2000 with Sharon's visit to the Temple Mount, the settlement movement's second generation of activists have continued the expansion of settlements, creating smaller "outposts" which look more like the settlements of the movement's first years. Under both Benjamin Netanyahu and Ehud Barak, the settlers continued to build new housing units in existing settlements, swelling the total number of Israelis living in the West Bank to more than 150,000. Huge numbers of troops are now required to protect the settlers' enclaves, their lives and their property. Billions of dollars have been spent to build bypass roads so that the settlers do not have to pass too closely to Palestinian population centers. But, the building of roads and infrastructure of the settlements also makes a contiguous space for a Palestinian state all but impossible.

The settlers are completing the re-territorialization of Judaism. What they are doing is completely consistent with the original political understanding of Judaism. Indeed, when they claim that the only legitimate reason to create a Jewish state in this land is found in God's revelation, and that to displace an existent population would otherwise be immoral, there is a certain logic to their position.

Although the settlers are themselves highly observant Jews, their theological differences with the haredim enabled them to co-opt and cooperate with secular nationalists who love the land just as much as they do. For Orthodox Jews, the commandments are all equally binding. Not so for these religious Zionist pioneers: For them, commandments related to settlement and possession of the land are supreme. By elevating these commandments above all others, they can both build a bridge to Israel's secular pioneering tradition and avoid confrontation with Israel's secular majority, who are unwilling to abide governmental enforcement of religious law but can be persuaded to support Jewish settlement. The settlers need not demand that those secular Israelis who wish to join them adhere to the Torah's other dictates. Thus, the majority of the largest original settlement, Ma'ale Adumim, just a few miles east of downtown Jerusalem, and which became the first municipality in the West Bank in the early 1990s when its population swelled beyond twenty-five thousand, is heavily secular.

Because possession of the land, in itself, is the highest value, the settlements are not established with an eye to self-sufficiency. Often, they are not engaged in any form of collective or cooperative production. Sometimes they engage in no production at all. Unlike the kibbutzim, which provided work for Jews, these Jewish outposts originally provided work for Arabs, who actually built the first generation of Jewish houses and roads. During the first intifada, the Palestinians' Unified National Leadership was able to slow the number of Palestinians building the settlements. However, the promise of the Oslo Process opened the gates for increased Palestinian employment. However, during the second intifada Palestinians who worked for the settlers were threatened with immediate execution, often in the most brutal ways. The labor supply dried up.

Unlike early Zionist settlements, which were predominantly rural, Jewish settlements in the West Bank are primarily bedroom communities for workers who commute to Jerusalem, Haifa, and Tel Aviv. Gush Emunim and settlement movement activists believe that one builds the sacred through the medium of the profane, that settling the land itself makes a Jew holy and extends the state's sacrality. This vision has enabled the movement to exploit the natural logic of suburbanization, not cynically, but as a practical messianic tactic perfectly consistent with their worldview (Aran 1991; Ravitzky 1996: 79–44).

As of 2004 approximately 190,000 Jews lived in the West Bank and Gaza, exclusive of Jerusalem, drawn by a mixture of messianic, materialist, and nationalist motives. The evidence indicates that Jews attracted to affordable suburban homes quickly moved toward the religious and right-wing territorial maximalist parties after taking up residence in the settlements. For a social movement to succeed, it must make extraordinary behavior ordinary. Success requires just such a weld of ideals and interests.

MAKING RELIGION POLITICAL AND THE POLITICAL RELIGIOUS

The creation of a Jewish state brought the world's Judaisms into one small territory, compressing divergent histories into one place, a kind of spiritual metropolis. If territorial separation was still possible, sharing sovereignty has not been so easy. This new apparatus of collective representation was up for grabs. Its formation forced the renegotiation of the relation between sovereignty, territoriality, and Judaism.

The irony is that the Jewish state was founded by men and women who were not religiously Jewish; they were secular, eastern and central Europeans, who understood themselves as a people, a state-less nation, not as a religious community. Indeed, given the shadow of the Holocaust in which Jewish sovereignty was secured, they naturally repudiated any racialization of the nation's new identity. They sought to harness Judaism to the national project. But their Judaism was not a religious system. For them Judaism was a mythic narrative, a redemptive historiography, leading back to this primordial place.

The secular nationalist establishment of this Jewish state not only created a symbolic space in which religious forces would be able to legitimately wrestle for a more explicitly religious definition of the polity, but it became the vehicle through which diverse forms of Judaism sought to legitimate themselves, to reach for resources and to adjudicate their relationship to each other. Not only did the Judaisms outside of Israel become increasingly joined to the Zionist project, but Israel itself became the religious center, the primary polity in which religious conflicts between the world's Judaisms are fought out. For example, one potent argument that has continued to be voiced among Reform Jews in the United States is that their form of Judaism will only survive in the long run to the degree that they are able to at least obtain a religious foothold in Israel, if not to secure ritual legitimacy, which is now denied them.

The exilic, nonterritorial global Judaism has also had a significant impact on the nature of Zionism. The legitimacy of the state using anything other than defensive armed force came relatively late in Israeli history, with Menachem Begin's doctrine of "war of choice" in Lebanon. Historian Anita Shapira argues:

"Zionist reticence toward armed conflict did not derive solely from the common wisdom that war was evil and should be avoided if possible. Its motivating causes ran deeper. For nearly two thousand years Jews had been a noncombative people. From the time of the Christianization of Rome, and especially after the rise of the feudal social order in Europe and the spread of Islam, Jews in the Mediterranean had been confined to the noncombatant classes. Even when other town dwellers began to carry weapons, Jews continued to be excluded from bearing arms. They accepted their weakness and dependence on others for protection as God's will, not to be challenged or questioned" (1992: vii).

This exilic Judaism, which understood itself in the context of utopian redemption through justice, was harnessed to Zionism, the Jews' own romantic nationalism. Unlike the German, who would ultimately seek the Jews' annihilation, the redemptive qualities of Jewish nationalism produced in the early Zionist theorists and activists a powerful self-understanding, in which they saw themselves as just conquerors whose own identity required them to share the land. A Judaism without a territorial state provided and still provide cultural materials critical for the Jewish state's sharing of the land with the Palestinian Arabs.

BIBLIOGRAPHY

Aran, Gideon. 1991. "Religious Zionist Fundamentalism: The Bloc of the Faithful in Israel." In *Fundamentalisms Observed*. Eds. Martin E. Marty and R. Scott Appleby, 265–344. Chicago: University of Chicago Press.

Bar-Moha, Yossi. 2000. "If You Wrong Us, Shall We Not Avenge?" *Ha-Aretz*, 11 February. Internet version.

Beyer, Peter. 1994. *Religion and Globalization*. Thousand Oaks, Calif.: Sage Publications.

Davis, Mike. 1998. *Ecology of Fear: Los Angeles and the Imagination of Disaster*. New York: Metropolitan Books.

Dowty, Alan. 1998. *The Jewish State: A Century Later*. Berkeley: University of California Press.

Friedman, Menachem. 1994. "Habad as Messianic Fundamentalism: From Local Particularism to Universal Jewish Mission." In *Accounting for Fundamentalisms: The Dynamic Character of Movements*. Eds. Martin E. Marty and R. Scott Appleby, 328–357. Chicago: University of Chicago Press.

Ravitzky, Aviezer. 1996. *Messianism, Zionism, and Jewish Religious Radicalism*. Chicago: University of Chicago Press.

Segev, Tom. 1986. *1949: The First Israelis*. New York: Free Press.

Shapira, Anita. 1992. *Land and Power: The Zionist Resort to Force 1881–1948*. New York: Oxford University Press.

Smooha, Sammy. 1978. *Israel: Pluralism and Conflict*. London: Routledge and Kegan Paul.

Soja, Edward W. 2000. *Postmetropolis: Critical Studies of Cities and Regions*. Oxford: Blackwell Publishers.

Soloveitchik, Haym. 1994. "Migration, Acculturation, and the New Role of Texts in the Haredi World." In *Accounting for Fundamentalisms: The Dynamic Character of Movements*. Eds. Martin E. Marty and R. Scott Appleby, 197–235. Chicago: University of Chicago Press.

Sprinzak, Ehud. 1991. *The Ascendance of Israel's Radical Right*. New York: Oxford University Press.

Sternhill, Zeev. 1998. *The Founding Myths of Israel: Nationalism, Socialism, and the Making of the Jewish State*. Princeton, N.J.: Princeton University Press.

Vital, David. 1982. *Zionism: The Formative Years*. Oxford: Oxford University Press.

CHAPTER 20

JEWISH COMMUNITIES IN NORTH AFRICA AND THE MIDDLE EAST

REUBEN AHRONI

THE Jewish world is generally lumped into two broad categories, *Ashkenazim* and *Sefaradim*, despite the marked differences that exist among the diverse Jewish communities around the world in terms of traditions, culture, language, customs, synagogue service, pronunciation of Hebrew, and the like. Although "Ashkenaz" is the Hebrew word for Germany, its connotation has been broadened to denote all Jews of European descent possessing a particular Jewish cultural complex including a Germanic dialect known as Yiddish. In contrast to "Ashkenaz," "Sefarad" is the Hebrew word for Spain. The adjective "Sefaradi" originally refers to the descendants of the Jews who were expelled in 1492 from the Iberian Peninsula. Their particular cultural complex includes Spanish cultural traits, songs, and the Judeo-Spanish dialect known as Ladino or Judezmo. The Sefaradi Jews were concentrated mainly in Italy, Turkey, Greece, and North Africa. Erroneously, all the Jews of the East, including Iraq, Yemen, and Iran, are often lumped under the term "Sefaradim." To avoid such a misnomer, the authorities in Israel refer to them by the term ʿ*edot ha-Mizraḥ* (the communities of the East).

Before the establishment of Israel, Jewish communities were to be found in almost all the Middle Eastern and North African countries. With the establishment of Israel in 1948, Jews emigrated from the Arab and Muslim countries in continuous waves, mainly to Israel. In this chapter I will provide an overview of the

Jewish Middle Eastern and African communities, focusing primarily on the Jews of Yemen and Ethiopia.

THE HISTORY OF MIDDLE EAST AND NORTH AFRICAN JEWISH COMMUNITIES

It should be noted that, except for the Jews of Iraq (ancient Babylonia), the origins of the Jewish communities of the Middle East and North Africa are clouded with obscurity. The lack of knowledge of the ancient history of these Jewish communities is to a large extent a function of the obscurity that characterizes the ancient history of the region itself. As is well recognized, our knowledge of the events that transpired in this region, particularly Arabia, as early as a few centuries before the rise of Islam is derived chiefly from epigraphic material, scanty historical notes, and embellished traditions. While credible records relating to the origins and antiquity of most of the Middle Eastern Jewish communities are sparse, each of them possesses a plethora of traditions which trace its origins back to biblical times, namely to the tribes of Israel who were exiled during the destruction of the First Temple (597 BCE) and the Second Temple (70 BCE), if not earlier.

Several modern scholars, however, suggest that a considerable number, if not the majority, of the Jews of the region are descendants of indigenous people who converted to Judaism before the advent of Islam. They point to the well-attested historical phenomenon of extensive Judaization among the inhabitants of southern Arabia in pre-Islamic times. Much has been written, for example, about the Judaized kingdom of Himyar, the last of the independent kingdoms that flourished in southern Arabia prior to the advent of the Prophet Muhammad, and particularly about Dhu Nuwas, the last of the kings of Himyar (ruled ca. 517–523 CE). The mass Judaization of Himyar has led some scholars to claim that the majority of the Jews of southern Arabia are not to be traced back to the tribes of Israel, as the Jews of Yemen claim, but are rather descendants of indigenous Arabs who had embraced the Jewish faith. Indeed, sociologists have long been puzzled by the distinctive features of the Yemeni Jews who, on the one hand, are similar to those of the tribesmen of Yemen and, on the other hand, defy classification within the parameters of the existing Jewish groups. Moreover, genetic studies conducted in Israel bolster the view that links the majority of the Yemeni Jews to indigenous Arabs. Nevertheless, Yemeni Jewish scholars and rabbis dismiss the story of the mass conversion of the Himyarites as totally fictitious, or at most, shallow and short-lived. All that the Himyarites received from the Jews, said the late Yemeni scholar, Rabbi Yosef Kafih, was the faith in one God, the God of heaven and earth. The Himyarites, he added, did not study the Torah nor maintain the Jewish precepts.

Our knowledge is rather scanty regarding the profundity of the Himyarites' conversion to Judaism with regard to their commitment to Jewish laws and customs. Although the historical episode relating to the conversion of Yusuf Ash ʿDhu Nuwas is the most well-known in the history of pre-Islamic Arabia, we know very little about the motivation for the Judaization of both this monarch and the multitudes of his people. Indeed, the life, family lineage, and the circumstances of the death of ʿDhu Nuwas are all cloaked in legend. Nevertheless, although the cumulative evidence thus far available does not conclusively support the view that the majority of the Jews of Yemen, or of any of the other Middle Eastern or North African countries, are of indigenous Arab extraction, the evidence which points to such a possibility is not to be ignored. The nascent genetic research of the Jews of the Arab lands is highly intriguing and should be vigorously pursued.

But what triggered the massive emigration of the Jews of the Arab world to Israel after they had for many centuries lived in the region? As indicated above, the Jews of the Arab world, like their brethren elsewhere, strongly believe that they are the descendents of the tribes of Israel and in the idea of the historic and spiritual connection between the Jewish people and its ancient homeland. They viewed their residence in exile as merely temporal. The idea of the restoration, as repeatedly stressed in the Bible and expressed in ritual and prayer, was for them a matter of dogmatic belief. While their body was in Exile, their heart was in the holy land. Thus, the establishment of the State of Israel was seen as fulfillment of the long-awaited divine promise and they responded with alacrity to the newly formed Israel's call for emigration.

Concomitant with the role that these primeval spiritual forces played in prompting this Jewish mass exodus was the ardent desire of the Jews to rid themselves of the inferior social status to which they were generally subjected and to be able, like all other nations, to seize the reign of their own destiny. The strong yearning for the return to the ancestral homeland which in Europe gave rise to the Zionist movement at the end of the nineteenth century was no less potent among the Jews of the Arab world.

Within Islamic societies Jews were regarded as second-class citizens. It is a matter of history that Islam imposed upon non-Muslims, Jews and Christians alike, certain restrictions aimed at demonstrating the superiority of Islam and perpetuating by legal means the alleged inferiority of nonbelievers. The general tenor of the various discriminatory laws and ordinances promulgated by Muslim states against non-Muslims was thought to be in accordance with various Qur'anic homilies and utterances which enjoin the Muslims to humble the nonbelievers and turn them into lowly tribute bearers. Thus, the *jizya* (poll tax) was imposed upon nonbelievers (see, for example, Qur'an 9:29).

The notorious pact ascribed to ʿUmar specifies the conditions by which non-Muslim minorities living under Muslim rule would be granted protection and religious freedom. In this pact the *dhimmis* (protected non-Muslims) obligated themselves, among other things, to refrain from building new houses of worship (churches and synagogues), holding public religious ceremonies, converting anyone to their religion, displaying signs or symbols of their religion in Muslim thoroughfares or marketplaces, raising their voices when reciting the service in their temples, building homes higher than those of Muslims, and wielding authority over Muslims. The Pact of ʿUmar also prohibits non-Muslims from any attempt to resemble the Muslims in their dress and their manner of appearance. These prohibitions laid the basis for the various distinctive signs (*ghiyar*) imposed upon non-Muslims for the purpose of humiliating the nonbelievers and to draw a sharp distinction between them and the Muslims.

It should be noted, however, that the degree of enforcement of these restrictive regulations in the vast and rapidly growing Muslim empire varied widely with time and region. Generally speaking, the Sunni countries of Islam in the Middle East and North Africa were tolerant toward non-Muslim minorities. Although the humiliating measures promulgated against *ahl al-dhimma* (the protected people) were never rescinded, they were generally disregarded, or at least not rigidly enforced and their degree of enforcement varied with time and locality. Despite the occasional outbreaks of fanaticism and spasms of intolerance, as in the period of al-Hakim in Egypt (996–1021), it can be safely concluded that Sunni Muslim rulers' policy toward non-Muslims was usually determined by practical considerations and by the force of circumstances, rather than by the provisions of the law. As a result, the dhimmis in Sunni Muslim countries were generally able to enjoy a broad religious and social freedom and lead a relatively secure life.

To some extent, this situation of occasional outbreaks of anti-Jewish pogroms, resulting mainly from political upheavals, was also true of the Jewish communities in North Africa. The exception was Egypt, in which the Jewish communities (totaling 65,600 in 1947) generally enjoyed until 1967 a peaceful co-existence, interrupted by rare cases of anti-Jewish riots.

In contrast to the countries dominated by Sunni Islam, the Jews in Shiʿi Muslim countries, Iran and Zaydi Yemen, were subjected to far more severe dhimmi regulations. The Shiʿis were notorious for their legalistic attitude with respect to religious matters. Hence, the religious restrictions which were enacted by Islam against non-Muslim minorities were generally rigorously enforced, often given a local twist for the worst. In Iran, the land which gave rise to the ʿIsawiyya Jewish sect and served as a prominent center for the Jewish Karaite movement, the Jew was viewed by Muslims as *najis* (impure); a Shiʿi Muslim regards food or drink touched by Jews as contaminated and would not partake of it. "In no other country of the Diaspora," writes Walter J. Fischel, "have the Jews suffered from so many centuries of unrelenting oppression and mortifying legal restrictions as did the Jews of Persia" (1950: 123). However, with the rise of Reza Shah Pahlevi to the Persian throne in 1925, the harsh condition of the Jews was considerably ameliorated. Under the late Ayatollah Khomeini, the Jews once again endured many hardships (Fischel 1950:119–60). As a result, they left Iran in waves, emigrating mainly to Israel and the United States, leaving very few remnants.

THE JEWS OF YEMEN

The condition of the Jews of Yemen was similar to those in Iran. Yemen was until 1962 a sectarian Muslim state ruled by the Zaydis (an offshoot of the Shiʿi sect), who were not hospitable to Yemeni Jews. For example, a decree, known as the Scrapers Edict, imposed upon the Jews the task of cleansing the country's public sewers and latrines of human excrement. It was also incumbent upon Jews to rid the markets, courtyards, Muslim quarters, and other public areas of the stench and carcasses of dogs, horses, camels, and other animals. Moreover, Jews were strictly prohibited from wearing ʿamama (headgear) or a jambiyya, the ubiquitous dagger worn at the waist by almost every Yemeni Muslim man. The avowed aim of this decree was to deprive the Jews, the only non-Muslim minority in Yemen, of any respectable appearance.

Most grievous in the eyes of the Yemeni Jews was the Orphan Edict, operative in Yemen until the 1950s, which imposed forced conversion to Islam on all dhimmis, male and female alike, who had not attained puberty before their fathers died. The effect of this decree on the Jews of Yemen was devastating. Unlike the laws of ghiyar and other degrading measures that affected their social status, this impacted on their religious convictions and posed a threat to their very existence as Jews. Due to constant decimation of Jewish families by famine, disease, and other calamities, children of minor age were often left without parents, or fathers. These were taken away and converted to Islam. The evasion or circumvention of this ordinance was considered by the Jews of Yemen as a sacred obligation that justified almost any means. Many of the orphans were smuggled out of Yemen to Aden, which was ruled by Britain until 1967. Others were adopted into other families who introduced them as their own children. Still others were quickly married off at a tender age in order to exempt them from the decree.

Given the fact that Islam is opposed to forced conversion, which was almost nonexistent in other Muslim countries, one wonders as to its origin and justification in Yemen. Most probably it stems from the obscure and disputed concept of *fitra* that occurs in Qur'an 30:30 and is elaborated upon in a ḥadith. According to this ḥadith, the Prophet Muhammad stated that every person is born according to his fitra (true nature), namely, a Muslim; it is his parents who make him a Jew, a Christian, or a Magian. While Muslim theologians differ widely as to the interpretation and practical implications of this saying, it was understood in Yemen in its narrow and literal sense, namely, as incumbent upon Muslim authorities to spread the wings of Islam on all Jewish orphans of minor age.

It should be noted, however, that these and other edicts persisted mainly in Sanʿa and other urban areas. Indeed, Yemeni Jewish writings (chronicles and poetry) emanating mainly from these areas read like scrolls of agony, presenting a dark and despondent picture of the Yemeni Jews. One should, nevertheless, be wary of sweeping generalizations and oversimplifications. Most of the Jews of Yemen were widely dispersed in small towns, villages, and hamlets. Yemeni Jewish folktales present the relationship between Muslims and Jews in the rural areas of Yemen as relatively congenial, even symbiotic. They depict the itinerant Jewish craftsman peacefully traversing wide areas, crossing tribal borders in the pursuit of his livelihood. This picture is not surprising. The protection bestowed upon Jews by tribal chiefs, local sheikhs or potentates, though at times frail and inconsistent, enabled Jewish life in the rural areas to be relatively secure. The Arab tribes considered the murder of Jews as most shameful and degrading; a murderer of Jews was in many cases severely punished by the tribal or local patrons. As long as a Jew managed to live outside the field of political contentions and to maintain a low and humble profile, he was generally safe.

It is noteworthy that Yemeni Jewry who continually lived in a country untouched by the Westernizing influences, is the only Jewry which preserved the Babylonian superlinear system of punctuation in their biblical texts. The Hebrew punctuation of the Jews of Yemen, remarked A. Neubauer, "is very minute and accurate according to the tonic accents." These Yemenis, concludes Neubauer, "possibly retain the old tradition of reciting Biblical passages" (1891: 604).

The wholesale transplantation of Yemeni Jewry to Israel was one of the most dramatic episodes in modern history. Motivated by messianic frenzy, they poured continuously into Aden, en route to Israel. They came on their own in overwhelming numbers, many of them on foot, undeterred by the prospects of the trials and tribulations which they knew would await them in the course of their travels. They arrived in Aden half-starved, destitute, and emaciated. Despite these and other inconveniences such as the stifling heat of the Aden camp, the gale-force winds, and the sand storms so characteristic of the Arabian desert, the Yemeni Jews hardly complained. With great anticipation, they awaited the day when they would be flown to Israel.

Indeed, in a gigantic operation known as "On Eagles' Wings" (often referred to as "Operation Magic Carpet"), which began in 1949, about fifty thousand Yemeni Jews were flown to Israel. The newly born Jewish state was then experiencing the fantastic phenomenon of the ingathering of the exiles from many countries in the world. This massive influx of immigrants came with different languages, cultures, clothing, complexions, and folklore. Nevertheless, the uniqueness of the Yemeni immigrants was the most pronounced. For hundreds of years, the Jews of Yemen had remained relatively intact and had existed with unbroken continuity in that same region, almost totally secluded from the rest of the world, veiled in mystery and myth. As a result of this isolation, it had developed specific cultural traits and peculiarities distinct from other Jewish communities. The *Palestine Post*, welcoming the first arrivals of the Yemenis with an editorial that highlighted the exotic nature of this historic saga, exclaimed in exultation that "no tale out of the Arabian Nights is so romantic and picturesque, so adventurous and exciting as the story of this homecoming of a whole community" (*Palestine Post* 1949:1).

The Yemenis, most of whom had never seen an airplane before, associated this "miraculous" operation with the biblical verse, "I bore you on eagles' wings" (Exodus 19:4). Indeed, as Shlomo Barer, who had accompanied them on their way from Aden to Israel, aptly indicated, the Yemeni Jews belonged for all practical purposes to biblical times, moving in the agitated whirlpool of their unfamiliar, modern environment "in a state of almost apocalyptic frenzy." They created an interesting sight indeed since they arrived with virtually no possessions. Some of their elders clung to holy parchments or scrolls. It is no wonder that this colorful, exotic, religious people with their dangling earlocks were viewed by one of the American captains of the airlift as "prophets stepping out of the Bible."

The drama of the "homecoming" of these Yemenis was heightened by the marked contrasts between their long-established, primitive ways of life and the highly developed civilization and technology of the new environment into which they were suddenly thrust. Thus they stared in amazement at the moving traffic and the "magic" of technology around them. Indeed, as it has vividly been expressed, the planes that carried them to Israel spanned "not only a thousand miles but also a thousand years."

THE JEWISH COMMUNITY IN ADEN

Within the widely divergent groups of the Jews of southern Arabia, the tiny Jewish community of Aden, situated on the southern coast of Arabia, at the entrance of the Red Sea, stood out as an exceptional and distinctive phenomenon. It is the newest of all the Jewish communities and it is also the most short-lived, its life span being some 128 years only. For although a thriving Jewish community existed in Aden during the Genizah period, this community increasingly diminished with the rapid decline of Aden as an international emporium, particularly from the sixteenth century onward, which eventually brought about the utter eclipse of Aden's role as a center of commerce. As a result, the once flourishing large Jewish community gradually shrank in numbers and significance.

With the conquest of Aden by the British in January 1839, the population of this newly founded British Crown Colony (which constituted only some seventy-five square miles) grew by leaps and bounds, attracting immigrants, mainly from Yemen and the diverse parts of the British Empire. This is also true of the Jewish community of Aden, which had witnessed a rapid growth from 250 in 1839 to 5,000 ((5,000 at its peak in 1947). Thus, the Jewish community of the former British Crown Colony of Aden is virtually a new phenomenon, at least in the sense that its great bulk did not live there before the British occupation. Mirroring the general population of Aden, this Jewish community constituted a composite and variegated ethnic-group society, a fact that accorded it a unique cosmopolitan nature.

Immediately following their occupation of Aden, the British authorities granted extensive civil rights to *all* the inhabitants of the new colony, Jews, Muslims, and other religious communities, according them equal footing before the law. As a result, the Jews were able to engage in every legal field of endeavor and to travel freely as British subjects with British passports. This development, a quantum leap in the social and civil status of the Jews, was a highly significant historical event. For the first time since the rise of the Prophet Muhammad, a Jewish community in the Arabian Peninsula could live freely without the stigma of the inferior dhimmi status and its manifold social disabilities, to which the Jewish communities of the sectarian Zaydi Yemen were subjected. Thus, the British occupation precipitated a process of far-reaching changes in the general character of the Jewish community of Aden, forming it and transforming it demographically, culturally, and socioeconomically. Another significant development resulting from the British occupation is the exposure of Aden and its Jewish community to European influence and education. Schools for both boys and girls were gradually opened; teachers were brought to Aden from England and from Palestine. Troops of Jewish boys and girls were organized under the umbrella of the Aden Scouts; the erstwhile attire gave way to modern European clothing; European, Sepharadi, and anglicized names, such as Howard (instead of ʿAwad), Sami, Simon, Adela, Mary, Susan, Regina, Flori, and Violet were adopted by many. As a result, the Jewish community of Aden gradually developed a culture and custom of its own, which sharply distinguished it from the other Jewish communities of Yemen. Certain differences in ritualistic detail and much larger socioeconomic and other lines of demarcation crept in; the social, financial, cultural, and educational horizons of this community were considerably widened and it no longer regarded itself as an integral part of Yemeni Jewry.

Except for occasional intermarriage with European or Sepharadi Jews, marriages in the Adeni Jewish community were essentially endogamous. Acculturated to the new norms, and exposed to a heterogeneous, multilingual environment, the Jewish community created a Judeo-Arabic dialect consisting mainly of a fusion of languages reflecting the multi-tongues spoken by the inhabitants of Aden, particularly incorporating words and phrases from the vernacular Arabic, Hebrew, English, Hindustani, Guzerati, Persian, Turkish, Greek, Somali, and others. These and other factors gave the Jewish community of Aden a cultural, social, socio-economic, and linguistic mold, quite distinct from that of other Jewish communities in Yemen and the British Protectorates of Arabia.

From the beginning of the twentieth century, the Jews of Aden did away with the custom of bigamy or polygamy, so prevalent among the Jews of Yemen and adhered almost strictly to monogamous marriages, except for the rare cases of *yibbum* (levirate marriage). Furthermore, the Jewish religious court (*Beit Din*) of Aden scoffed at requests for divorce and made the judicial process leading to divorce a discouraging and humiliating one. Thus, the women of Aden were essentially protected from a unilateral repudiation on the part of the husband and immune from the potential threat of a rival wife and its unpleasant ramifications.

One may, therefore safely say that the Jewish community of Aden was, to a large extent, the product of the British occupation, which lasted only 128 years (1839–1967). With the British evacuation of Aden in November 29, 1967, its pulsating life as a community came to an abrupt end, not leaving even a vestigial remnant. While most of the Adeni Jews emigrated to Israel, a sizeable number left for England.

The Ingathering of the Exiles in Israel

With the emigration of almost all the Jews who lived in Middle Eastern and North African countries primarily to Israel, a dramatic chapter of the history of a once thriving eastern Jewish diaspora ended. This included the Jews of Morocco and Iraq, the largest of the eastern Jewish communities. In Morocco there lived about a quarter of a million Jews. During the many centuries of its existence, Moroccan Jewry produced a considerable number of highly influential scholars and writers in the realm of Judaica, several of whom had an inclination toward mysticism and Kabbalah. The Jews of Morocco are also noted for their veneration of saints. Sainthood, namely the attribution of sanctity to individuals and their subsequent

veneration, whether in their lifetime or after their death, is a universal phenomenon. While the phenomenon of saint veneration is not alien to Judaism, it is
most notable among Moroccan Jewry which is marked by unparalleled proliferation of saints (the Hebrew term for "saint" is *qadosh* or *tsadiq*). This Jewry has
produced more than 610 Jewish saints, including 25 women. This is, however, not
surprising, in view of the fact that this community lived in a country dotted with
tombs of Muslim saints (*walis*) and maraboutic shrines. With the establishment
of the State of Israel and the end of French colonialism, the Jews of Morocco left
for Israel and the West in successive waves, leaving only a vestigial remnant.

Iraq (ancient Mesopotamia or Babylonia), the cradle of rabbinic Judaism, is
associated with the biblical patriarchs, the Prophet Ezekiel, Ezra, and Nehemiah.
It also served as the arena for the rise of Karaism and for the activity of prominent
Jewish institutions and highly influential Jewish personalities, like Saadiah Gaon.
In short, Iraqi Jewry's contribution to the shaping of Judaism was enormous.
Following the establishment of Israel, the Jews of Iraq (about 125,000) left their
country in successive waves, primarily in a massive airlift, known as Operation
Ezra and Nehemiah.

Upon their arrival in Israel, most of the Jews of the Arab world stayed for
months, even years, in Mᶜabarot (transit camps), in tents, and in corrugated iron
and wooden prefabricated shacks. From there they gradually established permanent residence throughout the country. In Israel they underwent a socioeconomic,
occupational, cultural, and intellectual transformation. Despite the overwhelming,
and at times traumatic, initial difficulties, they coped remarkably well with the
new conditions, contributing greatly to the dynamic, developing, industrial economy. While at the beginning they were heavily concentrated in unskilled and
semiskilled occupations, filling a wide range of jobs in industries, factories, and
construction, they ultimately managed to take advantage of the opportunities
offered by Israel's modern economy and welfare state. They attained a considerable
measure of well-being and educational and occupational mobility, moving rapidly
into positions of influence and importance in the political, military, and administrative system of the city and state. Subject to both centrifugal and centripetal
pressures, and by virtue of education, service in the military, and membership in
unions and political parties, they managed to attain a high degree of integration
in the fast developing Israeli society.

The process of the integration of Jews from the eastern diaspora into Israeli
society is accelerating. The increasing trend of movement from endogamous to
exogamous marriages, namely to Jews of other ethnic origins, is blurring the
differences between the ethnic groups. Indeed, there is hardly a single family that
has not experienced at least one mixed marriage, and no pattern of preference is
discernible. But this is in consonance with the highly cherished Zionist ideal of
the fusion of the exiles which is generally viewed by all Jews, despite some un-

derstandable apprehension of losing their ethnic and cultural identity and distinctiveness, as a blessing, the consummation of a devout longing.

THE JEWS OF ETHIOPIA

To the colorful heterogeneous, lingual, cultural, and folkloristic tapestry of the Israeli society some exotic threads have recently been added: the Ethiopian Jews, widely known as "Falasha." They, however, resent being called by this term, because they view it as pejorative. They prefer to be called "Beta Israel" (House of Israel).

Known as Cush in biblical times and Abyssinia in the Middle Ages, the Federal Democratic Republic of Ethiopia, one of the poorest and least developed countries in the world, lies between Muslim North Africa and the South Arabian Peninsula. Its official language is Amharic. This black African country is predominantly Orthodox Christian. Its monarchs traced their lineage back to Menelik I, the alleged son of King Solomon and Makeda, the Queen of Sheba. Thus, the last negus (king), Haile Selasie (ruled from 1930–74), referred to himself as the "Lion of Judah," and claimed to be 225th emperor of the Solomon-Makeda royal line.

The Jews of Ethiopia (Beta Israel) encountered absorptive difficulties in Israel, far more than any other Jewish community. Their major problem, it should be noted, did not necessarily lie in their black complexion. According to their own testimony, they were generally warmly received by the Israeli society, and all the relevant authorities strived with considerable success to integrate them into the Israeli social and cultural fabric as equal citizens. Their major, even painful, problem lay in the voiced skepticism relating to their origins and identity, hence their Jewishness. Exclusively written in Ge'ez, or old Ethiopic, their *Orit* (Ethiopic for Torah) comprised the Five Books of Moses, Joshua, Judges, Samuel, and Ruth, along with apocrypha and some pseudepigraphical books. They were ignorant of rabbinic halakha as well as sources of oral law, particularly the Mishna and the Talmud, including rabbinic commandments relating to *talit* (prayer shawl), tefillin (phylacteries), and *mezuzot* (parchment scrolls fixed to the door post). While they adhered to a rigorous observance of the Sabbath, they knew almost nothing of the celebrations of the Fast of Esther and Hanukkah. Moreover, their Rosh Hashana (Jewish New Year) service did not include the blowing of the *shofar* (ram's horn). Like their Ethiopian neighbors, they performed clitorectomies on their daughters. Strangely enough, they had a monastic system of monks and nuns, an institution alien to Judaism. In short, their traditions evolved in isolation from those that were initiated by the rabbis during the Second Commonwealth. They had no knowledge of Hebrew. Rabbinic authorities were gravely concerned about the halakhic status of the Beta Israel's marriages and divorces, hence their family lineage and their eligibility to intermarry with other Jews.

No wonder, some rabbis dismissed them as indigenous Ethiopians, whose Judaism was molded by Jewish influences, thus a mere reflection of rabbinic Judaism. Indeed, as late as January 1973, the Israeli Ministry of Absorption issued a report, stating that according to Jewish laws (Halakha), "the Falasha are not recognized as Jews and cannot immigrate to Israel under the Law of Return." That same year, however, the Sefaradi Chief Rabbi Ovadiah Yosef issued a responsum recognizing the Beta Israel as "descendants of Jewish tribes that moved south of Cush." He urged all authorities concerned to exert the utmost of efforts to hasten their immigration to Israel. Rabbi Yosef's ruling was subsequently endorsed by the Ashkenazi Chief Rabbi as well as by the Israeli government, thus paving the way for making the Beta Israel eligible for emigration to Israel under the Law of Return. The Israeli government, however, did not take immediate action in this regard and by the end of 1973 only 300 Ethiopian Jews had settled in Israel. A change in Israeli policy came by the end of 1984, when more than 6,500 Ethiopian Jews were airlifted to Israel through "Operation Moses," followed later by "Operation Solomon" (May 1991) which transported some 14,500 Jews. There are more than 75,000 Ethiopian Jews in Israel today.

It should be noted, however, that despite the recognition of the Beta Israel's Jewishness, doubts regarding their halakhic status and their marriageability continue to linger among rabbinic circles, though in a diminishing scale, to this very day. This evokes great distress and indignation among the Beta Israel, who view these doubts as an unjustified blemish upon their Jewishness. There also remains the issue of thousands of Ethiopians who had left Beta Israel and converted to Christianity. Many of their descendants known as Falashmura, have been seeking to return to their original Jewish fold and to emigrate to Israel under the Law of Return. Their request, however, poses thorny problems from the Jewish legal point of view, a controversy yet to be resolved.

BIBLIOGRAPHY

Ahroni, Reuben. 1986. *Yemenite Jewry: Origins Culture and Literature*. Bloomington: Indiana University Press.

———. 1994. *The Jews of the British Crown Colony of Aden: History, Culture, and Ethnic Relations*. Leiden. E. J. Brill.

Ben-Ami, Issachar. 1984. *Saint Veneration Among the Jews In Morocco*. Jerusalem. The Magnes Press.

Blady, Ken. 2000. *Jewish Communities in Exotic Places*. Northvale, N.J.: Jason Aronson.

Corinaldi, Michael. 1998. *Jewish Identity: The Case of Ethiopian Jewry*. Jerusalem: Magnes Press; Hebrew University, [Some Aspects of the Eastern Jewish Diaspora].

Fischel, Walter J. 1982. "The Jews in Mediaeval Iran from the 16th to the 18th Centuries: Political, Economic, and Communal Aspects." *Irano-Judaica* I: 265–291.

———. 1950. "The Jews of Persia, 1795–1940." *Jewish Social Studies* 12: 119–160.

Goitein, S. D. 1974. *Jews and Arabs: Their Contacts Through the Ages*. New York. Schocken Books.

Neubauer, A. 1891. "The Literature of the Jews of Yemen." *Jewish Quarterly Review* 3: 604–621.

CHAPTER 21

JEWISH COMMUNITIES IN EUROPE

SERGIO DELLAPERGOLA

THE Jewish presence in Europe dates back to the second or third centuries BCE. Archeological vestiges dating from the Roman Empire point to well-articulated Jewish religious, economic, and other activities along the Mediterranean regions of the continent. Later during the first millennium the Jewish presence expanded northward along the Rhein valley while other European regions, still sparsely settled or barely touched by advanced forms of civilization, did not yet a significant Jewish presence.

Between the twelfth and the twentieth centuries the overall course of the European Jewish community can be summarized as one of *demographic rise, hegemony,* and *decline.* During the Middle Ages the number of Jews in Europe increased substantially. So did their share of a global Jewish population that previously was mainly concentrated in the Middle East and neighboring areas. Between Benjamin of Tudela's travel memoirs of 1170 and the end of the fifteenth century, the Jewish presence steadily increased in Western Europe. This occurred in spite of mass expulsions from virtually all major European countries resulting in segregation in urban places, pressure to convert to Christianity, and in some cases unrestrained anti-Jewish physical violence. These problematic features epitomized the subordinate legal status of Jewish communities and their continuous dependency on economic and political concessions by European ruling authorities nationally and locally.

The major exodus from Spanish and Portuguese domains between the end of the fifteenth century and the first half of the sixteenth, and the conversion of many Jews who chose not to leave their countries, caused a significant downturn in the Jewish presence in Europe, although many of those who left the Iberian peninsula eventually resettled in other parts of the continent. It is only during the late Middle Ages that the Jewish presence in Eastern Europe grew to a significant component of European and world Jewry. Around 1700 it comprised about 80 percent of Europe's total Jewish population estimated at over 700,000.

During the eighteenth and nineteenth centuries, declining mortality and high fertility made Eastern European Jewry rise steadily to a predominant demographic and cultural role among world Jewry. The total number of Jews in Europe grew from 2 million in 1800 to 9.5 million in 1939. Over most of this period European Jews constituted 80 to 90 percent of the world total; more than 80 percent of them lived in Eastern Europe.

Since the 1880s, a massive outflow of migrants from Eastern and other parts of Europe increased the numbers of North American Jews and strengthened the then tiny Jewish community in Palestine. In spite of emigration, East European communities reached an all-time high of 8.1 million in 1939 and continued to constitute the demographic backbone of world Jewry.

The last two-thirds of the twentieth century witnessed a dramatic demographic decline for European Jewry. Most important, the holocaust—the *Shoah*—resulted in the annihilation of about two-thirds of the continent's Jewish population, which fell from 9.5 million in 1939 to 3.8 million in 1945. This involved the nearly total destruction of the large communities in Central and Eastern Europe (with the partial exception of the Russian Republic), the Balkans, and parts of Western Europe. After the war, many of the survivors emigrated to Israel and to America.

During the 1950s and 1960s substantial immigration from North Africa temporarily provided new vitality to French and other Western European Jewish communities. But growing intermarriage, identificational assimilation and population aging produced continuous erosion in the European share of world Jewry. Eventually, out-migration again became a major factor of Jewish population decline on the continent. For a short span during the early 1970s, and more resolutely since the end of the 1980s, the exodus of Jews from the former Soviet Union brought about a drastic decline in the number of Jews in Eastern Europe and on the continent.

At the turn of the millennium these diverse trends had brought back the size of the Jewish population in Europe to where it was at the end of the eighteenth century: 1.6 million. Europe's share of world Jewry—10 to 15 percent of the total 13 million—was back to Middle Age levels. After nearly four centuries, the majority of European Jews again lived in the western parts of the continent.

Jews in the European System

Jewish demographic trends do not occur in a vacuum. European countries and their Jewish populations are part of a worldwide political and socioeconomic system of nations whose individual components offer widely different qualities of life to local Jews. Historically, the balance of global socioeconomic forces tended to attract Jews toward the more developed and stable countries and regions—the world system's *core*—and away from the less developed and more unstable *periphery*. Legal limitations, however, long prevented European Jews from freely settling in the most desirable locations. The initial kernel and rapid growth of a Jewish population in Eastern Europe largely reflected a lack of opportunities in more developed Western European countries and the interest of Eastern European rulers to attract Jews there. It was therefore in Poland, Lithuania, Ukraine, and Belorussia that most Jews found a niche. After the end of World War II, Jews gradually moved from there to places more compatible with their socioeconomic skills and needs.

In Western European history, the leading center of Jewish life shifted from a leading late medieval power, Spain, to an emerging continental power of modernity, Germany, where it lasted until 1933. After World War II, the political freedom and improved standards of living in the Western countries attracted Jewish immigration from Eastern Europe and the Middle East. Until the early 1960s the United Kingdom had the largest Jewish population in Western Europe, but following de-colonization in North Africa, massive immigration turned France into the largest Jewish presence. Other Jews migrated to the United States, Israel, and other Western countries. Germany's strong economic standing after 1990 stimulated the re-building of its small post-Holocaust Jewish community into a larger presence.

An analysis of the data from the European Union's sixty-nine economic regions in the 1990s indicates the relationship between the Jewish population and economic development. Fifty-nine percent of the Jewish population lived in the top fifth of regions ranked by standard of living, whereas only 1 percent lived in the lowest fifth. The most attractive locations for Jews tended to be large capital cities, led by Paris, London, and, until the demise of the Soviet power, Moscow metropolitan areas. These were places with powerful transnational connections, high income in a highly differentiated economy, an emphasis on sophisticated tertiary and manufacturing activities, and strong cultural and research facilities.

JEWS IN EUROPEAN POLITICAL SOCIETY

The European legal and political system developed from roots in the Roman Empire, then to the Holy Roman Empire, later into several major empires surrounded by minor local domains, and eventually into a substantial number of national states. Jews did not always fit comfortably in these definitions of political society, however. They were among the most ancient settlers of the continent, nevertheless more often than not they were placed in the role of the feared and hated *other*. Strategies of exclusion included expulsions, territorial segregation, forced conversion to Christianity, and outright physical suppression. Yet Jews also provided indispensable specialized and efficient services, particularly in the economic domains of trade and the professions. Hence some European nations, social strata, and groups made efforts to incorporate the Jews as legitimate partners. Jews did not truly belong in any of the typical classes of the European social structure, but in some sense they were part of the continent's constituted social order. In light of the perennial conflict between church and state, powerless Jews were sometimes able to find shelter on one side as against the other, but it would be difficult to find a consistent pattern of allied interests.

Paradoxically, modern antisemitism rose along with the process of emancipation of the Jews allowed by a liberalization of Europe's political culture. This antisemitism was nourished by old forms of religious and lay prejudice but was also armed with an entirely new array of symbols and tools of aggression. This apparent contradiction between prejudice and political openness raises the question of which was the more authentic European attitude toward Jews, reserved inclusion or outright exclusion? The question is whether Auschwitz was a mere accident or a result of deeply ingrained European religious, political, and cultural perceptions? An intriguing corollary is whether the memory of Auschwitz will become a permanent feature of Europe's newly emerging civic conscience. Events such as the high-profile rememberance of the sixtieth anniversary of the liberation of death camps and the establishment of a European Day of Memory send promising signals in this direction.

Whatever the final outcome, Europe continued to need its share of Jews—to mistrust and persecute them but also to cherish and imitate them. An ambiguous relationship with Jews has been an enduring fixture of European history and society.

A UNIQUE JEWISH CONTRIBUTION?

Given these premises, the cultural contributions of Jews to Europe's history and culture cannot be reduced to a single pattern, but rather reflect the widely contrasting range of different options and constraints that characterized the Jewish experience in Europe. One type of contribution came from Jews in Europe who found ways to express fundamentally Jewish ways of discourse. Scholars such as Shlomo Itzhaki of Troyes (better known as Rashi, author of the great commentaries on the Torah and the Talmud); Moses ben Maimon of Cordoba (the Rambam, compiler of the greatest code of Jewish Law); Joseph Caro of Toledo, Adrianople and Safed, and Moses Isserles of Cracow (the compilers of Shulhan Arukh); Elijah ben Solomon Zalman (the Gaon) of Vilna; and Israel Ba'al Shem Tov the mystic of Miedzyboz, not only expanded upon previous layers of Jewish culture but actually defined fundamental normative pillars of Jewish culture for all subsequent generations.

The influence of these innovative interpeters was significant not only for the Jewish constituency but also for the European public at large. On the negative side, enhancing an assertive and distinct Jewish cultural identity and reinforcing unique cultural and community patterns could help to sharpen Jewish separatedness, hence hostile perceptions and behaviors by non-Jews. On the positive side, the gradual emergence of a more pluralistic and multicultural European society offered propitious room for having such Jewish contributions incorporated into an expanded concept of Europe's cultural richness.

At the opposite end, other cultural innovators reflected the encounter between Jews emerging from centuries of discrimination and exclusion and a European society opening up to universal values, technical innovation and a measure of multiculturalism. Such nonconformist Jewish thinkers included those who criticized major social and cultural paradigms routinely accepted in the broader European environment. They transfused Jewish intellectual premises and energies into new visions of religion and ethics (Baruch Spinoza), political thought (Karl Marx), the social sciences (Emile Durkheim, Sigmund Freud), and the natural sciences (Albert Einstein). These innovators did not restrict themselves to an exclusive Jewish frame of thought. Some were greatly estranged from it. Others did not deny their Jewish origins, and some were significantly involved with the Jewish community and its institutions. They were all leading interpreters of a general European paradigm of human progress, rationality, and enlightenment.

In between these extremes were those who operated from within the Jewish paradigm but made efforts to develop it into new directions, sometimes trying to reform some of Judaism's fundamental premises. Moses Mendelssohn led a movement for religious reform that from its initial European rationale and location later expanded overseas, primarily in the United States. Another strand for social reform was a secularized piety applied by European-based organizations such as the Alliance Israélite Universelle and the Jewish Colonization Association led by Isaac Adolphe Crémieux, the Rothschild family, and the Baron Hirsch. These movements were aimed at improving the educational level, material conditions, and political representation of European and other Jews. The ultimate expression of this new spirit was the emergence of political Zionism led by Theodor Herzl—a direct outcome of nineteenth-century Western European political thought. Zionism eventually transcended its European roots and became instrumental in the birth of the State of Israel, a watershed in modern Jewish history. The early generations of Israeli leaders, including Haiim Weizmann and David Ben Gurion, were mostly European-born and were imbued with an Eastern European Jewish ethos of exclusion and self-emancipation blended with a Western European ethos of progress and modernity.

In addition to these thinkers and leaders were hundreds of thousands of upwardly mobile European Jewish individuals who applied their professional skills in medicine, law, literature and the humanities, social sciences, natural sciences, visual and performing arts, economic and cultural entrepreneurship, and civil service. This is best illustrated by such political leaders as prime ministers Benjamin Disraeli, Luigi Luzzatti, Léon Blum, and Pierre Mendès-France. Together these skilled Jewish men and women offered an invaluable contribution to the progress of European society and civilization.

The prospects for European Jews in the future depend on a combination of emerging factors. Crucially important will be the fate of the new process of political integration throughout the European Union and the predicament of consolidation of an integrated European identity. An expanded European framework of socioeconomic change and more fluid options of identity and allegiance may offer a congenial context for Jewish life. On the other hand, the prevalence of rigid national identities would limit the options of Jews and others to feel genuinely incorporated within a new European identity. Another imponderable is the changing global system. Whether or not Europe moves toward an era of institutional build-up and socioeconomic prosperity in the global market may affect attitudes toward tolerance and multiculturalism.

Of equal importance is the question of whether European Jews will be able to express themselves as an autonomous *community of continuity*—generating from within their community an existential rationale and cultural originality—or whether they will be a mere *community of presence*, reflecting the variable and unpredictable circumstances of socioeconomic and political forces and bound to grow or disappear accordingly.

BIBLIOGRAPHY

DellaPergola, S. 1993. "Jews in the European Community: Sociodemographic Trends and Challenges." *American Jewish Year Book* 93: 25–82.

Gitelman, Z., Kosmin, K, Kovacs, A. ed. 2002 *New Jewish Identities: Contemporary Europe and Beyond*. Budapest: Central European University Press.

The Jewish People Policy Planning Institute 2005 "Europe and the European Union" *Annual Assessment 2004–2005: The Jewish People Between Thriving and Decline*, Jerusalem: The Jewish People Policy Planning Institute.

Marrus, M. 1997. "How Important Were the Jews?" *Jewish Studies* 37: 63–173.

Mendelsohn, E. 1987. *The Jews of East Central Europe between the World Wars*. Bloomington: Indiana University Press.

Pinto, D. 1994. *Beyond Anti-Semitism: The New Jewish Presence in Europe*. New York: American Jewish Committee.

Troen, I. S., ed. 1999. *Jewish Centers and Peripheries: Europe between America and Israel Fifty Years after World War II*. New Brunswick, N.J.: Transaction.

Wasserstein, B. 1996. *Vanishing Diaspora: The Jews in Europe since 1945*. London: Hamish Hamilton.

Webber, J., ed. 1994. *Jewish Identities in the New Europe*. London: Littman Library of Jewish Civilization.

CHAPTER 22

JEWISH COMMUNITIES
IN THE AMERICAS

J. SHAWN LANDRES

AMERICAN Judaism is a major element of global Judaism. Aside from Israel, more Jews live in North America than anywhere else in the world. Forty-one percent of the 13 million Jews worldwide live in the United States, and approximately 6 percent live elsewhere in the Americas—according to 2005 estimates, 372,000 lived in Canada, 185,000 in Argentina, and 213,000 elsewhere in Latin America. Though for many years the United States had the largest Jewish population in the world, the decline in the U.S. Jewish population and the relatively high birth rate of Jews in Israel likely will result in Israel's Jewish population exceeding that of the United States by 2010. The United States will retain the largest Jewish population outside Israel. There are still more than twice as many Jews in the United States as in Europe, for instance. After the United States and Israel, the next largest Jewish population center, France, can claim less than 4 percent of the worldwide Jewish population. Of the other ninety countries around the world in which Jews live (down from two hundred countries a century ago), only seven have a Jewish population that is greater than 1 percent of the worldwide Jewish population. As these numbers indicate, American Judaism plays a dominant role in global Judaism; and at the same time what happens in Judaism around the world directly affects the Jewish community in the United States.

Approximately 5.5 million people in the United States identify themselves as Jewish, but their importance in American life is disproportionately greater. There is a Jewish presence in approximately 4 percent of all U.S. households. While religious Judaism often is classified into seven streams—ultra-Orthodox, Modern

Orthodox, Conservative, Reform, Reconstructionist, Renewal, and nondenominational—this religion-based typology belies the complexity of a tradition that is simultaneously a religion, an ethnicity, and a nation. Over the past century, in a manner that might be called "global" or "transnational," the Jewish community in its various manifestations has evolved to become a significant player on the American and international religious, ethnic, and political scenes.

The year 2004 marked the 350th anniversary of Judaism in North America. Jews have been part of North American life since long before the United States, Canada, and Mexico were born as modern nation-states. Many members of Christopher Columbus's crew are believed to have been Jews fleeing the expulsion and inquisition in Spain and Portugal; New Christians (Jews who converted to Christianity) and crypto-Jews (New Christians who secretly maintained their Judaism) formed part of the Portuguese settlement in Brazil. One hundred fifty years later, these Jews launched a wave of migration to the religiously tolerant Dutch colonies—Curaçao in 1651 and New Amsterdam in 1654. A second, somewhat larger group of Jewish immigrants arrived in the United States from Germany in the early nineteenth century. From 1880 to 1920, the largest wave of Jewish immigrants to the United States fled persecution and socioeconomic instability in Central and Eastern Europe. Subsequent patterns of Jewish immigration to the United States are smaller in scale but no less striking: Jews fled Nazi-occupied Europe to Latin America in the late 1930s and early 1940s; survivors of the Shoah moved to the United States after World War II; and Iranian Jews moved to Long Island and Los Angeles after the revolution of 1978–79. Jews from the former Soviet Union arrived in the early 1990s; and, in the wake of severe economic crises, Argentinean and other South American Jews migrated north in the early twenty-first century. As of 2000–01, fully 8 percent of the adult Jewish population of the United States was born abroad; two-thirds of that group came from the former Soviet Union and half of the remainder from just three countries: Israel, Canada, and Iran.

The first wave of Spanish and Portuguese Jews who arrived in the New World were in a sense continuing a 1,500-year diaspora in search of religious freedom and socioeconomic stability. Their travel to North America was made possible by European colonial expansion. The second and third waves of German and East-Central European Jews were mostly economic migrants, spurred by the aftereffects of the Industrial Revolution and the birth pains of the modern capitalist nation-state. The most recent waves—Jews from post–World War II Europe, Iran, and the former Soviet Union—have been refugees and stateless migrants.

Since 1948, any analysis of Jewish transnational migration must account for migration to Israel, called *aliyah*, or "going up" in Hebrew. Since its founding, Israeli law has guaranteed entry and citizenship to any self-identified Jew (including applicants with even a single Jewish grandparent) and encouraged people to migrate to Israel. To "make aliyah" is a rhetorical priority (if not always an actual one) for American Jewish communal organizations. From a high of 8,100 immigrants to Israel from the United States in 1971, the number of Americans migrating to Israel fell to an average of 1,400 per year in the 1990s, with large fluctuations between 1,000 and 2,000 in the early twenty-first century. From the late 1990s through 2002, emigration from Latin America, particularly Argentina, Venezuela, and Uruguay, increased sharply from historic lows in the early 1990s, due to continued economic and political distress. In 2005, a record 23,000 Jews immigrated to Israel, with the largest increases from South America, Belarus, and France. In the wake of sporadic antisemitic violence in France, approximately 3,000 French Jews "made aliyah" each year from 2001 to 2005.

Emigration from Israel is called *yeridah*, or "going down." Complicating the political and theological logic of immigration to Israel is the more or less permanent presence in the United States of approximately 350,000–400,000 Israelis, mostly in Los Angeles and New York. If their emigration to the United States is problematic for Israel, it is doubly so for American Jewish communal leaders, who find their rhetoric of aliyah challenged by the presence of Israelis who seem to have rejected what many American Jews would regard as the "opportunity" to live in "the Promised Land."

The history of Judaism in the United States is in many ways an account of Jewish ambivalence about the homogenizing tendencies of both nationalism and globalism. American Jews—along with many of other faiths—have resisted the most extreme tendencies of American nationalism, appealing not only to their right to ethnic difference but also to the universalistic ethical demands of their religious tradition. At the same time, American Jews have resisted the totalizing strains of globalism, insisting on their religious, ethnic, and national particularity. The American Jewish relationship with Israel—as a metaphor, as a Zionist ideal, and as a political reality—is but one example of this latter resistance to globalization.

The word "pluralism" was coined by an American Jew, Horace Kallen, as was its counterpart, the term "melting pot," coined by Israel Zangwill. Both words entered the lexicon shortly after the turn of the twentieth century, as immigrants arriving from East-Central Europe coped with conflicting impulses to assimilate into American society and to preserve their religious and cultural heritage. That American Jews developed the basic vocabulary of integration, acculturation, diversity, and difference suggests that the Jewish experience in the United States has become paradigmatic. Indeed, many leaders of immigrant Arab and Muslim groups openly model their social, educational, religious, and political organizations on successful Jewish exemplars: the American-Arab Anti-Discrimination Committee is modeled on the B'nai B'rith Anti-Defamation League; the Los Angeles Bureau of Muslim Education is modeled on that city's Bureau of Jewish Education; the Islamic Society of North America has developed a fellowship program in nonprofit management and governance based on similar models for Jewish communal service.

Jews in the United States have had to make fundamental choices about how to balance the demands of American society (sometimes secular, sometimes Christian) with Jewish traditions and expectations. How to be Jewish in the United States? How to be an American within Judaism? And what about Israel? In many respects, a person or group's response to those competing questions is more revealing than that person or group's affiliation with a particular stream of religious Judaism. Thus, there are three main avenues of approach to exploring the nexus of the United States, Judaism, and globalization. First, there is the global in the local: American Jewish response to the global Jewish religious experience. Second, there is the local in the global: how specifically American forms of Jewish life are making their way across the globe. Finally, there is the transnational, that is, the relationship between American Jews and Israel, in both its ideal and real forms.

THE LOCAL IN THE GLOBAL

American Judaism—specifically American religious Judaism—has long been a proving ground for global Jewish religious innovation. The non-Orthodox Reform and Conservative movements, though born in Germany and Hungary, grew to maturity and dominance in the United States; the World Union for Progressive Judaism (Reform) and Masorti Olami (Conservative) depend on U.S.-based support for their global efforts. The organization called Hillel: The Foundation for Jewish Campus Life pioneered its university outreach program in the United States and has since exported its model to Israel, the former Soviet Union, and South America. The American Jewish summer camp movement has outposts in Hungary (funded by Ronald Lauder, heir to his mother Estée's perfume fortune) and Ukraine (funded by the Conservative movement).

American religious leaders have helped to shape global Judaism, in particular rabbis like Moshe Feinstein (ultra-Orthodox), Abraham Joshua Heschel (Conservative), Menachem Schneerson (Chabad-Lubavitch), Joseph Soloveitchik (Modern Orthodox), and Stephen S. Wise (Reform). Jewish liturgical music and popular songs composed by Americans such as Rabbi Shlomo Carlebach, Debbie Friedman, and Craig Taubman are sung worldwide.

Perhaps the most famous American Jewish export is the Chabad-Lubavitch network of synagogues, kindergartens, and community centers, which now span the globe from Norway to Namibia to Nepal. This Chassidic outreach movement, based in Brooklyn, New York, seeks to create and serve Jewish markets throughout the world while adhering at all times to an ultra-Orthodox vision of religious Judaism. The most visible sign of Chabad's global influence came in 2000, when the Chabad-sponsored Federation of Jewish Communities of the CIS secured official recognition from the Russian government and installed its rabbi as the Chief Rabbi of Russia, pushing aside the long-established Russian Jewish Congress and the Federation of Jewish Organizations and Communities of Russia. And every year, Chabad of Nepal sponsors a Passover meal for as many as fifteen hundred backpackers in the Himalaya mountains.

THE GLOBAL IN THE LOCAL

The processes of cultural detraditionalization and retraditionalization associated with late modernity have had an especially strong impact on Jewish life in America and Europe. The combination of migration and assimilation affects any community; but the genealogical break of the Holocaust meant that the postwar generation largely was cut off from what had been centuries of local and regional Jewish customs and practices. As both historians and anthropologists have noted, Jews seeking to rebuild their religious lives turned to the formal legal tradition, preserved in written texts, to fill the cultural vacuum. One result was the loss of local variation—perhaps inevitable because of the destruction of the actual physical places—in favor of a global uniformity of practice. Another result was the polarization of religious Judaism: as Orthodox Jews sought new legal strictures to take the place of vanished customs, non-Orthodox Jews took advantage of the cultural vacuum to reinterpret Jewish law, borrowing customs from Jewish communities around the globe. For example, for centuries, East-Central European Jews banned rice and legumes during the Passover week in addition to the five types of leavened wheat, whereas Mediterranean and Middle Eastern Jews legislated no such limitation. The Conservative/Masorti movement—largely populated by East-Central European Jews—has adopted the latter practice and lifted the ban on rice and legumes, dismissing it as merely a folk custom unsupported by the law.

Nowhere is globalization more a part of the American Jewish experience than in the development of what Reform Rabbi Isaac Mayer Wise called "Minhag America," or the "American school of practice." American Jewish ritual and music, particularly in non-Orthodox settings, has moved far beyond the confines of Ashkenazi (East-Central European), Sephardi (Mediterranean), and Mizrachi (Middle Eastern and Iranian) groupings. "Yemenite steps" were introduced into American Jewish "Israeli folkdancing" in the 1950s and 1960s, and Ugandan Jewish melodies were adopted in synagogue services in the early 2000s.

The first major cultural importation in the late twentieth century, American

Judaism was the legitimating of Sephardi and Mizrachi liturgical and musical practices. However, this was not so much a globalizing trend as a multicultural trend; that is, the Sephardi and Mizrachi traditions were acknowledged as valid Jewish traditions in and of themselves, but they were not integrated into the liturgy alongside Ashkenazi practices, nor were Ashkenazi practices adopted in Sephardi and Mizrachi congregations. In the past twenty years, however, synagogues such as Los Angeles's Sinai Temple have been host to an often awkward integration of Iranian and European cultural practices, and both Sephardi and Mizrachi congregations have adopted European Orthodox norms not found in their native traditions, such as a divider separating men and women.

While ethnomusicologists such as Jeffrey Summit have documented the history and breadth of Jewish musical folk traditions worldwide, it is only a relatively recent development that the full range of these traditions has found a place in the American synagogue. Much of the shift is due to the expansion of the religious Jewish summer camp movement, beginning in the late 1960s; campers who learned exciting new ways of praying and singing began to demand that their home synagogues incorporate these innovations. As synagogues themselves became sites for liturgical and musical experimentation, congregants looked farther and farther afield for inspiration, in many cases not limiting themselves to traditionally Jewish modes. Thus, Congregation B'nai Jeshurun in New York City has incorporated into its Friday Night Shabbat service music from the Sephardi tradition, the (Muslim) Sufi tradition, and from cultures as varied as Turkey, Bulgaria, Holland, Israel, and Pakistan. Congregations around the country have adopted these melodies for use in their services. Often, the melodies are mixed and adapted without regard to maintaining any regional or ethnic integrity, so it would not be inaccurate to suggest that "Minhag America" is in fact a global school of practice.

Israel and the Transnational

Since 1967, American Jewish philanthropic activity abroad has centered on two poles: Israel, on the one hand, and one or two diaspora communities, on the other. Throughout the 1970s and 1980s, for instance, American Jewish attention focused on Soviet Jewry. From the mid-1980s to the mid-1990s, Jewish attention turned to Ethiopian Jews and postsocialist Central European Jews. At the turn of the twenty-first century, communal efforts were aimed at Argentinean Jews, whose previously self-sustaining Jewish community neared collapse in the wake of the economic crisis there during the late 1990s. In the mid 2000s, some American

Jewish organizations, such as the American Jewish World Service, began to emphasize non-Jewish priorities, such as opposing the genocide in Darfur, Sudan, and aiding tsunami survivors in Southeast Asia alongside hurricane victims in the southeastern United States. Throughout this period, however, each of these interest groups—Soviet, Ethiopian, Central European, Western European, and Argentinean Jews, as well as concerns beyond the Jewish community—had to compete for attention with Israel.

The complexities of the American Jewish relationship with Israel arise from a deceptively simple set of dilemmas. Who is a Jew? What does "Israel" (real or imagined) mean to American Jews? What is—or should be—Israel's role in shaping diaspora Jewish communities? The peace process of the mid- to late 1990s, inaugurated by the 1993 Oslo Accords, marked the height of a period of American Jewish ambivalence about Israel's geopolitical situation. However, the so-called Al-Aqsa Intifada, which began in 2000, and the sharp rise in antisemitic expressions and attacks have shifted the ground of debate to the question of "Jewish security," a debate which peaked with the August 2005 Israeli withdrawal from Gaza. There is, however, a twist to this relationship: non-Orthodox American Jews demand a voice in Israel's internal religious politics but they largely remain silent when it comes to Israel's strategic choices. The irony is that from a global perspective, Jews in the United States and elsewhere have a greater physical and political stake in the outcome of the Israeli-Palestinian conflict than they do in Israel's "who is a Jew" debate.

Despite occasional claims to the contrary made by Jewish communal leaders, when American Jews speak, they do not do so with one voice about the future of the Israeli-Palestinian dilemma. Israeli withdrawal from settlements in Gaza and the West Bank elicited both support and opposition from American Jews. There are U.S.-based organizations supporting every Israeli political party and position, from American Friends of Peace Now to American Friends of Israel's National Union, as well as transnational groups spanning the sociopolitical spectrum, from Rabbis for Human Rights to the Jewish Defense League. These groups operate independently of and often in opposition to the stated policies of the U.S. and Israeli governments, not to mention the positions of "official" Jewish organizations.

Thus, American Judaism is global in diverse ways. The United States has exported many versions of Judaism around the globe. At the same time, Judaism in America is the site of global ritual practices that are not tied to a particular ethnic genealogy or geography. Ultimately, however, it may be more fruitful to consider American Judaism as a "transnational" religious tradition enmeshed in a network of two-way connections to other Jewish communities around the globe and to Israel. The Jewish diaspora is a specific type of transnationalism, one that links a homeland (both real and imagined) with a network of communities across the globe that are exilic with respect to that "homeland" but nonetheless at home with respect to the countries in which they are located. Inhabitants of the American Jewish diaspora may perceive the Diaspora itself as the local—Israel—in the global and their specific locations on the diasporic map as the global in the local.

BIBLIOGRAPHY

Ben Rafael, Eliezer, Yosef Gorni, and Yaacov Ro'i. 2003. *Contemporary Jewries: Convergence and Divergence, Jewish Identities in a Changing World, vol. 2.* Leiden and Boston: Brill.

Della Pergola, Sergio, Yehezkel Dror, and Shalom S. Wald. 2005. *Jewish People Policy Planning Institute Annual Assessment 2005: Facing a Rapidly Changing World.* Jerusalem: The Jewish People Policy Planning Institute.

Fishkoff, Sue. 2003. *The Rebbe's Army: Inside the World of Chabad-Lubavitch.* 1st ed. New York: Schocken Books.

Gold, Steven J. 2002. *The Israeli Diaspora.* Seattle: University of Washington Press.

Goldberg, Harvey E. 2003. *Jewish Passages: Cycles of Jewish Life.* Berkeley: University of California Press.

Haddad, Yvonne Yazbeck, Jane I. Smith, and John L. Esposito. 2003. *Religion and Immigration: Christian, Jewish, and Muslim Experiences in the United States.* Walnut Creek, Calif.: AltaMira Press.

Kosmin, Barry A., Egon Mayer, Ariela Keysar, and City University of New York. Graduate School and University Center. 2001. *American Religious Identification Survey 2001.* New York: Graduate Center of the City University of New York.

Lowenstein, Steven M. 2000. *The Jewish Cultural Tapestry: International Jewish Folk Traditions.* New York: Oxford University Press.

Mittleman, Alan, Robert A. Licht, and Jonathan D. Sarna. 2002. *Jewish Polity and American Civil Society: Communal Agencies and Religious Movements in the American Public Sphere.* Lanham, Md.: Rowman and Littlefield.

Sarna, Jonathan D. 2004. *American Judaism: A New History.* New Haven, Conn.: Yale University Press.

Shain, Yossi. 2002. "Jewish Kinship at a Crossroads: Lessons for Homelands and Diasporas." *Political Science Quarterly* 117, no. 2: 279–309.

Summit, Jeffrey A. 2000. *The Lord's Song in a Strange Land: Music and Identity in Contemporary Jewish Worship, American Musicspheres.* New York: Oxford University Press.

United Jewish Communities. 2003. *National Jewish Population Survey, 2000–01* [MRDF]. New York: United Jewish Communities (producer). Waltham, Mass.: North American Jewish Data Bank (distributor).

CHAPTER 23

JEWISH COMMUNITIES IN ASIA

NATHAN KATZ

PERHAPS for as long as two millennia, there have been Jewish communities throughout much of South, East, and Southeast Asia. Most have been in such port cities as Surat, Kochi (formerly Cochin), Mumbai (formerly Bombay), Calcutta, Yangon (formerly Rangoon), Singapore, Bangkok, Kobe, Hong Kong, and Shanghai. Others were found at major trading centers along the Spice Route, which meandered westward from South India through Kabul, Herat and thence Iran and Turkey. Yet other communities thrived along the Silk Route, the best known and longest lived of which was at its eastern terminus, Kaifeng.

Some of these communities are very old, dating at least from the early medieval period if not ancient times, while some of them emerged when merchant houses in India established branches eastward during the nineteenth century. Some are even newer: Bangkok's Jewish community dates from the first half of the twentieth century, and Shanghai's present community has existed only since the establishment of diplomatic relations between China and Israel in 1992. Many Asian diaspora communities have been in decline for the past half-century due to emigration to Israel. It is in the oldest of these Jewish communities that we find the most profound interactions with the host culture, and the best examples are Kochi in India and Kaifeng in China.

KOCHI, INDIA

According to local traditions, Jews first settled on India's southwest coast when the Second Temple was destroyed and the Romans exiled all Jews from Jerusalem in the year 70 CE. They fled along maritime trade routes, which had been in use since King Solomon's time and which had recently been speeded by the discovery of the monsoon winds by Greek navigators early in the first century. They settled at Cranganore, among other towns, where they were granted political autonomy by local monarchs and flourished as agriculturists, international spice merchants, petty traders, shipbuilders, and in government service and the military. During the fourteenth century they migrated to Kochi. Their numbers in the Malabar rose as high as three thousand at the time of independence, but fewer than fifty remain today. Where there were once nine flourishing synagogues with Jewish schools, scribes, scholars, mystics, and poets, today the Cochin Synagogue, built in 1568, fails to obtain a prayer quorum of ten adult males unless there are Jewish visitors from elsewhere in India or abroad.

The Kochi Jews, always part of the Jewish mainstream both commercially and culturally, were knowledgeable about their religion and savvy about affairs of state and currency fluctuations even in far-off Europe, not to mention among the plethora of princely states of South India. Knowing the languages of the subcontinent, the Middle East, and Europe, they played invaluable roles in both commerce and diplomacy.

Their religious life evidences a high degree of acculturation into their Indian context but not assimilation. For example, during their autumn holy days and at weddings, many Nayar (the local dominant caste) customs and symbols of royalty were adopted. At a wedding, for another example, the Jews would borrow an elephant from a neighboring Hindu temple to convey the bridegroom to the synagogue for nuptials. During the festival of Rejoicing in the Torah (Simhat Torah), Kochi's Jews added three elements to their celebrations found nowhere else in the Jewish world: they displayed their Torah scrolls on a temporary Ark on the days just prior to the festival; during the afternoon prayers, they made outdoor circumambulations of the synagogue with their Torah scrolls; and at the conclusion of the festival, they ritually demolished their temporary Ark to the accompaniment of unique Hebrew songs. All of these behaviors reflect Hindu temple festivals, when the deity (*murti*) of the temple is first displayed, then taken on procession, and then (often) disposed of. None of these practices violate Judaic law (halacha), so these borrowings from the local Hindu culture were judicious, reflecting their firm Jewish identity, based on Judaic learning. They were acculturated, which is to say they were culturally at home in their Hindu environment, without becoming assimilated, which involves a surrender of identity.

KAIFENG, CHINA

Such acculturation was not so with the Jews of Kaifeng, China, at least not in the long run, for they became quite assimilated indeed. Jews came to China following two routes. Persian Jews came via the Silk Route. Judging from a Hebrew manuscript on Chinese paper discovered in a Buddhist library in Dunhuang, as well as Muslim travelers' reports, Jews were established in China no later than the eighth century. Indian Jews came via maritime routes of the South China Sea and settled in port cities. The Kaifeng community is the only one that survived the Middle Ages, having been "discovered" as an isolated, moribund community by Jesuit missionaries during the early seventeenth century.

Jews lived in Kaifeng for nearly a thousand years where they were traders, agriculturists, artisans, physicians, and government officials. More than a few passed the rigorous civil service examinations and became Mandarins. They constructed a synagogue in Kaifeng in 1126 that included an ancestor hall, typical of Chinese temples.

Kaifeng's Jews increasingly identified with Chinese high culture. A 1488 inscription in their synagogue proclaimed: "Although our religion agrees in many respects with the religion of the literati, from which it differs in a slight degree, yet the main design of it is nothing more than reverence for Heaven, and veneration for ancestors, fidelity to the prince, and obedience to parents, just what is included in the five human relations, the five constant virtues, with the three principal connections of life."

To Western Jews, it is striking to hear Judaism described in such Confucian terms. Similarly, it is remarkable to see in the Cochin Synagogue reflections of Hindu temple behavior. But on the other hand, one can imagine that to an Indian or Chinese Jew it would be unnerving to know that their American coreligionists understand Judaism fundamentally as ethical monotheism; such a characterization might sound so very Protestant. The point is that Judaism, like any ancient religion, has many threads within itself, and that one or another of these threads becomes highlighted in response to the ethos of the host culture in which a particular Jewish community finds itself. Such a process could be indicated by using a concept borrowed from Gestalt psychology, that of background and foreground. In relation to a background (the host culture), certain elements in a perceptual field rise to the foreground (the particular Judaisms of India, China, or America). As Judaism, or any religion, moves from culture to culture, or as it moves through time, differing threads are foregrounded and others backgrounded, depending of course on the host culture and its vicissitudes.

INDIAN JEWRY TODAY

India had and still has the largest number of Jews of any country east of Iran. Their population peaked in 1950 at around thirty to thirty-five thousand, after which emigration to Israel and other places reduced their number to around four to six thousand today, more if the so-called Bene Menashe and Bene Ephraim are counted.

There have been three major distinct Jewish communities in India. The oldest group is found in and around Kochi in the southwestern state of Kerala, who today number less than fifty. Perhaps five thousand Cochinim, as they are called in Hebrew, live in Israel. The largest group is known as Bene Israel and is found chiefly in and around Mumbai, with active communities in Pune, also in Maharashtra state, in Ahmedabad in Gujerat State, and in New Delhi. All told, there are four to five thousand Bene Israel in India and forty to fifty thousand in Israel, where they make up a significant ethnic group (*edah* in Hebrew). The most recently arrived group is known in India as Baghdadis, Middle Eastern Jews, Arabic speakers mostly, who migrated to India since the late eighteenth century, about the same time as the British arrived, and who settled in India's port cities, especially Mumbai and Calcutta. Numbering about 5,000 at their peak, they have declined to a few hundred, most all of whom are elderly. The Baghdadis played a significant role in the development of British India's ports. Beginning as jewelers and opium traders, Baghdadi entrepreneurs soon moved into textiles and shipping in Mumbai, and real estate, jute, manufacturing, and tobacco in Calcutta. Of the three groups, only the Bene Israel remain viable as a community.

While Mumbai is home to most of India's Bene Israel, the nearby Konkan host is their spiritual home. Bene Israel trace themselves back to seven couples from Israel who survived a shipwreck off Navgaon, in the unknown, distant past. Somehow they clung to vestigial Judaic observances despite centuries of isolation. Their tenacity in maintaining the Sabbath, ritual circumcision, Jewish dietary codes, and the Hebrew Shema—the affirmation "Hear O Israel! The Lord is our God, the Lord is One"—set the stage for their unlikely transformation from an anonymous oil-pressing caste in the remote Konkan into modern, urban members of the world Jewish community. This evolution occurred over the span of two hundred years, beginning in the middle of the eighteenth century.

A Kochi merchant heard rumors of a Konkani caste that rested on Saturday and circumcised their sons on the eighth day, so David Rahabi visited them. After spending some time with the community, examining their dietary habits as well as eccentric (by Hindu standards) religious observances, he concluded that they were lost Jews. He took three of them back to Kochi where he educated them in Hebrew and the rudiments of Judaism and sent them back with the title of *kazi*, religious leader. This began a longstanding relationship between Bene Israel and

Kochi Jews; as Bene Israel prospered, they hired Kochi Jews to be their cantors, teachers, ritual slaughterers, and scribes. Bene Israel recall these events as their "first awakening."

Subsequent encounters with British and American missionaries and with the nascent Baghdadi community of Mumbai built upon their sense of Jewishness. This period is known as their "second awakening." They learned Bible stories from the missionaries, and they shared their synagogues (they built their first one in Mumbai in 1796) and cemeteries with the Baghdadis. Both the British and the Baghdadis offered opportunities in Mumbai, whether in the military, railway of civil service, or in the mills and docks of the illustrious Sassoons, and Bene Israel migrated to the new, glamorous city in search of their fortunes. It did not take long until there were more Bene Israel in Mumbai than in the Konkan.

Gradually the Baghdadis, in an effort to become accepted by the British as "European" rather than "Indian"—the former label with tangible economic benefits; the latter with social snobbery judgment—came to adopt British condescension toward all things Indian, including the Bene Israel Jews, who were unmistakably Indian in both appearance and culture. This condescension became all the uglier when the Baghdadis came to cast aspersions upon the very Jewishness of the Bene Israel. The heart and soul of their newly found and hard-earned identity was under attack.

In Mumbai the Bene Israel encountered both the Zionist and Swaraj movements for independence from Britain in Palestine and India respectively, and they were rent by the competing nationalisms. On the one hand, as Jews they had internalized the longing to return to Jerusalem and rebuild Zion. On the other hand, their unhappy experiences with the Baghdadis led them to mistrust foreign Jews, and as Indians they yearned for independence from the British. On yet a third hand, they were also fond of the British, their employers and often patrons, and wanted to support them as well. Mahatma Gandhi appreciated their ambivalence. Leaders of the Ahmedabad Jewish community (where Gandhi had headquarters at his Sabarmati Ashram) asked the Mahatma what should be the stance of India's Jews vis-à-vis the independence movement. He is said to have replied that the Jews should "stand aside" because as a microscopically small community, they would be crushed between the competing and overwhelming forces of the British Empire, Indian nationalism, and Muslim separatism. As a community, they did stand apart, although many Bene Israel became involved as individuals. The bottom line, however, is that the great majority of Bene Israel emigrated to Israel.

The Bene Israel community today has stabilized. Those who intended to emigrate have done so, and most of those who remain intend to stay. Most are in Mumbai, where they work in the professions, education, industry, the military, and commerce. Most are educated and in the middle class. Twenty-five years or so ago, the Organization for Rehabilitation and Training (ORT) established two schools in Mumbai, one for boys and one for girls, to provide vocational training.

The ORT schools became very popular among Jews and Gentiles alike. Soon services expanded to include classes in religion, Hebrew, and Israel studies. More recently, the Joint Distribution Committee (JDC) has become active in Mumbai, sending rabbis from America to help meet the community's religious and educational needs. The Israeli Consulate, too, serves as a community focus. Several of the synagogues in Mumbai have a full range of programs, from prayer services to singles groups to computer classes. Summer camps at a rural retreat center have provided an intense infusion of Jewish spirit to many of Mumbai's younger Jews. Kosher meat and wine, ritual objects, books, Indian Jewish calendars, and the accouterments of Judaic religious life are available, and India's generally tolerant approach to religions and religious pluralism bode well for the future of the Jewish community in Mumbai.

Smaller organized communities in Ahmedabad and Pune face more difficult challenges, but their synagogues are lively, and social and educational programs are well subscribed. In New Delhi there are only a handful of Bene Israel families, but they are augmented by Israeli and American diplomats and businesspeople. Regular prayers are held at the synagogue, and the Israeli Embassy helps out with the community's Passover Seder.

About fifty years ago, several shamans and leaders of tribal people in extreme eastern India (the states of Mizoram, Manipur, and Tripura) and western Myanmar (formerly Burma) began having dreams and visions which told them of their lost, true identity: that they were Jews of the Tribe of Menashe who had meandered from ancient Israel along the Silk Route to Kaifeng, China, then through Southeast Asia, finally settling in their current mountainous, remote homes. Their religious enthusiasm spread, such that today there are untold thousands of Kuki tribals on both sides of the border who are living as Jews. Some have gone to Israel, where they learned Hebrew, studied, and ultimately converted to Judaism, and have returned home as religious leaders. A number of synagogues have sprouted up, and now there are regular visits from Israeli and American coreligionists. A few now live in Israel, but most wait for their redemption. About a decade ago, a similar group emerged in Andhra Pradesh, a state on the Bay of Bengal on India's southeast coast, who call themselves Bene Ephraim.

Most demographics of Indian Jewry do not include these tribals, and there are no reliable estimates of their number, but it is incontestable that some of them have undergone conversion and are therefore Jewish. It is also the case that the vast majority are sincere in their beliefs and aspirations. Israeli immigration officials generally take an unsympathetic, skeptical approach, believing them to be opportunists who seek only a higher standard of living. Their passionate yearning for Israel has provoked controversy in Israel. Some accuse immigration authorities of racism, pointing out that many Russians who are not Jewish but who are white have been welcomed, but that these tribals who have at least some claim to Jewishness but who are not white, receive only scorn.

CHINA'S JEWS TODAY

The ancient community at Kaifeng was on its last legs when Jesuits first visited in the seventeenth century. Even then, local Jews bemoaned the withering away of traditions and observances: the dismal state of Hebrew learning, the lack of a rabbi. Their synagogue had been destroyed by a series of floods in during the seventeenth and eighteenth centuries and was subsequently rebuilt but in the aftermath of the 1857 flood, the community was to impoverished and isolated to rebuild it. Intermarriage was the rule and assimilation had worn down their sense of Jewish identity.

However, due to the interest of Jewish tourists and then to the establishment of diplomatic relations with Israel, the community has over the past twenty years experienced something of a rebirth. Where twenty years ago virtually no Jews or Jewish descendants were to be found, today there are hundreds of people in Kaifeng who claim to be Jews. Some petition the government to be allowed to list their ethnicity as Jewish on their identity cards. Others hope to learn something about the religion of their ancestors. One even went to rabbinical school in New York. There is talk of building a Jewish museum in Kaifeng, but it seems that the Chinese bureaucracy is reticent.

In Shanghai and Hong Kong, on the other hand, Jewish life seems to be on the rise. The former city is more significant from a historical point of view, whereas the latter has the more active Jewish life today.

Modern Jewish communities in China date to 1844, when one of the sons of Mumbai Jewish industrialist David Sassoon arrived. Elias Sassoon soon established his family's interests, mostly in opium, there and soon had offices in Guangzhou (formerly Canton) and Hong Kong as well. As soon as Japan was "opened" to Western trade in 1858, a branch office was opened in Tokyo. Jews from Calcutta, Iraq, and elsewhere soon followed.

Shanghai's synagogues were built during the late nineteenth century, and soon the city's Jewish community had its own newspaper and glossy magazine, a religious school, a secular school, a hospital, and chapters of the B'nai B'rith and Zionist organization at the same time as Shanghai's Sephardic community was coming of age and Ashkenazic Jews from Russia migrated east, following the overland trade route to Manchuria, especially the city of Harbin. These adventurers and furriers were soon joined by a wave of migration spurred by the 1917 Russian Revolution. Within a few years, Harbin had thirteen thousand Jews, and there were more in Tientsin and other cities. When the Japanese conquered Manchuria in 1931, most of these Ashkenazim moved to Shanghai, where they built their own synagogues and institutions. They were soon joined by German and Polish refugees from Hitler. At its peak, there were more than thirty thousand Jews in Shanghai—the only city in the world to remain open to Jewish immigration throughout World War II. The end of the war was followed by the Communist victory in China, at which time all but a handful of China's Jews left.

With China's opening to the West, and especially the establishment of diplomatic relations with Israel, commercial opportunities in Shanghai enticed a number of Jews to take up residence there, with the result that a Jewish community may be in the process of rebirth. The Chinese government recently refurbished one of the old synagogues in Shanghai, but only as a museum. Prayers are forbidden.

Hong Kong is home to a thriving, prosperous Jewish community of about five hundred families. The community itself dates to the Sassoon and Kadoorie families, who arrived during the middle of the nineteenth century. Jews played a significant role in the development of Hong Kong, having electrified the city and established the famous Star Ferry. Even the city's main thoroughfare, Nathan Road, is named for a Jewish governor of a century ago. The beautiful Ohel Leah Synagogue dates from the turn of the century, and the city has kosher facilities, a Jewish school, a historical society and library, and prayers are held at several locations. The question of economic inability facing Hong Kong's Jews is the same as that facing the entrepreneurial class as a whole, whose well-being is dependent upon the continued laissez-faire approach from Beijing.

There is also a small Jewish community in Taipei, led by an Ashkenazic native of Harbin. The community is composed of both Sephardic and Ashkenazic members as well as a handful of Jewish Chinese nationals.

JAPAN

Jews have lived in Japan since the Sassoons established themselves there in the mid-nineteenth century. Indian, Iraqi, and European Jews soon settled in Yokohama, Tokyo, Nagasaki, and Kobe.

Japanese attitudes toward Jews seem highly contradictory. Anti-Semitic literature enjoys great popularity among Japanese readers, who otherwise display no negative behavior toward Jews. During World War II, Japan was of course allied with Nazi Germany. Nevertheless, Japan afforded refuge to thousands of Eastern European Jews, including the entire Mir Yeshiva from Poland.

Among the Jews of Japan are Russian-speaking former residents of Manchuria and Shanghai, Indian and Middle Eastern Sephardim, and a variety of foreign Jewish temporary residents. There are synagogues in Tokyo and Kobe.

Since World War II, Japan has been especially fertile ground for the emergence of new religions, and Japan's longstanding, ambivalent fascination with the Jewish people had led to intriguing syncretic religious expressions. For example, there is a small but serious group led by Setsu Zau Abraham Kotsuji, who converted to Judaism. Another group, the fifty-thousand-plus strong Jewish-Christian Makuya, led by Professor Abraham Teshima, believes itself to be the lost tribe of Zevulun. Although they accept the Christian Messiah, they study Hebrew and visit Israel frequently.

SOUTHEAST ASIA

In the early nineteenth century, Baghdadis from Calcutta pursued their fortunes to Yangon in Myanmar, gradually joined by Bene Israel and a few Kochi Jews. Later that century they built their synagogue, which welcomes visitors to its well-maintained sanctuary today. Satellite communities emerged in many of Burma's trade and shipping centers: Mandalay, Myanmo, Moulmein, Bassein, Akyab, and Toungyi.

The community in Myanmar was virtually destroyed when the Japanese, suspicious of Jews as potential British sympathizers, conquered Burma and drove most of its 1,300 Jewish inhabitants to Calcutta. About five hundred returned after the war. Burmese Judaism enjoyed a brief flowering after independence and the establishment of cordial Israeli-Burmese relations, based on the warm friendship between prime ministers U Nu and David Ben-Gurion. After a military coup in 1962, the position of minorities in Burma degenerated, and most Jews left. A handful of Jewish descendants remain. Other Calcutta Jews migrated farther east, to Singapore, Malaya, Bangkok, Indonesia, and the Philippines.

As soon as Sir Stamford Raffles established a British settlement at Singapore in 1818, Indian Jews followed, mostly to pursue the opium trade. They settled in the Chinatown section that by the middle of the century had a synagogue and a cemetery. Twenty-five years later the community had migrated to what was then a suburban quarter, where they built the Maghain Aboth Synagogue, to be followed after another quarter century by Chesed El Synagogue and a religious school.

Out of a community, which at one time numbered two thousand, David Marshall was undoubtedly the first citizen. The island-nation's "father of independence," he was prime minister in 1955 and United Nations ambassador after that. Today about three hundred Jewish families, mostly Sephardim, can be found in the prosperous, tiny state, enjoying a full religious life under the leadership of an emissary of the Chabad-Lubavitch movement.

A handful of Jews reside in Bangkok as citizens of Thailand. In that country, law requires all nonethnic Thai citizens to adopt a Thai name, which has caused considerable distress among Muslims, the largest minority in Thailand. Jews have been the only group exempted from the law. The local community, comprising several hundred Sephardim and Ashkenazim, is augmented by a significant number of Jewish businessmen and young Israeli backpackers. Two synagogues are maintained, one in a residential area and the other in the business district, both led by a Chabad-Lubavitch emissary.

As the Inquisition reigned in Spain, Spanish Jews and marranos had an added impetus to join in Spanish voyages of exploration. They sailed to Mexico, the American colonies, Goa, the Philippines, and elsewhere. Sadly, the Inquisition followed them, and by 1580 an auto-da-fé was held in Manila.

By the last quarter of the nineteenth century, Jews from Alsace, Turkey, Syria, Lebanon, and Egypt began to settle openly in the Philippines. They were soon joined by Russian and central European Jews, who found their way to the Philippines via Harbin and Shanghai. After the Spanish-American War, American Jews added to Manila's community. In 1922 a formal congregation was established. Today about two hundred fifty Jews live in the Philippines on a permanent basis.

CONCLUSIONS

The study of Asian Jewish communities uproots several of our stereotypes. For example, the adage that "east is east and west is west" becomes transparent as a "colonizing myth" once a Jewish perspective is adopted. Their study also reconfigures our common understanding of Judaism and the Jewish people. It is commonly held that Judaism is one of the sources of Western civilization, and that Judaism is a Western religion. Such a view blinds us to Jewish experience in Asia; it silences the millennia-old rich cultural interactions between Judaic, Indic, and Sinitic cultures. On the other hand, Jews have traditionally spoken of themselves as an *am-olam*, a "universal people," a cultural and mercantile bridge in a world bifurcated in relatively recent times into an East and a West. The study of Asian Jewish experience debunks the Jews-as-Westerners view and confirms the traditional self-understanding as a truly universal people.

Jewish experience in Asia also provides the background to the ambassadorial-level relations established between Israel and India and between Israel and China in 1992. These relationships are becoming increasingly important for Israel. In 1999, for example, nonmilitary trade between Israel and India surpassed one billion dollars. Bilateral ventures in software development, transfer of agricultural technology, strategic and intelligence cooperation, as well as educational and cultural exchanges, are best understood as the most recent manifestation of very long friendships. While the economic and strategic benefits of these relationships may be obvious, their cultural impact may be the most significant for the long term.

BIBLIOGRAPHY

Elazar, Daniel J. 1989. *The Other Jews: The Sephardim Today.* New York: Basic Books.

Katz, Nathan. 2000. *Who Are the Jews of India?* Berkeley: University of California Press.

Katz, Nathan, and Ellen S. Goldberg. 1993. *The Last Jews of Cochin: Jewish Identity in Hindu India.* Columbia: University of South Carolina Press.

Lesley, Donald D. 1972. *The Survival of the Chinese Jews: The Jewish Community of Kaifeng.*Leiden: E. J. Brill.

Roland, Joan G. 1989. *Jews in British India: Identity in a Colonial Age.* Hanover, N.H.: University Press of New England.

PART IV

CHRISTIAN CULTURAL REGION

CHAPTER 24

THINKING GLOBALLY ABOUT CHRISTIANITY

HARVEY COX

SOME time around 1970 the demographic center of Christianity shifted. Since then the majority of the world's two billion Christians are no longer to be found in old European and North American precincts of Christendom, but in Asia, Africa, and South America. It is startling to realize that the two largest Christian countries in the world, after the United States, are Brazil and Mexico (with Russia and China close behind). Andrew Walls, the founder and director of the University of Edinburgh's Centre for the Study of Christianity in the non-Western World, contends that both the spiritual and intellectual center of Christianity has moved to "the southern world." Pressed about what this might mean for the Western church and its theologians, Walls, in an interview published in *Christian Century*, predicted that "it and they will be less significant for the future Christianity" (August 2–9, 2000: 795).

Walls is undoubtedly right. Still, I think that it would be premature to claim that the era of "Western" Christianity is over and the age of "global" Christianity is beginning. It would be more accurate to say that we entering an era of global Christianities in which the new ecumenical challenge will not be the relations between and among traditional Catholics and Orthodox and Protestant Christians, but the relations among them and the burgeoning new Christian communities that are now rooting themselves in Indic, Chinese, Inca, and African cultures.

This picture becomes even more complicated when one considers that even the Christianity of the Western world is changing. In two or three decades Western Christianity will increasingly have a Pentecostal and charismatic flavor. Not only will Euro-American Christians find themselves on the margin of global Christendom, but the "mainline" churches will find themselves there as well. How well equipped are Christian leaders and thinkers to address this new globalized situation?

The answer is not very promising. When I interviewed Christian leaders while researching my book on the rapid planetary growth of Pentecostalism, I found that these leaders viewed the rise of Pentecostalism with a mixture of bewilderment, fear, and condescension. They considered the emergent Christian theologies of the non-Western world as picturesque or exotic. The Euro-American theological obsession with "modernity"—a concern that is now nearly two centuries old—has not prepared them to grasp the most urgent theological issue of the day: how Christianity, especially the charismatic variety, can root itself in cultures steeped in Hindu, Buddhist, Confucian, and indigenous religious symbols and still remain Christian.

There are, however, some promising signs. Increasing numbers of younger theologians, from both northern and southern countries, are placing the task of developing a theology of "other religions" high on their agenda. Some of these theologians are Pentecostal.

Among the theological resources for thinking about Christianity in pluralistic cultures is a legacy of reflection that is often overlooked because of the way that Christian theology developed in the twentieth century, especially after Karl Barth. This was a current of Christian thought that took the emergence of world civilization and of globe-encircling religions seriously—something that Barth, despite his towering intellect, never did.

I first became aware of this legacy of global Christian thinking as a child in Sunday school when an overly cerebral young teacher told our fidgeting class about Oswald Spengler's *Decline of the West*. Our bespectacled mentor told us that the whole of Western Christian civilization was doomed to inevitable decline and would be succeeded by a new civilization from the East. In college, this impression was buttressed by a course on world history called "Centers of Civilization," which portrayed religious history in global perspective. In this course we jumped from Athens under Pericles (with Athena and Zeus) to Rome under Augustus (and the fading Roman pantheon) to Baghdad under Haroun al-Raschid (and a vigorous Islam), and then to Rome under Pope Innocent III (at the height of Medieval Catholicism), culminating with Washington under Wilson (whose deep-dyed Presbyterianism was passed over with little comment). We read secondary accounts, original sources in translation, and examples of the literature of these periods, and looked at slides of temples, cathedrals, and mosques. To some the course might have seemed superficial. But it kindled in me a lifelong love of the intertwined fields of religion and history.

With no formal religious study to guide me, I had to pursue my theological interests as a kind of auto-didact but with the help of some classmates who shared my enthusiasms. I was fascinated by writers such as F. S. C. Northrop, whose *The Meeting of East and West*, with its intriguing frontispiece of Georgia O'Keefe's "Two Blue Lines," offered a more hopeful scenario of East and West than Spengler had offered. I remember arguing with a Bryn Mawr student (they were all women then) about Toynbee. His *A Study of History* had just been reviewed by *Time* magazine, and we had both heard him lecture. It may be recalled that Toynbee thought only a revival of faith would prevent Western civilization from going down the drain foreseen by Spengler. On the basis of very little knowledge of his multivolume opus we debated energetically what we took to be his thesis. I thought it was wonderful. The Bryn Mawr student, a serious Presbyterian, said his theology was wooly. (She was probably right.)

In seminary I found the thinking to be much less global in scope. I entered just as the intellectual excitement of the "Neo-Orthodox" movement in Protestant theology, initiated by Karl Barth and represented in America by Reinhold Niebuhr, was making its impact. These theologians emphasized biblical categories and Reformation themes, and they did it with captivating flair and imagination. But to me something seemed missing. In doing their work so well, they concentrated on one particular tradition and tended to leave behind the musings of a previous generation of thinkers who had evidenced broader religious concerns. Despite my Neo-Orthodox formation, however, I never gave up my secret vice, and I still have those books on interreligious thinking on my shelf, replete with underlining and marginal comments.

When I began my doctoral work at Harvard in the late 1950s, the Barthian wind was still blowing. But there were other options. My doctoral mentor, James Luther Adams, a Unitarian, nursed an affection for this older, global way of thinking. While I was there both Christopher Dawson and Gabriel Marcel came to the Yard. I listened attentively to both, but since they were only visiting professors, they quickly passed through. Paul Tillich, with whom I took two advanced seminars, had started out as a philosopher of religion. He was then immersed in the writing of his *Systematic Theology* and somewhat preoccupied with rescuing his students from the influence of Barth. This was before his dramatic turn to an interest in world religions, which only happened after he moved to the University of Chicago and taught with Mircea Eliade. When, after my graduation, I returned to Harvard to teach I sometimes ate my brown-bag lunch with Wilfred Cantwell Smith who had come to direct the Center for the Study of World Religions. His book, *The Meaning and End of Religion*, though densely written, boldly took on some of the issues Neo-Orthodoxy had swept aside. He once actually had the audacity to offer a seminar on the possibilities of finding a "world faith." I suspect Smith welcomed me to our cheese-on-rye and coffee lunches even though I was a mere rookie, in part because there were not many other people around who appreciated the awesome scope of his projects.

But now we have globalization. Consequently, the somewhat suspect questions

that fascinated me in Sunday school, in college, and in graduate school are legitimate again, albeit in a somewhat different key. As an example of the heritage
worth retrieving let me cite a Harvard philosopher (who had already retired before
I arrived), William Ernest Hocking. He was the Alford Professor of Natural Religion, Moral Philosophy and Civil Polity until his retirement in 1943. His lifelong
preoccupation was the relationship of religions and civilizations. A serious Christian, as he matured in his career he became increasingly interested in Buddhism
and Hinduism but had an especially strong fascination for Islam. As early as 1934
he wrote an essay on "Christianity and Intercultural Contacts." In 1938 he deliv-
ered the Hibbert Lectures at the Universities of Cambridge and Oxford. They
were published in 1940 as *Living Religions and a World Faith*. In 1956 there appeared his *The Coming World Civilization*, which included a chapter entitled
"Christianity and the Faith of the Coming World Civilization." But, sadly, even
before Hocking died, both philosophy and theology had left his concerns behind.
Philosophy became absorbed with semantic analysis; and theology—Christian theology at least—was occupied with more manageable, tradition-specific issues.
True, Reinhold Niebuhr did publish a broadly conceived book toward the end of
his career, *The Structure of Nations and Empires*. But even his admirers concede
that it was one of his weakest efforts. He was more at home with the Hebrew
prophets, Augustine, Original Sin, and Calvin—as were most Christian thinkers
of his generation.

But there are some hints that the tide may be turning. Once again there is
lively public debate over the idea of civilizations. When Samuel Huntington published his famous essay, "The Clash of Civilizations" a few years ago, he was widely
criticized for pitting "the West against the rest" in the new post-cold war era. He
contended that civilizations would now become the major players, and—citing
Toynbee—that at the core of each civilization there was always a religious tradition. His gloomy analysis spoke darkly of "bloody boundaries" and implied the
real possibility of an ugly new era of holy wars.

Many of the criticisms of Huntington are quite valid, including the one made
by my colleague, Diana Eck, that Huntington's thesis does not take into sufficient
consideration the fact that the world religions are now no longer regionally defined as they once were. Muslims and Christians and Buddhists live everywhere
on the globe, interspersed with a variety of other peoples, creating a "marbling"
effect that raises serious questions about whether they could inspire religious wars
against another civilization. A second critique of Huntington is that all the various
civilizations of the world are being drawn relentlessly into the maw of market
culture and the religion of consumer consumption. Thus a unified, if tawdry,
single world civilization is emerging pasted together by MacDonald's and Hollywood, in which the classical religions may be reduced to folk artifacts and local
color. Even if these critiques are apt, however, Huntington's thesis has raised our
sights regarding religions and civilizations. He and his critics have re-opened an

intellectual Pandora's box—though it was never fully sealed. The older, larger questions are decidedly back on the table. It is no longer quaint to think about Hocking's fascination with "Christianity and the coming world civilization."

As we take up the agenda again, however, we must begin by recognizing that a few things have changed since Hocking, Toynbee, and the others. For example, the world religious traditions themselves are mutating faster than ever. Facilitated by their new proximity and "marbling," the on-the-ground interaction among the adherents of the various spiritual traditions has sped up. It takes place not just at conferences but at kitchen tables, barbecues, and in bars around the world. It has out-distanced the capacity of theologians within those traditions to guide or control it. Still, if somewhat futilely, they try. Ten years ago the Vatican was vexed about Latin American liberation theology. Today Rome loses sleep over Catholic theologians in Sri Lanka and Africa who are trying to re-think Christian theology within the categories of those ancient civilizations. The Sacred Congregation for the Doctrine of the Faith, it would seem, is now more worried about the incursion of karma than about the danger of class struggle.

Little by little the cheek-by-jowl cohabitation among the global faiths has begun to influence Western Christian thought. There was a time when Christian theologians could spin out a complete systematic theology, sometimes in many volumes, with no reference to other religions. Sometimes, when the last chapter (usually on eschatology) was finished, they might devote a kind of appendix to "other religions." Even those who took the dialogue with these alternative faiths seriously wrote as though one could round out a comprehensive Christian theology first, and then, fully equipped, enter it into the larger conversation. The possibility that the very pillars of Christian theology—Christology, revelation, sin and redemption, and the rest—should be re-thought in continuing conversation with analogous elements in other faiths had not yet seeped in.

But now the seeping has begun. It is becoming obvious to more and more Christian theologians, mainly younger ones, that it is simply idle to rehearse, for example, the Christian doctrine of Creation without reference to a tradition like Buddhism that flatly denies any such idea. How can one discuss traditional Christian teachings about death and resurrection without taking into account the fact that in America, for instance, an astonishing number of those polled tell interviewers (if not their priests and ministers) that they believe in some form of reincarnation? Or, can one proceed with Christian Christology—a topic that I have taught for the last ten years—without reference to the appreciative portraits of Jesus Christ now being sketched by Muslims, Jews, Hindus, and Buddhists?

I think not. It is also misleading to treat religion as an entity separate from other aspects of society and politics, as we still sometimes do in the West. Today movements that appear on the surface to be secular nonetheless demonstrate unmistakable religious characteristics. Both nationalists and Communists became infamous for their shrines, saints, holy books, hymns, and *rites de passage*. At the same time, movements that appear to be religious frequently exhibit patently secular purposes. Still, despite these changed parameters and confusing borders, the questions that Neo-Orthodoxy swept under the rug are heaving into view. Here are some of the premises on which they will have to be addressed, as we think globally about Christianity.

First, for blessing or for bane, we *will* have a world civilization. When Hocking and Toynbee and their cohort talked about a world civilization, it was still a surmise or a hope. Today we are there, or nearly so. Some perceive its arrival as a disaster, the ultimate triumph of multinational corporations. Others greet it as the golden dream of the centuries come true at last. Still others see it as a process whose end product is still indistinct but which is subject to mid-course correction. But no one disputes the actuality: the global world civilization is upon us whether we like it or not.

Second, religions will play some role in the coming world civilization. What role is unclear. In some places, the rootedness of indigenous traditions throws up a bulwark against the incursions of globalization at least for a season. At the same time, some historians claim that the religions such as Christianity that are already global have laid the foundation for a worldwide society. Were he alive today, Arnold Toynbee would no doubt contend that no civilization, including presumably a world civilization, can exist for long without a core of symbols, myths, and narratives that preserve and transmit its values and meanings. In other words, no world religion, no world civilization. But others contend that "the advent of modern science, mass literacy and instant global communication, have rendered religion superfluous." For Christians this argument raises the fascinating question that haunted Dietrich Bonhoeffer toward the end of his life, as he sat in the Gestapo prison, when he suggested that we were entering a "post-religious" age that would require a "non-religious interpretation of the Gospel." The deeper question implied by his comments is whether Christianity is essentially, or only accidentally, a "religion."

Given all these elusive factors, it is obvious that answers to all the questions wrapped in the topic of "Christianity and the coming world civilization" are not available. Still, short-range projections are possible. If we are scourged by nuclear war, a worldwide economic collapse, or an ecological disaster—none of which are out of the question—then all bets are off. But given present tendencies, this is what we might well expect of religion(s), including Christianity, and of civilization(s) in the near-term future.

First, the painful divisions within religious traditions will continue. Encounters between traditions open and closed, experiential and doctrinal, hierarchical and congregational, dialogical and dogmatic, will deepen. Fundamentalist Christians, Muslims, and Jews will continue to reserve their most scurrilous polemics not for adherents of other faiths but for their fellow religionists whom they view as traitors. (These internal divisions, incidentally, make the kind of clash of civilizations Huntington anticipates even less likely.)

Second, global communication will get faster while human attention spans get shorter, altering both civilization and religion. Technology has always had an effect on civilization. The Romans knit together their sphere of influence, which was nearly "global" for its time, with a then unparalleled system of highways. The British plied the sealanes. America unified itself, geographically at least, with shining rails and a golden spike. Today we have the Internet. But the burden of the information overload is already taking its toll on our limited capacity to absorb, process, and evaluate the multiple signals. Religion in the past has cultivated the long view, and has often encouraged people to slow down on occasion through meditation practices and institutions like the Sabbath. We may already be seeing the beginning of a backlash against speed and overload. The evidence can be detected in the popularity of meditation techniques and retreat centers. The danger is that religion could become no more than a service sector to the global civilization, no longer shaping its values but repairing the spiritual damage it inflicts.

Third, the current direction of global civilization will likely lead to nuclear or ecological calamities unless fundamental changes are introduced. Christianity, along with the other world religions, could play a role in altering the course of this direction. Experts differ on what the first global catastrophe might be—of water, air, climate, or arable soil—but few disagree that unless present consumption patterns change, it will occur sooner rather than later.

Perpetuating an economy whose logic is infinite expansion on a finite planet enhances the possibility of such a disaster. Moreover, the entrance of China into the world economy could strain the earth's resources even further. The idea of one billion new customers consuming petroleum and other hydrocarbons, and then expelling their residues into the atmosphere, is enough to terrify any ecologist. Religions have traditionally taught that restraint, and a recognition of limits, are virtues to be cultivated, not antiquated habits to be outgrown. But will Christianity, or any religion, be enough to challenge the inner logic of planetary market capitalism? So far the evidence is not entirely encouraging.

The capitalist market system has so far succeeded in making many promises of more wealth for all, but has produced instead more division and a wider gulf between haves and have-nots. Christianity has traditionally counseled the rejection of excess riches, especially when they are won at the expense of others. For the most part, however, religions have addressed economic disparity with alms and charity. They have not—with some important exceptions—confronted the structural sources of inequality. It now appears that those exceptions, like Islamic notions of a righteous economy, the medieval Christian doctrine of the just price, the social gospel movement and liberation theology, need to be brought from the past and from theology's edges into the center of reflection on the ethical responsibilities of a global civilization.

Fourth, as Christianity increasingly becomes a global faith, it will engage in the selective retrieval of components of other traditions. This is also true of the other religions. To most people, the major traditions appear less and less like discreet entities, hermetically sealed off from one another. Most people view them as wells from which to draw, or as tool kits from which to choose the elements that give meaning to their lives. This often infuriates the guardians of these traditions who cherish them as indivisible wholes—though one might question whether in fact, they ever have been.

The best scholarship today questions the idea of "religions" as discreet entities that sail through history like battleships in a fleet, with wide expanses of open sea churning between them, interacting at their edges if at all. Instead, historians suggest that the so-called "religions"—be they Christianity, Judaism, Islam, or Buddhism—are conceptual constructions projected on a past that in reality was characterized more by interaction than by separateness. Historians such as Daniel Boyarin and Karen King question whether there was something called "Judaism" in the first century CE, for instance, and something else called "early Christianity" that separated from it and was in conflict with it. They suggest that the actual picture at the time was far more complex. The same could be said for the history of what we now call "Buddhism," which many Hindus see as merely another variant of their heterogeneous tradition.

I am not one of those who believes, as some in Hocking's generation did, that a single world civilization will inevitably result in a single world religion. If anything, we may be headed in a very different direction. As globalization seeks to spread its web to every nook and cranny, it is—unexpectedly, perhaps—evoking resistance from local, indigenous religions some had thought to be moribund. It might amaze Cortez to know that five hundred years after his conquest of Mexico ("for gold and for souls" as he put it), the spiritual traditions he thought he had defeated are staging a recovery. How else are we to explain the fusion of Catholic and Mayan images that inspired the Zapatista uprising in Chiapas? What is especially intriguing about this revival is that it occurred not against but within Catholicism. This suggests another question for Christianity in a global age. Might the rebirth of local spiritualities—Native North America, Celtic, indigenous South American, black African—take place within, and even under the sponsorship of, historically mainstream Christianity? Might the same process also occur in other global religious traditions? There is some confirmation that it might.

The fifth point about Christianity in an era of globalization is in regard to the expanding role of women. In Christian churches everywhere women increasingly are exercising leadership. After millennia of marginalization, they are now involved in Christian teaching and research, and in ministerial and priestly functions. There is a parallel development in the other faiths, where women are active in teaching Torah, leading Buddhist retreat centers, and interpreting the Qur'an. The question is still open as to what impact this wholly new kind of liturgical and theological leadership will have.

This inventory could undoubtedly be extended. And it will change as new, unforeseen factors will emerge. Who knows what rough and unshaped beasts are slouching toward Bethlehem, Benares, Kyoto, and countless other places to be born? As they do, and as religions go global, I am content that Christian theological reflection will rise to wrestle with this ample agenda of global change.

BIBLIOGRAPHY

Eck, Diana. 2001. *A New Religious America: How a "Christian" Country Has Become the World's Most Religiously Diverse Nation*. San Francisco: Harper Press.

Hervieu-Leger, Daniele. 1993. "Permanence et devenir du religieux dans les societes europeenes." *Autre Temps* 38 (June): 33–34.

Hessel, Dieter T., and Rosemary Radford Reuther. 2000. *Christianity and Ecology*. Cambridge, Mass.: Harvard University Press.

Hocking, William Ernest. 1940. *Living Religions and a World Faith*. New York: Macmillan Publishers.

————. 1956. *The Coming World Civilization*. New York: Harper Press.

Huntington, Samuel. 1996. *The Clash of Civilizations and the Remaking of World Order*. New York: Simon and Schuster.

Northrup, F. S. C. 1946. *The Meeting of East and West: An Inquiry Concerning World Understanding*. New York: Macmillan Publishers.

Rouner, Leroy, ed. 1966. *Philosophy, Religion, and the Coming World Civilization: Essays in Honor of William Ernest Hocking*. The Hague: Martinus Nijhoff.

Smith, Wilfred Cantwell. 1991. *The Meaning and End of Religion*. Minneapolis: Fortress Press.

Spengler, Oswald. 1939. *Decline of the West*. New York: Knopf.

Toynbee, A. J. 1947–1957. *Study of History*. 10 vols. New York: Oxford University Press.

Walls, Andrew. 2000. "The Expansion of Christianity: An Interview with Andrew Walls." *Christian Century*, August 2–9: 795.

Yong, Amos. 1999. " 'Not Knowing Where the Wind Blows': On Envisioning a Pentecostal-Charismatic Theology of Religions." *Journal of Pentecostal Studies* 14 (April): 81–91.

CHAPTER 25

....

WESTERN EUROPEAN CATHOLIC SOCIETIES

....

KAREL DOBBELAERE

WESTERN Europe has historically been considered the heart of Catholic Christianity. Yet it is fair to ask whether there are still Catholic countries in Europe. France, which was once called "the oldest daughter of the Church," has become what might be described as a laicized republic with a Catholic culture. This suggests that, although laicized, its culture is still imbued with the Catholic meaning-system that is attested to by some of its symbols, mores, and folklore. In fact, only the Irish republic is not completely differentiated from Catholicism. In all other so-called Catholic countries—Austria, Belgium, Italy, Luxembourg, Portugal, and Spain—there is a separation of church and state: they are politically secularized. The laicization of the state, which is an antagonistic form of secularization, characterizes the difference between France and the other European Catholic societies. However, in the last decennium, we have noticed a laicization policy conducted by Belgian and Spanish governments supported by parties in which manners of atheistic lodges are prominent.

In France, the sociologic of laicization is characterized by a conflict that opposes *la République laïque* to the church resulting in anti-clericalism and the elaboration of an alternative meaning-system, i.e., a nonreligious vision of man and the world. Crucial in the elaboration of such a laicized doctrine was the formulation of universal moral principles replacing all religious and metaphysical creeds. This anti-religious civil religion permeated the state schools, whose teachers were its missionaries, in contrast to the secularized Catholic countries where the state and the state-schools are religiously neutral. Within the *République laïque* a split occurred between militant faith and militant unbelief and, as David Martin has suggested, the split was endlessly reproductive of itself down to the local level: *curé* (parish priest) against schoolmaster, even mother against father; it was transmitted from generation to generation through rival school systems; and it heavily reinforced other fissures such as social class. That this split is still latently present became manifest in recent conflicts. In 1984, thousands of French citizens marched in Versailles, with bishops leading the demonstration, against a government proposal to create a unified and laicized public service for national education. In 1994, large numbers of people marched through Paris in defense of state schools and in opposition to a government proposal to allow local communities to augment their financing of investment in private schools, until then limited to 10 percent.

In laicized France—contrary to other Catholic and duopolistic countries like Germany, the Netherlands, and Switzerland where Catholics are a large minority—no *pillarized* organizations emerged, since the French Catholics were divided between republicans and monarchists; the bishops, linked to reactionary politics, were weak; and Catholic mass organizations emerged only in the interbellum period, in response to a papal demand to organize Catholic action in response to the secularization of society. Consequently, French Catholicism lacked political and social organizations that were independent of the church and which might have established a pillar. Pillarization emerged in neither Spain nor Portugal, where the Catholic Right had succeeded in taking over the reins of power, calling their organic social order a "Christian civilization." Since the state used the church in so instrumental a manner, some segments of the church began to perceive this as a danger for its own mission and stimulated the church to regain its own autonomy by initiating the process of functional differentiation, thus producing the secularization of society.

All other Catholic and duopolistic Western European societies are characterized by vertical integration as a result of the emergence in the late nineteenth century of Catholic, Protestant, and Socialist pillars. The concept of pillarization refers to a process by which pillarized structures are erected. Such organizational complexes striving toward autarky, or self-sufficiency, are active, on a religious or ideological basis, in areas that are primarilly defined as secular. The more services a pillar renders, the more self-sufficient it is. A very good example of such an autarkic organizational complex is the Catholic pillar in Belgium. It embraces schools (from kindergarten to university), hospitals, old peoples' homes, youth movements, cultural associations, sport clubs, newspapers, magazines, book clubs, and libraries. It also has professional associations, a health insurance fund, a trade union, and a political party, the Christian People's Party. The Catholic pillar provides almost all possible services from the cradle to the grave. In contrast to social classes, which integrate people on a horizontal basis, pillars do so more on a vertical basis. Clearly, such structures may produce exclusiveness and an in-group mentality.

How is the emergence and the extension of such a process of pillarization to be explained? For Catholics and Protestants alike, pillarization was a radical reaction to the process of functional differentiation that accelerated in the second half of the ninetenth century. In the Catholic world, it was a reactive policy: the clergy and part of the religious elite started to create a world segregated from the secularized world. In fact, to check the impact of secularization and to preserve church control over the Catholic part of the population, they reverted to an older process of differentiation: segmentary differentiation, i.e., the duplication of services in those sectors that were functionally differentiated from the religious subsystem. If the state and the differentiated subsystems were no longer to be organized according to the Catholic doctrine, then the new civic liberties provided the opportunity for the establishment of separate Catholic organizations to protect believers from a secular, that is, an a- or anti-religious ideology. We may conclude, then, that it was the process of functional differentiation resulting in a proces of secularization that provoked Catholic pillarization: "dikes" were built to prevent the secularization of the church's flock, but in the Netherlands and Switzerland, the Catholic pillar also had an emancipatory function, and the same was true of the Dutch Protestant pillar. The Socialist pillars were first and foremost emancipatory. Through the integration of their organizations in one complex, they augmented their power, and the Socialist Party became the political expression of this organizational complex. In the first part of the twentieth century the Catholic organizations were also gradually organized into a more centralized pillar of which the emerging Catholic party was the political expression. Hence in Stein Rokkan's terms, we may speak about an institutionalized pillar, interlocking a corporate and a political channel. The quasi-omnipresence of Catholic pillars in Western Europe may be seen as a segmentary reduction of *omnia instaurare in Christo* (edify all in Christ). The organizational force and the populism of the Catholic Church, staffed by a large number of priests and religious people, allowed the church to adopt a strategy as a response to the modern world as a way of protecting its flock from secular influences. Was it a successful strategy? Did it prevent the effect of the secularization of society on individual religiosity?

Functional differentiation produced not only secularization but also the concomit-tant processes of functional rationalization and societalization and, as Niklas Luhmann has pointed out, the other side of the coin was the proces of individualization, a proces which, according to Robert Bellah, has a utilitarian and an expressive side. Liliane Voyé and I analyzed the impact of these modernization processes on Catholics and lapsed Catholics in all fourteen Western and Northern European countries covered by the European Valus Study (EVS) of 1990. We used age (the younger the people the more exclusively they have lived in a secularized world), level of education (which measures the extent to which people have been exposed to science and technical knowledge with their attendant de-sacralization of the content of learning), and sex (since women, until more recently, have been less instrumentally socialized) as proxy variables for secularization. On all dimensions of religiosity—religiousness (experiential dimension); orthodoxy and Christian worldview (belief dimension); membership, involvement, and rites of passage (ritual dimension); and confidence in church, sexual and bioethical morality, and civic morality (consequential dimension)—older people and women scored highest, the more educated lowest, and thus revealing the impact of secularization. Expressive individualism—operationalized in qualities of independence and imagination, which are basic to the "freedom to express oneself"—was also negatively associated with these different dimensions of religiosity. Age was the crucial variable: it had the highest total effect on all dimensions of religiosity, since it was negatively associated with the level of education and positively with expressive individualism.

In a study of Catholic and Protestant Europeans by Jagodzinski and myself, the impact of age on church involvement was also the most important single variable. Consequently, we asked ourselves what the sociological meaning of age was: did it express a life-cycle effect, period effects, or generational differences? Our analysis per country and per religion demonstrated that the contagion model of generational change fitted the data best. This model suggests that secularization gradually undermines the basic beliefs of traditional religion but that this does not immediately become manifest in behavioral change. Specific events are necessary before these internal doubts turn into overt protest and exit. For example, public criticism from theologians, public disapproval in the media of church documents and policies, or public controversies about synodal or concilliar resolutions, make it apparent that religious beliefs and the religious understanding of ethics and church authority are already very much undermined. A convergence of one's *public* behavior and *private* disbelief may then follow, which promotes both exit from the churches and a decline in church involvement of those who remain. The model predicts that the younger cohorts will react more rapidly to these specific events since they do not have to give up ingrained habits. Older cohorts might always remain at higher levels of church involvement, partly because they are less affected by the process of secularization and partly because some of them are unwilling to change their religious outlook. However, in general, a change in all cohorts is expected, but a differential one, within fairly short time periods. The criticism of churchly traditions, and the public discussions accompanying it, contagiously undermine the religious behavior of all generations but particularly of the younger generations. To be sure, this model postulates a generational change because, after the periods of rapid decay, all cohorts are much less religious than before. Does this major trend exclude small life-cycle effects? No: in the Catholic Church, parents, and especially mothers, may return for a short period to church on Sundays during the period that their children undergo one or two years of cathechism prior to confirmation; or some people in their old age may return to higher levels of church involvement.

How did the Catholic pillars react to these changes in affiliation and involvement? We may distiguish two models of adaptation, clearly exemplified by changes in the Netherlands and Belgium. In the Netherlands, the Catholic pillar started to totter as a consequence of crisis in the religious culture. Christian parties lost voters, and Protestant and Catholic parties merged into a new party, the Christian Democratic Appeal. National and local federations and mergers of Catholic, Protestant, and neutral organizations were also registered. Catholic newspapers abandoned their religious signature, and Protestant and Catholic radio and television stations lost large numbers of members. Related factors also contributed to the changes: the professionalization of services, a shortage of funds, and legal restrictions in the world of education and health. In Belgium, on the contrary, secularization and related processes did not break up the pillars. The absence of Protestant and neutral organizations and the antagonism between the existing pillars precluded mergers and the erection of federations such as occurred in the Netherlands: instead the *particular* Catholic legitimation of the pillar was *universalized* into a broader Christian legitimation. This resulted in a new collective consciousness: *sociocultural Christianity*, the formulae of which are less precise than the former church norms and consequently less imperative. Its core values entail, on the one hand, the legitimation of vertical pluralism on the basis of the constitutional right of freedom of assembly and choice, subsidiarity, private enterprise, and economic efficiency; and, on the other hand, the articulation of its own specific character, the so-called Christian identity, in evangelical values; that is, a humane approach toward members, clients, and patients, the *Gemeinschaftlichkeit* of Christian institutions, solidarity between social classes, stewardship, well-being, and self-development. This "sacred canopy" is still symbolized by a "C," referring more and more to Christian values and norms, i.e, evangelical ones, rather than to typical Catholic norms, since "Catholic" was considered to have a more restrictive appeal. The more economically oriented organizations of the pillar invoke especially that part of the legitimation which refers to vertical pluralism. The sociocultural organizations refer mainly to so-called Christian values. It might be argued, of course, that these values are not uniquely Christian, not even in their specific combination, but by backing them up with a religious source they acquire a sacred aura, which is occasionally solemnized with religious ritual. This universalization of its values was a successful innovation that not only consolidated but even extended the power base of the now Christian pillar. However, in the long run, the Christian pillar may become deinstitutionalized since the electoral appeal of its political channel is continually shrinking: the in-coming generations are not replacing the outgoing older generations.

Secularization and the ensuing loss of authority of the buttressing organizations making up the religious subsystem had a negative effect on the religious collective consciousness, which became less specific and more general. The new collective consciousness of the Belgian Christian pillar attests to that. And, according to the European Values Study Surveys, specific religious beliefs are also being replaced by more general notions: for example, a general belief (or is it only a hope?) in a hereafter is replacing the specific Catholic notions of heaven, hell, and purgatory. As Emile Durkheim already noted (1964: 167–73), if norms become less precise and are replaced by general principles, discussions extend even to articles of faith that were once beyond discussion. Being questioned, they lose part of their force, the collective conscience becomes less imperative, and for this very reason, it wields less restraint over the free development of individual varieties. Consequently, the individual may now develop unorthodox beliefs, various degrees of belief and unbelief, and engage in "mixing of codes." Referring to postmodernity, Liliane Voyé (1995:199–204) suggests that the individual religiosity of some Catholics is characterized by the "end of Great Narratives," a certain reenchantment of the World, and a "mixing of codes." This mixing of codes is, according to her, reflected in a three-fold manner: references and practices blending the institutional and the popular; occasional borrowings from scientific discourses as well as from religious sources; and inspiration sought in diverse religions, notably, oriental religions. In olden times, the church was able to impose its doctrines, at least publicly. What people thought we may only guess, but they would never publicly proclaim a "religion à la carte." Now bricolage is publicly accepted, notwithstanding the official opposition of the church (e.g., according to the EVS nearly 20 percent of Catholics mix some form of reincarnation with typical Catholic beliefs).

The decay of the Catholic religious consciousness has also opened up the religious market for sectarian and new religious movements, which are more in evidence in Italy and France than in the other so-called Catholic countries. Parliamentary commissions in France and Belgium—two countries without a religiously pluralistic past—have reacted very negatively toward their spread, especially under the impact of conservative Catholics and the atheistic lodges. Finally, studies in France and recently in Belgium have indicated that the waning of Catholicism's institutional influence has been a factor in contributing to the spread of astrology newspaper columns and the increase of the market of horoscopes, the belief in clairvoyance, witchcraft, divination, ghosts, and the development of beliefs and practices in the paranormal and occult sciences.

Do these trends allow us to predict the fading away of Catholicism in that part of the world that once was its stronghold? For sure, the number of nuclear Catholics has rapidly diminished since the sixties: in 1990, only 30 percent of the Catholics interviewed in the frame of the EVS attended mass at least once a week; France and Belgium are below and Italy and especially Ireland are above this average. At the same time the number of people not affiliated with a church was rapidly increasing in five of the so-called Catholic countries included in the 1981 and 1990 EVS (Belgium, France, Ireland, Italy, and Spain), from 12 to 21 percent. Other Catholics, who make up the vast majority, turn toward the church only for celebrations of rites of passage (baptism, confirmation, church marriage, and church funeral) and for incantations. The church functions, then, as a "service station": to give a sacred aura to changes in the life-cycle and to help people to overcome difficult moments in life. Candlelight, blessings, charms, and novenas are good examples of the latter, as are pilgrimages, which may inform us about the polysemic nature of religious rituals.

All countries have local and regional places of pilgrimage to venerate saints, but especially the Holy Mother. Regional sanctuaries near borders often have an international radiation. However, those with a real international appeal are Lourdes (France) and Fatima (Portugal), where the Blessed Virgin is said to have appeared. For individuals, pilgrimages to sanctuaries have different functions, which may or may not be combined. First of all, there is the function of a quest. According to several studies done in Belgium, people pray for health, the maintenance or the restoration of harmonious familial and friendship relations, success in examinations and on the job, but also for religious reasons, e.g., that their deceased spouse should find eternal peace. The beneficiaries of the quests are overwhelmingly family members and friends, but also the pilgrim her- or himself. Irregular churchgoers and marginal Catholics especially formulate such quests, as do nuclear Catholics, but the latter also go on pilgrimage to *worship*. Many also go to *thank* the Madonna for a received grace. Pilgrimages for *penance*, on the other hand, which were sometimes requested by religious authorities, are now largely a thing of the past. The most remarkable exception is St. Patrick's Purgatory in Ireland, where pilgrims still mortify themselves on Station Island for at least three days. However, it should be noted that for many Catholics, a pilgrimage may also be an occasion to go to confession. Pilgrimages may also have the function of *revivifying one's faith*. People go to places marked by the presence of the founder or his disciples, e.g., Palestine and Rome, and, as the Turners (1978) have pointed out, these places, better than others, are a reminder of the fundamental principles of the Bible and the church. They also seem to restore the *Communitas* and God's order in opposition to the order of the world. Liliane Voyé (1991) has suggested that this may be one of the reasons why the words of the pope are heard all over the world, since they come from a "liminal" place, an otherworldly place, expressing some basic values that are defined as "desirable."

But pilgrimages may also articulate the identity of a collectivity. Santiago de Com-postella (Spain), Europe's second most important place of pilgrimage, expresses its Christian identity. Identified with the *reconquista* of the Christian territories against the "infidels," i.e., the Moors, it has been famous since the eleventh century as a substitute for the pilgrimage to Palestine, which was considered a perilous destination because of the invasion of the Holy Land by the Turks. In 1989, during his pilgrimage to Compostella, the pope clearly articulated this idea: "The whole of Europe has again met around the memorial of Santiago as in those centuries during which Europe was being built, becoming an homogeneous and spiritually united continent" (Catholic Documentation, no. 1841: 1128); in other words, a *Christian* continent, which, according to the pope, means a Catholic Europe. This proclamation of, if not a Catholic, at least a Christian Europe, is favorably received by the authorities of the European Commission, which, according to Jacques Delors, its former president, is searching for its soul.

Pilgrimages may also express national, regional, and local identites. The Irish go to Knock, where the Blessed Virgin appeared in 1879, to express their faith but also to revindicate the reunion of Ireland; and the Portuguese emigrant workers, returning to their country, go on pilgrimage to Fatima to reaffirm their belonging to the Portuguese nation. The same is true of regional saints—like Saint Odile, patron of the Alsace, and Saint Anne, patron of the Bretons, in France—and the regional madonnas like the Virgins of Montserrat or of the *Desemparats* in Valencia or *del Pilar* in Zaragoza (Spain). According to Marlène Albert-Llorca (1994: 37–40) these Virgin Marys are particularized by the place and their names but also by their physiognomy and their clothes. They symbolize a particular place, although always being the Virgin Mary, mother of Christ and "Queen of the world." In fact, of all the saints, it is the Madonna who expresses best of all at the same time the universal pretentions of the Catholic Church and its capacity to particularize itself and even to express the existence of the local. These sanctuaries are like the totemic places where the clans unite to celebrate their "corrobbori" or religious ceremonies, (Durkheim); they express a national, regional, local, or even professional allegiance. One has only to observe the processions toward the sanctuaries: a number of pilgrims are dressed in local attire, carrying the national, regional, and local flags; the banners of their association or profession; and the statues of their saints, which are the emblems of their clan or the profession.

In Western Europe, Catholicism is an expression of institutional involvement only for a small minority: it survives for the vast majority as a service station capable of sacralizing important passages in the life-cycle, offering means for incantations, and providing symbols which express identities. It is involved in the secular world through its pillars: however, these refer to universal values which are given a sacred aura in reference to the Gospel, rather than to the particular rules of the church.

BIBLIOGRAPHY

Albert-Llorca, M. 1994. "La fabrique du Sacré: Les Vierges 'miraculeuses' du pays valencien." *Genèses*, no. 17: 33–51.

Davie, G., and D. Hervieu-Léger, eds. 1996. *Identités religieuses en Europe*. Paris: Éditions la Découverte.

Dobbelaere, K., and W. Jagodzinski. 1995. "Religious Cognitions and Beliefs." In J. van Deth and E. Scarbrough, eds., *The Impact of Values*, 197–217. Oxford: Oxford University Press.

Dobbelaere, K., and L. Voyé. 1996. "Europäische Katholiken und die katholische Kirche nach dem Zweiten Vatikanischen Konzil." In F.-X. Kaufmann and A. Zingerle, eds., *Vatikanum II und Modernisierung: Historische, theologische und Soziologische Perspektiven*, 209–232. Paderborn: Ferdinand Schöningh.

Durkheim, E. 1964. *The Division of Labor in Society*. Trans. George Simpson. New York: Free Press.

Gannon, T. M. 1988. *World Catholicism in Transition*. New York: Macmillan.

Jagodzinski, W., and K. Dobbelaere. 1995. "Secularization and Church Religiosity." In J. van Deth and E. Scarbrough, eds., *The Impact of Values*, 76–119. Oxford: Oxford University Press.

———. 1995. "Religious and Ethical Pluralism." In J. van Deth and E. Scarbrough, eds., *The Impact of Values*, 218–49. Oxford: Oxford University Press.

Martin, D. 1978. *A General Theory of Secularization*. Oxford: Basil Blackwell.

Roof, W. C., J. W. Carroll, and D. A. Roozen, eds. 1995. *The Post-War Generation and Establishment Religion: Cross-Cultural Perspectives*. Oxford: Westview Press.

Turner, V., and E. Turner. 1978. *Image and Pilgrimage in Christian Culture: Anthropological Perspectives*. New York: Columbia University Press.

Voyé, L. 1991. "Les jeunes et le mariage religieux: une émancipation du sacré." *Social Compas* 38, no. 4: 405–416.

———. "From Institutional Catholicism to 'Christian Inspiration': Another Look at Belgium." In W. C. Roof, J. W. Carroll, and D. A. Roozen, eds. *The Post-War Generation and Establishment Religion: Cross-Cultural Perspectives*, 191–206. Oxford: Westview Press.

CHAPTER 26

EASTERN EUROPEAN CATHOLIC SOCIETIES

SABRINA P. RAMET

THOUGH Catholicism is found worldwide, in Eastern Europe it is the predominant religious affiliation of the region. It is the majority religion of the national societies of Poland, Slovakia, Slovenia, and Croatia and it is the largest faith in the Czech Republic and Hungary. There are also smaller Catholic communities in other Eastern European countries. The largest Catholic population in Eastern Europe is Poland, with more than 36 million Catholics; the smallest Catholic communities in Eastern Europe are those of Bulgaria, Macedonia, and Serbia. In Bulgaria, for instance, there are about fifty thousand Catholics.

During the Communist era, beginning around 1945 to 1948 and continuing to around 1989–90, the Catholic Church labored under various limitations. In Albania, Catholicism, together with all other religious associations, was completely illegal from 1967 until 1990. In some other countries in the region, episcopal appointments were subjected to strict party control, Catholic newspapers were subject to censorship, seminary curricula were reviewed and controlled by party commissars, church construction and repair were controlled, and a steady propaganda campaign was waged against believers and their beliefs. After the collapse of the Communist organizational monopoly 1989–90, the situation of religious associations in the area changed dramatically. The Catholic Church, no longer compelled to be on the defensive, undertook to promote its own program for society. This has been especially noticeable in Poland, where the Catholic Church succeeded in having restrictions imposed on access to abortion, in establishing guidelines for the "protection of Christian values" in television and radio broadcasts, and in introducing Catholic religious instruction in public schools. Where believers were on the defensive in the Communist era, nonbelievers have complained of discrimination in Poland, Croatia, and elsewhere in the region since 1989.

ORIGINS AND HISTORY UNTIL THE 1800S

Christianity spread throughout the Mediterranean area by the fourth century, gradually suppressing its chief rival, the Cult of Mithra. Christianity became the dominant religion in the city of Zadar, for example, by around 300 CE. Czar Boris of Bulgaria converted to Christianity in 864 and brought that religion to the Romanians as well. Poland converted to Christianity in 966, although pre-Christian polytheist religion endured in the countryside for several centuries thereafter. Hungary accepted Christianity in the year 1000.

In the course of the first millennium the claims of the bishop of Rome to primacy became steadily clearer and more comprehensive, culminating in a drive to impose doctrinal and ritual uniformity in the tenth and eleventh centuries. In the eastern Mediterranean these claims were disputed, resulting in a growing dispute in the ninth through eleventh centuries. The Holy See was interested, inter alia, in seeing Latin established as the exclusive liturgical language and the Latin alphabet as the sole ecclesiastical alphabet. In this connection, a dispute arose in the mid-eleventh century between the Holy See and the Catholic community of Dalmatia, concerning the latter's use of the Glagolitic alphabet and preference of Old Church Slavonic as the language of liturgy. Gregory, bishop of Nin, led the resistance against Rome and at the Council of Split. In 1079, the pope relented and allowed the community to retain its traditional alphabet and liturgical language. With time, however, these local variations gave way to the Latin standard.

The Eastern and Western churches were, thus, already growing apart when the so-called *filioque controversy* in the eleventh century finalized the split between the Orthodox Church (to the East) and the Catholic Church (to the West and north). The date 1054 has been traditionally associated with this ecclesiastical schism, though it would be artificial to pin the long process of fissure on a single year. Even so, the short reign of Pope Leo IX (1049–54) is associated with the assertion of papal authority, including the sphere of dogma.

The Latin Church, as it was often called in those centuries, faced a new challenge in the early fifteenth century from Hussite-Taborite reformers in Bohemia, who denied the church doctrine of transsubstantiation (the doctrine that the bread and wine are transformed into the flesh and blood of Christ in the course of the Holy Mass). Although inspired by the martyred preacher Jan Hus, the Taborites were led in turn by Václav Koranda and Prokop Holy, and held off Catholic armies for some twenty years before they were finally subdued at the Battle of Lipany in 1434. In spite of this defeat, they were granted toleration in the peace treaty of 1436 (the so-called Compact of Iglau), enjoying the fruits thereof until the 1620s.

Pope Clement VI (reigned 1342–52) had already declared that indulgences might be granted for good works, drawing upon the treasury of merits won by Christ; an indulgence was understood as a release for part of the stain of sin, and hence from some of the penalty to be paid in the hereafter. In the early sixteenth century, Pope Leo X (1475–1521; reigned 1513–21) extended generous patronage of the arts, authorized a lavish building program, became embrangled in wars between France and Spain, and even planned a crusade against the Turks. In the process, he strained papal finances to the breaking point. He saw a solution in the sale of indulgences and, in the process, outraged clergy such as Martin Luther, provoking Luther's famous remonstration against the sale of indulgences. Luther and his allies protested and demanded reform, thus christening their revolt the "Protestant Reformation." The result was a wave of religious wars that set those protesting papal corruption against those loyal to Rome. This Protestant Reformation won adherents throughout the areas under Roman jurisdiction, making deep inroads into areas that are now firmly Catholic, including Poland, Slovakia, Slovenia, and Croatia, as well as Bohemia and Hungary where larger communities of Protestants remain active. In Silesia, the population was overwhelmingly Protestant until the late 1600s.

During the papacy of Paul V (1552–1621; reigned 1605–21), war broke out between German Catholics and Protestants. Paul V declined to provide any support to the Catholic princes in this war, however, which began in Bohemia. The conflict would later be known as The Thirty Years War (1618–48). Although it would end only with the Peace of Westphalia in 1648, it reached an early climax at least in the Bohemian context on 8 November 1620, when Catholic forces smashed the Protestants. Kaiser Ferdinand II (1578–1637; reigned 1619–37) was intent on snuffing out all traces of Hussitism and Protestantism in Bohemia and even declared that "a desert is better than a country with heretics." Ferdinand compelled Protestants of Lower and Upper Austria, and of Bohemia, to convert to Catholicism on pain of expulsion or death; in his Edict of Restitution of 1629, he forced Protestants to return all properties seized since 1552. It is, thus, with him that the Catholic Church may be said to have undertaken to reverse the course of the Reformation, in what it called the Counter-Reformation. This campaign included the burning of Protestant churches and libraries, the expulsion of unrepentant Protestants (e.g., in Bohemia), and the undertaking of an ambitious resocialization program which included not only fresh intellectual endeavors (as per Polish Catholic scholars such as Jan Laskii, Andrzej Frycz Modrzewski, and Stanislaw Hozjusz) but also a studied effort to display the glories of the divine in art, architecture, and music. The aesthetics of the Counter-Reformation came to be known as the Baroque and stood in sharp contrast to the stark simplicity of much Protestant art, architecture, and music. Fine examples of Baroque ecclesiastical architecture may be found throughout the region, from Poland in the north to Croatia and Romanian Transylvania in the south. It was during this period that the Holy See negotiated a series of agreements (such as the Union of Brest in 1596) which brought certain hitherto Orthodox communities into union with Rome; under these agreements, the communities in question were allowed to retain differences in ritual, song, architecture, and other externalia, but agreed to respect the authority of the pope in doctrinal matters and to accept Catholic theological and ecclesiological teachings. In exchange for such agreements, the communities were promised equal treatment with Roman Catholics. These Greek-rite Catholics are known under various names, including Greek Catholics, Byzantine Catholics, and Uniates. The term *Uniate* is sometimes considered derogatory, though one finds the term used in a neutral way in scholarly publications.

In the late eighteenth century, enlightened despotism was the prevailing system in Eastern Europe. The most important enlightened despots were Maria Theresa of Austria (1717–80; reigned 1740–80); Josef II of Austria (1741–90; reigned 1765/80–90); Friedrich the Great of Prussia (1712–86; reigned 1740–86); and Catherine the Great of Russia (Yekaterina Velikaya, 1729–96; reigned 1762–96). These rulers believed that their people had certain rights, among them the right to education. Josef II, in particular, issued an edict of toleration, granting toleration to the Jewish faith and certain Protestant churches and thus undercutting the Catholic Church's religious monopoly. Yet these same rulers undertook a series of partitions of Poland, beginning in 1772, which by 1795, had wiped Poland off the map. The first partition was the result of a crisis brought on by Catherine the Great, who was concerned about the discriminatory treatment of Orthodox believers in Catholic Poland. The years of partition, 1795–1918, saw a series of autonomous or nominally autonomous national reincarnations (such as the Duchy of Warsaw, 1807–46, and the Grand Duchy of Posen, 1815–49), but the lack of independence inflamed the souls of some Poles, and there were revolts against Russian rule in 1830 and 1863. Although the Holy See denounced these revolts, local parish priests took the side of the people and this contributed to the identification of the church with the Polish nation.

Catholic clergy played an important role in educating the people of Eastern Europe. In Slovenia, for example, the Augustinian monk Marko Pohlin (1735–1801) published a Slovene grammar book in 1768, while Franciscan friar Valentine Vodnik (1758–1819) pioneered Slovenian secular poetry. The church's contributions in education and culture continued in the nineteenth and twentieth centuries. In Croatia, for example, Bishop Josip Juraj Strossmayer of Djakovo (1815–1905) founded the South Slav Academy in 1876 and helped to reorganize the entire educational system of Dalmatia and Croatia-Dalmatia, while in Albania the Jesuits reopened elementary schools in 1855 and established the Saint Xavier College in Shkodrë in 1877. In Bosnia, the Franciscans enjoyed a monopoly among Catholic religious orders in the era of Turkish rule (1463–1878), operating with exclusive permission from the Sublime Porte, and made major contributions to the education of locals.

CATHOLICISM AND THE NATIONAL AWAKENING OF THE NINETEENTH CENTURY

The nineteenth century was, arguably, the most optimistic century since the time of ancient Greece. This "optimism" was connected with the growing conviction, among people—especially in the latter half of the century—that they were witnessing real progress in the sociopolitical sphere, in the scientific sphere, and even in the economic sphere. The names Comte, Fournier, Darwin, and Marx exemplify the spirit of the age. This spirit was by no means limited to Western Europe, though its echo was fainter in the East. Still, one can scarcely talk about nineteenth-century Croatia without recalling the towering figure of Bishop Strossmayer, who fought against the proclamation of the doctrine of papal infallibility at the First Vatican Council (1869–70) and who worked energetically to promote the idea of Catholic-Orthodox ecclesiastical rapprochement locally as a preparatory stage for Croat-Serb political union. Nor would an account of nineteenth-century Poland be complete without a mention of Fr. Stanislaw Staszic (1775–1826), who fantasized about Polish Catholicism playing a special civilizing mission in Europe and looked to the Russian czar to provide the military might for this Catholic mission. August Cieszkowski (1814–94), trained in the philosophy of Hegel at the University of Berlin, agreed with Staszic that Catholicism and the Polish nation had been ordained by God to play a special role in history; he even spoke of a glorious future which he called "the Era of the Holy Spirit."

THE TWENTIETH CENTURY

The years 1911–1923 were years of chaos, beginning with the Italo-Ottoman War and the Balkan Wars, culminating in World War I, and trailing off with Communist insurrections across Central and Eastern Europe; uprisings in parts of the newly established Kingdom of Serbs, Croats, and Slovenes; and outright war between Poland and Soviet Russia. The defeat of the Central Powers in 1918 set new frameworks for church-state relations, and in the following years, the Catholic Church tried to sign concordats (or agreements) with as many European states as possible. Concordats were signed with Poland (1925), Albania (1927), Czechoslovakia (1928), and Romania (1929); on the other hand, the Holy See declined to press for a concordat with Hungary, while its efforts to obtain a concordat with the Yugoslav government ended in failure. During the interwar years, 1918–39, the Catholic Church secured a preeminent legal position in Poland, while the Orthodox Church enjoyed clear preeminence in Romania, Bulgaria, and even, albeit in more complicated conditions, Yugoslavia. The situation in Czechoslovakia, Hungary, and Albania was more complicated. In the Czechoslovak case, this complexity was due to the resentment that some Czechs felt toward the Catholic Church as the Church of "the Oppressor"—the now-defunct Habsburg Empire. Indeed, upon obtaining their independence in 1918, many Czechs celebrated by smashing statues of the Blessed Virgin Mary.

Anti-Semitism was rife in the region during the interwar years, and most Catholic prelates were content, at most, to keep silence as anti-Semitism fed emerging fascist and Nazi currents. In the short run, the Catholic Church gained some ground in Poland, where it obtained the return of some church buildings that had been owned by Protestant churches, as well as some church buildings belonging to the Orthodox community. In Hungary, Catholic clergy joined Lutheran clergy in supporting official irredentism and blocked endeavors on the part of Catholic ethnic minorities to establish schools in their own languages. In the long run, the Catholic failure to take a stronger stand against anti-Semitism— Pope Pius XI's sharp anti-Nazi encyclical of 1937, "Mit brennender Sorge" and Pope Pius XII's repeated protests against Nazi atrocities notwithstanding—has continued to haunt the church down to the present day (Phayer 2000).

World War II posed its toughest challenges to clergy in nominally independent states under quisling regimes, in particular Slovakia and Croatia. In the former, Msgr. Jozef Tiso (1887–1947), who had become prime minister of an autonomous Slovakia in the newly federalized Czecho-Slovakia on 6 October 1938, agreed to serve as head of a Nazi puppet state in Slovakia, when the Nazis annexed rump Bohemia-Moravia in March 1939. Although Tiso's rule has been characterized as "clerico-fascism," it was neither fully clerical nor fully fascist; where its clerical credentials are concerned, one must note that, as the price for Hitler's patronage,

Tiso was not allowed to distribute all papal encyclicals in Slovakia ("Mit bren-nender Sorge" representing a particular offense to Nazi sensibilities as their re-peated protests to the Holy See in 1937 had made utterly clear). In Croatia, the leading Catholic prelates were Zagreb's Archbishop Alojzije Stepinac (1898–1960) and Sarajevo's Archbishop Ivan Sarić (1871–1960). But while Sarić had joined the fascist Ustase movement in 1934 and continued to give the Ustase his support during the genocidal war, Stepinac kept his distance from the quisling Croatian regime and, on the contrary, protested repeatedly in public against the racism, chauvinism, and atrocities of the regime. In spite of that, Stepinac found himself on trial at war's end on trumped-up charges of "collaboration." Stepinac was not alone. The new Communist regimes tried and imprisoned their leading prelates in Hungary (Archbishop Jósef Mindszenty of Esztergom), Czechoslovakia (Arch-bishop Josef Beran of Prague), and Poland (Archbishop Stefan Wyszynski of War-saw and Bishop Czeslaw Kaczmarek), once they realized that the prelates were not about to take their orders from the Communist Party.

The early years of Communism were years of great hardship for the Catholic Church in Eastern Europe in general, despite some local variations. The closure and confiscation of monasteries, convents, schools, printing presses, and vineyards severely weakened the church and put it on the defensive. From the late 1940s until the 1970s, the church contented itself with defending its "core values," which is to say, with protecting its clergy from harassment as far as possible and with endeavoring to assure itself of the possibility to perform Mass and provide after-hours religious instruction wherever there were Catholics. Pope Paul VI (1897–1978; reigned 1963–78) adopted a strategy he called *Ostpolitik*, which involved the promotion of Christian-Marxist dialogue, the reduction of tensions between the Catholic Church and Communist regimes in Eastern Europe, and the negotiation of such gains as could be obtained (in what Archbishop László Lekai of Esztergom called the "small steps policy").

The Catholic Church became bolder in the late 1970s as a result of at least three factors: the weakened position of the Communist Party in Poland in par-ticular; the accession of Karol Wojtya (b. 1920) to the papacy, as John Paul II, in 1978; and the emergence of openly dissident movements such as Charter 77 in Czechoslovakia and Solidarity in Poland. John Paul II, though conservative on issues such as women priests, contraception, and abortion, proved to be doggedly liberal when it came to human rights, independent trade unions, and democra-tization. The "Polish pontiff" challenged authoritarian regimes of both left and right, including the apartheid regime in South Africa and the Sandinista regime in Nicaragua. In the East European context there could be no mistake about the pope's determination to see the overthrow or collapse of the Communist political order. The Polish regime drew up lists of "enemy priests" and at least one such priest, Fr. Jerzy Popieuszko, was brutally murdered by Polish secret police in 1984. The Czechoslovak and Romanian regimes also manhandled their clergy; in the former, the popular forty-seven-year-old priest, Fr. Stefan Polak, was murdered by Czechoslovak secret police in 1987 while Catholic civil rights activist Augustin Navratil was confined to a psychiatric hospital. Toward the end of the Communist era, Pope John Paul II issued his programmatic encyclical *Sollicitudo rei socialis* (1988) in which, building on the foundation of the earlier papal encyclicals *Rerum novarum* (issued by Pope Leo XIII in 1891) and *Mater et magistra* (issued by Pope John XXIII in 1961), he subjected both Marxist collectivism and laissez-faire capitalism to sharp criticism, arguing that "the unregulated competition which so-called liberals espouse, or the class struggle in the Marxist sense, are utterly opposed to Christian teaching and also to the very nature of man" (John XXIII, 1961, 9).

THE POST-COMMUNIST CONTEXT

Since the collapse of the Communist organizational monopoly throughout the region during the years 1989-90, the Catholic Church has been able to rebuild its infrastructure. Vacant episcopal seats in Czechoslovakia and Albania have been filled; Catholic religious instruction has been introduced in public schools in Poland and Croatia; and throughout the region, the church has actively sought the return of property confiscated during the Communist era (being especially successful in this regard in Poland, Slovakia, and Hungary). In Slovenia and Croatia, the Catholic theological faculties, which had been forced to disassociate from the universities of Ljubljana and Zagreb respectively, have been reaffiliated with those universities. In Romania, the Greek-rite Catholic Church has been fighting an uphill battle for the restitution of facilities that had been turned over to the Romanian Orthodox Church. The new freedom enjoyed by the Catholic Church in Eastern Europe now that the Communist monopoly has ended is of course enjoyed by other religious associations as well. The result has been that the Catholic Church faces new challenges in the region, in the form of competition from often well-funded neo-Protestant and non-Christian groups based in the United States. There have also been some striking challenges indigenous to the area, such as the apocalyptic White Brotherhood of Maria Tsvigun, which built a following in Ukraine on its claim that the world would end in November 1993; the White Brotherhood also won some adherents in Poland.

In Poland there are currently more than three hundred religious groups competing for members, while in neighboring Slovakia about two hundred religious groups are represented. The burgeoning religious market depends on conversions, which is to say on locals abandoning the faiths in which they were raised. In

Poland, for example, at least 100,000 persons changed their religion in the years 1989–2002; most of these, presumably, were Catholics.

One of the consequences of the collapse of Communism was that formerly Communist states of the region applied for membership in the European Union; by spring 2004, Poland, the Czech Republic, Slovakia, Hungary, and Slovenia had been admitted to the EU, while Croatia was given active encouragement to hope for eventual admission. European Union membership became problematic in the eyes of Catholic hierarchs, however, when, in July 2002, the European Parliament called for the legalization of abortion in both current and prospective EU member-states. Then, in February 2003, the first sixteen articles of a draft constitution for the EU were released for public discussion. The preamble mentioned the humanistic values of ancient Greece and Rome, the liberal principles of the Enlightenment, and the rights trumpeted in the French Revolution, but said nothing about God or Christianity. This sparked controversy, with the Holy See leading Catholic opposition to the text—though not to the EU as such. Catholic pressure eventually induced EU leaders to make some small adjustments—removing the references to Greece and Rome but without adding any reference to God or Christianity. But the whole matter became moot when, in July 2005, French voters rejected the proposed EU constitution.

Past and Present

The Second Vatican Council (1962–65) exerted its impact in the region only very gradually. Among the earliest exponents of the new thinking wrought by the council were Fr. György Bulanyi whose grassroots movement so threatened Hungary's bishops that they released the good-natured cleric from his sacerdotal duties in 1982 as well as the clerics associated with the *Kršćanska sadašnjost* (Christian Present) publishing house in Zagreb, who experimented with a "self-managing" form of organization in the 1970s. By and large, however, the Catholics of Eastern Europe remained theologically, doctrinally, and socially conservative.

Pilgrimage sites have played a certain role in the life of the Catholic Church in the area. Here one may mention, in particular, Częstochowa (where the Blessed Virgin Mary is said to have intervened to save the Poles from destruction at the hands of the Swedes). Also worth mentioning are Velehrad in Moravia, the shrine at Levaca, and Marija Bistrica in Croatia; with the beatification of Zagreb's Archbishop Stepinac in 1998, there is a strong likelihood that his native village of Krašić may also become a pilgrimage center. The most famous pilgrimage site in the region, however, is undoubtedly Medjugorje, where the Blessed Virgin Mary is thought, by some, to have been making regular appearances since the early 1980s; the Holy See has declined to confer any official status on Medjugorje and at one point even ordered dioceses to desist from organizing any official church pilgrimages to the site. The Holy See has not, however, tried to dissuade believers from visiting Medjugorje.

Past rivalries and relations of superordination have left deep scars on the religious landscape. Relations between the Catholic Church, on the one side, and Romanian Orthodox, Polish Protestants (including the Seventh Day Adventists), and at least some Czech Protestants, on the other, remain deeply conflicted at best, if not outright hostile. In Croatia, the bitterness sown by the War of Yugoslav Succession (1991–95) has been associated not only with anti-Serbian but also with anti-Orthodox sentiments. This has only been compounded by Serbian expulsions of some of its Catholics from Vojvodina and Belgrade (in most cases, Croats). In Bosnia, on the other hand, the profound integrity displayed by Catholic Archbishop Vinko Puljić during the war did much to maintain and reinforce friendly ties between local Croats and Muslims, in spite of Croatian President Franjo Tudjman's irredentist course in Bosnia-Herzegovina during that war. In addition to Poland's 36 million Catholics, there are more than 6 million Hungarian Catholics, some 5 million Czech and Slovak Catholics, and up to 4 million Catholics in Croatia. Most of Slovenia's roughly 2 million inhabitants are Catholics, at least nominally. There are also about 2 million Catholics (both Roman and Greek) in Romania, alongside about 450,000 Roman Catholics in Albania. The Roman Catholic community in Bulgaria numbers only about 50,000, while those in Serbia and Macedonia are probably even smaller. There are some 625,000 Catholics living in Bosnia-Herzegovina today.

BIBLIOGRAPHY

Buchenau, Klaus. 2004. *Orthodoxie und Katholizismus in Jugoslawien 1945–1991.* Wiesbaden: Harrassowitz Verlag.

Byrnes, Timothy A., and Peter J. Katzenstein, eds. 2006. *Religion in an Expanding Europe.* Cambridge: Cambridge University Press.

Gardin, Giacomo. 1988. *Banishing God in Albania*, trans. from Italian. San Francisco: Ignatius Press.

Hainbuch, Friedrich. 1982. *Kirche und Staat in Ungarn nach dem Zweiten Weltkrieg.* Munich: Dr. Rudolf Trofenik.

John XXIII, Pope. 1961. *Mater et magistra*, N.C.W.C. translation. Boston: St. Paul Editions.

Kloczowski, Jerzy. 2000. *A History of Polish Christianity.* Cambridge: Cambridge University Press.

Michnik, Adam. 1993. *The Church and the Left.* Trans. from Polish by David Ost. Chicago: University of Chicago Press.

Modras, Ronald. 1994. *The Catholic Church and Antisemitism: Poland, 1933–1939.* Chur, Switz.: Harwood Academics.

Monticone, Ronald C. 1986. *The Catholic Church in Communist Poland, 1945–1985.* Boulder, Colo.: East European Monographs.

Phayer, Michael. 2000. *The Catholic Church and the Holocaust.* Bloomington: Indiana University Press.

Ramet, Pedro, ed. 1990. *Catholicism and Politics in Communist Societies.* Durham, N.C.: Duke University Press.

Ramet, Sabrina P. 1998. *Nihil Obstat. Religion, Politics, and Social Change in East Central Europe and Russia.* Durham, N.C.: Duke University Press.

Szulc, Tad. 1995. *Pope John Paul II: The Biography.* New York: Scribner.

Weigel, George. 1992. *The Final Revolution: The Resistance Church and the Collapse of Communism.* New York: Oxford University Press.

CHAPTER 27

EUROPEAN PROTESTANT SOCIETIES

FRITZ ERICH ANHELM

PROTESTANT Christianity originated in Europe and although it is now found throughout the world it is still characterized by its European origins. Its most distinctive social feature is its structural plurality. Though strikingly different from the social organization of Catholic and Orthodox traditions this plurality is hardly by design. It developed historically, largely because Protestantism neglected the issue of social organization, rather than consciously creating it. This experience with plurality, however, has enabled the Protestant churches to become the instigators behind the ecumenical movement. Despite their long history of division, the pluralism of Protestants has led them to search for an apparent unity within all Christian churches. Hence, plurality offers opportunities as well as obstacles and is a vital mark of Protestant self-identity in an era of globalization.

"To be Protestant" is an affirmation of unity that has both social and theological dimensions. The tension between Protestant unity and plurality creates a critical potential that leads to permanent self-reflection and reorientation. The *ecclesia semper reformanda*, or constant renewal of the church, aims at the true God-given church. Its social manifestation oscillates between reassurance and decampment, between preservation of traditions and openness toward social change.

THE PROTESTANT CHURCHES
AND THE STATE

The main Protestant confessions of Lutheranism, Calvinism, and Zwinglinism developed from small groups in the sixteenth century into established churches. At the same time, however, the pre-reformatory movements of the Waldensian and the Bohemian brothers as well as the post-reformatory Baptists, Congregationalists, and Methodists developed into free churches. Both developments are mirrored in their relation to the state. The main churches established themselves along the territorial principles set forth in the Counter-Reformation and the Thirty Years War and the resulting Peace of Westphalia. These principles led to the establishment of a union in nineteenth-century Prussia between the Lutherans and the Reformed churches. The churches adapted to the prevailing political system and developed their organizations along state lines. This is reflected even today in their methods of taxation, laws, and jurisdiction. The free churches on the other hand distanced themselves from the state format. In contrast to the main churches' territorial principle, they developed institutional structures that embodied their unique and voluntary nature.

The Enlightenment, the French Revolution, and American independence confronted the main churches of Western Europe with demands for human rights and freedom of religion. Both demands were met through the churches' internal reforms. Despite the exception of representative synods, however, the demands did not result in any other structural changes within the churches. Nevertheless, they did have direct consequences in regard to their relationship with the state.

Today there are three distinct types of church-state relationships in Europe: the state church, the cooperative church, and separation from the state; each is regulated by treaties between state and church. State churches exist only in Northern Europe where Lutheranism has been established as the majority church. This model is increasingly viewed as anachronistic. In many cases it has been, as in Sweden, transformed into the cooperative model. France has the third model. It sustained a strict separation of church and state with the exception of the Protestant region of Alsace-Lorraine. Forms of cooperation in which the state grants the church a status *sui generis* as opposed to other social organizations, are found in Germany, Austria, and Switzerland and since the 1970s in Spain and Italy as well.

The integration of Europe within the EU creates a particular problem for the state church model. The treaty of Amsterdam respects the unique national laws determining the relation between church and state. This, however, will be subject to change as there must be new regulations concerning the relationship between the churches and EU institutions. In this situation, whether even the cooperative model can be implemented is doubtful.

Since the time of the cold war, religious legislation in the Middle and Eastern European states seems to follow the cooperative model. Protestant confessions are in the minority compared to the Orthodox faith in Eastern Europe and the Catholic faith of Poland, Latvia, Hungary, and Southern Europe. Consequently, there are acute differences of interests regarding religious legislation that might privilege one group over others.

The state-church pattern of Western European churches, even in their cooperative forms, is up for discussion for two reasons. First, there is a general assumption that church and religion as a whole have gone through a loss of meaning in contemporary society. This is evident by the decrease of members and an individualization of religious options. Second, there is a decreasing homogeneity of the European Christian societies as a result of Muslim immigration. An official recognition of Islam, which in itself is not homogenous, would create a problem not only for the Protestant but also for the other Christian confessions, as they either would have to waive their privileged status with the state or expand state involvement in religious institutions to non-Christian associations. In this respect, though, other non-Christian communities such as Judaism have already been officially recognized.

Both factors merge in discussions about the role of religious instruction in schools, religious symbols in public spaces, and in the financing system of the churches. These issues seem to favor the privatization of religion and force the state-church tradition into the background. This trend aims at restructuring the main churches into the cooperative pattern of state-church relations. It affirms that churches in society are part of the "third sector," alongside state and economy. Even those within the church that hold to this view of church-in-society, however, often still hold on to existing laws governing the churches' status within the state.

PROTESTANTISM'S ROLE IN SOCIETY

Since the late nineteenth century many social organizations have developed at the periphery of even established Protestant state-churches. These clubs, associations, and foundations were often based on groups that regarded their interests neglected by both the church and the state. This affected the churches' mission and their leadership. The churches often served as umbrellas for many local and regional clubs, including men's, women's, and youth groups and occupational associations.

By the mid-twentieth century, the institutionalization of these movements resulted in their status as independently working services within the church. In the 1970s, social service, adult education, and journalism found their way into the church's internal organization. In Germany after World War II there were two specific institutions that had a social impact on Protestantism, the Kirchentag (literally "Church Day") and the evangelical academies. The Kirchentag reached the public through a four-day main event every two years, and the academies' meetings act as an ongoing input of public discourse and political culture into the churches.

The 1970s and 1980s saw new, ongoing processes of self-organization that eventually developed into a church reform movement. It covered the whole spectrum from the liberal to the pietistic. The movements formed in response to issues of peace, environment, women's rights, and international justice relating to the North-South discrepancy. These initiatives were characterized by an ecumenical sensibility and were found within the conciliatory processes for justice, peace, and respect for nature on local, regional, national, European-wide, and global levels. These movements are mainly a western European phenomenon as they originated in Germany, the Netherlands, and Switzerland, but activities and ideas from Northern, Southern, and Eastern Europe have been included. One cannot disregard the impact of this process on the democratic re-orientation of the middle and eastern European churches. At the same time one has to recognize that the conciliatory process has lost much of its public influence since the end of the East-West conflict.

The cold war and the resulting potential of self-organization represented a new perception of the church by society. Beginning in the early nineties, tendencies to reconfessionalize have hindered the ecumenical relationships among the main churches. In addition, financial crises have resulted in receding involvement in social activities and diminishing support for independently acting organizations. The churches' decreasing social involvement, though, is only temporary, and will eventually rebound.

In the newly conceived Protestant understanding of the church, social involvement is the obligation of both the formal church organization—community churches, regional church associations, and the wider church—as well as specific church initiatives. However, the church reform movements of the seventies and the conciliatory course of the eighties have shown how difficult it is for the new initiatives to be recognized by synodically represented main churches. Yet since the main churches are themselves increasingly under public scrutiny, the tensions between mainstream and reform have eased. The relation between institution and movement, an issue that dominated the seventies and eighties, is not on the daily agenda anymore. Instead, the question has become whether the smaller groups' activities can relate to the self-organized initiatives of their secularized counterparts. The distinction between state, economy, and civil society makes self-organized ecclesiastical forms of social service into recognized, faith-motivated aspects of social change. They can serve to intensify the "society pattern" of church-state relationship.

THE PROTESTANT HABITUS

The question of the nature of Protestantism has hitherto been answered on a theological-ecclesiastical level with the help of scientific theology and the field of history of religion, largely based on the confessional writings of the churches, such as the Augsburg Confession for Lutherans and the Heidelberg Catechism for the Reformed tradition. Increasingly, however, one has to consider the attempts that seek to transcend the confessional limits and rescind mutual condemnations of the past, such as the Barmer Erklärung of 1934 by Lutherans and Reformists; the Leuernberger Konkordie of 1973, which all Protestant churches have signed on to; the Lima Erklärung of 1982; or the most recent decree of Lutherans and Catholics for vindication (1999). These were all efforts to come to a common understanding.

It is questionable, however, how far these initiatives reflect the everyday reality of Christian existence. Analyses that examine the differences of the confessional cultures are suspect in their legitimacy. One must also take into consideration the sociological results of surveys and the evidence of a plethora of interconfessional communities. Thus one must assume that there is an individualization of Christian-religious lifestyles.

It is this trend of individualization that carries the opportunity for a more secularized Protestant social order and worldview—a "habitus" as the French sociologist Pierre Bourdieu has termed it. The Protestant habitus (insofar as there is such a thing) has lost its relation to the dogmatic form of faith in the reality of everyday life. Even the notion of individual spiritual transcendence is no longer dependent on it.

An understanding of the Protestant habitus still relies on Max Weber's thesis, *The Protestant Ethic and the Spirit of Capitalism,* which locates an ascetic core in the Calvinist, Puritan, and Methodist traditions that advanced the mentality of a capitalist way of life. This thesis has never really been challenged and is, in fact, beyond question. Moreover, the close affinity of neo-Protestantism (the "confession of bourgeois society") to political liberalism still reverberates. The theory that Protestantism's proximity to European modernity, as it developed during the nineteenth and twentieth centuries, reached its ambivalent height in "cultural Protestantism," is not challenged either.

As a religion, Protestantism seeks rational reasons to establish a relation to the transcendental. It thus helps to de-mythologize the world and provide the basis for the expansion of the realm of the available. In this way—even if unintended—Protestantism made secularization possible. The rediscovery of the spiritual dimension in Protestant communities can be regarded as a reaction to the secularized Protestant habitus.

New sociological studies differentiate the generalized thesis of an ever-accelerating secularization. Especially in the growing professional middle class of society, a new habitus is propagated that connects modernity with values such as community, solidarity, participation, and dialogue. Despite all the distance to the church as an institution, people neither seek nor refuse dialogue. Instead the church is expected to initiate a dialogue in people's terms. It is not so much the sacral-spiritual element but rather the social activities that offer contact with the community. In the declining traditional petit-bourgeois settings that make up the majority of the core communities, it is personal affirmation that counts more. These expectations represent the tension and the problems of orientation of the church's role in society.

Thus, modernity is increasingly influenced by Protestant ethics but decreasingly affected by the Protestant church organization as it expresses itself more privately than publicly. This trend of the individualization of faith is the main reason why a socially relevant fundamentalism within European Protestantism remains a rare phenomenon. Consequently, however, the church is in direct competition with secularized value systems.

PROTESTANTISM IN SECULAR SOCIETY

In view of the rapid growth of independent and mostly evangelical communities and free churches in Latin America, Asia, and Africa, Protestant Europe must be viewed as an exception. Globally, it is expected that these independent church movements will soon outnumber the mainstream churches.

Western European Protestantism's close affiliation with the Enlightenment and modernity comes to represent more a kind of ethical reasoning than spirituality. Essentially, Protestantism contains a secularizing dynamic. It therefore is all the more reliant on theological competence in interpreting sociological change, especially when politics, economic issues, science, and culture set secular trends that question Christian anthropology and social ethics. It is exactly this theological competence of interpretation that constitutes the importance of the Protestant confession. Where this confidence is lost, the church is reduced to an institution involved merely in individual religious concerns. Particularly useful for society is the central theological model of interpretation, "Justification by Faith Alone," found in Lutheranism that can warn a secularized society about concepts of self-redemption that result in illusions of omnipotence. Because the justification of one's own existence lies outside human domain, human acts are ultimately freed from determinism. Behind the strong normative force of the real world, the alternative becomes a real possibility.

Both Protestantism and a secular, democratically composed society thus share the attitude that civility and fundamentalism are not compatible. Of course, Europe is not entirely safe from fundamentalism, especially in the form of totalitarian political systems, such as Nazism with its organized preparation of war and genocide. Communism as a secular substitution for religion also defaced middle and Eastern Europe in the twentieth century. Fundamentalist positions continue to be violent in the pseudoreligious conflicts of Northern Ireland and in the ethnic-religious differences in southeastern Europe.

But despite all these involvements in the violent history of Europe, there is a willingness for critical self-reflection in Protestantism. It proves itself resistant against all forms of absolute control and quasi-religious ideologies of self-redemption. The Protestant faith does not tolerate secular absolutist pretensions in shoring up its credibility. It is exactly this ideological criticism that makes Protestantism appear as the religion of reason and ascribes to it a demythologizing function. Hence, Protestant ethics are obliged to a more balanced approach than are its dogma; it is more situational than doctrinaire.

The Protestant understanding of the individual, economic, social, and cultural rights of man can be related to theological interpretations. A theology similar to the humanistic-philosophical concept of the origins of these rights—where natural patterns of equal justice can go astray and are in danger of becoming perverted by political doctrines—gives a Protestant basis for human rights. It provides perspectives for a humanistic world and articulates ideals of freedom that are based on one's attitude toward transcendence.

The Protestant ethic assumes that there is a range of responsible freedoms, meaning the opportunity for individuals to be responsibly involved in shaping the world in the image of God. At its core, it has a positive relationship to plurality. In social ethics, Protestantism provides support for the poor, in peace ethics it offers a responsible pacifism that prefers civil rather than military solutions to disputes. Ecologically, it advocates an understanding of nature that reflects a culture of human responsibility for the works of Creation. Consequently, the Protestant ethic is constantly challenged by the struggle for truth in the public discourse of modern society, especially when the latter tries to free itself from religious claims.

PROTESTANTISM AND INTERRELIGIOUS DIALOGUE

It is not coincidental but rather inherent in its own pluralism that European Protestantism is skeptical about endeavors to create a "universal ethic." attempt to abide by a single ethic model—despite each of the world religion's claim that it possesses the one true faith—contradicts the historical experience of the Protestant plurality. Instead, Protestantism opts for a dialogical approach, with the help of interreligious hermeneutics, to understand the other and to bring its own religious identity in relation to the other. To understand means at the same time to accept differences.

Within all Christian confessions, dialogue and mission are separate and not easily resolved. Hence they require adjustment to each other. In this respect, Protestantism is less inclusive than Catholicism. But since it is more exclusive, it is all the more in need of dialogic interaction with other religious communities. A pluralistic theology that emphasizes the equality of all paths toward transcendence, however, will remain an impossibility in Europe.

Alongside the inner-Christian, confession-oriented ecumenical dialogue, which, despite all its problems, difficulties, and setbacks, has become an essential part of church understanding, interreligious dialogue also continues, albeit at a slower pace. An exception is the Jewish-Christian dialogue, which has been continual if not always harmonious. The so-called Jewish missions, however, have recently hampered this dialogue. Regarding Islam, one of the basic tenets of the document "The Christian Testimonial for Reconciliation" of the Second European Ecumenical Congress states that the members acknowledge the especially pressing issue of Islam, not only because there are thirty million Muslims in Europe but also because Christianity and Islam have had a long history of disparagement and hostility toward each other that have to be overcome in the spirit of reconciliation (*Dokumente der Zweiten Europäischen Ökumenischen Versammlung in Graz*, 48).

Concrete forms of interreligious dialogue with Islam can be found more on a local level as a result of self-organized initiations than from the churches themselves. In an ever-integrating Europe, all Christian confessions must enter into a dialogue with Islam if they want to learn to critically yet constructively deal with its religious and cultural influence. In the context of dialogue an inclusive view would be an obstacle, since it would presuppose that commonalities would have to be established before a reciprocal understanding could be created. Furthermore, the inclusive view would complicate matters because it might conceal differences, which, without addressing them could lead to a deepening of existing prejudices. The more thoughtful and continual the dialogue is conducted, the more a broad, societal acceptance can be ensured.

PROTESTANT CHRISTIANITY IN AN ERA OF GLOBALIZATION

European Protestantism's social plurality has prevented it from becoming an institutional form within Europe in general or the European Union in particular. Even global confessional associations such as the Lutheran or the Reformed Church do not appear as regional European institutional organizations. Yet each Protestant church has developed its own pattern of relationships with other Protestant, Anglican, and Orthodox churches in Europe through the Conference of European Churches and globally through the World Council of Churches.

Thus in an era of globalization, the social character of European Protestantism leads it in an ecumenical direction. In these ecumenical undertakings, European Protestantism will have to preserve and develop its constituent confessional identities. These identities that make up its plurality are, however, historical forms of one single Christian faith. Only through dialogue among themselves and other faiths will they grow ecumenically and interreligiously and find their niche in contemporary social life.

Note: Translated from German by Jochen Banasch.

BIBLIOGRAPHY

Anhelm, Fritz Erich. "Being a Christian in the Civil Society: Communitarists, Liberals, and the 'Conciliar Process.' " In *Consultation on Theology and Civil Society*. Loccumer Protokolle 23/95 s. 125ff.

———. "Soziologie der konziliaren Bewegung." In *Evangelische Kommentare* 1/91, S. 12ff.

Berger, Peter. 1992. *Der Zwang zur Häresie. Religion in der pluralistischen Gesellschaft.* Freiburg i. Breisgau.

Daiber, Karl F., ed. 1989. *Religion und Konfession.* Hannover

Dokumente der Zweiten Europäischen Ökumenschen Versammlung in Graz. "Versöhnung, Gottes Gabe und Quelle neuen Lebens." 1998. Hrsg. vom *Rat der Europäischen Bischofskonferenzen und der Konferenz Europäischer Kirchen.* Graz. Vien. Köln S. 48.

Hollenweger, Walter. 1997. *Charismatische pfingstliches Christentum.* Göttingen.

Huber, Wolfgang. 1998. *Kirche in der Zeitenwende: Gesellschaftlicher Wandel und Erneuerung der Kirche.* Gütersloh

Huber, Wolfgang and Heinz Eduard Tödt. 1988. *Menschenrechte: Perspectiven einer menschlichen Welt.* Munich S. 64ff.

Küng, Hans. 1991. *Projekt Weltethos.* Munich/Zürich

Robbers, Gerhad. *Vom Heiligen Römischen Reich zum Laizismus.* In Fritz Erich Anhelm, ed. *Europabilder. Die Bedeutung der Religionen für die europäische Integration.* Loccumer Protokolle 66/96, S. 39ff.

Schmidt-Leukel, Perry. 1998. "Skizze einer Theologie der Religionen." In *Religionen im Gespräch*, Bd. 5, Hrsg. Von R. Kirste u.a., Balve, S. 135ff.

Vögele, Wolfgang, ed. *Kirche und die Mileus der Gesellschaft.* Loccumer Protokolle 56/99 1.

Weber, Max. 1920. *Die protestantische Ethic und der Geist des Kapitalismus.* Tübingen (neuausgabe Munich/Hamburg 1969).

CHAPTER 28

ORTHODOX CHRISTIAN SOCIETIES

PHILIP WALTERS

THOUGH there are members of Orthodox communions found around the world, all of the branches can be traced back to the great split between Western and Eastern Christianity, between Roman Catholic and Orthodox, which became permanent in 1054 CE. Instead of retaining one spiritual leader and a single organization as did the Roman Catholic Church, the Orthodox community developed as a system of sister-churches. Those that are fully independent are called "autocephalous." The oldest are the four ancient patriarchates of Constantinople, Alexandria, Antioch, and Jerusalem. There are also five patriarchates of more recent origin (Russia, Serbia, Romania, Bulgaria, and Georgia); and the independent Orthodox churches of Cyprus, Greece, Poland, and Albania. There are also a number of "autonomous" churches, which are self-governing in most respects but do not enjoy full independence: the churches of the Czech Republic and Slovakia, Finland, Estonia, Latvia, Lithuania, China, Japan, and the monastery of Sinai. Some of the non-autocephalous churches are under the jurisdiction of the Moscow Patriarchate and some are under that of the Ecumenical Patriarchate—a fact that has led to interpatriarchal disputes in the past and continues to do so in the present. The Macedonian Orthodox Church regards itself as autocephalous but is not recognized as such by any other Orthodox church.

As a result of large-scale emigration from the 1920s onward, particularly by Greeks and Russians, there are now for example about three hundred thousand Orthodox in Britain and some 3.5 million in the United States. There is a Russian Orthodox Archdiocese in Western Europe under the jurisdiction of the Ecumenical Patriarch. The Russian Orthodox Church in America, with some one million members, is seeking to become autocephalous. The Russian Orthodox Church Abroad (ROCA) set itself up as an alternative jurisdiction to that of the Moscow Patriarchate in the early years of Soviet power. It makes no claims to autocephaly but recognizes no alternative jurisdiction and continues to function independently. Longstanding conflict between the Moscow patriarchate and the ROCA came to a head in the early 1990s when the latter was able to reestablish a presence on Russian soil and a number of parishes of the Moscow Patriarchate began to come over to it.

As well as the Chalcedonian churches listed above there are five churches that did not accept the conclusions of the Council of Chalcedon in 451, but nevertheless consider themselves part of the Orthodox community. Known as the Oriental Orthodox churches, they are: the Armenian Apostolic Church, the Coptic Church in Egypt, the Ethiopian Orthodox Church, the Malabar Jacobite Church (in India), and the Syrian Jacobite Church. The Armenian Church has throughout its history been the symbol and preserver of the national identity of the Armenian people; however, the Armenian homeland in the Caucasus has suffered continual occupation by foreign powers, culminating in genocide, and today the Armenian diaspora is at least as large as the population of its home republic. There are two church jurisdictions, one at Echmiadzin in the Armenian homeland and one in Cilicia (the region of today's Lebanon).

Since the fifth century the patriarchates of Alexandria, Antioch, and Jerusalem have steadily declined in numbers and importance; their area of geographical jurisdiction has largely been Islamicized. The patriarch of Alexandria, for example, has authority over up to two hundred thousand believers in Egypt and the rest of Africa. In the 1920s the territory of the Patriarchate of Antioch was divided between the two republics of Syria and Lebanon; some 280,000 Orthodox Arabs were left under its supervision, of whom one hundred thousand were in the diaspora, mostly in North and South America. The autonomous Church of Sinai consists of a single monastery and some local people: altogether a few hundred souls. The heart of the Orthodox world is today in Eastern Europe and the former Soviet Union. By far the largest Orthodox church is that of Russia, which claims as many as fifty million, sometimes even eighty million, members, followed by the Romanian Church with up to seventeen million.

Within Europe and the former Soviet Union, the Orthodox world is not to be identified with the "Slav" world. One of the largest and most spiritually fertile Orthodox churches is that of the Romanians, a non-Slav people; and Slav nations such as the Poles, Slovaks, and Croats are staunchly Catholic. However, the Orthodox churches virtually all lie beyond a fault-line that divides Europe into East and West and are to be found in that part of Europe with a distinctive pattern of political, economic, and cultural development. How far these have shaped religion and how far the reverse is true is a complex question. The Orthodox countries have also been cut off from the West by a series of historical experiences.

From the mid-thirteenth century Russia was under Mongol political domination for several hundred years; from the fourteenth to the nineteenth centuries the Balkans were under Ottoman control; and in the twentieth century Communism has divided Europe with an Iron Curtain.

AUTOCEPHALY

The Orthodox churches differ from Western European churches in the style of their liturgy and in certain doctrinal respects; but from a sociological point of view the most important difference is that the Orthodox world is a communion of more or less self-governing churches, each usually identified with a particular nation-state. Those with the most complete independence enjoy autocephaly.

There has long been debate about the meaning and implications of autocephaly. In particular, the question arises as to whether a particular Orthodox Church is the church of a people or the church in a particular geographical area. In the nineteenth century, as the Bulgarian church sought to achieve self-governance, it appealed to ethnic Bulgarians wherever they might live, and the Ecumenical Patriarchate accused it of the heresy of phyletism, or maintaining that autocephaly is defined ethnically rather than territorially. The Serbian Orthodox Church nourishes the doctrine of Svetosavlje, which sees a special religious role for the Serbian nation to be achieved through suffering. In the post-Communist period many Orthodox churches, most saliently the Russian Orthodox Church, began seeking to safeguard what they saw as their canonical territory against the incursions of Protestant missionaries and sects from abroad. The churches have a tendency to count as their members all their potential or nominal flock, defined ethnically or territorially. In the case of Russia, for example, as a result of seventy years of institutional atheism the vast majority of those whom the church is inclined to consider as members of its flock never visit a church and are ignorant of the faith. Foreign missionaries claim that what they are doing is converting the hitherto unreached rather than stealing Orthodox sheep.

ORGANIZATION

During the Ottoman period the patriarch of Constantinople had jurisdiction over all the Orthodox believers in the Empire. As the Balkan countries achieved independence in the course of the nineteenth century the area of jurisdiction of the Patriarchate of Constantinople shrank steadily, and before World War I comprised some eight million Christians. Political events in the early 1920s reduced this figure precipitously to some eighty thousand Greeks living in Istanbul, whom the government of the new Turkish Republic was bound by treaty to protect; Crete, Rhodes, some other Greek islands, Mount Athos, and the Greeks in the diaspora (totaling some five hundred thousand) continued to recognize the patriarch as their spiritual head. Under foreign pressure the Turkish government allowed him to continue to reside in Istanbul, but they imposed many restrictions on his movements, and only a Turkish citizen may become patriarch. As Ecumenical Patriarch, he is accorded a primacy of honor by all the Orthodox churches.

Four of the autocephalous Orthodox churches (the Russian, Romanian, Bulgarian, and Serbian) have a patriarch at their head. The Georgian Church has a catholicos-patriarch; the rest have a metropolitan or archbishop. Typically there is a synod of bishops and a bishops' council that meet more or less regularly. The highest authority in an Orthodox church is the local council of clergy and laypeople; such councils are convened infrequently. The higher administrative offices will typically be located in a monastery. The Russian Orthodox Church was handed back the ancient Danilov Monastery in Moscow by the Soviet authorities in good time for the celebration of the Millennium of Russian Christianity in 1988.

Monasteries, both urban and rural, have been of central importance throughout Orthodox history, the goal of pilgrimages and the residence of elders, who stand outside the church hierarchy but are revered for their holiness. The main monastic center for the Orthodox world is Mount Athos. In Moldavia a famous group of painted monasteries have nurtured spiritual creativity for centuries. Serbian monasteries clustered in Kosovo, now populated chiefly by Albanians, reveal where the historical core of Serbian orthodoxy was located.

THE WESTERN BORDERLANDS

The Western border of the Orthodox world in Europe has seen a good deal of religious mixing over the centuries. In Albania and Bosnia no one faith predominates to the extent of becoming identified with the nation. Farther north, in areas now mainly within Romania, Ukraine, and Belarus, Eastern-Rite Catholic churches (often called Greek Catholic or Uniate) date from the time of the Counter-Reformation. They are Orthodox in their liturgy, spirituality, discipline, and theology but are in communion with the Roman Catholic Church. They were founded as a result of political pressure on the indigenous Orthodox community exercised by the local dominant non-Orthodox power; but over the centuries they have acquired a distinctive character and a genuine identity. Nevertheless, whenever a state with an Orthodox majority church has achieved political power in Eastern-Rite Catholic areas, it has normally declared the local flock Orthodox and the Eastern-Rite Catholic Church both illegal and nonexistent. This was the situation in Soviet Ukraine from the 1940s. In 1989, however, the reformist Soviet government under Gorbachev suddenly re-legalized the Eastern-Rite Catholic Church, and immediately millions of nominal Orthodox in western Ukraine revealed their true allegiance, to the dismay and discomfiture of the Orthodox establishment. After the collapse of the Soviet Union, the Ukrainian Catholic Church became one of the major denominations in independent Ukraine. In post-Communist Romania the role of the Greek Catholic Church in Romania and its relationship to the Romanian Orthodox Church also became the subject of controversy and strife.

The emergence of newly independent states after the end of the Soviet Union had repercussions for the Orthodox churches. In 1995 President Lukashenka of Belarus placed severe restrictions on the work of the Roman Catholic Church and recognized the Orthodox Church, which is under the jurisdiction of the Moscow Patriarchate, as the leading religion, as part of his plan to bring his country back into a close political alliance with Russia. In 1996 a major dispute blew up in Estonia. An autonomous Estonian Orthodox Church, set up after World War I and in exile during in the Soviet period, was claiming to be the only legal Orthodox Church in Estonia. The church under the Moscow Patriarchate, which had functioned during the Soviet period, was denied registration, and this meant that it was unable to claim back property it felt was its own. Soon the quarrel involved the Moscow Patriarchate and the Ecumenical Patriarchate, the latter supporting the claims of the autonomous church, and for a matter of months the two patriarchates were out of communion with one another.

The Orthodox churches have traditionally engaged in missionary activity. The Orthodox churches in China and Japan, for example, are the result of nineteenth-century Russian Orthodox missions. In the post-Communist period, however, the Orthodox churches suddenly found themselves the unprepared targets for what they saw as aggressive proselytizing on the part of foreign Protestants, non-Christian sects, and the Roman Catholic Church, backed up with huge financial and technical resources which the local Orthodox Church could not hope to match. Rekindled Orthodox antipathy to Western Christianity, especially in a climate of growing nationalist self-defensiveness, led to a deterioration in ecumenical relations. Baptists and Pentecostals have been strong in Russia since the nineteenth century; yet material published in the 1990s with the imprimatur of the Russian Orthodox Church describes these well-established but minority denominations as "harmful sects."

Part of the explanation for the outrage with which the Orthodox churches generally responded to the large-scale arrival of foreign religions in the post-Communist period was that they were deeply suspicious of the motives of these rich organizations offering generous material inducements to convert: they seemed to be part of the juggernaut of Western-style capitalism which had arrived in the post-Communist world suddenly and in particularly virulent form and was causing widespread confusion and suffering. They were also genuinely shocked by the excesses, as they saw them, to which liberalizing tendencies had led in some Western churches, reducing them in their view to mere vehicles for heresy. The churches in Communist countries had been in enforced isolation from developments in the world outside, including the ecumenical movement and the consequences of the Second Vatican Council. Some of the Orthodox churches have now withdrawn from the World Council of Churches; others are considering doing so.

SUBDIVISIONS, SCHISMS, AND MOVEMENTS

Some Orthodox churches have experienced schism and inner division. In the seventeenth century the Old Believers, defending what they saw as genuine traditional Orthodoxy against patriarchal reforms, broke away from the Russian Orthodox Church; their church is still a significant one in Russia today. Various branches of the "True" or "Catacomb" Orthodox Church originated at various times in the Soviet Union when groups of believers went underground rather than follow the Moscow Patriarchate into what they saw as unacceptable compromise with the demands of the atheist Soviet authorities. Heavily persecuted by the Soviet authorities and highly secretive, they reemerged in the post-Communist period.

After the end of Communism an internal problem for the churches was how to overcome bitterness and distrust between those who "compromised" with the Communist authorities and those who resisted and who had been persecuted or discriminated against as a result. After 1989 the Orthodox Church in Ukraine experienced two major schisms, and soon three distinct Orthodox hierarchies were competing for the allegiance of parishes, clergy, and faithful: the Ukrainian Orthodox Church (Moscow Patriarchate), the Ukrainian Orthodox Church (Kiev Patriarchate), and the Ukrainian Autocephalous Orthodox Church. Paradoxically the result was that in the 1990s there was greater religious freedom in Ukraine than in many post-Communist Orthodox countries: no one church had the upper hand or recognition by the government as the national church. The Bulgarian Orthodox Church suffered a major schism in 1992; the original issue was the validity of the election of the patriarch in the Communist period. The schism, which produced two rival patriarchal structures, hampered the witness of the church and lowered its public reputation. In 1997 the Georgian Orthodox Church split amid internal controversy over its recent decision to withdraw from the World Council of Churches. The anti-ecumenical group tended also to support the nationalist Zviad Gamsakhurdia who was deposed in 1991 after a brief period as president of a newly independent Georgia.

In post-Communist times the regeneration of church work and witness tended to be hampered by internal disunity between conservatives and progressives, the former protectionist and traditionalist, the latter ecumenically open and committed to renewal. One area in which the Russian Orthodox Church was successful in reactivating itself in the post-Communist period was that of theological education; yet the dozens of new seminaries and academies tended to be divided into conservative and progressive as did the hierarchy of the church itself. The church was thus unable to speak with one voice on important issues.

At times of stagnation or turpitude, church renewal movements have regenerated Orthodox witness in several countries. The Zoe movement in the Greek Orthodox Church has been of lasting importance. The Lord's Army (Oastea Domnului) began within the Romanian Orthodox Church in the 1920s. It was persecuted by the Communists but was legalized in 1989 and began involving itself actively in educational and social work. In post-Communist Russia many small groups were activated by spiritual disciples of Fr Aleksandr Men,' the well-loved Russian Orthodox priest who was murdered in 1990 but whose legacy continued to have a growing influence both in Russia and in the West.

ORTHODOXY AND POLITICS

As the only European Orthodox Church in a non-Communist country, the Greek Orthodox Church continued after World War II to develop the implications of traditional Orthodox cooperation with the political establishment. This involved a delicate balancing act. Generally the church avoided sacrificing its principles for the sake of political accommodation, but during the dictatorship of the colonels (1967–73), for example, its collaboration was widely found offensive. Church-state links weakened after 1974. The new constitution of 1975 allowed proselytising by "recognized" non-Orthodox denominations, thus moving toward recognition of religious pluralism, but Orthodoxy was still recognized as the "dominant" religion, and clergy salaries were still paid by the state.

The Orthodox churches in the Communist countries suffered severe restrictions on their witness and were generally forbidden to involve themselves in social or political activity. Nevertheless, they knew where the boundaries were drawn and enjoyed the certainties of the status of second-class servant of the state. These certainties were destroyed in the late 1980s and early 1990s. It soon became clear that the post-Communist Orthodox churches were keen to learn from the Greek experience and also to achieve explicit protection, which would be enshrined in legislation. In 1997 the Russian parliament, with its nationalist and protectionist majority, passed a new law on religion placing restrictions on nontraditional denominations in Russia, replacing the liberal law on religion of 1990. Pressure from the Orthodox Church was important in assuring this outcome.

In the post-Communist period the Orthodox churches began to find themselves championed by nationalists and chauvinists, many of whom wanted a return to the old days of social and economic control but now under Orthodoxy rather than Communism. Many enthusiastic new converts to Orthodoxy, including new trainees for the priesthood, had formerly been active members of Communist youth movements and often now became xenophobic and isolationist church members. The Orthodox churches have generally tended to support those maintaining the status quo, and official church protests at political excesses such as the war between Russia and Chechnya are likely to take the form of generalized pleas for peace. An example of an Orthodox Church failing to disengage itself from an established political agenda is provided in post-Communist Serbia.

The Serbian Church was in a weak position throughout the Communist period, but it was prepared to oppose the government particularly when it perceived threats to Serbian culture and identity within the multinational Communist state. The Yugoslav government was, for example, eager for political reasons to see an independent Macedonian Orthodox Church and with its encouragement the Macedonian clergy unilaterally claimed autocephaly in 1967; but the Serbian Church has never recognized this claim. When Yugoslavia collapsed, the Milosevic government replaced Communist with nationalist rhetoric, and the Serbian Church suddenly found itself in the favored limelight. It had always been closely linked with the national aspirations of the Serbian people and was thus unable to make a principled stand as the government pursued its aim of a Greater Serbia, at moments of crisis doing little more than deplore the bloodshed involved.

ORTHODOXY, CULTURAL IDENTITY, AND WITNESS IN SOCIETY

The Orthodox churches have over the centuries produced a distinctive spirituality. The mystical insights of holy men and elders, a highly developed prayer life, rich monastic and charitable traditions, the veneration of icons, and sublime church music have enriched world Christianity. The Romanian Orthodox Church has produced vigorous theology. The Russian religious renaissance of the late nineteenth and early twentieth centuries had spiritual and cultural repercussions still being felt today.

Even during centuries of oppression, persecution, and hardship the Orthodox churches maintained the culture of their people, whose leadership at local levels often devolved on the clergy. For the people, Orthodoxy often became a cultural concept linking them with their historical roots. Social surveys in the 1990s showed that many Russians would be ready to identify themselves as Orthodox even if they did not believe in God.

In post-Communist Europe those with political power looked instinctively to the churches to help articulate the new national identity. Unfortunately the churches were by then generally ill-equipped to imbue the search for national identity with a lively spiritual content. Under Communism the Orthodox churches were allowed a limited institutional existence, able to train some clergy and to publish limited numbers of official journals and calendars and very small print runs of the Bible. Believers could attend the liturgy—if there was a church nearby—but parish newsletters, Sunday schools, discussion groups, charitable activity, and social involvement were typically prohibited. What these churches might have been capable of achieving had they had vigorous international support is a matter of speculation. It is interesting that the Armenian Church was perhaps the freest in the Soviet Union. The fact that the Armenian diaspora was so large helped to restrain the Soviet authorities from curtailing the activity of the church at home. In the late 1970s some 90 percent of Armenian babies were being baptized, pilgrimages to holy sites attracted huge crowds, and Armenia was the only republic where Bibles could sometimes be found on open sale. A fundamental difference between the Orthodox churches and the Roman Catholic Church is of course the latter's international nature. Catholicism in Poland remained strong and vigorous throughout the Communist period and eventually nurtured the Solidarity movement.

From 1989 the Orthodox churches in Eastern Europe suddenly found themselves with complete freedom; churches and monastic buildings began to be handed back in large numbers. Most of the Orthodox churches began making valiant efforts to initiate large-scale educational, publishing, and social activity. However, the deficit in all areas was huge. Parish life had ceased to exist under Communism. Khrushchev's antireligious campaign in the early 1960s, for example, involved the closure of two-thirds of the twenty thousand churches operating legally in the Soviet Union. The original total was still far from being reconstituted by the late 1990s. The churches were critically short of money, equipment, literature, and material resources of all kinds and also lacked trained clergy. In 1944, when the Communists came to power, the Bulgarian Orthodox Church had three thousand priests and four hundred monks to minister to a population of 6.5 million. By 1995 it had eight hundred priests and seventy monks, and the population had risen to eight million. The clergy that were gradually becoming available to the churches in post-Communist countries had all too often received no theological or pastoral training. They faced a fundamental problem in trying to communicate with their nominal flock, most of whom had had little or no contact with a church. We have seen that the Orthodox churches were outraged by the influx of foreign missionaries to their countries in the immediate post-Communist period. A central problem here, however, was their own inability to mount an effective witness to their nominal flock. It was arguably this failure, as much as the aggressive proselytizing activities of non-Orthodox denominations, which gave Orthodox denunciations of sheep-stealing their strident character.

BIBLIOGRAPHY

Alexander, Stella. 1979. *Church and State in Yugoslavia since 1945.* London: Cambridge University Press.

Attwater, Donald. 1961. *The Christian Churches of the East.* 2 vols. London: Thomas More Books.

Beeson, Trevor. 1982. *Discretion and Valour: Religious Conditions in Russia and Eastern Europe,* rev. ed. London: Collins.

Bourdeaux, Michael. 1969. *Patriarch and Prophets: Persecution of the Russian Orthodox Church Today.* London: Macmillan.

Brande, Benjamin, and Bernard Lewis. 1982. *Christians and Jews in the Ottoman Empire: The Functioning of a Plural Society.* New York: Holmes and Meier.

Betts, Robert Brenton. 1978. *Christians in the Arab East.* Atlanta: John Knox Press.

Bria, Ion. 1995. *Romania: Orthodox Identity at a Crossroads of Europe.* Geneva: World Council of Churches.

Davis, Nathaniel. 1995. *A Long Walk to Church: A Contemporary History of Russian Orthodoxy* Boulder, Colo.: Westview Press.

Dvornik, F. 1994. *National Churches and the Church Universal.* Westminster: Dacre Press.

Ellis, Jane. 1986. *The Russian Orthodox Church: A Contemporary History.* London: Croom Helm.

———. 1996. *The Russian Orthodox Church: Triumphalism and Defensiveness.* Basingstoke: Macmillan.

Frazee, Charles A. 1983. *Catholics and Sultans: The Church and the Ottoman Empire 1453–1923.* London: Cambridge University Press.

Gasparov, Boris, and Olga Raevsky-Hughes, eds. 1993–1995. *Christianity and the Eastern Slavs.* 3 vols. Berkeley: University of California Press.

Hastings, Adrian 1997. *The Construction of Nationhood: Ethnicity, Religion and Nationalism.* London: Cambridge University Press.

Keleher, Serge. 1993. *Passion and Resurrection: The Greek-Catholic Church in Soviet Ukraine*. Ukraine: Stauropegion, L'viv.

Kolarz, Walter. 1961. *Religion in the Soviet Union*. London: Macmillan.

Magocsi, Paul Robert. 1993. *Historical Atlas of East Central Europe*. Seattle: University of Washington Press.

Meyendorff, John. 1962. *The Orthodox Church*. London: Darton Longman and Todd.

Mojzes, Paul. 1995. *Yugoslavian Inferno: Ethnoreligious Warfare in the Balkans*. New York: Continuum.

Pospielovsky, Dimitry. 1984. *The Russian Church under the Soviet Regime 1917–1982*. 2 vols. New York: St Vladimir's Seminary.

Ramet, Pedro, ed. 1988. *Eastern Christianity and Politics in the Twentieth Century*. Durham, N.C.: Duke University Press.

Ramet, Sabrina Petra, ed. 1993. *Religious Policy in the Soviet Union*. London: Cambridge University Press.

Rinvolucri, Mario. 1966. *Anatomy of a Church: Greek Orthodoxy Today*. London: Burns and Oates.

Runciman, Steven. 1971. *The Orthodox Churches and the Secular State*. London: Oxford University Press.

Senyk, Sophia. 1993. *A History of the Church in Ukraine*. Rome: Pontificio Istituto Orientale.

Simon, Gerhard. 1974. *Church, State and Opposition in the USSR*. London: C. Hurst.

Stamoolis, James J. 1986. *Eastern Orthodox Mission Theology Today*. New York: Maryknoll.

Thual, François. 1993. *Géopolitique de 1'Orthodoxie*. Paris: Dunond.

Ware, Timothy. 1993. *The Orthodox Church*. London: Penguin.

Zernov, Nicolas. 1961. *Eastern Christendom*. London: G.P. Putnam's Sons.

———. 1963. *The Russian Religious Renaissance of the Twentieth Century*. London: Darton, Longman and Todd.

CHAPTER 29

RELIGIOUS COMMUNITIES IN RUSSIA

ALEXEY D. KRINDATCH

(Note: Unless otherwise cited, all data with statistics of religious organizations, i.e., number of places of regular worship, refer to 2004.)

Most of the world's faiths are represented in Russia. Eastern Orthodox Christians, Muslims, and Buddhists predominate in different regions of the Russian Federation. Jews, Roman Catholics, Protestants, and adherents of various native traditions are dispersed throughout the country as ethnoreligious minorities. Out of fifteen republics of the former Soviet Union, Russia is the only one comparable with the Russian Empire and the USSR in its cultural and ethnic diversity.

Since the Communist atheistic policy and restrictions on religious activities were lifted in the late 1980s, Russia has experienced a religious revival and a multidimensional return of religion to the social realm. Today, religious institutions form a significant component of Russian civil society. However, religious consciousness in Russia is one of secularized religiosity. On the one hand, many Russians regard religious organizations to be strongholds of moral values. On the other hand, religious self-identification frequently reflects neither a personal belief system nor a regular religious practice. Religion is perceived by many simply as part of the traditional cultural environment and as a component of ethnic identity and style of life: "I am Russian and, therefore, Orthodox" or "I am Tatar and, therefore, Muslim." The results of social surveys look paradoxical because they indicate a higher total of respondents identifying themselves as Orthodox, Muslims, and Buddhists than the proportion of those who answer "yes" to the general question "Do you believe in God?" or "Are you a religious person?" These religious identities are rooted in Russia's rich historical past.

ORTHODOX CHRISTIANITY

Orthodox Christianity became the state religion of Kievan Rus in 988 CE, when Grand Prince Vladimir decided to convert his principality to the Christianity of the Byzantine Rite. Initially the Russian Orthodox bishops came under the jurisdiction of the patriarch of Constantinople. However, as Moscow gained more political power, the Russian Orthodox Church (ROC) achieved its full independence ("autocephaly") from Greek Orthodoxy. The Patriarchate of Moscow was instituted in 1589 and the ROC became the national state church with its own titular head, the Patriarch of Moscow and All Russia.

The centralization of state power served to stimulate further territorial expansion of Russia southeast into the Volga basin (second half of sixteenth century), east into Siberia (mainly in the seventeenth century), south into Northern Caucasus (late eighteenth to nineteenth centuries). This expansion integrated within the growing Russian state vast territories with traditionally Islamic and Buddhist and pagan populations.

In the Russian Empire, until the revolution of 1917, Orthodoxy was both the state religion and part of the national ideology. With a few exceptions the followers of other faiths were considered second-class citizens. While most of them were tolerated, some religious groups were officially forbidden and thus persecuted (this was the fate of Orthodox Old Believers, Adventists, Molokans, and others). This situation changed only in 1905, when the Imperial Manifesto of April 17 declared religious tolerance and legalized conversion.

In spite of the privileged position enjoyed by the Orthodox Christianity, the relations between church and state were not easy and sometimes painful. In the late seventeenth century, a significant number of Orthodox believers and clergy refused to accept the church reforms that were supported by the Czar and during which the Orthodox liturgy was heavily modified. This caused a split in the official (reformed) ROC and many groups of the so-called Orthodox Old Believers, which were severely persecuted and outlawed until the twentieth century.

In 1700, Patriarch Adrian opposed the social and economic reforms instituted by Peter the Great, who—after the death of the patriarch—abolished the patriarchal system of church administration. Instead, in 1721, a Holy Governmental Synod was established composed of bishops and presided over by an emperor-appointed secular ober-procurator. The emperor was considered de jure the head of the church and ruled it through the Holy Synod. The institute of patriarchs was re-established only in August 1917.

After the revolution of 1917, the Communist policy of "militant atheism" was originally directed at the ROC in particular, as the symbol of monarchy. During 1918–41 more than 40,000 Orthodox clergy were executed or banished into concentration camps. Whereas in 1914 there were about 77,800 parishes of the ROC, by 1941 only 3,100 were still functioning. The majority of them were in the territories that were annexed to the USSR in 1939. In twenty-five administrative provinces (*oblast*) of the Russian Federation there was not a single functioning Orthodox parish. For two decades after the death of Patriarch Tikhon (1925) there was no patriarch, but in 1944 a few remaining Orthodox bishops were allowed to elect a new patriarch. This was part of Stalin's plan of rapprochement with the church which came at the price of the church's independence. The church affairs were controlled and in some cases administered by the USSR's Council for Religious Affairs which served de facto as the ministry for religious affairs.

After the onset of Gorbachev's policy of political liberalization the ROC began to revive rapidly. In 1988, the ROC had about 6,900 parishes, 21 monasteries, and 5 theological schools. Its clergy comprised 74 bishops and about 6,800 priests and deacons. By 2004, on the territory of the former USSR, the Moscow Patriarchate had about 23,350 parishes, more than 600 monasteries, and over 60 theological educational institutions. Its clergy comprised 162 bishops and 19,500 priests and deacons.

Today, Orthodox Christianity is the largest religion in the Russian Federation. No questions about personal religious affiliation have been asked in the 2002 census, but various sociological surveys and expert estimates indicate that 50 to 60 million Russian citizens identify themselves as Orthodox. In other words Orthodoxy is a religion for 33 to 40 percent of the total population or for about two-thirds to three-fourths of all believers in post–Soviet Russia. Most Orthodox believers belong to the ROC–Patriarchate Moscow (10,767 state-registered parishes in the Russian Federation in 2004), with only a proportion belonging to the diverse groups of Orthodox Old Believers (267 state registered parishes), to the Russian Orthodox Church Outside of Russia (41), to the Russian Orthodox Autonomous Church (36), to the True Orthodox Church (19), and some others.

The ROC must also be seen as an important actor in Russia's foreign affairs. Whereas in the Russian Empire and in the USSR the ROC was a predominantly national church, after the breakup of the USSR it became a truly international organization. The headquarters of the ROC remains in Moscow, but today more than half of its parishes and clergy are no longer in Russia itself but in the other former Soviet republics. In the Ukraine, Byelorussia, and Moldova, the branches of the ROC are the largest religious organizations of these currently independent states.

The official position of the ROC regarding its social role was declared in the "Bases of the Social Concept of the Russian Orthodox Church," which were adopted by an all-church Council of Bishops in 2000. According to this document and to the other decrees of the Bishop Councils, the main goal of the ROC is religious along with moral and educational work with special emphasis on evangelism. In relationship to the broader society the ROC considers itself to be a unifying and reconciling power.

The ROC does not show preference to any particular state system or political party. Clergy cannot be candidates in political elections or be involved in electoral campaigns. Such strong restrictions regarding political activity does not exclude, however, the signing of agreements about cooperation between the Moscow Patriarchate and various federal state institutions as well as between individual dioceses and the state authorities of administrative provinces. Generally, the position of the ROC was clearly formulated by Patriarch Alexei the Second: "The church is separated from the state, but not from the society."

PROTESTANT CHRISTIANITY

There are about one million Protestant Christians and about 5,000 state-registered Protestant congregations in Russia. Of all the religious groups, Protestantism has undergone the greatest changes during the twentieth century. Geographically, it spread from the limited areas of the northwest of the Russian Empire and from territories around Samara and Saratov in the Volga basin and from the Black Sea coast to all regions throughout Russia. This spread was accompanied by an increased diversity of Protestant denominations. At the end of the nineteenth century, "Protestant" and "Lutheran" were virtually synonymous, insofar as Lutherans comprised 95 percent of all Protestants in the Russian Empire, with Calvinists, Mennonites, and Baptists comprising respectively only 2.3 percent, 1.8 percent, and 1.0 percent of the Protestant population. Today Protestantism is represented in Russia by numerous denominations (Pentecostals, Baptists, Adventists, Jehovah's Witnesses, Lutherans, Presbyterians, Calvinists, New Apostolics, etc.) which in turn are divided into independent churches.

The largest Protestant churches in Russia are the Pentecostal Union of Evangelical Christians in Russia (300,000), the Union of the Evangelical Christian Baptists of Russia (about 280,000 members), the Russian Pentecostal Union of Christians of Evangelical Faith (180–200,000), the Church of Jehovah's Witnesses (130–140,000), and the West Russian Union of Christians—the Seventh Day Adventists (120,000).

The first Protestants who settled in Russia were German Lutherans. They were brought to Moscow in 1558 as POWs during the Livonian war. The banks of the Yauza River were known as the German Sloboda (Quarter). The first Lutheran church was erected in 1576. However, the first massive wave of Protestant immigrants to Russia was associated with the epoch of Peter the Great who invited many specialists from Western countries at the start of the eighteenth century to implement his socioeconomic reforms. Later, at the close of the eighteenth century and during the first half of the nineteenth century, upon the invitation of Catherine II and Alexander I, tens of thousands of German-speaking colonists moved into Russia to farm the virgin lands of the Volga basin, Southern Russia, and the Northern Caucasus. Most of them were Protestants. In the beginning of the twentieth century the secondary migration flow from these old colonies was directed to Siberia and dozens of German villages arose around the cities of Omsk and Barnaul.

In spite of its long historical existence in Russia, Lutheranism remains mainly a non-Slav religion. The two major Lutheran organizations in Russia are the Evangelical Lutheran Church and Ingermanland Lutheran Church. The first one is the successor-church to the Lutheran Church in Russia originally instituted in 1832 and re-established in 1991. It has about 120 state-registered congregations with an estimated 60,000 members who are mainly Germans, and persons of German ancestry, and the members of the mixed Russian-German families and some other "Western" ethnicities (Letts, Estonians) living in Russia. The language of worship is German and Russian.

The history, geography, and ethnic composition of the second, Ingermanland Lutheran Church, is different. The majority of its congregations are in northwest Russia, in the provinces of Sankt Petersburg and Karelia, and the members of this church are ethnic Finns living in Russia. Historically this church existed since 1641 when its first bishop was appointed. Under the Soviet regime the Ingermanland Lutheran congregations formed a part of the Estonian Lutheran Church. In 1992, they formed an independent church which has today in Russia 68 state-registered congregations and about 10,000 members. By theology and liturgy the Ingermanland Church is close to Swedish–Finnish Lutheran traditions. The languages of worship are Russian and Finnish.

Although the "ethnic" Lutherans have deep historic roots, they form today only a small segment of the Russian Protestant community. Unlike Lutheranism, the Baptist, Adventist, Pentecostal, and the Jehovah's Witnesses churches gained currency among the Slavic population thanks to the missionary work.

Russian Baptists emerged in the 1860s and 70s in agricultural populations in Ukraine, North Caucasus, and the Volga basin. In many cases the Baptist communities grew out of old Russian sects: the Molokans and the Dukhobors. In 1884 the Union of Russian Baptists was founded. Side by side with the popular rite of baptism, the ideas of evangelical Christianity, similar to those of the Baptist faith, spread among the aristocracy in St. Petersburg in the late 1870s. In 1944, a united Church of Russian Baptists and Evangelical Christians was formed: the Union of Evangelical Christians-Baptists. However, in 1961 a schism resulted from the government's anti-religious campaign, and the separate Council of Churches of Evangelical Christians-Baptists was founded. In comparison with the Union, the members of the Council of Churches are stricter in their religious practices. Under the Soviet regime they have refused any form of cooperation or compromise with the Communist state. For this reason the communities of the Council of Churches were deemed illegal and existed underground until 1988. Even in the post-Soviet era, most congregations of the Baptist Council of Churches refuse to be registered with the state. Membership in the Baptist Council of Churches is estimated at fifty thousand.

The followers of Adventism in Russia were originally German agricultural colonists in the North Caucasus and Volga basin, but in 1890 the first Russian Adventist community appeared in the south of Russia, in the city of Stavropol. The initial spread of Pentecostalism was due to efforts of missionaries from the United States, and the first community of Russian Pentecostals was founded in St. Petersburg in 1913. The Church of Jehovah's Witnesses started in the territories of Western Ukraine, Western Byelorussia, Bukovina, and Bessarabia, which became part of the Soviet Union after annexation in 1939–40.

The significant recent changes on Russian's religious map are associated with an increasing presence of Protestantism in the vast territories to the east of the Ural Mountains—in Siberia and the Far East. In the former Soviet Union, these territories featured a much higher proportion of agnostic population compared with the European part of the country. After the "death" of the Communist atheistic state policy, the Protestant churches have aimed their efforts especially at these "godless" areas. In 2002, four major Protestant religious organizations— the Union of the Evangelical Christian Baptists of Russia, the Pentecostal Union of Evangelical Christians in Russia, Russian Union of Christians of Evangelical Faith (Pentecostal), and West Russian Union of Christians, the Seventh Day Adventists—have formed the Consultative Council of the Leaders of Protestant Churches with the purpose of coordinating their further work.

ROMAN CATHOLICS

The Catholic Church has always been viewed as the "foreign church" serving Poles, Lithuanians, and other Western ethnic minorities resident in Russia. About one-third of Russian Germans are also Roman Catholics. The data on the numbers of Roman Catholics in today's Russia are controversial. The estimates vary from fifteen to twenty thousand regularly practicing believers up to five hundred thousand "virtual" Roman Catholics—counting all persons of Lithuanian, Polish, and German origins, for whom Roman Catholicism can be seen as a traditional religion of their ancestors. Most experts agree on the figure of 150,000.

The history of Roman Catholicism in Russia differs from Protestantism. Generally, compared with the Protestants the attitudes toward the Catholics have been more hostile both in the Russian Empire and in the USSR. In the medieval past, Russian national self-consciousness and statehood were formed on the base of opposition to the West, and the West at that time was equated with Roman Catholicism. Accordingly, Russian Orthodox spirituality has been perceived as an antinomy to the "Latinic world." Unlike Protestantism, Catholicism has been seen by the Russian Orthodox Church as a danger, and the Catholics were suspected of seeking to propagate Papism. Relations were especially harsh during the fourteenth to seventeenth centuries because of armed confrontations between the Russian State and the Catholic Livonia and Poland. The situation changed slightly under the reign of Peter the Great, who allowed the Catholics in Russia to build their first church in 1705. The nineteenth century witnessed the conversion to Catholicism of a number of Russian intellectuals and aristocrats (Prince Gagarin, the poet Chaadaev, the philosopher Solovjev) whose religious choice has been associated with their European cultural orientations, with the protest against Russian backward civil order, and with embracing Western culture.

After the revolution of 1917, in the atheistic Soviet Union, the Roman Catholic Church was perceived to be an agent of world imperialism. In Communist Russia, the Catholic Church did not exist as a religious institution. The few functioning Catholic parishes were de jure under supervision of the Catholic bishop of Latvia, but de facto they were fully autonomous. However, during World War II, "popular" non-institutional Catholicism infiltrated Russian Siberia because of the mass deportation of Russian Germans and Poles by Stalin.

In post-Soviet Russia, Roman Catholicism experienced a dynamic but difficult development. During 1991–2004, the number of state-registered Roman Catholic parishes in Russia grew from 34 to 248. While the Catholic theological seminary in St. Petersburg produced its first graduates in 1999, the vast majority of Catholic clergy in Russia are foreign nationals. Therefore many Catholic parishes have a certain ethnic "coloring" depending on the priest's national background and the traditions of church life in his home country. At the same time, there is a growing tendency toward conversion to Catholicism by the Slavic population. This is especially true among younger, well-educated populations in the larger urban centers. Similar to the past, conversion to Catholicism is seen by youths today as an opportunity for joining a community that shares Western cultural and political values and offers a spiritual atmosphere.

The reviving of Catholicism in Russia would not have been possible without the restoration of the administrative church structures. In 1991 two apostolic administrations (provisional dioceses) were established with headquarters in Moscow (for European Russia) and in Novosibirsk (for Catholics in Siberia). Two more Catholic bishops were appointed in 1998 with their residences in Irkutsk and in Samara. In 2002, the Vatican elevated the provisional administrations to established ecclesiastical structures—dioceses.

This action caused a strong negative reaction by the leadership of the Russian Orthodox Church who accused Catholics of proselytizing among ethnic Slavs on the canonical territory of the Russian Orthodox Church. The Russian political establishment and state authorities intervened openly in the interchurch conflict by backing the position and lobbying for the interests of the Russian Orthodox Church. The Ministry of Foreign Affairs produced a statement, which stressed the fact that the Vatican's decision about creation of the dioceses was not coordinated with the Russian Orthodox Church. A number of Catholic clergy (including the Bishop of Irkutsk, Ezhi Mazur) have been denied Russian entrance visas. Today, in spite of the church growth, the future of Roman Catholicism in the context of Russia's religious and political landscapes remains uncertain.

ISLAM

Islam is the second largest religion in the Russian Federation. More Muslims live in Russia than in Saudi Arabia, Islam's country of origin. There are two main Islamic areas: the Northern Caucasus and the lower Volga basin. Substantial Muslim minorities are present in the Southern Ural and in Western Siberia and also in the capital, Moscow.

The penetration of Islam into the Eastern Caucasus began in the epoch of the Arabic conquest. In 685, the Arabs captured the seaport of Derbent (currently in the Russian republic of Daguestan), and in 722–723 they occupied the internal areas of Daguestan. However, it was not until the eighteenth century that the Islamization of the entire Caucasus was completed, when Islam had finally taken root among the ethnically diverse peoples of the Western Caucasus: Adygs, Kabardins, Cherkess, Balkars, and Karatchai. The spread of Islam into the Volga basin in the eighth century was the result of frequent trade between Khazarian Kaganat and Central Asia. In 922, King Almush declared Islam the state religion of what was then known as Volgo-Kama Bulgaria after a visit of the delegation from the Baghdad Caliphate.

There are over 3,500 officially state-registered local Islamic religious communities in Russia, but neither the real number of de facto functioning mosques nor that of the actual Muslim believers is known. The expert estimate of the number of mosques in Russia is about seven thousand. Evaluating the number of Muslim believers is complicated by the fact that the term *Muslim* is frequently used in the broad ethnic rather than in a religious sense and encompasses therefore not only practicing believers but all the members of ethnicities of traditionally Islamic religious background: Tatars, Bashkirs, and the culturally and linguistically various peoples of the Caucasus. The estimates range therefore from twelve to twenty million Muslims. Today, "ethnic Muslims" form a majority of the population in seven out of eighty-nine administrative provinces of Russia: the republics of Bashkortostan, Tatarstan, Dagestan, Chechnya, Ingushetia, Kabardino-Balkaria, and Karatchayevo-Cherkessia. Demographic prognoses expect the Muslim component in Russia to continue to increase as the ethnically Russian population decreases. There are about seventy state-registered Islamic theological educational institutions. The most important of them are in Moscow, Kazan (capital of Tatarstan), and in the republic of Dagestan.

The Muslim community of Russia consists of almost forty ethnic groups, who speak different languages and have various cultures and life styles. The forms of Islamic religious practices in Russia differ strongly as well. The majority of Russia's Muslims are Sunnis, but the Tats and Azerbaijanians in the North Caucasus are Shiites. Most of Russia's Sunnis follow the Hanafite rite, but the adherents of the Shafiite *mazkhab* (school) constitute the majority of Chechens, Ingushs, and Dagestan Avars. Alongside "official Islam," the mystical Sufism represented by Naqshbandiya and Quadiriya religious orders is widespread in Chechnya, Dagestan, and in Ingushetia. The remains of pre-Islamic tribal beliefs and the norms of the customary law—*adat*—are mixed into Islamic practices of the Adyg ethnolinguistic family (Adygs, Kabardinians, Tcherkess peoples) in Western Caucasus.

By level of religiosity the Muslims of the Volga basin (Tatars, Bashkirs) in the Central European part of Russia are more secularized than the stricter followers of Islam from the Caucasian republics of Chechnya, Ingushetia, and Dagestan where, during the decade of the 1990s, several attempts were made to restore the system of Sharia'h law.

There is no single centralized Muslim religious organization in Russia. Numerous so-called Spiritual Administrations of Muslims are autonomous. Some are organized by territory, others by ethnicity. The repeatedly declared aspiration for some sort of unification of all Russian Muslims is overwhelmed by the ethnic tensions and political ambitions of various Islamic leaders.

The subdivisions within Russia's Muslim community are visible when one compares two big macrocultural Islamic regions, the North Caucasus and the Volga-Ural area. In the Caucasus, the relationship to Islam is rather superficial among the Adyg peoples in Western Caucasus. Here Islam co-exists peacefully with elements of Christianity and with remains of various pagan practices and beliefs. By contrast, in Chechnya and in Dagestan in Eastern Caucasus, the social and political impact of Islam is much more evident.

Even within individual administrative provinces the inner diversity of Islam might be great. For instance, the mountainous republic of Dagestan in the Caucasus region is a peculiar case of ethno-cultural mosaic combined with a variety of local Islamic religious practices, which demonstrated an amazing persistence even under the Communist regime.

The Dagestan town of Bujnaksk is widely recognized as the main Islamic educational and theological center for the entire North Caucasus. In the Russian Federation, it is only in Dagestan that the Islamic religion has been taught as an ordinary subject in the state schools since 1992. It was also in Dagestan that the radical-conservative Wahabi movement, advocating a return to an original "pure Islam," made its first appearance in Russia in the early 1990s, spreading fast in other parts of the North Caucasus.

Despite such strong Islamic traditions, the idea of Islamic unity has neither become the basis for the creation of a new post-Soviet identity for Dagestan's diverse population nor prevented latent and open conflicts in this republic. The seven major ethnic groups—Avars, Dargins, Kumyks, Lezgins, Laks, Tabassarans, Azerbaijanians—number 100,000 to 750,000 each. There are historical tensions among these ethnic clans and competition for representation in the local state administrations. These inter-ethnic contradictions caused the split of Dagestanian Islam into several administrative structures (muftiats, quadiats) that co-exist in the same territory and play a significant role in the process of political mobilization within respective ethnic groups. In May 1997, the armed conflict between followers of the Sufi brotherhood Naqshebandiya and the Wahhabites in Dagestanian villages Tchaban Makhi and Kara Makhi became a first example of an open confrontation based on inter-Islamic religious differentiations.

The relations between the Muslim and Christian (or broadly speaking "Slavic") populations in Russia is a sensitive issue. In the state-controlled mass media, and by federal authorities and by religious leaders, these relations have always been presented as tolerant and mutually respectful. However, the continuing military conflict in Chechnya and the numerous terrorist acts in Russian major cities have seriously tarnished the image of Islam. In the survey completed in June 2003, 49 percent of respondents defined the influence of Islam on the modern world as "negative" and only 14 percent believed it to be "positive."

BUDDHISM

There are about one million Buddhists in Russia and—similar to Islam—Buddhism has been historically a religion of certain ethnic minorities: the Buryats (445,000 as of 2002 census); Kalmyks (174,000); and Tuvinians (243,000). These ethnic groups are concentrated in the republics of Buryatia (where Buryats comprise 28 percent of the population); Kalmykia (where ethnic Kalmyks are 57 percent of the population); and Tuva (where Tuvinians are 77 percent of population). They are also to be found in the Ust-Ordynsky Buryat autonomous area (54,000 Buryats, 40 percent of local population); and the Aginsky Buryat autonomous area (45,000 Buryats, 63 percent of local population). Outside of traditional Buddhist areas, the organized groups of Buddhist worshippers are to be found in the major urban centers, especially in Moscow and in Saint-Petersburg.

The majority of Buddhists in Russia belong to the Gelug-Pa (Virtue) school that is a part of Tibetan Lamaist Buddhism. In Russia the Gelug-Pa school combines elements of both Mahayana and Vajrayana teachings. Buddhism was introduced in Buryatia and in Kalmykia from Tibet and from Mongolia. It spread there mainly during the seventeenth century due to the missionary efforts of Tibetan lamas and because of a migration influx from Eastern Mongolia. As for Tuva, Buddhism came there initially in the thirteenth century (at that time Tuva was a part of Tchingiskhan Empire) through the migration of about ten thousand Chinese, but it did not grow extensively until 1753 when Buddhism was officially declared the state religion of Tandy Urjankhaj (the name of Tuva at that time), competing with the deep-rooted local shamanism. Today, the religious tradition of Tuvinians still combines Buddhism with shamanist practices.

Although the history of Buddhism and the details of the religious practices of Tuvinians, Buryats, and Kalmyks are different, the religion has played an important role in the process of ethnic consolidation of all these peoples. After the lifting of the Communist antireligious policy, the revival of Buddhist traditions and the restoration of various Buddhist institutions has become for Buryats, Tuvinians, and Kalmyks one of the symbols of their ethno-cultural development and consolidation.

By 2004, there were 207 state-registered local Buddhist religious communities and organizations in the Russian Federation. Buddhist religious activity is usually concentrated around Buddhist monasteries: *dazans* in Buryatia, *khuruls* in Kalmykia, *khure* in Tuva. The largest centralized Buddhist organization in Russia is the Buddhist Traditional Sangha (church) of Russia with headquarters near Ulan-Ude, the capital of Buryatia. Many local Buddhist organizations outside of traditional Buddhist areas are subordinated to the Sangha of Russia. This means that they are to a large extent under the influence of the Buryatia variant of Buddhism rather than Tuvinian or Kalmyk. The most established Buddhist theological school in Russia is the Buddhist Institute Dashychojnhorlin in Buryatia. It has students from Russia and from Southeast Asia, from Thailand and Myanmar in particular.

Side-by-side with the revival of religious life of Buryats, Kalmyks, and Tuvinians, the conversion to Buddhism of ethnic Russians can be seen as another tendency in the development of Buddhism during the post-Communist period. The recent converts are mainly youths and intellectuals from urban centers who are interested in Buddhist philosophy and the practice of meditation. Many of the newly established Buddhist organizations do not belong to (Russia's most traditional) Gelug-Pa school. There are, for instance, communities of Theravada, Zen, and Won Buddhists, and followers of the Chan school of Chinese Buddhism. By 2004, 40 percent of all Russia's Buddhist local religious organizations and places of worship were outside of traditional Buddhist areas—named above—in comparison with only 15 percent in 1990.

JUDAISM

The first Jewish communities appeared in the current Russian territory in the early Middle Ages through the influx of Jews from Asia Minor to the north coast of the Black Sea and to the Lower Volga basin. The seventeenth and eighteenth centuries comprised an important period of mass migration for Jews from Germany to the Russian Empire. In fact, prior to the revolution of 1917 the Russian Empire was a worldwide cultural and religious center for the Jewish people and the home of some 5.2 million Jews. However, the anti-Semitism which was widespread in the Russian Empire and its successor the Soviet Union led to the several waves of emigration of Russian Jews: to the United States (at the end of the nineteenth and the beginning of the twentieth centuries) and to Israel (in the late 1960s and in the 1970s, when, after beginning the Israeli-Arab war of 1967, the Soviet authorities showed increasing hostility toward the Jewish community). Most recently, in the 1990s, special favorable regulations for Jewish immigration in Germany encouraged mass emigration of Russian Jews into the country. The tragic events of World War II when over one million Soviet Jews were massacred by Nazis also contributed to the dramatic decline of the number of Jews living in Russia.

As of the 2002 census there were 230,000 Jews remaining in the Russian Federation in comparison with 536,000 according to the previous 1989 census. However, these figures are questionable. They are based on the self-definition of respondents during the census. It is likely that antisemitism discouraged many Russian Jews from revealing their ethnic and religious backgrounds (especially in mixed families). By estimating the number of religious Jews in Russia one should keep in mind a further complication: there is no clear distinction between religious and ethnic identities within the Jewish community. Not all Russian Jews who are Jewish by ethnic background are practicing believers in a religious sense. Furthermore, the Jews in the Russian Federation demonstrate a high level of cultural assimilation with the Slavic population. Only 13 percent of them can speak Yiddish or Hebrew and more than 90 percent recognize Russian as their mother tongue.

As for Jewish religious life, the followers of Orthodox Judaism dominate over adherents of Reformed Judaism. There are 256 state-registered synagogues in Russia and 190 of them belong to Orthodox Judaism. In both Orthodox and Reformed Judaism, charitable foundations, various educational institutions (from kindergarten up to college level) and various ethnocultural associations are closely linked with religious organizations.

Similar to Islam, the Jewish religious community is split into several competing and even hostile factions. These divisions are based on both political ambitions and religious disagreements among their leaders. The two largest religious organizations of Russian Jews are Congress of Jewish Religious Communities and Organizations of Russia (founded in 1993, led by Rabbi Adolf Shaevich) and the Federation of Jewish Communities of Russia, which is strongly influenced by the Lubavitch Khasisds (founded in 1999, led by Rabi Berl Lazar).

Geographically, the Jewish communities are to be found primarily in larger cities: only 2.3 percent of Jews are living in the countryside (compared with 26.6 percent in the case of the total population), and half of all of Russia's Jews live in Moscow and Saint Petersburg.

POST-SOVIET RELIGIOUS REVIVAL

The broad term *post-Communist religious revival* covers several main trends. First, the rise in personal religiosity is astonishing if measured as a proportion of persons who identify themselves as "religious" or as "believers in God" or as followers of a particular religion. According to surveys, by the mid-1990s about 50 percent of Russian citizens declared themselves religious while before Gorbachev's policy of political liberalization (1985) this figure was only 25 percent. Although not as rapidly as in the early 1990s, this growth continues: 62 percent of respondents said they are "believers" in the 2004 national survey. These percentages are higher among ethnic groups of traditionally Islamic religious background, especially, among ethnically diverse Muslims of Northern Caucasus: Tchechens (97 percent),

Ingushs (95 percent), Karatchaevs (88 percent), etc. As for the Slavic population, the level of religiosity differs significantly from one geographic area to another. There is a higher proportion of believers in the Southern European part of Russia—a rural area of old-settlements. By contrast, the vast territories of more recent settlement with a predominantly urban and industrial population east of the Ural Mountains are generally more "godless." Gender is also a significant differentiating factor: today about 68 percent of women in Russia say that they are religious, but only 46 percent of men identify as such. Interestingly enough, in comparison with the obvious ethnic, geographical, social, and gender differences, surveys show that differences in religiosity among the various age groups are tending to decline. So are those among groups with different educational levels.

One should notice, however, the share of actually practicing believers—those who attend church on a regular basis and fulfill other religious requirements—remains very low: 5 to 8 percent according to various estimates. In this regard, Russian society remains by and large agnostic.

The second trend in post-Soviet religious awakening is the increasing social influence of organized churches. The decade of the 1990s has been marked by the dramatic decline of public confidence in the institutions of state power, mass media, public and political associations, and by the high popularity of religious organizations, with the Russian Orthodox Church in first place. Today, about half the population declares their trust in the Russian Orthodox Church and, in this context, the popular confidence in this country's largest religious organization is stronger than in any other state or public institution. Only a small number of Russians support the idea of the participation of the Orthodox Church and clergy in political activities and—according to 2003 survey—only a quarter of the population believes that the current social and political impact of the church in Russia is substantial. Nevertheless, the latent influence of the church on society is greater than it may seem. For example, in 2002, in the wake of the sudden conflict between the Orthodox and the Roman Catholic churches (caused by the establishment in Russia of the Catholic dioceses), almost half the respondents were of the view that that President Putin should not invite the pope to Russia if the Orthodox Church opposed it.

The third post-Soviet religious trend is the dynamic institutional growth of various religions and churches. During 1991–2004, the total number of the state-registered religious organizations increased from 6,600 to 21,600. This number includes local places of regular worship such as Christian parishes and congregations, Islamic mosques, Jewish synagogues, etc. (20,400), monasteries (361), administrative centers of religious organizations (428), and theological educational institutions (157). This quantitative rise was accompanied by an increasing diversity of the Russian "religious landscape." New religious organizations emerged that are mainly foreign in origin and were brought into the country by missionaries from the United States, South Korea, Germany, and elsewhere. Among the most active of the new religious organizations are Presbyterian, New Apostolic, and various charismatic churches as well as Church of Jesus Christ of the Latter Day Saints (Mormons). The geographic distribution of religious organizations of foreign origin is typically inversely proportional to the areas of strength of Russia's traditional religions and churches. The "newcomers" tend to fill a "religious vacuum" in the most godless areas of the country such as Siberia or the Far East.

The Evolution of Church-State Relations

After the revolution of 1917, Lenin's decree of the separation of church and state inaugurated seventy years of a consistent atheistic state policy. The Constitution of the Soviet Union guaranteed equality of all religions and freedom of worship, but there is little question that religion was repressed under Communist rule. The forms of repression changed significantly from outright persecutions during the 1920–30s to grudging toleration with considerable civil discrimination against clergy and openly practicing believers from the mid-1940s until the mid-1980s (while many religious organizations were still entirely outlawed).

In today's Russia the basic principles of church-state relations, as well as the rights of freedom of conscience, are outlined in the constitution's articles 14 and 28. In detail, the religious life of society is regulated by federal legislation, "About freedom of conscience and about religious associations." This was adopted in 1997 and has replaced the previous law of 1990 "About freedom of belief." In brief, the 1990 law focused on various freedoms and rights granted to religious organizations and it considered the religious life of society as a free market regulated only by natural competition. The present legislation emphasizes the idea of cooperation between the state and religious organizations depending on the social significance and on the historical contribution of various religious communities in the context of Russian society. In many ways the 1997 legislation is more restrictive in relation to religious organizations which are recently founded or which have foreign origins. For example, it has implemented a fifteen-year census for the newly established religious groups that will allow them to obtain recognition by the state as a "religious organization"—a status which is not required but provides essential privileges. In 2002, several further amendments to the legislation of 1997 have been proposed with the goal to define a limited number of so-called traditional religions and to grant them various legal privileges over all other religious organizations. While not adopted yet, these amendments are still pending in the Russian parliament.

The legal developments in church-state relations reflect to a certain extent the changes in public preferences and orientations. The late 1980s and early 1990s were characterized by a general passion for religion per se and by an essential interest in different foreign and new (for Russia) religious movements. By the mid-1990s, this situation changed significantly. The growing negative public attitude toward so-called nontraditional religious organizations became evident. Although in a national survey in 1997, 96 percent of Russians agreed with the general principle of freedom of personal choice of belief, only 40 percent of respondents supported the full legal equality of all religions and churches; and 28 percent of the population stood up for direct restrictions on the activity of nontraditional religious organizations in Russia.

With the rise of the xenophobic sentiments in the late 1990s, the sudden expressions of religious intolerance are increasingly associated with growing inter-ethnic tensions. In Putin's Russia, "religious freedom" has generally been seen not as a fundamental and unconditional principle, but rather something that can be granted or taken away by the state depending on circumstances.

BIBLIOGRAPHY

Borshev, V. V., and M. M. Prussak, eds. 1996. *Religioznyje objedinenija Rossijskoj Federacii* (Religious organizations of the Russian Federation). Moscow: Respublika.

Gammer, M. 1995. "Unity, diversity and conflict in the Northern Caucasus." In *Muslim Eurasia: Conflicting Legacies.* Ed. Yaacov Ro'I, 163–87. London: Frank Cass.

Krindatch, A. 1996. *Geography of Religions in Russia.* Decatur, Ga.: Glenmary Research Center.

Malashenko, A. 1998. *Islamskoe vozrozhdeniev sovremennoj Rossii* (Islamic revival of contemporary Russia). Moscow: Moscow Carnegi Center.

Pospelovskij, D. 1995. *Russkaja Pravoslavnaja Cerkov v XX veke* (Russian Orthodox Church in XX century). Moscow: Respublika.

Russian Academy of Governmental Service. 1997. *Religija, svoboda sovesti, gosudarstvenno-cerkovnyje otnoshenija v Rossii* (Religion, freedom of conscience, state-church relations in Russia). Moscow: Russian Academy of Governmental Service.

Russian Orthodox Church–Patriarchate Moscow. The official Web site at http://www.mospat.ru/index.php?lng=1, accessed 10 February, 2006

Russia's Research Institute of Cultural and Natural Heritage. 1996. *Islam v Rossii* (Islam in Russia). Moscow: Russia's Research Institute of Cultural and Natural Heritage.

CHAPTER 30

THE COPTIC COMMUNITY

JUAN E. CAMPO

JOHN ISKANDER

THE Copts, the indigenous Christians of Egypt, are early examples of the global spread of Christianity. Their name comes from *qibt*, which Arabic-speaking Muslims used to designate first the native population of Egypt, and subsequently Egyptian Christians. The Arabic name is a derivative of *aigyptos* (Greek "Egyptian"), which may be based on one of the ancient hieroglyphic names for the pharaonic city Memphis, home of the creator deity Ptah. Though Copts claim descent from the ancient Egyptians, most belong to the monophysite Coptic Orthodox Church, which attributes its origins to the missionary activities of Mark the Evangelist in the first century CE. As a result of the Islamic conquest in the seventh century and gradual conversion to Islam thereafter, they now constitute a small Arabized Christian community in an Arabic-speaking Muslim majority milieu. However, Copts remain the largest Christian population in the entire North African–Middle Eastern region. The key issues they face involve how to maintain communal viability and identity in the face of the powerful forces of nationalism, secularism, emigration, and postcolonial Islamic radicalism.

HISTORY

Coptic tradition traces the founding of the church back to the first century CE, when Saint Mark the Evangelist, arrived in Alexandria and became the first patriarch. Although this tradition is difficult to verify, there was certainly a substantial Christian population in Egypt by the second century CE. Two factors in the early period exerted a profound influence on the history of the church. The first was the persecution that the church suffered at the hands of various Roman emperors, and particularly during the reign of Diocletian. It is with the accession of Diocletian in 284, in fact, that the church begins its calendar, known as the "Era of the Martyrs." The second factor was the Christology espoused by the Alexandrine patriarchs who rejected any separation between the divine and human elements of Christ's nature. At the Council of Chalcedon, in 451 CE, the position of the Alexandrines was rejected; the independent existence of the Coptic Church begins from that date.

Egypt was Christianized by the time the Muslim conquest in 640–642 wrested the province away from the Byzantine Empire. The new Islamic regime had the advantage, from the Coptic perspective, of being uninterested in the theological disputes of the various Christian communities. For the new lords of the land, what was of interest was the substantial and timely payment of tribute, both in the form of the *kharaj,* or land tax, and *jizya,* or poll-tax on non-Muslims. Conversion to Islam, in the early period, was strongly discouraged, as it would lead to a diminution of the tax base. By the Abbasid period (beginning in 750 CE), conversion to Islam on the part of Egyptian Christians was on the rise. In addition, upon suppression of a number of Coptic peasant revolts in the Nile Delta (the last of which was suppressed in 832 CE), large numbers of Arab tribesmen were allowed by the Abbasid governors of Egypt to settle in the Delta, forever changing the religious (and ethnic) makeup of the population. Coptic Christians, however, remained a substantial part of the population, perhaps the majority, until the twelfth and thirteenth centuries, when increased conversion to Islam reduced the Christian population to approximately the percentage it remains today. Throughout the Middle Ages, Copts for the most part lived in relative security as *dhimmis* (protected "peoples of the book," possessing a sacred scripture). During economic downturns or under the threat of foreign invasion, however, the Copts occasionally became the targets of popular anger expressed in pogrom-like attacks on the quarters of the city where they were concentrated. Many churches and monasteries—central to the organization of the community—were destroyed during such outbreaks, and the major wave of conversion to Islam in the fourteenth century was directly linked to a series of massive popular attacks on the Coptic population.

The modern history of the Copts, as with the Egyptian population as a whole, begins with the weakening of Ottoman rule and especially Napoleon's conquest of Egypt (1798–1801). Although that conquest was of extremely short duration, it ushered in a period of modernizing Egyptian governments beginning with Muhammad Ali, which resulted in a substantial change in the relationship of the Coptic community to the larger Muslim society. Christians and Muslims, starting in 1856, were declared citizens with equal rights and responsibilities. During the late nineteenth and twentieth centuries, the church itself underwent what some have called a "revival" or "renaissance" that resulted in giving the laity more of a voice in ecclesiastical affairs, educational reforms, and reaffirmation of the monastic tradition. Since the 1952 Free Officers' Revolution, the church has increased its wealth—largely through the remissions of Copts in the diaspora—and as a result has seen an increase in its power within the Christian community and Egypt as a whole. Under the dynamic leadership of the much-loved Patriarch Kyrillos VI (d. 1971) and the current patriarch Shenouda III, the church has positioned itself as the guarantor of the rights and freedoms of Egyptian Christians, while maintaining friendly relationships with the government and even such groups as the Muslim Brotherhood.

DEMOGRAPHICS

There are conflicting estimates for the size of Egypt's Coptic population. As is often the case with minorities, official counts tend to underestimate their size, while the minority group inflates its own numbers. In the early 1970s the government count was about 3.5 million, or about 10 percent of the total population. The church claimed a membership of close to 7 million (20 percent of the total). The 1986 census said that Copts comprised 6.3 percent of the population. By 1997, the total Egyptian population reached 61.5 million, of which almost 6 percent (3.6 million) were Copts according to the official count, perhaps as few as 5.7 percent. Some Coptic sources claim, however, that there were more than 9 million Copts (about 15 percent of the population) at this time. Other estimates say that they still constituted about 10 percent of the population. Copts remain by far the largest Christian population in North Africa and the Middle East, and they are growing in number. Nevertheless, it appears that they are actually diminishing in proportion to Egypt's Muslim population. This can be attributed to emigration, a declining birth rate, and conversion to Islam; but as long as we lack accurate data it is difficult to assess the extent to which any one of these factors actually affects the size of the Coptic population.

Members of this community have strong ties to rural areas in Upper Egypt, but they are concentrated in Nile Valley cities and towns. This has been the case since the Islamic conquest. According to a comparative analysis of census data published in the 1970s (Chitham 1986: 38–48); the Cairo governorate has the largest share of Christians in the country (22 percent); followed by the Upper Egyptian governorates of Minya (17.2 percent); Asyut (14.6 percent); and Sohag (11.8 percent). No governorate or city has a Coptic majority, but these same cities have the largest proportion of Christians within Egypt's total population. Few inhabit the Delta, but concentrations are evident in Alexandria and the Suez Canal towns. In Cairo, Copts can be found in all districts, living together with Muslims, and until the 1950s and 60s, with Jews; they are not confined to a Christian quarter per se. They are especially numerous in the former middle-class districts (now more working class, with small-scale industries) located north of downtown Cairo, such as Shubra and Rod al-Farag; in central commercial districts such as Ezbe-kiyya, Zahir, and Qasr al-Nil; as well as in the newer middle-class suburbs of Heliopolis and Nuzha on the northeastern edge of the city (Chitham 1986: 89–95). All of these areas are also connected historically with the European presence in Egypt. Few Copts remain in the districts of medieval Cairo (for example, Gam-aliyya and al-Darb al-Ahmar), and surprisingly few live in Old Cairo (formerly known as Fustat), where a number of medieval Coptic religious buildings are located, in addition to the modern Coptic Museum.

Prior to the modern era, Copts were known for their prowess in agriculture, finance, administration, and craftsmanship. They are still employed in these areas, but they are also strongly represented in modern professions such as medicine, pharmacy, engineering, and architecture. Indeed, the level of education among Egypt's Christians is higher than it is for the population as a whole, largely because of their openness to European educational reforms, starting in the late nineteenth century and the influence of foreign Christian missionary schools. Copts also undertake tasks that are shunned by Muslims and foreigners; garbage collection and disposal in Cairo is controlled by Coptic families who live in squalor on the city's outskirts.

Obstacles to determining the size of the Coptic community as a whole with precision make it even more difficult to estimate the size of subgroups within it. The overwhelming majority identify themselves with the Coptic Orthodox Church. Since the nineteenth century, Copts have also joined minority Roman Catholic, Greek Orthodox, Greek Catholic churches, as well as a variety of Prot-estant and evangelical Christian denominations. This was a result of missionary activities, dissatisfaction with the dominance of the Coptic clergy, the establish-ment of church-affiliated schools with Western-style curricula, and intermarriage. Nonetheless, many of these converts have maintained their Coptic ethnic identity, unlike those who converted to Islam. Thus, while it is possible to find Coptic Catholic and Coptic Protestant churches in Egypt, there is no evidence for any-thing like a Coptic Muslim mosque, church, or religious order.

RITUAL PRACTICES

Ritual activities are instrumental to the formation and maintenance of Coptic identities. Bound together with strong Trinitarian Christian beliefs and widespread faith in the manifestation of miraculous forces in everyday life, the Copts engage in three interconnected forms of ritual practice: sacramental, monastic, and devotional.

The Orthodox Church recognizes seven sacraments (*al-asrar al-muqaddasa*): baptism (*ma'mudiyya*), confirmation (*masha* or *mirun muqaddas*), penance (*tawba* or *i'tiraf*), Holy Communion (*afkharistiyya* or *qurban muqaddas*), unction of the sick (*mashat al-marda*), marriage (*zawaj*), and holy orders (*kahanut*). Each requires the services of an ordained priesthood, which claims to have inherited its authority from Jesus through the apostles. It is organized as a hierarchy consisting of a patriarch (also called a pope), bishops, priests, and deacons. The seat of the patriarch is now at the Cathedral of Saint Mark (*al-Murqusiyya*) in Cairo. Most of the sacraments are performed in a church, though Copts often prefer to conduct baptisms and confirmations at a monastery or shrine. In addition to their spiritual benefits, the sacraments contribute significantly to maintaining communal solidarity—allowing baptism, confirmation, and communion for infants brings individuals promptly within the folds of the church; requiring marriage with other Orthodox Copts limits attrition through mixed marriage. Non-Copts must convert before marriage, and if they are Christians from other denominations they should be rebaptized. Although fasting is not a formal sacrament, it is required prior to receiving the Eucharist and is widely practiced by laity and clergy alike in accordance with the liturgical calendar, which recognizes over two hundred days of fasting annually. It normally involves abstaining from consuming all meat and animal products, no food or drink during daylight hours, as well as suppression of other bodily appetites.

Coptic identity is also formed and sustained by monasticism (*rahbana*), the second aspect of their ritual activity. This institution was created by the desert saints, Anthony and Pachomius, in the late fourth to early fifth centuries, and has played a pivotal role in maintaining the continuity of the church in good times and bad. It has provided the church with most of its leaders and exemplary saints and guided the church's "revival" during the nineteenth and twentieth centuries. Late in the twentieth century there were some 1,500 contemplative nuns, monks, and novices living in the eighteen convents and monasteries in Egypt that have been officially recognized by the Coptic Church (Doorn-Harder 1995: 34–37, 39). The monasteries are fortress-like compounds located in the country's arid deserts, while convents tend to be situated in traditional urban neighborhoods, mainly in Cairo. A monastic career begins with a probationary period of study and residence in the monastery, followed by admission into the novitiate through formal consecration rites, when the candidate is said to become dead to the outside world. Although nuns and monks may participate in daily communal meals, prayers, and liturgical celebrations, emphasis is placed on individual vigils, prostrations, prayer, and other ascetic activities performed in the solitude of the monastic cell (*qallayya*) or a secluded spot in the desert or mountains. The significance of this activity is aptly conveyed in the words of one of the monks: "Go and sit in your cell; the cell will teach you everything" (quoted in Doorn-Harder 1995: 47). Indeed, monasticism offers the Coptic community an idealized self-representation as a spiritual counterculture that cogently reflects its minority status in an Islamic milieu.

The devotional aspect of Coptic ritual life centers on the cult of the saints and pilgrimages to their shrines. Saints have the power to intervene at any moment in one's life; many Copts claim to have encounters with them in their dreams. Icons and saintly portraits adorn churches, homes, businesses, and vehicles. In seeking a blessing or cure, averting evil, or in penitence or thanksgiving for an answered prayer, devotees flock to shrines throughout the year, especially on the saint's feast day (*mulid*). Many go to have their children (males and females) baptized and circumcised, or to have crosses tattooed on their right wrists—a public symbol of Christian identity in an Islamic context. According to one estimate there are some sixty Coptic pilgrimage centers in late twentieth-century Egypt (Atiya 1991: 1968), in addition to those in the Holy Land that Copts have visited on only a very limited basis since the Arab-Israeli wars of 1967 and 1973. The most popular saints are the Virgin Mary, whom many claim to have seen in apparitions, and Saint George. They are venerated at sites throughout the country, but their shrines at Dayr al-Muharraq (near Asyut) and at Riziqat (near Luxor) respectively draw the large numbers of pilgrims on their annual feast days (fifty to one hundred thousand). In June 2000, Muslim and Christian officials and religious figures gathered at the Church of the Holy Virgin in a south Cairo suburb to celebrate the second millennium anniversary of the Holy Family's flight into Egypt. Other pilgrimage centers commemorate the archangel Michael, martyrs, and Coptic Church fathers. In recent decades, Coptic authorities have had some success in quelling the more carnivalesque, nondevotional activities that accompany the mulids, like their Muslim counterparts.

New shrines were established during the twentieth century at ancient Coptic holy sites, such as those of Patriarch Kyrillos VI (d. 1971) at Mari Mina's monastery in Maryut, Farous at St. Paul's monastery in the mountains of the Eastern Desert, and Abuna Yustus (d. 1976) at St. Anthony's monastery nearby. One of the most famous new shrines is the Church of the Virgin in Zeitun on the northern edge of Cairo, where widely reported Marian apparitions and miraculous healings occurred in the wake of Egypt's defeat in the 1967 Arab-Israeli war. With the support of church authorities and private donations, this modest church grew into a shrine complex consisting of a cathedral, health clinic, day care center, and housing for the elderly and unmarried girls.

LIVING WITH MUSLIMS

Relations between Copts and Muslims are frequently subject to distortion and misunderstanding. The prevailing nationalist discourse in Egypt sees both communities as contributing together to the common good of the nation, with all citizens holding equal rights and responsibilities. In the Egyptian cinema, historical dramas portray Coptic priests and Muslim shaykhs locked arm in arm, leading the masses in protest against British occupation. On the other hand, religious extremists in both communities—vociferous, though small in number—see the religions as largely incompatible, even to the point of regarding the others as infidels. Members of radical Islamist groups (jama'at) avoid associating with Christians, and in their call for the creation of an Islamic state, some would like to revive the subordinate dhimmi status for them. Militant Islamists attack Coptic-owned businesses and threaten individual Christians who do not conform to their codes of conduct and dress. Coptic extremists are not in a position to advocate for the creation of a Christian state, but instead exaggerate claims of religious persecution and retreat to a ghetto-like existence. Coptic émigrés in the West have embraced aspects of this discourse to the extent that they threaten to undermine the balance of relations between the two communities in Egypt. This situation is exacerbated by the occasional intervention of the Christian Right in the United States and the sometimes uninformed commentaries that appear in Western media which reduce incidents of socio-political violence to timeless interfaith hostilities.

A more fruitful way to view Coptic-Muslim relations is to look for their points of interconnection and discontinuity alike, within the wider framework of Egyptian culture, politics, and economics. Muslims and Copts look to the figure Maria the Copt, a favorite concubine or wife of the Prophet Muhammad (d. 632) and the mother of his son Ibrahim, as a symbol of historical harmony between the two communities. Both communities share a common language (the most prevalent word for God among Christians and Muslims alike is the Arabic "Allah"), a largely common ethnicity, and have experienced the costs and benefits of colonization, nationalism, urbanization, secularization, and industrial development. Both know the pains of defeat in modern war and embrace the progress made toward living in peace with neighboring countries. Copts hold substantial positions alongside Muslims in parliament, ministries, and public sector companies; and they work together in private sector businesses and trades. Butrous Butrous Ghali, the former secretary general of the United Nations, is a Copt and a former Egyptian minister of foreign affairs. Copts, like Muslims, are also required to serve in the armed forces.

In their ritual life, Copts and Muslims customarily exchange greetings on major religious holidays and attend each other's weddings and funerals. When Shaykh Muhammad Sha'rawi, a popular Muslim religious figure, died in June 1998, Patriarch Shenouda III eulogized him in the Egyptian press. Muslims visit Coptic saints' shrines and mulids, tattoo crosses on Coptic wrists, and turn to Coptic priests when seeking to exorcise a demonic spirit—although their participation in all of these activities is in decline. Both acknowledge the sacred status of Jesus, Mary, and other biblical figures, although not in the same way. They recognize similarities (as well as differences) in religious activities such as fasting, prayer, and the memorization of scripture. Both communities segregate the sexes during worship, though Coptic women do not practice veiling and gender segregation to the extent that Muslim women do. Copts and Muslims in Egypt alike practice male and female circumcision. Key disjunctions in the area of religious belief and practice include Muslim rejection of Jesus as the God incarnate, iconic representation of holy figures, the meaning of the Eucharist, the sacramental use of wine, and monasticism. Copts do not usually frequent mosques and Muslim saint shrines for religious purposes, nor do they accept the Islamic understanding of Jesus as "the son of Mary," which implies denial of his divinity.

Since the death of Gamal 'Abd al-Nasir in 1971, Egyptian affairs have been infused with a more Islamic spirit. The government recognizes Islam as the official religion of state, and the Shari'a has become the principle source for the law of the land. To counteract leftists in the 1970s, the Sadat government encouraged the Muslim Brotherhood and the formation of Islamic youth groups on university campuses. Copts began to experience more discrimination in school and at the work place, driving some to turn to Coptic-only employers, institutions, and voluntary associations, and others with sufficient resources to emigrate to Christian majority countries in Europe, Australia, and North America. Having played the "Islamic card" at that time, the government found itself faced with growing Islamic radicalism and began to take steps to contain it, resulting in sporadic cycles of violence between agents of the state and armed Islamists. Egyptians as a people, Muslims, and Christians, have since paid a high price in this war: hundreds have been killed and wounded, tens of thousands have been imprisoned, President Anwar al-Sadat was assassinated in front of his own ministers and troops in 1981, and billions of dollars in tourist revenues have been lost. Restoring the peace at home and establishing more equitable relations between Muslims and Christians must clearly be among the most serious challenges facing Egypt at the beginning of the twenty-first century.

LIVING IN DIASPORA

The church established outposts in Sudan and Ethiopia, as well as in Jerusalem, long ago. In recent times, however, Copts—like their Egyptian Muslim compatriots—have begun to migrate in relatively massive numbers to North America, Europe, and Australia. Since many of these émigrés were well-educated professionals in Egypt, emigration to the industrialized nations has been an attractive and mutually beneficial situation. No precise count of the Coptic émigré population has been undertaken, and numbers given range from the hundreds of thousands to over a million. Several hundred churches have been built abroad, which serve as important centers for Coptic social as well as religious life. Some have succeeded in winning new converts, and others play host to annual Egyptian cultural pageants.

Some Copts in Egypt consider emigration to be a betrayal of the community as a whole, both because the best educated and wealthiest are often the ones who can emigrate, and because every Copt who emigrates weakens the population of Copts that remains in Egypt and further upsets the balance of Copt-Muslim relations. The church, however, has taken the stand that this emigration is only a result of natural circumstances and is neither a flight into exile nor a threat to the strength of the home church. Pope Shenouda III, in particular, has strongly supported the emigration of Copts and visits the émigré churches regularly. Certainly the Coptic Church in Egypt has benefited tremendously from the émigré population. As Copts abroad become wealthier, and are able to donate financial resources to the church, the home church has become progressively wealthier and better established. One could say, in fact, that the renaissance currently under way in the Coptic Church has been partly funded by the Coptic émigrés.

Although tied in many ways to the Egyptian mother church, Copts abroad are beginning to define a distinctive identity. While their priests tend to be Egyptian born and trained, there are increasing numbers of émigré Copts joining the priesthood. Moreover, the Coptic community has become increasingly independent of the church politically. While the church holds to a government-sanctioned line that emphasizes the unity of the Egyptian nation without regard to religion, Copts in the United States have very publicly accused the Egyptian government of complicity in the murder—actually carried out by militant Islamist groups—of Copts in the southern part of Egypt. As émigré Copts bring pressure to bear upon the Egyptian government, reaction in the Egyptian press and of many in the public has been to accuse the Copts—without differentiating between those in Egypt and émigrés—of dividing the nation. Many Copts in Egypt, including many in the church hierarchy, have, as a result, strongly opposed the actions of émigré Copts (such as publishing strongly worded advertisements in major U.S. newspapers and staging demonstrations during the Egyptian president's visits to the United States) that draw attention to the various forms of persecution and discrimination that most Copts consider to be a part of everyday life in Egypt. As Coptic émigrés continue to increase in numbers and wealth, we can only expect this sort of independence to increase, although it is not likely to lead to a break with the church in Egypt.

BIBLIOGRAPHY

Atiya, Aziz Sourial, ed. 1991. *The Coptic Encyclopedia*. 8 vols. New York: MacMillian.

Bestavros, A. 1998. *Encyclopedia Coptica*. Available on the Web at: http://www.coptic.net/EncyclopediaCoptica/.

Chitham, E. J. 1986. *The Coptic Community in Egypt: Spatial and Social Change*. Durham, England: University of Durham.

Doorn-Harder, Pieternella van. 1995. *Contemporary Coptic Nuns*. Columbia: University of South Carolina Press.

Doorn-Harder, Nelly van, and Kari Vogt, eds. 1997. *Between Desert and City: The Coptic Orthodox Church Today*. Norway: University of Oslo.

Kamil, Jill. 2002. *Christianity in the Land of the Pharoahs: The Coptic Orthodox Church*. London: Routledge.

Meinardus, Otto F.A. 2002. *Coptic Saints and Pilgrimages*. Cairo, Egypt: American University in Cairo Press.

CHAPTER 31

LATIN AMERICAN CATHOLIC SOCIETIES

PAUL E. SIGMUND

A large majority of Latin Americans identify themselves as Roman Catholics. But to what extent are Latin American societies Catholic? If regular church attendance is the measure, a larger percentage of the population attends Mass on any given Sunday morning in the United States than in most Latin American countries. Countries like Uruguay have very low rates of Catholic religious practice, and until recently Mexico and Cuba had anti-Catholic laws and policies. Anticlericalism has been strong in Latin America, at least since the nineteenth century and probably earlier. In the last two decades, conversions to evangelical Protestantism have accelerated, and Pentacostalism is the fastest-growing religion in Latin America. There are now more Mormons in Latin American than in the United States. The remnants of state support for Catholicism are rapidly disappearing in the wave of constitutional reforms that has followed the transition from military rule to elected civilian governments in the eighties and nineties.

Yet the history, culture, and public ceremonials of Latin America are profoundly Catholic, and even those who, except for weddings and funerals, have never been near a Catholic Church since baptism think of themselves as Catholic. The number of adherents of evangelical Protestantism and other religions is growing, but Brazil and Mexico have the largest Catholic populations in the world. (With sixty-two million Catholics, a growing number of them of Hispanic background, the United States is in third place.)

Like most Catholics worldwide, those in Latin American accept the teaching authority of the pope and bishops, although they will disagree with individual teachings, and often their practice departs widely from church teachings, especially in the area of sexual morality. The doctrines of the Trinity, the Incarnation, the Death and Resurrection of Christ, and the Immaculate Conception and Assumption into heaven of the Blessed Virgin Mary are core beliefs, as are the central position of the sacraments, especially Baptism, Confirmation, and the Holy Eucharist. The major Catholic feasts are observed as national holidays in many Latin American countries and most of the continent closes down from Christmas until the Feast of the Three Kings (Epiphany) in late December and early January, and for Holy Week before Easter. Villages often have colorful festivals on the feasts of the saints after which they are named, and many countries are dedicated to Mary under various names. In the cases of the Our Lady of Guadaloupe in Mexico and the Virgin of Mount Carmel (Carmen) in Chile, she is a symbol of national identity, and in the late 1980s the Shrine of the Black Virgin of Esquipulas was the site of the agreements that ended the Central American civil wars.

The identification of Latin America with Catholicism goes back to the colonization of the area by Spain and Portugal. The conquistadores were accompanied by Franciscan and Dominican missionaries ("the cross and the sword") and the conquest of Latin America was justified as an effort to convert the Indians to the true religion. In the Aztec and Inca regions of present-day Mexico and Peru, pagan temples were destroyed and Catholic houses of worship built over them. The church tried to mitigate the exploitation and enslavement of the Indians, and a few churchmen even questioned whether the conquest of the Americas was morally justified, but the Indian religions were extirpated and the Inquisition was established in Peru and Mexico. Through the institution of the *patronato real* or royal patronage, granted to the Spanish monarchs by the papacy in 1508, royal control of the appointment of bishops and clergy, preaching, missionary activity, and the collection of the tithe or church tax was assured. The church carried out a wide range of educational and welfare activities and possessed some autonomy, but at the highest levels the Spanish government exercised a decisive influence.

The superimposition of Catholicism in the Aztec and Inca areas was not difficult, because as in Spain, the native cultures closely linked religion and politics and were highly centralized. The militancy of Spanish Catholicism and the close ties between church and state were influenced by the centuries-long struggle to reconquer Spain from the Moslems that had ended in 1492, and in the sixteenth century by the effort of the Catholic Counter-Reformation to combat the spread of Protestantism. The only partially successful effort of the Hapsburg monarchs to control and coordinate the guilds and other corporate groups that had developed in late medieval Spain also influenced the organization of the Spanish colonies. In contrast to their North American counterparts, Latin American societies in colonial times were conservative, centralized, racially and socially hierarchical, composed of corporate groups and extended families, and characterized by religious uniformity (Wiarda 1981; Veliz 1988). While local governing bodies such as the *cabildo* were developed, the ultimate authority was the viceroy or royal governor or his representative.

These ideas and institutions, largely Catholic in their inspiration and uninfluenced by the Reformation, the Enlightenment, and the scientific and industrial revolutions, continued to mold Latin American culture down to the present. In this century they influenced various corporatist or organic theories of society that were developed by Catholic conservatives as an alternative "third position" between liberalism and socialism (Stepan 1978).

Liberalism came to Latin America in the nineteenth century from France and Spain rather than England and America and therefore differed from the Anglo-American liberal tradition. Although the term *liberal* was first employed in Spain in the 1820s, liberalism was viewed by many Catholics as contrary to their religion. As in Latin Europe, it was often linked to the spread of freemasonry and favored the abolition of the privileged position of the Catholic Church. Indeed, the basic political division in most Latin American countries throughout much of the century was between pro-church conservatives and anticlerical liberals. When liberal forces controlled the government, they would often confiscate church lands; limit or end its influence over education, hospitals, cemeteries, and the conversion of the Indians; and extend legal recognition to, mostly foreign-based, Protestants. (The best-known example of these programs is La Reforma of Benito Juarez in 1857, after which the principal boulevard of Mexico City is named.) The quasi-religious character of the differences between the two groups helps to explain the intensity of the political struggles of the time and the resulting political instability. Their effects were felt in the twentieth century in the anticlerical policies of the Mexican Revolution, including the strong, although often unenforced, limits on Catholicism contained in the 1917 constitution of Mexico, most of which were removed only in 1994.

In the mid-twentieth century, a political split developed within Catholic conservatism that produced Christian Democratic parties in many countries of Latin America. Drawing on the social teachings of the papal labor encyclicals and the writings on democracy and human rights of the French neo-Thomist philosopher, Jacques Maritain, the Christian Democrats argued that the Catholic tradition supported rather than opposed democracy, religious freedom, and human rights. Criticizing liberalism for its excessive individualism and commitment to free enterprise, the Christian Democrats initially argued for a corporative or functionalist legislative representation in the legislature and worker participation in factory ownership and profit sharing. Over time, however, they came to differ chiefly in their religiously based rhetoric and personal links to the church from the welfare-state liberals and social democrats with whom they were competing. Initially facing opposition from the Vatican and some members of the hierarchy, their support for democracy and human rights was finally adopted by the church as a whole in Pope John XXIII's encyclical, *Pacem in Terris* (1963) and the declaration of the Second Vatican Council on Religious Freedom and its endorsement of democracy in its decree on *The Church in Modern World* (1965).

That shift to democracy and human rights came just before most of Latin America succumbed to a wave of military coups. In most countries—Argentina was a notable exception—the church organized human rights groups and opposed military repression. In the transitions from military rule of the 1980s, as well as the ending of the Central American conflicts, the church took on a leading role. After the establishment of democratic rule and the emergence of competitive politics, it moved away from political participation and placed more emphasis on moral issues opposing abortion, divorce, materialism, and hedonism, although it continued to be critical of the adverse effects of the international economic system on the welfare of the poor.

A further broadening of the ideological spectrum within Latin American Catholicism took place with the emergence of liberation theology in the late 1960s and early 1970s. Quoting the biblical passages on the special religious status of the poor, and espousing a more partisan political commitment by the church, the liberation theologians, led by Gustavo Gutierrez of Peru, argued that capitalism was responsible for Latin American poverty and that socialism—in extreme cases revolutionary socialism—was the appropriate political position for Christians. They also favored the use of social theory, especially Marxism and dependency theory, to analyze the root causes of Latin America's problems. Their links to Marxism and promotion in several Latin American countries of alliances of Left Catholics and Marxists led to criticism by the Vatican, especially after the election of Pope John Paul II in 1978. In the mid-1980s the Vatican issued two statements on liberation theology. The first was critical of those versions that were based on Marxism and promoted revolution, while the second argued that a biblically based liberation theology in communion with the church that was oriented toward the problems of both spiritual and material poverty was not only useful but necessary for church teaching. With the collapse of the Soviet Union and the ensuing economic difficulties of Cuba, as well as the failure of the Sandinista experiment in Nicaragua, liberation theology lost influence, although the liberation theologians were successful in persuading the Latin American bishops at their 1979 Puebla conference to adopt what they called "the preferential option for the poor" as a central element in the agenda of the Latin American church. In addition, the organization in many Latin American countries of Christian Base Communities, centers for the application of biblical teaching to the day-to-day problems of the poor, was associated with the influence of liberation theology (Sigmund 1990).

On the right, a more modern version of Catholic conservatism has emerged with the extension of the influence of Opus Dei, a conservative Catholic religious group, originally established in Spain in the 1930s. While Opus Dei was influential in the last days of the Franco government, it now supports democracy and free enterprise and recruits its membership from the technical, financial, business, and professional elites, although it also does extensive work among the poor. It attempts to extend Catholic influence to modernizing sectors of Latin America, shifting the church's base from rural and landowning sectors to the more modern sectors of a continent that has become predominantly urban and industrial.

What has resulted is much greater pluralism within Latin American Catholicism in attitudes toward politics and society with conservatives, liberals, and radicals all finding a basis in the Catholic tradition for their views. Contributing to this pluralism are the policies of the Vatican, under Pope John Paul II, which has promoted religious and moral conservatism but accepted liberal democracy and capitalism (subject to moral and legal constraints imposed by concern for "the common good"), while making radical criticisms of the widening gap between rich and poor countries.

The cultural and moral influence of Catholicism in Latin America is still strong, although it has diminished as a result of the competition of Protestantism, especially of the evangelical and Pentecostal variety, secularism, and materialism. The degree of Catholic influence and practice varies from country to country. Uruguay is probably the most secular, while Chile, Costa Rica, and Colombia are the most Catholic. There is also variation on the basis of social class—with strong influence among the upper classes, many of whom have attended exclusive private schools run by Catholic religious orders, and in the lower classes where a popular Catholicism, often linked to devotion to Mary and the saints, is widespread. In the Indian areas, indigenous religions have survived, and sometimes they have influenced a syncretic Catholicism that has identified Catholic saints with earlier pagan deities. In Mexico, the miraculous appearance of Our Lady of Guadaloupe is commemorated at the site of an earlier Aztec temple. In general, devotion to the Virgin Mary is stronger in Latin America than elsewhere and provides an obstacle to the expansion of Protestantism. Feminists have criticized the veneration of Mary for promoting a dichotomous version of the female as "virgin or whore" and supporting Latin American patriarchalism and machismo, the exaggeration of supposed male qualities and the subordination of women. Other cultural characteristics of Latin America that have been linked to Catholicism include the strength of family ties, commitment to moral values—in theory, if not in practice—as well as a willingness to recognize human fallibility and weakness, based on a belief in original sin. Catholic influence is partially responsible for the fact that abortion is outlawed in all Latin American countries despite being widely practiced. Church opposition, along with the availability of a convenient but fraudulent annulment procedure blocked efforts to repeal the prohibition of divorce in Chile until 2004.

There have been changes, however, in the legal and constitutional position of Catholicism in Latin America. Among the constitutional reforms that accompanied the movement to civilian elected governments in the 1980s and 1990s has been a reduction in the special legal or constitutional position of Catholicism so that, for example, it is no longer required that the president of Argentina be Catholic. In Chile and Columbia there have been successful efforts, only Argentina, Bolivia, and Costa Rica, while guaranteeing religious freedom for all, distinguish in their constitutions between Catholicism and other religions, and in the first two countries there have been strong arguments for the repeal of those clauses. In Chile and Colombia there have been efforts to modify or generalize the special position of Catholicism resulting from earlier concordats with the Vatican. Evangelical Protestants have organized political parties in several countries and are pressing for equal treatment.

However, the historical and cultural tradition and the many institutions operated by, or linked to the Catholic Church, ensure that its influence on Latin American society will continue to be strong. There are Catholic universities in many countries, elite primary and secondary schools operated by the religious orders, active efforts to compete with evangelicals in shantytown areas, missionaries working with the Indian population, radio stations, newspapers, and media coverage of church programs and policies, and charitable institutions and activities in many areas. Most important, the network of parish priests and churches, organized under the bishops or archbishops of each diocese, and the large numbers of priests, women religious, and dedicated laypersons ensure that Catholicism will remain a presence in Latin America. The forces of secularism, religious pluralism, and globalization are strong, but Latin American societies will continue to be predominantly Catholic for the foreseeable future.

BIBLIOGRAPHY

Cleary, Edward. 1985. *Crisis and Change: The Church in Latin America Today*. Maryknoll, N.Y.: Orbis Books.

Dussell, Enrique. 1981. *A History of Church in Latin America*. Grand Rapids, Mich.: Eerdmans.

Gill, Anthony. 1998. *Rendering unto Caesar: The Catholic Church and the State in Latin America*. Chicago: University of Chicago Press.

Gutierrez, Gustavo. 1973. *A Theology of Liberation*. Maryknoll, N.Y.: Orbis Press; reprinted with new introd.,1988.

Lernoux, Penny. 1982. *Cry of the People*. New York: Penguin Books.

Levine, Daniel H., ed. 1986. *Religion and Political Conflict in Latin America*. Chapel Hill: University of North Carolina Press.

Sigmund, Paul E. 1990. *Liberation Theology at the Crossroads*. New York: Oxford University Press.

———, ed. 1999. *Evangelization and Religious Freedom in Latin America*. Maryknoll, N.Y.: Orbis Press.

Stepan, Alfred. 1978. *State and Society: Peru in Comparative Perspective.* Princeton, N.J.:
    Princeton University Press.
Veliz, Claudio. 1988. *The Centralist Tradition of Latin America.* Princeton, N.J.: Princeton
    University Press.
Wiarda, Howard J. 1981. *The Corporatist Tradition in Latin America.* Boulder, Colo.:
    Westview Press.

CHAPTER 32

NORTH AMERICAN RELIGIOUS COMMUNITIES

WADE CLARK ROOF

RELIGION in contemporary North America reflects the dynamic interplay of two widespread modernizing trends: pluralism and privatization. The societies of both the United States and Canada took shape culturally and religiously by migrant streams and continue to be shaped by them. The immigrants came first from Protestant and Catholic areas in Europe and more recently from many other parts of the globe. These patterns of immigration have been closely linked to the economic and political alliances of the modern era, resulting in lasting structures of religious pluralism that were superimposed upon a preexisting pluralistic indigenous religious life. At the same time, modernity with its enhanced individualism and subjectivity has led to highly privatized religious styles—in keeping with an underlying, broadly based shift in contemporary societies from ascriptive loyalties to greater personal choice.

Among other things, this privatization has meant a more voluntary approach to religious belonging and interpretation, thereby enhancing the diversity of belief, practice, and outlook among and within religious communities. In both countries, religious cultures carry the strong imprint of the Enlightenment. Constitutionally, religion is separate from the state. The individual enjoys sovereignty in matters of faith and practice, and religious polities—even those of the most hierarchically organized bodies—are sensitive to the wishes of local congregations. Democratic ideology intersects with tradition to create highly adaptable, popular-based faiths.

Historically, Catholic and Protestant strongholds in Canada assured a dominant Christian influence. A strong evangelical Protestant tradition in the United States conveyed through revivals and reform movements in the nineteenth and twentieth centuries was and still is an influential moral and religious force. This tradition has given rise to what Max Weber and Ernst Troeltsch described as the "church-sect" pattern of dissidents breaking away from established churches and organizing new movements that were less accommodating to the dominant culture of society and thereby religiously more faithful. Scores of evangelical, fundamentalist, holiness, and charismatic Protestant bodies, mostly in the United States but also often spreading northward, owe their existence to the playing out of this sectarian pattern.

Yet from the beginning there was far more religious pluralism in both countries than history books would suggest. Though the dominant culture was Christian and Christian churches were institutionalized and enjoyed a large following, there was nonetheless a rival Theosophical and New Thought movement manifesting itself in a variety of ways. They brought to American culture elements of spiritualism, nature worship, holistic thinking, and mind-cure. Less visible and less driven to proselytization, these movements have exerted greater influence than often has been acknowledged, and particularly so in urban centers. Also, there has been a fair amount of religious and cultural exchange among traditions as a result of encounters between Angles and Africans, Protestants and Catholics, Euro-Americans and indigenous people. There has also been an importation of Eastern spiritual teachings onto North American shores. Since the 1960s especially, several developments have led to a reconfiguring of the religious scene: an older religious and cultural hegemony lost much of its influence; growing numbers of "new immigrants" added to the religious diversity; and widespread evangelical Christian and New Age movements attracted mounting attention among the younger generations. While these latter movements are at odds theologically, they are brought closer together by popular cultural interpretations and eclectic religious practice. Both the evangelical and New Age movements respect the individual as responsible for making religious choices and emphasize the inner, subjective aspects of faith. Both of them stress healing and look upon health and prosperity as blessings. Both movements cut across religious institutional lines. Hence in contemporary culture, with its emphasis upon self-actualization and popularization of belief, not surprisingly the normative religious style in North America is increasingly that of the individual who—whatever the religious tradition—believes, practices, and cultivates a spiritual life, drawing upon resources available much to his or her own choosing.

In the United States, the demographics reveal a gradually declining majority population of Protestant Christians over most of this past century. The country entered the twenty-first century with a Protestant majority, but barely so, down considerably from earlier levels as recently as forty years ago. The religious population was also polarized into "evangelical-fundamentalist" and moderate-to-liberal "mainline" constituencies. An erosion of the white Protestant hegemony over the culture is reflected in loss of members and influence among the old-line, established religious denominations (Episcopalians, Presbyterians, United Church of Christ) as well as among the more moderate mainline groups (Disciples, United Methodists, Lutherans). During this same period evangelical, fundamentalist, and charismatic Protestant bodies, such as the Adventists, Assemblies of God, Nazarenes, Churches of God, Churches of Christ, and Southern Baptists have all continued to grow. More than just having grown, these more conservative constituencies have gained in middle-class standing, social respectability, and public visibility; to a considerable extent, they comprise the religious mainstream of the country today and set the cultural and political mood of the times.

Taken as a whole, this shift—demographic and cultural—amounts to a major restructuring of religion and its normative styles. Based upon national surveys of religious identification, the institutional breakdown for Protestants in the late 1990s is as follows: Oldline Protestant, 9 percent; Moderate Protestant, 24 percent; Conservative Protestant, 16 percent; and Black Protestant, 9 percent. Among the hundreds of Protestant bodies, Southern Baptists make up the largest single denomination with 15,600,000 members, concentrated in the Deep South but increasingly spreading across the Sun Belt. United Methodists are the second largest Protestant denomination with 8,500,000 members largely in the South and Midwest and are probably the most dispersed across the country of all religious groups. The National Baptist Convention, USA, historically African American, is the third largest with 8,200,000 members, concentrated in the South and Northeast. The Church of God in Christ is the fourth largest with 5,500,000 members, located heavily in the South, the Midwest, and increasingly on the West Coast. The Evangelical Lutheran Church in America is the fifth largest, with 5,200,000 members concentrated in the Upper Midwest. The Presbyterian Church (U.S.A.) is the sixth largest Protestant body, with 3,700,000 members mainly in the Northeast and Midwest. Both the National Baptist Convention of America Inc. and the African Methodist Episcopal Church claim 3,500,000 members each, both historically black communities and located mainly in the South, Midwest, and Northeast. Other sizable Protestant constituencies include the Missouri Synod Lutherans with 2,600,000 members, a Midwestern denomination; the Episcopalians with 2,500,000 members, located mainly on the Eastern Seaboard and in Texas and California; the Progressive National Baptist Convention and the National Missionary Baptist Convention of America with 2,500,000 members each, residing largely in the South and Northeast; the Assemblies of God with 2,300,000 members, concentrated in the South, the Midwest, and on the West Coast; the Churches of Christ with 1,650,000 members, in the South and Midwest; American Baptist Churches in the USA with 1,500,000 members, largely in the Northeast; and the United Church of Christ with 1,500,000 members, located primarily in the Northeast, the Midwest, and the West. Hundreds of small splinter denominations, some regionally concentrated, many of them ethnic in character, exist as do many evangelical, holiness, pentecostal, charismatic, and nondenominational fellowships and associations, all claiming to espouse some version of the historic Protestant faith.

In terms of organizational centers, Nashville, Tennessee, is a major center for southern-based, conservative-to-moderate Protestants, for Baptists and Methodists in particular. Over the past decade several liberal denominations have moved out of New York City, trying to reclaim a grassroots identity in heartland places like Cleveland, Ohio, and Louisville, Kentucky. Los Angeles is rapidly emerging as a center for global evangelical missions, on the part especially of nondenomination Protestants and sixties-style religious groups like Vineyard Fellowship and Calvary Chapel. The United States is one of the most religiously diverse countries in the world, and particularly since 1965 when the immigration laws were liberalized. Roman Catholics now have an estimated 60,200,000 members, making it the largest single religious community. Benefiting from a continuous in-flow of migrants into the United States, the Catholic population is becoming more diversified largely along Latino ethnic lines; areas of greatest Catholic concentration are the Northeast, the Midwest, California, and Texas. The Mormons claim 4,600,000 members, located largely in Utah and surrounding western states. The Jewish community remains relatively small at 2 percent, or less, of the total American population, its members residing mainly in the states of New York, Florida, and California. The Orthodox Church in America estimates its membership at 2,000,000 and the Greek Orthodox Diocese at 1,950,000, their followers residing mainly in the Northeast and Upper Midwest. Jehovah's Witnesses report approximately 950,000 members, widely scattered across the country. All other religious groups are relatively small, one-half of a percent of the American population or less. Muslims are estimated to have in excess of 500,000 members, around 40 percent of whom are African Americans and the remainder largely tracing their ancestry to Arab countries, great numbers of whom live in New York City and Los Angeles. Unitarian-Universalists number about 500,000 members, followed by roughly 400,000 Buddhists, 235,000 Hindus, 67,000 Quakers, and 50,000 Native Americans of various tribal traditions. The Amish, the Bruderhof, and other small German Pietist communities are scattered throughout the Northeast and Midwest. Other constituencies identified in surveys, all with less than 50,000 followers each, include Scientology, Baha'i, Taoist, New Age, Eckankar, Rastafarian, Sikh, Wiccan, Shintoist, and Deity. New Age's influence is much greater than these self-reported identities suggest since much of its heterogeneous mix of teachings is absorbed by other religious communities and as a religious option is not always very distinct.

With a much smaller population, Canada is a less religiously pluralistic society than the United States, but it is rapidly beginning to match it. Its faith communities reflect historically the heritages of the British and the French plus the more recent immigrants; as of the last national census in 1991 the remaining "aboriginal" population was only 1.7 percent of the nation, about a half-million people, half of whom are now Catholic, a third Protestant, and the remainder belonging mainly to the so-called "First Nations," or tribal peoples. For the country as a whole, Roman Catholics are the largest single religious constituency, amounting to more than 40 percent of the population with an estimated membership of 12,500,000. Roughly half of all Catholics reside in the province of Quebec, and another fourth in Ontario. Because of its size, the region of Ontario has large representations of most major religious traditions in Canada. Among Protestant bodies, the United Church of Canada (a merger in 1925 of Congregationalists, Methodists, and some, but not all, Presbyterians) is the second largest of all groups with a reported membership of 1,900,000, concentrated in Ontario and the Prairies. The Orthodox Church claims a membership of 1,000,000, living mostly in Ontario and the Prairies. Anglicans number approximately 850,000, found mostly in Ontario but are fairly well-dispersed across the country. United Pentecostals have a membership of 550,000, largely in the Ontario and Atlantic regions. Major Protestant groups with less than a half-million members include: the Presbyterians with 236,000 members, highly concentrated in Ontario; the Greek Orthodox with 230,000, mostly in Ontario and Quebec; the Pentecostal Assemblies of Canada with 226,000, highly dispersed across all regions except in Quebec; and Evangelical Lutherans with 144,000, scattered throughout the Prairies more than anywhere else. The Jewish population numbers 370,000, down somewhat over the past several decades, its members found mainly in the urban centers. Small pockets of Quakers, Baha'is, and other historic faith communities are dispersed across the country.

Over the past thirty years, large numbers of Asians, Middle Easterners, and Latin Americans have settled in Canada. An estimated 400,000 Muslims now reside there, mostly in the region of Ontario. Asians have brought with them Buddhist traditions, estimated at 300,000 followers concentrated largely in British Columbia and in the large urban centers elsewhere in the country; Hindu traditions, estimated at 200,000 followers largely in Ontario; and Sikh traditions, estimated at 200,000 followers especially in British Columbia. However, the presence of non-Christian faiths is not as great as might be expected since one in three Asian migrants reportedly identify with Christianity; likewise, immigrants from Latin America, largely from Central America, South America, and the Caribbean, tend to arrive as Roman Catholics. The result is an expanding pluralism, but also a reinforcement of Catholic and Protestant communities, though in this latter instance largely within its conservative wing. As in the United States, to the extent we can speak of Protestant growth since mid-century, it is among evangelicals, fundamentalists, and charismatics, many of whom belong to nondenominational community churches. Other groups growing are the Mormons and

Jehovah's Witnesses, with reported memberships of 130,000 and 110,000, respectively. Canadian cities, as in the United States, have great varieties of new religious movements and communal groups such as Scientology, Wiccan, Rastafarian, and Eckankar.

A word of caution is necessary about the statistical information on populations and memberships. Survey and census estimates of religious populations are one thing, organizational memberships as reported by those bodies are something else. Moreover, definitions of membership vary from one religious body to another. Evangelical Protestant groups tend to count only baptized members; Roman Catholics and mainline Protestants report inclusive memberships (both the nonconfirmed and full communicants). The age at which young people are confirmed, and thus counted as full members, also varies to some extent across traditions. And to add to the misreporting, there can be overlapping memberships. With a relatively high degree of religious switching from one religious denomination to another among Protestants and movement across parishes for Roman Catholics, membership rolls easily get inflated.

Not reflected in such statistics are many types of religious structures such as house churches, prayer groups, Eucharistic communities, and small groups that generally have only tangential ties to established religious communities. In both countries, religious identity takes on features distinctive to a pluralistic context. Religion is a source of belonging for the vast majority of the people, even for those who are religiously inactive in virtually all other ways; in this respect, the United States and Canada are "denominational societies" in the sense that religious communities provide a basis of social location. To be a Roman Catholic, a Muslim, a United Methodist, or whatever, is to possess a cultural and religious identity in a large pool of possibilities. As ethnic identities have receded in significance, particularly for those of European ancestry (Quebec being an exception), religion as a voluntary affiliation may have increased in importance in providing such identities. Despite a good deal of switching from one tradition or denomination to another, resulting often from intermarriage, there is surprisingly little exodus, as compared with many other modern societies, from religious identities altogether. People may drop out, quit attending religious services, no longer contribute financially, even denounce its teachings or its leaders, but they continue to return to religious communities for rites of passage, most notably, for weddings and funerals.

In the absence of a state church, or a highly regulated religious market, religious groups survive through voluntary memberships. This has the effect of keeping churches, synagogues, temples, and mosques fairly well mobilized, always seeking new recruits. Pluralism generates competition that, in turn, promotes innovation in religious interpretation and in strategies for reaching out to new people. Aside from the obvious importance of new immigrants for religious growth, faith communities all benefit from well-planned recruitment methods, deliberate efforts at relating to younger generations, highly specialized "niche min-istries" oriented to people of a similar circumstance or lifestyle, the construction of megachurches (in the case of evangelicals) offering religious options, and cre-ative use of the media. In this sense, pluralism is a continuing source of religious vitality.

Yet at another level of analysis, religion in these countries shows signs of a weakening of denominational loyalties. Energies displaced from these bodies are mobilized around parachurch, or special purpose, groups. Hundreds of these newly organized, largely single-issue groups now exist, divided along liberal-conservative ideological lines. Conservative coalitions have seized upon abortion, pornography, and homosexuality as major causes; liberals concern themselves mostly with environmentalism, women's issues, and lifestyle tolerance. As a result, the religious scene is often polarized. Religious communities themselves suffer from cross-pressures: Catholics and Southern Baptists who oppose abortion on demand may find themselves having more in common than they do with mem-bers of their own faith communities who hold different views. At all levels—from congregations up to national governing boards—tensions frequently erupt. Reli-gion's public face thus easily shifts depending upon the issues at stake and how they are mediated. In neither country is there a strong, uncontested religious voice holding a monopoly over public opinion, a situation described in the United States as a "naked public square." The lack of a strong, unified public religious presence follows as well from trends toward privatization. By this is meant a diminishing of religious influence, particularly in the realms of work and the economy, and a simultaneous enhancement of religious symbols and values within the personal and familial spheres. Spirituality, for example, is a topic of widespread interest at present. With increased attention to the private realm, and more and more opportunity to "construct" a religious self, individuals enjoy considerable latitude in picking and choosing among religious themes and practices, both from within the tradition in which they are a part and, increasingly, in a global world, from an expanding menu of possibilities, including other world religions, feminist and womanist ideologies, journey and recovery spiritualities, Native American spirituality, and New Age teachings. More than one-fourth of Christians in the United States, for example, report now believing in reincarnation. In Canada, this same fragmentation of traditional faith and mixing of religious and spiritual themes is referred to by one commentator as "religion a la carte." At the beginning of the twenty-first century, North Americans are clearly in a reflexive posture, exploring traditions and searching for sustainable faiths. They are not abandoning religion, but their religious identities are in flux.

BIBLIOGRAPHY

Bedell, Kenneth B., ed. 1996. *Yearbook of American and Canadian Churches*. Nashville: Abingdon Press.

Bibby, Reginald. 1987. *Fragmented Gods: The Poverty and Potential of Religion in Canada*. Toronto: lrwin Publishing.

Finke, Roger, and Rodney Stark. 1993. *The Churching of America 1776–1990: Winners and Losers in our Religious Economy*. New Brunswick, N.J.: Rutgers University Press.

Hewitt, W. E., ed. 1993. *The Sociology of Religion: A Canadian Focus*. Toronto: Butterworths.

Kosmin, Barry A., and Seymour P. Lachman. 1993. *One Nation Under God: Religion in Contemporary American Society*. New York: Crown Trade Paperbacks.

Melton, J. Gordon, ed. 1996. *The Encyclopedia of American Religions*. Fifth Edition. Detroit: Gale Research Company.

Roof, Wade Clark, and William McKinney. 1987. *American Mainline Religion: Its Changing Shape and Future*. New Brunswick, N.J.: Rutgers University Press.

Wuthnow, Robert. 1988. *The Restructuring of American Religion*. Princeton, N.J.: Princeton University Press.

CHAPTER 33

EVANGELICAL CHRISTIAN COMMUNITY IN NORTH AND SOUTH AMERICA

RANDALL BALMER

THROUGH missionaries and the communications media, Evangelical Protestant Christianity has spread its tentacles around the world. A recent estimate put the number of evangelicals worldwide at two hundred million. Its roots, however, are in the European Protestant Reformation and in a kind of primitivist yearning for New Testament purity. Evangelicalism has also been the most influential social and religious movement in American history.

EVANGELICAL DEMOGRAPHICS

The term *evangelicalism* refers to an internally diverse religious movement, which includes fundamentalists, neo-evangelicals, charismatics, and pentecostals. Evangelicals inhabit a variety of denominations as well as churches with no denominational affiliation, and many evangelicals do not recognize themselves by that label, preferring to call themselves simply *Christian* or Bible-believing Christian. For these reasons, evangelicalism has eluded quantification—even though pollsters have become more sophisticated in recent years in attempting to define it. A 1998 Gallup poll placed the number of evangelicals at 39 percent of the population of the United States, using the three-fold definitional criteria of personal conversion, belief in the Bible as the Word of God, and a desire "to lead nonbelievers to the point of conversion." The poll found that, among the African American population, the percentage rose to 58 percent, and 21 percent of Roman Catholics fit the definition of evangelical, up from 12 percent in 1988. Gallup also identified large numbers of evangelicals in every region of the country, from a low of 26 percent in the East to 54 percent in the South (Gallup 1999).

Lyman A. Kellstedt and John C. Green (1996) lay out four criteria for locating evangelicals: belief that salvation comes only through faith in Jesus, conversion experience, belief in the importance of missions and evangelism, and "belief in the truth or inerrancy of Scripture." Only 14 percent of Americans, they found, met all four tests, but 31 percent affirmed the importance of being born again, 37 percent said it was essential to witness to the faith, 44 percent said the Bible was true, and 46 percent insisted that Jesus was the only way to salvation. Kellstedt and Green also sought to get at the question a slightly different way, dividing the population into five groupings: white evangelical Protestant, Roman Catholic, black Protestant, white mainline Protestant, and others. Using this tool, they found that white evangelical Protestants made up the largest percentage at 26 percent, followed by Roman Catholics at 23 percent, and mainline Protestants at 17 percent.

A survey conducted by Christian Smith, Michael Emerson, Sally Gallagher, and Paul Kennedy (1998) asked Americans to classify themselves according to different religious identities. Mainline Protestants numbered 27 percent of the population, and the category "theologically liberal Christian" claimed 20 percent. Nineteen percent said they were fundamentalists, and 21 percent were evangelicals.

The Angus Reid Group of Canada conducted a poll in 1996 that compared religious affiliations in the United States and Canada. The poll found that while 55 percent of the population in the United States "believe the Bible is God's word, to be taken literally word for word," only 28 percent of Canadians agreed. As for reading the Bible, 21 percent of Canadians said they did so at least weekly, while the number rose to 43 percent in the United States. As for the number of evangelicals overall, the survey identified 15 percent of the Canadian population as "non-black evangelical Protestant," whereas the percentage in the United States was more than double: 33 percent.

Beyond North America the figures are more sporadic and less reliable. In 1998 the evangelical magazine *Christianity Today* published figures prepared by David B. Barrett, who gave the population of evangelicals, defined as "all persons of evangelical conviction who are active in spreading the gospel," broken down according to continents. Barrett pegged the percentage of evangelicals in North America at 27 percent, and the number in Latin America, which includes Mexico, at 14 percent (pentecostalism has made substantial inroads in Latin America in recent decades). In Europe, 23 percent were evangelicals, 13 percent of Africans, 5 percent of Asians, and 28 percent of those in Australia and New Zealand (Oceania) identified as evangelicals. In every continent, Barrett found that the percentage of evangelicals had risen over the course of the twentieth century, and he estimated the percentage of evangelicals throughout the world at 11 percent (Barrett 1998).

Sociologist David Martin puts the number of evangelicals in Latin America between 40 and 50 million, about one in ten. In Peru evangelicals make up only about 7 percent of the population, while the number rises to 15 percent in Brazil, nearly 20 percent in Chile, and 30 percent in Guatemala, where evangelicals have become a major force in Guatemalan politics (two evangelicals, Efraín Rios Montt and Jorge Serrano, have held the office of presidency since 1982). Elsewhere, evangelicals have amassed cohorts large enough to influence the political process in Portugal, Hungary, Zimbabwe, Liberia, Nigeria, India, the Philippines, and (to a lesser degree) Korea (Martin 2000).

History of Evangelicalism

The term *evangelical* refers to the gospel of the New Testament and to the evangels, the authors of the first four books of the New Testament: Matthew, Mark, Luke, and John. Evangelical took on another layer of meaning in the sixteenth century with Martin Luther's "recovery of the gospel" from what he considered centuries of corruptions and accretions at the hands of the Roman Catholic Church. Luther's complaints against Rome triggered the Protestant Reformation; the Lutheran church in Germany to this day is known as Evangelische.

Evangelicalism, then, traces its lineage from the New Testament, through the Protestant Reformation, and then through the various Lutheran, Reformed (Calvinist), and Anabaptist traditions in early modern Europe, and then, finally, to North America, where it assumed unique characteristics. American evangelicalism emerged from three strands, Continental Pietism, Scots-Irish Presbyterianism, and the remnants of New England Puritanism, which became intertwined in the middle decades of the eighteenth century. The combustion of these three elements (to shift the metaphor) ignited the revival fires of what historians call the Great Awakening, a massive spiritual movement that swept through the Atlantic colonies.

Already in the eighteenth century some of the distinctive characteristics began to emerge: the emphasis on introspection and warm-hearted piety; the importance of preaching, especially persuasive oratory; and the assault on clerical and ecclesiastical pretensions. American evangelicalism was refined further in a subsequent revival in the decades surrounding the turn of the nineteenth century, the Second Great Awakening, which convulsed the new nation in three theaters: New England, especially northwestern Connecticut; the Cumberland Valley, recently opened to settlement by the Louisiana Purchase; and western New York, where the construction of the Erie Canal gave rise to a booming frontier. During the course of the Second Awakening, evangelical theology shifted decisively from the Calvinist doctrine of election—God has elected *some* for salvation, regardless of merit—to a theology called Arminianism, which emphasized the ability of individuals to initiate the salvation process. Among a people who had only recently taken their *political* destiny into their own hands, Arminianism assured them that they controlled their *spiritual* destiny as well, a notion that proved to be overwhelmingly popular in the antebellum period. The Second Awakening also unleashed various reforming impulses—abolitionism, the temperance crusade, missions, women's rights, the female seminary movement—as evangelicals sought to bring about the kingdom of God here on earth and, more particularly, here in America.

Evangelical enterprises suffered a setback later in the nineteenth century when urbanization, industrialization, and waves of immigrants diminished expectations that America would become the New Jerusalem anytime soon, but the pentecostal revival at the Azusa Street Mission in Los Angeles, beginning in 1906, rekindled optimism that God was indeed at work, and one of the most notable legacies of Azusa Street was a renewed missionary impulse. Pentecostals—those who believe in the gifts of the Holy Spirit, including divine healing and speaking in tongues—left Los Angeles and fanned across North America and eventually to Latin America and the rest of the world, where they joined other evangelical missionaries in spreading the gospel, or "good news," of the New Testament.

Over the course of the twentieth century, American evangelicals, battered by Darwinism, liberal theology, and by scholarly assaults on the Bible, retreated into their own subculture—a vast and interlocking network of congregations, denominations, Bible institutes, colleges, seminaries, mission societies, and publishing houses—after the infamous Scopes trial of 1925. They remained safely cosseted within the subculture until the mid-1970s, when they began to venture into the larger world and to reinsert themselves into the arena of public discourse. The success of the Religious Right in the 1980s signaled an important shift for evangelicals. They were still part of the evangelical subculture, but their comfort with the larger world meant that they were no longer a counterculture in the way they had been during the middle decades of the twentieth century.

DEFINITION

The general definition of an evangelical is threefold. First, an evangelical is some-one who believes in the centrality of a conversion or "born again" experience as the criterion for salvation; this is taken from John 3:3, where Nicodemus approaches Jesus at night to inquire how he can enter the kingdom of heaven. The second characteristic is that an evangelical, taking a cue from Luther's notion of *sola scriptura*—the Bible alone is the source of authority—approaches the Bible seriously as God's inspired revelation to humanity. Many even go so far as to insist on literal interpretations of the entire Bible, from Genesis and the account of Creation to the Book of Revelation, which they claim provides a blueprint for understanding the end of time. Finally, an evangelical affirms the importance of *evangelism*, or telling the "good news," to others.

Within that broad and general definition of evangelicalism, however, there are several variants. *Pentecostals*, as indicated earlier, believe in the gifts of the Holy Spirit, and their worship is often lively, even ecstatic, as they acknowledge of the importance of speaking in tongues. *Fundamentalists* take their name from a series of pamphlets called *The Fundamentals*, published between 1910 and 1915 in an effort to arrest the slide toward what conservatives reviled as "modernism" in many Protestant denominations; fundamentalists tend toward militancy and separatism from those they regard as insufficiently conservative. The *neo-evangelicals*, symbolized by Billy Graham, emerged at the middle of the twentieth century; unlike the fundamentalists, whom the new evangelicals regarded as too starchy and legalistic, they sought to speak the language of the larger culture, and they jumped on newly emerging media to help them do so. *Charismatics*, who bear a strong resemblance to pentecostals in their embrace of the spiritual gifts, are those who maintain their evangelical presence in the Episcopal Church or the Roman Catholic Church or other venues not generally known for their hospitality toward evangelical or pentecostal expressions of faith. There are other strains that might be added beneath this general rubric of evangelicalism—Southern Baptists, particular Hispanic and African American traditions, holiness people—but all fit the larger definition of evangelicalism.

EVANGELICALISM IN GLOBAL PERSPECTIVE

The third characteristic of evangelicalism—the impulse to spread the gospel or *evangelize*—helps to explain the worldwide reach of the movement. While North

America once was viewed as a mission field, especially by European settlers who sought to Christianize the Native Americans, evangelicals beginning in the nineteenth century sought to propagate their understanding of the faith to the rest of the world. Intrepid missionaries set sail for distant places, supported and encouraged by fellow believers. An array of missionary societies—such as the Student Volunteer Movement for Foreign Missions, denominational mission boards, and China Inland Mission, among many others—provided financial, organizational, and logistical support. The single event that provided the greatest twentieth-century impetus for missions was the famous Azusa Street Revival, which took place in Los Angeles from 1906 until 1909. This pentecostal awakening, complete with speaking in tongues and divine healing, had a ripple effect on evangelical missions. Not only did those affected by Azusa Street carry the message across North America, many also embarked on careers as foreign missionaries.

While missionary activity emanating from North America helps to explain the presence of evangelicalism throughout the world and the Azusa Street Revival accounts for the extraordinary growth of pentecostalism in Latin America and elsewhere, evangelical communities themselves tend to be remarkably self-sufficient and indigenous. They respond to the needs and appeal to the aspirations of the grass roots. Like politics, evangelicalism is local—perhaps even more so because it honors the Reformation notions of *sola scriptura* and believer's priesthood (each individual is directly accountable to God, not to some ecclesiastical tribunal).

EVANGELICAL ATTITUDES TOWARD SOCIETY

Evangelicals are, in theory at least, otherworldly, in that their ultimate concern is preparation for the next world rather than accommodation to the present world. That equation, however, has varied considerably with time and circumstance. Evangelicals in antebellum America, for instance, assumed responsibility for a broad range of social reforms, confident that their efforts could usher in the kingdom of God. Later in the century, however, faced with overwhelming social problems, they retreated into a theology called premillennialism, which posited the imminent end of human history and thereby absolved them from responsibility for social amelioration.

One of the most persistent myths about evangelicalism is that it is implacably opposed to modernity and seeks shelter in some earlier, halcyon age of innocence. While there is some reason to believe that myth, judging from the agenda perpetrated by the Religious Right in the United States in the final decades of the twentieth century, that conclusion is misleading. Many evangelicals are indeed chary of modernity insofar as modernity carries a moral valence, but that should not be confused with a suspicion of innovation. Evangelicals have been remarkably adept at using innovations in technology and communications to propagate the gospel, which helps to account for its global reach. Throughout American history, from the eighteenth century to the present, evangelicals have appropriated new forms of communication—open-air preaching, camp meetings, colporteurs, radio, television, cyberspace—and the relative absence of ecclesiastical hierarchies, entrenched institutions, or theological rigidity have made it infinitely easier for evangelicals to compete in the marketplace of ideas.

Finally, evangelicalism, in the United States and elsewhere, has endured and flourished because of its entrepreneurial nature. The First Amendment to the United States Constitution, with its guarantee of "free exercise" and its proscription against religious establishment, set up a free market of religion. American history is littered with examples of religious entrepreneurs who have struck out on their own, galvanized a popular following, and offered alternatives to the existing religious options. As often as not, those entrepreneurs have been evangelicals, taking full advantage of the religious marketplace, and as religious establishments have lost their hold in other parts of the world, evangelicalism, a religion exquisitely attuned to popular sentiments and aspirations, has made inroads. The protean character of evangelicalism lends itself to meeting the challenges of the marketplace, and its adaptability to popular whims has ensured both its appeal and its durability throughout the world.

BIBLIOGRAPHY

Balmer, Randall. 1999. *Blessed Assurance: A History of Evangelicalism in America*. Boston: Beacon Press.
Barrett, David B. 1998. "A Century of Growth." *Christianity Today*, November 16: 50–51.
Gallup, George, Jr., with D. Michael Lindsay. 1999. *Surveying the Religious Landscape: Trends in U.S. Beliefs*. Harrisburg, Pa.: Morehouse Publishing.
Kellstedt, Lyman A., and John C. Green. 1996. "The Mismeasure of Evangelicals." *Books & Culture*. January/February: 14–15.
Marsden, George M. 1980. *Fundamentalism and American Culture: The Shaping of Twentieth Century Evangelicalism: 1870–1925*. New York: Oxford University Press.

Martin, David. 2000. "The People's Church: The Global Evangelical Upsurge and Its Political Consequences." *Books & Culture*, January/February: 12–15.

Smith, Christian, Michael Emerson, Sally Gallagher, and Paul Kennedy. 1998. "Findings from the Evangelical Identity and Influence Project." Paper presented at the ISAE Summer Consultation, June 25–27.

CHAPTER 34

AFRICAN CHRISTIAN COMMUNITIES

DAVID CHIDESTER

As a global religion, Christianity is also an African religion, and increasingly so. During the twentieth century, the number of Christians in Africa rose from an estimated 10 million to 350 million, a dramatic increase from less than 10 percent to nearly 50 percent of the continent's population. It is likely that at some point during the twenty-first century, more Christians will be living in Africa than on any other continent. Both ancient and modern, African Christian communities have given global Christianity a distinctively local character in Africa. While ancient churches maintain forms of Christian Orthodoxy in North Africa, a rich, complex variety of Christian communities in sub-Saharan Africa emerged out of the contacts, relations, and exchanges of five hundred years of European colonialism. The majority of African Christians belong to churches, whether Catholic or Protestant, with historical roots in Europe. During the twentieth century, however, substantial and widespread Christian commitment was generated by new forms of African Christianity that have been variously identified as African independent, indigenous, or initiated churches. Revitalizing traditional African culture, these local innovations in Christianity have also responded to global forces—conquest, colonization, capitalism, and urbanization—while participating actively in the twentieth-century transatlantic expansion of intensely experiential forms of Christianity. While briefly recalling the history of Christian formations in Africa, this chapter focuses on two forces in that history—intercultural translation and economic exchange—that continue to operate in African Christian responses to the challenges of globalization.

Within the predominantly Muslim region of North Africa, ancient Christian communities survive. The Coptic Church, which traces its origin back to the first-century mission of Mark the Evangelist, has preserved an ancient orthodoxy in Egypt. The Ethiopian Church, once the state religion of the ancient African kingdom of Abyssinia, maintains a distinctive form of African Christianity that features certain religious practices, such as circumcision, dietary regulations, and observance of Saturday as Sabbath, that Ethiopian Christians regard as signs of their authentic roots in ancient Israel. In Sudan traces remain of the once powerful Nubian Church, although Sudanese Christians have struggled to maintain their religious identity within an Islamic state. Testifying to the long historical continuity of Christianity in Africa, these North African Christian communities are also situated in the inter-religious relations of the Middle East, especially within the occasional tensions arising between Christians and a Muslim majority. Increasingly, however, North African churches, particularly the Coptic Church, have been looking south to establish new links with African Christianity.

In sub-Saharan Africa, Christian communities emerged out of the more recent history of European interventions in the Atlantic world. The historical formation of African Christianity involved two processes—translation and exchange—that reveal important facets of Christianity as a global religion in the modern world. Although Christian missionaries from Europe insisted that they were bringing light into a region of darkness, their gospel of sin and salvation was experienced by Africans as a local problem of translation. When the Portuguese Catholic missionaries succeeded in converting the ruler of the BaKongo in central Africa in the 1480s, they set out to destroy the power of traditional religious leaders, the diviners and healers known as *nganga*, and to abolish the use of ritual objects known as *nkisi*. In the local idiom, however, BaKongo Christians referred to the missionaries as nganga, the crucifix as an nkisi, and the Bible as *mukanda nkisi*, the most powerful ritual object. From the fifteenth century, therefore, African Christian communities have been engaged in an ongoing process of intercultural translation, moving back and forth between indigenous religious knowledge and the terms of Christian doctrine, practice, and authority.

Although European missionaries tried to control this process, a small group of foreigners could not possibly have managed the work of translation. During the nineteenth century, as southern Africa became the most missionized region in the world, missionaries intervened in local languages, producing grammars, dictionaries, catechisms, and biblical translations. In the process, they appropriated terms from local religious vocabularies. The Scottish missionary Robert Moffat, for example, took a local Tswana term for extraordinary power, *Modimo*, and redefined it as the God of Christianity. At the same time, Moffat took the Tswana term for ancestors, *badimo*, the ancestral spirits who were venerated in traditional ritual, and redefined that term as "demons" within a Christian symbolism of evil. Such translations profoundly altered the religious terms of both indigenous religion and Christianity in Africa. According to the missionaries, Christianity was in fundamental opposition to the indigenous religious heritage. Intercultural translation, however, often produced an Africanization of Christianity. In the consolidation of the late nineteenth-century Ngwato Christian kingdom in southern Africa, for example, foreign missionaries might have introduced the ritual of baptism as a fundamental mark of opposition between two ways of life, Christian and heathen. The Tswana term for that sacramental "mark of God," however, was the same word that was used for the ear-brand or cutting that identified the ownership of cattle. Accordingly, the sign of baptism was understood as a mark of inclusion, not merely within the Christian church but also within the polity of the Ngwato king, the titular owner of all cattle. In this respect, Christian symbols registered less as signs of personal salvation than as focal points for gathering a community. This ongoing work of translating Christianity into local African idioms remains crucial to the formation of Christian communities in Africa.

While developing new ways of translating the "spirit" of the Word into indigenous African terms, Christian communities in Africa also formed around new material relations of exchange. With the emergence of the west coast of Africa during the seventeenth century as a mercantile trading zone, intercultural translation was entangled with the problem of determining value in relations of economic exchange. According to European travelers and traders, Africans lacked any religion that might provide a framework for assessing the value of material objects. While undervaluing trade goods, Africans allegedly overvalued trifling objects—a bone, a rock, a bunch of feathers, a bundle of sticks—that they apparently regarded as containing extraordinary power. Adapting the Portuguese term for a magical object used in witchcraft, *feitiço*, European traders reported that Africans had no religion but instead persisted in the superstitious worship of fetish objects. As a result, Africans supposedly had no stable system of values that would allow them to assess the relative worth of trade goods. According to this mercantile theory of religion, Christianity was necessary to provide a system of value, both spiritual and material that would facilitate trade.

During the nineteenth century, as European Christian interests in Africa were advanced under the slogan, "Christianity, Commerce, and Civilization," the link between religion and economic exchange became firmly established. Christianity was promoted as the religion of economic prosperity. Ironically, during the early nineteenth century, European missionaries in southern Africa periodically complained that they were having no success because Africans were too prosperous. Nevertheless, Christianity increasingly registered as a religion that was based not only on the ancient authority of the Bible but also on new disciplines of work, wage labor, and production for markets. According to the nineteenth-century missionary Robert Moffat, two objects, the Bible and the plow, both of which inevitably appeared in their African context as Christian sacred objects, promised to redeem Africa. Christian converts to mission churches, both Protestant and

Catholic, occasionally became successful entrepreneurs. More often, however, by entering into new systems of wage labor, Christian converts became converted into exploitable labor. In this process, Christianity in Africa was intimately entangled with relations of exchange within a capitalist economy. Promising prosperity, the advance of "Christianity, Commerce, and Civilization" had resulted by the end of the twentieth century in the massive exploitation, underdevelopment, and impoverishment of Africa.

During the twentieth century, the formation of new African Christian movements was particularly revealing about the ways in which Christianity has operated as a global religion with local effects in Africa. Through local African initiatives in dealing with the problems of intercultural translation and economic exchange raised by Christianity, African initiated churches developed different strategies for engaging indigenous African structures of religious, cultural, and social authority. On the one hand, some African initiated churches have adopted the stance of opposition to traditional religion and culture. For example, the Harrist churches of West Africa, inspired by the early twentieth-century work of the prophet William Wade Harris, embraced and extended the missionary rejection of the entire indigenous religious heritage. As the prophet Harris insisted, all traces of indigenous religion, the ancestral shrines, sacrificial altars, ritual masks, and ceremonial objects, had to be destroyed to make way for Christianity. At the same time, Harris rejected the authority of the European Christian missionaries who had failed to protect Africans from military conquest, political oppression, and economic exploitation. Although independent of foreign missionary control, Harrist churches nevertheless continued the missionary strategy of forming African Christian communities in strict opposition to traditional African religion.

On the other hand, some African initiated churches have actively sought to weave together the resources of Christianity and African heritage in a new synthesis. Also in West Africa, for example, the Aladura movement, a constellation of new Yoruba Christian churches that began to emerge during the 1920s, consciously sought to draw elements of local indigenous religion, such as Yoruba proverbial wisdom, an indigenous understanding of the soul's destiny, respect for ancestors, divination, healing, and protection from the evil forces of witchcraft, into a dynamic Christian context. Meaning "owners of the prayer," Aladura represented a strategy for building religious communities by affirming the sacred power of both African ritual speech and Christian prayer. Rejecting both foreign missions and traditional structures of religious authority, such independent Christian communities have forged new forms of African Christianity by appropriating the religious resources of both. Although Christian theologians have accused them of the heresy of syncretism, the illicit mixing of "pure" Christianity with African indigenous religion, the Aladura Christians have used the term "struggle" for the spiritual and practical work of prayer through which they have made Christianity an indigenous African religion.

In over 8,000 denominations, with perhaps as many as 50 million members, these independent churches have often been regarded from the outside as if they were distinctively, perhaps even strangely, African in character. More recently, however, African initiated churches have been recognized as part of the most significant demographic development in twentieth-century Christianity, the global expansion of pentecostalism. In southern Africa, for example, the largest African initiated church is the Zion Christian Church (ZCC), founded in 1910 by the prophet Ignatius Lekganyane, with its headquarters at Moria, the mountain of God, that represents the sacred center of the Christian world for over three million members who meet weekly in local house churches throughout southern Africa. For the annual Easter pilgrimage, thousands of Zionists gather at Moria to affirm their religious commitment to ethical discipline, ritual purity, and spiritual healing. Although often depicted as a distinctively African Christianity, the history of the ZCC can be traced back to the arrival in southern Africa during the 1890s of American missionaries from Zion City, Illinois, the faith-healing community established near Chicago in 1893 by the evangelist John Alexander Dowie. Like Dowie's Zion City, the ZCC stressed moral discipline, including the avoidance of alcohol, tobacco, and pork, in support of a Christian practice based on the power of prayer, faith healing, and dramatic spiritual experience.

Throughout Africa, independent Christian communities emerged by translating and deploying the transatlantic spirituality of pentecostal, holiness, Adventist, and other recently formed American churches into local African situations. In addition to adapting practices of faith healing, they translated other elements of this global religious mix, such as speaking in tongues or anticipating the millennial end of the world, as religious strategies for creating separate social enclaves in a world dominated by the colonial state. During the waning years of colonialism in twentieth-century central and southern Africa, colonial officials regarded speaking in tongues as a challenge to their control over the language of rule; prophetic predictions of the end of the world represented dangerous threats to their rule over the territory they controlled. Surviving the often-violent colonial repression of new religious movements, African initiated churches had to adapt to new challenges after the 1960s in the shifting context of post-independence African states. While some independent churches mobilized political support for new African leaders and parties, others were perceived as subversive or divisive forces by African nationalists. Suspicion of creating divided loyalties between a separatist church and a tenuously unified nation has led in some recent cases to the repression of independent churches. During the 1990s, the Holy Spirit Movement of Alice Lakwena was repressed in Uganda for allegedly organizing legions of troops protected by spiritual medicine, and the leadership of the Tent of the Living God was arrested in Kenya on the charge of illegally fomenting "tribal" divisions within the unified nation. In these and other cases, tensions between independent churches and the modern state have carried over from the colonial to the post-colonial era.

In the case of the ZCC and many other independent churches, the process of creating a separate enclave of religious authority, spiritual power, and faith healing has resulted in unexpected social consequences by providing new means for adapting to the challenges and opportunities of the capitalist economy. While the leadership of the ZCC in Moria stands as a model of capital accumulation, with its centralized bureaucracy drawing vast resources from a dispersed network of local "franchises," the local membership, often representing the "poorest of the poor" in urban townships, has internalized a this worldly asceticism of self-discipline and self-denial that seems to follow Max Weber's classic formula for the Protestant work ethic. Accordingly, Zionist Christians have generally been valued by employers as disciplined, sober workers. As the new Puritans of a twentieth-century African Reformation, Zionist Christians have effectively demonstrated that translating Christianity into African contexts can also have implications for Africans struggling to survive the harsh realities of the labor market. At the same time, Zionist and other African Christian churches have developed mutual aid schemes, from burial societies to pension funds, for pooling and redistributing resources. Not only adapting to the demands of wage labor, African Christian communities have found ways to accumulate capital under difficult conditions.

During the last decade of the twentieth century, the link between Christianity and economic activity was explicitly advanced by conservative evangelical or fundamentalist missions, usually from the United States, that proclaimed a "gospel of prosperity" for Africa. Rather than stressing the self-discipline and self-denial of the Protestant work ethic, many of these missions promised miraculous wealth by the grace of God. In this promise, many African Christians have been drawn into what anthropologists Jean Comaroff and John L. Comaroff have called the global "occult economy" of late capitalism in which material wealth is expected from spiritual modes of production. In 1999, for example, one of the biggest events in global Christianity, especially within the transatlantic network of pentecostalism, was the miracle of the gold teeth. Reportedly, during a worship service in February 1999 led by John Arnott of the Toronto Airport Christian Fellowship at the Hatfield Christian Church in Pretoria, South Africa, people suddenly found their mouths miraculously filled with golden fillings, crowns, and inlays. Although a local South African dentist who examined the mouths of people involved in this event found that God was using outmoded techniques of dentistry, this "miracle" was widely interpreted in America and Africa not only as the "outpouring of the Holy Spirit" but also as a sign of the untold wealth that could be achieved through a specific kind of Christian faith.

Whether historically rooted in Protestant or Catholic missions or locally initiated by new religious movements, African Christian communities have operated in different political contexts. In general terms, after independence, Christian communities in Africa found themselves in three different types of states, Muslim in North Africa; Marxist in Ethiopia, Mozambique, and Angola; or pluralist, with principled separation between religion and the state, within most other independent nations. However, relations between religion and independent African states cannot be understood merely by referring to constitutional principles. In the case of African Christianity, the role of religion in political culture has been complicated by the broad diffusion of Christian education in Africa. For the generation of national leaders who drove the struggle for African independence into the 1960s, even an explicitly Marxist struggle could carry a Christian aura. In Zambia, Kenneth Kaunda drew upon his Presbyterian background in shaping an African Humanism. In Tanzania, Julius Nyerere found in Catholicism support for developing an African Socialism. Even Kwame Nkrumah in Ghana presumed a wide diffusion of Christianity in African political culture when he adapted a New Testament injunction to declare, "Seek ye first the political kingdom."

By the end of the twentieth century, African leaders continued to assume that Christianity was an integral part of sub-Saharan African political culture. In the last African nation to achieve liberation with its first democratic elections of 1994, South Africa instituted a Truth and Reconciliation Commission (TRC), under the leadership of the Anglican Archbishop Desmond Tutu, to forge national unity out of the conflicts and divisions of the past. At the opening of the commission, Archbishop Tutu explicitly drew upon the resources of the Christian tradition by proclaiming the TRC as a process of national contrition, confession, and forgiveness. As a pervasive system of symbols, myths, and rituals, therefore, Christianity has been integrated into African political culture. However, as a separate institution in relation to a broader social environment, Christianity has not always exercised a measurable impact on events in Africa. For example, during the Rwandan genocide of 1994 in which nearly 1 million people were killed, Christians were both perpetrators and victims in a country that was 90 percent Christian. In this instance, membership within a Christian community did not represent an independent social variable in relation to the carnage.

Looking to the future, South African President Thabo Mbeki has drawn upon religious imagery that is broadly Christian in character to call for an African Renaissance. In this initiative, Mbeki has been actively participating in the long tradition of intercultural translation and economic exchange that have characterized the historical formation of African Christian communities. In prophetic terms, Mbeki has rejected the "god of the market" and the "deification of arms" in order to base his political project on the emergence of what might be regarded as a new spiritual identity, the rebirth of the spirit of Africa. As Africa becomes the largest Christian continent during the twenty-first century, African Christianity, whether institutionalized in specific communities or diffused in political culture, will play a significant role in the future of Africa.

BIBLIOGRAPHY

Chidester, David. 2000. "African Prophets." In *Christianity: A Global History*. London: Allen Lane/Penguin, 446–68.

Comaroff, Jean, and John L Comaroff. 1999. "Occult Economies and the Violence of Abstraction: Notes from the South African Postcolony." *American Ethnologist* 26: 279–303.

Fields, Karen E. 1985. *Revival and Rebellion in Colonial Central Africa*. Princeton, N.J.: Princeton University Press.

Gifford, Paul. 1998. *African Christianity: Its Public Role*. Bloomington: Indiana University Press.

Haynes, Jeff. 1996. *Religion and Politics in Africa*. London: Zed Books.

Isichei, Elizabeth. 1995. *A History of Christianity in Africa*. Grand Rapids, Mich.: Eerdmans.

Mbeki, Thabo. 1998. *Africa: The Time Has Come*. Tafelberg, South Africa: Mafube.

Sindima, Harvey J. 1999. *Drums of Redemption: An Introduction to African Christianity*. Westport, Conn.: Praeger.

CHAPTER 35

CHRISTIAN COMMUNITIES IN SOUTH ASIA

AINSLIE T. EMBREE

THE many Christian communities of South Asia—some as old as the ancient churches of the first Christian century from which they originated, some as recent as new arrivals from North America—were all deeply embedded in the complex civilizations of the subcontinent. Today these communities number some thirty million people in India, Pakistan, Sri Lanka, Nepal, and elsewhere in the region. Because of the complicated origin of Christian communities and their interaction with the civilizations of the region, it is impossible to write of them in a consecutive, coherent narrative, as it is indeed to write such a narrative of the social and political history of India itself.

South Asia is the modern term, dating to the end of World War II, for the territory, or subcontinent, that has been referred to in the West (but not in the area itself) for at least two and a half millennia as "India." It is quite sharply defined on two sides by seas and on the other two by mountain ranges, and it has been the site of many kingdoms and great empires, some of which have been indigenous in origin and some, since the twelfth century of the Christian era, established from outside. South Asia has been deeply influenced by three great historic civilizations: the Indian, with its period of growth and development taking place within the region; the Islamic, developing outside and brought in by traders and conquerors; and the Western European, also brought in by traders and conquerors. All three have left indelible imprints on the civilization of the region and all are part of the living inheritance of the modern nation of India, which came into formal existence with the declaration of its independence. Christian communities have been related to each of these, and have their own histories as well.

To give some clarity to this complex story, it helps to think of four historical phases or periods of the history and development of Christian communities of India over a very long stretch of time, with India referring to the subcontinental territory, and only after 1947 to the modern nation. In all of these, the Christian communities have been closely linked with the churches of the Middle East, Europe, and North America but not significantly with churches in other parts of Asia. The first phase begins, according to the Thomas Christians as they are known, with the arrival of the apostle Thomas sometime in the middle of the first Christian century. The second begins with the arrival of the Portuguese in 1497, and the third, in a formal sense, begins in 1813, when the East India Company was compelled by the British Parliament to admit missionaries into its territories. The fourth begins in 1947, with the ending of British rule in the subcontinent and with a marked suspicion on the part of the Indian government for Christian activity. Like all attempts at periodization, these dates can be challenged, but they are not being used to represent the closing of one era and the opening of another, for the institutional experiences of the Christian communities continue from one period to the next up to the present, and all are interlinked with each other in some fashion. Space permits consideration of only a few of the many Christian communities throughout the subcontinent in these different time periods, and with little separate attention to the two countries, India and Pakistan, that emerged from the British empire of India in 1947, or to Sri Lanka or Bangladesh. The Christian communities are all closely linked, however, by the same political developments. To explicate something of the nature of Christian communities in India, brief references will be made, as relevant to the different periods, of the Thomas Christians of South India, the Roman Catholic Church in Goa, the relation of the government of India to institutional religion, denominational institutional-building by Protestant European and American churches, mass movements and the conversion of Dalits, the conversion of tribal groups in the Northeast, church union, Indianization of the churches, and the effect of nationalism on Christian communities in India and Pakistan.

In the first period in the history of Christian communities in India, we enter on very contested questions of historicity. The Thomas Christians, located mainly in South India, believed that, following the crucifixion of Jesus, the apostle Thomas went to India in 52 AD, preached the gospel, founded a church, and was martyred at Mylapore, south of what is now Chennai. Although there is neither contemporary archaeological nor documentary evidence for such an early date for the founding of a Christian community in India, it is not impossible as there was a considerable trade between the west coast of India and the Mediterranean world. The *Acts of St. Thomas* (c. 225), a work regarded as apocryphal by the

Western churches, written in Syriac, the ancient language of some of the Eastern churches, in Edessa, reports that India was assigned to Thomas when the apostles divided the world among themselves for evangelization, and the early church fathers accepted this account. By the fourth century, however, there is good evidence of Christian communities in the Kerala region, making them older than many of the churches of Northern Europe. The liturgy of their services was in Syriac, indication of their early relations with the ancient churches of Mesopotamia from which they received bishops. Little is known in detail of the life of the church or its members until the arrival of the Portuguese in the early sixteenth century, but they had flourished through the centuries, holding positions under the local rulers and as successful merchants and traders. There is no information about the groups from which they were initially recruited, but the respect with which they were treated suggests that they were not converts from the lowest castes. They apparently did not seek converts either in their own regions or elsewhere in India, and family customs in regard to marriage, commensality, and occupational customs seemed in many ways to follow patterns that would be understood and accepted by their neighbors. Mention of developments in these Thomas Christian communities will be noted when the later phases of other Christian communities impinge upon them.

One other intriguing connection of the ancient Christian world with India is the legend in Kashmir, in the extreme north, that Jesus did not die during the crucifixion by the Romans, but that he fled to Kashmir, where a tomb has long been regarded as his burial place. The explanation of this strange story is that Muslims, who revere Jesus as one of the greatest of the prophets before Muhammad, insist that he would not have permitted himself to die such an ignominious death.

The second phase of Christian communities starts with the arrival of the Portuguese as a territorial power in Goa in 1510, accompanied by the Roman Catholic Church. Portuguese rulers always insisted that their motivation in building their mighty empire, of which Goa was the center in Asia, had been to serve God and make a profit for themselves, and there is little reason to doubt it (Lach 1965: 229–44). Politics, religion, and economics were part of a seamless web woven by the Creator himself. In the first thirty years in Goa, little attempt was made to convert the people, but after 1542 there was a dramatic change with the arrival of the Jesuits, "the shock troops of the Counter-Reformation," led by St. Francis Xavier, the most famous of missionaries. Hindus were discriminated against in many ways, including taxation and the confiscation of temple lands and the destruction of temples, while converts were favored. The Inquisition was established to punish converts who showed signs of heresy, and while non-Christians were not subject to it, they could be punished for trying to prevent conversion or encouraging converts to relapse.

Relations of the Roman Catholics and the Portuguese with the ancient Thomas Christians in the south were cordial at first, as they seemed to be willing to accept the primacy of the pope. The Portuguese bishops, however, kept demanding that they follow the rites of the Latin Church and change some portion of their creeds, which they said taught the doctrines of the Nestorian heresy. The Thomas Christians were supported by the local rulers, who feared that the power of the Portuguese over the local Christians would lead to increased takeover of their lands by Goa. Finally, through pressure and intimidation, the leaders of the Thomas Christians were forced at the Synod of Diamper in 1599 to acknowledge the supremacy of Rome, deny the Nestorian heresy, and abandon long-standing customs relating to marriage and inheritance, which the Portuguese clergy declared to be Hindu in origin. By the middle of the seventeenth century, the Thomas Christians had become increasingly resentful of the dominance of the Jesuits and about a third of them formed the Malankara Syrian Orthodox Church, with two jurisdictions under an Indian catholicos. In 1970, the smaller of the two broke with the catholicos and formed a church under the Syrian patriarch of Damascus. The two factions have instituted hundreds of lawsuits against each other in the Indian courts.

To return to Goa: the physical witnesses to the symbiotic relationship of church and state in these years are the number of parish churches throughout the Goan territory; the immense cathedral, the splendid sanctuary where the uncorrupted body of St. Francis Xavier is venerated; numerous convents and monasteries; and schools. By 1600 there were perhaps 150,000 Catholic converts, including 100,000 low-caste fishermen along the coast south of Goa, and in Goa itself there were about 50,000 Christians. It is from this group, many of whom married Portuguese, that the large Roman Catholic population of Goans, as they are popularly known, has come, which plays an important role in many of the cities and towns of India, principally Mumbai. The first Indian cardinal, Valerian Gracias, came from the Goan community. Goa remained a possession of Portugal until 1962 when it was forcibly annexed by India. The Christian presence is, however, visible everywhere, in the beautiful parish churches as well as in the grand churches of old Goa; in the great festivals, especially at Christmas and Easter; and in the crowded processions at the decennial display of St. Francis Xavier's body, all asserting the presence of a unique Christian community.

The third phase marks the arrival of missionaries from the modern West early in the nineteenth century, mainly from the English-speaking world, but also in smaller numbers from virtually every country in Europe, as part of the triumphal movement of Western political and economic power in the nineteenth and twentieth centuries. Steamships, railroads, postal service, telegraphs, were all part of the industrial revolution that was changing relationships between societies, and they all favored the arrival and work of foreign missionaries. At the same time, in the Protestant religious world three related movements were effecting dramatic changes: Pietism in Germany, the Great Awakening in the United States, and, especially important for India, the revivalism in the Church of England associated with Charles Wesley. These movements are often referred to as "evangelical," but this is somewhat misleading as they should not be equated with modern American fundamentalism or biblical literalism. These movements had four characteristics in common that shaped the modern Christian communities founded by Western churches in India beginning in the nineteenth century. One was that a Christian must have an inward, personal experience of the saving power of Christ, known as conversion, a fundamental aspect of the growth of Christian communities in India. A second characteristic of these movements was that, while religious observances were no proof of this inward salvation, a change in social behavior was necessary toward a Christian lifestyle, often defined in terms of conventional European mores. This was obviously of great importance in India, for it meant changing customs that were deeply ingrained in the society; that is, abandoning ways of life that were part of everyday existence. Related to this was a third characteristic: true Christians were dedicated to uprooting what they regarded as evil customs, not just in their own lives but in society in general. This attitude is quite foreign to Hinduism and has been the cause of much mutual misunderstanding. It is not accidental that the same people who were involved in the antislavery movement were often the promoters of mission work in India, for the fourth characteristic was the conviction that true Christians must be actively engaged in preaching the Protestant version of the gospel to those in foreign lands who had not heard it. These religious changes in the West were taking place at a time of great political change in India, for by the beginning of the nineteenth century Great Britain had become the dominant political power in the subcontinent through the East India Company, the great multinational with its headquarters in London.

When the East India Company was in the process of establishing its power in India, it had forbidden missionaries to settle and preach in their territories out of fear that they would attack Hindus and Muslims and arouse their anger, thus threatening the position of the British. This was the reason that William Carey (1761–1834), the first English missionary, was forced to live and work at Serampore, the small Danish settlement outside Calcutta, and where he began his work of having the Bible translated into Indian languages. The evangelicals, led by the most prominent official in the Company, Charles Grant (1746–1823), who had worked for many years in Bengal and had been converted there, began to demand that not only should the Company permit missionaries to go to India but it should assist them. He was opposed by many of his fellow officials in the Company and by politicians, who feared Indian resentment, and by some of the bishops of the Church of England who feared the spread of what they called "religious enthusiasm." Finally in 1813, with the assistance of his friend, William Wilberforce, the British government forced the East India Company 1813 to accept, as the price of having its trading charter renewed, that in order to promote the happiness of the inhabitants of the British dominions in India, they would agree to measures for the introduction "of useful knowledge, and religious and moral improvement" (Embree 1962: 270–72). This did not mean, of course, that Christianity could now be introduced into India, for that had been done at least fifteen hundred years before, but that new forms of Protestant activities would be introduced into the fabric of Indian society.

One result, quite separate from the work of missionaries, was the appointment of a bishop of Calcutta and numerous chaplains, with salaries paid for by the government. Their function was not to work with Indians but to provide for the instruction of its British employees according to the principles of the Church of England. The bishop was paid a salary of £5000 a year, and, as a concession when protests were made by the Roman Catholics, their bishop was given an allowance of £20, with £5000 to be distributed among seventy-eight priests. The bishops and clergy of the Church of England were government employees, paid from the accounts of the Public Works department. The salaries of the Church of England missionaries were, on the other hand, paid by the groups that sent them. The many beautiful churches the government built were often referred to as "white" churches, recognizing a racial reality; Indians went to the plainer "Indian" churches built by the missionary societies for their converts.

The spread of Christianity is directly related to the great uprisings in North India against the British, known to the British as the Mutiny of 1857 and to some modern Indian nationalists as the First War of Independence. In the search for causes of the outbreak, one popular explanation, by both Indians and some British, was that Muslims and Hindus had both been offended by the activities of missionaries, believing that it was an attempt by the government to destroy both Hinduism and Islam. An opposite view, put forward by a prominent missionary, was that the outbreak was God's doing to teach the British government a lesson for not having used its power to convert the heathens. When it was over, Queen Victoria issued a proclamation that most Indian nationalists as well as the British accepted as a reasonable solution to the complicated question of modern societies: how to govern a pluralistic society of numerous religious communities. It was the royal will, the proclamation read, that "none be anywise favored, none molested or disquieted, by reason of their religious faith or observances" (Philips 1962: 11). The religious neutrality of 1858 was more or less adhered to for the rest of British rule and after much debate was essentially affirmed in its constitution in 1950 by the government of India and in 1976 by the amendment that declared India a secular state, a decision that was bitterly contested in later years by Hindu groups that argued that this was tantamount to saying that all religions had equal rights in India, when this was obviously not true, since Hinduism was the religion of 80 percent of the people.

A peculiar feature of the new Christian communities that grew up in India as a result of nineteenth-century missionary work was that the missionaries brought with them the denominational divisions of the Protestant world as well as their national identifications. Thus there were two American Presbyterian groups, reflecting divisions in American church life, as well as Irish, Canadian, and New Zealand Presbyterian churches. The mainline churches did not actually compete for converts but practiced what was known as "Comity of missions," that is, not establishing work where others were at work. The multitude of such denominational and national units was one of the problems faced by Christian communities in India in the twentieth century as they united to form Indian churches.

The activities of the missionaries who came to India can be conveniently noted under the three categories that the missionaries themselves used in describing their work: evangelical, educational, and medical. All three were intended to win converts but through different methods and techniques. Evangelism was meant to win converts through preaching the gospel, but this required more than proclamation, it required the pointing out of the evils and weaknesses of Hinduism, resulting in one of the least attractive features of this new enterprise, a fierce denunciation of Indian religions, especially of Hinduism. Anti-Islamic rhetoric is part of Western attitudes to other religions, but confrontation with Hinduism was new and startling. Idolatry was the most obvious evil to Christians well versed in the denunciations of the blasphemous practice in the Hebrew scriptures; in addition was the alleged obscenity of the behavior of many of the Hindu gods. Caste, Christians believed, stunted human dignity, preventing social change; women were oppressed by their husbands and families; truth and honesty were unknown. The point of these denunciations was not to imply that Indians as people were inferior, but rather it was their religion that had degraded them. Changing their religion, then, would release them from the intolerable burdens of false beliefs and they would become new people, enjoying not only a better life in eternity but here and now.

Aside from the question of numbers, which were relatively modest in proportion to the effort expended, whom did they convert and from what segments of society did they come? There were a number of well-known converts from among the higher Hindu castes, including Brahmans, who made outstanding contributions to the development of Christian thought and gave leadership in the church, but it seems that most Christian converts came from the lower castes or from outcaste groups. Often conversion required that the convert give up cultural symbols and practices that the missionaries identified with Hinduism, but it is not clear how much economic change Christian conversion brought in the life of the convert, despite the frequent charge by Hindus that low-caste people were bribed by offers of jobs. Furthermore, becoming a Christian did not change one's status in society; relations between Christians of high- and low-caste origins remained a vexing problem. Nor did it change the way neighbors regarded the convert—indeed, it very often led to ostracism and scorn. In terms of the converts' descendants, however, it can scarcely be doubted that in many cases, perhaps in the majority of cases, conversion did lead to more opportunities in terms of education and employment.

Conversions in two special groups illustrate the growth of Christian communities in India. One group resulted from what are known as mass movements, when thousands of people from the lowest caste groups were converted very quickly and without much instruction; other Christian communities came from the tribal peoples, chief among them being the people of Northeast India.

Mass movements refers to the large numbers of low-caste people—including the groups formerly called untouchable, now more appropriately Dalits, the oppressed—coming into the churches in the late nineteenth and early twentieth centuries. These conversions were the subject of controversies both within the churches themselves and among outsiders and have become a target of militant Hindu groups that seek either to reconvert them or to harass them as dupes of foreigners. One of the best known of the mass movements took place in the Anglican diocese of Dornakal in South India, where the number of Christians increased from 56,681 in 1912 to 225,080 in 1941, almost all of them drawn from the "untouchables." Christianity had had little contact with these people, and the enormous influx was connected with the work of V. S. Azariah (1874–1945), the first Indian to be appointed a bishop of the Anglican Church. Pious Christians like Azariah believed the movement as proof of God's will, but they also explained it as the desire of the Dalits to escape from the burdens of untouchability imposed by the Hindu caste system. Hindus, however, saw it as due to the promises made for health and education services offered by the Christian church. Many Indian Christians as well as many missionaries disapproved of the mass movement as an abandonment of what had long been the strategy of evangelization from above, that is, winning over the upper castes who would lead the lower castes, having educated them first and instructed them in Christian belief. Sociologically sophisticated Christians, however, saw the mass movement as something known within Indian society, where low-caste groups often attempted to change their status by the whole group adopting new forms of social and religious behavior within *bhakti*, or Hindu devotional cults.

Azariah required the new Christians to take some instruction before receiving baptism and to give up beliefs, practices, and community customs associated with Hinduism. This rejection of old roles was interpreted by the upper-caste villagers in the Dornakal area as a challenge to the established order, but Azariah believed that this was the only way the new, uneducated, poverty-stricken Christians could find an identity and a respected place in society. Great emphasis was placed on providing education and health services to the new Christians among groups that had been deprived of both.

It is one of the ironies of modern Indian history that Bishop Azairah's work earned him the enmity of Gandhi, since he, too, sought to uplift the outcaste and marginalized of Hindu society, using, like Azariah, the mantra of cleanliness and godliness and stressing health and education but with an interpretation that drew upon Indian models. Azariah called them the people of God, uniting them with all Christians, while Gandhi called them Harijans, people of an Indian God. Gandhi claimed that Azariah, by baptizing the untouchables and other low castes, was depriving them of their rightful place in the new national society, which he was laboring to build. Azariah also annoyed many foreign missionaries for seeking to give the Indian church its own Indian leadership without Western patronage.

Azariah's construction of a new kind of Christian community has suffered from internal quarrels and factionalism. While the increase in numbers of converts of the earlier years and the vigor of the community has not been sustained, their descendants have managed, despite the liabilities of their social origins, to achieve a measure of respect in Indian society that they almost certainly would not have had without the mass movement.

The successes and failures of the Christian community in Dornakal provide an interesting comparison with the development of Christian communities in Nagaland, a small Indian state in the northeast region of hills and mountains between the Indian state of Assam and Myanmar. The growth of the Christian community in Nagaland is closely bound up with its political history. The people of the hills are made up of many tribes, quite distinct in language and customs from each other as well from the rest of India, and the area had never been incorporated into any of the great powers that controlled the Indian subcontinent until its formal takeover by the British in 1826. At first the region was part of Bengal Presidency but the riverine plains area became the province of Assam in 1874. The tribal people in the hills, however, were not brought directly under all the laws and political structures of British India but left under their tribal leaders. The Nagas had a reputation as a fierce, warlike people, who had once been head-hunters. The Naga people were intermingled with other tribes, but under the social and political changes brought about by the British they began to develop a sense of Naga cultural and national identity that led them to rebel against the new government of India in 1947. In this process, the Christian community that had grown up in the previous fifty years played a decisive role that was not matched elsewhere in India by any Christian community. For the Nagas, it was Christianity that helped them unite and realize that they were a people with a destiny to be a nation, whose land had been seized by the Indians whose army forces brutally oppressed them. For the Indian government, it was Christianity, through the machinations of foreign Christian missionaries, that led the Nagas to believe that they were a separate people from the Indian nation, with the right to self-determination, leading to a bloody, wasting rebellion led by duplicitous Christian Nagas.

This makes for a tangled story, without any agreed-upon plot line, and all that can be attempted here is to present a brief interpretation of why and how

Christian communities played a unique role by helping the Nagas preserve their sense of identity when confronted by the changes instituted by the British as rulers and then, much more systematically, by the Indian government. The preservation of identity by one group within a larger political structure often leads to undermining of national identity, and this, according to the careful analysis by Frederick Downs (1992), is what happened among the Nagas.

A number of attempts were made in the nineteenth century to begin Christian work among the tribal peoples in the hills, sometimes with the encouragement of British officials, despite the policy of religious neutrality, because they saw the Christian missions useful in providing education and working for peace among the tribes. American and Welsh Baptists were the most active groups working in the northeast, but denominationalism was not a particularly strong force in establishing Christianity in the hills. In Nagaland, 80 percent of the population is estimated to be Christian, making it second to Mizoram, also a northeastern state, among the Indian states in terms of percentage of Christians. The percentage of growth has been much greater in the fifty years since independence than in the similar preceding period, indicating that the growth is not due to the activities of foreign missionaries, few if any who have been allowed to work in the area, but instead to the vitality of the local churches. One remarkable change in lifestyle was that a very large percentage, as much as 70 percent of both men and women, became literate, far higher than in most parts of India.

The involvement of Christian Nagas in the militant movement against Indian rule is often cited by the Indians as the evidence that Christianity, especially among Dalits and tribals, is anti-national and destabilizing, and, as noted above, Christianity does appear to have given the Nagas a sense of shared identity. This involved antipathy to "the people of the plains," whom they regarded as economic exploiters because they came to their region as traders and officials. It also probably increased their sense that India, with its vast Hindu majority, was the enemy of their isolated Christian community.

While the evangelistic work of winning converts and nourishing the development of Christian communities was central to the mission enterprise, and probably had the most enduring impact, in the nineteenth century a very prominent aspect of evangelism was the establishment of hospitals and colleges. These institutions were much better known to non-Christian Indians than were the churches themselves. Both the medical and educational institutions reflected the changing humanitarian and religious visions of the period in which they were created and had their counterparts in institutions in the national homelands of the supporting churches. Establishing colleges was opposed by many Christian leaders, both in the churches abroad from which money came and from within church groups in India itself who argued the money could be better spent on evangelism. The great pioneers in Christian higher education in India were William Carey, who founded the first college at Serampore, and Alexander Duff (1806–1878), the Scottish missionary who had a leading role in the founding of Calcutta University in 1854, the first Indian university. Duff used three arguments for Christian colleges. The first, and most important, was that Western education in English was, in the Latin phrase he used, *praeparito evangelica*, a preparation for the gospel, for the light of Western learning in itself would dispel the darkness of Hinduism, opening the students' minds to truth. In almost all of the colleges, most of the students were non-Christian, mainly upper-caste Hindus, many of whom became leaders in the professions and in the nationalist movement. Another argument was that as the Indian church grew it would need educated leaders and the colleges provided them to a considerable extent, although in most of the colleges Christians made up only 10 percent of the student body. The third was that Christian teaching at the colleges would lead to conversion, although this rarely happened.

There were about forty Christian colleges of Protestant origin, and a smaller number of Roman Catholic ones, most of them founded after the setting up of the universities system on the model of the University of London, with the various universities (at first Calcutta, Madras, and Bombay, and later in other provinces) establishing the curriculum in all subjects, setting the examinations, grading them, and awarding degrees. All colleges, both government and private, including the Christian ones, were affiliated with the universities and so had little opportunity in this highly centralized system for much innovation or leadership.

A searching inquiry was done by a distinguished commission in 1930–31 (A. D. Lindsay, et. al, *The Christian College in India: The Report on the Commission on Christian Higher Education in India*) on the place of the Protestant Christian colleges in modern Indian life. (It is an important comment on Christian communities in India that virtually no mention is paid to Roman Catholic colleges; equally, in accounts of Christianity in India by Roman Catholic writers, scarcely any mention is ever made of Protestants.) The commission judged that a few of the Christian colleges were among the very best in the country; most of them compared favorably with the better ones in the university system, and a few had sunk to the mediocrity of the majority. The commission found, as did almost all observers, that teaching in all colleges in India was driven by the examination system, with its emphasis on memorizing "right" answers, and that there was very little emphasis on research. They agreed that where the Christian colleges had made a special contribution was in women's education. While the colleges once made a useful contribution to Indian life, it was not clear that the Christian colleges were doing anything very distinctive now that the university system had such an iron grip on higher education. Since the students were overwhelmingly non-Christian, as were the majority of the teachers, it was difficult for them to serve as Christian communities themselves or as service centers of other communities. What the commission was saying in effect was that the more integrated the Christian colleges were into the general community, the less value they were to Christian communities in India. This evaluation held with even more force at the beginning of the twenty-first century.

The need for modern medicinal work had attracted the attention of Christians from early in the nineteenth century, and almost all the foreign societies had established hospitals in the areas where they worked. They drew crowds of patients, desperate for help, and they made a very important contribution in training generations of nurses. In contrast to the Christian colleges, which graduated mainly non-Christians, virtually all nurses in India up to 1947 were Christians. The apparent explanation of this phenomenon is that Hindus and Muslims considered nursing an unsuitable occupation for women because of the tasks they had to perform. Only a few of the hospitals achieved the prestige that the Christian colleges had, although in some provincial towns they had a far higher reputation than government ones. Much of their popularity came from the special attention they paid to women and children, especially for maternity cases. They also trained medical aides, known as "compounders," who, though they had very little professional skill, were often the only service available in the villages. Two hospitals, one at Ludhiana in Panjab, the other at Vellore in Madras Presidency, were also centers of well-known medical schools, which are still thriving despite many new government and private ones that have opened in recent years.

Toward of the end of the third phase of the history of Christian communities in the Indian subcontinent, the question of unifying the many denominational churches became a subject of intense interest for a number of reasons. A divided and fragmented Christianity seemed a poor witness to the rest of the country of a faith that emphasized the equality and unity of all humankind. Second, for a number of years there had been a demand, both from Indian and foreign Christian leaders, that the churches in India should move toward self-support and that Indians should replace the foreign leaders. Finally, the nationalist movement was leading India inexorably toward independence, and it was becoming increasingly obvious that with the departure of the British as rulers it would be a debilitating anachronism to have foreigners leading the church.

The result was a movement toward church union, watched over with great interest not just by Christians in India but by many in foreign countries. In the proposed union of the churches in South India, the main issue was a theological one concerning the ordination of clergy, with the most powerful of the churches in South India, the Anglican or Church of England, holding that their bishops were in the apostolic succession and only clergy ordained by such bishops could validly perform the sacraments. The reformed churches, such as the Presbyterian, reject this doctrine, but the issue was finally worked out, and in 1947 the Church of South India came into existence. This smoothed the way for the churches in North India, Pakistan, and eventually in Bangladesh to form their own national unions. In this period, Indian Christians were very active in the ecumenical movement, especially in such manifestations of the new spirit as the World Council of Churches and the World Student Christian Movement.

In the fourth period, after the coming of independence in 1947, the Christian communities faced new problems. One surfaced very quickly in India as the debates over the constitution began. The relation of religion to the state had been a contentious and divisive issue, and Nehru and other leaders in the ruling party, the Indian National Congress, had hoped to settle the issue by a constitutional guarantee of religious freedom, which resulted in Article (25:1) of the Constitution, which guarantees religious freedom, stating that "all persons are equally entitled to the freedom of conscience and the right freely to profess, practice and propagate religion" (*The Constitution of India,* Article 25:1). There was little objection to guaranteeing freedom of worship, but the right to propagate one's religion was inserted only after very bitter debate. Christians and Muslims demanded its inclusion, arguing that propagation of their faiths was a central command of their religion. Very strenuous objection came from many Hindu groups and individuals, who argued that conversion to another religion is destructive, breaking the bonds of social intercourse and national unity.

Despite the occasional questioning of their place in the national polity because of their alleged ties to foreign organizations, Christian communities continue to have a respected position in the professions, especially education and medicine, and the Albanian nun, Mother Theresa, was regarded as a saint by Hindus as well as Muslims for her work among "the poorest of the poor." In the context of India's lively democracy, approximately 22 million Christians (according to a 2001 census) are too few and too geographically scattered to form confessional political parties as have the Hindus, Muslims, and Sikhs. Yet, Christians have been active in politics, especially in Kerala, where they form nearly 40 percent of the population, and in Nagaland and Mizoram, where they are in the majority. Generally speaking, Christians supported the Indian National Congress, believing that it would be the best support for freedom of religion.

With the increasing growth of Hindu nationalism in central and regional politics, the charge that Christians were anti-national and that they had been bribed by foreigners to become converts, began to assume serious proportions. The most vocal attacks on the Christian communities came from the powerful Hindu nationalist organization, the Rashtriya Swayamsevak Sangh (RSS), and its affiliates, the Vishva Hindu Parishad (VHP), or World Hindu Council, as it is known outside India, and its militant youth wing, the Bajrang Dal. Many of the leaders and supporters of the major political party, the Bharatiya Jan Sangh, come from these groups, making the position of Christian communities problematic. While for some time, there had been both verbal and physical attacks on Christians, late in 1998 hostility centered on the small Christian communities among the tribal people in the Dangs district of Gujarat, where Roman Catholic workers had established small schools, medical dispensaries, and organizations. The attacks on the local Christians soon passed from verbal abuse to burning of churches, beating up of local Christians, attacks on priests, and attempts to close schools. As one group, allegedly affiliated with the VHP put it, they were determined to protect Hindu religion and "to teach the bold Christian priests a lesson and to put them in their place" (*Report of the Citizens Commission* 1999: 41). The other and encouraging side of this picture is that an organization from Indian civil society, the National Alliance of Women, began an investigation and provided evidence for the complicity of the police and politicians with the destructive mobs. While urban Christian communities, with their prestigious schools and colleges and a respected place in civil society, were not physically attacked, the events in Gujarat made them aware of their fragile place in a society where nationalism and patriotism was being increasingly defined in terms of Hinduism, the dominant element in Indian culture.

Because India is a functioning democracy, such issues as the extent of religious freedom that should be permitted and what role religion should have in the determination of public policy have been freely, even fiercely, debated. Such debate has, unfortunately, seldom been possible in Pakistan, which shares so much in common with India but which has had a very different political experience since it was created as an independent state in 1947. Although Pakistan's constitution has been revised a number of times, one constant has been its self-definition as an Islamic state, unlike India's declaration that it is a secular state. Pakistan's constitution has, however, assured freedom of worship to its two small religious minorities, Hindu and Christian, both numbering around a million. Both are poor communities, but the Christian community fared somewhat better in the early years of the state, with a Christian having served as Chief Justice and a number of other Christians serving in government positions. The Christian colleges have fared much less better, however, than they have in India, with the government taking control of most of them. Most Christian communities are very poor, and there have been many cases of complaints of attacks on them, in some cases leading to murder. They have especially suffered under the rigorous blasphemy laws: the customary claims that Christians make for the truth of their doctrines and their scriptures have been interpreted as blasphemous because their claim to truth denies the truth of Islam. So severe have been some of the attacks on Christian groups that a bishop of the Roman Catholic Church felt called upon to make the dramatic protest of committing public suicide by burning himself to death. A report by the U.S. State Department has referred to widespread claims of discrimination and violence in Pakistan, noting that the lack of an adequate government response contributed to an atmosphere of impunity for acts of violence and intimidation committed against religious minorities. Burnings of churches and killings of members of congregations increased in 2000, apparently because Christians were associated with American attacks on Muslims in Afghanistan and elsewhere.

Ending with accounts of persecution of Christian communities in India and Pakistan may seem like a grim warning for the future, but Christian communities have reason for concern; both countries are showing signs of the growth of religious nationalisms that identify Christian communities as alien and enemies of the nation. Christians find some comfort, however, in a number of developments. One is that the accusation that they are alien to their host countries, which is certainly a detriment, suggests that their relationship to worldwide Christian communities gives them a measure of protection through that connection. Another is that in India Christians have a standing in the professional life of the country and have made political alliances that afford them a measure of protection. A third source of assurance for the future is that Christian communities have been embedded in the social fabric of South Asia since the very early years of Christianity itself. Furthermore, for believers there is comfort in the text, often heard in Indian churches, especially for those who have come from marginalized social groups, such as the Dalits and the tribal groups, "Once you were not a people, but now you are God's people"(1 Peter 2:10). This can be translated into secular language as, "Through membership in a Christian community you have found a sense of identity."

BIBLIOGRAPHY

Brown, Judith M., and Robert E. Frykenberg. 2002. *Christians, Cultural Interactions, and India's Religious Traditions*. Grand Rapids, Mich.: Eerdmans.

Christianity in India: Collection of Pamphlets. 1998. 18 Microfiches. New Delhi: Library of Congress.

Clarke, Sathianathan. 1998. *Dalits and Christianity*. New York: Oxford University Press.

Constitution of India. 1949. New Delhi: Government of India Press.

Downs, F. S. 1992. *North East India in the Nineteenth and Twentieth Centuries*, vol. 5, part 2, *History of Christianity in India*. Bangalore: Church History Association.

Embree, Ainslie T. 1962. *Charles Grant and British Rule in India*. London: Allen and Unwin.

Hambye, E. R. 1976. *A Bibliography of Christianity in India*. Bangalore: Church History Association of India.

Harper, Susan Billington. 2000. *In the Shadow of the Mahatma: Bishop Azariah and the Travails of Christianity in British India*. Grand Rapids, Mich.: Eerdmans.

Kanjamala, Augustine. 1966. *Integral Mission Dynamics: An Interdisciplinary Study of the Catholic Church in India*. New Delhi: International Publications.

Lach, Donald E. 1965. *Asia in the Making of Europe*, vol. 2, book 1. Chicago: University of Chicago Press.

Neill, Stephen. 1984. *A History of Christianity in India: The Beginnings to AD 1707*. New York: Cambridge University Press.

————. 1985. *A History of Christianity in India: 1707–1858*. New York: Cambridge University Press.

New Testament, New Revised Standard Version. 1994. New York: Oxford University Press.

Philips, C. H. 1962. *The Evolution of India and Pakistan, 1858–1947*. Oxford: Oxford University Press.

Report of the Citizen's Commission on Persecution of Christians in Gujarat. 1999. New Delhi: National Alliance of Women.

CHAPTER 36

CHRISTIAN COMMUNITIES IN CHINA

RICHARD MADSEN

CHRISTIANITY in China is a relatively new import from the West. Although a few Nestorian communities were established in Western China in the seventh century and Franciscan missionaries made at least thirty thousand converts among the Mongols in Beijing around 1300 during the Yuan Dynasty, these early communities have disappeared. During the seventeenth century, European missionary orders, especially the Jesuits and Dominicans, entered China and began impressive missionary efforts. The Jesuits in particular made some very high-ranking converts and gained considerable favor within the imperial household. However, a bitter "rites controversy" emerged between the Jesuits and the Dominicans over how much the Christian faith could be adapted to correspond to Chinese culture. In the early eighteenth century, the pope sided with the Dominicans, who rejected any compromise with Chinese religious practices. As a result, the emperor expelled missionaries and proscribed Christianity. Although there are still a few Catholic communities which claim descendance back to the seventeenth-century missionaries, the great majority of present-day Chinese Christian communities were established by European and American missionaries who arrived under the protection of imperialist powers after the Opium Wars of the mid-nineteenth century.

The legacy of nineteenth- and early twentieth-century imperialism still affects Chinese Christian churches. Under the protection of foreign powers, Western missionaries felt relatively little pressure to adapt their faith to Chinese culture.

Churches were mostly built in Western styles. Catechisms and hymnals were mainly straightforward translations of European or North American works. Christian schools, universities, and hospitals were all in the Western style. Until the establishment of the People's Republic of China in 1949, the leaders of most denominations in China were foreigners.

When the Communists came to power, they began to impose tight restrictions on and eventually attempted to suppress all religious communities, foreign and indigenous. But the connections of Christian communities with imperialism gave the Communists an added excuse to attack them. Since the end of the Maoist era, the harshest forms of repression have been lifted. However, some Christian leaders still feel defensive about their connections with imperialism in the past. On the other hand, other Christians—and some non-Christians as well—are attracted to the churches precisely because of their origins and continued connections with advanced industrial societies. Some Europeans and North Americans have been eager to reestablish contact with their former mission churches and to help these communities with money. They sometimes lobby politically to get their governments to sanction China for allegedly persecuting Christians. Thus, the legacy of imperialism continues, though its effects are extremely ambivalent. Whatever its effects, that legacy has not stopped Christianity from growing in China. Before 1949, there were about three million Catholics and less than a million Protestants. At the end of the twentieth century, there are about ten million Catholics and perhaps more than twenty million Protestants in China. Christians account for only a tiny part of the Chinese population—no more than 2 or 3 percent. But the growth rate for Chinese Christianity is currently one of the fastest in the world. Most of this growth has occurred since restrictions on religious practice were reduced in 1979. Although foreign aid has helped the growth to some degree, most of it has taken place through the efforts of indigenous evangelists drawing on local resources.

There are Christian communities in virtually every region of China and among all the ethnic groups that make up Chinese society. Christianity often found warm acceptance among "national minority" groups—i.e., relatively small, tribal societies—in southern China, for whom missionaries developed writing systems so that the Bible could be translated into their own languages. In some cases, as among the Miao in Yunnan and among the Plains aborigines in Taiwan, Christianity was accepted by ethnic minorities partly as a way to distinguish themselves from the dominant Han culture, and it remains today tightly connected with ethnic identity.

In general, nineteenth- and twentieth-century Catholic missionaries focused most of their attention on the countryside, Protestants from the major denominations focused on the cities, while interdenominational organizations (like the China Inland Mission) and independent missionaries representing Western sectarian currents like the Holiness or Pentecostal movements worked in the interior.

The legacy of these patterns remains visible today. Perhaps 90 percent of Catholics live in the countryside, often in village communities that are entirely Catholic. In such a context, villages become like tiny Christendoms (a word that was actually used to describe them by French missionaries in the eighteenth century), places in which Catholicism is so intertwined with all major social institutions that one cannot shed one's Catholic identity, even if one wanted to. The theology connected with this worldview is the conservative, Counter-Reformation theology that disappeared in much of Europe and North America after the Second Vatican Council in the early 1960s. There is also a strong emphasis on Marian devotion. Many Catholics tell of apparitions of the Virgin Mary, who usually comes in her role as protector of communities beleaguered by outside forces. There are major pilgrimage sites in Donglu in Hebei Province and in Sheshan, near Shanghai, where the Virgin is believed to have appeared and to continue to work miracles.

Mainline Protestantism, on the other hand, is a more vigorous presence in the cities and seems more adapted to urban realities. According to principles put forth by government-supervised Protestant leadership bodies, the churches are supposed to be postdenominational, that is, there is no distinction between Anglicans, Presbyterians, Lutherans, etc. (As government pressure relaxes or becomes less effective, however, older denominational distinctions are beginning to assert themselves.) But whatever their official designation, urban Protestant congregations follow the sociological model of denominationalism. Congregations are more like voluntary associations with relatively easy entry and exit. Theology stresses a personal relationship with Christ, expressed in lives of personal rectitude.

Meanwhile, a strongly evangelical Protestantism, sometimes taking the form of idiosyncratic, independent sects, is rapidly growing in the countryside. This form is the fastest growing in China. It stresses a born-again conversion experience and evokes an intense emotional commitment from its members. Theology is pietistic, stressing individual experience rather than intellectual interpretation of doctrines. Often, faith is believed to lead to miracles of bodily healing.

Besides the legacy of imperialism, a second important legacy of Christianity in contemporary China is the history of persecution under the Communist regime. In the Constitution of the People's Republic of China, there is a guarantee of freedom of religious belief but not of assembly. Churches are allowed to function openly only if they are registered with the government. Under the Maoist regime, from 1949 to 1966, the government tried to use this policy to diminish and destroy Christianity. Especially during the Cultural Revolution era, all religious practice was fiercely attacked, clergy members were imprisoned, lay leaders persecuted, all church building were closed and many destroyed. This time of trial produced many heroic martyrs, whose example inspires Chinese Christians to this day. But it also left a heritage of bitterness and mistrust that complicates the relations between Christians and outsiders and among Christians themselves.

Under the reform policies begun by Mao's successor, Deng Xiaoping, in 1979, the government's policy has been more to co-opt and control rather than to repress and destroy. But there is considerable division among Christians about how to react to the government. Some Christians are opposed in principle to abiding by the government's regulations. Many Catholics, for instance, believe that registering with the Communist-led government is inconsistent with their need to be loyal to the pope. Some Protestants believe that their conscience forbids them to accept any direction from the state, especially a Communist one. Other believers might be willing to cooperate with the government in principle, but are unable to do so in practice because the government restricts the number of groups it is willing to register and limits registration only to groups it can adequately supervise. As a result, there have developed a large number of extralegal Christian communities. Among Catholics, these go by the name of the "underground Church," and among Protestants they are often called "house Churches" because worship takes place in homes rather than approved church buildings. Other Christians find the government's conditions for registration acceptable. This sometimes leads to severe conflicts within Christian communities. The conflicts are especially bitter between some underground Catholics and members of the "public Church."

The situation is further complicated by the fact that the government's policies are unevenly implemented. In some places, government officials actively persecute extra-legal Christians; in other places, they turn a blind eye to such activity. Where one group of Christians is harshly suppressed, they will harbor resentment not only toward the government but toward those fellow Christians who are living in relative comfort while cooperating with the government. Where no one is being persecuted, the relations between "underground" and officially approved Christians can be very fluid. Sometimes, the difference between being a member of an underground or house church, on the one hand, and an officially approved congregation on the other, is not a matter of principle but of accident—of one community's good fortune, perhaps, in falling under an informal quota of groups the government is willing to register. Under such circumstances, relations between extra-legal and officially approved Christians can be quite amicable.

Practicing Christians in China often exhibit an extraordinary level of devotion compared with their counterparts in North America and Europe. The social and political obstacles to practicing the faith keep the weakly committed from practicing at all. A heritage of martyrs provides high standards to emulate. And the moral vacuum caused by the ideological (though not institutional) collapse of Communism makes some people hungry for the larger meaning that faith can provide.

The enthusiasm, however, is not necessarily matched by systematic doctrinal formation. During the Maoist era, most seminaries were closed and it was almost impossible to train and ordain new clergy. By the time restrictions on religious practice were relaxed after 1979, most surviving clergy were elderly. In the last two decades of the twentieth century, a modest number of Catholic and Protestant seminaries have been opened, producing a small but steady stream of clergy. But the seminaries have lacked resources to train their students in the latest theological education. And aspiring ministers or evangelists who refuse to participate in government registered churches receive only informal training. The shortage of clergy and the thinness of their training lead toward rather uneven patterns of belief and practice. Widely scattered communities exhibit very diverse forms of spirituality, often involving some mixture of Western Christian and Chinese folk religious beliefs.

Since Catholicism is heavily dependent on an ordained clergy, its growth in China is inhibited by the shortage of clergy. Various forms of Protestantism grow much more rapidly because they can depend on lay preachers. It is hard to predict, though, how long the growth will continue. Both Protestant and Catholic leaders often express fears that their efforts to preach the faith will fail not because of political repression but because of competition with the materialism of a rapidly developing consumer society. Internal conflicts and institutional disarray within the various churches also repels some people who might find the faith attractive. Nonetheless, among Chinese intellectuals at the beginning of the twenty-first century there has arisen a small movement of "culture Christians" who have learned about Christian history and theology through personal study and have become convinced that it provides answers to life's ultimate questions. Most of these, however, stay away from the institutional church.

BIBLIOGRAPHY

Aikman, David. 2003. *Jesus in Beijing.* Washington, D.C.: Regnery.

Bays, Daniel H., ed. 1996. *Christianity in China: From the Eighteenth Century to the Present.* Palo Alto, Calif.: Stanford University Press.

Hunter, Alan, and Kim-Kwong Chan. 1993. *Protestantism in Contemporary China.* Cambridge: Cambridge University Press.

Madsen, Richard. 1998. *China's Catholics: Tragedy and Hope in an Emerging Civil Society.* Berkeley: University of California Press.

Uhalley, Stephen Jr., and Xiaoxin Wu, eds. 2001. *China and Christianity: Burdened Past, Hopeful Future.* Armonk, N.Y.: M.E. Sharpe.

Ziming, Yuan, et al. 1997. *Soul Searching: Chinese Intellectuals on Faith and Society.* Wheaton, Ill.: China Horizon.

CHAPTER 37

CHRISTIAN COMMUNITIES IN SOUTHEAST ASIA

TARA VILLALBA MUNSON

CHRISTIANITY in Southeast Asia is part of a rich tapestry of global religious traditions that include Buddhism, Hinduism, and Islam. In mainland Southeast Asia, Christianity competes with Buddhism, which has been enshrined as the state religion in Myanmar and Cambodia, and is widely practiced in Vietnam, Laos, and Thailand. Christianity first came to mainland Southeast Asia through the French in Vietnam. Although Christianity started to arrive in Vietnam in the 1300s, proselytizing from the Roman Catholic missionaries began in earnest in the 1500s. A Roman Catholic priest transliterated Vietnamese into Latin letters, the letters still in use in modern Vietnamese. In the mid-1900s the Christian and Missionary Alliance sent missionaries (many of whom moved from China) to evangelize Indochina. Vietnam's population is approximately eight 8 percent Christian, the majority of whom are Catholic.

In the same way that China served as the initial base for Western missionaries to evangelize in Indochina and the Malay Archipelago, Vietnam served in a similar way for missionaries proselytizing in Laos, Myanmar, and Cambodia. Thus, Christianity in nationalist Laos, Myanmar, and Cambodia was seen as foreign because it came from two groups of outsiders: the European colonizers and missionaries, and the Vietnamese who spread it further farther into Indochina. Many Christian communities in Laos, Myanmar, and Cambodia are found in ethnic minority groups such as the Karen and the Kachin in Myanmar. These groups, freedom to perform their own religious practices is complicated by oppressive government policies that target ethnic minority groups who also happen in many cases to be Christian.

Elsewhere in mainland Southeast Asia smaller Christian communities may be found. About .5 percent of Thailand's population is Christian, while 95 percent are Buddhist, and 3 percent are Muslims. Meanwhile, 1.5 percent of Laos' population is Christian, 4 to 6 percent of Burma's population is Christian, while 89 percent are Buddhists, and 4 percent are Muslims. Finally, 0.16 percent of Cambodia's population is Christian and 86 percent are Buddhists. National councils and conferences as well as some individual churches in Southeast Asia are members of the Christian Conference of Asia including Myanmar, Cambodia, Indonesia, Malaysia, and the Philippines.

Larger Christian populations are found further farther east. Malaysia's population is about 8.6 percent Christian. Singapore has one of the highest percentages of Southeast Asian Christians, about 14 percent of its population, while the sheer numbers of Christians in the huge population of Indonesia is impressive even though the percentage of Christians in Indonesia is around 9 percent, compared with a 60 percent Muslim population. Islam arrived and became established in Indonesia in the twelfth century, and Roman Catholic Christianity was introduced in 1530 by the Portuguese in the Molucca region. Protestantism was introduced into Indonesia in 1605 by the Dutch who took over from the Portuguese after Spain annexed Portugal. Whereas Protestant clergy were initially intended to serve the needs of the Dutch East India Company, by 1930 it had become the state church. Furthermore, the Catholic Church has been active in political life and is represented by the Catholic Party in government. Presently, Christianity is one of five faiths recognized by the Indonesian government as an official religion. Previously part of Indonesia, East Timor voted for independence from Indonesia and in 1999 became established as an independent country with a Christian majority.

In addition to Roman Catholic and Protestant forms of Christianity in Southeast Asia, Eastern Christian communities seem to have traveled from India and settled as far east as Java in Indonesia before the 1500s. According to two written eyewitness accounts and dated artifacts including inscriptions, frescoes, and physical ruins, Christian churches appear to have been established as far east as Sumatra and Java as early as the seventh century to the twelfth century. As members of Nestorian, Jacobite, and Armenian churches moved from Persia through India, they also continued to travel and move into Southeast Asia, at times even becoming attached to the royal courts of the local kingdoms. European explorers and travelers, including Marco Polo, report encountering Christians from what is now Myanmar and Thailand. Although research is just beginning to unfold the extent of Christian communities for before 1500, it is believed that Persian, Arab, and

Indian traders traveled and witnessed and thus brought Eastern Christianity to Southeast Asia.

CHRISTIANITY IN THE PHILIPPINES

The Philippines is the only Southeast Asian country with a Christian majority. Its population is comprised of comprises roughly 80 percent Roman Catholics, 8 percent Protestants, and 10 percent Muslims. Christianity first came to the Philippines in the tow of colonial explorers. Roman Catholicism was introduced in 1521 with the arrival of Spain's Ferdinand Magellan and the first churches were built after 1565 with the establishment of the Spanish colonial rule secured by Miguel Lopez de Legazpi. Before the establishment of Roman Catholicism by Spanish friars, the islands of the Philippines were organized into local kinship communities led by a *datu* who belonged to local elite families. The communities, called *barangays*, coexisted with the expanding sultanates of Sulu and of Borneo. By the time the Spaniards arrived in the Philippines, Islam had already been established for about two hundred years in Mindanao and other southern islands, and the sultanates had outposts as far north as Manila on the island of Luzon. In addition to Islam, local animist and spirit worship was practiced widely by the inhabitants of the islands.

Although the Filipino natives were often characterized as simple, lazy, and sometimes recalcitrant wayward converts, the Spanish friars nevertheless considered them easy easier converts to Christianity. Such was not the case for the indigenous tribal peoples in the mountain regions of Northern Luzon, nor for the rebellious and inauthentic Muslims of Mindanao and Sulu (whom the Spaniards called Moros after the Moors of Iberia). Furthermore, the Spaniards relied on their experiences with Iberian Muslims to interpret the Muslims they encountered in the Philippines. According to the Spaniards comparing Mindanao Muslims with Muslims they had encountered elsewhere, the Spaniards considered, the Islam practiced by the most Mindanao Muslims was inauthentic, rendering Mindanao Muslims as mostly nominal Muslims who were fair game for conversion (instead of the few real Mindanao Muslims who should be killed or enslaved, according to the Spanish king).

While the friars were Christianizing and Hispanizing the Indios of Central Luzon and the Visayas, the Northern Luzon tribal peoples and the Muslims separately resisted Spanish efforts at conversion. The mountainous terrain in Northern Luzon helped to protect the resistant tribal peoples there. Tribes in

Northern Luzon actively resisted the Christianizing friars, while the Muslims fought back in armed encounters with the Spanish, subsequently characterized by Spaniards as instances of Moro piracy and slave trading. Thus, neither the Northern Luzon mountainous regions nor Mindanao and Sulu were ever Christianized and Hispanized during the three hundred years of Spanish colonial rule. However, the legacy of attitudes instilled during the Spanish colonial period about the harassing, recalcitrant, and ungodly Moros continue to haunt present political relations between the post-colonial Philippine government in Manila and many Muslim communities in Mindanao.

The colonial enterprise was justified in two ways: the conversion and salvation of native souls and the growth and protection of the Spanish Crown, particularly against its European rivals: Portugal and the Netherlands. As it turns out, the Spanish friars had a large role in the realization of both intentions. Legazpi brought Spanish friars with him on his expedition not only to serve the Spanish conquistadors who accompanied him but more importantly to spread Roman Catholicism as directed by Rome and by the Spanish Crown. The pope in Rome had earlier divided the East Indies between Portugal and Spain. Thus Spain's King Philip II was delegated by the pope with the power to appoint religious leaders (including bishops) in the new colonies and charged with providing for their livelihood and financial support. Many of the early religious limited their mission to the conversion of non-Christians to Roman Catholicism and to the education of the converted. Some of the early friars attempted to learn the languages of those they were attempting to convert, and while living within the local communities, tried to understand and tolerate the local customs and traditions.

Initially, the Spanish Crown forbade the friars and other religious to own property in the colonies. However, as the friars began to organize themselves into communities rather than living separately and far from each other, they also abused the privileges accorded to them by the Spanish Crown. Emboldened by the successful campaign of the religious in Mexico to acquire land and property, friars in the Philippines requested and were granted land and estates so that they could become self-supporting in their missionary efforts. The friars justified their request by emphasizing their desire not to be a financial burden to their local communities. Subsequently, the friars amassed property in various ways: from grants and donations by local wealthy elite, by purchasing land from local owners, by foreclosing on the land of their mortgagees, and sometimes by outright land grabbing. Thus, in addition to the portion allotted to the religious from the tributes collected by the *encomiendas* (parcels of land assigned and managed, but not owned, by Spanish colonial administrators), friars secured economic power in their local communities, adding to the religious power they already wielded.

Many friars and missionaries shifted their attention from just converting the local inhabitants to increasing their own wealth. As friars became landowners they increasingly treated their tenants and sharecroppers harshly, forbidding tenants and local inhabitants from using land and its features including lakes and rivers that had previously been available for the use of the local community. Along with the abuses the friars routinely committed on their local communities, the Spanish military were also committing abuses on the local populations. The 1896–98 revolution was both a nationalist movement striving to form a nation-state, and a protest movement against the abuses committed by the Spanish friars.

From 1896 to 1902 native Filipino clergy, after presenting their criticisms and grievances about the Spanish friars to the Spanish Crown, resolved to break away from the Roman Catholic Church and its Papal papal authority. They formed the Philippine Independent Church (Iglesia Filipina Indipendiente) whose liturgy continued to closely follow the Roman Catholic one, but also expressed vocal support for the aspirations of the nationalist Katipunan movement, and opposition to continued Spanish colonial rule. The goals of the revolution included the expulsion of friars from the Philippines, the redistribution of the friar property to the local communities, and the opening of the religious hierarchy in the Philippines to Filipino leaders. Gregorio Aglipay became the first supreme bishop of the Iglesia Independiente in 1902.

The United States acquired the Philippines as a colony after the United States defeated Spain in the Spanish-American War. American colonial rule brought with it missionaries from major Protestant denominations in the United States to the Philippines. As often happened in other parts of Southeast Asia, the Protestant missionaries found warmest reception to their message in the ethnic minority populations. Along with the conversions in ethnic minority communities that previous Roman Catholic missionaries did not reach, many Catholic Filipinos also converted to numerous Protestant denominations as a result of the unpopular policies and abuses of the Roman Catholic institution.

In addition to the Protestant missionaries who flooded into the Philippines during the American colonial period, many of the teachers working to set up the public education system in the Philippines also acted functioned as missionaries. Just as the educational system left by the Spanish colonists and indeed the entire essence of the Spanish endeavor to civilize the Filipinos was tied to the Roman Catholic faith and the quest to save the souls of the natives so the American colonial enterprise was also colored by the Protestant values and ideals evident in American political and economic life. The American colonial administrators professed to instruct Filipinos in rational nation building and to enlighten Filipinos in modern political and religious thought. While the Spanish colonial rule was characterized by the union of religious and political authority and power, the American colonial period proclaimed the freedom of religious practice and provided for the separation of church and state. Therefore, the American colonial period appeared more benevolent than the Spanish colonial period. Additionally, instead of using religion as the means to subjugate the Muslims, the Americans attempted to co-opt their leaders instead by enticing them with economic and educational opportunities such as sending Muslim princesses to study in American universities with the hope of bringing their American-learned values back to their home communities. At the same time, Protestant missionaries continued to enjoy the freedom to work and convert Muslims, Catholics, and Tribal Peoples.

When the Republic of the Philippines was proclaimed on July 4, 1946, the government groomed by the Americans modeled itself after its followed the model of American government progenitor. Separation of church and state continued, but the preeminence of Christianity also continued. The difficult relationship with the Muslims in Mindanao, initiated during the Spanish colonial period and continued throughout the American colonial period, also persisted in the post-colonial life of the Philippines.

The interaction of different Christian communities also yielded positive outcomes. Presently, the Roman Catholic Church in the Philippines, claiming about 80 percent of the population, runs more than 1,500 schools and universities as well as a number of hospitals, orphanages, health clinics, and offers other social services. One of the most significant contributions of the Roman Catholic Church in the Philippines is the privatized private parochial Catholic school system.

Whereas Roman Catholicism began as a religion wholly imported from Western Europe, Catholics in the Philippines have now continued to indigenized it. One way this indigenization is particularly evident is in the incorporation of local and popular religious practices into Roman Catholic traditions. For example, the word Bathala was previously used to denote the creator and supreme being and is now often understood as the native Filipino word for the God of the Bible (equivalent to Dios, closer to the Latin Deo). Another example of this syncretism is the belief that Catholic religious symbols have a supernatural power (like a talisman) to ward off evil or bad events and that this power can be accessed on certain holy days like a saint's feast day or Christmas. Philippine heroes, Jose Rizal in particular, have also been presented as the Christ and Savior of the Philippines. He is the object of veneration for a religion that believes he is the second son of God.

Furthermore, a new church was founded in 1914 by Felix Manalo called Iglesia ni Kristo (Church of Christ). It claims to be neither Catholic nor Protestant. Rather it claims that it is the true and uncorrupted mystical body of Christ, revealed to God's chosen people (the Filipinos) and that it alone is the way to salvation. It has a following of over 600,000 Filipinos with striking churches throughout the archipelago. It runs a hospital and a college in Quezon City, offering free healthcare and education to its members. The Iglesia ni Kristo is a wealthy church and has a conservative doctrine. It is run by an authoritarian leadership strictly enforcing its rules and policing its members.

Protestantism started out in the Philippines with the establishment of numerous denominations. After World War II, two developments led to the concerted efforts of the many Christian communities in the Philippines to transcend factionalism and move towards ecumenism. Firstly, in May 1948, the United Church of Christ in the Philippines (UCCP) was formed through the union of the Disciples of Christ, Evangelical United Brethren, Philippine Methodist (independent from the American denomination), Presbyterian, and Congregational churches. Most notably absent from this union were the larger Methodist Church and the Convention of Philippine Baptist Churches. The UCCP is the largest Protestant denomination in the Philippines, listing over 2,500 churches and about twenty church-owned or related schools and universities.

Secondly, the National Council of Churches in the Philippines (NCCP) was convened in 1963 to further advance the ecumenical works of the UCCP, the Methodist Church, the Convention of Philippine Baptist Churches, the Evangelical Methodist Church, the Iglesia Evangelica Unida de Cristo, the Philippine Episcopal Church, and the Philippine Independent Church. Overall, the churches affiliated with the UCCP and the NCCP strongly believe in the indigenization of the clergy ranks and the self-sufficiency of the local Christian communities. Thus, they strive to support their own ministries and some, like the UCCP, even actively refuse the long-term tenure of missionaries from overseas. Both the UCCP and the NCCP are members of the Christian Conference of Asia that is affiliated with the World Council of Churches. The Christian Conference of Asia is committed to the unity of the Christian communities in Asia and in the continued ecumenical work of the Christian communities.

Among the other Protestant denominations present in the Philippines are: Seventh Day Adventists, Church of Latter Day Saints, Churches of Christ, Assemblies of God, Foursquare Gospel, and the Southern Baptist Convention. There are a number of fast-growing evangelical and fundamental Protestant denominations in the Philippines, and the more established Protestant denominations as well as the Roman Catholic Church recognize that the competition for the membership, if not faith, of their parishioners/members is becoming more intense.

An important aspect of Christian ecumenical work in the Philippines is in the area of social justice and peace dialogues. During the troubled years of the Marcos presidency, the UCCP and NCCP and some Catholic communities supported the calls for fair and clean elections. They also voiced concerns pertaining to land reform and other labor issues in solidarity with industrial and agricultural works and the urban poor. In addition, the Bishops-Ulama Conference (BUC) was spearheaded by a Catholic bishop, a UCCP bishop, and a Muslim ulama. Together their religious communities discuss and hold dialogues with each other about the coming and importance of peace in conflict-ridden troubled Mindanao. The BUC strives to encourage dialogue between the Muslim and Christian inhabitants of Mindanao. These priorities and outspoken actions do not always prove to be popular with some Christian leaders and many of the more conservative congregations. For example, leaders in the UCCP were recently accused of being fronts for the Communist Party of the Philippines. Despite denials from different levels of the UCCP institution, some congregations have threatened to withhold their financial support from the national conference because of the actions of the some politically active leaders. The UCCP, as with other Christian churches, continues to struggle between conservative, progressive, and in-between understandings of social justice, sexuality, and the role of religion within politics.

Although some parishes and congregations openly support progressive politics, most Christian communities in the Philippines remain politically conservative. Furthermore, even if the social justice actions of particular denominations or parishes are more open to liberal politics, those same churches may still tend to be quite conservative on other issues matters such as issues about sexuality. These attitudes are carried over by Filipino migrants and immigrants to their new homes in host countries. In addition to the existence of Catholic communities with large Filipino memberships, there are also a number of UCCP congregations in the United States.

CHRISTIAN ADAPTATION IN SOUTHEAST ASIA AND ABROAD

Christian communities in much of Southeast Asia Asia are following the pattern of Christianity in the Phillipines where the religion has been indigenized and Filipinos are making it their own continue to make their Christian faith their own. Although Christianity came and grew to its present levels under the presence of Western European merchants and colonialists, From the western edge of Burma to the eastern borders of the Philippines, and from the northern reaches of Vietnam to the southern islands of Indonesia, Christianity came and grew to its present levels under the presence of Western European merchants and colonialists. However, far from the simple vision of Westernizing and modernizing the backward and unenlightened Southeast Asians, Christian communities adapted and formed in response to and awareness of local communities and their local needs and cultures. There is no one story of Christianity's coming to and subsequent growth in to Southeast Asia. Merchants and travelers from Eastern Christian Churches came to Asia prior to 1500. Christian missionaries came from outside Asia: France, the Netherlands, England, Portugal, Switzerland, Spain, and the United States from the 1500s continuing to the present. Many Christian missionaries also moved from closer parts of Asia into Southeast Asia: China, India, and later Vietnam and the Malay Archipelago. This pattern of Christian diversity continues as Southeast Asian Christians are now dispersed around the globe.

BIBLIOGRAPHY

Anderson, Gerald H. 1968. *Christ and Crisis in Southeast* Asia. New York: Friendship Press.

Carro, Daniel, and Richard Wilson, Richard (eds.). 1997. *Contemporary Gospel Accents: Doing Theology in Africa, Asia, Southeast Asia, and Latin America.* Macon, Ga.: Mercer University Press.

Cummins, J. S., (ed.). 1997. *Christianity and Missions 1450–1800.* Aldershot, U.K.: Variorum.

England, John C. 1996. *The Hidden History of Christianity in Asia.* Hong Kong: Christian Conference of Asia.

Gillman, Ian, and Hans-Joachim Klimkeit. 1999. *Christians in Asia Before 1500.* Ann Arbor: University of Michigan Press.

Historical Conservation Society. 1965. *The Christianization of the Philippines.* Manila: M. Sanchez.

Spickard, Paul R., and Kevin M. Cragg. 1994. *A Global History of Christians: How Everyday Believers Experienced Their World.* Grand Rapids, Mich.: Baker Book House.

CHAPTER 38

MORMON COMMUNITIES AROUND THE WORLD

JAN SHIPPS

THE global center of the Mormon faith is Salt Lake City, which since its earliest days has been the headquarters of the Church of Jesus Christ of Latter-day Saints (which is often called the LDS Church). It has also been such a reflection of this ecclesiastical body that changes in the church are reflected in the city. Many of the international visitors to the 2002 Olympic Games traveled to Salt Lake City expecting to find an insular provincial city inhabited by quaint but narrow-minded Mormon folk. Instead they discovered that today the metropolis founded by pioneer members of the Church of Jesus Christ of Latter-day Saints in 1847 is surprisingly cosmopolitan. To some degree this reflects an influx of modern electronic industries and financial organizations as well as the development of a successful tourist industry. But it reflects religious change even more.

What visitors to the city now find mirrors a new religious reality: the Church of Jesus Christ of Latter-day Saints has become an international institution. Historically, the greatest proportion of the church's membership resided in the United States. In 1996, for the first time ever, the number of church members living outside the United States slightly exceeded those living inside the nation. In less than a decade later, the relative proportions continued to move in an international direction. In 2003, out of a total membership of 11,340,522, slightly more than 53 percent (6,029,924) lived outside the United States. Almost 65 percent of the international members lived in Central and South America; a little more than 22 percent lived in the Pacific (the Philippines, the Pacific Islands, Australia, New Zealand, Japan, Korea, and other parts of South Asia), with smaller numbers living in Europe, Africa, and Canada.

Mormons are keenly aware of the reality of their church's global presence. Whenever they read church publications or participate in local church activities, church members are steadily reminded of their church's international commitment. Additionally, and of far greater significance, the church convenes church-wide conferences in Salt Lake City twice a year. Representative Saints from every place in the world where the church has missions or established congregations travel to the headquarters of the church to attend General Conference in April and Semi-annual Conference in October. Held in a huge new twenty-one thousand seat Conference Center (completed in 2000) that has translation facilities that would make the United Nations proud, these two-day meetings take on the character of worldwide forums. Broadcast on closed-circuit television to the general membership of the church, these semi-annual conferences create a virtual community that makes the fact of Mormonism's escalating universality visible to members all across the globe.

The spotlight trained on Utah during the 2002 Olympic Games played a big part in helping to undercut a long-standing non-Mormon perception that Mormonism is a provincial religious system whose adherents are concentrated in the state of Utah. During the games, journalists placed a great deal of emphasis on the Mormon presence in parts of the world other than the United States. This emphasis is continuously underscored by various church media venues, including its official Web sites. As a result, the LDS Church's worldwide reach is becoming ever more apparent both inside and outside the church.

Almost from the start, the church had members who were not native to the United States. But by no means has the church always been a multinational body. As recently as 1960, the Mormon Church, as it was generally known throughout the nineteenth and well into the twentieth century, was still very much an American institution. The diaspora that would lead to congregational units being established all across the nation and around the world was just getting underway. But the possibilities and implications of the Mormon diaspora were by no means obvious back then, even to the Latter-day Saints themselves. Although they surely hoped for such success, few people realized that, within forty years, the ensuing spatial diffusion would lead to this form of Mormonism's becoming a significant national and even worldwide religious force. Yet, at the outset, most insiders and nearly all outsiders regarded this formidable ecclesiastical body not even as a uniquely American institution, but rather as a Utah church.

By and large, they were correct. The church's membership was concentrated in Utah and the surrounding areas of the intermountain region of the Western United States, an area where the Mormon presence was so pervasive it was called the "Mormon culture region." Long-standing organizational units existed in

Southern California and in a few other areas in the Pacific coastal region. The church was strong in Hawaii, and it had well-established congregational units in several of the larger metropolitan areas in the United States. But fewer than 10 percent of the church's members resided outside the United States, with most of them living in such English-speaking countries as Canada, England, Australia, and New Zealand, or they lived in Mexico and Northern Europe.

If Mormons lived anywhere away from the Western United States, even in foreign lands, they tended to think of the Great Basin, and most especially Utah, as their homeland. Thus, it is not surprising that many non-Mormons thought this religion was a Western phenomenon—somewhat akin, in the secular realm, to cowboys and Indians. Mormons, of course, did not share this popular perception.

The members of the LDS Church headquartered in Salt Lake City were generally aware that another form of Mormonism was headquartered in Independence, Missouri. Although it was a much smaller ecclesiastical body, the mountain Saints realized—at least vaguely—that there were prairie Saints as well. Moreover, both sorts of Saints learned in Sunday School that their churches evolved out of a movement of Christian Restoration that started in western New York state in the late 1820s, and they were very conscious of the story of Mormon beginnings.

Besides thinking that the movement was distinctively Western, many Gentiles (the term used for non-Mormons) were not sure whether Mormonism fit into Christianity, and if so, how. Actually, it is likely that most Mormons knew very little about the structure of the Christian tradition. But their experience told them they were as surely Christian as they were Mormon. It also told them that their church was distinctly different from other Christian churches.

It always has been different, even though the first Mormons had much in common with the members of many other indigenous Christian movements that came into being in the United States during the early national period. Yet by the time Mormonism took institutional shape as the restored Church of Christ in 1830, this particular group advanced three distinctive beliefs that separated them not only from all other versions of primitivist and millennialist Christianity then present in the nation, but also from all other existing forms of Protestantism, Catholicism, and Orthodoxy.

The first and most important in this trio of beliefs was that a living prophet led their church. The other two truly distinctive beliefs were that their priesthoods were the restored priesthoods of Aaron and Melchizedek. In addition, besides the Old and New testaments, they had a complementary work of scripture.

The members of the first Mormon group followed a twenty-four-year-old visionary farm lad, Joseph Smith, Jr., whose words and actions persuaded them that he was a modern seer, translator, and prophet. They believed the restoration of the church and the ancient priesthoods came through his prophetic agency. Of even greater significance, Smith's followers accepted the claim that, with divine assistance manifested in the form of seer stones known as the "Urim Aurim and Thummim," Smith had translated the Book of Mormon from etchings engraved on a set of golden plates that he found buried in a hill not far from his home in Manchester, New York.

To believers, this was modern scripture, a marvelous work and a wonder that signified the nearness of the end of time. Unbelievers, however, facetiously and dismissively described this work as Smith's "golden Bible." They also called Smith's followers "mormonites," a nickname the members of the new church rejected, instead calling themselves Latter-day Saints.

Notwithstanding their possession of a new work of scripture and their other distinctive beliefs, these Latter-day Saints shared with other Christian bodies much more than many people realize. Indeed, a substantial portion of the Mormon pattern of belief came from the Bible, the Old Testament as well as the New. But the Saints' concern for going into the world to preach the gospel to every creature seems not to have come from the "Great Commission" to preach the gospel to all nations that the disciples received at the end of the Gospel of Matthew. Although the text of the Book of Mormon included a charge similar to "go ye into all the world and preach the gospel," the Saints' fervent and powerful missionary impulse came not from that directive so much as from the title page of their new scripture.

The text of this work asserts that it is a record of Hebrew peoples who traveled from the Near East to the Western Hemisphere before the Hebrews were carried off to captivity in Babylon. Their history, including an account of their hearing the Christian message from Jesus himself, was preserved by a man named Mormon, the only survivor of the internecine warfare that destroyed them and their culture. Hence the title, The Book of Mormon, which since 1981 has been subtitled "A New Testament of Jesus Christ." While overstating the importance of this new scripture to the LDS tradition would be difficult, with regard to the story of Mormonism in global perspective, the Book of Mormon was singularly important because its title page set the agenda for Mormon missions.

Appearing there was a declaration about the dual purpose for the book's coming forth. This unambiguous message is that the book was written for Native Americans (here called "Lamanites") to tell them they were a remnant of the House of Israel. It was also written "to the convincing of the Jew and Gentile that JESUS is the CHRIST, the ETERNAL GOD manifesting Himself to all nations." Seeing it as their duty to do so, the Saints accepted responsibility for delivering this information to these particular target audiences. Thus their church faced a dual task: carrying the message to the Indians and going into all nations in the world to convince both Jews and Gentiles that Jesus is the Christ.

To the Saints, the coming forth of the Book of Mormon had been a sign of the times, signaling that the end was near. This made their missionary obligation a priority, one that was accentuated by revelation. Less than six months after the organization of the church in April 1830, the Mormon prophet said that he had received a revelation that four members of his fledgling flock should undertake a mission to the Indians (here called Lamanites). They were charged with preaching the gospel and with establishing the church among those who received it.

Few, if any, Native Americans were thoroughly converted to Mormonism as a result of this first Lamanite mission. But this undertaking was terribly important because it resulted in the establishing of what they called a "stake in the tent of Zion" in Independence, Missouri, a settlement that stood on the border of "Indian country" where Native Americans at that time were being forced to go in response to the nation's Indian Removal Policy. This initial Indian mission was exceedingly significant to the history of the Latter-day Saints for another reason. As they wended their way west, the missionaries not only preached to the Indians but also to anyone else who would listen. In Ohio, the missionaries converted a Camp-bellite minister and his entire congregation to the new faith. Not long after Joseph Smith Jr. heard about the missionaries' success, he announced that he had received a revelation that he, too, should go to Ohio and that the New York Saints should go with him. This led to the organization of a second stake in Zion's tent.

This was the not the first revelatory mention of the concept of assembling the Lord's elect in one place, but it was the first time the Saints made this critically important gathering concept operative. From 1831 forward, the command that converts to Mormonism should leave their homes and go live in close proximity with other Saints took precedence over the revelation that said missionaries should preach the gospel and establish the church among those who received it. This "gathering" principle would further separate Mormonism from most other forms of Christianity. In addition, it would have a profound effect on how long it took for Mormonism to become a global movement.

For much of the 1830s the Saints in Ohio were more fortunate than the church members in Missouri. The town of Kirtland was both the administrative head-quarters of the church and its principal base for missionary activities. In 1838, however, for a variety of secular as well as sacred reasons, the hostile actions of northeastern Ohio mobs of old settlers caused Smith and other church leaders as well as most of the church's members to flee to the gathering place in north-western Missouri that the Saints had established after similarly being driven by old settlers from their homes, first from the frontier town of Independence and then from nearby Clay County.

Before the Saints left Kirtland, two events occurred that would eventually have immense significance for the globalization of Mormonism. The first was the construction of the Kirtland Temple and its dedication in 1836, a Pentecost-like occasion in which the temple built by the Saints received divine warrant as the house of God and the place for the performance of ancient ordinances that the Saints believed had once been performed in the temple at Jerusalem. This was exceedingly important because it was the first in a series of temples the Saints built that would not only become sacramental centers but also places of pilgrimage, beacons signaling a [stet] presence in particular geographical areas. Its significance for the nineteenth-century Mormon experience was intensified because the ordinance of celestial marriage (which was given by revelation and which held that marriages performed in LDS temples united couples for eternity as well as time) provided warrant for plural marriage.

The other occurrence critical to the globalization of Mormonism was the revelation on priesthood that included the organization of the Council of the Twelve, a body that would serve as a "Traveling High Council" that could preside over the church in regions where Saints were not gathered into stakes and wards. Aside from the first Lamanite Mission, most of the missionaries sent out from Kirtland between 1831 and 1837 were assigned to go to areas within the United States or eastern Canada. But soon after the Kirtland Temple was dedicated, a key Council of the Twelve member was called to initiate missionary work outside North America.

Despite the horrific suffering the Saints had to face in the next decade—arrest of the prophet and several other church leaders; dissension and apostasy among the Twelve, and a Mormon War in Missouri; the flight of the entire body of Saints back across the Mississippi River to Illinois; the building of a kingdom on the Mississippi at Nauvoo; and the prophet's murder—successful missionary work went forward in Great Britain. Before the church's English mission had been functioning for two years, 1,500 converts were baptized. Then, even as the Saints in the United States struggled to overcome the trauma of the Missouri Mormon War and labored to create a new gathering place, nine different members of the Council of the Twelve served missions in Great Britain.

Their efforts paid off handsomely in numbers of converts, with 4,000 more being baptized during those two years. Rather than establishing the church among those who accepted the gospel in Britain, however, the missionaries preached the gathering doctrine as a central element of the millennialist Restoration message. The result was that rather than establishing congregations for the long term, one dimension of the missionary task turned out to be arranging ocean passage so that converts could gather with the Saints in their American Zion.

And gather they did. By 1841, more than a fourth of the total membership of the church was made up of English converts, many of whom sacrificed virtually everything to travel to the land of Zion where they could join their co-religionists in preparing for the Second Coming. In spite of demanding and difficult ocean passages no millennial bliss materialized, and the immigrants, many of them destitute, were further tested and tried as they struggled to find places to live and the means to sustain themselves in Nauvoo and the surrounding areas on both sides of the Mississippi River.

The murder of the Mormon prophet was an additional stumbling block. But the tribulations of the ocean crossing and the difficulties the new Saints faced in the United States had little effect on the convert stream. In point of fact, the momentum of convert arrivals increased as the gathering continued in the Great Basin after members of the LDS community were forced to abandon the city-state they had fashioned in Illinois. In addition to the English, substantial numbers of converts came from Scandinavia and other parts of Northern Europe.

Many people, including a fair number of scholars, reckon that a large majority of LDS church members followed Brigham Young to the valley of the Great Salt Lake where they again created a kingdom, this one more fully realized and fleshed out. This estimate may be mistaken. While the Twelve took charge and kept the community together for almost three years before the Saints were compelled to flee, what actually happened after the prophet's murder is that the movement split apart, atomized. Henceforward there would be many Mormonisms, not just one.

A few Saints remained in Nauvoo and a substantial number stayed in Illinois and Iowa. In 1860, some of them "reorganized" the church under the leadership of the prophet's eldest son, Joseph Smith III. In the years between the death of the prophet and 1860, others established Mormon churches in Wisconsin, northern Michigan, Texas, Pennsylvania, and even New York. Only one, the Strangite group, called for a gathering of Saints, and that movement did not last long. None of the others treated the gathering principle as critical to what being Mormon meant.

But this was not the case with the Council of the Twelve and Brigham Young (who became the president of the church in the Great Basin). Keeping in mind that the gathering was a revealed principle, and perhaps recalling the appeal it had for British converts, they made coming to live in the kingdom one of the first principles of the Mormon gospel. Often with the assistance of the church's Perpetual Emigrating Fund, so many Saints from Europe were added to the numbers who made the pioneer trek from Nauvoo that the LDS settlement in the intermountain West rapidly became the form of Mormonism that had more adherents than any other.

Those who gathered there lived through a period of fullness, if not of time, then of living in a literal "Kingdom of God in the tops of the mountains." But it was not a kingdom totally isolated from the world because the intermountain West was serving as a catch basin into which immigrant converts were funneled. Only in Hawaii and Samoa were there more or less permanent congregational units that the church established among those who accepted Mormon gospel claims.

Two things happened to bring to an end what many Saints remembered—and what today's Saints commemorate and celebrate—as a difficult yet halcyon pioneer period. One was external and the other internal. First the external: backed by legal fiat and political reality, the federal government moved from outside the culture to insist that if Utah wanted to take its place as a sovereign state alongside other sovereign states in the United States, the territory would have to prove that it could pattern itself after the political, economic, and social systems of the other states in the nation. The effort to do so initiated dramatic alterations in politics and the economic system, and it required the cessation of the practice of plural marriage. But it was successful enough for Utah to become a state and for the boundary between Zion and Babylon to become quite porous.

The internal change came some fifteen or twenty years later when it became obvious to church leaders that as long as agriculture and mining were the principal means of earning livelihoods, the mountainous and desert region that had served them so well during the pioneer period could not support an infinite number of gathered Saints. As a result, the church changed its position about the necessity of continuing the gathering.

This change was gradual. First gathering was de-emphasized when the church president told European converts that, at present, they did not need to "trouble themselves too much about emigration." The time frame for gathering was extended indefinitely in 1921 when, on the basis of economic rather than religious reasons, the church issued an official statement urging missionaries to stop preaching immigration. Just prior to World War II, Saints in foreign lands were urged to gather out of "spiritual Babylon, out of the midst of wickedness," but they did not need to go so far as to gather in Utah. And soon after the war, the reinterpretation of the gathering revelation was carried forward when President Spencer W. Kimball told the Saints to "[R]emain [in their own lands] and build up a people to the Lord." This advice has been repeated again and again by General Authorities of the church.

This twentieth-century reinterpretation of the gathering revelation can be stated in another way: Zion is where the people of God are. Stated in this manner the theological ground shifts, returning Mormonism to its earliest revelation in which the Lord told the Saints who were sent on missions to "Go [unto the unconverted] and preach my gospel unto them; and inasmuch as they receive thy teachings thou shalt cause my church to be established among them." This also causes the pragmatic ground to shift. For almost an entire century the church's global perspective was centripetal, so directed toward the center that in the gathering process converts were Christianized, "Mormonized," and Americanized all at the same time.

After the reinterpretation of the various gathering revelations, things shifted, thereby causing the church's global perspective to become centrifugal. The center remains strong, but the church is clearly moving outward through a process in which missionaries, church leaders, and indigenous Saints are working together to create multiple centers. This, however, is not a move simply leading to a new definition of Zion. What is different is that church organization leading to the formation of branches, wards, and stakes follows as soon as a sufficient number of indigenous Saints are ordained to the Melchizedek priesthood to make up a competent leadership cadre. Of greater significance, wherever enough Saints are gathered together in close proximity, an LDS temple is being constructed. Once this happens, Zion is truly there in areas all across the world.

Enormous consequences followed the turn from gathering centripetally to gathering centrifugally. This ecclesiastical institution has always been hierarchal in nature and it has a highly structured system of lay priesthood that is led by a president who, by virtue of his position, is also the Mormon prophet, and by a body of "General Authorities" that presides over the whole church. Because it is headquartered in Salt Lake City, in "the tops of the mountains" as early Mormon leaders put it, thinking of the LDS Church as one that is ruled from the top down has always been easy. Surely this was the way the Mormon system worked in the nineteenth and well into the last decades of the twentieth century. To a great extent, it still works this way, but because of the diaspora, the church often works from the center out rather than the top down. In time, this might cause some dilution of the top-down concept.

But that this might be happening is not obvious. The General Authorities still make the important decisions including those about materials and programs. Members of the robust church bureaucracy that has come into existence in the past half century produce the LDS materials, see to their distribution, and assist as needed as the members of the priesthood hierarchy see that the church's doctrines, policies, and programs are carried out. To guarantee that the programs and materials are consistent with church doctrine and practice, to prevent duplication, and to keep things running smoothly, the church initiated "Correlation," a process of oversight that up to now has been crucial to the creation of a successful worldwide church. While this oversight is sometimes experienced as overbearing and repressive, it serves the clear purpose of locating and clarifying where authority rests in the LDS system.

This is critical because the Church of Jesus Christ of Latter-day Saints has obviously undergone dramatic change as church growth and geographical expansion became normal conditions. Perhaps it makes some difference whether change is the result of positive or negative conditions. No matter what the cause, however, change always causes the ground to shift in unexpected ways. This happened when the prophet Joseph Smith was murdered. In the absence of a clear stream of authority, the church faced dissension, division, and breaking apart, the product of which was a multiplicity of Mormonisms. The dramatic changes the LDS Church is currently experiencing as Mormonism goes global could pose a similar loss of clarity about where authority rests, not at the very top of the hierarchy, but at penultimate levels where indigenous leadership and cultural variation often make adapting one-size-fits-all policies and programs exceedingly difficult. So far, correlation has been a central factor in preventing a repetition of the creation of multiple Mormonisms. Whether it will continue to be effective is an open question simply because the current rate of change in Mormonism may be too rapid to permit leaders in Salt Lake City to anticipate the complexity and complicatedness that are imbedded in "Mormonizing en masse."

In noting the hardship and distress that converts had to face as they traveled to Zion, Brigham Young once said that the trek, i.e., the very process of gathering, was for "making Saints." Now that gathered congregations made up primarily of converts "do church" in virtually all the nations of the world, will carrying out correlated policies and programs turn enough of the baptized initiates into Saints to make wards and stakes truly Mormon all over the world? It is too soon to know. What is clear is that the face of the Church of Jesus Christ of Latter-day Saints has been radically altered. Until the Saints conclude that the real winding-up scene is nigh and they return to Jackson County to await the Second Coming, Salt Lake City will surely remain the center place. But the likelihood that this church will ever again be simply described as an American institution or a Utah church is rapidly fading into history.

BIBLIOGRAPHY

Arrington, Leonard J., and Davis Bitton. 1979. *The Mormon Experience.* New York: Knopf.

Encyclopedia of Mormonism. 1992. Edited by Daniel H. Ludlow. New York: Macmillan.

Knowlton, David C. 1996. "Mormonism in Latin America: Towards the Twenty-first Century." *Dialogue* 29 (spring): 159–76.

Mauss, Armand L. 1994. *The Angel and the Beehive: The Mormon Struggle with Assimilation.* Urbana: University of Illinois Press.

Shipps, Jan. 1987. *Mormonism: The Story of a New Religious Tradition.* Urbana: University of Illinois Press.

Tullis, F. LaMond, ed. 1978. *Mormonism: A Faith for All Cultures.* Provo, Utah: Brigham Young University Press.

PART V

ISLAMIC CULTURAL REGION

CHAPTER 39

....

THINKING GLOBALLY
ABOUT ISLAM

....

SAID AMIR ARJOMAND

VIRTUALLY from its inception, Islam has been a global religion. It is the youngest of what Max Weber calls the world religions of salvation. Far more than with Christianity, the old dynamics of the expansion of Islam as a world religion have remained in full vigor, even in the twenty-first century when Islam now has a billion adherents around the world. In the last quarter of the twentieth century a new variety of religious movements arose in Islam—as in Christianity and Judaism—that have been called "fundamentalist." Although such movements have been a distinctive aspect of contemporary Islamic society they by no means comprise all aspects of the contemporary expansion of Islam as a universalist religion of salvation.

According to Max Weber, the world religions of salvation are in principle universalistic: they have a tendency toward missionary expansion and intensive penetration of social life. Weber saw their emergence as the first epochal step in the rationalization of life. Although this process of rationalization can proceed in different directions—related to different concepts of salvation and different solutions to the problem of the meaning of life—it is always universalist. The universalism of the world religions gives them a built-in tendency to overcome many forms of particularism and expand beyond familial, ethnic, and national boundaries.

The missionary expansion of a world religion among nations and across the frontiers of empires can be considered the prototype of the process of globalization. In this old pattern, religion is the motive force of universalization. Contemporary globalization, however, is a much broader process. It is set in motion not by religion but by new cultural and technological forces that are entirely secular. The emergence of fundamentalist movements is often attributed to the impact of globalization on the religious sphere. From this perspective, fundamentalism is to some degree a consequence of globalization. Though this is partly true, other forms of social change besides globalization are also causes of the contemporary resurgence of Islam, including its fundamentalist extremes. The impact of these processes of social change and globalization on Islam has its own dynamics, complicating the old pattern of the universalist expansion of Islam, but by no means obviating it. Indeed, one of the things that makes contemporary Islam theoretically interesting is the intertwining of the dynamics of the old universalism and the new fundamentalism. In what follows I shall analyze these interwoven patterns in contemporary Islam by first examining how some new factors reinforce the old pattern, and then turning to these other, contrary, factors that open deviant paths and new patterns of development.

THE UNIVERSALIST EXPANSION OF ISLAM

The Islamic era begins with the migration of Muhammad from Mecca to Medina in 622. It was in Medina that Muhammad built a society on the basis of Islam, the new religion he had preached to a small number of Meccan followers as the final revelation in the Abrahamic tradition of monotheism. In the last years of his life, Muhammad conquered Mecca and unified the tribes of Arabia. After his death in 632, his successors, the caliphs, fought the refractory tribes in Arabia and conquered vast territories of the Persian and Roman empires. The major step in the institutionalization of Islam after Muhammad's death was the establishment of the text of the Qur'an under the third caliph. The canonization of the text of the Qur'an as the Word of God made Islam the religion of the book, even more than the other Abrahamic religions. As the literal Word of God, recited by his prophet, the Qur'an was a holy scripture par excellence. Its transcendent authority made possible the development of sectarian and mystical variants of Islam that diverged in their interpretation of the faith from the mainstream.

In addition to studying the Qur'an, several schools of pious learning began to collect and transmit the Traditions—reports of the sayings and deeds—of the prophet. The influence of this pious religious learning on legal practice grew during the first two centuries of Islam. Consequently, the institution that emerged as the main embodiment of Islam by the end of its second century was neither a church, as in Christianity, nor a monastic system, as in Buddhism, but the

Islamic law (*shari'a*). The law became the central institution in Islam, as had been the case with rabbinical Judaism. The Islamic law was in principle based on the Qur'an, the Traditions of the prophet, and the consensus of the jurists, and remained, in Weber's terms, a "jurists' law." The jurists formed schools of law and engaged both in teaching students and in legal consultation. Their compiled opinions acquired the force of law. With the consolidation of Islamic law as the main institutional embodiment of Islam, the scholar-jurists, the *ulema*, emerged as its guardians and authoritative interpreters.

The contribution of sects and heterodoxies to social transformation in the Islamic civilization has been considerable. Modern historical scholarship of the past hundred years has significantly altered our picture of the expansion of Islam in the seventh century and its penetration into the ancient societies that became parts of a vast Arab empire of conquest. As a result of modern scholarship, we know that Islam, as distinct from Arab domination, was not spread swiftly by the sword, but rather gradually and by popular missionary movements, often in defiance of the fiscal interest of the state. During the first three centuries of Islamic history, three important groups of sectarian movements—Kharijism, Murji'ism (which later merged with mainstream Islam), and Shi'ism—played a very important role in the conversion of the non-Arab subjects of the empire to Islam.

The Arab confederate tribes which ruled a vast empire of conquest were not keen on the conversion of its subject populations. It was only with the 'Abbasid revolution—Islam's social revolution beyond Arabia in the mid-eighth century— that the universalist potential of Islam as a world religion of salvation was fully released from the superordinate interest of Arab imperial domination. With the 'Abbasid revolution, a society based on the equality of Arab and non-Arab Muslims came into being. It was in this society and during the first century of 'Abbasid rule that the institutionalization of Islamic law was achieved. Meanwhile, from the mid-ninth century onward, a movement known as Hanbalism sought to unify sundry traditionalist groups, first against philosophical and theological rationalism and later against Shi'ism. Among the movements that account for the spread of Islam in the formative period, Hanbalism acted as an important force in the intensive penetration and consolidation of Islam among the urban population. It opposed rationalism in matters of faith and insisted on the unconditional acceptance of the Qur'an and the Prophetic Traditions as its unalterable scriptural fundamentals. Hanbalism can therefore be regarded as the prototype of Islamic fundamentalism. Furthermore, by branding sectarian movements as heretical, the Hanbalites accelerated the process of mutual self-definition between the sects and the mainstream. The mainstream Muslims increasingly came to see themselves as standing against all schism and division and advocating the unity of the Muslim community on the basis of the Tradition (*Sunna*) of the Prophet, hence the term Sunnism as the designation for the mainstream Islam.

In the subsequent centuries, however, the pattern of institutionalization of

Islam through Islamic law showed its definite and rather rigid limits. Intensive Islamicization through the law could not facilitate Islam's missionary expansion, nor could it penetrate deeply into society. The mission to convert the population of the frontier and rural areas increasingly fell upon a new mass movement, Sufism (Islamic mysticism). Popular Sufism became the instrument to spread Islam both into the geographical periphery of the Muslim world and into the lower ranks of Muslim society, especially in the rural areas. For centuries, popular Sufism offered a distinct variant of Islam that was in many ways the opposite of the scriptural fundamentalism of the Hanbalites. From the fifteenth century onward, popular Shi'ism adopted many of the practices of the Sufis such the veneration of the holy Imams and their descendants, in place of the Sufis saints, and pilgrimages to the shrines.

Since the beginning of the early modern period, a number of Islamic movements have responded to the challenge of popular religiosity by advocating the revival or renewal (*tajdid*) of Islam by returning to the Book of God and the pristine Islam of the prophet. These movements can be classified as orthodox reformism, as their aim was the reform and purification of religious beliefs and practices with close attention to the Qur'an and the Prophetic Tradition as the scriptural foundations of Islam. An important movement grew from within the Hanbalite fundamentalist tradition in Arabia to take up this challenge of popular Sufism and Shi'ism in the eighteenth century. It is known as the Wahhabi movement, after its founder Muhammad b. 'Abd al-Wahhab (d. 1792) who had visited Shi'ite Iran and come into contact with popular Sufism in Arabia and considered both as disguised polytheism. His followers sacked the Shi'ite holy shrines in Iraq and destroyed the Sufi orders in Arabia. Wahhabi fundamentalism rejected popular religious practices as polytheistic and aimed at returning to the pure monotheism of early Islam with the cry, "Back to the Book and the Tradition of the Prophet!"

Since the nineteenth century, Islam has faced the political and cultural challenge of the West. The Muslim response to this challenge can be simplified into three main types of reaction: secularism, Islamic modernism, and Islamic fundamentalism. Since World War II, this cultural and institutional response to Western domination has been deeply affected by an increasing vitality of Islam that has been firmly rooted in processes of social change. Throughout this time, the evolution of Islam as a universalist religion has continued. This evolution has been quite obvious in conversions to Islam in Black Africa and Southeast Asia but much less obvious in the form of intensive penetration of Islam within Muslim societies. The vitality of Islam caused by the social change of the last half century has created major advantages for scriptural fundamentalism over Sufism in popular religion, with the consequence of greater penetration of scriptural Islam into the social lives of the Muslims.

CONTEMPORARY ISLAMIC REVIVAL

Three processes of social change have been conducive to a broad revival of religious activity throughout the Muslim world and encouraged the growth of orthodox reformist and scriptural fundamentalism. They are interrelated and overlap chronologically, but can be separated for analytical purposes as urbanization; the growth of a religious public sphere with the development of transportation, communication, and the mass media; and the spread of literacy and education (Arjomand 1986). In addition, political change in the twentieth century has had a tremendous impact on Islam.

There is a strong historical connection between congregational religion and urban life in Islam. In its classic pattern, cities with their mosques and centers of religious learning have constituted centers of Islamic orthodoxy, while the tribal and rural areas were a superficially penetrated periphery. Movement from the tribal and rural periphery to the urban centers was associated with increasing religious orthodoxy and a more rigorous adherence to the central tradition of Islam. The late Ernest Gellner (1981: ch. 4) offered a model for this process. The scriptural, legalistic Islam of the ulema did not penetrate into rural areas where the Sufi holy men developed an alternative—a more personal and emotional—popular Islam. The puritanical, legalistic Islam of the cities would penetrate into the rural areas through the rise and fall of tribal dynasties from the periphery in alliance with puritanical ulema, making a "permanent reformation" a distinct feature of Islam. With the permanent concentration of the political life of modern states in the cities and the spread of literacy, the pace of this permanent reformation has been accelerated and scriptural Islam has become accessible to groups in the rural periphery of Islamic societies without the mediation of Sufi holy men.

This historical relationship between urbanization and the growth of scriptural Islam also holds for the period of rapid urbanization after World War II. In general, social dislocation—migration from villages to towns—is accompanied by increased religious practice and movements of religious revival. During the two decades preceding the Islamic revolution in Iran, the expanding urban centers of that country sustained an increasing vitality in religious activities: visits and donations to shrines and pilgrimages to Mecca greatly increased, while religious associations mushroomed among laymen, and the number of mosques per capita in the rapidly expanding Tehran doubled between 1961 and 1975. A similar association between urban growth and increased religious activities, such as the spread of Qur'anic schools, religious activities of guilds, growth of the religious associations, can be found throughout the Middle East and the Sub-Saharan Muslim Africa.

Considerable spread of literacy and expansion of higher education have occurred in all Muslim countries at the same time as rapid urbanization and have independently contributed to Islamic revivalist movements. An increase in the publication and circulation of religious books and periodicals and the growth of Islamic associations in the universities are correlates of this process. The growth of Islamic associations among university students throughout the Muslim world has been striking. It should be noted that university students and graduates in technical fields and the natural sciences predominate in these Islamic university associations. Physicians, pharmacists, engineers, and university students were assumed to be secular types but are now shown to be the backbone of Islamic fundamentalism.

The advent of books, periodicals, and newspapers creates a public sphere in which the literate members of society can participate. The institution of public debates and lectures adds to the vigor of activity in the public spheres; their boundaries are thus extended to include some of the semi-literate. It has long been taken for granted that the enlargement of public spheres is conducive to the rise of socio-political movements. However, it is just as possible that it is the arrival of the communications media in conjunction with these spheres that gives rise to religious movements. This has been the case with many Islamic movements since the nineteenth century.

An interesting aspect of the phenomenon of Islamic activism among the intelligentsia is created by the recent expansion of education. With urbanization and migration into metropolitan areas, many young people move from small towns and rural areas into the cities. There they attend universities and become Islamic activists in the newly expanding public sphere. The public sphere centers around universities, which is the scene of a new and highly politicized generation of students attracted to Islamic fundamentalism.

POLITICAL ISLAM

The resurgence of Islam sustained by urbanization and the spread of literacy has occurred in the context of the modernization of Muslim states and the incorporation of the masses into political society. The rise of secular, modernizing states, national integration and political mobilization have politically conditioned this religious revival. Observers who highlight the sharp political edge of the current Islamic revival have referred to it as "political Islam."

The Islamic revolution of 1979 in Iran was the most spectacular reaction to the modernization of the state. The Shiʿite religious institution had retained its independent authority but lost its influence as well as its judiciary and educational functions as a result of the concentration of state power and of the secularization of the judiciary and educational systems in the 1920s and 1930s. Taking advantage of the independence of the Shi'ite religious institution from the state and using the mass media effectively, Ayatollah Ruhollah Khomeini (d. 1989) was able to harness the religious revival generated by urbanization and the spread of literacy and education to a revolutionary movement that overthrew monarchy and established a theocratic Islamic republic in Iran.

Nowhere is the impact of modern politics on Islam more evident than in the emergence of contemporary Islamic ideologies. For at least a hundred years a variety of entrenched and aspiring Muslim elites have produced what might be called an Islamic modernism. Though their political ideologies have been termed Islamic, Islam has in fact played a subsidiary and sometimes only a decorative role. These ideologies include pan-Islam, Islamic nationalism, justifications of parliamentary democracy in Islamic terms, and Islamic socialism.

Since World War II, however, with the Muslim Brotherhood in Egypt and the Jama'at-i Islami in Pakistan, a distinct type of Islamic political organization and ideology has grown out of scriptural fundamentalism. The major ideological breakthrough was the work of Abu'l-A'la' Mawdudi (d. 1979) in the Indian subcontinent. The Muslim Brotherhood in Egypt was groping in the same direction but did not achieve anything like Mawdudi's ideological consistency until the 1960s. In the following decade, the main features of Islamic political ideologies were adopted by Khomeini's militant followers with a heavy clericalist twist—incidentally not so much before, as during and after the Islamic revolution.

Until the demise of Communism in 1989, Islamic political ideologies tended to adopt totalitarian models of society and focus on the constitution of an Islamic state. Where Islamic fundamentalists could participate in the political process, as in Pakistan, their ideology was gradually modified. Where they were excluded from the political process, as in Nasser's Egypt, Islamic fundamentalist ideology became revolutionary. A case in point is Sayyid Qutb (d. 1966), who formulated a Qur'anic justification of revolutionary violence that stands in sharp contrast to the conservative authoritarianism of traditional Islamic political thought. While Qutb's revolutionary version of political Islam continues to have adherents, especially under regimes that do not allow political participation, a pragmatic fundamentalist ideology has grown in the last decade. It encourages participation in competitive politics and shifts its focus from the seizure of the state to the control of civil society. The model for this most recent Islamic political literature is no longer the discredited totalitarian one but the currently fashionable discourse of democracy, civil society and, to a lesser extent, the model of the global market.

ISLAM AND GLOBALIZATION

Continuous improvement and declining cost of transportation since World War II has greatly increased the number of pilgrims to Mecca—and of missionaries from Africa and Asia to the main centers of Islamic learning in the Middle East. It should be noted that this aspect of globalization reinforces Islam's old universalism institutionalized around the Hajj—the pilgrimage to Mecca. In fact, improved sea transportation since the seventeenth century had encouraged international contact among Muslims and stimulated transnational movements for orthodox reformism and renewal (tajdid).

The postcolonial era has witnessed massive immigration of Muslims into Western Europe and North America where sizeable Muslim communities were formed. Meanwhile, there has been unprecedented global integration of Muslims through the mass media. The media contributed to the success of the Islamic revolution in Iran by enabling the Iranian opposition abroad to orchestrate widespread mass mobilization inside of Iran. Khomeini's aides abroad and his followers in Iran were able to coordinate their nationwide protests by using telephone lines. Khomeini's revolutionary speeches were disseminated by cassettes through the networks of mosques and religious associations. The Persian program of the British Broadcasting Corporation sympathetically reported Khomeini's activities and proclamations, and these reports were avidly received by millions of households in Iran to the dismay of the Shah and his political elite.

The international repercussions of the Rushdie case also illustrates the impact of the media on a globally integrated Muslim world. The protests and burning of his *Satanic Verses* by indignant Muslims began in Bradford, England. These were broadcast throughout the world and stimulated violent protests in Pakistan, which were in turn internationally broadcast. This media exposure gave Khomeini the opportunity to reassert his claim to revolutionary leadership of the Muslim world in the last year of his life. Only a few months after accepting the cease-fire in the war with Iraq, which had been like "drinking a cup of poison," he had the final satisfaction of issuing, on February 14, 1989, an injunction (*fatwa*) sanctioning the death of Salman Rushdie, a non-Iranian writer who lived in England, for apostasy.

The effects of globalization on Islam are interpreted variously. Eickelman (1998) sees the combined effect of globalization, the growth of education, and vigorous discussion of Islam in books and in public debates as the making of an Islamic Reformation. According to Eickelman, the Islamicization of social life has been far reaching but also dispersed, lacking any focus or single thrust. Barber, by contrast, puts Islam in the front line of the global clash between "Jihad vs. McWorld." He sees the effect of globalization concentrated in a sharply focused and vehement "anti-Western anti-universalist struggle" (Barber 1995: 207). Barber obliterates the distinction between Islamic fundamentalism and Islam. It is not just Islamic fundamentalism but Islam, tout court, that nurtures conditions favorable to Jihad: "parochialism, anti-modernism, exclusiveness and hostility to 'others' " (Barber 1995: 205).

I believe Barber's view on Islam and globalization, which is widely shared by journalists and commentators, is fundamentally mistaken. Not only is there variety in Islamic fundamentalism (Arjomand 1995), but Islamic fundamentalism is by no means identical with all the contemporary manifestations of Islam as a universalist religion. Urbanization, development of roads and transportation, the printing revolution, and other contemporary processes of social change, including globalization, all reinforce trends toward expansion and intensive penetration of society that are typical of Islam as a universalist religion. These trends are not exclusively fundamentalist. One would therefore have to agree with Eickelman on the dispersion of the current trends in Islamicization, whether or not one concurs with his value judgment that they constitute Reformation. One important question remains to be answered, however: How does globalization affect the old forms of Islamic universalism?

An interesting feature of globalization is the unfolding of antiglobal sentiments in particularistic, variety-producing movements that seek local legitimacy but nevertheless have a global frame of self-reference. Global integration induces Muslims to emphasize their unique identity within their own frames of reference—cultures that can be at once universal and local. There can be no doubt that global integration has made many Muslims seek to appropriate universalist institutions by what might be called Islamic cloning. We thus hear more and more about "Islamic science," "Islamic human rights," and "the Islamic international system." There are also a variety of organizations modeled after the United Nations and its offshoots, most notably the Organization of the Islamic Conference, which was founded in 1969 and whose meeting in Tehran in December 1997 was attended by the representatives of the fifty-five member countries, including many Muslim heads of state. This phenomenon is a direct result of globalization. To confuse it with fundamentalism is a grave mistake. It is, however, a reactive tendency and I would call it defensive counteruniversalism.

The dynamics of Islam as a universalist religion therefore includes a fundamentalist trend, alongside many others, that has been reinforced by some of the contemporary processes of social change, including globalization. Islam also has acquired a new and sharply political edge under the impact of political modernization. It would be misleading, however, to speak simply of a shift from universalism to fundamentalism. For one thing, missionary traditional Islam continues to flourish and has adopted modern technology to its growth. More important, the main impact of globalization on the Islamic world has not been the growth of fundamentalism but what I call defensive counteruniversalism. Fundamentalism can reasonably be characterized as selectively modern and electively traditional; it is therefore assimilative despite its intent. The assimilative character of defensive counteruniversalism is more pronounced. It has already resulted in the assimilation of universal organizational forms and, albeit restrictively, of universal ideas such as human rights and rights of women. It is difficult to escape the conclusion that, despite its intent, defensive counteruniversalism is inevitably a step toward the modernization of the Islamic tradition.

Last but not least, globalization has had a drastic impact on political Islam, especially as elaborated by Sayyid Qutb. With the declaration of Jihad against the Soviet Union and the Soviet-backed regime in Afghanistan and the recruitment of Muslims from South Asia, the Middle East and the West, the international use of violence was widely legitimized. The globalization of political violence and international terrorism is completed with the disintegration of Yugoslavia and the anti-Russian rebellion in Chechnya after the break-up of the Soviet Union. Osama bin Laden applied Sayyid Qutb's idea of the "vanguard" of the Islamic movement to a global counterelite who would be methodical and follow a set of rules or "the principle" (*al-qā'ida*) in waging Jihad. The worldwide use of violence of Islamic groups and individuals against the global order is by no means confined to al-Qaeda, which is not so much a hierarchical underground organization as a "Holy War Foundation," which considers applications for well-planned projects from Muslims throughout the world, including Western Europe (Burke). It is remarkable that the target of the new Jihad or Islamic terrorism was not just the United States as the sole global superpower but the whole order of globalization, which for bin Laden's lieutenant, al-Zawahiri, includes the United Nations, multinational corporations, international media, and international relief agencies.

BIBLIOGRAPHY

Arjomand, S. A. 1986. "Social Change and Movements of Revitalization in Contemporary Islam." In *New Religious Movements and Rapid Social Change*. Edited by James Beckford, 87–112. New York: Sage Publications.

———. 1995. "Unity and Diversity in Islamic Fundamentalism." In *Fundamentalisms Comprehended*. Eds. M. Marty and R. S. Apple, 179–198. Chicago: University of Chicago Press.

Barber, B. R. 1995. *Jihad vs. McWorld*. New York: Random House.

Burke, J. 2003. *Al-Qaeda. Casting a Shadow of Terror*. London: I.B. Tauris.

Eickelman, D. F. 1998. "Inside the Islamic Reformation." *Wilson Quarterly* 22, no. 1: 80–89.

Gellner, E. 1981. *Muslim Society*. New York: Cambridge University Press.

CHAPTER 40

ARAB ISLAMIC SOCIETIES

SAAD IBRAHIM
RICHARD C. MARTIN

ISLAM is often identified as the religion of Arabs, and the Arabs are commonly assumed to be Muslims. Although this chapter will focus on Arab Islamic societies, it is important to recognize that the Arab-Islam equivalence is not total. It is misleading historically and geographically—especially from a global perspective—to make this assumption. It is true that under the leadership of the Prophet Muhammad in the seventh century (610–32), under the guidance of a generation of Arab leaders (caliphs) who followed him, known as the Rightly Guided ones (632–61), and then under the dominance of the Umayyad Kingdom of Syria (661–750), Islam was predominantly a religion of Arabs in Arab lands. Nonetheless, in the seventh and eighth centuries, Islamic rulers were pursuing global ambitions, marching westward across North Africa to the Iberian Peninsula and eastward to Iran and Central Asia. Increasingly, the lands and peoples under Muslim rule were not Arab. Today, the majority of Muslims live east of Karachi, Pakistan—far from Arab lands. For all that, the Arabs and the Arabic language have played an enormously important role in Islamic societies. At the same time, Islam has transformed Arab society, a fact that becomes apparent when one considers pre-Islamic and non-Muslim Arab religions.

Prior to the rise of Islam, many Arab tribes in the Arabian peninsula worshiped a plurality of local gods and astral deities, reflecting ancient religious ideas and practices common in the Near East since the Sumerians and Babylonians in the third and second millennia BCE. Others in Arabia, Syria, and Iraq were Nestorian, Monophysite, or Orthodox Christians, reflecting the growth and sectarian differentiation of Christian monotheism during the age of the great Eastern church councils, from the fourth to the sixth centuries.

Muslim scripture, the Qur'an, incorporated this plurality of religious ideas and practices into its own global vision of religion, in which the Qur'an was the final revelation of God to humankind and Muhammad was the 'Seal of the Prophets" sent to humankind, from Adam to Jesus and including several Arabian prophets. Christians, Jews, other sects, and later Zoroastrians were regarded as People of the Book or scriptuaries, and thus accorded protection and minimal control when they fell under Islamic rule. Polytheists constituted the most serious threat to the oneness and unity of God, Allah, and thus they could be forced into conversion, expulsion, or even death—at least in theory. In modern times, non-Muslim Arab minorities, predominantly Christians, have shared a common language, culture, and political fortunes with Arab Muslims.

Thus Islam evolved as a global religion following the Arab Muslim conquests of large parts of North Africa and West Asia in the seventh and eighth centuries. This enabled the Arabic language, as the medium of scripture, worship, theological, and juristic discourse to attain global importance well beyond the ethnic and geographic borders of Arab society.

SITUATING ARAB MUSLIMS

Arabs are usually defined as a cluster of groups or peoples that share a common language and territory. People speaking Arabic inhabit a contiguous area that extends from the Atlantic coast of Mauritania and Morocco in the west to the shores of the Arabian Gulf in the east, from the shores of the Mediterranean and the slopes of the Anatolian plateau in the north to the Indian Ocean and the Sahara desert in the south. Approximately two hundred million people live in this immense area. Arabs are the majority ethnic population in twenty countries. Most of the Arab region is desert and consequently has very low population densities, though there are striking concentrations of people in some of the cities and river valleys. The major economic resources of the area are oil and agriculture; the major economic activities, at least until modern times, were farming, herding, and trading.

This broad band is marked by considerable geographical, social, and cultural diversity. Arab society has traditionally been viewed as a trinity of Bedouins, peasants, and urban dwellers, who live together in some kind of symbiosis. Detailed studies have tended to stress the differences between these categories of people, differences which the social and economic politics of Arab and foreign regimes have long tended to exacerbate. The area is divided into some twenty different states ranging from the city-states of the Gulf (Bahrain, Qatar, Kuwait) through the agrarian states of the Maghreb (North Africa) and the Fertile Crescent to the overpopulated Nile valley state of Egypt. Many of these states have long individual histories. Egypt has its Pharaonic past; Tunisia follows on Carthage; Morocco goes back at least to Roman times in North Africa; and Iraq has roots in Sumeria, Babylonia, and Assyria. Other states are recent creations with arbitrary boundaries resulting from the colonial period, such as the desert states of Mauritania, Libya, Saudi Arabia, and Jordan. At present the different regimes are divided between republics, some military in origin, and various kinds of monarchies. The diversity of the population of many of these states reflects the ebb and flow of empires and the refugees of the past—thus the concentration of Berber speakers in the Maghreb; the inclusion of Nuer, Dinka, Azande, and others in the Sudan; and the combination of Christians and Druze in Lebanon.

The colonial period of the nineteenth and twentieth centuries affected the various parts of the Arab world differently: At the beginning of the nineteenth century, most of the Arab world was under at least nominal domination by the Ottoman Turkish Muslim empire. The Ottomans tried to reinforce their hold in Iraq, Yemen, and Libya during that century. The Maghreb, on Western Europe's doorstep, fell under colonial domination by France fairly early (Algeria from 1830, Tunisia in 1881, Morocco by 1912) and Egypt was absorbed into the European economic and then political sphere at the same time as a result of its cotton potential and strategic location (British occupation in 1882). The Sudan escaped Egyptian domination under the Mahdi (1881) only to fall under Anglo-Egyptian rule after 1898. But most of the Arabian peninsula never fell under direct European colonial rule, and the Fertile Crescent states of Iraq, Syria, and Lebanon all spent less than a generation under European rule after having remained under the Ottomans until the Allied victory in World War I. Palestine is a special case, for it has suffered from multiple spheres of control—after the Ottomans, the British held a mandate from 1920 to 1948, and then came Israeli rule. The cultural influence resulting from colonial expansion was either French or British (or both as in Egypt), with smaller areas experiencing Italian or Spanish influence. But many countries and the interior parts of most others were only marginally affected by such cultural influences.

For the purposes of this analysis, it is useful to think of the Arabs and their respective "sovereign states" as one cultural area, that is, the Arab society. There are several reasons for such treatment. First, Arab political regimes, on the normative prescriptive level, consider their states as parts of one nation. No Arab regime in any of the twenty sovereign states has dared formally to go against this proclaimed national self-identification. None, in theory, equates its present legal status of a "sovereign state" with that of a "sovereign nation-state." Despite many practices to the contrary, the explicit or implicit assumption is that the present state of affairs, i.e., separation into several sovereign countries, is only "temporary." The prescribed goal, in theory again, is for these separate Arab states ultimately to unite in one nation-state. This is not asserted today as much as it was in the 1950s and 60s, but neither has any leader or government gone the other way to negate the prescribed norm. The belief in one Arab Nation to which all Arabs belong is still nominally observed—though not always practiced—by most regimes at present.

Second, this belief in one Arab Nation is shared by most people in all countries, classes, and subgroupings of the area extending from Iraq to Morocco. In a recent attitudinal survey conducted in ten Arab countries (Kuwait, Qatar, Yemen, Jordan, Palestine, Lebanon, Egypt, Sudan, Tunisia, and Morocco), about 80 percent of a cross section of the adult population identified themselves as Arabs, belonging to one Arab Nation. Of course, there were intercountry variations, but in no country did the percentage of people holding this belief fall below 60 percent (e.g., Lebanon, Morocco, and Sudan); it was about 90 percent in others (e.g., Yemen, Kuwait, and Jordan). Underlying this common belief is people's perception of shared language, religion, way of life, and problems. Islam especially was considered crucial in forging the Arab Nation. The majority of those surveyed aspired to see the Arab countries united politically, although only a minority thought that would happen in the near future.

Third, it is because of both governmental and popular belief in being part of the same nation that several pan-Arab organizations have been created to foster closer cooperation, if not outright integration. The League of Arab States was established in 1945, and some twenty specialized agencies have sprung up over the following five decades in nearly every field of human endeavor. Even countries that have been blessed with oil wealth have found it morally obligatory and politically expedient to set up individual and collective funds to extend aid for development in "poor sister states." Many of these efforts fall short of what "ought to be" in the views of ardent Arab nationalists. Nevertheless, they have given this region of the world an appearance of a unity of sorts, hardly matched in any other region of the Third World. Such unity has particularly asserted itself in times of regional crisis (e.g., the Arab-Israeli wars, the 1956 Suez Crisis, the resignation of Nasser in 1967 and his death in 1970).

Fourth, the increased volume of human movement and interaction across state lines in the last forty years has added a sociological dimension to both the pan-Arab political norms and institutional arrangements. In the 1950s and 1960s, the bulk of interstate human movement was for study and tourism. In the 1970s and 1980s, most of such movement was for employment.

The above reasons, and others, justify looking at the Arab world as one cultural area or as one societal unit. In this respect, it stands socioculturally at a midpoint between, say, Europe and the United States, i.e., more culturally homogeneous than the former but less politically united than the latter. Thus, while almost no Italians or Frenchmen would identify themselves abroad as simply Europeans, Syrians or Saudis would readily describe themselves as Arabs. At the same time, few U.S. citizens would identify themselves abroad as Californians or New Yorkers, but many citizens of Arab countries would identify themselves as Egyptians, Yemenis, or Tunisians. In other words, there are concentric political-cultural-legal identities for most Arabs, all of them equally or nearly equally salient and readily used. The broader political-cultural identity as an Arab is invoked when the person is outside the Arab world. The particularistic-country-legal identity (Syrian, Egyptian, Saudi, Iraqi, etc.) is used mostly within the Arab world itself or when crossing sovereign state borders.

Treating the Arab world as one single cultural area or as one Arab society implies an emphasis on the broad cultural unifiers, e.g., language, religion, shared traditions, common history, and common aspirations. But there are as many cultural diversifiers. Thus within the common language there are different dialects; and within the common religion there are denominations and sects. Times of Arab strength and glory are those in which the unifiers dominate. Periods of weakness or decline are those in which the diversifiers are manipulated by indigenous or external forces to divide the Arabs. Much of Arab history can be viewed as an interplay between periods of unity and diversity. The great heroes in Arab history are those who stimulated the cultural unifiers, especially in times of external challenge (e.g., Saladin during the Crusades and Gamal 'Abd al-Nasser during the Suez Crisis at mid-twentieth century). Individual and group loyalties in such times are to Islam, the Arab Nation, or the Motherland. On the other hand, the bleak moments in Arab history are when the diversifiers get magnified out of proportion and appropriate the passions and behavior of individuals and groups to primordial and local loyalties, e.g., ethnicity, sect, and tribe. The concerted Arab action in the October War of 1973 was an example of invoking broad unifiers. The Civil War in Lebanon (1975–1985), on the other hand, is an example of stimulating and manipulating narrower diversifiers.

Unity and diversity are two of the parameters of Arab society. Another is the interplay between forces of continuity and forces of change, indigenous forces and external forces. Some of these parameters are worth mentioning here. The first is by Abd al-Aziz A1-Duri, an eminent Iraqi historian, who has stressed the spiritual role of religion and common historical experience, the various moments in history when the "Arabness" of the Arabs was cast into doubt and which caused the Arabs to re-assert themselves (Al Duri 1987: 40–41). Samir Amin, an Egyptian scholar, has looked at the material role of trade and other economic activities in shaping Arab society. He argues that the Arab Nation corresponds to a pre-colonial and pre-capitalist social formation based on long-distance trade, and that the unity of this nation has been challenged but also reinforced by the more recent experience of foreign colonial domination (Amin 1984). The anthropologist Leila Al-Hamamsy recounts the emergence of a new form of Egyptian identity as the result of the intersection of several parameters and forces of change—economic, political, and cultural. However, she is always keen to show how this uniqueness is a sub-identity of a broader Arab Nation to which Egyptians belong. What Hamamsy says could be paralleled by similar socio-historical investigations of such other particularistic sub-identities as Moroccans, Tunisians, Yemenis, and Iraqis (Hamamsy 1977).

It is clear that all these are approximations. They help us to raise and refine the issues, but the definitive answer is not yet forthcoming. It is theoretically possible to give objective answers to the perennial question "what is an Arab?" by relying on citizenship or language. Yet in the end it is the consciousness of the individuals that matters. Do people feel themselves to be Arab in the appropriate situations? Beyond that, there lies the construction of a society or a series of linked societies based on Arab consciousness.

ARABS AND GLOBALIZATION

The Arabs, their language and culture, are a global phenomenon politically and religiously and thus to a certain extent culturally. Oil has brought the Arabs into contact with the rest of the world, particularly since the 1970s. Following upon the rest of the world's thirst for the liquid gold beneath the sands of the Gulf states, many nations—in particular regimes in Western Europe and the former Soviet Union, and the United States—have frequently intervened in the political affairs of Arab countries since the end of colonialism in the mid-twentieth century. The Arab-Israeli conflict has also fostered a global awareness of the Arabs, particularly the Palestinians, since 1947. Indeed, the Palestinians have been one of the largest Arab diasporas in search of political acceptance and economic opportunity. More recently, the Gulf War of 1991 brought international coalition military forces into Saudi Arabia, Kuwait, and Iraq. The stationing of American troops in particular near the sacred precincts of Mecca and Medina during and after the Gulf War was strongly offensive to conservative, traditional-minded Muslims living mainly in Saudi Arabia and other Gulf states. Known as Wahhabis after the eighteenth-century puritanical reformer, Muhammad ibn 'Abd al-Wahhab, the term Salafi is more broadly acceptable among those who have adopted this identity. Growing Muslim anger over foreign, non-Muslim intervention in Muslim lands, such as the Soviet Union in Afghanistan in the 1980s and the American-led Gulf War with Iraq in 1991 and again since 2003, drew Arabs especially into transnational Islamic resistance movements such as al Quaida founded by 'Ab-dallah 'Azzam and led by Osama bin Ladin. September 11, 2001, was an important moment in the rise of the transnational Islamic and largely Arab political move-ments that have fostered a global identity accepted by a small number of Muslims worldwide who are prepared to use violence in pursuit of their ideological and political convictions. The appearance of Arabic-language cable television networks and Web sites reaching Muslim (and non-Muslim) audiences around the world has added another global dimension to the Arabs and their religion, culture, and politics.

The global reach and significance of Arab Islamic society, however, has a strong pre-modern history, extending back to the seventh century. The connection between Islam and Arabic language is stated in God's voice: "We have sent it down as an Arabic Qur'an" (Q. 12:2, 17:82, 20:113, and other loci). One under-standing of the significance of the revelation to the Arabs in their own tongue is that even as other nations of antiquity received messengers and scriptures, so too did the Arabs. They now had their own prophet and scripture and could interact with Byzantine, Sassanian, and other larger religious civilizations beyond the level of trade. The vehicle for carrying this new world vision in the Qur'anic idiom was the *hajj*, the annual Muslim pilgrimage to Mecca that soon brought Muslims from across Asia and Africa into an intense Arabic religious and cultural experi-ence at Mecca and Medina in Arabia. Pilgrims would often stop at lesser shrines of saints, where the universal Arabic ritual performances blended with local cul-tural practices. The hajj was also an occasion for stopping at the great teaching mosques and *madrasas* in North Africa, Central Asia, Iran, and the Middle East. In all such places, the language of instruction about the Qur'an, the sayings of the Prophet Muhammad (*hadith*), Islamic law and theology was Arabic. The dic-tation method by which Islamic knowledge was transmitted throughout the Mus-lim world combined both speaking and writing skills.

Since the colonial period, the emphasis on maintaining a curriculum based on the religious sciences and the value placed on learning and writing about them in Arabic has come under intense pressure for educational reform, not just in Europe, the Americas, Africa, and Asia, but in Arab states as well. Fields such as science, technology, and modern medicine have been imported into modern Is-lamic schools and universities, primarily in English. During the postcolonial ex-perience in the twentieth century of most Arab and other Muslim states, national governments assumed control over schools and infused them with curricula mod-eled on Europe, the Soviet Union, or the United States.

The late twentieth and early twenty-first centuries have seen a returning global Muslim awareness of the historic Arab and Arabic basis of Islamic identity. This is perhaps the maturation of what some political scientists call a world system, bound loosely together in a larger imagined community by the elements discussed above. That it constitutes a civilization destined to clash with America and the

West is perhaps to place too much weight on the idea of a worldwide religious or cultural identity, facing off against all others. The other is now deeply embedded in Arab society, even as the Arabs in both their religion and region now have a considerable public awareness well beyond their ancestral lands.

BIBLIOGRAPHY

al-Duri, Abd al-Aziz. 1987. *The Historical Formation of the Arab Nation*. London: Croom Helm.

Amin, Samir. 1984. "Self-Reliance and the New International Economic Order." In *Transforming the World Economy? Nine Critical Essays on the New International Economic Order*. Ed. Herb Aldo, 204–19. London: Hodder and Stoughton.

Berger, Moroe. 1964. *The Arab World Today*. Garden City, N.Y.: Anchor Books.

Hamamsy, Leila. 1977. "The Assertion of Egyptian Identity." In *Arab Society in Transition: A Reader*. Eds. Saad Eddin Ibrahim and Nicholas S. Hopkins. Cairo: The American University, Cairo.

Hourani, Albert. 1991. *A History of the Arab Peoples*. Cambridge, Mass.: Harvard University Press.

Ibrahim, Saad Eddin. 1982. *The New Arab Social Order: A Study of the Social Impact of Oil Wealth*. Boulder, Colo.: Westview Press.

Ibrahim, Saad Eddin, and Nicholas S. Hopkins, eds. 1985. *Arab Society: Social Science Perspectives*. Cairo: University of Cairo Press.

Weekes, Richard V., ed. 1984. *Muslim Peoples: A World Ethnographic Survey*. 2 Vols. Westport, Conn.: Greenwood Press. Esp. "Arabs," Vol. 1: 35–45.

CHAPTER 41

NORTH AFRICAN ISLAMIC SOCIETIES

EBRAHIM MOOSA

THE North African region is multicultural in that although most North Africans are ethnically of Hamitic stock there are also sizable numbers of Arabic-speaking communities, Berbers, Arab-Berbers, and some persons of European descent. The region includes five countries—Egypt with a population of around seventy million, Libya with around five million, Tunisia with ten million, Algeria with thirty-two million, and Morocco with around thirty-one million, with a total population of more than 146 million people. Islam dominates the region, but there are also minority communities of Christians, especially in Egypt. The Jewish presence in North Africa rapidly dwindled after the creation of the state of Israel and by the beginning of the twenty-first century had virtually disappeared. Most Muslims in the region adhere to the Sunni theological creed. Followers of the Shiʻite and Khariji creeds can also be found in smaller numbers in Egypt and Algeria. In terms of religious rites and rituals, the Sunnis follow the Maliki school of law that is predominant in the region. Substantial numbers also follow the Shafiʻi school, especially in Egypt. Most Shiʻa in the region follow the Jaʻfari school of law, while the Kharijis follow the Ibadi school of law.

All the legal schools trace their guild-like character, as sources of canonical authority in matters of law, to seventh- and eighth-century developments in Islam. However, with the rise of pragmatic revivalist discourses in the twentieth century wresting away authority from traditionalist interpretations, there has been a tendency to eschew the premodern legal schools in favor of more generic, almost protestant-like interpretations of Islamic law. Modernization, even though it occurs haltingly, in the shape of new forms of knowledge and epistemology, accounts for some of the radical flux and instability of religious discourses.

In several parts of North Africa, old-style Islamic traditionalism or orthodoxy, for the lack of a more precise formulation, represented by the *'ulama'*, the *marabouts,* and the *shaykhs* of the Sufi brotherhoods has been displaced by modernist revivalist discourses of two types: Salafiyya doctrines espoused by some 'ulama' groups and the organized revivalist political movements. Before the penetration of European colonialism the 'ulama' and the Sufi brotherhoods were part of the sociopolitical leadership of the premodern states and represented different class interests. The fortunes of these classes began to decline during the colonial interregnum and their role was totally transformed in the postcolonial nation-states and reduced to the margins of sociopolitical discourse.

The Salafiyya *'ulama'* leadership were scholars well versed in traditional Islamic scholarship but who under the shock of Western colonial encroachment responded to modernity with an Islamic synthesis, a response that at times stretched their classical methodologies. They argued that the true spirit of the pious ancestors—*al-salaf al-salih*—to whose heritage they laid claim, was a progressive and rational approach. Therefore, they argued, Islamic rationality and the rationality of modernity were compatible. The model of modernity and progress they had in mind was that of European nation-states, politics, economics, military power, and technology.

Among the earliest Salafi reformers—who were later viewed as liberal reformers and modernizers of the nineteenth and early twentieth century—were figures like Jamal al-Din al-Afghani (d. 1897) and his disciple Muhammad Abduh (d. 1905) and Rashid Rida (d. 1935). They had espoused Salafism as a progressive ideology or strategy in order to counter their more conservative fellow traditionalists whom they believed had stifled the dynamic and prophetic voice of Islam under the weight of tradition. So in its earliest guise Salafism in the hands of the modernizing 'ulama' was an emancipatory move. It advocated that ordinary laypersons should interpret the scripture and read it in their vernacular languages for edification. Previously, interpretation of the Qur'an was the preserve of the 'ulama.' The modernizing 'ulama' thought that in empowering laypeople to understand religion would lead to individuals shouldering greater autonomy and agency in order to affect progress and change in the world around them.

The new Salafi orthodoxy had to contend with a more prevalent older orthodoxy that was very diverse and constituted a complex intellectual canvas. However, over the years this older orthodoxy too underwent change in response to two main influences: the Islamic rationalism of Salafism and the ideologically charged political expressions of Islamic revivalism or Islamism. While the al-Azhar University in Cairo looms large as the bastion of both old traditional and new Salafi orthodoxies in the region, one can hardly discern any major differences between the rhetoric and content of the traditional 'ulama' and that of the politicized Islamists. Both are equally ideologized, although the 'ulama are less effective in social engineering compared to the Islamists who are better equipped for the modern bureaucratic and media-intensive public space.

New orthodoxy and political Islam have both identified *maraboutism*, the charismatic Sufi practices that flourished in urban and rural areas of North Africa, as its very antithesis and have gradually displaced it. Both groups view maraboutism as the purveyor of superstition and un-Islamic practices. They blame it for the political misfortunes and setbacks Muslims had experienced in the nineteenth and twentieth centuries.

'Abd al-Hamid Bin Badis (d.1940) exemplifies the new Salafi orthodoxy. He was a tireless scholar-writer and the dominant figure in Algerian Islam for the first part of the twentieth century. He summarized his life's work in the following words: "I am a sower of love, but on the foundation of justice, equity and respect towards everyone of whatever race or religion." The Moroccan 'Allal al-Fasi (d.1974) made a more serious attempt to formulate an Islamic response to modernity and the new nation-state by discussing issues of land ownership, alcoholism, and prostitution. But even here there was a predilection to blame history rather than offering workable solutions. In Egypt Rashid Rida made similar efforts but balked at the negative influences of secularism and took a conservative turn.

In the post-independence phase the Islamic hope that the new orthodoxy held out for the nation-states of North Africa, like elsewhere in the Muslim world, fed into the nationalist consciousness of the Muslim masses and their leadership. But since the new orthodoxy did not eclipse the older orthodoxy as a group, and was unable to produce workable political and economic programs nor contribute to the crucial stages of national liberation, they did not succeed in having a say in the determination of the new independent states (Abun Naser 1985).

Broadly speaking, Salafism is Islam's equivalent of Calvinism. It has distinct features such as doctrinal puritanism and sometimes rigid juroethical scripturalism that some of its proponents claim to trace back to the founding moments of the tradition. It either dismisses the historical developments of postformative Islam as perversions of the faith or selectively appropriates certain aspects and figures of the historical tradition. Salafi ideology is attractive to many modern educated Muslims since it has an aura of authenticity and a coherent scriptural rationality that appeals to the ideologically minded. Therefore it readily avails itself to the modern revivalist movements in North Africa from the Muslim Brotherhood and other Islamist movements in Egypt to the Islamic Salvation Front (FIS) in Algeria. In the custody of politicized non-'ulama' activists, Salafi ideology in its later mutation has turned into the radical fundamentalism that has been viewed as extremely menacing in several instances.

The 'ulama' in post-independence North African states have become quasi-officials of the state. Some are officially employed by the state and have limited autonomy. Few institutions for training 'ulama' remain within the region; where they do exist, the educational system, philosophy, and curricula are viewed as anachronistic. Al-Azhar University in Egypt and Qayrawan University in Morocco still remain traditionalist strongholds with little influence on national life. The famous Zaytuna, a traditional university, has effectively been dismantled in Tunisia. With the exception of Egypt where the 'ulama' still have a visible social role as a religious group, in most of the other North African states the traditional 'ulama' have almost no visibility in society except as figureheads in performing ceremonial roles.

In Libya, Tunisia, and Algeria, the 'ulama' as a class have been marginalized and are said to be the representatives of a tamed and state-sponsored Islam. In Tunisia, for instance, the state took the lead in affecting far-reaching reforms in the traditional social structure by changing the family law codes derived from the religious law, Shari'a, in order to make them compatible with modern and egalitarian norms. *Ijtihad*, the license to undertake juristic innovation, once the exclusive preserve of the master-jurists (*mujtahidun*), has now become the domain of the modern state. In short, Shari'a prescriptions have become subordinate to the interests of the nation-state.

If elements of Islamic orthodoxy and new orthodoxy have worked to modernize Islam, then political Islam has struggled to Islamize modernity. Islamism challenged the legitimacy of the nationalist state, calling into question its right to affect religious reforms, and accused it of ignoring the obligation to implement the Shari'a in all spheres of life and failing to protect Muslim societies from the harmful effects of westernization and secularization.

For much of the twentieth century North African societies have been exposed to modernizing influences from nearby Europe. Identitarian religious and political movements have replaced yesteryear's identity markers based on creedal and legal affiliations (Hermassi 1994: 97). Religiopolitical identitarian movements derive their impetus from new forms of social segmentation occasioned by the failure of the modern secular nation-state to meet the expectations of their societies. Some countries like Morocco and Libya experimented with monarchies, while Tunisia, Algeria, and Egypt adopted versions of socialism. Libya got rid of its monarchy and implemented a version of Arab socialism. The region, with the exception of Morocco, was caught in the crossfire of the cold war with pro-Soviet sympathies, but there was also a marked deterioration of the state with abysmal human rights records and political authoritarianism, as each country raced to embrace forms of market capitalism.

In each country from the 1960s onward the Islamist counterelites—heirs of the Salafi legacy—challenged the hegemony and legitimacy of the secular state and presented themselves as the brokers of both the sacred and the political. The end of the cold war and the triumph of global capitalism coupled with the rise of Euro-American global power, created new opportunities for Islamism to challenge the power alliances of the postcolonial ruling elites as well as their European and American backers. In its earliest mutation Islamism was a benign threat in all of North Africa, grafting itself onto the nationalist will for autonomy and cultural identity, as part of a nineteenth-century and early twentieth-century trajectory of anti-colonial resistance. With the collapse of the nationalist states in the 1980s, a range of Islamist tendencies begin to challenge the state and pose as alternatives—much to the alarm of the secular bourgeoisie and their Euro-American allies abroad.

Radical Islamist movements like the Islamic Jihad and the Jama'at Islamiyya legitimated jihad, armed struggle against secular regimes in order to implement Islamic rule with the Shari'a as its jurophilosophical centerpiece. In Egypt several uprisings were brutally suppressed, but they also produced instability. Egypt's president Anwar Sadat was assassinated by Muslim militants. Several high-ranking government officials also became targets of violence. Islamists in pursuit of their guerrilla struggle have attacked Western tourists, Christian minorities, and members of the security forces. Independent human rights agencies have also acknowledged that, in their treatment of Islamic political dissidents in Egypt as well as elsewhere in North Africa, governments have violated the human rights of prisoners—many of whom are sentenced by special military courts, akin to kangaroo justice.

In Algeria, the Islamist alliance known as the Islamic Salvation Front (Front Islamique du Salut or FIS) captured the popular imagination and won local municipal elections. They were poised to win power after the first round of elections, when the military abruptly aborted the democratic process with a coup d'etat in 1990 and cancelled the elections. Since then, both radical Islamist extremists as well as elements within the military government have inflicted spectacular acts of violence on the civilian population—particularly in the rural areas but also in urban sites—resulting in thousands of deaths. In Morocco, several Islamist leaders have been suppressed by the monarchy, even though some of the leading figures did not advocate social change through violence. Despite long spells of imprisonment and house arrests for Islamist figures, Morocco did not descend into a spiral of violent conflict. In Tunisia, the state has outlawed one of the more progressive Islamist parties in the Muslim world, the Renaissance Party, and has faced very little opposition. Libya is also a highly segmented society that has been ruled by Colonel Mu'ammar Qaddhafi who came to power in 1969. The country underwent two distinct phases, a quasi-Islamist phase until 1974 and then a form of secular socialism—largely due to the changes in the mindset of its ruler. Since the September 11, 2001, attacks on New York and Washington by al-Qaida, Libya has gone to great lengths to regain credibility with the U.S. government and its European allies after several decades of isolation.

In many parts of the Muslim world, and North Africa in particular, authoritarian regimes criminalize secular political activities and force disaffected groups to seek out religion as almost the only means to express social grievances. Sham democracies, one-party states, dictatorships, and monarchies consider democracies to be inimical to their objectives. The state presumes to be the repository of all truth and the only truth, mimicking an ancient Islamic claim that in the sectarian milieu of myriads of political and theological schisms only one sect will be redeemed. This has led a prominent Egyptian philosopher to sarcastically comment that the state in North Africa truly believes that its ideology was that of the "saved sect" and compels people to adhere or else fall victim to the ruthless outlaw of alternative views with religious zealotry (Hanafi and Al-Jabiri 1990:23). The choices of citizens are thus severely limited to either affiliation with the authoritarian state and compliance with its abusive practices or identification with the absolutist and militant discourses of the Islamists. In combating militant Islamism, several states from Algeria, Tunisia, Libya, and Egypt have been guilty of human rights abuses and brutalizing entire communities. This has led to further polarization between the state and a citizenry that spans several social classes. Elections in several North African states in the early part of the twenty first century have yet to usher in democractic conditions for the betterment of the citizenry of these states.

Contestation over religion in the twentieth century has resulted in the radical ideologization of Islam. The contest is not a simplistic one, as pitting modernity against tradition or Islam versus secularism. Rather, it is a contest fraught with contradictions and paradoxes. This is the direct result of the process of acculturation and development occasioned by modernization that occurs within a relationship of multiple dependencies. Thus, contemporary Muslim thought has experienced a shift from being a religious field known for its emphasis on juristic and theological concerns to one that is intensely ideological in the modern period.

In the premodern period when Islam was the leitmotif of empire, a de facto secularism was in place. The state took care of governance while the scholars, the 'ulama,' in addition to offering religious guidance and moral advice, were also part of the socio-political realm. Scholars at times had different political interests and became pro-state actors and at other times were vocal critics of political authority. Contemporary Muslim thinkers in North Africa are not entirely comfortable with the nation-state political model. Some intellectuals still view it as an extra-Islamic edifice, lacking in Islamic legitimacy, while other Islamists believe that the state can be Islamized with the application of Shari'a. In this illustration modern and pre-modern traditions co-exist with some tension but nevertheless also create an opportunity for hybridity and creativity.

Given the social context, the content of modern Islam is driven by economic and political concerns, while the mythical and spiritual aspects of the tradition are overshadowed by the existential conditions that a civilizational amalgam known as "Islam" is required to address given the failure of the state after independence. The absence of civil society and the preeminent role of the state as the sole agent of legitimization, means that the state defines Islam itself. Even though the state may claim to be secular, it still requires religious discourse in order to legitimate itself and often receives that blessing from the quasi-official 'ulama.' Opponents to the government also employ religious discourse in order to contest its legitimacy. Fierce competition over religious discourse becomes the distinctive hallmark of most North African societies.

The state is largely patronized by elites consisting of former feudal families, military and secular bureaucratic nationalist elites whose adherence to Islam is cultural. Religion is but one element of identity formation, but not the totality. Nationalism largely informs the identity of the secular elites in general terms. For the secular elites religion remains a distinct sphere, separate from the logic of statecraft. However, in the last decade of the twentieth century even this sector felt compelled to exhibit their religious credentials in order to compete with the influence of the Islamist counterelites. The secular elites prefer certain forms of traditionalism of the 'ulama' and would be tolerant of the popular religion (maraboutism) of the charismatic saints. Contrary to what may have been expected, modernist Islamic interpretations with their emphasis on rationality have had an uneven appeal for the secular Muslim elites.

There are three ideological strands that permeate forms of Islamic expression in North Africa and effectively define the subgroups of North African Islam. Salafism started out as a modernizing attempt to discover Islam's "protestant ethic." A bid to overthrow traditionalist orthodoxy in the nineteenth century paradoxically turned out to be the sword of impalement when militant Islamists appropriated it at the beginning of the twenty-first century. Islamic nationalism desperately (and barely) holds on to power without a coherent ideology that can provide it with the necessary legitimacy and thus relies on international powers for both legitimacy and survival.

Under the impact of modernization all groups and actors, pro-state and anti-state groups, had to scurry into the Islamic heritage in order to find legitimating credentials to engage modernity. These discourses ranged from efforts to Islamize modernity while others tried to modernize Islam, with several intermediate and hybrid articulations also coming into existence. In all justifications for their respective projects there is an engagement with the past intellectual heritage in order to reinvent an authentic tradition.

Defining groups in terms of shifting ideological commitments is possibly the beginning of new but unconsciously held understandings of the historical creed and law. But these definitions have yet to be distilled into clear formulations in the manner that the creedal statements of antiquity manifested themselves.

BIBLIOGRAPHY

Abun-Nasr, Jamil M. 1985. "Militant Islam: A Historical Perspective." In *Islamic Dilemmas: Reformers, Nationalists and Industrialization.* Ed. Ernest Gellner. Berlin: Mouton.

Hanafi, Hasan, and Muhammad 'Abid al-Jabiri. 1990. *Hiwar al-Mashriq wa 'l-Maghrib.* Cairo: Maktaba Madbul.

Hermassi, Abdelbaki. 1994. "The Political and the Religious in the Modern History of the Maghrib." In *Islamism and Secularism in North Africa.* Ed. John Ruedy. New York: St. Martin's Press.

CHAPTER 42

SUB-SAHARAN AFRICAN ISLAM

ABDULKADER TAYOB

THINKING globally about Islam in sub-Saharan Africa means trying to juggle at least two contradictory phenomena. On the one hand, it appears that the relentless rush toward a global world threatens to leave Africa on the sidelines. With regard to Internet connections, a significant indicator of participation in the global community, Africa lags far behind the rest of the world. As of July 2000, African online participation represented only 0.8 percent of the world total (NUA Internet Services 2000). On the other hand, global forces affect African social processes in a variety of ways. The flow of information, goods, and arms is relentless in drawing Africa into the effects of globalization. Religious trends in Africa—especially regarding Islam—also reveal the effects of globalization. Consequently, even for Africa, globalization provides a useful frame for understanding changing Islamic patterns in Africa south of the Sahara.

ISLAM AND MODERNIZATION

Writing long before the recent return of religion to the public space, Ernest Gellner has suggested that Islam "alone may maintain its pre-industrial faith in the modern world" (Gellner 1981: 4). He suggested that modernization was an urban phenomenon and that the revitalization of Islam would emerge from the centers of power. Such a prospect will reverse the pattern identified first by Ibn Khaldun that Islamic piety movements originated in the hinterland. While religious traditions have had a more checkered history than Gellner's model would suggest, the major issues in African Islam are directly or indirectly linked to issues of state and modernization. In particular, the patterns of African Islam are dominated by national representation of Muslims in secular states, Islamic reformist movements, and ideological clashes between secular and Islamic conceptions of the state.

All Muslim communities in Africa have faced the problem of representation in a nation-state. This must be seen in the light of the artificial boundaries imposed by colonial rule and also in the new challenges of defining a Muslim community for political purposes. Given the absence of a centralizing authority in Islamic leadership, the question of national representation has bedeviled both the new states and Muslim communities. In East Africa, for example, the state has recognized the role and presence of Muslims as an integral part of a religiously plural society. However, informal leadership patterns representing a variety of ethnic groups and religious tendencies has not made it easy for the state to negotiate with Muslims as a national group. As a result, the states encouraged and then formed supreme councils representing Muslims: Supreme Council of Kenya Muslims; Baraza kuu Waislamu wa Tanzania; Uganda Muslim Supreme Council; and Muslim Association in Malawi. According to Constantin, the major motivation for the formation of these organizations came from the state, which tended to reinforce a client relationship with Muslims (Constantin 1993: 48). He goes on to argue that the councils lacked financial and symbolic resources to translate such representation into legitimate national leadership (Constantin 1993: 55).

Nigeria and its experience of Muslim representation on a national level confronts similar challenges. In Nigeria it is not only a question of imposing a Muslim organization from above but also the internal problem of self-definition within the Muslim community. Loimeier's study of the career of Abu Bakr Gumi records the rise of a Muslim religious and political leader and his championing of a pure, universal understanding of Islam (Loimeier 1997). However, the struggle for the definition of Islam free of cultural practices was also a struggle for a national conception of Islam. This becomes clear when we link Gumi's own approach with the approach of the prime minister of Northern Nigeria, Ahmadu Bello from 1954 to 1966. Bello had tried to unite the Muslims of Nigeria under a new Sufi order, called Uthmaniyyah, to recall the jihadist leader of the nineteenth century. This particular order would unite Muslims in a nation-state under the symbol of a historical figure associated with the area. The particular construction of a national Sufi order would be reminiscent of constructing a nation in historical and symbolic terms. At the same time, the Uthmaniyyah aimed to diminish the political and social roles of the older Qadiriyyah and Tijaniyyah orders. When Bello was assassinated in 1966 and the Nigerian state collapsed soon thereafter, Abu Bakr

Gumi emerged as the most important Islamic leader with a religious message that had similar goals.

On the religious level, Gumi's approach reflected many international Islamic trends of removing cultural elements from Islam. On the social and political level, however, Gumi's message of Islamic revivalism was directed against traditional Sufi leaders whom Bello had previously tried to weaken or at least incorporate under the Uthmaniyyah. Gumi was supported by the Yan Izala movement led by Mallam Ismailia Idris (b. 1937), a former imam (prayer leader) in the Nigerian army. Intense religious discord between their groups and the older Sufi orders was a battle for leadership over Nigerian Muslims as a national group. For example, the Tijani leader Dahiru Bauchi opposed Gumi's appointment as the grand mufti of Nigeria in 1985. And finally, conflict among Muslims only came to an end when Muslims in Nigeria realized that they were losing support to Christians in national politics. The point being made here is that religious conflicts in northern Nigeria had a marked national significance. Even though Muslims in East and West Africa did not endorse the nation-state from a religious point of view, many of the issues arising within Muslim communities had direct and indirect national implications. The major issue here seems to be Muslim leadership on a national level.

From an entirely religious perspective, the second issue raised in the context of modernization concerns the emergence of so-called orthodox Islam. This issue has been raised in the context of Gumi and the Yan Izala attempting to purify Islam from cultural traditions. More generally, however, we can only recall here Gellner's prognosis that the modernization of Islam will emerge from urban Islam and its emphasis on a scripturalist interpretation of Islam. This has certainly been a major issue in Islamic communities in Africa. Usually, both Muslims themselves and critical observers have related this phenomenon to the influence of international Islamic trends. Thus, Brenner relates the emergence of Wahhabi Muslims in Mali in the 1940s and 1950s to influences from the Middle East. Such new Islamic trends were opposed to traditional Muslims who supported the French status quo as well as the new secular state. Brenner, unlike many other observers, locates the Wahhabis in Mali in the context of an emerging mercantile class taking advantage of the new trade opportunities in the colonial era. Continuing to build their institutions in the postcolonial period, the Wahhabis became a distinctive Islamic trend between traditional Muslims and the secularists (Brenner 1993). Analyses that do not go beyond the international connections of Islamic change overlook two important dimensions. First, the turn to Islamic scriptures within a strong egalitarian ethos cannot be extricated from the modernizing forces of science and socio-political egalitarianism. Scripturalist Islam rejects Sufi leaders who enjoy special access to God, or Islamic law that depends on a complex history of legal philosophy. Scripturalist Islam is austere, simple, and transparent in its methodology, ritual demands and membership. This understanding of Islam may sometimes appear backward and retrogressive in content, but it is premised on modern foundations. Second, critical appraisal of reformist Islam tends to ignore its particular location in context. What is very clear from the examples of Islamic purification groups in Nigeria and Mali is that such practices have unique social and political consequences.

The third issue that dominates Islam in the context of the nation-state is that of the nature of the state itself. This issue has been most clearly articulated in countries with large Muslim majorities in Asia, but it is also present in some African countries like the Sudan, Nigeria, and to a lesser extent South Africa. This debate revolves around the question of the sovereignty of the state. The Indian ideologue Abu al-A'la Mawdoodi was the first to raise the issue when he compared the sovereignty of the modern state to the sovereignty of God. He argued that the modern state was usurping the sovereignty of God by assuming final authority in all social and political affairs of the nation: "No person, class or group, not even the entire population of the state as a whole, can lay claim to sovereignty" (Mawdoodi 1976: 159). Mawdoodi's formulation has become a popular slogan against the modern state in Muslim societies. It has some popularity among African Muslims and may be more closely observed in the conflicts of the Sudan. Turabi, the leading ideologue in the Sudan, led its Islamist movement from the 1960s. However, as Mahmoud reminds us, the Islamist ideology under al-Turabi and Sudanese history was offered "within the framework of the country's liberal democracy which provided for a multiparty system; the country's religious and cultural diversity was recognized; a decentralized, federal system was advocated; other laws, besides sharia, were recognized and were even accepted on a territorial level in areas where non-Muslims were a majority . . ." (Mahmoud 1997: 185).

The Islamist ideology clearly begins to take on a different shape in the context of the nation-state in Africa. But Islamic political thought in the context of a nation-state takes on another form as well. In contrast to Turabi, another leading Islamic figure, Sadiq al-Mehdi, a descendent of the Mahdi who revolted against Egyptian and British colonization of the Sudan, also argues for an Islamic system of government. However, his approach to Islamic government reveals a deeper appreciation of the history of Islamic legal thinking and a greater sensitivity to the diverse needs of contemporary society: ". . . we need a scholarly-cum-lay-effort to review the whole corpus of law on the basis of the texts of the enlightened by the formulations of the schools, and conscious of current problems and of other legal systems, in order to prepare a contemporary Islamic legal system to act as a source for our legislators. Only then can we expect a revival of the Islamic legislative credibility" (Al-Mehdi 1978: 130).

These two contrasting approaches to the state clarify the third issue that dominated Islamic thought and practice. Together with Muslim national representation and movements of religious purification, the nature of the modern Islamic state forms a rich and varied tapestry of Islamic patterns and questions

in modernity. These three questions are closely interrelated and have been interpreted as part of a general Islamization of society. I have shown, however, that
they cannot be extricated from global patterns of modernization. Moreover, in
different localities in Africa, one of these elements may be appropriated in a
particular social and political context.

ISLAM AND GLOBALIZATION

Modernization and nation-state formation have shaped Islamic patterns and discourses in a distinctive manner. In some respects, these patterns appear hardly
discernible from earlier patterns. Keeping in mind that contemporary globalization is a form of deterritorialization, however, we detect new possibilities within
the old.

As a system of belief, it is much easier to relate to Islam as a global religion.
The concept of the religious community, *ummah*, seems to be an ideal candidate
for thinking about Islam in global context. We must remember, though, that we
are here concerned with Islamic practice in the context of a unique form of
globalization (deterritorialization). In this past, the ummah was clearly manifested
in vast political empires, intricate trade networks, global religious rituals, and
scholarly connections. Contrary to Scholte's assertion that "adherents of the world
religions have for centuries affirmed a national unity with their co-believers everywhere, even though these long-distance communities usually never in practice
had direct contact with one another" (Scholte 2000: 172), contact between Muslim
communities was made real in a number of ways. While it is true that better
forms of communication have made this idea of a global ummah more accessible
to a greater number of people, the deterritorialization of contemporary globalization creates opportunities for subtly different patterns of Islam. The particular
definition of globalization presents us with an opportunity to understand how
even global concepts, of which there are many in Islam, are experienced in an
age of globalization through vast, digital, communication networks.

Like everywhere else, Muslim communities in Africa have recorded a significant rise in Islamic observance. A greater degree of participation in the annual
pilgrimage (*hajj*), fasting, and daily worship is noticeable in most communities.
Greater coverage of Islamic issues in international media ensures a cross-
fertilization and sharing of styles and modes that tend to create a global Islamic
identity. This identity is most clearly reflected in the style of dress, particularly
for women, that dominates the discourse of Muslims as well as the media. For
the media and outside observers generally, the Muslim identity is a compelling

sign that is worth more than a thousand words. For Muslims, local symbols of Islamic identity are affected and transformed by those presented in the very media. In general, then, a greater sense of Islamic identity is part of what Akbar Ahmed called the ubiquity of cultural flows that tends toward a degree of homogeneity. Much has been said about the globalization of neoliberal and market-centered values, but a similar process seems to be at play in the globalization of Islamic identity. And in this sense, Islam in Africa is not immune to the greater sense of Muslim self as reflected in common, visible symbols easily identified and categorized.

The Islamization of identity, however, is equally subject to diversification as much as it is to homogenization. As a mark of the increasing awareness of Islam, for example, mosque building has taken off in an unprecedented scale. Barkindo has documented a significant increase in the number of Friday mosques in Kano city in Nigeria. Until 1970, one Friday mosque served the entire city. However, between 1980 and 1990, a further ten Friday mosques were built. Barkinda has situated the rise of Islamism in the city in the context of rapid urbanization and modernization. Islamic observance was part of the "frustration with the failure of 'modern' measures to cope with the worsening social and economic problems" (Barkindo 1993: 105). However, Barkindo has also recorded the multiplicity of Islamic voices, from the radical Maitatsine rebellions of the under classes as well as state functionaries who supported Islamic ventures. Thus, increases in Islamic institutions do not only measure the degree of Islamization but also its variety. The centralization of Islam in a city at a Friday mosque must be contrasted with the multiplicity of nodes where worship takes place at the same time, each sustaining a different form, purpose, and social purpose. This particular feature of diversity can be multiplied manifold as Islamic groups, parties, and movements take on a variety of causes in the name of Islam. The explosion of Islamic voices will continue in a global world, even if it may appear sometimes as if the voices everywhere are the same.

The globalization of Islamic practice and discourse can be seen in the appearance of competing global Islamic voices. At the very least, deterritorialization engenders a decontextualized ideology of Islam. Eickelman and Piscatori have correctly identified how ". . . these nonstate organizations, particularly through their formal presentations of Islamic issues and standardization of language and approach, help to create incipient ideological communities that do not overlap neatly with those of state frontiers. This process of objectification is unfolding in the transnational arena as well as within national and local contexts" (Eickelman and Piscatori 1996: 144).

As shown earlier, Islamist ideology in the history of the Sudanese state was clearly and inextricably linked with the history of the country. Under the impact of local history and politics, the Islamic state was rendered diffuse and diverse. Similarly, the rise of Wahhabi Islam in Mali may similarly be linked to a new economic engagement. The presence of global media and the Internet, however, has created a significant opportunity for the acceleration of the Islamic ideology as a decontextualized, global movement, something which Eickelman and Piscatori noted in the description of Muslim politics above. This new global, decontextualized Islamic ideology, born in the context of intense conflict, is now floating free, and is apparently supported by the flow of global funds, weapons, and plans. This ideology is ranged against equally global forces, symbolized by the most global of powers, the United States of America.

Being the least connected, African Muslims are not at the forefront of this revolution. However, the 1998 United States Embassy bombings in Nairobi and Darussalam present a case of how a global Islamic ideology forces itself on Africa. On the one level, such bombings were immediately linked to the ubiquitous Osama bin Laden, now living in Sudan, now in Afghanistan, but allegedly carrying out his plan on a global scale. Muslims in Kenya came to know of this global force when it was alleged that he was also using Islamic relief efforts as front organizations. The Kenyan government immediately ordered six nongovernmental organizations to cease their activities (Bonner 1998). As in many other contexts, it seems that local Islamic organizations must prove themselves innocent of the international, global network of Osama bin Laden. Thinking globally of Islam in Africa would mean how local, cash-strapped, and embattled Muslim communities struggle against the global ideologies of Islamism and a global political order that has declared them the usual suspects.

Since globalization is inherently diverse, there are signs that competing Islamic conceptions and movements are also at play in African Islam. Based in America and Europe, a number of Sufi orders are taking on a leading and innovative role in the Internet. Greatly maligned during the era of modernization, Sufi orders are now finding a voice on the Internet. There are at least two such African groups that may present an alternative Islamic presence as regional, global forces. The Mouridiyyeh of Senegal are well known for their economic miracle of work and peanut cultivation during the French period. In the postcolonial period, they joined the intellectual trends in the cities of Senegal (O'Brien 1988). Since then, the order has encouraged their adherents to follow their economic dreams in a number of European and American cities. When South Africa became independent in 1994, the Mouridiyyeh established circles (*dairahs*) in Cape Town and Johannesburg as well. With an active support network by the order, the Mouridiyyeh has become a model of a global African Islamic community. Even more advanced, in terms of global communications, may be the Tijaniyyah of the Niyasse branch whose leader Hassan Cisse has become a global figure in Islam in Africa. The order has a modest Web presence on the Internet (http://www .tijaniyya.com/hassancisse.htm). The site cannot compare in sophistication with other sites such as that of the Hizb al-Tahrir (http://www.hizb-ut-tahrir.org) and the Naqshbandiyyah Sufi order (http://www.naqshbandi.org), but the profile of the shaykh certainly presents him as a global leader from an African context. While his spiritual chain is clearly located in Senegal, he is also educated in Mauritania, Egypt, England, and the United States. He has a visible presence in the United States as founder and chair of the Board of the African American Islamic Institute Inc., and plays an active part in the United Nations where, according to the Web page, he expounds an "enlightened Islamic perspective on human rights, women's rights, marriage, alcohol and other drugs and children" ("Hassan Cisse" 2005). Clearly Shaykh Hassan Cisse has a global profile as an African Islamic voice. It remains to be seen how the competing global voices of Islam will relate to each other on the African continent.

BIBLIOGRAPHY

Al-Mehdi, Sadiq. 1978. "The Concept of an Islamic State." In *The Challenge of Islam.* Edited by Altaf Gauhar, 114–33. London: Islamic Council of Europe.

Barkindo, Bawuro M. 1993. "Growing Islamism in Kano City Since 1970." In *Muslim Identity and Social Change in Sub-Saharan Africa.* Ed. Louis Brenner, 91–105. London: Hurst and Company.

Bonner, Raymond. 1998. "Public Face of Terror Suspect: Low-Key Family Man." *New York Times,* September 27.

Brenner, Louis. 1993. "Constructing Muslim Identities in Mali." In *Muslim Identity and Social Change in Sub-Saharan Africa.* Ed. Louis Brenner, 59–78. London: Hurst and Company.

Constantin, Francois. 1993. "Leadership, Muslim Identities, and East African Politics: Tradition, Bureaucratization and Communication." In *Muslim Identity and Social Change in Sub-Saharan Africa.* Ed. Louis Brenner, 36–58. London: Hurst and Company.

Eickelman, Dale E., and James Piscatori. 1996. *Muslim Politics.* Princeton, N.J.: Princeton University Press.

Gellner, Ernest. *Muslim Society.* Cambridge Studies in Social Anthropology. Cambridge: Cambridge University Press, 1981.

"Hassan Cisse" Web site. 2005. http://www.tijaniyya.com/hassancisse.htm. Accessed August 5.

Loimeier, Roman. 1997. "Islamic Reform and Political Change: The Example of Abubakar Gumi and the Yan Izala Movement in Northern Nigeria." In *African Islam and Islam in Africa.* Eds. Eva Evers Rosander and David Westerlund, 286–307. London: Hurst and Company.

Mahmoud, Muhammad. 1997. "Sufism and Islamism in the Sudan." In *African Islam and Islam in Africa: Encounters Between Sufis and Islamists.* Eds. David Westerlund and Eva Evers Rosander, 162–192. London: Hurst and Company, in cooperation with the Nordic Africa Institute, Uppsala, Sweden.

Mawdoodi, Abul A'-la. 1976. "Political Theory of Islam." In *Islam: Its Meaning and Message*. Edited by Saleem Azzam, 147–171. London: Islamic Council of Europe.

NUA Internet Services. 2000. "How Many Online." Accessed July 2000. http://www.nua.ie/surveys/how_many_online/index.html.

O'Brien, Donal B. Cruise. 1988. "Charisma Comes to Town: Mouride Urbanization 1945–1986." In *Charisma and Brotherhood in African Islam*. Eds. Donal B. Cruise O'Brien and Christian Coulon, 135–55. Oxford: Clarendon Press.

Scholte, Jan Aart. 2000. *Globalization: A Critical Introduction*. Houndmills: Macmillan.

CHAPTER 43

EUROPEAN ISLAM

AMILA BUTUROVIC

EUROPEAN and Islamic cultures began to interact—volatilely—as early as the seventh century, mainly along the southern borders of the Byzantine Empire and in the Iberian Peninsula. While the Reconquista campaigns brought an end to Islam in Spain by 1492, the consolidation of the Ottoman rule in southeastern Europe occasioned the formation of new Muslim communities whose ongoing dynamic presence in the European region testifies to a successful convergence of Islamic and local values. More recently, the growing and assertive presence of Muslim immigrant communities throughout Europe, in addition to the indigenous European Muslim groups, indicates that any discussion of Europe today can hardly be complete without taking into account its Islamic constituency.

Islam is often perceived as a complete system, self-contained and static, and, as such, a hurdle to modernity. Yet the very idea of a "European Islam" indicates that the role of Islam in determining cultural identity cannot be described in a continuous or unitary way. By focusing on four countries—Albania, Bosnia-Herzegovina, Turkey, and Russia—this essay suggests that neither being Muslim nor European is a sufficient determinant to explain the complexity of this identity. European Muslims negotiate their beliefs and practices along several trajectories that cannot be separated from other players and collectivities. "European Islam" is thus seen as a textured interplay between the unifying ethos of Muslim *umma* and the modernizing trends and demands of contemporary European nation-states.

ISLAM IN THE BALKANS: THE CASE OF BOSNIA-HERZEGOVINA AND ALBANIA

The Muslims of Bosnia and Albania have much in common since they were both products of the Ottoman period. Divided in medieval times between Catholicism and Eastern Orthodoxy (and, in the Bosnian case, the local Bosnian Church), large numbers of Albanians and Bosnians converted to Sunni Islam of Hanafi legal orientation following the consolidation of the Ottoman rule in the Balkan peninsula in the fifteenth century. In both cases, conversion was a gradual and mainly voluntary process, involving first the local nobility and then common folk. Unlike Bosnia where conversion took place mainly in the sixteenth and early seventeenth centuries, Albania continued to be Islamized well into the eighteenth century. Here, however, local records suggest that the late conversions were an attempt on the part of local Catholics to improve their social status without changing their religious practices and beliefs (they were hence referred to as crypto-Catholics or *laramane*).

Islamization was assisted by both Ottoman administrators and missionaries, primarily Sufi groups (Helveti, Mevelvi, Qadiri, Rifa'i, and, especially in the case of Albania, Bektashi). In both regions, therefore, Sufi practices coexisted with normative Sunni practices. Furthermore, in both cases mass conversion facilitated a rapid integration of the new Muslim nobility into the Ottoman high culture that led to a privileged sense of selfhood vis-à-vis other subjects of the empire and an identity crisis after the demise of the empire. After World War II both Bosnian and Albanian Muslims were absorbed into the Communist system of governance. Yet the difference between the two Communist regimes and their politics of national identity set the Muslims of Bosnia-Herzegovina and Albania on different routes in the second half of the twentieth century.

Albania

Current estimates hold that approximately 70 percent of the overall population of Albania is Muslim, while 20 percent is Eastern Orthodox and 10 percent Catholic. That makes Albania, next to Turkey, the only European country with a clear Muslim majority. Internally, the Muslim population is divided between Sunni (ca. 80 percent) and Bektashi (ca. 20 percent) denominations. The Bektashis, a community formed at the intersection of Shi'i, Sufi, and Turkic folk practices, broke away from Albanian Sunnis (mainstream and Sufi) in 1925. Ethnonationally, the Muslims of Albania are predominantly Albanian, though the 1999 estimates suggest the presence of some fifty to ninety-five thousand Roma Muslims who constitute the most underprivileged cultural minority in the country.

The Albanian state was declared atheist in 1967. Isolated quite decisively from the rest of the world, the Communist government engaged in an aggressive policy of internal "religious cleansing." All religious activity was severely punished and many religious leaders were killed in order to prevent decentralization of authority. The four official "national churches" that had been active until 1967—the Orthodox Church, the Catholic Church, the Sunni Community, and the Bektashi Community—suffered severe persecution of their leaders and membership at large and the confiscation of institutional and material possessions. For nearly three decades all religious practice had to be performed secretly. In the early 1990s the religion ban was relaxed and the freedom of religious expression was introduced, albeit hesitantly, by the new government.

Today, Muslims, just like Christians, must work hard to minimize the consequences of religious repression suffered under the Communists. As regards the Muslim community, the question "what now?" is as acute as "who are we?" The (re)discovery of Muslim identity for a whole generation of atheist Albanians needs to be addressed in relation to the Albanian state in particular and the global Muslim umma in general. In combination, they determine the future of Muslim life in this impoverished European country.

As expected, the Sunnis, unlike the Bektashis, have had better opportunity to improve ties with Muslims abroad. With internal funds practically nonexistent, the Sunnis have mobilized resources of several affluent Muslim organizations, including the Organization of Islamic Conference (OIC), that have allowed them to set a course toward the rebuilding of the ritual and spiritual life with international help. In light of their previous Ahmadiyya-oriented tendencies, moving toward normative Sunnism points to their need for support and recognition, as well as doctrinal re-orientation. A number of new mosques and *medreses* have been opened since the early 1990s. Much effort has been put to disseminating knowledge about Islam through education, local community centers, and media. Hafiz Sabri Koçi, the great mufti of Albanian Sunnis, has frequently praised the high quality of Islamic education in Albania in the post-Communist era. Given the fact that the majority of Albania's population is Muslim and in light of the growing Christian missionary presence, the more assertive Sunni Muslim leaders have even raised the question of declaring Islam the official national religion. Though this did not imply turning Albania into a theocracy, assertions of political Islam have been greatly toned down after non-Muslims voiced their discontent.

As the mainstream Sunni community struggles for wider recognition, the Sufi orders of Albania face organizational problems. The importance of internal structure and hierarchy in Sufi tradition requires that Albanian orders re-establish and stabilize the broken chains of authority. Though assisted by their fellow Sufis from abroad, the Albanian branches can ensure survival only if local membership is strengthened and ritual patterns re-established within the country.

This is especially important for the Bektashis who re-stated their difference from other Muslims in 1993. The order has for a long time lost its international character and, except for its North American branch, it is associated primarily with Albania and Kosovo. The death of the senior Bektashi in his Detroit home in 1995 signaled a need to expand human and other resources both at home and abroad so as to maintain spiritual lineage. To that end, despite their narrow networks and slim finances, the Bektashis have succeeded in reopening a few *tekkes* (monastic centers) including one in the capital Tirana, restoring some shrines (*türbes*), and have generally increased membership. Internationally, the support for Albanian Bektashi is scarce, coming from the Bektashi diaspora mainly in North America and, somewhat surprisingly, from Shi'i Iran.

Bosnia-Herzegovina

The end of Communism and the outbursts of nationalism in the former Yugoslavia placed Bosnia-Herzegovina in the limelight of world politics. The campaigns of "ethnic cleansing," designed and directed primarily against Bosnian Muslims, raised international awareness about the vulnerability as well as resilience of Islam in this region.

Contemporary Bosnian Muslim identity traces its roots in the policies of the former Yugoslavia to which Bosnia-Herzegovina belonged until 1992. Pressured into defining themselves against the threats of assimilation by Serbian and Croatian nationalists, Bosnian Muslims were granted the status of separate "ethnicity" in 1961 and then of separate "nationality" in 1969. Configured as a secular, ethnically South Slavic, and local nationality, Bosnian Islam was to pose no challenge to the secular principles of Communist Yugoslavia. Roughly 40 percent of the Bosnian population was Muslim before the outburst of the 1992 war. While the recognition of their ethno-national distinctiveness strengthened a sense of cohesion, it also led to a feeling of isolation from Muslims elsewhere.

The relationship between the Communist government and Bosnian Muslims had been relatively untroubled until the mid-1970s. The immediate Communist policies included taking over various religious offices, ending the *shari'a*-based court system, replacing religiously based education of mektebs and medresas with public schools, turning a significant number of mosques and Sufi tekkes into "cultural" monuments, and nationalizing the land and *vakf* (charity) resources. At the same time, the Yugoslav government set out to maintain a unified Muslim community by centralizing its spiritual life. In 1947 they founded a supreme council and appointed its leader, the *reis-ul-ulema*, entrusting him with spiritual education, which as the official phrase went, "would not carry out any political goals." Given that all religious offices and affairs were under the supervision of the *reis*, the surveillance over spiritual matters of all practicing Muslims in Yugoslavia was in the hands of the supreme council and, by extension, the federal government.

As long as he did not promote political activism, the reis was given relative freedom to chart out religious practices which led, throughout the 1960s and 1970s, to spiritual awakening among Muslims. Islamic press was readily disseminated, hundreds of new mosques were built, religious education at the secondary and post-secondary levels was animated (including a school of theology in Sarajevo and a secondary school for women) and, internationally, the vitality of the Muslim community was flaunted so as to maintain friendly ties with many Muslims countries of the nonaligned movement.

But following the establishment of the Islamic Republic in Iran, the Yugoslav government exerted pressure on Bosnian Muslims to denounce ties, real or imaginary, with fundamentalism in Iran and elsewhere. The fear of political Islam led in 1983 to the trial of thirteen Muslim intellectuals who were accused of disseminating Alija Izetbegovic's "Islamic Declaration," which had been published in 1970. Though avoiding explicit references to Yugoslavia's Muslims, the document promoted Islamization, denounced Marxist ideology and the cult of personality, and advocated a revival of the global umma. On that account, the thirteen Muslims were charged with attempting to turn secular Bosnian Islam into a chauvinistic Muslim nationalism, and were given a combined sentence of ninety years, ironically, by an atheist judge from the Muslim community. Following their release, a number of these intellectuals became active in the demise of Communism. Alija Izetbegovic, the current chairman of the Bosnian Federation, founded the Stranka Demokratske Akcije (SDA), Party of Democratic Action, The SDA party had a clear Islamic platform intended to protect and promote Islamic values in Bosnia. In 1992 Izetbegovic became the president of Bosnia-Herzegovina as it declared independence from Yugoslavia. His election, albeit democratic, was used as a pretext by Serbian nationalists to launch expansionist policies of "ethnic cleansing" against Muslims of Bosnia-Herzegovina in the 1992–1995 war.

Despite the heavy loss, Islamic life is being revitalized in the postwar period. The office of reis-ul-ulema is still in effect, and the current reis, Dr. Mustafa Ceric, continues to enjoy the central and politically empowered role in the promulgation of Islamic life in Bosnia-Herzegovina. This involves strengthening ties with Muslim countries that are eager to help Bosnian Muslims reconstruct the mosques and other destroyed Islamic objects (e.g., some six hundred mosques were demolished by either Serbian or Croatian nationalists between 1992–1995). The most recent show of Muslim solidarity was the opening of Europe's largest Islamic complex in Sarajevo in September 2000. Financed by the Saudis, the King Fahd Mosque and the Islamic cultural center signal that the Muslim community in Bosnia is now eager to reach out to Muslims abroad to overcome the scars of the recent aggression and thus position themselves within the umma at large.

TURKEY

Turkey's population is estimated to be 99 percent Muslim, with the great majority, both among ethnic Turks and Kurds, being Sunni/Hanafi. Though there are no official statistics on denominational differences, informal estimates suggest that as many as 20 percent of Muslims may be of Alevi Shi'i persuasion. Because of a series of persecutions by Sunni Muslims, only partial acceptance by the main-stream Shi'i communities, and now repression by the Turkish state, the Alevis have for centuries remained on the fringes of the umma. Furthermore, we now know that the ethnic composition of the Alevi minority in Turkey is Arab and Kurdish as well as Turkish. While traditionally the Alevis used to inhabit the southeastern regions of Turkey, rapid urbanization has occasioned the increased Alevi presence in most major cities in Turkey. However, their relationship with the Turkish state and the Sunni majority continues to be volatile.

Established in 1923 under Mustafa Kemal Atatürk, Turkey is officially a secular state. Through a series of swift political interventions, Atatürk cut off ideological ties with the Ottoman Empire on whose theocratic debris the Turkish republic was founded. These measures included abolishing the shari'a system, banning Sufi activities, closing down Sufi tekkes and charitable *waqf* organizations, adopting Latin script in place of Arabic, and, for a while, demanding that prayer be conducted in Turkish.

The assertive policies of secularization, intended to bring Turkey closer to Western Europe, confined religious practices to private space. But the ongoing discontent about the absence of religion in public life and the state's alleged disrespect of Islamic values propelled a more active demand for religious freedom and involvement. One of the early responses to that grievance was the founding of the Divinity School at Ankara University in 1949 and, two years later, special secondary schools (*imam hatip okullari*) for the training of religious officials. These and other interventions were implemented by Diyanet, the Turkish Directorate of Religious Affairs, which, set up in 1925, continues to function as the main department of administration of religious life. Some observers consider the Diyanet to be the "official" Islam of Turkey and point to its particularly successful involvement with Turkish emigrants in Western Europe. But for the most part the Diyanet's activities have been criticized by both secularists and Islamists: the former argue that its very existence runs against the foundations of the Turkish state, while the latter sneer that the Diyanet symbolizes the secularist appropriation of Islam and has nothing to do with its values.

These opposing views of the Diyanet epitomize the generally ambivalent relationship between Islam and the Turkish state. In many respects the case of Turkey illustrates well the unsettled accounts between secular and religious currents facing many modern societies. The lack of will to establish the common ground has perpetuated the rift between the "Islamists" and "secularists." While occasionally accommodating each other, both sides have used Islam as a rhetorical tool to fight political opposition. For example, the parties on the center and center-right often resorted to Islamic values and idiom to counteract the extreme left. Similarly, in light of the 1990s' economic recession and the popular disenchantment with Western Europe's treatment of Turkey, many Turks questioned the state's staunch secularism and called for more cooperation with the Islamic world. Exploiting such sentiments, Islamic activists have become rhetorically bolder and politically more assertive. The explicitly political Fethullahi movement tried to penetrate the very bastion of Turkish secularism by setting out to recruit military cadets. In 1995 the Islamist Welfare Party (RP) led by N. Erbakan came to power, underscoring the growing popular support for Islamic values in the face of the country's problems. The Welfare Party's triumph was short lived: in 1997 Erbakan was ousted and in 1998 the party was closed down allegedly for economic and political scandals. The ousting of Erbakan testifies to the ongoing discomfort of the secular establishment in dealing with overt Islamic agendas. In 1999, another Islamist party, the Virtue Party (FP), was subjected to humiliation when one of its members tried to take the oath in the parliament while wearing a headscarf. She was forced out of the ceremony and was subsequently stripped of her Turkish citizenship. This was not an isolated incident of women's dress becoming a site of contention. An increase in the number of young Muslim women wearing headscarf and long, concealing overcoats in early 1980s led to the prohibition of such fashion at universities in 1987. Several universities eventually lifted the ban after a series of protests by Muslim students and university staff. The issue persists as one of the central symbols of the freedom of religious expression in Turkey.

The querulous interaction between secularists and Islamists has become both more intense and tragic in the past decade. An incident of religious extremism claimed the lives of thirty-nine secular Turks during a cultural festival in Sivas in 1993. This form of activism is certainly more distressing than the activities of the Ticani Sufi of the 1950s that had primarily targeted the material symbols of Kemalism. After the Sivas incident that shook the nation, another wave of religious violence, this time by the Turkish Hezbollah group against both secularists and liberal Islamists, has heightened the urgency for a more constructive dialogue between the two sides. Furthermore, although posited as an internal matter, the Islamic awakening in Turkey has inevitably carried international implications on several fronts: an increased involvement of international Sufi orders (especially Qadiri, Nakshbandi, and Mevlevi) in promoting Islamic values, and the Saudi, even Iranian, financial support of some religious activism, indicate that the debate can no longer be confined within the borders of Turkey.

In spite of the intensity of emotions and actions on both sides, at least some steps have been made toward mutual accommodation. The construction of new mosques, community centers, health and financial institutions, as well as the increased number of media avenues promoting Islamic content, facilitate a more open understanding of the parameters within which Islamists can contribute to Turkish culture and society. The intellectual dialogue has also been strengthened: for example, the Islamist writers Ali Bulaç and Rasim Ozdenoren have offered a new perspective on Turkish culture and society. Combining both Western philosophical thought and Islamic teachings, they have been critical of extremists on both sides while emphasizing, quite selectively, the Islamic values in which they find hope for a more constructive solution for Turkey's unresolved dilemma.

RUSSIA

The majority of Muslims living in European Russia are of Sunni/Hanafi persuasion, but their ethnic composition is very diverse. Their geographical distribution is also wide, spreading across the regions between the Black Sea and the Caspian Sea (Adyghs, Balkars, Bashkirs, Chechens, Cherkess, Ingush, Kabardins, Karachay, and various Dagestani groups), the middle Volga Basin (Tatars, Udmurts), and the *oblasts* of Ul'yanovsk, Samara, Nizhniy Novgorod, Moscow, Perm', and Leningrad. Sufism is present in most areas, but it is most notable among the Chechens. During the recent troubles in Chechnya, the prominence of Sufism as the source of bonding and vigor within the anti-Russian movement has shed new light on the vitality of the mystical branch of Islam in this part of the former Soviet Union. Moreover, the Chechen resistance to mainstream Islamic teachings, which have tried to infiltrate the region in recent years, proves that Sufism is the central venue through which Islam has endured as a collective identity in Soviet and pre-Soviet times.

The collapse of the Soviet Union gave the Muslims a momentum to explore new depths of Islamic identity that had been carefully curtailed during the Communist regime. To that end, new mosques have been built, religious schools and institutes established, newspapers with Islamic content published, copies of the Qur'an distributed, and overall, much effort has been invested, mainly under the guidance of the imam Hatib Mukaddas of the Union of Muslims, to spread knowledge about Islam among Muslims and non-Muslims alike.

Politically, however, the end of Communism isolated the Muslims of Russia from the large Muslim groups of Central Asia and Transcaucasia. Despite the tension arising from doctrinal and cultural differences among the various Soviet Muslim groups, the four Moscow-run muftiates had successfully functioned as both a means to control Muslim activities and a safety valve vis-à-vis other religious groups. After the breakup of Soviet Union, the Muslims of Russia, though accounting for almost 20 percent of the population, have found themselves threatened by the burgeoning ties between the government and the Orthodox Church. As early as 1992 Sheikh Gainurtdin of the Council of Muftis complained openly about the unabashed show of favoritism of Orthodoxy over other religions, fearing that the pillars of czarist ideology were fueling the new generation of clergymen and politicians. Most recently, Gainurtdin refused, on behalf of the council, to meet Moscow's request to ban Wahhabism on Russian territory. His criticism was directed at the general lack of understanding of the term and its popular reference to any public display of Islamic sentiments. Given such uncritical usage of the term, the mufti fears that the government could use such a ban to intervene in any aspect of Muslim life. Moscow's alleged animosity toward Islam was already addressed during the war in Chechnya, which even if not strictly religious, fueled the sense of distrust between Muslim and Orthodox Russians. In a similar vein, the Russian explicit support of Serbia, another Orthodox nation, in fighting the Muslims of Bosnia, added a new dimension to that distrust. According to a number of Russian Muslim intellectuals, with this latest appeal to cleanse Russia of Wahhabism, the government is creating its own nemesis.

Indeed, the convening of an Islamic conference in Saratov in 1992 with the proposal to unite the Muslims of the former Soviet Union in an umma of sorts, was condemned as a pan-Islamist ploy. A similar reaction is emerging at the latest news that Turkic and Finno-Ugric activists in the region between the Volga and the Urals are trying to revive the idea of "Idel-Ural." A confederation of the peoples of Tatarstan, Bashkurtistan, Chuvashia, Mordvinia, Mari, and Udmurtia and other adjacent regions, "Idel-Ural" is conceived along ethnic, not religious, affinities, but its strong Islamic component is nevertheless perceived as a potential threat to the Orthodox foundations of Russia.

But the Russian Muslims have also perpetuated a series of internal problems and disputes. Although two of the four Soviet-made muftiates remained in the hands of Russian Muslims, seemingly enabling them to preserve a sense of continuity during the turbulent breakup of the Soviet Union, the transition of authority has been neither automatic nor smooth. In 1992 Bashkurt and Tatar Muslims broke away and set up their own muftiates, shattering the hopes for (or, from the non-Muslim perspective, fears of) wider Muslim bonding. The doctrinal differences, in addition to the numerous ethno-linguistic differences among various Muslim groups, indicate that in Russia too, Islamic identity cannot overarch other forms of collective sentiments—ethnic, national, social, or regional—that make up contemporary identities.

BIBLIOGRAPHY

Benningsen, A., and S. Enders Wimbush. 1986. *Muslims of the Soviet Empire*. Bloomington: Indiana University Press.

Clayer, N. 1990. *L'Albanie, pays des derviches*. Wiesbaden: Otto Harrassowitz.

Dawisha, K., and B. Parrot. 1994. *Russia and the New States of Eurasia*. Cambridge: Cambridge University Press.

Friedman, F. 1996. *The Bosnian Muslims*. Boulder, Colo.: Westview Press.

Ozdalga, E. 1998. *The Veiling Issue, Official Secularism and Popular Islam in Modern Turkey*. Richmond, Surrey: Curzon.

Poulton, H., and S. Taji-Farouki, eds. 1997. *Muslim Identity and the Balkan State*. New York: New York University Press.

CHAPTER 44

SHI'A ISLAMIC SOCIETIES

MANSOOR MOADDEL

THE center of Shi'a Islam is to be found in three countries where over half the population is identified with the Shi'a branch—Iran, where 90 percent are Shi'I; Iraq with 57 percent; and Bahrain with 54 percent. Other countries with significant percentages of Shi'i are Lebanon (30 percent); Kuwait (19 percent); Pakistan (14 percent); and Afghanistan (6 percent). In addition, 3 percent of the population of Turkey is Shi'i, and around 2 percent of India and Saudi Arabia. Of the total world Muslim population of more than seven hundred million, about 10 percent, adhere to Shi'ism.

The Arabic word *Shi'i* literally means followers or party. The Shi'is disagreed with the Sunnis over the issue of succession and considered Prophet Muhammad's spiritual heritage to devolve on his son-in-law, Ali, and his male descendants through the blood lineage to the prophet provided by Fatima, the prophet's daughter. The debates and dissension over the issue of succession following the prophet's death and the broader question of secular politics were crystallized into three different sects in early Islam. The Kharijis demanded a clear-cut separation of the constitutional question from the religious one. In Shi'ism, on the other hand, the two were intertwined. The Sunnis took the middle line.

Shi'ism consisted of different Muslim groups who commonly recognized Ali as the legitimate imam (leader or caliph) after the death of Prophet Muhammad. In this Islamic sect, only Imam Ali and his successors were endowed with the divine quality and necessary Islamic credentials to be the leaders of the Muslim community (*umma*). On the question of the divine status of the imam and the idea of epiphany (the manifestation of the divine in man) and the intercession of the imam, the Shi'is, however, were divided from the outset. The Zaidis limited God's manifestation in the imam to mere divine "right" guidance, without being bestowed with the power to perform miracles. For the extremists (the Ghulat), on the other hand, the epiphany is completely inhabiting. They believed in the descent of God or the Spirit of God into a person. Among the Ghulat were those who believed that Ali was God (*Ali allahi*). For the imamis, the imam remains mortal, but a divine light-substance is partially inherent in him and passes onto his eldest son after his death. Each of these three divisions was further divided into many subdivisions in the course of history. The most dominant group among them is Twelver Shi'ism, the belief in the succession of twelve Imams, beginning with Ali and ending with Mahdi, or the Imam of the Age, who is in occultation (Gibb and Kramers 1995).

SUNNI-SHI'I RELATIONS

The followers of Shi'ism were initially a small group. Living under the Sunni rule and in a predominantly hostile environment, the Shi'is opted to deny legitimacy to the existing ruler while abstaining from any overt political action. Under the Abbasids (750–1722) and more extensively under the Buyids (945–1055), their political conditions began to improve, and important Shi'i centers of learning were established in Iraq and Iran. Shi'ism gained a nationwide and lasting recognition under the Safavids (1501–1722) when it was declared the state religion of Iran in 1501. This announcement was followed by a ruthless religious policy that involved the abolition of millenarian extremism, persecution of Sufism, and suppression of Sunnism (Arjomand 1984). The Safavid religious extremism angered the Sunni Ottomans, leading to the outbreak of a major war between the two countries in 1514 and intense anti-Shi'i bigotry under the Ottomans and Sunni intolerance in Iran. In 1555, Tahmasp signed a peace treaty with the Ottomans and moved his capital from Tabriz to Qazvin. In 1597, Abbas I transferred the capital to Isfahan. From this period on, Isfahan grew to become another center of learning in Shi'ism.

The Shi'i-Sunni relationship grew tense as Arabia came under the influence of the reformist fundamentalism of Muhammad Ibn Abdul Wahhab, who had rejected Shi'ism. His followers in the early nineteenth century sacked Karbala and stripped the gold and ornaments from the shrines of Imam Hussein and his brother Abbas, killing many Shi'is in the process. In the modern period, the Sunni and Shi'i conflicts considerably subsided and the relationship gradually gave way to a mutual recognition of each other's faith by the ulama of both sects. Tensions have resurfaced, however, in post-Saddam Iraq.

Except for the problem of succession, there is no serious difference in articles of faith between the two sects. And in the course of history, the Shi'i and Sunni ulama ended up accepting the reality of secular politics and considering legitimate the differentiation between political and religious leadership. In the modern period, Islamic modernists downplayed the Shi'i-Sunni political differences. Shi'i Amir Ali, for example, developed a formula that considered the caliphate and the imamate as legitimate yet varying forms of leadership in Islam. He made a distinction between the Shi'i notion of apostolical imamate and the pontifical caliphate of Abu Bakr, Omar, and Osman who preceded Ali. For Amir Ali, the two forms of leadership, apostolic and pontifical, can coexist and even play positive functions for the Muslim community as evidenced by Ali being the principal adviser to Abu Bakr and Omar. He disagreed with the traditional Shi'i position that considered the caliphate of the first three caliphs as illegitimate. For him, these caliphs were elected by the unanimous suffrage of the Muslims, and, for protecting the unity of the Muslims, Ali was perceptive in forfeiting his claim and pledging allegiance to Abu Bakr. Amir Ali thus provided a basis for a closer relationship between the Sunnis and the Shi'is (Amir Ali 1922).

IRAQ AND ARAB STATES

Iraq has been one of the most important centers of Shi'i learning since the early days of the tradition. The holy cities of Najaf and Karbala, known as the *atabat*, are where the shrines of Imam Ali and Imam Hussein, the first and third imams, respectively, are located. These cities have always attracted pilgrims, theological students, and high-ranking Shi'i theologians. The Iraqi Shi'is have also been active in the politics of their country. In the twentieth century, they at first welcomed the British as deliverers from the yoke of Turkish domination, but later on became suspicious of British objectives in Iraq and began to express their opposition to their presence in the country and to the establishment of the Mandate of the League of Nations. Being predominantly of poor socioeconomic status, they supported the 1958 coup that brought the socialists and the Communists to power. When the Ba'ath party came to power in the coup of 1963, they constituted 53 percent of the party. But gradually the Sunni element in the party predominated and by 1968, the Shi'i portion of the party membership had fallen to 6 percent. In the 1970s, the Ba'ath party's discriminatory policies resulted in the Shi'i population abandoning secular politics and participating in religious oppositional movements against the regime. These Shi'i political parties were repressed under the regime of Saddam Hussein, but have since flourished after the fall of his regime in 2003.

The Shi'is in Bahrain are even more repressed than in Iraqi. A Sunni ruling family, the al-Khalifa, dominated an autocratic political order that excluded Shi'i from participation in public life and discriminated against them economically. Likewise, the Shi'i population of Saudi Arabia has been subject to the government's discriminatory policies. Their community is the least integrated into the Sunni society and they are almost entirely denied the public expressions of their religious traditions. The Shi'is of Kuwait, on the other hand, are better off than any other Shi'i community in the Persian Gulf region. They have encountered little visible persecution at the official and social levels. Unlike the Shi'i minority in Saudi Arabia, the Kuwaiti Shi'is are allowed to build mosques and community centers, observe their religious rituals, and teach their religion at school. The situation of the Shi'i minority in Lebanon is unique compared with the rest of the Arab world. While they have always been among the poorest and least-educated groups, they managed, in recent years, to amass considerable political power and influence. Their persistent resistance against the Israeli occupation of Southern Lebanon, which successfully forced the Israelis to withdraw from the country, enhanced their popularity among the Muslim Arab population (Momen 1985; Fuller and Francke 1999).

THE POLITICAL POWER OF THE SHI'I ULAMA IN IRAN

The political power of the Shi'a community in Iran is due in large measure to the role played by the ulama—the learned religious scholars, jurists, and interpreters of the law. At the apex of the Shi'i clerical hierarchy were the few who attained a certain fame, the approval of a great body of jurists, or a level of intellectual competence to be able to settle differences and decide questions of general discipline, and thus enjoyed the honorific title of Shaikh ul-Islam or *ayatollah al-ozma* (grand ayatollah). Like their Sunni counterparts in the pre-modern Islamic world, the Shi'i ulama owned considerable landed property, which was partly a Safavid legacy and partly the result of pro-ulama practices of Qajar rulers in the nineteenth century, and enjoyed a fairly close relationship with the ruling elite. Unlike their Sunni counterparts in other Muslim countries, however, the Shi'i ulama not only increased their power in nineteenth-century Iran but also managed to play a crucial part either in favor of the ruling monarch or in opposition to him in all significant political events that transpired in the country in the nineteenth and twentieth centuries.

The rise in ulama power is attributed to the interplay of several historical factors. One was the weakness of the Qajar state in the nineteenth century. Another was the ulama's close ties to the bazaar merchants, the craft guilds, and the landowners. These classes often supported them financially in the form of gifts, donations, and religious taxes (khoms and zakat). They also received payments for performing various functions related to general economic and social exchange. Finally, doctrinal development and religious contention in Shi'i hierarchy also enhanced ulama power. In the late eighteenth century, a long-standing controversy in the discipline of jurisprudence was concluded at the center of the Shi'i learning in the Atabat—the Shi'i holy places in Iraq. At that time, the ulama were divided into three competing schools. The first was the Akhbari school, which denied any independent ruling on the part of the ulama above and beyond the tradition of the prophet and the imams. The Usuli school, on the other hand, asserted the legitimacy of the function of the mujtahids in the interpretation of law and in making independent judgment. For the Akhbaris, the ulama's basic function was the transmission of doctrine (naql), which was given precedent over the application of reason ('aql), and ijtihad or independent reasoning was considered unlawful innovation. While for the Akhbaris, all believers should be the followers (muqallid) of the imam, who is in occultation; for the Usulis, all believers should choose a living mujtahid to follow his judgment, hence the divisions of the Shi'is into followers (muqallid) and the spiritual leader (marja'). Finally, there was Sufism. The Sufis were attached to the esoteric rather than to the law. Sufism basically rejected the validity of any interference of the ulama in worldly affairs, while claiming that the Sufi doctrine was identical with the esoteric knowledge of the imams. The leading proponent of the Usuli position was a certain Aqa Muhammad Baqir Bihbahani (1705–1803), who ended the supremacy of the Akhbaris in the Atabat. He vigorously championed the Usuli position, and attacked both the Akhbaris and the Sufis by formally denouncing them as infidels (i.e., takfir). The means Bihbahani employed were often brutal. He was known as Sufi-killer (Algar 1969; Keddie 1972; Moaddel 1986).

Yet despite their organizational and social resources, the ulama seldom displayed a unified political action. They were subject to conflicting interests emanating from their ties to the state, landowners, and the bazaar. The emergence of opposing political tendencies among these social forces at different historical junctures often resulted in the emergence of politically diverse factions among the ulama, undermining their ability to control and supervise culture production. This disunity was particularly visible in virtually all the political movements that emerged in Iran in the nineteenth and twentieth centuries.

RELIGIOUS DISPUTES IN IRAN'S
CONSTITUTIONAL REVOLUTION

While the ulama were divided in the Tobacco Movement of 1890–92, their division was most pronounced during the constitutional revolution in Iran when they debated over the Islamic nature of the Fundamental Laws ratified in 1906 and the Supplementary Fundamental Laws ratified in 1907. The absolutist ulama were led by Shaikh Fazlullah Nuri. He attacked the constitution as a great sedition (*fitneh-yeh kubra*) which from its emergence, rise, and decline went through three stages: (1) discourse and presentation (*taqrir va unvan*); (2) writing and declaration (*tahrir va i'lam*); and (3) practice and test (*'amal va imtihan*). The first stage was presented in such a pleasant way that it attracted the learned and the common people. In the second stage, the constitutionalists first confined themselves to obscure statements, then began writing laws and regulations so that they could write freely against religion, religious leaders, and the ulama. In the third stage, the constitutionalists began to practice whatever oppression they could. The constitutionalist ulama, on the other hand, rejected Nuri's argument. Prominent among them was Ayatollah Na'ini, who formulated a defense of constitutionalism from the Shi'i standpoint. In his view, a despotic regime displayed three negative aspects. It had usurped the authority of God, hence injustice to Him. It had oppressed the imam for usurping his authority. Finally, it was based on the oppression of the people. A constitutional government, on the other hand, was free of the first and third oppression. It had only usurped the authority of the imam. Thus there was no doubt that a constitutional government was far superior to a despotic one (Hairi 1977).

THE ULAMA UNDER THE PAHLAVIS

The constitutional revolution did not lead to political democracy. After about two decades of ethnic and group conflicts, Iran experienced the rise of a new centralized authoritarian regime under Reza Shah who was capable of establishing order and security in the country. Under the Pahlavis, decisions about culture were the sole prerogative of the monarch, who in an authoritarian manner opted to promote secularism by undermining the Shi'i institutions, controlling their financial resources, imposing "feminism" from above by passing a law in 1936 that prohibited women from going public with veil, expanding modern secular education, and glorifying pre-Islamic Iranian kingship and culture. Under Reza Shah rule and during the decade following his downfall in 1941, the ulama's opposition to the state was not ideological. The 1940s and early 1950s were a period of extensive political activities by diverse groups. Yet the religious establishment was not nearly as influential in politics as it became in the 1960s and 1970s. Although there were some influential ulama who supported Mosadeq's nationalism, a good section of high-ranking ulama either ended up supporting the shah in the 1953 coup or remained aloof from participating in politics.

The overly secularist ideology of the second Shah in the 1960s and 1970s pushed the ulama into the opposition. At the same time, the decline of liberal-nationalism and various forms of secular ideologies during the same general period contributed to the popularization of Shi'ism as the dominant oppositional discourse. Lay intellectuals began to express their opposition to the shah's authoritarianism in religious terms. Within this context, Khomeini's theory of *vilayat-i faqih* (the rule of jurisprudent or Islamic law) in which he empowered the ulama to take power and rule on behalf of the imam gained considerable currency. Although Khomeini claimed that his political view was rooted in the tradition of Shi'i jurisprudence, some of the prominent ayatollahs disputed his view. They, however, were silenced by radical revolutionaries after the overthrow of the monarchy in 1979. For example, Ayatollah Shari'atmadari argued that the rule of Islamic law (faqih) applies when there is not a legitimate ruler in society, such as after the fall of the Shah. But when there is a president and a parliament, it is their responsibilities to rule the country. The followers of Ayatollah Khomeini tended to give absolute power to the faqih (Moaddel 1993).

THE SHI'I POLITICS IN THE POST-REVOLUTIONARY PERIOD

If the secularism of the state in pre-revolutionary Iran generated an Islamic opposition, the fundamentalism of the Islamic Republic in post-revolutionary Iran appeared to have generated a new form of oppositional discourse. Far from transcending the narrow ideological boundaries of the Pahlavis, the Islamic Republic imposed a system of religious rules on society that rested on a particular, not universal, understanding of the *shari'a*. To be sure, during the revolutionary period of 1977–79, Islam transcended social differences among the participants in communitarian relations. The universalism of the Islamic revolutionary discourse, however, did not mean that there was a shared understanding about the nature of the post-revolutionary government, the social status of women, the sociopolitical function of religion, and the country's relationship with the outside world. It was universal precisely because it meant different things to different people. The political unity that transpired during the revolutionary movement was produced by a factor external to Islam: as long as the shah, i.e., the common enemy, was present, diverse Islamic groups were united and the Islamic alternative to the ideology of the monarchy seemed uniform and consistent. This unity, however, proved ephemeral and fleeting, and as soon as concrete plans emerged about the nature of the post-revolutionary regime, disputes replaced harmony.

This is not to argue that Islam was incapable of furnishing a set of universal concepts to build a national consensus about Iran's post-revolutionary society. It was certainly possible for Ayatollah Khomeini and associates to follow the project of the Islamic modernists of the earlier period, showing a more positive orientation toward democracy and rational rule making, a more egalitarian attitude toward gender relations, a less belligerent attitude toward the West, and a more inclusive understanding of Islam. Instead, they took an overly fundamentalist orientation. Through effective and large-scale repression of the opposition, they were able to establish a theocracy, whose central institution was the governance of the jurisprudent. The ruling clerics attempted to transform the institution of Shi'ism into a monolithic religion controlled and guided by the state through the absolutist power of the spiritual leader. They brought the entire educational institutions under the government's control to promote the ethics and morality of revolutionary Shi'ism. The mixing of the sexes was prohibited, and the universities and governmental offices were rearranged to ensure gender segregation. An Islamic dress code was imposed from above. Men were discouraged from wearing certain clothes deemed too Westernized, and women were not allowed to be seen in public without the veil or a headscarf. Nor were they permitted to wear brightly colored dresses in public (appropriate colors being brown, black, blue, and gray). The moral police rigorously enforced the observance of the government's codes of conduct. The portraits of the spiritual leader substituted that of the shah, and the Islamic revolutionary slogans came to replace the propagandistic statements of the pre-revolutionary regime in public places. And the mass media turned into the organ of the state's propaganda machine.

Nevertheless, the authoritarian nature of the state was moderated by a host of historical and religious factors. Contrary to the Pahlavis, who came to power through military coups, the Islamic Republic was the result of a popular revolution. The public demand for inclusion and political representation and the religious leaders' desire to establish a theocracy were combined to produce a contradictory compromise in the structure of the Islamic Republic. Although considerably skewed in favor of the spiritual leader, the structural forces within the Islamic Republic were arranged in a fashion that would make the monopolization of power by the leader problematic. There are, for example, the offices of the spiritual leader and the constitutional guardians versus the office of the president and the parliament, the revolutionary guards versus the army, and the religious overseers in various governmental offices versus the secular members of the civil service. The Islamic Republic displayed an amalgam of religion and secularism. The office of the spiritual leader derived its sovereignty from the shari'a, the presidency and the parliament from the electorates. Further, from the religious viewpoint, we may consider the contradiction between the monolithic religious structure imposed from above after the revolution and defended by the office of the spiritual leader and the pluralistic historical tradition of the Shi'i ulama. The spiritual leader in Iran is not necessarily the most learned ayatollah in the country, and the most learned ayatollah in Shi'ism may not be interested in political involvement. The leaders of the Islamic Republic have thus far failed to force all the ulama to bow to the authority of the spiritual leader. Finally, the duality between the state and civil society, that is, the general conflict between the Islamic Republic and the demand of the public, particularly women and university students, for political power and inclusion yet generated another favorable context that undermined the concentration of power.

Thus this structural and ideological pluralism may explain the rise of the current Islamic reformist movement in Iran. This movement has tended toward Islamic transcendentalism rather than toward fundamentalism and extremism. The reformist leaders in fact tried to occupy the political positions within the pluralistic structure of the Islamic Republic in the presidential elections in May 1997 and in June 2001, municipal elections in March 1998, parliamentary elections in February 2000, and the run-off parliamentary elections in May 2000. The dynamics of this structural and ideological pluralism may be attributed to the ideological reorientation of a significant group of Muslim scholars moving in a reformist direction. We have seen that some of the key figures leading the reformist movement were among the architects of the Islamic Republic: Abdul Karim Sorush, who is now defending Islamic democracy, was the principal theoretician of the Cultural Revolution that dismantled the institutions of secular education in the country in the early 1980s. Some of the reformist newspapers were run by the activists who were involved in the anti-West demonstrations and the seizure of the U.S. embassy in Tehran. And some of the grand ayatollahs who were among the signatories of the institution of the governance of Islamic jurisprudence are now part of the opposition, demanding political reforms. What is even more astonishing is that all these reformist groups are defending their democratic position in terms of their reading of Islam; traditional liberal democratic discourse still plays a minor role in legitimizing the demands for personal freedom and the rule of law.

BIBLIOGRAPHY

Algar, Hamid. 1969. *Religion and State in Modern Iran*. Berkeley: University of California Press.

Amir Ali, Maulavi Sayed. 1922. *The Spirit of Islam*. London: Christophers.

Arjomand, Said A. 1984. *The Shadow of God and the Hidden Imam*. Chicago: University of Chicago Press.

Fuller, Graham E., and Rend Rahim Francke. 1999. *The Arab Shi'a: The Forgotten Muslims*. London: Macmillan.

Gibb, H. A. R., and J. H. Kramers, eds. 1995. *Shorter Encyclopedia of Islam*. Leiden, Netherlands: E. J. Brill.

Hairi, Hadi. 1977. *Shi'ism and Constitutionalism in Iran*. Leiden, Netherlands: E. J. Brill.

Keddie, Nikki R. 1972. "The Roots of *Ulama* Power in Modern Iran." In *Scholars, Saints and Sufis*. Edited by Nikki R. Keddie, 211–29. Los Angeles: University of California Press.

Moaddel, Mansoor. 1986. "The Shi'i *Ulama* and the State in Iran." *Theory and Society* 15: 519–56.

———. 1993. *Class, Politics, and Ideology in the Iranian Revolution*. New York: Columbia University Press.

Momen, Moojan 1985. *An Introduction to Shi'i Islam*. New Haven, Conn.: Yale University Press.

CHAPTER 45

ISLAMIC COMMUNITIES IN CENTRAL ASIA

RICHARD C. FOLTZ

CENTRAL Asia was for many centuries a center of global trade and a zone of major cultural transmission and interaction via the overland routes known as the Silk Road. For at least three millennia until modern times the socioeconomic dynamics of Central Asia were shaped by relations between oasis settlers and pastoral nomads. The region's settled populations are today found in the Muslim majority states of the former Soviet Union and Afghanistan. They have historically been mainly speakers of Iranian languages, though Turkic dialects have been progressively encroaching over the past thousand years with the settlement and urbanization of mainly Turkic-speaking nomadic populations.

Islam spread across Central Asia along the trade routes, beginning with the Arab conquests in the early eighth century. The urban areas were the first to be Islamicized as economic, political, and cultural institutions came under Muslim control. Increasingly the large Zoroastrian, Buddhist, Christian, and Manichaean populations in the urban areas of the region ceased to exist. By the fifteenth century, only Jewish communities retained their distinct identity.

Rural areas were Islamicized rather later than the towns, and indeed among such recently settled groups as the Kazakh and Kyrgyz one could say that the process continues even today. Markedly different forms of Islamic teaching were transmitted depending on context, with cities tending to be under the influence of the interpretations of legal scholars (*ulema*) while charismatic mystic teachers—the Sufi shaykhs—held sway in the countryside. In some cases, as with the Naqshbandi shaykhs of the fifteenth century, Sufis became important political and religious figures in the cities as well. The historical tensions between competing sources of religious authority that exist in most Muslim societies, such as legal scholarship versus mystical insight, were especially pronounced in Central Asia.

Central Asian Muslim elites had strong cultural and economic ties with India, Iran, and Asia Minor which were all often ruled by Turkic groups of Central Asian origin. The Mughals of India, for example (1526–1857), derived their political legitimacy from their Central Asian Timurid ancestry and consciously imported and maintained a wide range of Central Asian customs and symbols as reminders of their original homeland. Royal paintings often depict Mughal figures in the company of Timur (Tamerlane), and much of their monumental architecture was based on Timurid models.

By the nineteenth century when Russia and Britain made of Central Asia the chessboard of their "Great Game" for world hegemony, the native population of the region was one of the most completely Islamicized anywhere. But it had also become one of the most marginalized areas of the entire Muslim world. European sea trade had greatly diminished the importance of the Central Asian trade routes, and contacts to the west were impeded by religiopolitical divisions between the region's Sunni Uzbek rulers and the militantly Shi'ite Safavid empire of nearby Iran.

Although the rupture was not absolute, the diminished influence of Iran allowed for an accelerating Turkicization of Central Asia from the sixteenth century onward. Although variants of Persian continue to be spoken in Tajikistan, where it is the official language, in the cities of Samarkand and Bukhara in Uzbekistan, and in the north and west of Afghanistan, most of the populations of Azerbaijan, Turkmenistan, Uzbekistan, Kazakhstan, and Kyrgyzstan, as well as Xinjiang province in China, speak Turkic dialects. The entire region was generally referred to in pre-Soviet times as Turkestan.

The overwhelming majority of Central Asian Muslims are Sunnis who historically followed the Hanafi school of law. The Kazakhs and Kyrgyz retain many traditional pre-Islamic beliefs and practices and are often considered by other groups to be "superficial Muslims." There are small numbers of Sevener, or Isma'ili Shi'ites, in the Pamir mountains of Tajikistan, and the Hazaras of central Afghanistan are Twelver Shi'ites.

THE FORMER SOVIET REPUBLICS

From the second half of the nineteenth century until 1991 much of Central Asia was under Russian domination. The khanates of Bukhara and Khiva became vassal states and were eventually annexed, and following the October Revolution of 1917 their territories were gradually absorbed into the Soviet Union. The Soviet policy on nationalities, of which Josef Stalin was one of the architects, called for a max-imized differentiation among the various subject ethnic groups. Thus, Russian linguists identified regional dialects that differed the most from each other and constructed from them "official languages" such as Uzbek, Kazakh, and Kyrgyz (all variants of a language formerly known simply as "Turki") and used them as the formal basis for "national" identities. Persian-speakers were taught that they spoke a language called "Tojiki" and that it was a separate language from Persian.

By the late nineteenth century some Central Asian Muslim intellectuals had absorbed modernizing influences from Russia and Europe and were advocating educational, technological, and other social reforms. One expression of this was the so-called Jadidist movement (from the Arabic word for "new"), associated with figures such as the Tatar reformist Ismail Bey Gasprinskii. Some Jadidists, like the Tajik writer Sadruddin Aini, became early supporters of the Soviet state that they saw as a modernizing force.

Under the officially atheist Soviet regime all religions, Islam included, were actively discouraged. Mosques and seminaries were closed down and their build-ings turned to other purposes. Only a few religious institutions were allowed to remain open and these were closely supervised, their leaders being appointed by the government. A major result of this was that for seventy years throughout the twentieth century, the "official" Islam of the legal scholars was suppressed in a way that allowed the "unofficial" Islam of Sufis and shrine custodians to predom-inate and become the normative source for the religious life of Central Asian Muslims.

Among the popular expressions of religion for Central Asian Muslims, the most significant are the life-cycle celebrations—generically called *tuys*—of male circumcision and marriage. Both involve entire neighborhoods and are ruinously expensive for the sponsoring parents. As such these ceremonies were targeted for elimination by the Soviets as "backward" rituals, but to no avail. Islamist reform-ers today often oppose these celebrations as well, at least in their popular forms that tend to include the consumption of large quantities of alcohol.

Another important focus of popular religious life is shrine visitation. As else-where in the Muslim world, Central Asian Muslims visit the shrines of deceased religious figures—usually Sufi saints—in hopes of obtaining some of the divine blessing (*baraka*) believed to inhere in such sites. One may visit a shrine to pray for success, for children, or for any number of reasons. Although shrine visitation for religious purposes was suppressed under the Soviets, it was possible to disguise pilgrimages as "tourism," which Central Asians did on a massive scale. As a result of the effective removal of seminary-trained clergy during the Soviet period, the custodians of shrines acquired a virtual monopoly on religious authority, which largely escaped official control.

At the same time many Central Asian Muslims did successfully assimilate into Soviet society and came to adopt the ideologies and worldview of the Soviet state. Under the Soviets it was possible for women to become educated, to enter professions, and to lead public lives. (They often faced double duties, however, as traditional gender roles were maintained in the home.) Many Central Asian Muslims ceased to practice Islam and became Muslim in name only. It is somewhat ironic that the president of Uzbekistan, though named *Islam* Karimov, has seen resurgent Islamism as the primary threat to his neo-Stalinist state.

With the disintegration of Soviet power in 1991 this Islamic resurgence was dramatic, especially in parts of Uzbekistan such as the Ferghana valley and in the desperately impoverished new nation of Tajikistan. All over Central Asia new mosques went up by the thousands virtually overnight. Also, foreign agencies from Saudi Arabia, Iran, and elsewhere have sought to establish footholds of influence through the funding of new religious institutions and public works projects. Most visible perhaps has been the influx of religious teachers of the purist variety, often called "Wahhabi," after the eighteenth-century Arabian reformer Abd al-Wahhab. Today all forms of civil unrest and political dissent are routinely blamed by the secular, post-Communist Central Asian regimes on "Wahhabi agitators," though the realities underlying such conflicts are in fact much more complex.

Ethnic rivalries have been apparent among members of various Central Asian "nationalities," though it may be recalled that these identities were constructed mostly artificially during the twentieth century. Tensions also exist between Central Asians and Europeans and others who immigrated into the region during the Soviet period. Many of the latter have left for Russia since 1991, and those who stay face increasing pressure to accept new language laws and other restrictions. Europeans are estimated to account for around 15 percent of the current population in Uzbekistan, less than 5 percent in Tajikistan, and only 1 or 2 percent in Turkmenistan. Kazakhstan presents a special case in that Europeans still constitute more than one-third of the population, but in other republics the trend toward nationalization has been strong.

Despite the pressures on Central Asians of European origin, it would seem that among those suffering from nationalization policies none have been harder hit than the Persian (or Tojiki) speakers of Uzbekistan. The inheritors of Central Asia's long urban cultural tradition, which includes poetry and other literary forms as well as music, art, and architecture, Uzbekistan's Tajiks have found themselves embattled as never before as the nation strives to establish its Turkic identity.

While official figures downplay the numbers of Persian speakers, they likely account for 10 to 20 percent of the total national population and may actually be more numerous than in the formally Persian-speaking neighbor republic of Tajikistan, the total number being perhaps as much as ten million between the two countries. (Census figures are unreliable and many Persian-speakers in Uzbekistan outwardly claim Uzbek ethnicity.) Tajiks on both sides of the border complain that their nation was deliberately split in two under Stalin in the 1920s, and the historical centers of Persian-speaking culture, Samarkand and Bukhara, relegated to an officially Turkic-speaking republic. Tajiks explain their current status as the most impoverished of the former Soviet peoples by insisting that they are "a nation which has been decapitated."

AFGHANISTAN

The present nation of Afghanistan owes its existence as a distinct identity at least in part to the aims of European powers. Its territories were always part of larger empires—the Alexandrid, the Kushan, the Sasanian, and later Muslim states such as the Mughal, Safavid or Uzbek—until the 1750s when a Pukhtun tribal leader by the name of Ahmad Durrani managed to consolidate much of the area of the present state under his authority. The British and the Russians, who were progressively taking over the lands of Muslim empires in India and Central Asia, were content to allow a nominally independent Afghan state to exist as a buffer between them.

In fact this southern part of Central Asia, which comprises mainly arid, rugged, mountainous terrain and is inhabited by a wide range of disparate peoples, has never been fully under the control of any central government. Instead, successive regimes have focused on controlling the region's cities, while the outlying areas have usually been under the rule of local leaders. The cities of present-day Afghanistan were historically part of the broader Persian-speaking cultural sphere, but back-and-forth struggles between the Iranian Safavid and Indian Mughal empires in the seventeenth and eighteenth centuries reduced them to a condition from which they have not recovered. More recently, a decade of Soviet occupation followed by the brutal rule of the extremist Taliban and finally the U.S.-led invasion of 2001 have laid waste to virtually the entire country.

The largest of Afghanistan's many ethnic and linguistic groups are the Pukhtuns, or Pathans, who constitute about half the total population, and several Persian-speaking groups who make up about 35 percent. The Pukhtuns are the "true" Afghans in the sense that the very word "Afghan" is an onomatopoeic (and originally derisive) label applied by Persian-speakers, akin to the Greek notion of "barbarian." The Pukhtuns, whose language is a distant relative of Persian, are a clan-based society organized according to an ethical code known as *pukhtunwali*, which requires that every insult be avenged and every guest be extended hospitality.

This code of honor is enforced through revenge (*badat*), normally in the form of killing the offender. This is similar to the Islamic "law of retaliation" (*qisas*), and is the basis of law enforcement and social stability in Pukhtun society. Honor (*izzat*) is principally understood to reside in the chastity of a family's female members. One visible expression of this concern is the complete covering of women with the burqa and their general exclusion from public life.

The pukhtunwali code also provides offenders with the option of "seeking refuge" (*tanawatay*) and guarantees them protection if they do. (Seeking tanawatay is seen as highly dishonorable, however.) Pukhtunwali can be seen as the basis for much of the recent social history of Afghanistan, from the domestic policies of the Taliban regime to the hospitality extended to foreign Muslim militant groups. The Taliban (literally, "the students," that is, of their teacher Mulla Mohammad Omar) applied an interpretation of Islamic tradition that was heavily informed by pukhtunwali.

Apart from the Sunni Pukhtun majority (who exist in roughly equivalent numbers in adjacent areas of Pakistan), Afghanistan is home to Iranian-speaking groups, mainly Sunnis, such as the Tajiks, the Parsiwan, and the Baluch. Numerous Turkic-speaking groups, including Uzbeks, Turkmens, and others exist mostly in the north, along with small numbers of Arabs descended from the first Muslim conquerors. Twelver Shi'ite communities exist especially in the center of the country, and some Sevener (Isma'ili) groups in the northeast. The complex ethnic and linguistic makeup of the country, a cultural tradition of strong local autonomy, combined with the rugged topography and lack of connecting infrastructure, together suggest that any attempts to build a unified state in Afghanistan will prove extremely challenging.

BIBLIOGRAPHY

Aini, Sadruddin. 1998. *The Sands of Oxus.* Trans. John R. Perry and Rachel Lehr. Costa Mesa, Calif.: Mazda Publishers.

Foltz, Richard C. 1999. *Religions of the Silk Road: Overland Trade and Cultural Exchange from Antiquity to the Fifteenth Century.* New York: St. Martin's Press.

———. 1998. *Mughal India and Central Asia.* Karachi: Oxford University Press.

Hopkirk, Peter. 1994. *The Great Game: The Struggle for Empire in Central Asia.* New York: Kodansha.

Khalid, Adeeb. 1998. *The Politics of Muslim Cultural Reform: Jadidism in Central Asia.* Berkeley: University of California Press.

Poliakov, Sergei. 1992. *Everyday Islam: Religion and Tradition in Rural Central Asia.* Armonk, N.Y.: M. E. Sharpe.

Rashid, Ahmed. 2003. *Jihad: The Rise of Militant Islam in Central Asia*. New York: Penguin.

Roy, Olivier. *The New Central Asia: The Creation of Nations*. New York: New York University Press, 2000.

Sagdeev, R. Z. et al., eds. 2000. *Islam and Central Asia*. Washington, D.C.: Eisenhower Institute.

CHAPTER 46

....

ISLAMIC COMMUNITIES
IN SOUTH ASIA

....

SCOTT KUGLE

In sheer numbers South Asia is the global center of Islam. It is the host to over 350 million Muslims: 128 million in India (13 percent of the total population), 124 million in Pakistan (97 percent of the total population) and 103 million in Bangladesh (87 percent of the total population). Muslims in South Asia have a deep and rich cultural history and have long-founded and complex relationships with other religious traditions. In India, for instance, despite their enormous numbers, they are the minority religious community. The vast and varied regions of South Asia have fostered a multiplicity of Muslim communities, providing a home for a diverse collection of Muslims from different sectarian allegiances and theological orientations.

South Asia is commonly known as the "Indian subcontinent" or the "Indo-Pak subcontinent." Its core is the landmass south of the Himalaya and Hindukush mountain ranges: the Ganges and Indus river plains and the peninsula (consisting of the nations of India, Pakistan, and Bangladesh). Closely related to South Asia are the mountainous regions that define its core (including the nations of Afghanistan, Nepal, Bhutan, Burma, and the region of Tibet) whose societies have been in close contact with the Indus and Ganges plains. Also in the South Asian cultural zone are the islands of the Indian Ocean (Sri Lanka, Lashwadweep, and the Maldives).

South Asia is a distinctive area with complex cultural relations to other parts of Asia: it is separated from China, the Central Asian steppes, and the Iranian plateau by the world's highest mountain chains; yet mountain passes have always provided conduits for trade of material goods, exchange of religious and cultural ideas, and invasion and migration of peoples. By sea, South Asia is connected by trade to the Middle Eastern lands of the Persian Gulf and Red Sea and to the Southeast Asian islands of Indonesia and the straits of Malaysia. Geographic relations between mountains and ocean create a unique monsoon season of heavy rainfall. South Asia developed complex agrarian societies, expansive political empires, and highly developed religious systems (from local goddess cults to Brahmanical Hinduism, Buddhism, and Jainism). These geographic boundaries and connections shaped the growth of Muslim communities in the region.

Muslims have been present in South Asia for almost as long has they have been present in the Arabian peninsula. The first mosque in South Asia was built in Kerala not long after the death of the Prophet Muhammad in 642. Nevertheless, Western scholars, often bound by the Orientalist tradition, have often considered South Asia to be "marginal" to the discipline of Islamic studies (similar to the intellectual myopia that has obscured the importance of Muslim communities in Southeast Asia and China, as aptly described by Mark Woodward and Dru Gladney in this volume). Western scholars who work on Islamic subjects tend to learn Arabic or Persian, neglecting the literary and spoken languages of South Asian Muslims: Punjabi, Pashto, Urdu, Bengali, Sindhi, Gujarati, Malayalam, and Tamil.

Early Contacts and Coastal Communities

Three factors led to the growth of Muslim communities in South Asia: commerce, conquest, and conversion. Maritime relations of commerce first established a Muslim presence in South Asia. The western coast of South Asia had intimate commercial and political relations with the Middle East long before the time of Muhammad. The southwest coast of South Asia, known as Ma'bar or Malabar (Arabic for "Place of Crossing," now Kerala) housed merchants and settlers from pre-Islamic Arab, Jewish, and Christian communities from the Middle East. All three communities established trade networks, patronized and promoted by the local Hindu rulers, as described by Ainslie T. Embree in this volume. With the establishment of the early Muslim community in Arabia, Arab settlers became Muslim settlers. At first this did not dramatically change their relation with rulers or local populations in South Asia. Arab merchants married local women and were absorbed into local kingdoms as a distinct caste with high status. As Arab trade communities became Muslim trade communities, they built mosques and acted as overseas trade partners with local rulers and perhaps as political advisors (Bayley 1989).

Arabic literacy through Qur'anic study may have raised their status in South Asia, as did the rapid political expansion of the Islamic empire in the Middle East and the Iranian plateau that established Arabic as the lingua franca of commerce in the Indian Ocean basin. Children of marriages between Arab merchants and local South Asian women were raised as Muslims, creating the nucleus for a more indigenous Muslim community. Some evidence suggests that Hindu rulers of the Malabar coast appointed certain children to be raised in Arab families in order for them to learn sailing and promote interregional trade. There is a legend that, during the lifetime of the Prophet Muhammad, a Hindu ruler on the Malabar coast converted to Islam and traveled to the Hijaz (the Arabian region encompassing Makka and Madina). When he never returned to South Asia, his descendents ruled as Hindu kings who were delegates for the authority of the disappeared Muslim king. This legend may reflect less historical reality than mythic explanation of the cooperative relationship between Hindu kings and Arab-Muslim trade communities that formed the basis for the wealth and power of this coastal kingdom. Whether such stories are origin legends or contain traces of historical events, Muslim communities flourished in the southern regions (now the Indian states of Kerala and Tamil Nadu) due to seafaring and trade. The local languages were written down in Arabic script, creating rich and complex Islamic literary traditions that are only recently coming to the attention of scholars and translators (Narayanan 2000).

The Muslims of contemporary Kerala are called Mappila, and numbered almost 7.5 million in the 1990 census. They follow the Shafi'i legal school due to their close cultural ties to Arabia (in contradistinction to most other Sunni Muslims in South Asia who follow the Hanafi legal school with cultural ties to Turkic Central Asia). The Mappilas continue to foster close ties to Arabian Gulf states, as migrant workers and skilled professionals in Saudi Arabia and the Gulf states, like Kuwait and the United Arab Emirates.

Isma'ili Syncretism and Maritime Trade

Unlike the southwest coast of the Arabian Sea, the northwest coast was not hospitable to Arab and Persian merchant settlers. The Hindu communities of Sindh and Gujarat were already engaged in sea-faring trade and looked upon Arab settlements as competition, not complement. These coasts were too close to Middle Eastern empires that threatened to dominate them even as they engaged in interregional trade. The first Arab-Islamic dynasty, the Umayyad, entered into maritime relations with Sri Lanka and the Indonesian archipelago. This dynasty quickly came into conflict with local Hindu rulers in Sindh over piracy and interference in sea routes with these islands. When a ship with a royal gift bound from Sri Lanka to the Umayyad ruler in Damascus was pirated, the Arab-Islamic empire mounted a naval expedition that led to the conquest of Sindh in 711.

The leader of those naval expeditions, Muhammad ibn Qasim, established the first Arab-Islamic polity in South Asian territory. Sectarian and political feuds in Sindh facilitated the conquest; Mahayana Buddhists were a sizable part of the local population and were losing a battle for political supremacy against Brahmanical Hindus. Evidence suggests that Sindhi Buddhists may have even colluded with Arab invaders in order to displace Brahmanical rulers. Muhammad ibn Qasim extended *dhimmi* status (as protected religious groups) to Brahmanical Hindus and Buddhists. This is the first example in Islamic history of dhimmi status being extended to groups not specifically mentioned in the Qur'an (such as Jews and Christians). At the same time, this state was initially justified with a "call" for the population of Sindhi Buddhists to convert to Islam. However, there is no evidence of sustained effort to convert local populations. This confirms to the patterns of the wider Near Eastern Islamic Empire in the Umayyad period (Bulliet 1994). After initial military conquest, local Hindu communities were responsible for large areas of administration, like taxation and revenue, and temples were allowed to function.

The Arab conquerors founded Mansura, which functioned from approximately 730 as the capital of Islamic Sindh, first as a garrison then as a full city (Maclean 1989). The Arab conquest of Sindh increased the cultural, religious, and scientific contact between South Asians and Muslims in the Middle Eastern Islamic lands. Indic numerals and decimal-based mathematics, chess, astronomy, and literature were transmitted to the Islamic capital at Baghdad and translated into Arabic. Many Sindhi scholars traveled west, lived in Baghdad, and were employed by the Abbasid court.

Sindh was drawn into political strife that tore through the Middle Eastern Islamic lands. The Fatimid insurrection gained force in North Africa and a Shi'i counter-caliphate was established by 910. The Fatimids were one branch of the Isma'ili movement, which was a potent variation of Shi'ism that engineered a political and spiritual revolution. Isma'ilis are known in the West as "Sevener Shi'ites" because they diverged from the mainstream Shi'ite community over conflicts about the identity of the seventh Shi'ite imam; they elected to follow Isma'il, one son of the sixth imam, from whom they take the name of their movement. The Isma'ili movement was both secretive and populist, expounding an esoteric Islamic doctrine comparable to Gnosticism in Christian and Jewish traditions.

This doctrine encouraged covert rebellion against Islamic law and the Sunni imperial rulers who upheld it.

The repercussions of this spiritual and political movement were felt in Sindh. There Isma'ili missionaries engineered a coup at Mansura, driving underground the Sunnis who were loyal to the Abbasid caliphate. As a result, Sindh became a satellite of Fatimid rule based in the newly established capital of Cairo. Isma'ili missionaries were highly creative in adapting to the South Asian environment. They drew equivalence between Islamic beliefs and those of the native populations in order to facilitate conversion and also to give their movement a stronger hold outside the urban centers. For instance, Allah was pictured as equivalent to Brahma, while Adam was an incarnation (or avatar) of Shiva and 'Ali was an incarnation of Vishnu. Beyond the realm of political strategy, this eclectic and syncretic theology promoted the idea that Hindu forms of monotheism were compatible, even equivalent, to Islam. Their poetry and devotional hymns are rich resources for scholars of comparative literature and religious studies (Kassam 1992).

Although they were driven from political control by 997, Isma'ili communities continued to thrive in South Asia, especially in Sindh and Gujarat. They divided into different sectarian communities (the two major divisions are Khojas or Nizaris who follow the Agha-Khan, and Bohras or Tayyibis with ties to Yemeni spiritual leaders); these communities became self-contained social groups that excelled in trade, through which they spread in an international diaspora (Nanji 1978). During British colonial rule, Isma'ilis adapted to new educational opportunities and trained as lawyers to serve as important mediators between colonial rule and wider Muslim communities. As merchants, Isma'ilis were especially influential in East Africa (after the independence of African states like Uganda and Kenya, these communities increasingly moved to Canada and the United States).

SUNNI RESURGENCE AND EMPIRE BUILDING

Although the initial contact between Muslims and South Asians was via sea routes, more sustained contact came though land routes that provided not just trade but conquest as well. Central Asia, Khurasan, and Afghanistan became more important regions of the Islamic Empire during the Abbasid period. Abbasid rulers built a standing army consisting mainly of Turkic slaves who were raised as soldiers and court administrators. When central rule became weak in Baghdad, Turkic "slave soldiers" assigned as governors of outlying territories asserted their independence as sultans. In this way, the Sultanate of Ghazna (based in Afghanistan) became an important state that bridged the land routes between the Central Islamic lands and South Asia.

Mahmud of Ghazna ruled this sultanate from 998–1030. He created a Turkic ruling aristocracy with Persian court rituals and a strong emphasis on Sunni religiosity. Through continuous warfare, he expanded westward into Iran and Central Asia and eastward into the Punjab. He established Lahore as a frontier garrison town and important local center of Islamic scholarship in South Asia. Mahmud's court patronized the scholar al-Biruni who authored a detailed study of the religions, philosophies, and sciences of South Asia (al-Biruni 1964), which is probably the first explicitly comparative study of religions.

Mahmud of Ghazna was also drawn into larger political and religious rivalries. He justified his invasion of Sindh as opposition to the Isma'ili and Fatimid presence there. His armies raided far into the Ganges plain, and political chronicles attribute to him a policy of stripping Hindu temples of the wealth stored in their treasuries. These plunder campaigns were to fund his westward expansion into Central Asia and the Iranian highlands rather than to rule directly in South Asia beyond Lahore. Historians still argue over the true extent of his plunder of temples and whether iconoclastic desecration was part of a religious justification of his military campaigns (Eaton 2000). During this time, Sufi organizations began to move into Ghaznavid-controlled territories in greater numbers and acted as missionaries for Sunni allegiance. Sufism will be discussed below, as it was the theological, mystical, and literary heart of the Sunni community governed by imperial sultanates.

Direct Ghaznavid rule did not last long, but it set up a pattern of invasion by ambitious Turkic slave-soldier regimes. In 1175, Muhammad ibn Sam led an invasion from Afghanistan. Unlike the Ghaznavids, this new wave of invaders conquered Delhi and set up an administration that would last in the South Asian heartland (Lawrence 1999). This administration was known as the Sultanate of Delhi and was ruled by a succession of "slave-soldier" regimes, lasting from 1193–1526. These sultans set up a stable political structure justified by championing Sunni Islam. In their rhetoric "Islam" meant the political dominance of the Sunni Turkic and Afghan elite. This rhetoric (preserved in coinage, monumental architecture, and historical chronicles) should not obscure the fact that local Muslim communities were growing outside the purview of this Islamic state. In fact, local Muslims were employed as soldiers by Hindu kings (rajas) who fought against the Turkic dynasties, just as Hindu soldiers were an integral part of the Turkic standing armies. The political conflict between expanding Turkic dynasties and local Hindu rajas should not be interpreted as a clash between two religions (Islam and Hinduism) or two incompatible civilizations (Islamic and Indic), despite colonial-era historiography and contemporary nationalist histories that put forward this picture.

Rulers of the Delhi Sultanate made important contributions to South Asian culture, introducing new forms of administration, military organization, architecture (for both secular and sacred buildings), coinage and trade, and court patronage of literature, painting, and music. These last two were spheres that involved intensive syncretic creativity between Hindus and Muslims. The system of North Indian (Hindustani) classical music was shaped by Muslim innovations through court patronage; the name of Amir Khusro stands out as an important innovator in Hindustani music who was deeply involved in both Sufism and court life, as discussed below.

From their base at Delhi, the sultanate expanded eastward to Bihar and Bengal, westward to Rajasthan and Gujarat, and southward into the Dekkan region of peninsular South Asia. Their most profound military success was deflecting the Mongols, who had devastated the central Islamic lands and leveled most major cities, including Baghdad in 1255. As the Sultans of Delhi fought off Mongol incursions, South Asia became a haven of continuity for Islamic rule as most Middle Eastern Islamic lands were thrown into chaos. Immigration of skilled artisans, intellectuals, and religious leaders into South Asia caused fluorescence in Sufism, Islamic scholarship, and literary and fine arts. From this point onward, South Asian Muslims inhabited a heartland for Islamic civilization rather than an outpost.

SUFI ORDERS AND RELIGIOUS FLUORESCENCE

Official structure of the sultanate included religious leaders. The ruler appointed a shaykh al-Islam, who was the most authoritative Islamic scholar in each city or region, presiding over Qadis who acted as judges and notaries, who were drawn from the ranks of scholars trained in jurisprudence and theology. Religious life outside the purview of the state was more active and vibrant. Sufis established mosques and hospices in smaller towns, which functioned as devotional, educational, and charitable centers. Discourses of Sufi masters often introduced new intellectual disciplines and scholarly knowledge into South Asia. Official religious leaders and Sufi religious leaders did not always see eye to eye. The two sides debated the issues of listening to devotional music, visiting tombs of saints, and public displays of devotion to one's saintly master (Lawrence 1978). Sufis criticized scholars and judges in official positions for being subservient to the government, hypocrisy, and unjust accumulation of wealth. However, the two groups were not diametrically opposed; especially outside the capital, tacit cooperation between Qadi and Sufi leaders was the norm.

This dynamic of cooperation and competition between Sufis and sultan is aptly demonstrated by the Sufi master, Nizam al-Din Awliya (1244–1325). His life is exemplary for South Asian Sufis, and under his guidance, the Chishti Sufi order became the most characteristically "South Asian" of Sufi organizations; in the present, it continues to play a vibrant role. Nizam al-Din Awliya was the most renowned Sufi saint of his age in South Asia. He systematized the core practices of the Chishti Sufi community and spread its institutions throughout the region.

Nizam al-Din's teachings are in continuity with his saintly predecessors, the Chishti masters. Mu'in al-Din 'asan Sanjari (d. 1236) brought this Sufi lineage from Afghanistan as he settled in Ajmer, Rajastan, on the frontier of Islamic rule. He taught that to be a Muslim one must become a true human being by cultivating "generosity like the generosity of the ocean, compassion like the compassion of the sun, and humility like the humility of the earth" (Ernst and Lawrence 2002: 150). He distilled universal teachings from the Islamic religion, attracting many Hindu devotees even as he extolled Muhammad the Prophet as the primordial human being and Imam Ali as the exemplary Sufi master. He adopted devotional hymns from his Hindu environment and freely mixed Persianate music with Indic melodies and instruments. A lineage of great masters expounded these Chishti teachings after Mu'in al-Din's death, including: Shaykh Qutb al-Din Bakhtiyar Kaki who died in the midst of ecstasy inspired by listening to Persian Sufi poetry; Shaykh 'amid al-Din Nagawri, a gentle advocate of social justice who adopted the lifestyle of impoverished vegetarian peasants; and the rigorously ascetic Shaykh Farid al-Din.

Nizam al-Din's teachings can be summarized in three short statements. First, service to the needy is better than ritual worship. He used to teach that, although there are innumerable ways leading to God, the surest way to intimate knowledge of God is bringing happiness to others. Second, the presence of God is found among the destitute and needy. Third, egoistic chauvinism is real idolatry, to be combated by loving compassion, open-hearted acceptance of others, and religious tolerance. Nizam al-Din advocated three practical means to realize and internalize these teachings. First, one had to find a spiritual master and devote oneself to his loving service. Second, one must embrace voluntary poverty and renounce saving and hoarding. Third, one should revive the life of the heart through listening to devotional music. For Nizam al-Din, devotional music consisted mainly of singing poems, accompanied by drumming and occasionally stringed instruments in gatherings that could erupt into ecstatic states and enraptured dance.

Despite his aloofness from material livelihood, Nizam al-Din was a skilled organizer who maintained an active devotional center and brought into his disciples' circle people of all classes and education levels. He codified the rules of living at devotional centers, stressing strict financial management, which must rely on voluntary gifts rather than royal largesse. Nizam al-Din refused to bless the rule of particular sultans, accept valuables from them, or meet them face-to-face. Yet he oversaw expansion of the Chishti Sufi community in parallel with the expanding Islamic empire, sending his delegates to all corners of the Delhi Sultanate to set up devotional centers based on the model of his center in Delhi. Nizam al-Din's disciples included courtiers who were the best poets of their age. Amir Hasan Sijzi (1254–1336) wrote down Nizam al-Din's oral discourses on Sufism in a unique record, entitled *Morals for the Heart* (Lawrence 1992). This book spawned a whole genre of Sufi literature that came to dominate Sufi literature in South Asia and left us intimate portraits of their saints' daily lives and spiritual teachings. His friend, Amir Khusro (d.1325), created Persian ghazals of great depth, Hindawi poems in praise of Nizam al-Din based on Krishna-devotion imagery of the female lover awaiting her beloved, and musical settings of Islamic prayers and praise that defined the tradition of Qawwali singing (Qureishi 1995). Qawwali singing has reached "world music" audiences since Peter Gabriel popularized the voice of Nusrat Fateh Ali Khan, who has recorded traditional Sufi singing as well as experimented with genre fusions and sound tracks to films like *Dead Man Walking*.

SHI'I COMMUNITIES AND
REGIONAL BRILLIANCE

Central rule of the Delhi Sultanate became weak in the mid-fourteenth century. Regional governors began to assert their independence, creating local Islamic dynasties. In the Dekkan, the Bahmani dynasty threw off the rule of Delhi in 1347, then split into five small Islamic states: Golkonda, Khandesh, Bijapur, Ahmadnagar, and Berar. Scholars tend to overlook these smaller Islamic dynasties, but they created distinctive regional Islamic societies and literature in local languages beyond Persian (Ernst 1992). Some of them justified independence from Delhi by adopting Shi'i loyalty (Ithna-'Ashari, the same Shi'ite group that came to dominate Iran and Lebanon). This sectarian identity solidified in religious terms their independence from the Sunni dynasty centered upon Delhi and fostered cultural and commercial relationships with the Shi'i Safavid dynasty that ruled Iran. The Qutb Shahi dynasty of Golconda and Hyderabad cultivated especially close ties

with Iran, as evidenced by their style of miniature painting, their artistry with
Persian Gulf pearls, and their building of shrines to house Shi'i battle-standards
used in rituals of mourning for the death of Hussayn and other Shi'i imams.
Islamic ritual sites that are not formal mosques, such as tombs of Sufi masters or
shrines with Shi'i relics, were important sites of religious devotion in South Asia
(Cole 1988). They were highly venerated places with intense syncretic potential.
Local Hindus were free to engage in worship there in an Islamic environment,
transferring Hindu devotional practices onto Islamic foci of devotion. Most likely,
these were important channels for "conversion" into Muslim communities, which
was a slow process of acculturation over generations rather than a dramatic individual transformation.

These heterogeneous Dekkan kingdoms also sheltered other Muslim splinter
groups like the Mahdawis. They are followers of a medieval Muslim reformer,
Sayyid Muhammad of Jawnpur (1443–1505), who took Sufi ideas to a chiliastic
and millennial extreme. He declared himself the long-awaited Mahdi, a savior
whose coming at the end of time would mirror the coming of the Prophet Muhammad (Qamaruddin 1985). Many Muslims expected this event in the tenth
Islamic century (the end of the first millennium according to the Islamic calendar). Sayyid Muhammad encouraged followers to purify their ritual life of legalistic formality, embrace communal life, and reject routine work in a dynamic
strangely similar to Protestant movements in Europe. After a period of enthusiastic evangelism and violent oppression by Sunni governors, the Mahdawi community developed into a puritan but settled sub-sect of the Sunni Muslim community, in which form it persists.

ISLAMIC COSMOPOLITANISM AND
CONVERSION IN MUGHAL TIMES

The breakdown of centralized power accelerated when Timur (Tamerlane) invaded South Asia and sacked Delhi in 1389, carrying off its wealth to his Central
Asian capital of Samarqand. Later, a chieftain of Chaghatai Turks who claimed
descent from Timur came to stay. This was Babur, a warlord from Ferghana (now
Tajikistan), who lost his control and invaded South Asia to bide his time until he
could retake his home region. He extinguished the last vestiges of the Delhi Sultanate. Babur's descendents created the Mughal (or Timurid) Empire and brought
centralized rule back to South Asia and ruled from 1526–1857 (Richards 1993).

Babur's descendants built the largest and strongest agrarian empire of the early-modern world. Mughal rule reached stability and ideological maturity under Akbar (ruled 1556–1605). Later Mughal rulers pushed their empire steadily southward into the Dekkan and eastward toward Burma. From the time of Akbar, local Rajput Hindu rulers were absorbed into the Mughal ruling class through court promotion and marriage. Akbar's mother, for instance, was a Rajput princess. The Mughal Empire was more ideologically open to sharing power with Hindu elites and also with Shi'i nobles (many of whom were joining the Mughal court from Safavid Iran). The Mughal Empire diffused the emphasis on Sunni triumphalism and Turkic supremacy that had sustained the Delhi Sultanate.

In order to manage the multiethnic and multireligious composition of the court elite, Akbar elevated the person of the emperor into a divinely guided figure (through an eclectic blending of Sufi, Mahdawi, and Shi'i ideas). His courtiers experimented with a new cult of personal devotion to the emperor, the Din-i Ilahi or Universal Religion of God; scholars still debate about the nature and scope of this cult and its relation to Islam as a religious orientation (Nizami 1989). Later emperors discontinued this experiment and ruled with reference to more canonical Islamic titles and symbols. Perhaps they were responding to the protests of certain Islamic scholars and Sufis that Akbar's experiment was heretical, but it seems more likely that once Rajput and Shi'i nobles were integrated into court life, the experiment was no longer needed.

Persian was the major literary language of court chronicles, secular poetry, and Sufi devotional literature in Mughal times as in the Delhi Sultanate. Some Mughal courtiers patronized or composed poetry in the Braj Bhasha dialect of Hindawi with its rich imagery of Krishna devotion, while Hindustani music continued to develop in close synthesis between Hindu and Muslim practitioners; Tansen stands out as the major innovator in court music of the Mughal period and was a Hindu musician with a Muslim spiritual guide. Music had a special spiritual significance in South Asian Islamic culture, whether in form of sung praise for the Prophet Muhammad (*na't*), requiems for slain Imams (*marthiya*), Sufi ecstatic singing (*qawwali*), or the more abstract and nonconfessional tradition of Hindustani classical music nurtured by court patronage.

Closer cooperation and intermarriage between Muslim and Rajput Hindu elites led to new syncretic possibilities in language and literature. Urdu, or the language of the army camp, was a newly formed language in which the grammar base of Hindawi absorbed words and phrases from Persian and Turkish. It became the common language of the Gangetic plain and from the seventeenth century would become a literary language to complement Persian. Sufis innovated in composing devotional literature in vernacular Indic languages. Shah Hussayn initiated Sufi poetry in Punjabi that rapidly became a regional tradition while Sayyid Sultan composed the Nabivamsa, a mythic retelling of the Prophet Muhammad's life in Bengali. Such vernacular literatures bridged the gap between more elite Persian poetry and folk traditions, while drawing equivalencies between Islamic theological concepts and local Indic images (Lawrence 1984). These vernacular compositions provide evidence of increasing conversion of local Indians to Islam. Scholars of Islam in Bengal have provided the most theoretically astute analyses of conversion as a process of acculturation (Roy 1983; Eaton 1993). Castes of artisans (like weavers) formed new additions to Muslim communities and gave rise to syncretic and iconoclastic religious leaders like Kabir of Benares and Guru Nanak in the Punjab (Lawrence 1987). Nanak's followers forged a new Sikh religion, at first in cooperation with Punjabi Sufis and later in violent conflict with Mughal governors and Muslim jurists. While many Sufis, like the jurists, advocated the inviolability of the *shari'a*, the Mughal era witnessed a rise of Sufis who ignored or disparaged the shari'a and Islamic communal norms. Shah Hussayn of Lahore is an example of an Islamic theology student who rebelled through music and dance to advocate a more universal spirituality that attracted Sufi and Hindu devotees and angered official Muslim scholars (Kugle 2000). Members of the Mughal elite cultivated ties to Sufi communities, and some Mughal nobles were outspoken "Unifiers" (Muwahhid) who believed that Islamic and Hindu theology were compatible and not contradictory, a position informed by theosophical ideas associated with the Andalusian Sufi, Ibn al-Arabi. Prince Dara Shikoh (1615–1659) is an example of this trend. He was the eldest son of the Emperor Shah Jahan and a disciple of the Qadiri Sufi master, Miyan Mir. Besides governing and being groomed to inherit rule of the Mughal realm, he wrote numerous books arguing the ultimate identity of Hindu and Islamic theological concepts. The Mughal court patronized translations into Persian of Hindu literature, like the Upanishads, Ramayana, and Mahabharata, some of which Dara Shikoh translated himself.

In contrast, this environment of synthesis and relaxation of communal boundaries roused Muslim reformers who called for a return to the shari'a. Many scholars see this reformist trend as the exclusive contribution of the Naqshbandi Sufis, like Ahmad Sirhindi (1562–1624). This reformer became most famous since he worked in Delhi and focused his efforts on Mughal nobles (Friedman 1971). However, reformers arose in many communities. Ali Muttaqi (1480–1575) strove to reform Sufism and advocated the centrality of the prophet's example in Ahmadabad, just as the Mughals invaded Gujarat. His disciple in the Qadiri Sufi order, Abd al-Haqq Dihlawi (1551–1642), set up a reformist madrassa in Delhi and composed a manual of religious advice on just and pious rule for the emperor.

The impulse toward reform came into dominance under the Emperor Aurangzeb. After imprisoning his father, Aurangzeb killed his elder brother, Dara Shikoh, in a fratricidal struggle for power. As if in compensation, Aurangzeb advocated shari'a-oriented piety and legalistic righteousness. Aurangzeb's long rule is crucial, for it laid the groundwork for forces that would come to characterize South Asian Muslim communities in the modern period: reformist activism, communal defensiveness, confrontation with European military and commercial power (followed by grudging accommodation to modernist ideals). In this environment, the Naqshbandi Sufi community led a revival of scriptural and theological studies with Shah Waliullah (1703–1762). Waliullah strove to integrate Sufism with study of Qur'an, hadith, and Islamic law in order to strengthen the hold of the shari'a over Islamic culture in South Asia (Baljon 1986). He also urged Muslims to avoid sectarian extremes and blind allegiance to legal schools while reviving *ijtihad,* or independent legal reasoning. His project was made more urgent by the over-expansion and internal weakness of Mughal rule (after Aurangzeb's conquest of the Dekkan). His son, Shah Abd al-Aziz (1746–1823), continued this work in Delhi, translating the Qur'an into Urdu as part of a reformist program. The voluminous and brilliant writings of Shah Waliullah form the constant reference for reformers into the twentieth century.

In hindsight, the reformist impulse would prove most influential on modern Islamic movements, but its dominance should not be exaggerated. Many Sufis continued to cherish Ibn al-Arabi's ideas and did not perceive any conflict between the Islamic shari'a and the "Oneness of Being." Other Naqshbandis, like Mirza Mazhar Jan-i Janan, continued the project of syncretic devotion in cooperation with Hindus which stressed meditation, devotional music, and theosophical poetry; his disciples forged a Sufi Order that gradually attracted Hindu devotees who "Hinduized" it completely by drawing equivalence between Persian terms from Islamic theology and Sanskrit terms from the Upanishads and Bhakti mysticism (Dahnhardt 2002).

COLONIAL EXPANSION AND MUSLIM REACTION

Aurangzeb was an ambitious emperor who focused his energies on military conquests, especially of the Dekkan kingdoms with Shi'i ruling families. After the death of Aurangzeb in 1707, Mughal rulers were weak strategists. Decentralization allowed local powers to grow (like Sikhs in Punjab, the Hindu Marathas in the Dekkan, and Shi'i rulers in Awadh centered in Lucknow). Lucknow in particular created a vibrant fluorescence of Islamic scholarship and Indo-Islamic arts, like Urdu poetry, Hindustani music, and Kathak dance. Sentimental appropriations of Lucknow culture, many penned in Urdu by Muslim poets and in cooperation with Parsi (Indian Zoroastrian) dramatists, supplied many of the lyric images that drove Hindi cinema in Bombay in the 1950s and 60s; Bollywood musical extravaganzas, now absorbing disco and hip-hop inflections, have become a truly global cultural production.

Political and military chaos in the Mughal capital facilitated European expansion in South Asia. The British East India Company grew from a commercial trading post to a regional military power based at Fort William in Calcutta. By 1765, the leader of the East India Company had assumed the title of Diwan of Bengal with rights of taxation and fiscal administration. Though he was a nominal "vassal" of the Mughal emperor, the governor of the Company began military expansion into and commercial exploitation of neighboring regions of South Asia (C. Bayly 1987). Many East India Company administrators were also scholars of religion, and Fort William was the base of early Orientalists, like William Jones and Charles Hamilton, who translated legal and historical texts from Persian and Arabic into English. After 1793, the East India Company systematically administered Islamic law to Muslims in the territories it controlled, and over the next century synthesized Islamic and British legal norms, called Anglo-Muhammadan Law (Kugle 2001).

By 1840, the British controlled most Mughal dominions directly or indirectly. After conquering the Punjabi kingdom of the Sikhs in 1849, the British began to integrate the local kingdoms under their control, constructing railway and telegraph lines. They deposed the ruler of Awadh in 1856, sparking rebellion against the now more visible political aspirations. Muslim and Hindu soldiers in the British East India Company army revolted; the British called it the "Sepoy Mutiny" but South Asian historians know it as the First War of Independence. The Mughal emperor, Bahadur Shah II, served as the rallying point of the rebel soldiers and nobles, though he was an ineffectual leader. A proclamation issued in his name declared that the people of Hindustan, both Hindus and Muslims, were being ruined under the tyranny and oppression of the infidel and treacherous English, so that it was the duty of all wealthy people of India to stake their lives and property for the well being of the public. By the fall of 1857, the British army had reconquered Delhi, executed or exiled the Mughal royal family, and declared India integrated into the British Empire, transferring East India Company rights to the British crown.

Some Islamic leaders opposed the British and tried to restore Muslim rule militarily. Sayyid Ahmad "Shahid" (1786–1831) was a Sufi leader and soldier who declared South Asia to no longer be Dar al-Islam, a realm in which Muslims rule. He allied his movement with the family of Shah Waliullah and was known as *ghayr muqallad* (independent in legal and ritual rulings), having abandoned conformity with the Hanafi legal school. For this, the British misleadingly labeled his followers "Wahhabi"; in contrast, they call themselves "Ahl-i Hadith" (Followers of the Prophet's Example). Having organized his Sufi disciples into a militia, he emigrated to Afghanistan and from there waged a military struggle, which he called jihad, against the Sikh kingdom in the Punjab as the first step in the restoration of Muslim rule in South Asia. He was killed fighting against the Sikhs in 1831, along with his theologian lieutenant, Shah Isma'il. Independently, Hajji

Shari'atullah (1721–1840) organized a similar movement among peasants in Bengal, known as the Fara'idi (The Obligatory Duties) Movement. He declared Bengal to no longer be Dar al-Islam since it was ruled by the British through landlords who were increasingly Hindus since British land and taxation reforms in 1793. He urged his followers to reform their religious practices to conform more closely to the example of Muhammad, which he identified with the Arabian practices of Mecca, where he went on hajj pilgrimage and spent twenty years. Hajji Shari'atullah's son politicized the movement, attacking Hindu landlords and resisting British taxation demands while forbidding his followers from seeking redress in British adminis-tered Anglo-Muhammadan courts. Elsewhere, many Sufis and Islamic leaders par-ticipated in the 1857 rebellion against the British. The Sabiri-Chishti Sufi leader, Hajji Imdadullah, fought against British forces and then fled after orders for his arrest; he lived out the rest of his life in exile in Mecca from where he continued to guide disciples in South Asia, many of whom founded the Deoband Academy (see below).

In the twentieth century, sectarian labels developed to reflect the positions of these Sunni movements: reformers who retain an allegiance to Islamic law call themselves "Deobandi," and revivalists who reject traditional Islamic law call themselves "Ahl-i Hadith," while traditionalists who eschew reform and revival in favor of Sufi and folk practices call themselves "Barelwi." This final group is the least formally organized and represents the vast majority of South Asian Mus-lims into the present.

Other Islamic leaders did not oppose British colonization, especially after the War of 1857. Many "modernist" Islamic scholars joined the Aligarh movement and founded the Muhammadan Anglo-Oriental College (now Aligarh Muslim University) under the inspiration of scholar, journalist, and community leader, Sayyid Ahmad Khan (1817–1898). He strove to prove the loyalty of the Muslim educated classes to British rule, arguing that Muslims could, in good conscience, cooperate with Christians, politically and theologically, even as they competed with the accelerating critiques of Protestant missionaries (Lelyveld 1978). Through his Urdu journal, "The Refinement of Morals," he sought to reconcile rationalism, natural science, and Islamic theology while promoting the social liberation and education of Muslim women. Since he broke open the question of South Asian Muslim women's role in a modernizing society, many Western scholars have fol-lowed his example (Jeffery 1979; Papenek and Minault 1983). Sayyid Ahmad Khan also oversaw translations of British scientific literature into Urdu (Troll 1978). More conservative Islamic scholars founded the competing Deoband Academy as a way to preserve Islamic law and education as the custom of the "Muslim com-munity" rather than as the rule of the Mughal state (Metcalf 1982).

Political modernists like Jamal al-Din Afghani (1838–1897) and Muhammad Iqbal (1876–1938) criticized both the Aligarh movement's acceptance of British colonial domination and the Deoband movement's traditionalist "obscurantism."

They tried to agitate for cultural revival and political self-rule for Muslims in South Asia through the rhetoric of "nationalism" and "Pan-Islamism" (Keddi 1968). In Urdu, the epic poems of Altaf Hussayn Hali ("The Ebb and Flow of Islam" in 1879) and Iqbal ("Complaint and Answer" in 1909) popularized these sentiments more widely. Islamic modernists blamed "despotic" Mughal rule, Sufi mysticism, and "effeminate" Persian culture for the political weakness of South Asian Islam (Shackle and Mujeeb 1997).

With World War I, these sentiments became more sharply focused in a politically viable anticolonial movement. South Asian Muslim elites reacted negatively when the British Empire fought Ottoman Turkey (which allied with Germany) and imposed the humiliating treaty of Sevres in 1920. The "Khilafat Movement" in support of Turkey and in hopes of preserving the authority of the caliph there spread anti-British sentiment and led some Muslim leaders into Gandhi's "Non-Cooperation Movement" (Minault 1982). Muslim theologians organized a novel body, Jami'at-i 'Ulama'-yi Hind, "The Indian Congress of Islamic Scholars," that supported the political protest of the Khilafat Movement. New Urdu newspapers also spread anticolonial ideals. Students and faculty withdrew from Aligarh Muslim University in protest and founded a Muslim Nationalist University in Delhi, Jami'a Milliya Islamiya.

Islamic anticolonial activity was split between two groups: those advocating "Indian Nationalism" and those advocating "Muslim Nationalism." The first group felt Muslims should join with Hindus, Sikhs, and other South Asians to rid South Asia of British domination and create a "secular" and multi-religious India. They can be called "Islamic integrationists." These included Abdul Ghaffar Khan (known as Baccha Khan, 1890–1988), a Pashto-speaking educator in the Northwest Frontier Province who led the Khudai Khidmatgar movement, "The Servants of God," for nonviolent resistance (Easwaran 1999). His colleague, Abul Kalam Azad (known as Maulana Azad, 1888–1958), an Urdu-speaking theologian and journalist from Calcutta, acted as president of the Indian National Congress. Such leaders cooperated with Gandhi and Nehru in the activities of the Indian National Congress (Douglas 1988; Hasan 1992).

The second group felt that Muslims should form an exclusive community based on their own religious identity and communal ethics and that Muslims could not coexist in an independent nation with a Hindu majority. They can be called "Islamic exclusivists." This group included the leaders of the Muslim League, a political party organized in 1906 by upper-class and land-holding Muslims to seek concessions from the British for the Muslim community (Qureishi 1962; Robinson 1974). In reaction to the Indian National Congress, it was reorganized in 1936 by the brilliant Shi'i lawyer, Muhammad Ali Jinnah, in order to stand for the Provincial elections in 1937. In 1940 the Muslim League adopted the program that a constitutional government for Independent India was not possible, and demanded the contiguous Muslim-majority provinces be formed into "autonomous and sovereign" states.

INDEPENDENCE, COMMUNALISM, AND PARTITION

British colonial policies tended to force Muslims and Hindus into two separate and irreconcilable "communal" groups. British histories and ethnographies since the eighteenth century have portrayed these two groups as opposites in racial terms. In the wake of the rebellion in 1857, British policy suppressed the upper-class Muslim communities while promoting Hindus who embraced colonial education in the government bureaucracy. British policy recognized "Urdu" and "Hindi" as two distinct languages, each associated with an exclusive religious community, Muslims and Hindus respectively (Lelyveld 1993). Finally, the creation of a parliamentary system of representation for South Asians within the colonial administration raised the vexing question of "proportional representation" and quotas, further polarizing communal relations between Muslims and Hindus.

With these assumptions, the British colonial government experimented with policies of partition to organize colonial subjects by their communal religious identity. As the anticolonial movement gained momentum after World War I, the British used concerns over the threatened rights of "minority" communities to stall discussions of impending independence. The Nehru Report of 1928 recommended that, after the proposed independence of India, Muslims be granted 26 percent representation in parliament, whereas Muslim communalist parties advocated a 33 percent representative reservation. In reaction, the Muslim League proposed that Muslim-majority provinces become autonomous regions within a federal government of independent India, so that Muslims would not become a disempowered minority in a democracy dominated by a Hindu majority. As the Indian National Congress resisted this proposal, the Muslim league advocated the "two-nation" solution, in which British India would be partitioned and Muslim-majority provinces would form the separate state of Pakistan.

Despite opposition by the Indian National Congress and some Islamic leaders, the plan for partition became a political reality in 1947. The idea seemed simple in rhetoric, but a national border proved impossible to draw in advance. Partition uprooted millions of people as Sikhs and Hindus fled Muslim-majority areas of the Punjab and Sindh, while Muslims in Hindu-majority areas of Punjab, Uttar

Pradesh, and Bihar experienced a similar displacement; the same process happened between East and West Bengal. Communal riots erupted on both sides, resulting in murder, looting, and destruction of homes, the extent of which is still being documented (Pandey 1992). Partition did not solve the political complexities of South Asia's multi-religious population. Many Muslims refused or were unable to move to Pakistan, and Muslims are still the largest religious minority in independent India (estimated at 13 percent of the total population). Those who chose to remain in India include: Muslims loyal to the Indian National Congress's vision of a "secular" Indian democracy, those more rooted in their local community than in a modernist vision of Islamic nationalism, and those without the economic resources to move.

Pakistan began in 1947 as one nation with two noncontiguous territories. Its western territory included West Punjab, Sindh, Baluchistan, part of Kashmir, and the Afghan-dominated Northwest Frontier; its eastern territory included East Bengal. The population of East Pakistan developed a separatist political movement stressing the Bengali language and cultural distinctiveness over against Urdu-speaking Muslims who dominated the national administration. The military forces of the Pakistani state, controlled mainly by West Pakistan, put down a popular uprising in East Pakistan with great violence, leading to a civil war in 1972. The Indian military intervened, allowing East Pakistan to declare independence as Bangladesh.

Partition created major geopolitical controversies that have yet found no solution—the major example is Kashmir. The British colonial government ruled most of South Asia directly but ruled many regions indirectly through "princely states." The largest of these were Kashmir in the north (where a Hindu ruler governed a population that was 75 percent Muslim) and Hyderabad in the south (where a Muslim ruler governed a population in which Hindus were a wide majority). Both local rulers, the Dogra of Kashmir and the Nizam of Hyderabad, tried to negotiate for local autonomy after independence. However, the British gave all princes the ultimatum to choose between becoming a part of India or Pakistan. The ruler of Kashmir faced a Muslim leader, Shaykh Muhammad Abdullah (born 1905), who demanded democratic representation and an uprising by Muslim peasants. The ruler ultimately declared Kashmir to be part of India without a popular referendum for his majority-Muslim population. The Pakistani government saw this as a betrayal of the principle of partition, while the Indian government saw it as legal annexation of integral territory. War broke out, and military stalemate created a "line of control" (with Pakistan occupying the one-third of Kashmir and India occupying the two-thirds that includes the heavily populated valleys of Srinagar and Jammu). There have been three subsequent wars between India and Pakistan over control of Kashmir. The "line of control" exists up until the present, though both nations claim the entire territory. The UN has mandated a popular referendum about Indian annexation of the territory, but the

Indian government has never allowed a referendum. Since the 1980s, Kashmiri Muslims have increasingly risen up against Indian military occupation. The Indian government accuses Pakistan of sending agents across the line of control to organize the uprisings.

In contrast, the princely ruler of Hyderabad negotiated for independence until 1948, when the Indian army occupied the territory. Since then, Hyderabad became the capital city of the southern state of Andhra Pradesh. Many upper-class Muslims of Hyderabad had emigrated to Pakistan or the West (especially to Chicago). While there is still a large Muslim minority in Hyderabad, they no longer control local politics as they did during the days of the princely state. With the educated and economic elite Muslims choosing migration, those Muslims left in Hyderabad struggle with poverty and educational deprivation. This local drama in Hyderabad represents an extreme example of the social forces of community disintegration against which other regional Muslim communities in India also struggle.

RELIGIOUS COMMUNALISM
AND RADICALISM

Despite the violence of partition and the continual preparations for war with Pakistan, the state of India was able to build a multi-religious and multiethnic democratic state. Under the leadership of Jawaharlal Nehru (1889–1964) the ruling Indian National Congress party articulated a "secular" ideology where the state ideally supported the development of all religious communities. However, communalist Hindu forces advocated a Hindu India in which Muslims and other religious minorities would be excluded full citizenship.

A member of one such organization, the paramilitary RSS (Rashtriya Svayamsevak Sangh or "National Self-Service Society"), assassinated Gandhi in 1948, claiming that the nationalist leader capitulated to Muslim concerns. Though the RSS was outlawed, its leaders came to rule the state of Maharastra, giving rise to Hindu communal politics. The BJP (Bharata Janata Party) organized as a national political party combining Hindu communalist ideology (commonly called "Hindutva"), neoliberal capitalist economics, and opposition to the Indian National Congress. Such communalist forces steadily gained power in the 1980s and increasingly compromised the promise of democratic citizenship to all Indians regardless of religious community.

In their political drive to capture power in the national parliament, the BJP raised a controversy over the Babri Mosque, claiming that it was built (in the sixteenth century) over the site of a destroyed Hindu temple commemorating the birthplace of Rama at Ayodhya, in Uttar Pradesh. Calling for destruction of the mosque and rebuilding of the temple, the BJP led a successful campaign in national elections and came to power in Delhi. A coalition of Hindu communalist organizations demolished the Babri Mosque in 1993, sparking protests by Muslim citizens of India and leading to communalist riots in which Muslims were systematically targeted and killed. Militant action of Hindu communalist organizations and political support of them by a rising Hindu middle class is the major threat to religious minorities in India (foremost among them Muslims but increasingly including Christians, as discussed by Embree in this volume). In the state of Gujarat, the Godhra Massacre (in February and March, 2002) has sparked further anti-Muslim riots protected by local government collaboration.

Muslims in South Asia have also formed communalist organizations. The Jama'at-i Islami or "Islamic Party" was organized in 1940 by the journalist turned theologian, Mawlana Mawdudi (1903–1979). At first he rejected the idea of Pakistan, but later migrated there and set up the Jama'at as a radical political party aimed at forging Pakistan into an "Islamic State." The party has never succeeded in parliamentary elections but is a major voice of protest and formulator of "Islamist" ideology in Pakistan (Nasr 1996). The Jama'at has also spread internationally to Bangladesh, Britain, and North America. Along with al-Ikhwan al-Muslimun in Egypt and Syria, the Jama'at is the oldest and most institutionalized radical political association calling for Islamization of a postcolonial nation-state.

TRANSNATIONAL MOVEMENTS IN THE GLOBALIZATION AGE

Another communalist organization began locally in South Asia but has rapidly morphed into a transnational Islamic movement. The Tablighi Jama'at or "Missionary Party" is largely apolitical. It began as a missionary movement to properly "Islamize" Indian Muslims in rural areas south of Delhi, in reaction to Hindu missionary movements that viewed Indian Muslims as "lapsed Hindus" who should re-convert to Hinduism. Its initial leader was a Deobandi activist from a Sufi family, Maulana Muhammad Ilyas (1885–1944). The movement grew rapidly after Indian independence, fueled by Indian Muslims' uncertainty over their place in the new nation-state. The movement advocates religious revival, suspicion of modern education and intellectual reason, and abandoning participation in "secular" projects. It is now an international movement, claiming the largest membership of any Islamic organization globally (Masud 2000; Sikand 2002). Both the Jama'at-i Islami and Tablighi Jama'at have questioned the legitimacy of parliamentary democratic governments of Pakistan and Bangladesh, especially since the election of women as prime ministers, such as Benazir Bhutto in Pakistan and Khalida Zia in Bangladesh. Whether modernist or anti-modernist in intellectual orientation, both organizations reinforce patriarchal values with regard to women's social roles, even as they attract women activists as members.

British colonialism created new interregional connections and global flows of people and ideas. South Asians, both professional and working class (including Muslims, Hindus, and Sikhs), have become the largest ethnic minority in Britain itself (Lewis 1994). South Asian Muslims moved as laborers to South Africa, Burma, and the Caribbean (especially to Trinidad and Tobago, Guyana, and the Dutch colony of Suriname). More wealthy Isma'ilis constituted an interregional merchant class that has spread internationally and ethically engaged modernity through the Agha Khan's development projects. Sufi orders, too, have also spread internationally through diaspora communities. The Sabiri-Chishti order spread from Pakistan to Malaysia and the West, through the spiritual leadership of a Sufi master who was also an airplane pilot, Capt. Wahid Bakhsh; it has spread primarily through Pakistani and Indian Muslims living or traveling outside their home region but has also attracted some Western converts. In contrast is the Sufi movement of Inayat Khan, a Chishti spiritual guide and musician who moved from South Asia to Europe and then to North America; he forged the Sufi Order of the West, a global Sufi movement that emphasizes the universal nature of Islamic teachings and stresses their continuity with Christianity, Judaism, Buddhism, and Hinduism (Khan 2001). Because it does not require participants to formally convert to Islam, it has a wide following in the United States and Canada. It is based in New Lebanon, New York, and organizes popular Sufi Dances for World Peace programs.

Comparable in its syncretic potential is the Sufi community known as the Bawa Muhaiyadeen Peace Fellowship (based in Philadelphia, Pa.). Bawa Muhaiyadeen was a Sufi leader who migrated from Sri Lanka in the 1970s. He came from the Muslim minority of ethnic Tamil Sri Lankans, who were caught in the cross-fire of the civil war between Hindu Tamil separatists and the Buddhist Sinhalese majority. His spiritual teachings from the Qadiri Sufi tradition attracted many American followers, who did not at first associate them with Islam as a formal religious allegiance. Upon his death, Bawa Muhaiyadeen did not nominate a formal successor to spiritual leadership but instead delegated committees to oversee important aspects of community life, providing a fascinating example of South Asian Muslim adaptation to a Western environment that stresses individual volunteerism, democratic decentralization, and meritocracy.

The events of Sept. 11, 2001, have overshadowed these quiet and gradual attempts to build diasporic communities based on the teachings of South Asian

Muslims. Since then, the Taliban has become the most notorious Islamic movement to emerge in South Asia. The Taliban, meaning "Pious Students," is a local variation, indigenous to Afghanistan and Pakistan, of a global fundamentalist Sunni movement, loosely known as Wahhabis (after the movement which formed the national government of Saudi Arabia that inspires and funds local variations internationally). They emerged from the Afghan civil war to fill a vacuum of authority created by the Soviet-supported Communist take-over in 1978 and Mujahidin resistance supported by the United States and Pakistan through the 1980s. This covert operation during the cold war between the superpowers and their local allies led to political instability, dire poverty, and civic violence in Afghanistan and the Northwest Frontier Province of Pakistan. The Taliban advocated an extremist form of Sunni militancy. They rejected all modernist forms of government and also Islamic forms of social organization developed in medieval and early-modern times, such as Hanafi Islamic law, conventional Sunni theology, and respect for Sufi communities. Such a movement is more atavistic than traditionally religious. Their utopian goal was an Islamic "Amirate" based on a simplistic notion of recreating the original Islamic community of the prophet and his earliest followers. Their revolution was fueled by rhetoric that is virulently anti-Shi'ite, anti-female, anti-Christian, and anti-Western (including both Soviet and American forms of Western modernism). It appealed to the latent chauvinism of the Pashto (Pukhtun) ethnic group in the ethnic multiplicity of Afghanistan and Pakistan.

Because the Taliban movement's shock troops were made up of impoverished young Pashto men who found some institutional stability in Madrasas, Western journalists and political scientists have erroneously labeled the movement "Deobandi." While it is true that many Madrasas had been established by the Deobandi movement in Northern Pakistan and Afghanistan since the late nineteenth century, their curriculum had been emptied since the 1970s of traditionally Deobandi content; Deobandis adhere to moderate forms of Islamic law and theology coupled with reformist politics (Zaman 2002). The revolutionary anti-intellectualism of the Taliban is a significant departure from traditional Deobandi teachings and is more a response to violence and poverty than it is an outgrowth of South Asian Muslim tradition. Long before 1996, when the Taliban formed a national government in Afghanistan through military conquest and gave safe-haven to the al-Qaeda organization, Pakistani journalists and educators were warning of the threat of "Talibanization" of Pakistani youth as a reaction to the failures and false promises of the postcolonial Pakistani state. Though it took shape in the dire local conditions of civil war in Afghanistan, the Taliban ideology is capable of rapid exportation: Muslims in Indian-occupied Kashmir as well as the Central Asian states of Uzbekistan and Tajikistan face local variations of the Taliban, probably strengthened by refugees from the United States' war against the Taliban regime in 2002 and its continuing military activity in the region in the years following. When the fighting has spilled over into Pakistan, this has created a religious-political crisis for Muslims and non-Muslims alike.

BIBLIOGRAPHY

Ahmad, Aziz. 1964. *Studies in Islamic Culture in the Indian Environment.* Oxford: Oxford University Press.

al-Biruni. 1964. *Alberuni's India.* Edited and translated by Eduard Sachau. New Delhi: S. Chand Popular Edition.

Baljon, J. M. S. 1986. *Religion and Thought of Shah Wali Allah Dihlawi, 1703–1762.* Leiden: Brill.

Bayley, Susan. 1989. *Saints, Goddesses and Kings: Muslims and Christians in South India.* Delhi: South Asia Press.

Bayly, C. A. 1987. *Indian Society and the Making of the British Empire.* New York: Cambridge University Press.

Bulliet, Richard. 1994. *Islam: The View from the Edge.* New York: Columbia University Press.

Cole, Juan. 1988. *Roots of North Indian Shi'ism in Iran and Iraq: Religion and State in Awadh, 1722–1859.* Berkeley: University of California Press.

Dahnhardt, Thomas. 2002. *Change and Continuity in Indian Sufism.* Delhi: D. K. Printworld.

Douglas, Ian Henderson. 1988. *Abul Kalam Azad, an Intellectual and Religious Biography.* New York: Oxford University Press.

Easwaran, Eknath. 1999. *Nonviolent Soldier of Islam: Badshah Khan, a Man to Match His Mountains.* Tomales, Calif.: Nilgiri Press.

Eaton, Richard. 1993. *The Rise of Islam on the Bengal Frontier.* Berkeley: University of California Press.

———. 2000. "Temple Destruction and Indo-Muslim States." In *Beyond Hindu and Turk: Rethinking Religious Identities in Islamicate South Asia.* Eds. Bruce Lawrence and David Gilmartin. Gainsville: University of Florida Press.

Ernst, Carl. 1992. *Eternal Garden: Mysticism, History and Politics at a South Asian Sufi Center.* Albany: SUNY Press.

Ernst, Carl, and Bruce Lawrence. 2002. *Sufi Martyrs of Love: The Chishti Order in South Asia and Beyond.* New York: Palgrave Macmillan.

Friedmann, Yohanan. 1971. *Shaykh Ahmad Sirhindi: An Outline of His Thought and a Study of His Image in the Eyes of Posterity.* Montreal: McGill University, Institute of Islamic Studies.

Hasan, Mushirul. 1992. *Islam and Indian Nationalism: Reflections on Abul Kalam Azad.* New Delhi: Manohar Publications.

Ikram, Muhammad. 1964. *Muslim Civilization in India.* Ed. Ainslie T. Embree. New York: Columbia University Press.

Jeffery, Patricia. 1979. *Frogs in a Well: Indian Women in Purdah.* London: Zed Press.

Kassam, Tazim. 1992. *Songs of Wisdom and Circles of Dance: Hymns of the Satpanth Isma'ili Muslim saint, Pir Shams.* Albany: SUNY Press.

Keddi, Nikki. 1968. *Islamic Response to Imperialism: Jamal al-Din Afghani: Political and Religious Writings of Sayyid Jamal al-Din al-Afghani.* Berkeley: University of California Press.

Khan, Zia Inayat. 2001. *A Pearl in Wine: Essays on the Life, Music and Sufism of Hazrat Inayat Khan.* New Lebanon, Pa.: Omega Press, 267–321.

Kugle, Scott. 2000. "Haqiqat al-Fuqara: Poetic Biography of 'Madho Lal' Hussayn." In *Same Sex Love in India: Readings from Literature and History.* Eds. Ruth Vanita and Saleem Kidwai, 145–56. New York: St. Martin's Press.

———. 2001. "Framed, Blamed and Renamed: The Recasting of Islamic Jurisprudence in Colonial South Asia" *Modern Asian Studies* 35, no. 2: 257–313.

Lawrence, Bruce. 1978. *Notes From a Distant Flute: the Existent Literature of Pre-Mughal South Asia.* Tehran: Imperial Academy of Philosophy.

———. 1984. "Early Indo-Muslim Saints and Conversion." In *Islam in Asia. Volume I: South Asia.* Edited by Y. Friedmann. Boulder, Co.: Westview Press.

———. 1987. "The Sant Movement and North Indian Sufis." In *The Sants: Studies in a Devotional Tradition of India.* Edited by K. Schomer and W. H. McLeod, 359–376. Delhi: Motilal Banarsidass.

———, trans. 1992. *Morals for the Heart: Conversations of Shaykh Nizam al-Din Awliya Recorded by Amir Hasan Sijzi.* Mahwah, N.J.: Paulist Press.

———. 1999. "The Eastward Journey of Muslim Kingship: Islam in South and Southeast Asia." In *The Oxford History of Islam.* Edited by John Esposito, 395–432. New York: Oxford University Press.

Lelyveld, David. 1978. *Aligarh's First Generation: Muslim Solidarity in British India.* Princeton, N.J.: Princeton University Press.

———. 1993. "Colonial Knowledge and the Fate of Hindustani." *Journal of the Comparative Study of Society and History* 35, no. 4: 665–82.

Lewis, Philip. 1994. *Islamic Britain: Religion, Politics, and Identity among British Muslims.* London: I. B. Taurus.

Maclean, Derryl. 1989. *Religion and Society in Arab Sind.* Leiden: E. J. Brill.

Masud, Muhammad Khalid. 2000. *Travelers in Faith: Studies of the Tablighi Jama'at as: A Transnational Islamic Movement for Faith Renewal.* Leiden: E. J. Brill.

Metcalf, Barbara Daly. 1982. *Islamic Revival in British India: Deoband, 1860–1900.* Princeton, N. J.: Princeton University Press.

Minault, Gail. 1982. *The Khilafat Movement: Religious Symbolism and Political Mobilization in India.* New York: Columbia University Press.

Nanji, Azim. 1978. *The Nizari Isma'ili Tradition in the Indo-Pakistan Subcontinent.* Delmar, Calif.: Caravan Books.

Narayanan, Vasudha. 2000. "Religious Vocabulary and Regional Identity: A Study of the Tamil Cirappuranam." In *Beyond Hindu and Turk: Rethinking Religious Identities in Islamicate South Asia.* Edited by Bruce Lawrence and David Gilmartin. Gainsville: University of Florida Press.

Nasr, Seyyed Vali Reza. 1996. *Mawdudi and the Making of Islamic Revivalism.* New York: Oxford University Press.

Nizami, Khaliq Ahmad. 1989. *Akbar and Religion.* Delhi: Idarah-i-Adabiyat-i-Delli.

Pandey, Gyandendra. 1992. "In Defense of the Fragment: Writing about Hindu-Muslim Riots in India Today." *Representations* 37: 27–55.

Papanek, Hannah, and Gail Minault, eds. 1983. *Separate Worlds: Studies of Purdah in South Asia*. Delhi: South Asia Books.

Qamaruddin. 1985. *The Mahdawi Movement in India*. Delhi: Idarah-i Adabiyat-i Delhi.

Qureshi, Ishtiaq Husain. 1962. *The Muslim Community of the Indo-Pakistan Subcontinent*. The Hague: Mouton and Co.

Qureishi, Regula Burkhardt. 1995. *Sufi Mustic in India and Pakistan: Sound, Context and Meaning in Qawwali*. Chicago: University of Chicago Press.

Richards, John. 1993. *The Mughal Empire*. New York: Cambridge University Press.

Robinson, Francis. 1974. *Separatism Among Indian Muslims: The Politics of the United Provinces Muslims, 1860–1923*. Cambridge: Cambridge University Press.

Roy, Asim. 1983. *The Islamic Syncretistic Tradition in Bengal*. Princeton, N.J.: Princeton University Press.

———. 1996. *Islam in South Asia: A Regional Perspective*. Delhi: South Asian Publishers.

Schimmel, Annemarie. 1980. *Islam in the Indian Subcontinent*. Leiden: E. J. Brill.

Shackle, Chirstopher, and Javed Majeed. 1997. *Hali's Musaddas: The Flow and Ebb of Islam*. Delhi: Oxford University Press.

Sikand, Yoginder. 2002. *The Origins and Development of the Tablighi Jama'at (1920–2000): A Cross-country Comparative Study*. Hyderabad: Orient Longman.

Troll, Christian. 1978. *Sayyid Ahmad Khan: A Reinterpretation of Muslim Theology*. Karachi: Oxford University Press.

Wink, Andre. 2002. *Al-Hind: The Making of the Indo-Islamic World*. Leiden: Brill.

Zaman, Muhammad Qasim. 2002. *The Ulama in Contemporary Islam: Custodians of Change*. Princeton, N.J.: Princeton University Press.

CHAPTER 47

ISLAMIC SOCIETIES IN SOUTHEAST ASIA

MARK WOODWARD

SOUTHEAST Asia is home to a large variety of Islamic societies and cultures, including those in the world's largest Muslim country, Indonesia. A basic distinction can be drawn between the cultures of the Southeast Asian islands and the mainland. Malay-speaking Muslims numerically and culturally dominate much of insular Southeast Asia, including Indonesia, Brunei, Malaysia, and the southern Philippines. Quite different cultural traditions are found in the diverse Muslim minority communities of mainland Southeast Asia in Burma, Thailand, and Cambodia. Islam is virtually absent in Vietnam and Laos. In Indonesia nearly 90 percent of its population of over 200 million profess some form of Islam. The languages of Indonesia's largest ethnic communities, Malay and Javanese, are major Islamic literary languages in much the same way as Persian, Turkish, and Urdu are. While Islamic literatures exist in Burmese, Thai, and Khmer, they are largely derivative of Urdu, Arabic, and Malay sources.

Islam came to Southeast Asia in the thirteenth century. It was brought to the Malay world by Arab and South Asian Muslim traders who dominated the Indian Ocean trade during that period. Muslim states were established on both sides of the straits of Malacca and later spread southward to Java and as Far East as the southern Philippines. Largely owing to the power of coastal sultanates it rapidly became the dominant religion in the Malay-speaking world. Muslim communities in Vietnam and Cambodia and southern Thailand originated in similar ways but never displaced the political dominance of the Indianized and, in the case of Vietnam, Sinicized states of the region. Islam came to Burma from two additional sources in the precolonial period, from Bengal in the west and from Southern China. During the period of British rule large numbers of South Asian Muslims migrated to Rangoon, Mandalay, and other Burmese urban centers.

THE MALAY WORLD

The Muslim Malay world includes the indigenous Malay population of the peninsula and most of what is now Indonesia and the southernmost portions of the Philippines. Despite enormous diversity, all of these groups speak Malay-Polynesian languages and adhere to the Shafite school of Sunni Muslim law. Shi'a Muslims are virtually unknown in the region. For centuries the Malay Muslims were known collectively to Middle Eastern Muslims as "Jawi." In the Malay world there is a significant tension between Islam as practiced by traditional royal courts, which adapted many elements of Hindu and Buddhist culture and literature, and the more strictly orthoprax Islam of the commercial classes. Court-centered Islam, which for centuries influenced the development of Islamic cultures in rural areas, was also heavily influenced by the theosophical Sufism of Ibn al-Arabi and his school and is often not especially concerned with the ritual system mandated by Islamic law. The Islam of the commercial classes, while also strongly influenced by Sufi mystical thought, tends to be more concerned with legal questions. If the royal courts were the centers of imperial and popular Islam in the region, the more orthoprax tradition is centered on *pesantren* and *madrasah*, which are centers for the study of Islamic law and classical Arabic texts. Until the establishment of the Wahabi state in 1926 there were strong social, economic, and kinship ties between Islamic scholars in the Malay world and Mecca. These theological differences underlie a basic sociological and often political distinction between "orthodox" and "nominal" Muslims described by Clifford Geertz (1960). More recent scholarship has tended to focus on "how" rather than "if" the rural populations are Muslim (Woodward 1989; Bowen 1993).

The introduction to modernist and fundamentalist theologies in the early decades of the twentieth century resulted in further sociological divisions within the "orthodox" community. Reformist organizations of which the Indonesian Muhammadiyah movement is by far the largest were inspired largely by the writings of the Egyptian reformer Muhammad Abduh. Southeast Asian Islamic modernism rejects many traditional ritual practices associated with the pesantren tradition and is radically opposed to all forms of mystical thought and practice. Modernists also tend to emphasize the religious value of work and other secular activities. This dual agenda is linked by the theological claim that it was the decline of Islam as a "pure" faith that lead to domination of Muslim societies by European colonial powers and the related claim that restoring Islam to its pristine condition was a necessary condition for social, political, and economic progress. The introduction of Modernism sparked an intense and highly polemical discourse, much of which concerned the details of ritual performance, which continues to the present day. These debates have important sociological implications. The divisions are often so deep that traditionalists and modernists will not pray together. For many years they were endogamous communities. While these tensions have diminished in recent years, questions concerning ritual are still debated and hinder the ability of modernist and traditionalist organizations to work cooperatively even when they share a common social, economic, or political agenda.

Modernism is primarily an urban phenomenon, appealing primarily to middle-class merchants, artisans, and professionals. It has made little progress in rural areas that continue to cling to some combination of traditional orthodoxy and palace Islam. During the colonial period Modernism made important contributions to the development of education and social services including clinics, hospitals, and women's and youth organizations. Traditionalists regard these institutions as *haram* (forbidden) because of their resemblance to those of the colonial state. In the postcolonial period traditionalists have, however, developed parallel institutions.

ISLAM AND POLITICS IN THE MALAY WORLD

The role of Islam in the political systems of the majority Muslim nations of the region—Indonesia, Malaysia, and Brunei—differ fundamentally. Malaysia, for instance, is officially an Islamic state, although little more than half of its citizens are Muslims. Political parties compete to appear more Islamic than the others. The United Malay Organization (UMNO), which has long been the ruling party, embarked on the self-conscious program of Islamizing the state and society in 1981. Malaysian Islamic Party (PAS), which governs the state of Kelantan, advocates an even stronger Islamist program including the institutions of corporal and capital punishment advocated by classical Islamic legal texts.

Despite the fact it is the world's most populous Islamic nation, Indonesia defines itself as being neither a religious nor a secular state but rather as one guided by the state ideology Panca Sila (The Five Principles). These principles include: belief in the one true God, a just and civilized humanity, national unity, democracy based on consensus of the people, and wise leadership and social justices for all Indonesian people. Islamic parties, several of which advocated the creation of an Islamic state, played significant roles in Indonesian politics until 1973 when political parties based on religion were outlawed. The largest Muslim organizations, the modernist Muhammadiyah and the traditionalist Nahdlatul Ulama, now define themselves as nonpolitical social and religious organizations but continue to have substantial political influence.

Brunei is by far the smallest of the Muslim states of Southeast Asia. It is, however, the wealthiest in terms of per capita income because of enormous oil reserves. It is officially defined as a Malay Islamic Monarchy. Power is located with the sultan and members of his immediate family. The current sultan is known as a pragmatist and has sought to limit the influence of Muslim scholars and fundamentalists.

Throughout the region *ziarah*, the visitation of graves, is a significant element of Islamic practice, except among modernists who denounce the practice as unbelief. There are thousands of such shrines spread throughout Indonesia and Malaysia, most of which are the tombs of either Islamic scholars, Sufi saints, or monarchs, who are often regarded as saints. Perhaps the most impressive of these is Imo Giri, the cemetery of the Javanese Mataram dynasty located near the modern city of Yogyakarta.

Muslim Minorities

With the exception of Vietnam, all of the other nations of Southeast Asia have significant Muslim minorities. There is, however, considerable variation in the social and economic status of Muslim minority populations. A basic distinction exists between immigrant and native Muslim communities, i.e., between those who define themselves in terms of ethnic categories indigenous to the region and those of Arab, Persian, and South Asian origin. The largest communities of native Muslims are found in the Southern Philippines and Southern Thailand.

While Muslims make up less than 10 percent of the Philippine population, they are concentrated in the Sulu archipelago and the southern island of Mindanao. The great majority are farmers or fishermen. Philippine Muslims are culturally and linguistically related to those of eastern Indonesia and the Indonesian/Malaysian island of Kalimantan (Borneo). They fiercely resisted both Spanish and American colonialism and have never been fully integrated into the modern Philippine state. The conquest of these territories was not completed until 1914. The modern state has continued the anti-Islamic policies of Spanish and American colonialists and encouraged Christian immigration to Muslim majority areas. The result has been continued armed struggle between the army and the Moro National Liberation front.

Muslims make up approximately 10 percent of the population of Thailand and are of diverse ethnic origin. Most of the Muslim population of the southern provinces reside in Malay, although there are significant Muslims of Thai origin. Most are farmers and fishermen. Much of this area was not part of the Thai state until the mid-nineteenth century. There are still periodic outbreaks of resistance to Thai rule. In the vicinity of Bangkok there are diverse Muslim communities of Malay, Thai, Persian, and Cham (Cambodian) origin. In the northern area there is a substantial community of Chinese Muslims originating in Yunan. In general the Thai Muslim community is not well organized and faces continuous pressure to assimilate Thai cultural norms and Theravada Buddhism.

Prior to the Khmer Rouge persecutions, there were approximately 500,000 Cambodian-origin Muslims. Most are the descendants of Muslim refugees from the kingdom of Champa which was destroyed by the Vietnamese in the fifteenth century. Many retain distinct Cham ethnic and linguistic identities, while others speak only Khmer and have assimilated many aspects of Khmer culture. In the precolonial period and again after the reestablishment of independence in 1953 members of the Muslim elite played significant military, political, and economic roles in the Cambodian state. Others were farmers, merchants, and petty traders. Relationships between Muslims and the Buddhist majority were usually harmonious. When the Khmer Rouge came to power in 1975 the Muslim community was decimated. Mosques were destroyed and religious books burned. While many fled to Malaysia untold thousands suffered persecution reminiscent of that inflicted on Jews in Nazi Germany. Many were forced to eat pork, drink blood, and perform other acts prohibited by Muslim law before being brutally executed. Others died of disease or starvation attempting to flee. The community of religious scholars was virtually destroyed. With the fall of the Khmer Rouge many members of the community have returned. Some mosques have been rebuilt, but it will take generations for the community to return to its former status. Other Khmer Muslims were resettled in the United States. There are now active communities in California and Washington state.

The Muslim community in Burma makes up approximately 4 percent of a total population of over forty million. It is, however, among the most complex and diverse Muslim communities, including indigenous Burmese Muslims, many of who played significant roles in government and politics in the precolonial period. There are numerous immigrant communities from Yunan in southern China and all parts of South Asia, Persia, and Arabia. These communities can be found in most urban areas. Most Burmese Muslims are engaged in trade or commerce. In the southern state of Arakan there are large Muslim peasant communities called Rohinga. They have faced repeated and sustained persecution since the eighteenth century. In other regions relationships between Muslims and the Buddhist majority have been generally harmonious. Muslims often dominate sectors of the economy including the slaughter of cattle and goats and pest control, which Buddhists shun for religious reasons. The xenophobic policies of Burmese governments since 1963 have caused serious problems for the Muslim community. The citizenship act put in place in the early 1980s denied Burmese nationality to those who could not establish an unbroken history of family residency dating to 1826, the time of the first Anglo-Burmese war. This left many of Burma's Muslims as stateless persons. Beginning in 1989 the self-designated "State Law and Order Restoration Committee," which crushed the pro-democracy movement, has singled out Muslims for persecution. In the south many fled to Bangladesh. Many mosques have been destroyed or defiled with pig blood. Most of the world, including supporters of the democracy movement, has remained silent about these gross human rights abuses. Burmese Muslims continue to live in great peril.

ISLAM AND ETHNICITY IN SOUTHEAST ASIA

Religion plays a central role in the definition of ethnic and national identities throughout Southeast Asia. In Malaysia, Islam is central to Malay ethnic identity. There is considerable discrimination against non-Muslim Chinese and South Asian Hindu communities. In Indonesia, Islam as a religion transcends ethnic distinctions, binding culturally diverse Muslim communities together. There is considerable tension in Indonesia between the Muslim community and Christians, particularly Christians of Chinese origin who dominate the commercial sector of the economy. Conversion to Islam is often mentioned as the solution to the "Chinese problem." In mainland Southeast Asia, Buddhists lump indigenous and immigrant communities together, defining all of them as simply "Muslim." Muslims reject this equation of Islam and ethnicity and are themselves separated among many distinct ethnic communities that in many cases have their own mosques.

BIBLIOGRAPHY

Bowen, John R. 1993. *Muslims Through Discourse, Religion and Ritual in Gayo Society.* Princeton, N.J.: Princeton University Press.

Geertz, Clifford. 1960. *The Religion of Java.* Glencoe, Ill.: Free Press.

Ketani, Muhammad. 1986. *Muslim Minorities in the World Today.* London: Mansell Publishing.

Woodward, Mark R. 1989. *Islam in Java: Normative Piety and Mysticism in the Sultanate of Yogyakarta.* Tucson: University of Arizona Press.

CHAPTER 48

CHINESE ISLAMIC COMMUNITIES

DRU C. GLADNEY

THE nearly twenty million Muslims of China constitute a diverse community that is both multi-ethnic and, within Islam, multireligious. Indeed, it is arguable whether they should be described as a "community" at all, since they rarely cohere corporately and almost never act in unison (Gladney 1996: 1–23). There are ten official Muslim nationalities of China, including the people known as the "Hui"— the "Muslim Chinese" proper. The other nine Muslim nationalities do not speak Chinese as their native language and are derived more from Central Asian than Chinese origins. Even the Hui are difficult to describe as a unified Islamic community, except that they have been identified by the government as a single nationality.

The Hui, the most numerous of the ten Muslim nationalities in China, are spread across the length and breadth of the country. But the Hui often share nothing in common with each other except Islam, or the memory of it as handed down to them by their ancestors. The other Muslim peoples in China maintain linguistic, territorial, and historical affinities that led to their special nationality identification in the 1950s by the early Communists, influenced by Soviet Stalinist nationality policies. While it also might be argued that most of the other Muslim minorities are on the borders of China proper and are historically and culturally more attuned to the regions and peoples outside of China, the Hui are unique in that they inhabit every city, town, and 97 percent of all counties in China. They boast a thirteen-hundred-year internal history within China. Perhaps because the non-Hui Muslim minorities are concentrated in more politically sensitive and remote border areas, there has been less access to outsiders and fewer important publications in general. Nevertheless, while this chapter will focus primarily on Islam among Muslims classified by the state as Hui, conclusions reached will have wider implications for all the Muslim communities in China.

The reasonably accurate 2000 census reported that there are a total of 20.3 million members of the ten mainly Muslim nationalities. Each of the state-recognized Muslim nationalities include: Hui (9,816,805); Uyghur (8,399,393); Kazak (1,250,458); Dongxiang (513,805); Kyrgyz (160,823); Salar (104,503); Tadjik (41,028); Uzbek (14,502); Bonan (16,505); and Tatar (4,890). The Hui speak primarily Chinese languages; Turkic language speakers include the Uyghur, Kazak, Kyrgyz, Uzbek, and Tatar; combined Turkic-Mongolian speakers include the Dongxiang, Salar, and Bonan, concentrated in Gansu's mountainous Hexi corridor; and the Tadjik speak a variety of Indo-Persian dialects. Religion is not a stipulated category on the Chinese census, similar to the U.S. census, so this figure only reveals how many individuals are identified by the state as belonging to nationalities whose majority identify as Islamic. The figures therefore include some members of these nationalities who may not actually believe in or practice the Islamic religion (such as a Uyghur Communist party member), as well as excluding Han and other minority nationalities who might believe in Islam (such as a Thai Muslim living in Yunnan, who might be categorized either as Hui or as Thai, or a Tibetan Muslim who would generally be categorized as a Hui or Tibetan).

The debate over Muslim population figures in China is quite controversial. Some members of Muslim nationalities, especially the Uyghur, have claimed that their numbers have long been under-reported in the Chinese census in order to minimize their demographic strength in certain regions. This reflects and supports the forty-year-old debate over a pre-Communist estimate of "50 million" Muslims in China that is still widely repeated and debated in the international Muslim press. This debate continues to influence Muslim perceptions of Islam in China, despite the fact that independent non-Chinese evaluations of Chinese census-taking have been extremely positive in general. It is interesting to note, however, that state figures do reveal a substantial increase of 1.2 million Muslim nationality members between the two most reliable censuses of 1982 and 1990, indicating a 13 percent increase, surpassing the general Han population increase of 10 percent. Furthermore, even the categories of "religion" and "nationality" are especially problematic for Muslims and other minorities in China, as they are derived from Japanese and Soviet policies and ill-suited for China's heterogeneous make up.

The vast majority of Hui are to some extent linked together by the fact that they exclusively practice Sunni Islam, belonging to the Hanafi School of jurisprudence, but they are also divided internally among a multitude of traditionalist, Sufi, and reformist Islamic factions. While Raphael Israeli posits that there is also Shi'ism among Hui Muslims in China, there is clearly no institutionalized expression of this branch of Islam and only traces of influences may be detected among the Hui due to early Persian migration and Islamic heritage. Although there are no official figures, one northwestern Hui scholar estimates that over half of China's Hui Muslims practice what became known as "Gedimu" traditionalist Islam, meaning that they do not belong to any Islamic organization or order beyond their local mosque community; one quarter identify themselves with the "Yihewani" (Chinese for the Ikhwan, Muslim Brotherhood, a Wahabi-inspired movement which entered China at the turn of the nineteenth century); and the last quarter is divided into numerous Sufi brotherhoods, including the Naqsh-bandiyya, Qadariyya, and Kubrawiyya. In the past, the state has tended to support the Yihewani Ikhwan in China as it has been the most "modernist" and scrip-turally reformist, promoting education, accommodation to the government, and nonpolitical spiritual activities. By contrast, particularly during the late 1950s and Cultural Revolution period, the state has tended to suppress all Sufi and tradi-tionalist Hui Muslim associations that it regarded as "feudal" and too well or-ganized or perhaps threatening to local state authority. Joseph Fletcher has argued that these communities entered China on three "tides" of Islamic influence that washed across China as Islam expanded into Asia, and China either opened itself up or sealed itself off to outside cultural influence (for political or economic reasons)(Fletcher and Manz 1995). As Chen Dasheng has so beautifully displayed, the early archaeological evidence of substantial Islamic communities along the southeast coast and in inland capital cities such as Xi'an, Luoyang, and Beijing, based on Muslim tombs and epigrapha dating from the ninth century, suggests that Islam had an early and widespread influence along China's important mar-itime and overland trade routes (Chen 1984). Thus, the rise and fall of the Silk Road characterized the increasing and decreasing influence of China's Muslim communities and their relative isolation from the Chinese mainstream. Recently, I have proposed a "fourth tide" of Muslim activism in China due to increasing contacts with the Middle East, globalization, and China's growing reliance on Muslim nation trade for oil imports and military or consumer exports. This has produced not only Islamic revivalism but Muslim separatism (especially among the Uyghur) and increasing Han-Muslim conflicts particularly in the border regions of Xinjiang and Yunnan, as well as in the Gansu, Ningxia, and Qinghai frontiers where Muslims are concentrated. It has also produced a more thorough permeation of Chinese society by Muslim traders, small urban communities, res-taurants, and Islamic cultural traditions. Few Chinese schoolchildren today grow up without learning a Uyghur dance or two, and memorizing the fifty-five mi-nority nationality names and homelands, including the ten Muslim nationalities.

Jonathan Lipman once distinguished the Muslim communities in China as "patchwork" and "network," with the earlier traditionalist Islamic groups living in rather isolated patchworked villages and towns, quite distinct from the broader Han Chinese society, and more importantly, from other Muslim communities (Lipman 1997). Network societies characterized mainly Sufi groups that proliferated in the sixteenth to eighteenth centuries and linked groups across China to their all-powerful shaykhs and ritual centers. Today, globalization and freedom of movement within the country have linked China's Muslims even more closely to each other, as well as to the wider Muslim world community. The Salman Rushdie case, the Iran-Iraq war, the Gulf War, and the more recent Pakistan-India nuclear rivalry have put China's Muslims into the national and even international debate more than ever before.

If Islam has had such a long history among the people now identified as Hui in China proper, and continues to be so widespread and multi-varied in its expression, one must ask why it has been so absent from both the scholarly literature on Islam and Muslim societies in general, as well as ignored by the bulk of traditional China scholarship. The answer may be found in what Lila Abu-Lughod termed "zones of theory" in the general Western scholarship of Islam, in which studies of the Middle Eastern "core" have been privileged over Islam on the so-called periphery (Abu-Lughod 1989). So, too, Muslims in China have been relegated to the distant frontiers of both Sinological and Islamic scholarship, rarely receiving much academic attention precisely because they were by definition marginalized. Ironically, Muslims in China were either regarded as so "Islamic" that they were indistinguishable from other Muslims and therefore not worthy of study (except as potential rebels to a non-Muslim regime), or so "assimilated" (the term employed was "Sinicized") that they were virtually indistinguishable from the Han Chinese, and thus not worth studying. The idea that the Muslims in China were an isolated religious enclave, stigmatized by the broader Chinese population to the extent that they were pushed to either rebellion or assimilation led Protestant missionaries in China to regard them as a potential pool of willing converts to Christianity, giving rise to a series of missionary publications by Marshall Broomhall, G. Findlay Andrew, Mark Botham, Isaac Mason, Claude L. Pickens, Jr., F.W. Martin Taylor, W. A. Saunders, and others. Additional works in the pre-PRC era by Isaac Mason, Rudolf Löwenthal, and Owen Lattimore, to name but a few, were less interested in Islam per se, than in the sociological data on Muslims in China and in the adventures of the "Great Game" politics on China's northwestern frontiers. Interestingly, Muslims in China were subjected to two very different kinds of peripheralization, Islamic and Sinological, with the result that they were generally of interest only as pools of potential converts or rebels. The sociological predilection toward center-periphery typology wreaked havoc on outside understanding of Islamic communities in China. In addition, Chinese scholarship, which also tends to privilege the so-called "center" of either Confucian propriety (ignoring non-Chinese traditions) or Communist censorship (denying social activities that might oppose the Party), also limited understanding of China's Muslim communities.

Studies of Chinese Islamic communities between 1949 and the early 1980s have been primarily confined to archival research abroad and in Taiwan due to restricted access to the China Mainland. The best historical work on Muslims in China during this period has been carried out by Françoise Aubin, Joseph Fletcher, Andrew Forbes, Donald Leslie, and Jonathan Lipman. Insightful field-work on Muslims in Taiwan by Barbara Pillsbury gave Western scholars a further glimpse into their ethnic and cultural complexity. Again, few of these works dealt with Islam per se, concerning themselves primarily with questions of ethnicity, history, politics, and cultural practice. Raphael Israeli's attempts at examining the historical context of Islam in China were hampered by an uncritical bias toward Islamic "rebelliousness," arguing that if Muslims in China did not succeed at secession, then they must have completely assimilated (Israeli 1994).

Chinese scholarship on Muslim communities in China has been so diffuse and prolific in recent years that it is impossible to briefly and adequately summarize. In the late 1950s, a profusion of Marxist-oriented studies led by Bai Shouyi and state-sponsored studies sought to explain the rise of the Hui national minority and other Muslim ethnic groups in terms of class-based theories of nationalism and religion. Islam in most of these studies was seen to have had a negative but galvanizing influence on the construction of Muslim identity and was thus never seriously examined. More recently, historical and contemporary studies have attempted to address Islam more positively, and a profusion of publications have provided a wealth of information, though still from a Marxist perspective. Of these, a few Muslim scholars from China, such as Ma Tong, Ma Shouqian, and Yang Huaizhong have provided the richest information regarding the wide variety of Islamic movements, Sufi orders, and Muslim religious practices among the Hui. A historical novel, *The History of the Mind* by the Hui Muslim writer Zhang Chengzhi, published in 1990, depicted in extraordinary detail intra-Sufi factionalism among the Jahriyya Naqshbandi Sufi communities in the arid northwestern regions of Ningxia and Gansu. This was the first internal glimpse of the complexity of Islamic community life offered to outside readers (albeit, so far only Chinese readers). Interestingly enough, the novel was extremely popular in China, Taiwan, and Japan, indicating a rising interest in the internal dynamics of Muslim communal life in China.

In addition, two state-sponsored serials published by the China Islamic Society, *China's Muslims* and *Arab World*, both of which started in the late 1950s and were interrupted by the Cultural Revolution, have reappeared and are becoming increasingly independent in their coverage of Islam in China and abroad. On a more academic level, all state-sponsored encyclopedias and "dictionaries" are now employing trained Hui authors and including nationality articles that are more sympathetic to Muslim and ethnic views. A new journal, *Hui Nationality Research*, sponsored by the Ningxia Academy of Social Sciences under the editorship of Mohammed Usiar Yang Huaizhong, also offers a much more reliable source of scholarly information on Islamic communities in China.

Since the early 1980s, Western scholars have enjoyed increased access to travel in China and research on Muslims in China, leading to my own book-length study and a UCLA dissertation by Pang Keng-fong on a Hui Muslim village in Hainan Island, as well as a recent Harvard dissertation on the Xi'an Muslim community by Maris Gillette focusing on their interesting food culture. Most of these studies have dealt less directly with Islam per se among China's Muslims, than the sociological and historical nature of Islam and the Muslim communities and individuals under consideration. One limitation in this regard is that most Western scholars have approached Islam in China with training primarily in Sinology, and few possess the linguistic (Arabic, Persian, and Turkish) and theological training in Islamic studies required for in-depth access into the "inner" nature of Chinese Islamic communities. For the Turkic speakers, it is even more demanding in that Turkic and its many dialects (Uyghur, Kyrgyz, Kazak) are critical for access to the Muslim communities. For example, an extensive study of the important historical and mystical connections between Daoism and Sufism that pervades much of Muslim Chinese communal life would reveal much of the history of ideas and the interrelations between the two traditions but would require thorough training in Islamic and Chinese religious studies, as well as the necessary languages for each field. While important questions of demographics, distribution, public policy, and the stickier issues of national identification and ethnic conflict will continue to characterize studies of Islam and its adherents in China, it is hoped that further training and access will allow more in-depth research into China's unique contribution to Islamic thought, ideology, and practice, and perhaps Islam's transformation of and centrality to the Chinese world as well. Now that Muslim communities in China have begun to capture the interest of Chinese and outside scholars, there is the potential for them to become a field of study of their own and perhaps challenge long-held assumptions about the nature of Chinese society itself, or even the wisdom of exiling any Islamic community to the periphery.

BIBLIOGRAPHY

Abu-Lughod, Lila. 1989. "Zones of Theory in the Anthropology of the Arab World." *Annual Review of Anthropology* 18: 267–306.

Broomhall, Marshall. 1910. *Islam in China: A Neglected Problem*. New York: Paragon Books.

Chen, Dasheng, ed. 1984. *Islamic Inscriptions in Quanzhou*. Trans. Chen Enming. Yinchuan: Ningxia Peoples Publishing Society and Quanzhou: Fujian People's Publishing Society.

Forbes, Andrew D. W. 1986. *Warlords and Muslims in Chinese Central Asia*. Cambridge: Cambridge University Press.

Gillette, Maris. 1997. *Making Hui Community: Food and Society among China's Muslims.* Ph.D. diss., Harvard University.

Gladney, Dru C. [1991] 1996. *Muslim Chinese: Ethnic Nationalism in the People's Republic.* Cambridge: Harvard University Press.

Fletcher, Joseph, and Beatrice Forbes Manz, eds. 1995. *Studies on Chinese and Islamic Inner Asia.* Hampshire, England: Varorium Press.

Israeli, Raphael. 1994. *Islam in China: A Critical Bibliography.* With assistance of Lyn Gorman. Westport, Conn.: Greenwood Press.

———. 1978. *Muslims in China.* London: Curzon and Humanities Press.

Leslie, Donald Daniel. 1986. *Islam in Traditional China: A Short History to 1800.* Canberra, Australia: CCAE.

Lipman, Jonathan N. 1997. *Familiar Strangers.* Seattle: University of Washington Press.

Pang, Keng-Fong. 1992. *The Dynamics of Gender, Ethnicity, and State Among Austronesian-speaking Muslims of Hui-Utat of Hainan Island.* Ph.D. diss., University of California, Los Angeles.

Pillsbury, Barbara. 1973. *Cohesion and Cleavage in a Chinese Muslim Minority.* Ph.D. diss., Columbia University, New York.

Rudleson, Justin. 1997. *Bones in the Sand.* Durham, N.C.: Duke University Press.

Zhang, Chengzhi. [1990] 1997. *A History of the Mind (Xin Ling Shi).* Taipei: Fengyunshi Publishing.

CHAPTER 49

AMERICAN ISLAMIC COMMUNITIES

JANE I. SMITH

MUSLIMS who live in regions such as Europe and the United States that are outside the sphere of dominant Islamic culture face a steady array of choices. Some Muslims decide that their primary goal is the full public and private practice of Islam. Others make cultural compromises: they do not pray, fast during Ramadan, pay the alms-tax, or attend the mosque on a regular basis, although they consider themselves Muslim. Some families insist that their children socialize according to Islamic expectations and hope especially that their daughters choose to dress and comport themselves conservatively. Others fear that too much strictness will drive their young people away from Islam and therefore allow them to share fully in the social life of other youth. While race and ethnicity are not matters of choice, an individual may decide whether such factors are or are not a primary focus and determinant of identity.

Underlying the lifestyle decisions of many American Muslims is what is often posed as a fundamental choice between being first an American or first a Muslim. Earlier generations of Muslim immigrants often sought acculturation and tried to blend into American society, playing down distinguishing elements of religion and culture. Some of those who arrived more recently, on the other hand, have struggled to maintain their Islamic identities by distancing themselves as much as possible from the common culture and attempting to adhere to the traditional norms of their own heritage. Now Muslims appear to be moving into another stage of identity in which these kinds of either/or decisions are being resolved in new and creative ways. The result may well be that a truly American Islam is in the process of emerging.

Muslims who currently make their home in the United States represent a great number of movements and identities—immigrant and indigenous, Sunni and Shi'i, conservative and liberal, orthodox and heterodox. Numbers are difficult to determine with exactness, in part because U.S. census figures do not include religious affiliation, and in part because some belong to movements that claim for themselves Islamic identity but are not recognized as part of Islam by other groups. The issue of who is and is not Muslim, and by whose determination, is an important part of the current conversation within the Islamic community. Over the last three decades numbers of Muslims in the United States have grown from fewer than half a million to an estimated six million. American Muslims can be clustered into three general groups, although this is not to suggest that they necessarily live or operate discretely: Muslims who are recent immigrants or children of immigrant families, including students; African American Muslims, both Sunni and sectarian; and other Americans who have converted to Islam.

IMMIGRANT ISLAM

The first of a number of identifiable waves of Muslim immigrations came from what is now Syria and Lebanon in the Middle East during the last part of the nineteenth century. For the most part they were young men coming West looking to make their fortune and then return home. Many of them stayed, however, finding jobs as laborers, farm workers, peddlers, and petty merchants. They settled in the East, moved across the Middle West, and made their way as far as the Pacific coast. Other waves of immigration occurred with the break-up of the Ottoman Empire after World War I, during the 1930s and 1940s, and after major upheavals such as the partition of India in 1948, the 1967 war in Israel/Palestine, the Iranian Revolution in 1979, and various uprisings in Asia and Africa. Among the many factors contributing to these waves, in addition to U.S. immigration policies, have been economics, political unrest, and the desire for advanced technical education. In the last decades of the twentieth century the largest numbers of Muslim immigrants have been from Southeast Asia, although Muslims in America now represent all Islamic nations of the world. While in the earlier part of the century Muslim immigrants generally were low on the education and economic scales, today they often represent some of the best-educated and most professionally successful Americans.

The interaction among members of immigrant Muslim communities in

America has fluctuated. In earlier decades they were forced to come together for worship and even for social occasions because their numbers were relatively small. As more immigrants arrived in various parts of the country, national and ethnic groups were able to meet and worship separately as Arabs, or Pakistanis, or Turks, or Somalis. These associations continue, although with the rise in consciousness of being Muslim in the American context more immigrant Muslims of differing nationalities are living in proximity and worshiping together. Some areas of the United States, such as greater Detroit and Southern California, have significant numbers of both Sunni and Shi'i Muslims living in the same area and cooperating on common causes. Shi'ites, who account for about one-fifth of the American Muslim community, observe some rites and holidays distinct from Sunnis and usually worship separately. Generally they continue to look to Iran, Iraq, or Lebanon for religious leadership.

AFRICAN AMERICAN ISLAM

In the early decades of the twentieth century, several black nationalist movements began to claim Islamic roots and identity. Typical of these was Noble Drew Ali's Moorish American Science Temple, established in New Jersey in 1913. Ali preached that Americans of African descent should discard the identities forced on them by whites and understand that their true heritage is Asiatic, or Moorish. The Nation of Islam (NOI) became the most prominent African American freedom movement to identify with Islam, beginning in the 1930s with the teaching of W. D. Fard in Detroit that American blacks are members of the lost, and now found, ancient tribe of Shabazz. Fard's chief minister was to become the Honorable Elijah Muhammad, later to claim the title Messenger of Allah. In 1932 Elijah Muhammad moved the main headquarters for the Nation of Islam to Chicago, and temples soon appeared in many of the major eastern cities. He combined economics and ethics into a structure in which NOI members were required to be personally abstemious and professionally industrious. Many of the doctrines of the NOI as developed by Elijah Muhammad are irreconcilable with the tradition of Islam. Sunni Muslims today actively dissociate themselves from the current Nation under the leadership of Louis Farrakhan for a number of reasons, including his continuing recognition of the prophethood of Elijah Muhammad, considered heretical, and his espousal of racial separation, which is antithetical to the Islamic affirmation that all persons and all races are equal before God. It was primarily his understanding of the brotherhood of all Muslims acquired while on pilgrimage that motivated NOI minister Malcolm X to leave the Nation of Islam and begin the Organization of Afro-American Unity. An unidentified assailant assassinated Malcolm X in 1965.

Meanwhile the organization was continuing to grow, and by the middle of the 1970s it claimed a million members. When Elijah Muhammad died in 1975, his son Wallace succeeded him. With that new leadership came momentous changes within the movement as the political millenarianism of the earlier Nation gave way to a visible move toward orthodox Islam. A highly educated Muslim, Wallace began to rethink publicly the ideology that had earlier characterized the Nation. Central to his preaching has been the rebuttal of the doctrine of black superiority. Wallace focused on Islam as a spiritual force rather than a political tool, playing down the nationalism that in different ways had characterized the preaching of both his father and Malcolm. He changed his name to Warith Deen Mohammed, and the name of his followers changed several times. They are now identified as members of the American Muslim Society, or simply as Sunni Muslims.

In the course of separation from the earlier doctrines of the Nation of Islam and bringing his followers into Muslim orthodoxy, Imam Warith Deen has emerged as a significant, recognized, and respected leader of American Islam, one whose vision highly influences both Muslim and non-Muslim American blacks. Several other African American groups also identify themselves as Sunni, such as the Hanafis who have attracted several prominent black athletes. A number of other movements have grown up espousing heterodox beliefs and practices, again challenging the character of what can be called genuine Islam. African Americans constitute some 40 percent of the American Muslim community.

CONVERTS TO ISLAM

The third major grouping of American Muslims, far smaller in number than the immigrants or African Americans, is made up of others who have decided to adopt Islam as a faith and an identity. Many of them prefer the designation "revert" to convert, indicating that they are coming back to what is their natural and innate faith. They are composed of persons affiliated with Sufi movements, of those (mainly but not exclusively female) who change their faith on marriage, of some who find the straightforwardness of Islamic faith and practice reasonable and persuasive, and of growing numbers of Hispanics and Native Americans. The *da'wa*, or Islamic missionary movement, is strong in America, and Muslims are active in making conversions in prisons, in the academic world, and in various minority communities.

MOSQUES AND ISLAMIC ORGANIZATIONS

Islamic identity was not a major concern of the early immigrants. Yet as children appeared and families wished to inculcate in them some of the essentials of Islamic faith and culture they began to organize for prayer and study. For many years they functioned with little or no trained leadership and without meeting space that could be called a mosque, sometimes gathering in individual homes or renting space from local churches. Several places claim to be the site of the first American mosque, although the honor is usually given to Cedar Rapids, Iowa. Other mosques were built in New York, Massachusetts, and the Middle West in the 1920s and 1930s. The mosque movement began to gain momentum by the middle of the twentieth century, highlighted by the completion of the Islamic Center in Washington, D.C., in 1957, built as a cooperative venture between U.S. Muslims and Islamic governments overseas.

As the numbers of new Muslims arriving in America have swelled, adherence to Islam has often taken a more public face. Flourishing communities are now found in most major cities of the United States, and the number of mosques and Islamic centers has grown to over twelve hundred. For the past several decades much of the funding for building Islamic establishments, and for providing trained leadership (imams) for Muslim congregations, has come from oil-producing countries of the Middle East. Now extensive efforts are underway in many parts of the country to secure internal funding for building mosques and establishing new programs. Large mosques and Islamic centers provide for a great range of activities aside from worship, including education after school and on weekends, Islamic libraries, contexts for social engagement, gymnasiums, facilities for the elderly, and other means of full-service accommodation. Many Muslim groups, of course, continue to worship and meet in much smaller facilities, often converted houses or storefronts. This is particularly the case for many African American congregations, for whom finances often remain a major consideration. While significant numbers of imams trained overseas are providing leadership to American mosques, increasing attention is being paid to the need for educating indigenous leadership.

Imams in America are called on to function in capacities far beyond what is expected in Islamic societies. Paralleling the roles of Christian and Jewish clergy, imams not only preach and teach but also provide counseling services, lead in fundraising activities, perform weddings and funerals, and communicate with the public for purposes of educating about Islam and countering anti-Muslim prejudice. Trained imams are present, though in limited numbers, in the armed services and in the prison system, where they lead worship, counsel service personnel and inmates, and work to assure that the religious rights of Muslims are protected, especially in terms of dress, appropriate meals, and the opportunity to observe prayer and fasting. Some imams are now active on college campuses as part of the educational ministry of the schools.

Beginning in the 1960s with the establishment of the Muslim Student Association (MSA) to strengthen ties among international Muslim students, the United States has seen a steady growth of Muslim organizations at the local and national levels. Some are specific to professions and interests while others serve as umbrella organizations. Of the latter, the two largest are the Islamic Society of North America (ISNA) and the somewhat smaller and more conservative Islamic Circle of North America (ICNA). The American Muslim Council, begun in 1990, devotes itself to advancing the political presence of Muslims in America, while others such the Muslim Women's Lawyer's Committee (KARAMA) function to support women's rights. Youth organizations like the Muslim Youth of North America (MYNA) sponsor summer gatherings and work opportunities so that young American Muslims can meet and share common cause.

BEING MUSLIM IN AMERICA

Many of the Muslim organizations are now publishing journals with articles designed to aid Muslims trying to live Islamically acceptable lives in the context of what they see as an essentially secular society. These, along with rapidly growing resources on the Internet, services provided by mosques and local communities, and the mushrooming literature and media information available on Islam, offer a range of solutions to the concerns of everyday life.

Muslims ponder how to raise their children to respect and practice their faith in the face of peer pressures and in a culture that exhibits deep societal problems. They are concerned about matters of dating, meeting prospective marriage partners, whether interfaith marriages are acceptable, what kind of health care is appropriate, and how to keep their elderly from feeling lonely and isolated without an extended family structure. Many Muslim families, concerned about the nature of public school education, opt to educate their children either at home or in the growing numbers of Islamic schools. At the same time they worry about socialization, financing expensive private education, and the quality of teaching available. While many Muslim families need the extra income provided by women working, often they are concerned about the appropriateness of such public exposure. Sometimes decisions about female participation in the public arena are directly related to matters of dress and decorum. Increasing numbers of Muslim women and men, like their counterparts in many other parts of the world, are adopting forms of modest Islamic dress, especially in public. Often this leads to overt forms of prejudice against women who may not find employment or may be passed over for promotions because of their attire. Many Islamic stores and supply houses are now advertising appropriate forms of Islamic dress for males and females.

Economics is an issue that raises serious questions for many Muslims. Strict Muslim law prohibits the accumulation of interest on financial investments, and individuals often struggle to make wise financial decisions that honor those strictures. Some communities, for example, have insisted on raising the entire amount to pay for the building of a new mosque so as to avoid involvement with banking. Observing the religious duties required by the faith can cause particular problems in American society. Fasting during the month of Ramadan or praying five times daily are often very hard to carry out in the American work scene. Most places of employment do not provide facilities to wash before prayers or to carry out the physical prostrations and do not acknowledge the special difficulties experienced by those who do not eat or drink from sunrise to sundown.

Some in the American Muslim community feel that the best way to maintain their Islamic faith and identity in the American context is to avoid socialization with those who are not Muslim. This may also extend to not participating in, or allowing their children to be part of, any festivities associated with traditionally Christian or Jewish holidays such as Christmas or Hanukkah. Others are equally convinced that the only way to earn recognition and a rightful place in American society is to be involved with others so as to better explain and exemplify what being Muslim really means. Countering what is perceived to be a continuing and even growing prejudice on the part of Americans in general to Islam and Muslims is a constant challenge. Organized efforts are now being launched to protest unfair media coverage, incidents of perceived prejudice in the public arena, biased presentations of Islam in textbooks and public school materials, and other ways in which a prejudicial or sensationalist pictures of Islam further complicates life for American Muslims.

A NEW AMERICAN ISLAM?

Muslims are in the process of determining the nature and validity of an indigenous American Islam. In this task they often find that international political realities impinge. Immigrant Muslim communities in particular are subject to a range of international influences. Part of the task of American Muslims is to determine when interpretations of Islam in different political and cultural contexts are or are not appropriate to the practice of the faith in the West. This can become particularly complex when foreign financial support of American Muslim religious and educational institutions is tied to the ideological interpretations and political interests of the donors. Internally, Muslims who traditionally have not been active in American politics are awakening to the reality of a great potential for political power, and many are working to build coalitions and PACs and to make sure that more Muslims are candidates for political office.

As the children and grandchildren of immigrant Muslims find themselves increasingly distant from their international, cultural heritage, they are engaging more strenuously in the task of emphasizing commonality over distinctiveness. The search for, or the creation of, an American *umma*, or community, must also result in bringing together in effective ways immigrant and indigenous Muslims, converts and those with a long heritage of Islam. To the extent to which Muslims succeed in this task, they may find themselves not only an important power bloc on the American political scene but able to contribute significantly to the international discourse about Islam in the contemporary world and the role to be played in it by Muslims in diaspora.

BIBLIOGRAPHY

Bukhari, Zahid, and Sulayman Nyang. 2004. *Muslims' Place in the American Public Square.* Walnut Creek, Calif.: Altamira Press.

Haddad, Yvonne, and Jane Smith. 2002. *Muslim Minorities in the West.* Walnut Creek, Calif.: Altamira Press.

Haddad, Yvonne Y., and John L. Esposito. 1998. *Muslims on the Americanization Path?* New York: Oxford University Press.

Leonard, Karen. 2003. *Muslims in the United States: The State of Research.* New York: Russell Sage Foundation.

Schmidt, Garbi. 2004. *Islam in Urban America.* Philadelphia: Temple University Press.

Smith, Jane I. 1999. *Islam in America.* New York: Columbia University Press.

CHAPTER 50

RELIGIOUS MOVEMENTS WITH ISLAMIC ORIGINS

ALI S. ASANI

NEW movements have emerged in Muslim society that have developed separate traditions and communities of their own, often with a global expanse. Several of these originated in the Islamic world of the nineteenth century, a period that was characterized by fervent revivalist/reformist activity in almost every region inhabited by Muslims. Sparked by a complex combination of factors, including the spread of European colonial rule, proselytizing by Christian missionaries, and growing trends toward Westernization, Muslim activists sought a revitalization of Islam and Muslim societies through programs of religious and social reform. In some instances, the reformers perceived themselves to be messianic individuals on a divinely sanctioned mission to herald a new Islamic millennium. Among these reformers, Bahaullah (1817–1892) of Iran and Mirza Ghulam Ahmad (c. 1838–1908) of India, are of particular significance, for their teachings led to the emergence of the two most highly controversial movements in modern Islamic history, the Bahai and Ahmadiyya movements. Although Bahaullalh preached in a Twelver Shii context and Mirza Ghulam Ahmad in a Sunni context, their prophetic and messianic claims seemed to many Muslims to contradict a fundamental precept of the Islamic creed—the belief in the finality of Muhammad's prophethood. Their claims also undermined the authority of Shii and Sunni *ulama* as custodians of Islamic learning and interpreters of the faith. Not surprisingly, both movements came to be viewed by Muslim religious and political authorities as heresies that were no longer part of Islam. Subject to intense persecution in their homelands, the Bahais and the Ahmadis began to propagate their beliefs on a global basis,

particularly in regions such as North America and Europe that did not traditionally have significant Muslim populations. As their beliefs and doctrines evolved,
the Bahais eventually came to consider themselves as adherents of a new global
religion that had superseded Islam. On the other hand, the Ahmadis have persis-
tently claimed that they still belong within the fold of Islam, notwithstanding the
edicts declaring them to be non-Muslim.

THE BAHAI MOVEMENT

The origins of the Bahai movement can be traced to messianic expectations in
Twelver Shiism concerning the return of the hidden Twelfth Imam. On 22 May
1844, a thousand years after the disappearance of the Twelfth Imam, Sayyid Mi
Muhammad, a pious businessman claiming descent from the Prophet Muhammad declared himself to be the Bab or "gate" between Hidden Twelfth Imam and
the Shii community. Initially, his followers, called Babis, seemed to have understood him as an intermediary figure between them and the imam, but gradually
the Bab claimed that he himself was the long-awaited imam and the bearer of a
new divinely revealed scripture, the *Qayyumu'l Asma*. The claims of the Bab and
the growing appeal of his teachings created a great deal of consternation among
the Shii ulama whose authority he openly challenged. Consequently, they embarked on a prolonged campaign of persecution of the Bab and his followers,
which culminated in the Bab's execution by a firing squad in July 1850. The Bab
had nominated the scion of a wealthy aristocratic landowning family, Mirza Yahya
Nuri, to be his successor. On account of their new leader's reclusive and intro-
verted nature, however, the Babis gradually turned to his more dynamic younger
brother, Mirza Husayn Mi Nun, for guidance. Mirza Husayn, who later adopted
the title Bahaullah, "Glory of God," was himself imprisoned in Tehran for four
months on account of a Babi conspiracy to assassinate the shah of Iran. While in
prison, Bahaullah received the first intimations of his unique spiritual status. After
his release in 1853, he and his family were exiled to Baghdad. During the next
decade, his influence over the Babi community completely overshadowed that of
his brother with a growing number of Babis calling themselves *ahl-i Baha* "the
people of Baha." Finally, on 23 April 1863, Bahaullah declared himself to be "he
whom God shall make manifest," the messianic leader foretold by the Bab in his
book *Bayan*.

Under Bahaullah's leadership, the movement began to distance itself theologically from the Shii Islamic context within which it arose. Incorporating the millenarian traditions of other religions, Bahaullah claimed that not only was he the

messianic leader of the Babis but that he was also the Christ returned, the messiah of the Jews and the Shah Babram of the Zoroastrians. Perhaps influenced by the thoughts of the controversial thirteenth-century Sufi Ibn Arabi (d. 1240), he claimed that he was the divine manifestation (*mazhar-i ilahi*) through whom humanity could engage in the quest for the unknowable God and transform itself to reflect divine attributes. As the latest divine manifestation, he was continuing the mission of the previous divine manifestations who included Abraham, Zoroaster, Moses, Christ, and Muhammad. Through these manifestations, God fulfilled the promise that creation would never be without divine guidance. Bahaullah's mission was to establish peace on the earth by fostering a realization of the essential unity of all humanity, eliminating all forms of prejudice, discrimination, and social and economic injustice. So strong was the emphasis on peace and quietism that, in marked contrast to the earlier more aggressive Babi stance, Bahaullah's teachings advocated pacifism and loyalty to even a tyrannical government. Bahai aspirations for the unity of humankind included the promotion of a common international language and a single world government. The ultimate goal was the establishment of the "Most Great Peace" on the earth through the spiritualization of humanity that would be united under Bahai rule.

Bahaullah's teachings, particularly the proclamation of his status as divine manifestation, resulted in further charges of heresy and apostasy being leveled against him. He was exiled first to Istanbul, then to Edirne in what is now present-day Turkey, from where he wrote letters to major heads of state of Europe announcing his mission. In 1868 he and his followers were moved to Acre in Palestine where he was imprisoned in the fortress. After nine years he was allowed to move to a country house and then to Baliji, near Haifa in what is now present-day Israel, where he died in 1892.

Bahaullah appointed his son Abbas Effendi (1844–1921) to be the head of the Bahai faith after him. Under Abbas, who chose for himself the title Abdu'l Baha, "the servant of Baha," the Bahai faith witnessed an expansion beyond Iran and the Ottoman realms. A community of immigrant Iranian Bahai merchants settled in Ashkhabad, Turkestan, where, under protection afforded to them by Russian authorities, they established a variety of Bahai institutions, such as schools, a hospital, a printing press, and the first Bahai House of Worship. Small communities, mostly consisting of immigrant Iranian families and a sprinkling of converts from elite local families, were also established in the Caucasus and India where they were reasonably free to practice their faith. Even more significant was the spread of the Bahai faith in the West and the establishment of a small Bahai community in Chicago in 1894. Gradually, more Bahai communities mushroomed in other American cities as well as in Europe. Between 1911–1913, Abdu'l Baha undertook trips to Europe and America with the aim of strengthening the community, traveling across the United States and delivering lectures. Although small in number, the Bahais in the West enjoyed a freedom of religion that their Eastern counterparts had rarely experienced. Since they were mostly from the middle and upper echelons of society, they also had access to financial and other resources. Consequently, they had a profound impact on the future character of the Bahai faith.

On Abdu'l Baha's death in 1921, the mantle of leadership fell on the shoulders of his eldest grandchild, the twenty-four-year-old Shoghi Effendi (1897–1957), who at the time was a student of political science and economics at Oxford University. According to his grandfather's will, Shoghi Effendi was to be the "Guardian of the Cause of God" to whom was due the obedience of the entire Bahai community. Although initially overwhelmed by his responsibilities, Shoghi Effendi pursued an active agenda on many fronts. He personally translated into English many Bahai works, including those written by Bahaullah. Building on an informal system instituted by Bahaullah and Abdu'l Baha, he formalized the administrative structure of the Bahai community by introducing membership rolls and creating local and national spiritual assemblies wherever Bahais lived. Membership to these assemblies, which were responsible for looking after various aspects of Bahai life in their areas of jurisdiction, was through election. Once these assemblies were established, they were given systematic plans to undertake the expansion of the Bahai faith, both nationally and internationally. In 1953, under Shoghi Effendi's direction, the assemblies began a ten-year Global Crusade aimed at further promoting the faith on a worldwide basis. One indication of the crusade's dramatic success was the increase of the number of local assemblies from 4,437 in 1953 to 14,437 in 1963, many of them in the developing world. Shoghi Effendi also initiated the building of the Bahai world center and headquarters, housing various Bahai institutions as well as shrines, in the Acre-Haifa area, currently in Israel.

Shoghi Effendi died unexpectedly in 1957 without explicitly appointing a successor. A group of individuals he had designated as the "Hands of the Cause of God" and entrusted with responsibility of propagating the faith, took over leadership. In 1963, under instructions from the "Hands of the Cause of God," elections were held in the Bahai community for positions in the Universal House of Justice. This institution, which had been mentioned by Bahaullah in one of his writings, constitutes today the supreme authority of the Bahai world. Its members are elected every five years from among the representatives of the national spiritual assemblies around the world. In the absence of the guardian, the Universal House of Justice provides infallible interpretation on matters of faith to Bahais worldwide. It communicates its guidance to Bahai communities by means of letters that are considered to be divinely empowered. Many of these have been compiled into published volumes. To prevent cults developing around individuals, no member of the House of Justice holds authority on an individual basis; authority is based in the collective membership. Under the Universal House of Justice are the local and national spiritual assemblies, which are responsible for matters of governance. Membership in these assemblies is based on annual election. Matters related to the propagation and defense of the faith are the responsibility of the Continental Boards of Counselors and other boards working under their direction. Membership in these institutions is by appointment.

As the Bahai community has evolved and responded to the changing circumstances in which it found itself, the charismatic authority of Bahaullah and his descendants has been institutionalized into a model of governance that can be best described as a "theocratic democracy." The elections ensure that the leadership reflects changes in the racial and ethnic composition of the community. Various crusades have dramatically increased the number of Bahais in the Third World (sub-Saharan Africa, Latin America, and India) so that they now form the predominant majority of the world Bahai community. Iranian and Middle Eastern Bahais, who once formed the majority, are now a distinct minority. The expansion into the Third World, in contrast to the initial expansion into the West that attracted mostly "elite" populations, has taken place mostly among socially underdeveloped rural populations. This has led to increased emphasis and concern with social and economic development in contemporary Bahai teachings.

The Ahmadiyya Movement

The Ahmadiyya movement emerged in the late nineteenth century in Punjab in northern India. Under British colonial rule, the region experienced a sharp rise in religious communalism and nationalism. A number of reform movements among the Sikh, Hindu, and Muslim communities of the province actively sought to defend their respective traditions against not only the onslaught of Western culture and Christian missionaries but also the competing truth claims of other religions. As a result, levels of interreligious acrimony were at an all-time high. The interreligious conflict was reflected in the numerous newspapers and journals published by religious organizations with the aim of engaging in polemical attacks against rivals. Some organizations even sponsored public forums in which representatives of rival religions were invited to debate before audiences that sometimes numbered in the thousands. Among the most prominent spokesmen for the Islamic cause was Mirza Ghulam Ahmad, a member of a prominent aristocratic landowning family from the town of Qadiyan in India. Well-versed in traditional Islamic learning, particularly the Qu'ran, Mirza Ghulam Ahmad first engaged in debates with Christian missionaries in the area who were active in an intense proselytizing campaign. In a 1872 newspaper article, he challenged any non-Muslim to debate the truth of Islam, with the winner being offered a prize. A few years later, in 1880, he published a four-volume book, *Barahin-i Ahmadiyya,* in which he defended Islamic beliefs by disproving the claims of particularly the right-wing Hindu Arya Samaj whose members had also intensified their activities in the area. Later, he came into confrontation with the Sikhs as well when he claimed that Guru Nanak, the founder of the Sikh religion, had been, in fact, a Muslim.

Although a vocal champion of Islam against non-Muslims, Mirza Ghulam Ahmad was a controversial figure among Muslims because of the various claims he made about his personal religious status. Already in the *Barahin-i Ahmadiyya* (1880), he claimed that he was a *muhaddath*, "a person spoken to by God." Furthermore, he asserted that he was a divinely appointed *mujaddid*, or reformer, sent in fulfillment of God's promise to the Muslim community that a leader would emerge at the beginning of every century to renew and revive the faith. As the mujaddid of the fourteenth Islamic century, which commenced on November 12, 1882, it was his duty to raise Muslim society from the depths to which it had sunk. This was a situation for which the arrogant, materialistic, and self-centered *ulama* (religious scholars) were responsible. In 1890 he declared that he was the *mahdi*, "the rightly guided one," and the Promised Messiah who, according to popular Muslim belief, would be Jesus himself. Integral to Mirza Ghulam Ahmad's notion of the messiah was his radical departure from the generally accepted Muslim teaching concerning Jesus' fate after the crucifixion. He held that, instead of ascending to heaven, Jesus, with God's help, escaped from the cross and made his way to Afghanistan and Kashmir where he preached to the lost tribes of Israel. Jesus, he asserted, died at the age of 120 and was buried in Srinagar, Kashmir. Since the historical Jesus was mortal, he could not return in person. However, he, Mirza Ghulam Ahmad, possessed the spirit and power of Jesus. Later, Mirza Ghulam Ahmad extended his messianic claims to the Hindu tradition as well by claiming that he was also Kalki, the long-awaited tenth incarnation of the deity Vishnu. Most controversial, however, was his claim to be a prophet. Influenced by the mystical prophetology of Ibn Arabi (d. 1240), Mirza Ghulam Ahmad claimed that while "legislative" prophecy ended with the Prophet Muhammad, there would always be "non-legislative" prophets chosen from among his devout followers to guide the community. He was one of these prophets.

Mirza Ghulam Ahmad's claim to prophethood created a great deal of controversy among Sunni ulama and conservative Muslims who saw in it a challenge to the Islamic doctrine of prophethood. According to orthodox belief, Prophet Muhammad, as the "seal of the Prophets," was the final prophet sent by God. Therefore, after him there could be no more prophets in any form or shape. To the ulama, Mirza Ghulam Ahmad's distinction between "legislative" and "non-legislative" prophets and his other claims were clearly heretical. Not surprisingly, as early as 1891, the first of many *fatwas* or religious edicts was issued declaring Mirza Ghulam Ahmad and his followers to be apostates and non-Muslims. In subsequent decades, the religious status of the Ahmadiyya continued to be the subject of a great deal of acrimonious debate in all sorts of forums, including newspapers and journals, with right-wing religious groups leading the attack. The creation of Pakistan in 1947 as a Muslim nation and the injection of Islamic ideology in its political discourse further exacerbated the situation. The presence of the Ahmadiyya headquarters in Rabwa, a town in Pakistan specially built by members of the sect on land granted by the state, and the prominence of Ahmadiyya in the armed forces, civil service, and the government generated a climate in which religious parties, such as the Abrar and the Jamat-i Islami, instigated riots against the Ahmadiyya in the early 1950s and pressured the government to declare them non-Muslim. The government refused. In 1974, after clashes between Ahmadis and non-Ahmadis in Rabwa, the religious groups renewed their agitation, threatening to call a general strike. This time the government of Zulfikar Au Bhutto capitulated and allowed the matter to be debated by the National Assembly. On 7 September 1974, after lengthy debate, a clause was added to the Pakistani constitution stating that a person who does not believe in the finality of Muhammad's prophethood or claims to be a prophet, "in any sense of the word or of any description whatsoever, after Muhammad . . . or recognizes such a claimant as Prophet or religious reformer, is not a Muslim." Following the action of the Pakistani National Assembly, anti-Ahmadiyya resolutions were adopted throughout the Muslim world by various religious organizations, including the World Muslim League, the African Islamic Congress, and the Fifth World Islamic Conference. In Pakistan, the campaign against the Ahmadiyya "distortion of Islam" continued. In 1975 the Pakistani minister of religious affairs issued an order forbidding members of the group to perform the pilgrimage to Mecca, a city which only Muslims may enter. Almost a decade later, in 1984, Pakistan's military ruler Zia ul-Haq, under his Islamization program, issued an ordinance according to which the Ahmadiyya were forbidden to refer to their faith as Islam and to call themselves Muslims. They were not allowed to call their places of worship mosques, nor were they allowed to propagate their ideas. Violations could lead to imprisonment and fines.

The Ahmadi doctrine of prophethood, the theological status of Mirza Ghulam Ahmad, and the nature of community leadership generated controversy within the Ahmadi community itself, eventually resulting in a schism. Internal tensions first became apparent in the period after Ghulam Ahmad's death when one of his closest disciples, Hakim Nur ad-Din (d. 1914), took over leadership of the community. The majority of the Ahmadiyya held firm to Mirza Ghulam Ahmad's teachings about prophethood and believed that his authority was to be inherited by an individual who was to be elected by members of an electoral college. This individual was to be Khalifat al-Masih "successor to the Messiah." Although in principle succession was not by genealogical inheritance, all three Khalzfas elected after Nur ad-Din have in fact been the founder's male descendants: his son Mirza Bashir ad-Din Mahmud Ahmad (1914–1965) and grandsons Nasir Ahmad (1965–

1982) and Tahir Ahmad (1982–). The majority group, who came to be called Qadiani (after the town of Qadian, which served as the headquarters for the movement in pre-partition India), considered all non-Ahmadi Muslims who did not accept the leadership of the Ahmadi khalifa to be *kafirs*, or infidels. On the other hand, a smaller group, the Lahori (after the city of Lahore in Pakistan), sought to downplay the central doctrinal difference that separated the Ahmadiyya from other Muslims by claiming that Mirza Ghulam Ahmad was more of a reformer than a prophet. Being keen on emphasizing commonalities rather than differences, they were reluctant to consider other non-Ahmadi Muslims to be infidels. On the question of leadership, they refused to accept the leadership of khalifas, claiming that Mirza Ghulam Ahmad intended to provide collective leadership of the Ahmadi community through the Central Ahmadiyya Association. The polarization of Ahmadiyya movement into the Qadiani and Lahori positions has persisted to this day with no sign of reconciliation.

As with many minority religious movements that have found themselves oppressed, the intense persecution and controversy that have surrounded the Ahmadiyya movement have only served to strengthen the commitment of its adherents, both morally and financially, to the cause and created a sense of solidarity. The attention and publicity from the controversy attracted new converts. Most significantly, the determination to survive led to the rise of a strong activist zeal focused on propagating Ahmadi beliefs in South Asia and abroad. The missionary character of the movement was undoubtedly accentuated by Mirza Ghulam Ahmad's interpretation of the term *jihad*, which was developed in the context of his polemical debates with non-Muslim religious leaders in the Punjab. Disavowing classical interpretations of jihad in the militaristic sense, he proclaimed that in modern times jihad meant, in fact, the propagating of Islam through "the tongue and the pen." Translated into action, this interpretation led to the evolution of the Ahmadiyya into one of the most active and vocal missionary groups to emerge from the Muslim world in modern times. Within Muslim majority areas, such as those of the Middle East, Central Asia, and Southeast Asia, Ahmadiyya missions met with limited success as a result of the opposition they faced from the Muslim religious establishment. They were more successful, however, in areas of sub-Saharan Africa, particularly in the West African countries of Nigeria and Sierra Leone. England was one of the first Western countries in which the Ahmadiyya began their mission, with mosques being established in Woking and in London. The success of the English mission, particularly the conversion of a Lord Headley in 1913, was highly publicized in Ahmadiyya publications. The Ahmadiyya were also active in America in the early decades of the twentieth century, particularly among the African American population. Mosques were set up on the East Coast and Midwest where courses were offered on the formal study of Qu'ran and Islam. The Ahmadiyya missionaries played a very important role in making available copies of the Qu'ran to African Americans, many of whom were in the process of establishing their political and religious identity. The movement was in its heyday until the 1960s, counting among its adherents prominent African American jazz musicians such as Talib Daud, Art Blakey, and McCoy Tyner. In the later decades of the twentieth century, some of the adherents, disillusioned by attitudes of the Indo-Pakistani missionaries, left the movement. Wallace D. Fard, the founder of the Nation of Islam, is also believed to have had connections with the Ahmadiyya.

BIBLIOGRAPHY

On the Bahai

Cole, Juan. 1998. *Modernity and the Millennium: The Genesis of the Baha'i Faith in the Nineteenth-Century Middle East.* New York: Columbia University Press.

Smith, Peter. 1987. *The Babi and Bahai Religions: From Messianic Shi'ism to a World Religion.* Cambridge: Cambridge University Press.

———. 1996. *The Baha'i Faith: A Short History.* Oxford: One World Publications.

On the Ahmadiyya

Fisher, Humphrey. 1963. *Ahmadiyya: A Study of Islam on the West African Coast.* Oxford: Oxford University Press.

Friedmann, Yohanan. 1989. *Prophecy Continuous: Aspects of Ahmadi Religious Thought and Its Medieval Background.* Berkeley: University of California Press.

Lavan, Spencer. 1974. *The Ahmadiyyah Movement: A History and Perspective.* New Delhi: Manohar.

McCloud, Aminah. 1995. *African American Islam.* London: Routledge Press.

PART VI

AFRICAN CULTURAL REGION

CHAPTER 51

....

THINKING GLOBALLY ABOUT AFRICAN RELIGION

....

JACOB K. OLUPONA

THE global dimensions of African religion sweep across the plains of the African continent and into the African diaspora. Contemporary "African religion" is itself a product of globalization, for it is less a single tradition than a sociological context in which the elements of a variety of indigenous religious experiences are combined with Islam and Christianity. All three of these dimensions—indigenous religion, Africanized Islam, and Africanized Christianity—are part of the interactive, globalized African religious experience.

Some of the products of this growing interconnectedness of African and Africanized religions are new religions. As Max Weber has observed, the charismatic becomes routinized, and new faiths become accepted as established traditions. Following Ernst Troeltsch's categories, a breakaway sect can be characterized by the presence of doctrinal or ritual differences among the church's membership, and the new African religions have elements of both. These new religious structures reflect emerging values and the adoption of new practices in a changing social context. In the case of the African religions, this process reflects a growing pluralism among African religious institutions.

As globalization affects African religion both within Africa and throughout the African diaspora, new identities emerge. In the African Christian church, the Islamic mosque, and the Santeria temple, a new pluralism in African identity links the values, memories, and civil associations of a variety of African worldviews and moral systems. These are affected by their interactions with each other and with the cultures of the Western world.

The very language we use to describe the diverse religious experiences of people of African origin and descent is not only recent but also heavily dependent upon non-African paradigms and Eurocentric views. Terms such as Africa, black, and Pan-African all derive from recent conceptual periods in history where parts of the geographical area we now so readily call Africa interacted with Europe. It is this interaction beginning with trade and followed by the latter horrors of slavery and colonialism, that led to the Eurocentric idea of African religious cultures and worldviews.

As a consequence, it is difficult to come up with a distinct notion of African religion that is independent of the shaping tendencies of the paradigms and terms of the Western world. A truly indigenous understanding must include not only the history of Africa before colonialism but also aspects of living African communities that have derived from diverse heritages. Although the effort to define African religion can be challenging, a number of scholars, writers, and theologians have made the attempt. Writers associated with the Pan-African movement, for instance, which dates back for over three centuries, have sought to refine their sense of common being by looking at the totality of African religions within the global environment.

GLOBALIZATION

In looking at the relationship between African religion and globalization, we should not assume that globalization is an inevitable force that will one day replace all traditional values within the world with one common consumerist mass culture. In Africa globalization has had a significant impact upon traditions and cultural values, but at the same time African traditionalism retains a resiliency and adaptability that enables it to maintain cohesion both in non-Western environments and in the context of faiths such as Christianity and Islam.

African traditions are adaptable. Instead of offering inflexible dogmatic beliefs, often they provide frameworks for viewing and processing information. If a new piece of information does not fit an existing framework, it can modify but not necessarily reject the framework. For example, a form of taboo observed by an African people can be maintained until the old framework adapts, and it changes. What is interesting to ask about African immigrant religions is not so much what aspects of their traditions have been abandoned as how the frameworks of the traditions have adapted.

An interesting case in point is the changing roles of women within African religious communities. Such women are commonly expected to preserve culture and traditions. As a consequence, a significant proportion of African church members are women. Yet these largely female congregations demonstrate a wide variety of attitudes toward the participation of women, from very limited to active leadership roles.

Another impact of globalization on African religion affects the nature of African civil societies. Both within Africa and worldwide, African religious institutions serve as a source of identity and legitimacy. Across Africa religious leaders have challenged authoritarian and dictatorial political and military leaders such as the Abacha military dictatorship in Nigeria and in Moi's Kenya. During South Africa's apartheid era, the church played a critical role in racial reconciliation, and more recently Archbishop Desmond Tutu chaired a committee on reconciliation. Within the African diaspora, African religious communities have actively participated in the social life of their communities as well.

African Christianity

In describing African religion, we have to include the versions of Christianity and Islam that interact with traditional forms of African religion. Christianity in Africa is authentically African, but it is also global in that it is found in various forms in African communities in Africa, Europe, and the Americas. It is diverse not only in its geography but also in its three main strands: the African independent church movement, charismatic or Pentecostal churches, and the mission or mainline churches.

African Independent Churches

African independent churches include the Celestial Church of Christ, Christ Apostolic Church, and Cherubim and Seraphim in West Africa; Zulu Zionist churches in South Africa; and the Simon Kimbanque Church in Zaire. These churches reflect the nexus between African indigenous beliefs and Christianity. Converts to Christianity in Africa, like those in Latin America, retain significant aspects of indigenous culture. Many of the first mission converts were socially marginal members of their communities who, with the rise of colonialism, became the new local elites. The social dominance of these African Christian elites led to the emergence of new religious rebels: new spiritual leaders who claimed they had been called by God to begin authentic African churches.

These new African leaders relied upon both Christian and indigenous traditions as the source of truth and authority. Thus the African independent churches retained aspects of indigenous tradition and belief. Christian images of divine leadership, the Holy Spirit, and faith healing, for example, were integrated into African ideas of community, ancestor worship, and revelation. Moreover, individuals could engage in a form of religious pluralism by participating in Christian and indigenous traditions at the same time, combining aspects of both. A naming ceremony, for example, could be utilized to incorporate significant aspects of indigenous and traditional beliefs. Hymns in African languages incorporated indigenous sayings and values. Special Africanized church services were created to supplement existing English sermons.

These syncretic processes, however, were not coordinated with one another, and the African independent church movement was often divided. To some extent these churches were separated from other African churches. They had difficulty in expanding their efforts beyond their original ethnic base. They were plagued with many of the same ethnic and political divisions that have separated the wider African society and created a series of contemporary political crises.

AFRICAN PENTECOSTAL OR CHARISMATIC CHURCHES

African Pentecostal or charismatic churches are a rapidly growing sector of the African Christian communities. Unlike the African independent churches, which incorporate elements of indigenous African tradition, the charismatic church reflects the values of modernity, including Western rationalism and scientific/logical reasoning. Aspects of African spirituality such as divination, witchcraft, and polytheistic beliefs are strongly discouraged and are even portrayed as a product of the devil's influence. Yet these same churches often tolerate spirit possession as consistent with the Pentecostal tradition of "speaking in tongues." Pentecostal or born-again styles of worship are prominent in African immigrant communities as well as in Africa itself.

Charismatic churches place a strong emphasis on the reality of the devil, a concept that is defined in a variety of ways among African societies. Concern about the devil leads to the importance of exorcism and the practice of deliverance by the Holy Spirit. In some ways these practices—and such elements of Pentecostal spirituality as fervent prayer, pragmaticism, and proximate salvation—are close to African styles of spirituality. Yet born-again adherents in fact give very little recognition to the values of African indigenous traditions, and they critique traditional African beliefs as evil, superstitious, and contrary to the teachings of Christianity.

MAINLINE MISSION CHURCHES

The European and American mission church denominations remain the largest and the most organized churches in Africa, in spite of the recent upsurge of the Pentecostal-charismatic communities. The Methodist Church, for example, boasts many centuries of presence in Africa. Though patterned after their mother churches abroad, the mission churches have adapted to their local situations. The 1960s—a time when most African nations became independent—was a watershed in the social history of these denominations, for they began to put in place innovations adapting their European practices to African spiritual sensibilities. More recently they have had to adapt to the increasing popularity of charismatic-Pentecostalism in the African scene. A number of mainline mission churches have adopted charismatic services as a way of preventing their youth from abandoning the churches as they did in the 1960s and 1970s when the mission churches lost a sizable number of their congregations to the African independent church movement.

Loyalties to mainstream mission church identities persist in the diaspora communities of African immigrants in America and Europe. Episcopal, Baptist, and Catholic churches increasingly offer services that reflect the interests and concerns of these immigrant communities. Churches in the United States have developed ethnic ministries that minister to a wide range of immigrant communities, including Africans. Among their accommodations are the use of African languages in hymns. They sometimes conduct services entirely in African languages. Often these services are held on Saturday or Sunday evenings in addition to the Sunday morning services. Since not all Africans speak the same language, only where there are significant concentrations of such African language speakers as Igbo, Yoruba, or certain Ghanaian and Ethiopian communities will special language services be provided.

Accompanying the rise of ethnic and national congregations in Europe and America is the increasing number of African clergy ministering solely to African congregations. Such priests and ministers are found especially in the Catholic Church, with a growing number in Episcopal, Anglican, and Methodist mainstream churches. These African priests offer evidence that Africa has become a global center of Christianity and is able to send its own missionaries abroad.

AFRICAN ISLAM

The second heritage of African religion is the global faith of Islam. Unlike Christianity, which entered Africa primarily as a conduit for the disavowed and outcasts of African communities, Islam came to Africa as a religion of trade and commerce. Its pragmatism, scholarship, and globalizing linkages encouraged the development of vast trade empires across North Africa throughout the Middle Ages. Since no Muslim could become a slave, many Africans converted to Islam for protection as well as advancement.

Sub-Saharan Africa encapsulates the history of Islam, especially its contribution to knowledge, politics, and culture. The history of the western Sudanese empires of Ghana, Mali, and Songhi remain the most coveted phase of African history. Mali and Senegal, especially, were great centers of Islamic culture and intellectual discourse. The ancient cities of Timbuktu, Gao, and Genne were centers of Islamic education, science, and culture as they maintained close links with the Mediterranean world.

At the same time, Islam contributed greatly to the growth of East African civilization, especially along the coastal region where trade with the Arab world flourished. One result of this was the development of such linguistic cultures as the Swahili (based on a synthesis of Arabic and Bantu languages); another was the growth of maritime commerce long before colonialism entered the region.

Islam, like Christianity, has been able to adapt, capitalize, and even exploit the technologies of modernity in favor of expanding its own faith as a global religion. Like African Christianity, the growing presence of expatriate African Muslims worldwide has begun to alter many of the largest cities in the Afro-Atlantic world. In London, New York, Washington, D.C., and Atlanta, Ghanaian Islamic communities are becoming prominent. Mosques in these cities that were once dominated by Arab and Pakistani communities are now beginning to witness a strong influx of Islamic Africans from West Africa. Within these African Muslim communities abroad, however, divisions based on ethnic and traditional origins remain.

AFRICAN INDIGENOUS TRADITIONS
AND FAITHS

Globalization takes on a slightly different form when it comes to indigenous African religions. Although the vast majority of Africans are Christian and Muslim, those who are followers of indigenous faiths have had a disproportionate impact abroad. Globalization has also become a powerful impetus in the worldwide expansion of African traditions such as the Yoruba faith of Ile-Ife and Oyo in Nigeria and as the Fon in the republic of Benin. These variant forms of African traditions share many of the core beliefs as their African predecessors but the indigenous nature of them have been masked as they have been adapted to Christianity.

Yoruba religion, expressed in Afro-Cuban Santeria, Afro-Brazilian Candomble, Shango tradition in Trinidad, and to some extent Vodou in Haiti, continues to refashion the culture and religious landscape of the New World. In the United States, the Yoruba-derived Orisha tradition is becoming an alternative devotional practice for thousands of Africans and even a growing number of Europeans and European Americans. This rich tradition has for over a century been the subject of scholarship in several fields: the humanities and social sciences; African, Caribbean, and American religious studies; and artistic and literary creativity and criticism. The steady stream of scholarly and popular works on Yoruba religion— both as it is practiced in West Africa and as it influences the African-based religions of the New World—suggests that this religion especially can no longer be viewed as a local ethnic tradition but one that has in many ways attained the status of a world religion.

This globalization of African religious traditions embraces both African immigrants and Caucasian and Latino converts. They retain ties to Africa by importing priests such as Nigerian Youruba-Ifa holy men. Indeed a sizable number of Ifa priests have developed a strong clientele and semi-permanent homes in many of America's largest cities.

In some cases African immigrant religion intersects with African American culture. African immigrants have helped to revitalize African indigenous religion in black American communities. Some of these communities have formulated a mythic linkage with traditions such as the Yoruba kingdom of Oyo or the cities of Ile-Ife and communicate regularly with these cultural centers for the purpose of expanding and reinforcing these traditions within American society. A major American center for this revitalization is the Yoruba community of the Oyotungi Village in South Carolina, whose leader and Oba (king) Oseijami Adefunmi I, has created a pan-African–U.S. traditional Orisha society. These Orisha devotees regularly visit Nigeria during the Ifa and Oshun festivals, and through their financial support they help to maintain cultural practices that are in the decline in Africa itself.

AFRICAN CIVIL RELIGION

The fourth category of African religion is a trend that can be loosely described as a kind of African civil religion. Many traditional religious myths, rituals, and symbols have been embraced by secular institutions and leaders as a means of developing greater legitimacy for themselves within African societies. Many members of indigenous elite social strata within Africa and throughout the African diaspora have adopted religious practices to enhance their political influence, taking on symbols that would link them with notions of sacred kingships, ritual power, and historical-mythic legitimation.

CONCLUSION

The globalization of African religion, therefore, entails not only the death of African traditional values but also in many cases their expansion and promotion. This is the product of an innovative and somewhat unpredictable reshuffling of many of Africa's cultures, faiths, and traditions—which have become a force for change in both Western and non-Western societies. This is nowhere more evident than in the crosscurrents between contemporary religious communities in the Americas and the expansion of African religions within the African continent itself. These movements are sources of cultural continuity, stability, and authority and demonstrate the remarkable resiliency and strength of character of African cultures. They have also at times been sources of tension, division, and conflict. These characteristics of innovation and diversity will continue to evolve as African religions expand from their roots in the three pivotal traditions of Christianity, Islam, and indigenous faiths.

BIBLIOGRAPHY

Abdul-Raheem, T., ed. 1996. *Pan Africanism: Politics, Economy and Social Change in the Twenty-first Century*. London: Pluto.

Cesaire, Aime. 1971. *Return to My Native Land*. Paris: Presence Africaine.

Clifford, James. 1997. *Routes: Travel and Translation in the Late Twentieth Century*. Cambridge, Mass.: Harvard University Press.

Espin, Oliva. 1999. *Women Crossing Boundaries: A Psychology of Immigration and Trans-formations of Sexuality*. New York: Routledge.

Gilroy, Paul. 1993a. *Small Acts: Thoughts on the Politics of Black Cultures*. London: Serpents Tail.

———. 1993b. *The Black Atlantic: Modernity and Double Consciousness*. London: Verso.

Green, R. 1998. *A Salute to Historic African Kings and Queens*. Chicago: Empac.

Harris, Joseph. 1993. *Global Dimensions of the African Diaspora* (2nd ed.). Washington, D.C.: Howard University Press.

Hefner, Robert. 1998. "Multiple Modernities: Christianity, Islam, and Hinduism in a Globalizing Age." *Annual Review of Anthropology* 27: 83–104.

Jules-Rosette, Bennetta. 1989. "The Sacred in African New Religions." In *The Changing Face of Religion*. Edited by James Beckford and Thomas Luckman, 147–162. London: Sage Publications.

Kearney, M. 1995. "The Local and the Global: The Anthropology of Globalization and Transnationalism." *Annual Review of Anthropology* 24: 547–565.

Olupona, Jacob. 2002. *African Immigrant Religious Communities: Identity Formation in America's Pluralistic Society*. Ford Foundation.

Pereira de Queiroz, Isaura. 1989. "Afro-Brazilian Cults and Religious Change in Brazil." In *The Changing Face of Religion*. Eds. James Beckford and Thomas Luckmann, 88. London: Sage Publishers.

Redkey, E. S. 1969. *Black Exodus: Black Nationalism and Back to Africa Movements*. New Haven, Conn.: Yale University Press.

Segal, R. 1995. *The Black Diaspora*. London: Faber and Faber.

Warner, Stephen, and Judith Witter, eds. 1998. *Gathering in Diaspora: Religious Communities and the New Immigration*. Philadelphia: Temple University Press.

CHAPTER 52

TRADITIONAL AFRICAN RELIGIOUS SOCIETY

KOFI ASARE OPOKU

AFRICAN traditional religion is inextricably linked to the culture of the African people. In Africa religion has been understood as an integral part of life in which every aspect was knit together into a coherent system of thought and action, giving significance and meaning and providing abiding and satisfying values. Religion, culture, politics, and society were part of a seamless whole and no part of it could stand on its own.

The absence of a specific word for "religion" in many African languages is an indication of this African holistic understanding of life. Words related to the concept of religion may be translated as "custom," "tradition," or "way of life." The Akan word, *amammre* (Yoruba, *asa*; Ga, *kusum*; Ewe, *konu*), for example, is an all-inclusive category that includes the ideas of tradition, way of life, beliefs, practices (religion), etiquette, customs and usages, ways of organizing society, and the norms that govern the relationships between members of society with each other, as well as those which guide the relationships between members of society and their environment, both spiritual and physical. The religious aspects of this totality of the African experience has, like all other religions, sacred texts, iconography, rituals, and a philosophy or worldview, puts all other aspects of this experience coherently together in a way that makes sense to African people, giving the African tradition an integrity of its own.

These ideas and practices have been passed down to succeeding generations not only orally but also through symbols and art, rituals and festivals, names of people and places, songs and dances, proverbs and wise sayings, myths and legends. That the transmission of the heritage was not in written form does not make it less true than traditions that were written down in other parts of the world. In fact there exists a body of knowledge and traditions dating from antiquity that continues to guide human life and conduct in Africa, albeit in modified form today. When the traditions were passed down orally, they were not forgotten or lost, as the Akan proverb assures us: "When a person dies, his/her tongue does not rot." Each succeeding generation has related what was passed down from the past to its present circumstances.

Africa is a large continent characterized by great diversity of peoples and cultures, but beneath this diversity lies a core of ideas that are fairly uniform. To describe the religious heritage as African is not to "invent" or suggest that there is complete uniformity with respect to belief and practice; it is only to suggest that the heritage has an African provenance. But even where there is great diversity, the differences arise out of the African experience and can therefore be legitimately described as African. The existence of diversity not only with regard to religious beliefs and practices but also to other aspects of life, derives support from the African proverb: "Difference is better than resemblance."

The scholars who first wrote about the religious heritage of African societies were mostly Westerners—explorers, missionaries, colonial officials, and anthropologists—who brought their own preconceptions to bear on the matter under discussion. And while some writers found no evidence of what they called "religion" in Africa, others demonstrated that the continent was governed by what they described as "insensible fetish." Missionary studies left readers no doubt that the traditional religion had no abiding and satisfying values, and on the whole the European studies were based on the fundamental assumption that there was a permanent disjuncture between the minds of Africans and Europeans and whatever was found in Africa was bound to be the very opposite of what prevailed in Europe. Even where some familiar ideas and practices were found, the early writers were quick to attribute them to a source external to Africa.

Later scholars adopted special terms to designate the religious practices and beliefs found in Africa, all of which combined to show that the perspective of the African practitioners of their ancestral religion was not worth considering. As a result, the African religious traditions became synonymous with the idea of "otherness." The views of the observers and outsiders have tended to crystallize ideas about the religious traditions of Africa. As the African proverb puts it: "Until the lions have their own historians, tales of hunting will always glorify the hunter." The African soil abounds with profound religious and theological insights; the insiders' views and their own self-understanding should be a guiding factor in the interpretation of the African religious heritage.

Worldview

The traditional African worldview is of a created universe with visible and invisible aspects. This universe characterizes everything that exists. Nature, the community, and society all have aspects that are both visible and invisible. The universe is characterized by order, not chaos. There are forces—religious, moral, mystical, and natural (in nature) that are observed to be at work. Between all that exists, there is an interconnectedness and a dynamic correspondence among these forces, whether visible or not.

Social Organization and Religion

Membership of society includes not only the living but also the dead and the unborn. This has practical consequences for attitudes toward the land; for the land belongs to the ancestors who bequeathed it to the living to pass on to the next generation. The organization of society itself is based on the concept of the human person. The Akan of Ghana, for example, organize their society on their understanding of who a human being is. Every person has an *okra*, which links the individual directly with Onyame, Divinity; *sunsum,* an intangible element which accounts for a person's character, disposition, and intelligence; *ntoro,* which is inheritable from the father and accounts for a person's inherited characteristics; and the *mogya* or blood, which comes from the mother and is the basis of one's *abusua* or matriclan. On the basis of the mogya, the Akan divide themselves into eight clans: Aduana, Agona, Asona, Asakyiri, Asenee, Bretuo, Ekoona, and Oyoko. These clans form the basis of Akan social organization.

Kinship is at the basis of the political structure and each kin group is directly linked to its ancestors through its head. At the apex of the political structure is the *ohene*, king or chief, who derives his authority from the fact that he occupies the stool of the ancestors and is the intermediary between the ancestors of the society and the people. The stool that the ohene occupies is the *akonnwa tuntum,* black stool of the ancestors, which is the source of the ohene's power. The religious duties of the chief or king include the celebration of the Adae festival, which involves the feeding of the ancestral black stools, a periodic festival which brings all the lineages together as a political entity. The Adae festival is celebrated nine times during the year to bring the year to full cycle; therefore, the calculation of the Akan calendar is intimately tied up with the periodic feeding of the ancestral stools. At the end of the Akan year, the chief or king celebrates the Odwira, a cleansing festival as well as the offering of first fruits to the ancestors and divinities. This and other rituals performed by the chief or king ensure the welfare of the people and the society.

The ohene's office is a sacred one and the ceremonies surrounding it venerably accentuate it. The ritual of enstoolment takes place in the Stool House, where the ancestral black stools are kept; after the election of a chief or king, he is confined for a period of time, usually forty-two days, in Apatam, where he undergoes ritual instructions which transform him from an ordinary member of the royal family into a king or chief. After his enstoolment, his person becomes sacred for having been brought into contact with the royal ancestors. Many taboos surround his person to remind the community that the king or chief occupies a special position and for this reason he is treated with the highest approbation.

The king or chief combines his religious duties with administrative, executive, judicial, and, in the past, military duties. All these functions are rolled into one in the person of the king or chief and are not separated from each other. But when he abuses his power, the special relationship between him and his royal ancestors is formally severed and his sanctity is violated. This renders him palpably unfit to occupy the stool of the revered ancestors. Once this happens, the king or chief loses his right to perform all the other functions of his office. The removal from office in case of abuse of power is buttressed by the proverb: "No one sits for ever on the stool of time." A ruler does not rule forever, and those who placed him on the stool have the right to remove him from office when it becomes necessary.

Of all the sacred stools of the Akan, the Golden Stool of Asante stands out as the most preeminent and incomparable. It came into being, according to both history and legend, during the reign of King Osei Tutu, founder of the Asante nation. Before King Osei Tutu, what is now Asante was a collection of autonomous chiefdoms which were not particularly strong. They were all under the rule of the king of Denkyira, the most powerful state at the time. But King Osei Tutu was able to bring the autonomous chiefdoms together to defeat the king of Denkyira and demonstrate the strength that comes with unity in the proverb: "When spider webs unite, they can tie up a lion."

The bonds of unity that had been forged through war needed to be strengthened in order to give it lasting permanence, and it was at this point that Okomfo Anokye, the king's astute and perspicacious adviser, came up with the ingenious idea of the Golden Stool. At a gathering of the chiefs and people of Asante on a certain Friday, Okomfo Anokye commanded the Golden Stool, Sikadwa Kofi, from the heavens, amid thunder and lightning, and placed it on the lap of the king. He prepared a concoction with the hair and nails of the king, and the leading chiefs and queen mothers gathered there and mixed it with some herbs and sacred water. This was smeared on the Golden Stool and the rest was drunk as a medicinal, sacramental drink. Okomfo Anokye then solemnly and with utmost conviction announced that the soul of the Asante nation was in the Golden Stool and that the strength and bravery of the nation depended on the safety of the Golden Stool. The loss or capture of the Golden Stool would bring about the collapse of the nation. Through the Golden Stool, the Asante became conscious of themselves as a nation with a common religious bond. The Golden Stool is a sacred object that should never be sat upon nor be allowed to touch the ground, and it is the ultimate sanction of the laws of the nation.

The Asante throughout their history have gone to war to defend the Golden Stool and even allowed their king to be deported in 1896 rather than risk a war in which they feared they might lose the Golden Stool. It is the Golden Stool that became the secret of the military prowess of the Asante that led to the creation of an empire which, at its zenith, covered an area between 125,000–150,000 square miles, with a land area much larger than present-day Ghana and a population of nearly five million, made up of people from forty-seven ethnic groups.

Stools continue to be the symbolic source of royal power and prerogative, and the reverence, sacredness, and venerable mystery surrounding the Golden Stool has maintained a political structure in which the people continue to have not only cultural but also ritual links with the government. Even in areas without centralized political structures, such as among the Vagala, Sisala, and Konkomba of West Africa, there is an official called Tendana, custodian of the land, who officiates at annual festivals, performs sacrifices at the local shrines, and prays for the people and the community in times of danger and disaster. This person has extensive powers that come from respect for his religious power rather than from fear of physical punishment.

CHARTER MYTHS

The Yoruba treasure their sacred myth of Oduduwa, son of Olodumare, the Almighty. Oduduwa is also the mythical founder of Ile-Ife and the ancestor of the Yoruba. Ife is the symbolic center of the world where creation began as well as the center of Yoruba *asa* and social life. Oduduwa as the historical and political founder of Ife is said to have descended from the sky on a chain and wrested the crown from Obatala. Oduduwa was a historical figure, a warrior king who led his people to conquer the original inhabitants of the area and was deified after his death. The annual public wrestling festival when the Oni (king) of Ife, representative of Oduduwa, wrestles with the chief priest of Obatala and captures his crown, reenacts this historical event and celebrates the victory of Oduduwa. Not only is the conquest of Oduduwa dramatized but the religious basis of Yoruba traditional political authority is validated.

The direct descendants of Oduduwa are the principal rulers of Yorubaland and they must be able to trace their relationship to the Alafin of Oyo, who is the direct descendant of Oranyan, who was the son and successor of Oduduwa, the founder of Yorubaland. Shango, the son of Oranyan, was the fourth Alafin of Oyo who was deified after his death and became the *orisha* of thunder and lightning and the manifestation of the wrath of Olodumare. In Yoruba religious tradition, Shango is believed to be against lying, stealing, and poisoning among his worshipers. Shango therefore contributes to the maintenance of high moral standards in Yoruba society. Shango is also referred to in many Yoruba praise songs as the master, grandfather, and uncle of twins.

The Oni of Ife, who traces his descent to Oduduwa as other Yoruba kings, is responsible for the annual Egungun festival, meant to dramatize the continued presence of the Yoruba ancestors, who appear periodically, as masked figures, to communicate with the people. The Egungun are believed to turn away evil or misfortune that may befall the society and also watch over it. The Egungun also have the power to discipline unbearingly despotic kings in their Igbole, the Egungun grove, and also remove undesirable elements from the society. The maintenance of social peace, therefore, is not the responsibility of the living only but also of the dead, and the Egungun and Oro societies function in Yoruba society as instruments of discipline and execution to express the continued interest of the dead in the affairs of the living.

RELIGION AND PUBLIC MORALITY

One of the orders undergirding the universe according to African worldviews is the moral order established by the Creator and is the source of the prohibitions, taboos, customs, regulations and laws, notions of right and wrong, as well as what is beautiful or ugly, what people's rights and duties are, all of which make life in society livable and tolerable. The Creator's concern with morality can be seen from some of the Creator's names, such as the Akan name, Brekyirihunuade, the One who sees all even that which is behind, which refers to a judge who sees all and brings everything to book. The Ugandan name, The Great Eye, conveys the same idea. The Creator is so interested in justice that the proverb says: "To avoid fraud, Onyankopon [Divinity] gave each creature a name," so that there would be no injustice and every creature or person would be responsible for his or her own deeds.

While morality can be said to originate from common sense and human society, there is no gainsaying the fact that, to a considerable extent, morality derives from religious or supernatural sources. The divinities (Yoruba, *orishas*; Akan, *abosom*; Fon, *vodu*) have the responsibility of guarding public morality. Ani, the earth goddess of the Ibo, is believed to be the source and judge of morality and homicide; kidnapping, poisoning, stealing farm products, and adultery are all regarded as offenses against her. Laws are made and oaths are sworn in her name, and Ani's priests in Iboland are charged with the responsibility of guarding public morality. And in Akan society, the prohibition against suicide is in the name of Asase Yaa, Mother Earth, who abhors the spilling of human blood on the soil, which defiles her. Enormous sacrifices of appeasement are offered in instances of suicide to avert Mother Earth's retribution against the entire society.

Social and Religious Change

African societies have not remained static or unchanged through time. Since religious and cultural traditions are tied up with African people and their histories, they have undergone many changes as a result of human experiences and insights. Reflections on these changes have exerted their influences on the beliefs and practices of African people. These changes predate Africa's contact with the outside world, but they have been rapid since contact with the external worlds of Islam, Christianity, and the introduction of Western education. The spread of Islam and Christianity has been due not only to the "new" things they brought but also to the "points of convergence" between traditional religion and the ideas presented by these new religions. Where these religions have been accepted, they have been understood on the basis of the old and there have been conflicts and rejections as well as accommodations.

As the source of life and meaning, African traditional religion continues to influence the lives and thoughts of millions of people not only in Africa but also in the Americas where millions of Africans were involuntarily transported during the era of slave trade. These people were sustained by their own religious and cultural heritage before they were integrated into the new societies that were to emerge in the Americas. African religious and cultural heritage has continued to be a potent instrument of culture formation in the Americas, and the religions of African provenance, such as Candomble, Umbanda, and Macumba in Brazil;

Santeria in Cuba and the United States; Vodou in Haiti and the United States; and others continue to speak to the needs of millions of people from all walks of life and from many ethnic backgrounds.

BIBLIOGRAPHY

Abimbola, Wande. 1997. *Ifa Will Mend Our Broken World: Thoughts on Yoruba Religion and the Diaspora.* Roxbury, Mass.: Aim Books.

Blakely, Thomas D., Walter E. A. van Beek, and Dennis L. Thomson. 1994. *Religion in Africa: Experience and Expression.* London: James Currey and Heineman.

Busia, K. A. 1968. *The Position of the Chief in the Modern Political System of Ashanti.* London: Frank Cass.

Diawara, Manthia. 1998. *In Search of Africa.* Cambridge, Mass.: Harvard University Press.

Ford, Clyde W. 1999. *The Hero with an African Face: Mythic Wisdom of Traditional Africa.* New York: Bantam.

Harding, Rachel E. 2000. *A Refuge in Thunder: Candomble and Alternative Spaces of Blackness.* Bloomington: Indiana University Press.

Johnson, Samuel. 1966. *The History of the Yorubas.* London: Routledge and Kegan Paul.

Magesa, Laurenti. 1997. *African Religion: The Moral Traditions of Abundant Life.* Maryknoll, N.Y.: Orbis Books.

Mbiti, John S. 1969. *African Religions and Philosophy.* London: Heinemann.

———. 1991. *Introduction to African Religion.* Second Edition. London: Heinemann.

Olupona, Jacob K., ed. 1991. *African Traditional Religions in Contemporary Society.* New York: Paragon House.

Opoku, Kofi Asare. 1978. *West African Traditional Religion.* Singapore and Accra: FEP.

———. 1997. *Hearing and Keeping: Akan Proverbs.* Pretoria: UNISA Press.

Pinn, Anthony B. 1998. *Varieties of African Religious Experience.* Minneapolis: Fortress Press.

Ray, Benjamin. 2000. *African Religions: Symbol, Ritual and Community.* Second Edition. Upper Saddle River, N.J.: Prentice Hall.

Some, Malidoma Patrice. 1994. *Of Water and the Spirit: Ritual, Magic and the Spirit in the Life of an African Shaman.* New York: Penguin, Arkana.

———. 1998. *The Healing Wisdom of Africa: Finding Life Purpose Through Nature, Ritual and Community.* New York: Tarcher, Putnam.

Soyinka, Wole. 1992. *Myth, Literature and the African World.* Cambridge: Cambridge University Press.

Zahan, Dominique. 1979. *The Religion, Spirituality and Thought of Traditional Africa.* Chicago: University of Chicago Press.

CHAPTER 53

AFRO-CARIBBEAN RELIGIOUS SOCIETIES

KAREN MCCARTHY BROWN

THE product of an early and involuntary globalization of African culture, Haitian Vodou is arguably the most misunderstood and maligned world religion. The reasons for this are not so much theological as they are historical and political. The historical reasons are rooted in Haiti's revolution. Haiti was the first black independent republic. It achieved that status through a long and violent revolution led by slaves as well as free men of color. Haiti's revolution (1791–1804) occurred at a time when the United States and several countries in Europe were slaveholders. News of the slave revolt in Haiti spread like wildfire through the colonial world. Groups of free and enslaved blacks throughout the Americas took intense interest in what was happening in Haiti. Slaveholders were deeply threatened. The transatlantic colonial world responded strongly to news of the defeat of Napoleon's army in Haiti and of Haiti's declaration of independence on January 1, 1804.

The political repercussions of these events then contributed to misconceptions of Haitian Vodou. Multiple efforts were made to isolate and disempower the new black republic. Europe and the United States threw up a trade blockade around Haiti, and the Catholic Church in Rome withdrew all priests and severed its ties with the country. A remarkably nasty propaganda campaign with Vodou at its center completed the response of the so-called civilized world. A consensus was reached: Haitian blacks were too primitive to govern themselves and Haitian Vodou was the most convincing evidence for that argument. Vodou was characterized by white colonials, travel writers, politicians, and journalists as primitive, violent, irrational, and sexual. Its ritualizing was said to cause people to lose control (Moreau de St. Mery 1797/1958). On every point, this image of Vodou was fashioned from a simple reversal of Enlightenment values. Vodou was also diagnosed as satanic, the opposite of Christian behavior, and thus Vodou became the enemy of the church. At this time, Christian and Enlightenment rhetoric were still used to justify slavery and the hegemony of white men in the colonial world.

Haitian Vodou was born from the interaction of groups of people brought to Haiti to work as slaves, people who had been taken from several areas in West and Central Africa. The most obvious African influence in Haiti is that of the former Kingdom of Dahomey located in what is now Benin. There is also discernable influence from groups which surrounded the old Dahomean slave-trading empire, such as the Evhe, Adja, Mahi, and the Nago or Yoruba peoples. And finally, there is considerable cultural input from Central Africa, from areas now known as the Democratic Republic of Congo and Angola. Slaves from Central Africa tended to come in the later years from the slave colony, and these "Kongo" people became the largest ethnic group among Haiti's slaves.

Slaves were brutally forced to work the productive sugar plantations, as well as the smaller coffee, tobacco, and cotton plantations. Over time, these people blended spiritual insights and practices from a dozen or more traditional African religions. It was necessary not only to remember but also to recalibrate African religious beliefs and practices so that Vodou could address issues arising from the suffering and social distortion of chattel slavery on St. Domingue (Haiti's colonial name). Catholicism was included in this African religious mix, as was Free Masonry, and, in some ways, these spiritual systems also became resources for slaves and free people of color.

From the beginning Haitian Vodou was a religion of resistance. All Vodou practices reflect both European and African influences, but they also are marked by the trauma of plantation culture. Vodou is a religious healing system that, from the beginning, gave high priority to survival and also to resistance and even rebellion. Contemporary Haitian herbalists have preserved knowledge of poisons likely to have been used against white people in the slave era. Also, Vodou's social structures, and the secrecy they afforded, made it possible for blacks and mulattoes to plan the August 1791 attack on plantations in Haiti's northern plain, a violent event that started the revolution.

Two centuries have passed since the consensus on Vodou was formed in reaction to Haiti's slave revolution. Yet significant dimensions of it persist today among journalists who talk about "voodoo economics"; filmmakers who never tire of putting a zombie or two in their horror films; politicians who insist Haiti needs to be rescued from itself; and Protestant missionaries who think conversion is what Haitians, who live in the poorest country in the Western hemisphere, need more than anything else. Uncovering the true story of Haitian Vodou points to the importance of knowing the historical and political contexts of the world's religions.

Vodou, whether in Haiti or in diaspora communities in New York, Miami, New Orleans, and Montreal, is still characterized, more often than not, as a primitive religion involved in magic. In an attempt to undermine this persisting consensus about the nature of Haitian Vodou, I have chosen to introduce the religion via one of its most misunderstood aspects, the manufacture of charms, or *wanga*, as they are called in Vodou. (I encountered such a love charm in the Kalfou cemetery, more than a decade ago. It echoed the wanga Lola made for the woman with the unfaithful husband. One of the prayers requested that the woman who commissioned the charm would be the only one before whom the man involved would bow his head.)

The Charm Called *Mare Djol*

In the fall of 1994, Mama Lola, a well-known Vodou priestess living in Brooklyn, produced a *mare djol*, a charm called "close the lips" or "shut the mouth," for a young man who had come to her seeking help. Inside a terra cotta pot, she put *sabliye* leaves to foster forgetting (in Haitian Kreyol *bliye* means "to forget"), salt (a prophylactic), molasses (a sweetener), the name of an electronics company on Long Island, and the name of a female employee of that company. She covered up the small pot with a white cloth ("you tie the mouth with a white cloth") and then wrapped yard after yard of cotton string around the vessel until it looked like a mummy. Lola hung the mare djol from a heating pipe that crossed the ceiling of her basement altar room, the small crowded room where she consulted with a more or less constant stream of clients with problems concerning such things as health, love, jobs, and money. In the course of her workday, whenever Lola thought of the mare djol, she reached up and set the charm swinging. This activated the charm's ingredients. What she did is called "working the wanga," a ritual practice that includes such things as praying, and burning candles before a charm, spraying it with rum or perfume, or even thrashing it with a dry palm frond from last year's Palm Sunday services.

The mare djol was created for a man (let us call him Patrick) having trouble with his supervisor at the electronics plant where he worked. The supervisor was jealous because Patrick's work attracted the attention of "the higher-ups." She gossiped about Patrick in ways that damaged his reputation and could have seriously endangered his job. Lola created a wanga designed to keep the supervisor's mouth shut.

The Function of the Wanga in Healing Practices

In Vodou healing practices, priests and priestesses objectify troubled relational situations. A *manbo* (priestess) turns existential problems into accessible objects in the physical world and then "works the wanga," that is to say, changes those objects and the life situations they configure, in this case, by introducing more desirable ingredients into the social-emotional mix. When making the mare djol, Mama Lola put sabliye leaves into the red clay pot to make the supervisor and those she influenced forget the entire affair. Salt and molasses were also added; the first functioned as a cleanser and the second as a pacifier of office tension.

Healing work in Vodou is carried out in private, one-on-one sessions involving card readings that diagnose the presenting problem and its spiritual origins, along with treatments such as taking herbal baths and manufacturing wanga. The mare djol Lola made is a common type of wanga. It is based on a bound and tied vessel filled with ingredients both active and metaphoric. This type of wanga uses material objects to construct a narrative of problem-and-cure. This psychological / spiritual "work" moves powerful emotions and embarrassing problems from the secret and guarded spaces of individuals and families out into a larger social arena, where they can be "worked" on.

Haitian wanga have African ancestors and among them is a group of bocio figures from Benin in West Africa. These are austere human figures carved in wood and clothed in dense layers of raffia, herbal pouches, sacrificial blood, candle wax, animal teeth, and horns—all concrete signifiers. Art historian Suzanne Blier says these images "wear the inside on the outside" (Blier 1995: 133). In some cases the wanga similarly expose things painful and private. For example, a woman whose husband was unfaithful made a cloth doll (with Lola's assistance) from a piece of her husband's clothing, and then, after seating the doll in a small wooden chair, she "tied the man down" with copper wire and even added a padlock. A burning wick floating in a shallow bowl of oil was placed in front of the doll whose face turned to the wall. On that wall was a mirror. (Perhaps her husband needed to get a good look at himself.) Tucked behind that mirror was a picture of Santa Clara with her head bowed. This "work" was intended to induce humility in a proud man and to clear his eyes (a pun on the saint's name) so he would "see" only his wife.

Tying and Binding Wanga

It is common that wanga of almost any type are finished off by being tied and bound. After diagnosing a client's problem (a collaborative enterprise between manbo and client) a manbo may prescribe "binding" or "tying down" a person who is giving her client trouble. This will involve making a wanga. The role of the wanga is causal, not symbolic. It is not constructed to symbolize change in a troubled relationship; its role is to make that change happen. This Vodou sense of how "magic" works was, and perhaps still is, an unforgivable offense to Enlightenment rationalism. In Haiti, for a century, the making of wanga was so great an offense it was intermittently outlawed and those who broke these laws were jailed, tortured, and killed. Laws against the pretense of being able to change the material world through magic were first introduced by the government of an independent Haiti. The country's leaders were eager to prove themselves worthy of consorting with good Christian nations. Decades after the revolution, both church and state in Haiti sought to improve the country's international reputation by staging "anti-superstition campaigns." In their most extreme form, Vodou temples filled with people were burned to the ground.

The Ethics of Wanga

In Vodou there is a pervasive contrast between what is bound or tied and what has been let loose or allowed to flow. This should not be confused with the good-and-evil binary opposition. In general Vodou ritual healing practices aim at making things flow by untying knots and removing blockage, locks, and chains. Yet "tying a person down" is not innately destructive. In certain circumstances it can be a responsible social act. Such was the case with the mare djol Mama Lola made for Patrick. Also, the wanga created to change an unfaithful husband was certainly a worthy effort from the perspective of the woman who married him and had his children to worry about, yet that same wanga could easily be experienced as an illegitimate use of power by the husband. Once aware of the "work" affecting his life, a husband in that position might try to find another Vodou priest or priestess to counter the power of the one who made the wanga.

The ambivalent moral valence of spiritual strategies that allow one person to control another cannot be denied in the making of Vodou love charms. Love charms are the most common type of wanga. When dolls are bound back-to-back with ribbon or rope and then hung upside down in a tree, someone intends to get free of a troubled relationship. When two dolls are bound face-to-face and up-ended in a drinking glass, along with a cigarette, a candle, and a scribbled prayer or two, a closer connection is being demanded of one person by another. In this intimate context, Vodou reveals its complex and nuanced view of the moral life, including a sense of the importance of compromise in almost every human context, and the existential conviction that the value of survival tends to trump all other values.

Another insight into the nature of wanga concerns the difference between supplication and demand. The one who makes or commissions a wanga does not throw himself or herself on the mercy of God. Persons who make or commission wanga draw on their own inherited spiritual powers. Recognizing these powers and learning how to use them well, which usually means using them for the good of the community and not for selfish purposes, are central themes in the initiation processes of this African diaspora religion.

ALL HEALING IS ABOUT THE HEALING OF RELATIONSHIPS

In the Vodou view of things, human beings are not so much defined by the web of personal relationships that surrounds them as they are created out of it. There is a sense in which the individual person is composed from inherited ancestors and spirits. The relational web, which provides identity and character to those who "serve the spirits," has both temporal and spatial dimensions. It connects persons to living family members no matter how far away they are, as well as to ancestors, and lwa, Vodou spirits.

A word about ancestors: in Vodou, the dead do not go to heaven. Instead, they descend to what is called the bottom of the water, a place of chill and dampness. After a year or more has passed, it is up to the living to retrieve the souls of the dead, or at least the souls of those who were spiritually important during their lifetimes. A Vodou ceremony called *retire mo nan dlo*, "Remove the Dead from the Water," is often a lengthy and expensive ceremony, but without it, the ancestors can do nothing more constructive than harass their descendants. This ceremony warms the souls of the dead and raises them up from the water. Many emerge complaining of cold and hunger. (This communication is accomplished through a kind of ventriloquism that is also a form of possession-trance.) The hungry souls are fed and eventually installed in consecrated *govi*, large clay pots, on Vodou altars. They can always be consulted there, when wisdom is needed. It is understood that without this type of attention from the living, ancestors could not perform as their protectors. It is usually an ancestor who brings a warning of impending danger and these warnings often come through dreams.

A word about the Vodou spirits: the majority of the lwa were brought to Haiti from Africa, and they are central to the practice of Vodou. The lwa are not to be confused with ancestors, or with God. The single and incomparable God is recognized, but this God is "too busy" for individuals to make demands on Him. A person cannot plead with Bondye, "The Good God," or demand things from

Him. If it is determined that an illness is "from God," then the Vodou healer can do nothing about it, but the lwa are different from God. Like the ancestors, they have a symbiotic relationship with the living. They both need and enjoy the food prepared for them and the attention given them through the feasting, song, and dance of Vodou ceremonies. In return, the lwa can be coaxed into "riding" one of the faithful, using that person's body and voice to communicate directly with members of the *sosyete*, temple family. At Vodou ceremonies, through possession, the lwa sing, dance, eat, give advice, and, when it is needed, chastise the reluctant *sevite*, servant.

Some Vodou spirits, such as the trickster Gede, are treated like intimate family members who can be easily cajoled. Others, like the warrior Ogou, or the strong mother, Ezili Danto, are fiercer and demand more rigorous attention. It is built into the characters of all lwa that they can be both constructive and destructive. Even though the lwa are called "*sen-yo*," the saints, and even though each is associated with a Catholic saint, they are not saintly types in a Catholic sense of the term. They are not so much moral exemplars as they are models of different dimensions of life. So while Gede performs acts related to death, sexuality, and humor, Ogou explores aggression. And Ezili Danto, among other dimensions of her complex character, gives presence to both the rage of the mother and the power of the soldier.

Simple hierarchical schemes cannot easily be applied to the complicated re- lationships between humans and spirits. Spirits have dense personalities, just as human beings do. They also have good days and bad days, just like humans. People who serve the Vodou spirits have been known to explode in anger at a spirit's behavior and threaten to cut off the flow of gifts and honors to that spirit.

Interaction with the lwa by means of possession-trance is frequent, powerful, intimate, and central to Vodou. Possession can also be an aspect of the one-on- one healing sessions discussed above. Possession-trance makes it possible to cross barriers between the living and the dead, the human and the divine. Thus the religious practices connected to possession strengthen the relational web that sus- tains life in Haiti. From the Vodou perspective, people, their ancestors, and their spirits are caught up in a dense and dynamic relational web, one that is sustained by appropriate and ongoing reciprocity in all relationships.

BACK TO THE MARE DJOL

When Lola tied the mouth of Patrick's gossiping supervisor, she sought to clear blockage in the relational network sustaining her client. It is important to note that the problem was not conceptualized as an essential flaw in either one of the persons involved. Instead, the problem was located in the relational space between them. Yet, the block in that relationship proved to be indicative of other, more serious problems. Lola knew Patrick's job would never have been threatened if he had no spiritual problems. If the lwa and the ancestors had been properly cared for, they would have prevented his trouble on the job before it began. Thus Patrick's dilemma had to be diagnosed and treated on two different levels. Since spirits were found to be part of Patrick's problem, Lola first showed him how to feed the lwa and strengthen his spiritual protection. Then she turned to Patrick's presenting symptom, the gossiping supervisor, and chose to treat that problem with a mare djol. Several months after the wanga was assembled, Patrick told Lola that his supervisor had been promoted and, at the same time, transferred to another branch of the company outside New York. Both Patrick and Lola pronounced the "work" successful.

BIBLIOGRAPHY

Blier, Suzanne Preston. 1995. *African Vodun: Art, Psychology, and Power.* Chicago: University of Chicago Press.

Brown, Karen McCarthy. 1987. "The Power to Heal: Reflections on Women, Religion and Medicine." In *Shaping New Vision: Gender and Values in American Culture.* Eds. C. Atkinson, C. Buchanan, and M. Miles, 123–141. Ann Arbor, Mich.: UMI Research Press.

———. 1995. "Serving the Spirits: The Ritual Economy of Haitian Vodou." In *Sacred Arts of Haitian Vodou.* Ed. Donald J. Cosentino, 205–223. Los Angeles: UCLA Fowler Museum of Cultural History.

———. 1998. "The Moral Force Field of Haitian Vodou." In *In Face of the Facts: Moral Inquiry in American Scholarship.* Eds. Richard Wightman Fox and Robert B. Westbrook, 181–200. Washington, D.C.: Woodrow Wilson Center Press and Cambridge University Press.

———. 2001. *Mama Lola: A Vodou Priestess in Brooklyn.* Berkeley: University of California Press.

Dayan, Joan. 1995. *Haiti, History and the Gods.* Berkeley: University of California Press.

Deren, Maya. 1983. *Divine Horsemen:The Voodoo Gods of Haiti.* New York: McPherson.

Fick, Carolyn E. 1990. *The Making of Haiti: The Saint Domingue Revolution From Below.* Knoxville: University of Tennessee Press.

Lawless, Robert. 1992. *Haiti's Bad Press.* Rochester, Vt.: Schenkman Books.

Moreau de Saint-Mery, M.E.L. 1797. *Description topographique, physique, civil, politique, et historique de la partie francais de l'isle de Saint-Domingue.* 3 Vols. Philadelphia: N.P.

MacGaffey, Wyatt. 1991. *Art and Healing of the Bakongo.* Bloomington: Indiana University Press.

————. 1993. "The Eyes of Understanding: Kongo Minkisi." In *Astonishment and Power*. Eds. S. H. Williams and D. C. Driskell, 21–103. Washington, D.C.: National Museum of African Art/Smithsonian.

McAlister, Elizabeth. 2002. *Raral Vodou, Power, and Performance in Haiti and Its Diaspora*. Berkeley: University of California Press.

Leyburn, James G. 1966. *The Haitian People*. New Haven, Conn.: Yale University Press.

Pietz, William. 1985. "The Problem of the Fetish I." *Res: Anthropology and Aesthetics* 9:5–17.

————. 1987. "The Problem of the Fetish II." *Res: Anthropology and Aesthetics* 13:23–45.

————. 1988. "The Problem of the Fetish IIIa: Bosman's Guinea and the Enlightenment Theory of Fetishism." *Res: Anthropology and Aesthetics* 16:105–123.

PART VII

LOCAL RELIGIOUS SOCIETIES

CHAPTER 54

THINKING GLOBALLY ABOUT LOCAL RELIGIOUS SOCIETIES

JUHA PENTIKÄINEN

GLOBALIZATION has affected indigenous peoples and their traditional cultures in significant ways. Throughout the world, some 190 million people are identified by religious cultures that are variously known as "native," "indigenous," "local," and "ethnic" religions. These are the native people of North and South America, Siberia and Northern Europe, and the tribal peoples of Africa, India, Central Asia, Southeast Asia, Australia, New Zealand, and the Pacific Islands. If these people were members of a single religious community it would comprise the sixth largest in the world. In an era of globalization great numbers of these people have been obliged to leave their rural home territories to live in urban milieus or to migrate as emigrants or refugees to foreign countries, where they live in new environments in newly established groups with strange neighbors. Globalization—with its universally disseminated flow of information and complicated economic and socio-cultural structures—has both created a global family network and also threatened traditional cultural values.

This global diaspora of native peoples greatly affects their religious life because their spirituality is ordinarily not conveyed through organizations and ideologies. Indeed, the languages of most indigenous peoples do not have a concept of religion in their vocabulary. In Siberia, for instance, they have the native concept of *saman* instead. When I asked a Nanay shamaness from the Lower Amur Region in southeast Russia about the topic of religion she replied, "Religion...? It is

Russian. We have our samans only." Samans are those "who know"—who are capable of shamanizing in shamanic cultures.

These are neglected traditions in the study of world religions. In general, there has been little knowledge of and interest in the huge diversity of the "ethnic religions" to be found around the world. These typically have no founder. During most of modern history, their map remained that of the grey area of territories of the unknown world, *terra hyperborea incognita*. It was considered the pagan world, a kind of no-man's-land with no religion, which for this reason could be conquered, missionized, and colonialized into the safe spheres of the Christian power structures of Western colonial domains.

LAND AND LANGUAGE

What has protected traditional cultures from these colonial assaults has been their deep associations with the land—with nature in general and with certain places in particular—and their maintenance of native languages. What is typical of the indigenous languages of the minority peoples of the Fourth World is their confrontation against Western ways of thinking and power mechanisms which overwhelmingly seem to overcome their local settlements, traditional ways of living, ecological environments, and languages.

Along the lines described by the anthropologist Robert Redfield, a division may be outlined between the "great," established religions of humankind in comparison to the "little" traditions"—those that mainly exist in small local communities (Redfield 1973: 1). The little religious traditions around the world are based on the people's memory of their local landscape, a natural or cultural place, a locality. This place becomes sacred when it is carried in the long, deep memory of an individual, a nuclear or extended family, a clan, an ethnic group or a people, or in some cases even a nation. Typically enough, borders and frontiers crossed by them have a great significance in the narratives retaining that knowledge.

Arnold van Gennep in his *Les rites de passage* (1909, English translation 1960) made an important observation about the significance of the territorial borders crossed by people when they migrate. These movements in his opinion follow a pattern: *séparation, marge, agrégation*. The same pattern is followed by the rites of passage related to the social steps made public by such rites of passage as childbirth, naming, initiation, marriage, death. What I want to emphasize here is the point of view, usually forgotten in the functional and symbolic interpretations of van Gennep's theory, that focuses on the borderline between "this world" and "the other-worldly." Van Gennep in my mind was a prestructuralist interested in

how crossing frontiers and territorial borders were similar to crossings of a religious nature: the door is the boundary between the foreign and domestic worlds
in the case of a temple—therefore to cross the threshold is to unite oneself with
a new world.

The meanings of locally based memory, as described in historical examples
by Simon Schama (1996), are carried along as a part of the inner mentality of
people who flee or migrate. It acquires religious significance abroad in foreign
milieus and is felt as a kind of a sacred Heimland, a hidden spot in the depths
of the mind that cannot be expressed under threat or exile. The significance of
these memories retains an identity of an ethnic religion, even as an islet of a local
"little" community, in Redfield's terms. Refugee studies have repeatedly shown
how native religious symbols have become strengthened under pressure, in refugee
camps, even among refugees whose attitudes toward religion used to be hostile,
alien, or indifferent in their home countries. Religiocultural symbols become manifest in the home altars of the emigrants and refugees, wherever in the world
people may have migrated or fled. The importance of religious rituals related to
native rites of passage has also increased in diasporic immigrant communities.
People who, of course, did not migrate or flee with an intention to die in a foreign
country, nevertheless become interested in finding a spot of land where they can
bury their dead; a place, or an islet, of their own if possible, as an important
symbol of the locality of their religion.

Like location, language also is central to traditional cultures and in many
ways the spirituality of traditional peoples is reflected in their cultural mother
tongue. Language conveys those spiritual meanings. In the last decade of the
twentieth century, UNESCO launched a research program to report on the endangered languages in the world and to propose measures for supporting them.
Such reports as *Arctic Languages: An Awakening* (1990) and *Endangered Languages*
(1991) showed that the greatest threats concerned many small languages indigenous to the Arctic regions, due to the simultaneous ecological revitalization processes. Comparative research on shamanism in various loyalties has revealed interesting follow-up about the phases experienced by shamans as leaders of their
peoples in the north. How one language dies while another survives is a question
related to the ethnic/national processes that should be carefully studied in the
contemporary world. This kind of comparative research is needed since there is
currently no comprehensive study on the special role that native religionational
shamanic leaders play in these processes. However, isolated shamanic studies in
different milieus have provided valuable comparative research about contemporary shamans in Siberia, Sápmi (Sami territories), and among the American Indian
and Inuit peoples in the New World.

Comparisons among the Sápmi or Sami, the Khanty people of Siberia, and
Mapuche Indian shamanism in Chile indicate how similar the worldwide problems of the indigenous peoples are. One key issue concerns their rights to land

and water resources they have used for many generations without ever having marked such resources as their own, unlike the people who invaded their territories have been so eager to do. The Sami national movement arose and developed an internationally recognizable strength when its leaders were imprisoned as part of its battle against the occupation of the Alta River in Northern Norway. Although the size of the Mapuche Indian population (ca. 1.2 million) is much greater than that of the Sami in the four countries in which they are found (Finland, Norway, Russia, Sweden) their cultural rights under Spanish rule have been even more restricted.

The Ralco River, the ancient border between Mapuche and Spanish domains in Chile, has at the turn of the third millennium become the symbol of the national battle of the Mapuche Indians. When the second dam was built at the Andes, a dozen shamanic families refused to leave their hills, even with the threat of being drowned. The processions of Indian demonstrators started from their holy mountains in January 2001 and were led by their native leader, Sara Imilgei. They were stopped by water tanks in front of the presidential palace in Santiago de Chile. In my interview with Imilgei she told me that their Andean gods would solve their problems.

The gravestone of a Mapuche shaman stands as the religious symbol of this national confrontation. It is located on the road leading to the dam builders' camp. It was to be moved but the transfer was stopped by an accident that killed the truck driver who was going to move it away. The building project became temporarily closed during our field tour in January 2001 after a Mapuche cemetery was found on the hill of the Ralco River. Since the common interests of the national and ecological movements have found each other, the Ralco movement is nowadays called the Bio Bio River project.

WORLDWIDE REVIVAL OF ETHNIC RELIGIONS

The diaspora of traditional native communities to new locations around the world has in many cases weakened their identities, but it has also brought an awareness of the need to protect traditional places and languages. The globalization of culture has made non-indigenous people also aware that the native traditions are part of a world inheritance to be protected and appreciated by all. The year 1993 was celebrated as the UN year of indigenous peoples around the world. Although the proclamation of the year was, in the minds of the Fourth World political leaders, more symbolic and a show of goodwill than an effort to bring actual achievements and practical results. But it did help to increase the solidarity of the indigenous peoples and to demonstrate that the different indigenous communities had common concerns around the world.

The election of Alejandro Toledo as the first Native American Indian president of Peru in 2001 is an interesting indication of reformations taking place in Latin American countries. The nomination of this learned economist—who still speaks his Ketsuan Indian language learned in the Andes, although educated at Harvard University and trained in the World Bank—was accompanied on July 29, 2001, by a sacred ceremony on Macchu Picchu holy mountain, eyewitnessed by Prince Felipe of Spain; Shimon Peres, Israeli foreign minister; and Ricardo Lagos, president of Chile, among others. He received a golden axe and hangings from two barefooted priests after their plant and food sacrifice to Apui, the mountain god, and Panchamama, Mother Earth. President Toledo, showing his loyalty to his native background, shared by the clear Peru majority, said: "I have come to give thanks for the strength and energy that Apui and the Earth have given to me." His speech was followed by one given by his wife, an anthropologist with a Belgian background, who said that the fortune and well-being of the ancient rulers will now return to Peru.

Russia with its abundance of minority populations—over a hundred discrete communities—has after Soviet rule created a ministry for the problems of its indigenous peoples. Shamanism has accordingly been listed as a religion and interest in its value as an example of cultural heritage has increased. In my field work in this region since 1988 I found that traditional shamanism has survived after the persecutions of Soviet exile. Among the Khanty, the Yakut, and the Manchu Tungusic peoples, who are at the very cradle of shamanism, the vocabulary of a network of native shamanic concepts has been retained. In Central Siberia, such republics as Sakha (Yakutia), Khakassia, Buryatia, and Tuva have proclaimed shamans as the bearers of their cultural traditions. They support the official organizations of registered shamans who practice in their shamanic clinics, as do shamans in contemporary Korea and China.

How and why such an archaic phenomenon as shamanism has overcome the pressures of the great ideological, religious, and ecological changes that have taken place in the twentieth century in various territories and cultures is an interesting target of research awaiting further exploration. Native traditions have endured despite the influence of modern ideologies, the pressures of urbanization, collectivization, and other forms of social change, and despite the ravages of oil, military, and other modern intrusions. Despite these impacts on their ethnic cultures and the ecological environment of their homelands, their cultures have survived. The fieldwork carried out in these regions will give evidence of the importance of the role of shamans and other traditional leaders in the ethnic revival and survival processes of indigenous peoples. Shamans were persecuted for ideological and religious reasons in many countries. Some of those who survived have become remarkable ethnic and national leaders, giving new meaning to their traditional authority roles and strengthening the revitalization processes of their peoples.

BIBLIOGRAPHY

Collins, Dirmid R. F., ed. 1990. *Arctic Languages: An Awakening*. Paris: Unesco.

Gennep, Arnold van. 1960. *The Rites of Passage*. Chicago: University of Chicago Press.

Pentikäinen, Juha. 1998. *Shamanism and Culture*. Helsinki: Etnika.

Redfield, Robert. 1973. *The Little Community and Peasant Society and Culture*. Chicago: University of Chicago Press.

Robins, Robert H., and Eugenius M. Uhlenbeck, eds. 1991. *Endangered Languages*. Oxford: Berg.

Schama, Simon. 1996. *Lanscape and Memory*. London: Harper Collins.

My sincere thanks for the cooperation in the Mapuche field to Mr. Petri Salopera and for the help in bibliographical work to Dr. Risto Pulkkinen.

CHAPTER 55

NATIVE AMERICAN RELIGIOUS SOCIETIES

NIMACHIA HERNANDEZ

THE traditional indigenous peoples of the Americas share much in common with indigenous peoples throughout the world who have been affected by the forces of globalization. At the same time the importance of their knowledge—spiritual, ecological, and social—retains its significance in this increasingly globalized world for myriad reasons. Among these are a respect for the natural environment and ecosystems that sustain life. Another is the quest for meaning in local traditions that is a counterpoint to modern development.

THE PROBLEM OF DEFINITION AND IDENTITY

Native American identity has been designated, decided upon, and forced upon Native Americans by social and political actions. Most of the estimates of numbers of Native Americans continue to focus on racial definitions of identity and rely on these parameters exclusively. This fact makes it impossible to produce numbers of "Native Americans" that have meaning, especially when the goal is to determine "cultural background" orientation. Many people of mixed racial ancestry still practice the traditional Native cultural practices. Meanwhile, many who identify as Native American, and whose families have not intermixed with non-Natives, do not practice—or even believe in—the traditional Native practices of their own ancestors.

It is also difficult to provide names and locations of Native American communities because of historical political reasons. The names of Native American tribes that are known to most Americans are the result of treaties offered to those who could still fight forcefully to resist colonization. It often excludes Native communities who were enfolded into the nation-making enterprise through other means after disease and warfare diminished their ability to defend themselves: through intermarriage, religious conversion, removal from sacred and tribally held homelands, and assimilation into cultural norms.

DIVERSITY OF NATIVE AMERICAN WAYS

There is diversity, however, among Native American ways. Traditional Native American teachings about the sacred focus on a relationship with the sacred that is seen as inhabiting a variety of manifestations. Native Americans consider it sensible that a variety of peoples could have a variety of sacred ways. For example, the Amazonian Kayapo from Brazil paint themselves with crushed ants, while the Aztecs of Mexico use gold, and the Blackfoot of Montana and Alberta, Canada, use body paint made of red ochre. For each group the contexts and materials are obviously very different, but the point of using them on the body is to acknowledge, in a very formal way, a Creator force or being and to establish recognition, in the form of a relationship, of that force.

Another example of diverse expressions of the sacred would be the different ways various astronomical bodies are studied and explained. Some South American Natives focus on the Milky Way, while the Northern Lights figure prominently in the lifeways of Native Americans from the northern hemisphere. Still others emphasize the sun, moon, and morning star (Venus) or other specific constellations that are less significant to other Native Americans. Across an enormous range of expressions, from different focal points in the sky, to the ways the body can be decorated, the similar purpose forms the vital point of many traditional Native American practices. Though the apparent differences result from very different ecological and spatial contexts, the practices are all means of connecting with the creative forces of the universe.

STORY AND CREATION

What is common to most indigenous people is a religious philosophy rooted in teachings related in creation stories. These establish the foundational underpinnings of an indigenous practice of knowledge, otherwise known as an indigenous way. The stories, with their concomitant ceremonies and the worldview they present, are based on a "cosmovision" that holds the nature of knowledge to be one part of all of the energies in the universe, which are all interrelated and very much alive. To know, according to indigenous ways, is to be aware not simply of oneself but also of the interrelationships between the source of life and all that is imbued with this force. This educational process is lifelong and requires adherence to specific protocols, expectations, attitudes, purposes, and responsibilities (among other things). Balanced relationships between the various levels of existence, or energies, are primary because indigenous peoples experience life in a multidimensional, distance- and time-spanning world where it is necessary, for example, to sacrifice in order to receive the blessings of knowledge. Most important, it is a world in which the important indicators about all knowledge relate to the task of achieving understanding and self-awareness that can be put to use for the survival of all people. The creation stories are the source of these teachings. Other stories, those seemingly unrelated, promote similar values (often by negative example) and model behavior that is deemed worthy of being retold.

Indigenous traditions concerning the nature of spirit and reality and the proper ways to handle this knowledge and its transfer to future generations have been altered by the experience of colonization, although they continue to characterize indigenous existence even in the postcolonial era. For many indigenous peoples, the pressure to give up old practices of educating the young to be prepared to take active roles in the perpetuation of the nations' traditional ways was intense enough to cause them to stop practicing their ways and speaking their languages. Indigenous peoples recognize that language is the force that holds together and expresses deep and complex thought about the nature of spiritual life, particularly through storytelling.

At the same time, the external threats to their ways of living are so persistent that many Native American peoples have taken their traditions away from public access and exposure. Moreover, many aspects of the traditional spiritual life have always been closed. More recently, however, the need to protect the privacy requirements of these traditions has forced even stricter restraints on participants and witnesses.

SACRED EARTH, SACRED SPACE,
AND SACRED SITES

Indigenous peoples' traditions are bound to the environmental, ecosystemic, and cosmic context in which they have been originally conceived and practiced. We can begin to understand indigenous peoples by considering how we regard natural geographical and astronomical surroundings. These entities are considered sacred by indigenous people and are the root of traditional indigenous systems of spiritual awareness. They are therefore central to the processes involved in indigenous ceremonies. One characteristic of the predominantly oral culture of many indigenous peoples is that many of the basic precepts and practices are transferred to younger generations by oral tradition and by practicing this tradition in its appropriate settings.

In the indigenous creation stories spirit and physical bodies constantly change and exchange forms: they transform. Many of these stories tell of the origins and acquisition of designs, the origins of songs, and ceremonial episodes such as those associated with particular ceremonies. Generally, energies of different forms or transformed states (e.g., animals) form an important part in these rituals and are alternately identified with different realms. These original forms of creators either taught or brought some of the most important ceremonies to the humans on earth. They then set a precedent for future relations which humans were charged with maintaining in a harmonious way. This includes specific ceremonial items and practices that were developed, followed, or taught on the journeys between earth and sky, as well as relationships with specific animals and plants. Geographical sites are associated with the people in the stories. Observations of the cosmos for ceremonial or other knowledge-based reasons have a central role among most indigenous peoples, for whom astral observations related ceremonial life to the astronomical calendar. By thus focusing the ceremonial life, indigenous peoples fall into synch with the life cycles going on all around, whatever the environment.

The earth-to-cosmos connection confirmed through the stories is based on important teachings, including how respect for the interdependence and mutuality of human interrelationships is reflected in the natural environment, whether earthbound or astronomically located. The human environmental dependency teaches respect for the interdependence of humans, all earth life, and the larger circle of the universe because they are inseparable. They are connected and their relationship is reciprocal. The respect for land and its sacredness is so crucial to the indigenous worldview that when indigenous peoples' land is destroyed, so is the culture, which proves detrimental to traditional ecological as well as societal processes. Interrelationships this close between the environment/land, stories, and indigenous peoples' health—physical and mental—are practically universal across many indigenous peoples' traditions, from the Winnebago to the Hopi. The location, purpose, and structure of stories are significant for storytellers.

The thorough knowledge of the environment that is contained in, and is the source of, many indigenous teachings and traditions has potential benefits for global environmental, social, and most important, spiritual health. This is significant at a time of conflicts between Western and Native worldviews with respect to the land. Specifically, indigenous peoples view the land (world) as a living, social being, with whom we create and define a social relationship and modes of acceptable behavior. The world is seen as having the power to exert itself and its expectations upon humans, who should learn to listen to and receive insights in order to survive. This knowledge is of course passed from one generation to the next through stories and the rituals each generation retains and uses for instruction.

Discussion of the landscape-based aspects of the indigenous stories' teachings focuses attention on the early settlers' Western concepts of land and nature as material, mechanical, and devoid of spirit, while Native traditions picture nature throughout as an extended family or society of living, ensouled beings. Rather than attempting to control nature, the indigenous outlook offers the prospect of a human society in harmony with nature, with moral and spiritual dimensions to this relationship. Traditional indigenous teachings emphasize an awareness of a great power—the energy or moving force of the universe a holy, sacred energy that moves throughout the universe and is known by a variety of names. This energy and the respect that the indigenous have for its power is communicated in story, formally acknowledged in ceremony, and recognized as guiding a way to live.

The stories take place at sites found all over traditional indigenous lands. The significance of the indigenous creation taking place on areas around the home of the indigenous from time immemorial is not lost on those who know the stories. They indicate the home-sites of uncounted ancestors and the longstanding relationship with the universe established and nurtured by the indigenous peoples' ancestors. In the traditional indigenous relationship with the land, all land is alive and filled with the ancestors of the entire people, and these are the powers that indigenous peoples seek to understand and maintain a relationship with, over time, but in the same traditional places.

IDENTITY THROUGH HARMONY WITH THE LAND AND LIFE'S CYCLES

To disrespect the land is to disrespect ones' identity as an indigenous person in the traditional (story) sense: indigenous identity is deeply rooted in the earth. The ongoing relationship with the traditional homeland, with the indigenous peoples' responsibility to care for the earth, is reaffirmed by many examples of what happens to humans when they disrespect it. These traditions demonstrate an understanding of, and a perspective concerned with, relationships. Concern for the proper treatment of the land and the powers that live within it has longstanding traditions in indigenous spiritual life.

Indigenous peoples' elders, through the telling of their peoples' stories, convey the background underlying their specific teachings about the nature of the reciprocal relationship between humans and the rest of the natural world. The stories express a responsibility to maintain good relations between the different parts of nature, including animals and plants, because all of it is considered to be alive, and all share in the power given to all of creation by the creator. There is an assumed respect and responsibility in the role of caretaker of that balance. The natural world is not considered separate from human existence. Knowledge or access to spiritual growth is attainable only through a practice of respect for that which is trying to be understood and for the process of learning to understand. Once levels of awareness are achieved, it is essential to maintain a sense of responsibility for the well being of the source of knowledge, in the hope that it will continue to teach humans. Landscape has such a central role in indigenous knowledge since it is the source of that knowledge. The indigenous sense of respect and responsibility toward the care of the land is based on a series of covenants with energies and life forms that are explained in the traditional stories.

There is a consideration of the balance in the macro sense of including everything in the cosmos. Prayer, through song, action, word, or even just intent, is believed to influence this delicate balance. The energies of the world find ways to make their presence known when they are disrespected or when humans have obligations or responsibilities they are not fulfilling. This is not anthropomorphism, but a respect for the "essence" of the world, the life force that flows through all beings, keeping them connected. This is evident in many stories that relate the incidents or occasions wherein interactions between humans and other beings are positive and reciprocal.

In the context of this cosmological framework and its associated sacred geography, a cosmic sanctioning of ethics ensures the continued future through the practice of spiritual stewardship, involving the ritual taking and use of natural resources according to cultural protocols established in tribal stories and validated within a cosmology that views human beings as part of an interacting life force continuum that includes animals and spirit beings. Animals and fish are viewed as intelligent, sentient societies having the power to influence events and, as such, must be treated with respect according to instructions encoded in the stories and teachings of the peoples' oral traditions. Observation of the cosmos encourages a practice of balance and recognition that humans must live in harmony with the earth and with each other. There are specific ways in which the creation stories relate these messages, and it is important to recognize the significance of the message inherent in these stories about balance between humans and the natural world that surrounds us, including the cosmos. In identifying and explaining the relationships that the stories highlight, indigenous peoples have inherited location-specific spiritual traditions. This spatialization of knowledge and religious philosophy is central to the stories and to the particular knowledge of indigenous peoples in each of our traditional homelands. Likewise, it also describes and demonstrates the result of sacred energy (life force) that is the root of the indigenous knowledge system—that is, built upon acknowledgment of this power—and of its flow through the universe, and of our relation to it.

These practices focus on the oral transmission of stories and how these stories might be understood as giving meaning and expression to an understanding of "the way" or a "sacred philosophy," based on a relationship between humans and their natural environment. Indigenous peoples have always had stories to tell about why and how things are the way they are and to explain these to the next generation.

What can attention to the ways in which this knowledge is structured, relayed, and practiced ultimately tell us about the background that informs what we can observe about indigenous peoples' religion? Creation stories serve as repositories of the foundational ideals, goals, processes, and purposes behind "knowing" in indigenous spiritual systems. The best understanding of the meanings of these stories, however, is accessible to those who choose to practice a way of life that is outlined and guided by the teachings offered by the stories. The indigenous language, geographical and astronomical homeland, musical traditions, and designs, for example, serve as some ways religious knowledge is manifested and transferred in the indigenous tradition. The indigenous tradition of spiritual knowledge expressly depends upon direct experience, not just theory or rhetoric and secondhand inference, to sustain what can be justifiably referred to as sacred knowledge. Therefore, those who live within the traditional indigenous homeland, who speak the indigenous language, and who practice the traditions of knowledge that have been handed down for generations necessarily have enhanced opportunities for learning. This does not, however, mean that when one does not have this type of access, it is impossible to attain insights. But such insights are more difficult to achieve with colonization, diaspora, and conversion to deal with.

CHRISTIANITY AND NATIVE TRADITIONS

The acceptance by Native American peoples of some aspects of the dominant culture, including Christianity, does not necessarily mean the rejection of their tradition. When something new or unexpected is introduced people do not always necessarily see it as an either/or equation: either being "traditional Native American" or in violation of tradition.

An example of the assimilation of Christianity into the Native worldview is to be found in a story about an elder, very respected for his knowledge of the traditional Blackfoot "way of being," who had a dream. In telling his dream and considering interpretations of it with other Blackfoot elders, he revealed that in it he had seen some Blackfoot elders—"holy people"—with Jesus Christ among them. In their consideration of the elders' dream, one issue was just how "traditional" having an appearance of Jesus in this dream was. In the Blackfoot tradition, however, the dream had simply included an additional holy person. While not from the Blackfoot homeland and tradition, he would nonetheless be regarded as a holy and meaningful participant, albeit within a Blackfoot framework of interpretation.

This is the type of interpretation that complicates notions of cultural impact. Even before the introduction of Jesus Christ, other holy people/beings would have been similarly welcomed into the Blackfoot understanding of the sacred. This understanding is based on a longstanding tradition in many Native American spiritual practices wherein the addition of other spiritual elements/beings brings more power to prayers. A Native American practice that likely began long ago and that continues today is an extension of that same belief about bringing power by adding new elements to what one already believes: the practice of getting baptized several times, into different denominations. Some indigenous people consider themselves to be members of the Evangelicals, Mormons, fundamentalist Christians, Baptists, and others, simultaneous to their membership in more traditional activities and affiliations, in an effort to increase their power, protection, and knowledge of the Creator.

KEEPING TRADITION INTACT IN AN ERA OF GLOBALIZATION

Native American spiritual practices are born of and into a multidimensional sense of the sacred and in a specific geographical location or setting. Working to keep alive this central aspect of the traditions, Native Americans face many obstacles. These include the violent approach to indoctrination that has been the religious inheritance of many Native American communities. Still more detrimental, however, is the forced removal from the traditional homelands where the traditions were born and transferred to the people: within these lands the language ties together the people and the physical nature of their surroundings; it maintains a coherence across seemingly unrelated contexts, tells of the sources of creators' powers, and of their role in this creation. These specific and very particular settings are credited with having been the original source of many of the language, songs, and stories that form the basis of particular, nation-specific ways of life and worldviews.

Unfortunately Native Americans have many things that non-Natives have valued, among them land, oil, water, animals, spirituality, and even genes. These have been made available to others through a combination of social consensus, political enforcement, appeals for religious conversion to "save souls," and through rationalizations that these goods deserved to be appropriated. Other nations have followed the tradition of colonization and appropriation that has existed in the United States between Native Americans and the larger dominant society, including Japan, Russia, African countries, the South Pacific islands, Australia, and New Zealand. In each of these areas Native peoples face the effects of colonization and "development" through appropriation.

The prophecies of indigenous peoples throughout the Americas tell of this time and situation. They tell that the process of appropriation is not over: The taking of material aspects represents the first phase, while the continued efforts to take Native American and other indigenous peoples' spirituality are still to come. The present concern with the status of the world's health, climatologically and geographically, has increased non-Natives' interest in learning how to save the earth, and many seek a return to Native American and other indigenous traditions as a source of information about how to do this. Many Native Americans see such New Age approaches as the dominant society's attempt to continue to mine the Native way of life for items it desires, not as a form of reconciliation or healing.

The foundations of the traditional ways of indigenous peoples' religions are best explained in the context of the natural world, but we can nonetheless learn a great deal about it by approaching it with a review of some of the stories and their concepts (e.g., balance, harmony, responsibility, and respect) that are central to the more general indigenous religious paradigm that exists in the longstanding, extensive similarities and connections among various traditions around the world (e.g., Misiminay, Maori, Menomonee). In this way there is a kind of global connection among indigenous peoples.

BIBLIOGRAPHY

General Works

Bunge, R., 1982. "Awareness of the Unseen: The Indian's Contract with Life," *Listening*, 19:181–191.

Cajete, Gregory. 2000. *Native Science: Natural Laws of Interdependence*. Santa Fe: Clearlight.

Dei, George J. Sefa, Budd L. Hall, and Dorothy Goldin Rosenberg, eds. 2000. *Indigenous Knowledges in Global Contexts: Multiple Readings of Our World*. Toronto: University of Toronto Press.

Deloria, Vine Jr., 2002. *Evolution, Creationism, and Other Modern Myths: A Critical Inquiry*. Golden: Fulcrum.

———. 1994. *God Is Red: A Native View of Religion*. Golden: Fulcrum.

———. 1999. *For This Land: Writings on Religion in America*. New York: Routledge.

Dooling, D. M. and Paul Jordan-Smith, eds. 1989. *I Become Part of It: Sacred Dimensions in Native American Life*. San Francisco: Harper.

Echo-Hawk, W. R., 1993. "Native American Religious Liberty: Five Hundred Years After Columbus." *American Indian Culture and Research Journal*, 17(3):33–52.

Feld, Steven and Keith H. Basso, eds. 1996. *Senses of Place*. Santa Fe: School of American Research.

Gulliford, Andrew. 2000. *Sacred Objects and Sacred Places: Preserving Tribal Traditions*. Boulder: University Press of Colorado.

Hirschfelder, Arlene B. and Paulette Molin. 2000. *Encyclopedia of Native American Religion*. New York: Checkmark Books.

Irwin, Lee, ed. 2000. *Native American Spirituality: A Critical Reader*. Lincoln: University of Nebraska Press.

Josephy, Alvin M. Jr., ed. 1991. *America in 1492: The World of the Indian Peoples Before the Arrival of Columbus*. New York: Vintage Books.

Maffi, Luisa, ed. 2001. *On Biocultural Diversity: Linking Language, Knowledge, and the Environment*. Washington, D.C.: Smithsonian Institution Press.

McPherson, Dennis H. and J. Douglass Rabb. 1993. *Indian from the Inside: A Study in Ethno-Metaphysics*. Thunder Bay: Center for Northern Studies.

Radin, Paul. 1937. *Primitive Religion: Its Nature and Origin*. London: Hamilton.

Sillitoe, Paul, Alan Bicker, and Johan Pottier, eds. 2002. *Participating in Development: Approaches to Indigenous Knowledge*, ASA Monographs 39. London: Rutledge.

Sullivan, Lawrence E., ed. 2000. *Native Religions and Cultures of North America: Anthropology of the Sacred*. New York: Continuum.

Suzuki, David and Peter Knudtson. 1992. *Wisdom of the Elders: Sacred Native Stories of Nature*. New York: Bantam Books.

Tedlock, Dennis, and Barbara Tedlock. 1975. *Teachings from the American Earth: Indian Religion and Philosophy*. New York: Liveright.

Waters, Anne. 2004. *American Indian Thought: Philosophical Essays*. Oxford; Blackwell.

Weaver, Jace, ed., 1998. *Native American Religious Identity: Unforgotten Gods*, Maryknoll, N.Y.: Orbis Books.

Williamson, Ray A. 1984. *Living the Sky: The Cosmos of the American Indian*. Norman: University of Oklahoma Press.

Community-Specific Studies

Anderson, Jeffrey D. 2001. *The Four Hills of Life: Northern Arapaho Knowledge and Life Movement*. Lincoln: University of Nebraska Press.

Basso, Keith H. 1996. *Wisdom Sits in Places: Landscape and Language Among the Western Apache*. Albuquerque: University of New Mexico Press.

Beck, Peggy V., Anna Lee Walters, and Lee Walters. 2000. *The Sacred: Ways of Knowledge, Sources of Life*. Tsaile: Navajo Community College Press.

Courlander, Harold, ed. 1971. *The Fourth World of the Hopis: The Epic Story of the Hopi Indians as Preserved in their Legends and Traditions*. Albuquerque: University of New Mexico Press.

Deloria, Vine Jr. and Lee Irwin. 1996. *The Dream Seekers: Native American Visionary Traditions of the Great Plains*. Norman: University of Oklahoma Press.

Farella, John R. 1984. *The Main Stalk: A Synthesis of Navajo Philosophy*. Tucson: University of Arizona Press.

Fire, John (Lame Deer) and Richard Erdoes. 1972. *Lame Deer Seeker of Visions: The Life of a Sioux Medicine Man*. New York: Simon and Schuster.

Hungry Wolf, Beverly, Beverly. 1980. *The Ways of My Grandmothers*. New York: Morrow.

Kawagley, A. Oscar. 1995. *A Yupiaq Worldview: A Pathway to Ecology and Spirit*. Prospect Heights, Ill.: Waveland Press.

Martin, Calvin. 1999. *The Way of the Human Being*. New Haven, Conn.: Yale University Press.

McCleary, Timothy P. 1997. *The Stars We Know: Crow Indian Astronomy and Lifeways*. Prospect Heights, Ill.: Waveland Press.

Meyer, Manulani Aluli. 2003. *Ho'oulu, Our Time of Becoming: Hawaiian Epistemology and Early Writings*. Honolulu: Native Books.

Neihart, John C. 1988. *Black Elk Speaks*. Lincoln: University of Nebraska Press.

Overholt, Thomas W. and J. Baird Callicott. 1982. *Clothed-In-Fur and Other Tales: An Introduction to an Ojibwa World View*. London: University Press of America.

Schwarz, Maureen Trudelle. 1997. *Molded in the Image of Changing Woman: Navajo Views on the Human Body and Personhood*. Tucson: University of Arizona Press.

Wissler, C., and D. C. Duvall. 1995. *Mythology of the Blackfoot Indians*. Lincoln: University of Nebraska Press.

CHAPTER 56

AUSTRALIAN ABORIGINAL SOCIETIES

JOHN HILARY MARTIN

GLOBALIZATION has affected all reaches of society, including small indigenous communities that are embedded in large national cultures and economies such as Australia. Indigenous societies are affected by globalization in two ways: the forces of the global economy and culture that come into their traditional homes and their own out-migration to new pluralistic settings, including urban centers and foreign lands. In the case of the Australian aboriginals in the outback their very survival involves compromises with the surrounding society by accepting an inflow of money in the form of government services, grants, and entitlement programs.[1] Their communities become remittance economies that are similar but also different from other indigenous remittance economies in small Pacific island states such as Tonga. Though some have migrated to Australia's cities, for cultural reasons Australian aboriginals are strongly disinclined to leave their own local areas, and when they have left their local region, they have not left the landmass of Australia in any significant numbers. A major factor in this reluctance to leave is a culturally religious one: the notion of the Dreaming.

The Dreaming is a powerful factor in the culture of all Australian aboriginals and has religious roots. According to traditional aboriginal understanding, in the beginning before all time, the eternally existing land was flat and empty, without the features that we know today or have known at any time. There were multiple sources of power in the earth, however. Ancestral beings broke through to the surface of the earth and moved over the landscape. In the course of their ancestral journeys they shaped and formed the land, generating all the particularities we are aware of today. These ancestral Dreaming figures created communities of human beings to maintain and care for the particular places which they had shaped and formed and gave them charge over it. Their action generated an eternal relation between a particular people and a particular place on the landscape. There is an old phrase sometimes used to help explain this relationship to outsiders: "the land does not belong to us, we simply belong on this land." For aboriginal communities other people's lands (such as white people's lands) may be a commodity to be bought and sold, but not their land. The local land given to each community in the Dreaming is definitely not a commodity. That land which is the root of their Dreaming must be preserved in all its critical aspects, although the land can be shared. It is immediately obvious that any schemes to offer land (acreage) in exchange for a community's Dreaming sites will never be acceptable. Also, sharing, which is sometimes possible, will require the thoughtful consent of the traditional owners whose ancestors hark back to the Dreaming and is not to be carried out by any central planning agency.

At this point it might be well to keep in mind the differences that the globalization processes make on the aboriginals who live in a community on their own lands in the outback and those found in towns and larger cities, like Brisbane and Sydney. Aboriginal communities have resided in what is now a city area long before contact with European settlers in 1788. Although new municipalities were constructed over their ancient sacred sites, the sites gave them a reason for continuing to live there. Although one was expected by tribal tradition to be found on one's own land, aboriginal men and women began to go off and live in the larger Australian cities almost immediately after the European contact. Individuals came in from the bush for a variety of reasons, sometimes to avoid conflicts at home or sometimes out of simple curiosity to see the wonders of an urban world, but not solely to get ahead economically. Wanderers into town were always expected by their kinfolk to return home to their own land and very often they did, yet in the course of events many did not. In urban areas newcomers often mixed with and married members of other aboriginal groups ("mobs") with the result that the Dreamings inherited by later descendants and their land obligations became uncertain and confused. Although urban-based aboriginals currently form a good percent of the aboriginal population as a whole, they form only a small minority of the overall population in any given urban area. Like members of any minority, not part of the establishment, less well educated and less skilled, they fall to the bottom rung of the economic ladder. They are likely to find work more difficult to get and without specialized skills they will be more quickly replaced. From a simple economic point of view they seem least likely to succeed.

Yet getting ahead in the Western economic sense was not traditionally a high priority in aboriginal life. Other elements of aboriginal culture—the family, the influence of the Elders, and sacred land—have traditionally held a mob together. To some extent these factors sustain them in urban areas irrespective of the forces of globalization. But their cultural values are also under severe pressure as a result of an indirect, but no less powerful, effect that the climate of globalization has generated. In urban settings the traditional extended family of aunties, uncles, half brothers, half sisters, and first and second cousins feels the burden as more and more members are added who are not related to each other in traditional ways. The dynamics of city life facilitate marriages across local tribal lines, across racial and ethnic lines, and what is of more significance across Dreaming lines. Even where marriages are happy and successful, succeeding generations find it increasingly difficult to transmit traditional cultural values to offspring who only partially or incompletely share a connection with their lands. Children of mixed, non-aboriginal parentage, of necessity, do not inherit a Dreaming heritage from both parents. Children of mixed aboriginal parentage may well inherit the Dreamings of both parents, but these mixed arrangements may make a traditional marriage difficult to manage. In any event there is a clear loss of the influence of tribal Elders. Grandparents and older uncles and aunts have importance in one way or another, of course, in almost all cultures, but in traditional aboriginal society one's proper Elders have particular significance for they have the ceremonial ability and duty to pass on the Dreaming stories and rituals which establish identity. These same Elders are also the ones who have authority to offer advice about how their offspring must conduct their lives, advice which cannot be rejected without serious consequences. As individuals move into an urban environment and as the Elders remain on the land, their influence and authority inevitably begins to dissipate. For members of succeeding generations it becomes more difficult to determine who one's Elders are. As a result, the intimate association with one's own proper country and its Dreaming ancestors becomes less clear, less present. The leveling effect of globalization affects community life in urban settings, and the tendency to integrate small units of culture and economy into larger, more homogenous systems affects aboriginal communities more sharply than most.

Globalization also affects aboriginals who continue to live on their own lands in outback rural areas. The cultural values of the family, the Elders, and the land with its Dreaming are still largely in place in these traditional outback communities. Central planning for such communities has not been very successful, as indicated by the scrapping of Australian and Torres Strait Islander Commission and its replacement with another government program.[2] Whether consciously or not, aboriginal attention has been shifting from economic development to a protection of traditional values. Attention to one's own land, in the form of the Outstation movement, gained force in the 1970s.[3] Although aboriginal families live tightly together, crowding and the preservation of privacy is an old problem.[4] Communities of five hundred or more seemed too large, too uncomfortable. A smaller Outstation was preferred with its small community of thirty to fifty blood relatives or close affines. The influence of the Elders seemed more secure in such a place. Elders could make their headquarters on it, when needed they could be located, and they could supervise the children more closely. An Outstation cannot be located on just any piece of land, however. It must be located on one's own Dreaming land, that is, on or near one's Dreaming place.

These efforts help explain the new interest in attempting to locate precisely where one's family land is to be found. The location is not always beyond dispute. Ancient stories told both in public and in private business ceremonies help but are not always decisive. As a result, the study of local languages and local music has undergone a kind of renaissance. The number of aboriginal languages had declined drastically since European contact in 1788, from hundreds to scores, but serious attempts are now being made to preserve and even revive some of them. Speaking one's own language is often helpful in preserving a sense of personal identity, of course, but it can do much more. The names of places, waterholes, soaks, trees, and the stories about them transmitted in local languages can provide unexpected but reliable clues about who was once living at such and such a place, who was removed from there, and perhaps when a mob moved itself to a newer location. In a community where a particular aboriginal language is spoken as a kind of lingua franca, there can be others spoken less frequently by a few. In one community in the Northern Territory there were at one time as many as seven independent languages spoken in the district. They were gradually dying out under the influence of a dominant aboriginal language commonly spoken at a central location. The surviving speakers of the less frequently spoken languages are currently being pressed to write down, videotape, or narrate what they can still remember since linguistic variations of ancient stories can contain clues of land and place. They often do this in conjunction with the support and the alert critique of speakers from rival language groups. This is not surprising since not only words and taxonomy but accurate transmission of Dreaming stories is also at stake. The current revival of music also shares in this pattern. Catherine Ellis believed that traditional aboriginal knowledge was a system of logic that was enshrined in music, and Linda Barwick and Allan Marett have gathered a number of observers who have found that aboriginal music performance offers many similar clues (Ellis 1992: 161; Barwick and Tunstill 1995). The result of these efforts will be to pinpoint the location of a particular mob more precisely (around its sacred area) and help it focus on a living situation more in line with a traditional aboriginal ethos, i.e., a small familial group on its own but able to share with similar groupings in a traditional regional neighborhood.

To illustrate the effect of the social and economic changes on aboriginal culture, let me give the example of a particular aboriginal community in Australia's outback, the N.T. (Northern Territory). This settlement is located on the sea with a current population of about 1,500 to 2,000. Permanent, ongoing contact with this grouping of aboriginals was not made until about 1935. This community was in fact made up of a collection of small populations (mobs), each with significant linguistic and some minor cultural differences. The population, then numbering perhaps 150 people, had come together for mutual protection and were, in consequence, prepared to gloss over their differences. Like many other aboriginal groups in the rural outback they accepted the food, clothing, and shelter offered by government agencies and missionaries. Since Australian aboriginals had no common language, English became their lingua franca as they learned to read and write and gain a modicum of other skills enabling them to get along with the outside world. For the N.T. the metropolis was Darwin (then c. 20,000) and so the community was within its shadow.

By the 1950s the people at the settlement were involved in a number of small businesses and light industry. They had some small sewing rooms to make clothes for themselves with the prospect of outside sales in the future. They had a garden that produced enough vegetables for themselves, and they hoped that its bananas might be marketable some day. They made bricks and other building materials for local use and built their own houses, roads, and prepared an airstrip. There was a bakery that was famous for its fine, nourishing bread. A few years later a nearby part of the community began running some stock that produced beef for the locals. (It could not be sold outside the area for health reasons, but those objections could be overcome.) On the land there were some exotic minerals that offered possibilities for mining. (There had been tin and copper mines in a nearby district in the 1880s.) And then there was art. Bark paintings large and small and some small carvings were offered for sale at *corroborees* the community put on every so often for the few tourists who found their way there. (Corroboree is a performance by aboriginals containing aboriginal singing and dancing put on for friends, acquaintances, and even tourists. It is public and does not contain any restricted religious material, but often includes significant cultural material and is more than a mere entertainment.) All these occupations were done under the watchful supervision and direction of a small number of outside white people. By the late 1950s the community was on the threshold of becoming a financially viable, independent social unit—as independent, that is, as any small town in a rural setting was likely to be.

A number of individuals at the settlement wanted to get out from under the tutelage of outsiders by the late 1950s and early 1960s, but others found the arrangements convenient enough. Daily routines were in place, their sacred land was theirs to enjoy, white folks' problems such as education, health, airplanes, and the like, were being handled by white folks. Individuals still living on the outskirts of the settlement in the bush continued following the old ways (i.e., a modified hunter-gathering routine) but they were in touch with the newly available amenities (guns, sugar, steel fish hooks, tobacco, and alcohol).

This community was not an idle, happy, carefree, feckless group living as parasites on the largess of the nation. That is an image which many Australians and other Westerners once had of tribal peoples. The community had many concerns, including shortages of food and shelter, lack of health care, early death, and inability to follow up on the educational opportunities being thrust upon them. There was little money and no pay. Nonetheless the mini-economies of these places, although spartan, were stable with the possibility of growth. A rudimentary infrastructure was being put in place, training was occurring, and in theory individuals could work and get ahead. In the late 1960s and early 1970s this was to change.

Australia in the sixties, as elsewhere, was a warm-hearted time. Its idealism called for integration and assimilation to break down barriers, to remove prejudice, and to allow individuals to fulfill what they saw as their personal destinies. The trouble with this vision for small tribally based societies is that they gauged success and destiny more in communal than in individual terms. Those in charge of the larger society, whether consciously or not, set out on a path to shore up and support individual destinies. In the Australian case the indigenous population was invited to stand up and to take its full place and move on with the great mass of the Australian people. In 1967 a constitutional referendum was passed setting up the process where citizenship and all of its benefits were conferred upon every aboriginal individual. The referendum was a widely popular measure, long overdue, and there are few regrets, but it did have some unintended affects on the communities it was designed to help.

With citizenship came benefits. The more important benefits were intangible (freedom to vote, to travel, to marry), but some benefits were quite tangible and not unworthwhile. They included new levels of health care and hospital access, child support, old age pensions, and unemployment wages. These benefits were well received by individuals living in these small familial indigenous communities. Where wants were few it became possible to live without having to do traditional work—in fact without having to do any work at all as the new benefits were shared communally. The desire to work did not disappear from aboriginal communities or psyches, but the desire to work on white projects and on white-directed projects, whose benefits were now accessible anyway (health care, schools, transport, access to manufactured goods), declined noticeably. The new government grants and entitlements were sometimes laughingly called sit-down money. The dissocializing effect of pay without employment did not pass without protest from some aboriginals themselves. An aboriginal Elder refusing his check said that, "if I accept this money without doing anything for it, I will become a non-person, a nobody." But in the end individuals and aboriginal communities had new needs and much more money to spend.

Other forces were also at work on small aboriginal communities in the 1970s and into the 1980s. They can be conveniently lumped together under the heading of much improved communication. Seasonal weather patterns and impassable dirt roads had kept small outback communities virtually incommunicado for months at a time every year. With the multiplication of local airstrips for small planes and a much-improved network of roads by the 1970s the communities of the outback were no longer the isolated places they had once been. Aboriginals were free to leave them on visits to town, but more significantly, for our interest in globalization, nonaboriginals, outside businessmen, were now free to *enter* aboriginal communities on a regular basis, bringing with them offers of all sorts of goods and services. Aboriginal leaders abetted by community advisers, not unreasonably, began making use of these new services. Sadly, it is a fact of economic life that small homegrown, cottage industries are not as efficient or as profitable as well-organized large-scale businesses. It became cheaper to purchase in town and have the bricks, tiles, cut lumber, and cement trucked in to build houses. It was noticed that the quality of these imported products was more uniform, delivery more reliable. Local brick making was gradually abandoned. Building houses with modern electrical wiring and pipes brought in the skilled electricians and plumbers who had the required know-how, and house building soon passed out of local control. Other local activities felt similar pressures. It is always possible to run stock on a small scale, of course, but profitable cattle raising now required very large herds, substantial capital, and trained management and marketing. Local communities could hardly compete. Even clothes could now be bought more cheaply in town than sewn at home. The sewing room used fewer hands and finally needed none at all. The communal garden was abandoned—it had not been popular anyway—when canned foods, fresh vegetables, greens, and fruit could be flown or trucked in on a regular basis and bought at the general store. One by one the village enterprises of the pre-1950s were abandoned. The local bakery seems to have been the last to go. Members of the community now had enough money to pay for the things they wanted, forming what we might call a government remittance economy, i.e., an economy based on government payments.[5]

In some ways the economic impact in this community was similar to the one described by Cathy Small in her book, *Voyages: From Tongan Villages to American Suburbs* (1997), where she analyzed the effect of external money flow on another small community, the island kingdom of Tonga. In the twenty years between 1980 and 2000 individuals and whole Tongan families left Tonga in large numbers for the United States, Canada, New Zealand, and Australia. This emigration is not unlike what has happened in many other small island nations as the Pacific as become part of an interregional and global economy. The specific reasons why emigration has occurred from such a well-organized and well-run kingdom as Tonga is not a particular concern for us, but what is interesting is Small's description of the effects which large inflows of money have had on Tongan life. Like other aboriginal groups, the people of Tonga are community oriented. Their culture expects and trains its members to share, i.e., to shoulder obligations and responsibilities, one's *kavenga*. While some persons may have more and some may have less, sharing assures that no one will go without. Even when they live abroad, Tongans still fulfill duties and obligations on a regular basis with the family members remaining at home. The numbers of migrants overseas living in wealthy countries like New Zealand and America has become so extensive that the sums of money sent back home to help have become an important, even a vital part of the island's economy. Tonga has become, in effect, a remittance economy.

Some good things have happened in Tonga as a result. School fees (even advanced school fees) could be paid, washing machines and other electoral appliances could be installed, at least one water reticulation system was set up, and houses could be refurbished. But some problems also were generated. Families lost their younger, and most qualified, members who went abroad either to get ahead or to sustain the family at home. With young, creative members overseas, the local family at home was often disrupted, and family ties and family ethos inevitably weakened. Nor did all families share equally in the new remittance wealth. Families with little supplementary income from overseas fell behind in their style of living; families without emigrating members often received nothing and found themselves among the poor. If too many family members began to live overseas permanently, the family property in Tongan sometimes became neglected or was even allowed to run down (Small 1997: 127–45).

Some of the negative effects of the new remittance economy generated by globalization are readily observable, but some of them are indirect and affect culture. Overseas remittances took the form of gifts of cash or exotic goods that the local economy obviously could not repay in kind, yet some recompense had to be made by the Tongas staying at home. One form of repayment was exchange gifts in the form of cultural artifacts. Tapa cloth, a cloth made of beaten bark, was a traditional form of wealth that could be used and was used in gift exchanges. This fabric, the tapa, was difficult to make and required skill and many hours of slow work to produce. It was highly prized for it showed the rank and status of those who received it as well as reflected the efforts of those who produced and gave it. The fabric was used in dances, ceremonies, and for display and was produced by traditional communal efforts (Small 1997: 23, 42–43, 172–78). Its value could be assigned a trading value, covertly of course. As more and more of this store of wealth was required to keep up with gift exchanges, greater efforts were made to produce more of it. At first longer hours were devoted to producing the tapa cloth, but after a while ways were found to shorten traditional procedures— e.g., smaller pieces were made to do for larger ones, the quality was reduced, local specialists took over the communal production. Cultural rupture was now under way. Although the whole Tongan community made every effort to retain what was called the Tongan way by those living abroad—including its sense of kavenga (family duties and obligations), its traditional dancing and meal celebrations and its church attendance (largely Roman Catholic)—these traditions began to fade among second- and third-generation Tongans now making a home in places like North America, Australia, or New Zealand. In Tonga itself the lifestyles associated with industrial products coming from abroad also began to be imported into

Tonga. To own a TV is to have the world TV culture, or at least to be exposed to it. Sometimes cultural import was even more direct and personal than TV. Teenagers who were sent back to Tonga to better absorb the old familial ways often enough influenced the local Tongan youth to adopt the ways of their North American, Australian, or New Zealand cousins instead. A remittance economy was becoming a remittance culture as well.

The same processes of acculturation to global culture are occurring among the Australian aboriginals. The current experiences would seem to indicate that the small aboriginal cultures of outback Australia will not be able to survive the onslaught. Yet aboriginal communities have existed for thousands of years, undergoing various kinds of physical and cultural changes. Part of their ability to survive is their exclusivity. While guests are often welcomed, even for long periods of time, it is necessary to be born into the family in order to be accepted fully. This means that aboriginal groups never plan to be large, never wish to be larger than the natural increase of their populations. There is really no need to be larger, or at least any larger than can fit and be accommodated around the sacred Dreaming land. That is why land and land rights are at bottom so essential to aboriginal people. It is the locus of identity, both personal and communal. If the aggressive use and the exhaustion of all available natural resources, which has so characterized contemporary economic processes, turns to occupation and the reshaping of aboriginal land, then the progress of globalization may very well extinguish this most ancient culture existing on the planet as it has done to so many others. But the future is still uncertain.

NOTES

1. *Entitlement programs.* The word is being used here in the U. S. sense of payments made through government agencies for unemployment, old age pensions, child endowment, social security, Social Security I, and the like. The payments are made in favor of particular groups in society as a result of government legislation or regulations and not as the result of direct earnings made by the recipients.

2. The Australian and Torres Strait Islander Commission (ATSIC) began work March 1990. It was a national agency operating under an Act of Parliament (1989) to coordinate government programs dealing with economic, social and cultural, corporate and strategic planning that affected all aboriginal peoples of Australia. It was designed to resolve issues, such as land, land management; indigenous rights, law and justice, indigenous disadvantage, and family matters. The *ATSIC Annual Reports* (Canberra, Australia Government Publishing Service) contained much useful information about aboriginal life and prospects. However, ATSIC came under increasing attack as being inefficient, bureaucratic, and fostering aboriginal separatism. It had critics in some aboriginal quarters, too, who saw it as a central bureaucracy trying to impose controls on local aborigi-

nal communities. It was replaced July 1, 2004, by an appointed advisory board, National Indigenous Council (NIC), and its former portfolio was distributed among various government agencies with the intention of giving aboriginal people, a whole-of-government-response. That is to say, each department or agency of government was to respond to aboriginal concerns as they responded to all other Australians in the hope that aboriginal needs could be more easily coordinated with general administration of government programs. It is too early to tell how these new government arrangements will work out for global or for central planning among aboriginal communities.

3. For a brief overview of the Outstation movement see Sexton (1976). A more structural approach to recognition of land tenure was the Land Rights Councils set up in the N.T. (Northern Territory) under the Aboriginal Land Rights Act (ALRA), 1976. The councils were designed to function as liaison between the government and the traditional aboriginal owners of land. Friction developed between local traditional owners and the Land Councils themselves and the larger councils were subdivided after a time. The important High Court Mabo decision of 1994 recognized that aboriginal title to land could exist in Australia. This action served to concentrate interest in land as property that would be recognized at law. Diane Austin-Broos gives a brief history in Saunders (2002) and B.W. Walker (2000–2001) gives some comparative statistics for small indigenous communities throughout Australia for the years 1992, 1999.

4. Stanner has an interesting reflection on how aboriginal communities preserved privacy when living closely together in the bush (Stanner and Martin 2000).

5. Australian agencies have long been concerned about a welfare economy and what to do about it (Sanders 2002). The Australian Institute for Aboriginal (and Torres Strait Islander) Studies (AIAS now called AIATSIS), www.aiatsis.gov.au in Canberra, is a research center that has undertaken and encouraged many studies of aboriginal culture, religion, and economy since the 1930s. The institute has generated numerous occasional papers, but these studies have had only limited circulation, and then only among specialists. On questions of economy the Centre for Aboriginal Economic Policy Research (CAEPR), founded in 1990 but an independent center within the Australian National University (ANU) from 1999, has produced many discussion papers that can be found on the Web through AIATSIS. Many papers concentrate on the fairness of outback store operations, the effectiveness of stores in introducing new needs and desires in small isolated aboriginal communities, government schemes to make these communities economically self-sustaining and less dependent on outside subsidies. In another vein there is also a good deal of anecdotal, popular material, like *An Aboriginal Mother Tells of the Old World and the New* (Roughsey 1984) or even, *My Place* by Sally Morgan (1989), which looks with sorrow on the shift from hunter-gathering culture to the present small township life that characterizes so much of current aboriginal living situations. All these materials predate globalization concerns, but are a kind of preview of them.

BIBLIOGRAPHY

Altman, J. C. 1987. *Hunter Gatherers Today: An Aboriginal Economy in North Australia.* Canberra: Australian Institute of Aboriginal Studies.

Altman, J. C., and John Nieuwenhuysen. 1979. *The Economic Status of Australian Aborigines*. New York: Cambridge University Press.

Barwick, L., A. Marett, and G. Tunstill. 1995. *The Essence of Singing and the Substance of Song: Recent Responses to the Aboriginal Performing Arts and Other Essays in Honour of Catherine Ellis*. Sydney: Oceania Publications, Oceania Monograph No. 46.

Bultin, N. G. 1993. *Economics and the Dreamtime: A Hypothetical History*. London: Cambridge University Press.

Crough, G., and C. Christopherson. 1993. *Aboriginal People in the Economy of the Kimberlely Region*. Darwin: North Australia Research Unit, Australian National University.

Crough, Greg. 1993. *Visible and Invisible: Aboriginal People in the Economy of Northern Australia*. Darwin: North Australia Research Unit, Australian National University.

Edwards, W. H., ed. 1987. *Traditional Aboriginal Society: A Reader*. Sydney: Macmillan Company of Australia.

Ellis, Catherine. 1992. "Living Preservation: Problems of Cultural Exchange." In *Music and Dance of Aboriginal Australia and the South Pacific*. Edited by Alice Moyle, 155–62. Sydney: University of Sydney, Oceania Publications.

May, Dawn. 1994. *Aboriginal Labour and the Cattle Industry: Queensland from White Settlement to the Present*. London: Cambridge University Press.

McCorquodale, John, ed. 1987. *Aborigines and the Law: A Digest*. Canberra: Aboriginal Studies Press.

Morgan, Sally. 1989. *My Place*. Fremantle: Fremantle Arts Centre Press.

Rose, Frederick G. G. 1987. *The Traditional Mode of Production of the Australian Aborigines*. London: Angus and Robertson.

Roughscy, Labumore Elsie. 1984. *An Aboriginal Mother Tells of the Old and the New*. Sydney: Penguin Books Australia.

Sanders, W. G. 2002. *The Indigenous Welfare Economy and the CDEP Schemes*. Canberra: ANU Research Monograph No. 20.

Sexton, Sean. 1976. "Homeland Movement: Highs and Lows." *Indigenous Law Bulletin* 3 (1 August).

Small, Cathy A. 1997. *Voyages: From Tongan Villages to American Suburbs*. Ithica, N.Y: Cornell University Press.

Stanner, W. E. H. 1979. *White Man Got No Dreaming*. Canberra: Australian National University Press.

Stanner, W. E. H., and J. H. Martin. 2000. *People from the Dawn*. Antioch, Calif.: Solas Press.

Walker, B. W. 2000–2001. *Responding to Market Perceptions: A Strategy for Sustainable Energy Services in Remote Australia*. Canberra: Centre for Appropriate Technology.

Young, Elspeth. 1995. *Third World in the First: Development and Indigenous Peoples*. New York: Routledge.

CHAPTER 57

PACIFIC ISLANDS RELIGIOUS COMMUNITIES

JOEL ROBBINS

WHEN one considers processes of globalization in the Pacific Islands, one is struck by the extent to which religion has been central to them. Indeed, if we define globalization both as the movement of cultural ideas and institutions (including cultural constructions of politics, economics, etc.) and as the processes by which people come to construe themselves as acting in larger worlds and relating to people across vaster distances than they have in the past, then there are grounds to argue that religion, and Christianity in particular, has been the single most powerful globalizing force throughout the Pacific Islands.

Although the region comprises such social, cultural, and historical diversity among the islands of Melanesia, Polynesia, and Micronesia that generalization is rendered treacherous, this claim about the importance of religion to globalization is one that holds very broadly. Urban politics are almost everywhere carried out in rhetoric rich in Christian allusions and assumptions; the sound of church bells can be heard daily even in rural areas that the capitalist market has hardly penetrated; and Pacific Island migrants to New Zealand, Australia, and the United States as often construct diasporic communities around shared Christian faiths as they do around traditional beliefs and practices.

There are at least two reasons why Christianity and religion more generally have been so important in the Pacific Island experience of globalization. First, the carriers of Western culture to the Pacific Islands have elaborated its religious aspects more fully than any other aspect. This was of course true of the missionaries who from the outset took a leading role in bringing Western culture to Pacific Islanders, often arriving before or alongside government representatives. But it was also in many cases true of the colonial administrators as well. Seeing little economic potential in most areas, colonial officers were relatively uninterested in training rural people in the secular aspects of Western culture. With little incentive to spread their secular culture, and cash-strapped as well, colonial officers often left oversight of key secular institutions such as health care and schooling to missionaries. The missionaries responded to having the colonial field so much to themselves by conveying a version of Western culture in which Christianity was capable of grounding the social world in its entirety.

For their part, Pacific Islanders were in many cases quick to grasp the explanatory value of Christianity as a key to the new global world they were coming to inhabit, and this is the second reason it has played such an important part in their experience of globalization. The cultures of the region, both traditionally and still today, generally give religion a prominent place, and none of them holds it separate from other domains such as politics or economics: all of social life in the Pacific Islands has religious aspects and most situations, whatever else they demand, require that people take religious considerations into account in formulating their responses. These are cultures that have neither been nor understood themselves to be disenchanted.

Coming from this background, Pacific Islanders who encountered missionaries were inclined to make the effort needed to construct versions of Christianity that they could comprehend and use to fashion lives appropriate to their changing worlds. And as they encountered other aspects of Western ideology—for example, those surrounding politics and economics—they were inclined to understand them as much as possible in terms shaped by their religious commitments. It is this indigenous tendency to elaborate religious understandings of all domains of life, as much as the predominance of missionaries among those who have brought Western culture to the Pacific Islands, that has put religion at the center of globalization in the region.

The statistical data bears out claims of the importance of Christianity in the region. Melanesia, the most recently colonized subregion of the Pacific Islands, and one which contains 75 percent of the region's population, is 90 percent Christian. The rest of the Pacific Islands, not including the settler societies of New Zealand and Hawaii, are 99 percent Christian. Yet it is also true that scholars rarely report such figures without qualifying them by noting that many people who identify themselves as Christian are Christian only in a "nominal" sense. The criteria scholars use in making this judgment are rarely specified, and the scholarly politics of such attributions demand study in their own right. Yet in the present context it is perhaps best to let the nominalism charge stand. For the cultural terrain that that charge opens onto, a terrain whose features consist of various kinds of syncretism, is a very fertile one for those interested in the globalization of culture.

One can find all kinds of syncretism in the Pacific Islands. In some Polynesian societies one can find people who are committed to various brands of mission Christianity that look in many doctrinal and ritual respects quite orthodox, except where islanders have modified them to make them fit with the elaborate traditional social hierarchies that are still a fundamental part of their social lives. Elsewhere, too, one finds situations in which people committed to change can yet be found to be carrying over much of their traditional belief. In other parts of the Pacific, by contrast, one can find self-conscious movements back to tradition or *kastom* (custom) that are unselfconsciously shot through with Christian beliefs and practices. And beyond these straightforward examples of syncretism, one finds that even those cases that seem to approach a kind of purity of traditional or Christian expression usually contain some mixtures.

In seeking to frame a discussion of these diverse situations, we immediately come up against the fact that we do not have as yet, neither for the Pacific nor, as far as I know, for anyplace else, a good typology of syncretisms, much less an argument about why each kind appears where it does. Such a set of analytic tools would surely be a boon to the study of globalization in the Pacific (and elsewhere). But even in the absence of a well worked-out analytic scheme, one can detect something of a general trend in the development of Pacific Island syncretisms; a trend we can approach by contrasting cargo cults and Christian revivals—two kinds of movements that have become emblematic of religious life in Melanesia in particular.

Cargo cults are movements in which people work through innovations on traditional religious ideas and ritual techniques to engage their ancestors to help them confront the challenges presented by their encounter with Western culture. The term *cargo cult* follows from the way many of these movements aim to convince the ancestors to bring large quantities of Western material goods to those who participate in them. Some of the movements go beyond this, however, also asking ancestral help in ridding their land of Europeans. Furthermore, all cargo cults seek to minimize reliance on European powers by virtue of the strong claims their leaders make to having their own sources of religious authority (usually taking the form of ancestral revelation) that make them completely independent of the missions.

As responses to globalization, and this is surely what they have been (albeit often avant la lettre), cargo cults have to be seen as efforts to encompass the global within the local. Unlike some of the anti-globalization protests that have gained notoriety in some parts of the world in recent years, cargo cults do not represent a blanket indictment of the new culture. Instead, cargo cult leaders paint for their followers pictures of worlds in which local people will be able to control the flow of Western goods and powers and put them to locally defined and in many ways traditional ends (such as the construction of social relationships through the reciprocal exchange of material objects). Movement ideologies explain the origin of such goods in local ancestral production, just as they elaborate stories of the originally local origin of Christianity. In the worlds that cargo cults seek to bring about, then, Western culture is fully encompassed within the local world.

The enduring appeal of cargo cults—and in many parts of Melanesia they continue to arise and attract followers even today, deep into the era of independence—is based on the way they render globalization as a drama that can be played out to a satisfactory resolution on a local stage by a local cast employing largely indigenous kinds of action. Considered as such, we might take them to represent one kind of limit case of cultural globalization: one in which people confront globalization, recognize change, but strongly assert that what this change entails can be worked out locally and to the advantage of those whose horizons remain local ones. As a kind of syncretism, cargo cults can be taken as a paradigm of those cases in which traditional understandings provide the structure on the basis of which the mixture of elements is organized.

Although Melanesia is best known in the scholarly world for its cargo cults, they are not the only religious movements in the region that bear on issues of globalization. Since the 1970s Christian revival movements have become at least as prevalent as cargo cults. So profoundly have these revivals transformed religious life in many communities that one might be tempted to describe them as something of a Melanesian great awakening. Because the revivals are recognizably Pentecostal or charismatic in character (emphasizing healing, tongue speaking, prophetic dreaming, and possession among other gifts of the Holy Spirit), and because they are also intensely millennial, observers have been tempted to describe them as movements that syncretize Christianity with indigenous religious beliefs and practices. Yet this is not how they are usually understood by local people (whose traditional cultures often lacked some of these religious practices).

Instead, local people strongly emphasize the extent to which revival Christianity conflicts with their traditional religious systems. Once touched by revival, they tend actively to condemn their traditional religions, destroying the temples in which those religions were practiced and disposing of the sacra upon which their rituals were based. Many communities emerge from periods of revival far more deeply engaged with Christianity than they had been. They also emerge with their traditional religion in disarray, leaving them with little interest in, or resources to bring to, projects of syncretizing Christianity with traditional religion.

Considered as responses to the globalization of Western culture, revival movements stand in stark contrast to cargo cults. In them, people reach out to grasp what they think of as orthodox Western forms of religion and attempt to purify their Christian lives by setting aside inherited traditions and previous syncretic formulations. Through this effort to adapt their religious lives to what they imagine to be a global Christian standard, revivalists aim to forge relationships with

Christians living elsewhere by joining with them in imagined transnational communities of shared practice. As I heard one Papua New Guinean attending a very remote church one Sunday morning put it in a prayer, "God, people everywhere are [at this moment] praying to you." The ultimate telos of the Christian life also expresses this desire for global connectedness, for revivalists work to earn a home in a heaven where they will join others who come from more central parts of the global system, transcending the peripheral place they now know themselves to occupy. Revival Christianity thus appeals for the links it promises to build between its practitioners and Christians from other locales.

If cargo cults represent an attempt to bring global culture home and thereby encompass the global in the local, revival movements express a yearning to leave the local behind and achieve full participation in global culture on its own terms. Considered as representative of a distinct kind of syncretism, revivals are the converse of cargo cults, for in them those mixtures that exist tend to be structured along Christian rather than traditional lines. Given that the popularity of revival movements has waxed as that of cargo cults have waned, the contrasts between these two types of movements, and between the kinds of syncretism that lie at their core, trace a key trend in the globalization of culture in Melanesia.

The contrast between cargo cults and revival movements directs our attention to the role of religion in what we might call popular globalization: people's everyday use of religion to ground their engagement with Western culture and its representatives. There is also, however, a story to tell about how the Pacific Island elites during the era of independence have put religion to use in state-level projects of globalization and nation-building. Indeed, the extent to which Christianity features in Pacific Island politics has only increased during the period of independence. Some of the states of the region have enshrined their commitment to Christianity in their constitutions. The preamble to the Papua New Guinea constitution reads "We, the people of Papua New Guinea pledge ourselves to guard and pass on to those who come after us our noble traditions and the Christian principles that are now ours," and Vanuatu's constitution contains similar language. Furthermore, the independent governments of the region have continued to welcome missionaries and have in many cases continued to rely on them to provide educational and health services in rural areas. While frowning on cargo cult activity (or even outlawing it, as has the Papua New Guinea state), they have allowed evangelists from New Zealand and elsewhere to preach millenarian versions of revival Christianity to huge audiences in packed sports arenas in the larger cities. Finally, Christian versions of civil religion have sprung up that give a Christian tinge to political rhetoric across the region. As in the West, Pacific Island politicians are now quick to ask their constituents to pray for peace and to ask God for guidance in times of trouble.

State commitment to Christianity in the Pacific Islands can in part be explained as an effort by those who formulate state policy to secure a place for their states in the emerging global order. This order challenges states as much as citizens to construct identities that are meaningful in more than local terms. In the face of this challenge, Pacific Island leaders' use of Christianity as something of an official religion affords them a way to claim for their states distinctly modern identities within the global political system.

Yet even as elites look outward to the global system of nation-states in forging their political commitment to Christianity, they also look inward to their relationship to their own constituents. Christianity constitutes the one set of ideas that is both widely shared and highly valued by the majority of the citizens of each state. This makes it a natural focus of nation-building efforts organized around attempts to represent the nation as a cohesive Christian community.

As a nation-building project, the Christianization of the state is not without its pitfalls, the most important of which has been placed in its path by the way Christianity supports popular globalizing tendencies. One of the most distinct trends in revival Christianity, for example, is the way its followers often imagine that their new faith allows them to identify themselves with Western Christians and in doing so to demote their national identities to a distinctly secondary place; in effect, many revivalists link the local to the global in an effort to render the national unimportant in their lives. The state, poor in resources and rarely present in daily life outside of the more urban areas, comes to represent for those who make this move all of the sinful qualities of the past: the violence, the worldliness, the untrustworthiness. In response, revivalists forge (imagined) transnational connections that allow them to transcend the state's evils as they transcend their own sins.

The state commitment to Christianity that is produced in response both to the demands of the global state system and out of the needs of nation-building projects creates an environment in which people's use of Christianity in projects of popular globalization can flourish. Some of these projects, as we have seen, end up undermining state efforts at nation-building. Yet the states of the region continue to draw heavily on Christianity in formulating their political culture, and thus both popular and state engagements with Christianity are likely to be central to processes of globalization in the region in the future.

Moving away form the nation-state framework, we should also consider the role religion plays in shaping processes of migration, another important aspect of globalization. As I have noted, Christianity promises many Melanesians a future migration to a heaven in which national divisions will be dissolved. For Polynesians and Micronesians in particular, migration in the here and now to New Zealand, Australia, the United States, and elsewhere is also very much a live option. As several scholars have pointed out, if in Western terms globalization means a shrinking of the globe, for many Pacific Island migrants it has meant that their worlds are only getting larger. From the point of view of the topic at hand, what is most distinct about the way Pacific Islanders migrate is that they tend to do so as Christians. In their new homes, they build solidarities with other islanders on the basis of membership in the same churches, and their ties to home are kept strong through return visits to celebrate Christian holidays. For some migrants, home becomes identified with a more pure Christian life, untroubled by the myriad religious and secular temptations of their new Western dwelling places. Marshall Islander members of the Assemblies of God Church in Enid, Oklahoma, for instance, find their visits home particularly spiritually rewarding because they feel that their kin there practice a more spirited and sophisticated kind of Christianity than the one they have been able to practice in Enid. True Christianity, for them, ties them to home.

To say that Pacific Islanders migrate as Christians is also to say that to a large extent Pacific Island religions do not themselves globalize, at least in the senses of picking up new adherents outside their original communities, forming the basis of solidarities across ethnic lines, or providing the organizing framework for migrant lives. Some cargo cults give the lie to this, having spread between Melanesians who previously did not share a religion. But at the very least, Pacific Island religions do not seem to have migrated well. In part, the cause of this is surely the history I have recounted here: having first experienced globalization as it came to them in the form of Christianity, Pacific Islanders who migrate are often already Christian and thus are little inclined to try to adapt their traditional religions to the new settings, themselves usually Christian, in which they find themselves. Yet beyond this explanation, one might also hazard the observation that Pacific Island religions were (and are) so intricately tied to local places and social structures that one could not detach them from the local without breaking them in ways that have proven difficult to repair. Ancestors were tied to families, spirits were tied to places, and creators were tied to customs. Break up the families, leave the places, or discard the customs and it is very hard to hang on to the religions. There is a lesson here about what it takes to be a world religion—about the extent to which some disenchantment in the form of differentiating out religion from other spheres of life is part of what allows the world religions to travel light. There is also probably a lesson here about the strengths and weaknesses of global culture considered more broadly as a set of meanings that facilitate the widest possible spheres of interaction and shared meaning but at the expense of much of the nuance that makes local cultures adequate guides for life. These lessons point to issues globalization raises both for Pacific Islanders and for everyone else, religious and non-religious alike. They may well also point to the issues around which debates about the globalization of culture are destined to be carried out and to which global religions, if they are to remain central to the lives of Pacific Islanders and others, will have to formulate a response.

BIBLIOGRAPHY

Barker, John, ed. 1990. *Christianity in Oceania: Ethnographic Perspectives*. Lanham, Md.: University Press of America.

Burridge, Kenelm. 1995 (1960). *Mambu: A Melanesian Millennium*. Princeton, N.J.: Princeton University Press.

Jebens, Holger, ed. 2004. *Cargo, Cult, and Culture Critique*. Honolulu: University of Hawai'i Press.

Lawrence, Peter. 1971 (1964). *Road Belong Cargo: A Study of the Cargo Movement in the Southern Madang District New Guinea*. Atlantic Highlands, N.J.: Humanities Press.

Miles, William F. S. 1998. *Bridging Mental Boundaries in a Postcolonial Microcosm: Identity and Development in Vanuatu*. Honolulu: University of Hawai'i Press.

Otto, Ton, and Ad Borsboom, eds. 1997. *Cultural Dynamics of Religious Change in Oceania*. Leiden: KITLV Press.

Robbins, Joel. 2004. *Becoming Sinners: Christianity and Moral Torment in a Papua New Guinea Society*. Berkeley: University of California Press.

Robbins, Joel, Pamela J. Stewart, and Andrew Strathern, eds. 2001. *Charismatic and Pentecostal Christianity in Oceania*. Special issue, *Journal of Ritual Studies* 15, no. 2.

Swain, Tony, and Garry Tromp. 1995. *The Religions of Oceania*. London: Routledge.

Tuzin, Donald. 1997. *The Cassowary's Revenge: The Life and Death of Masculinity in a New Guinea Society*. Chicago: University of Chicago Press.

PART VIII

UNDERSTANDING GLOBAL RELIGION

....

CHAPTER 58

RELIGION IN GLOBAL PERSPECTIVE

....

MARTIN RIESEBRODT

In recent decades the dramatic global resurgence of religious movements—many of them fundamentalist in character—has caught many people by surprise. Most of us believed that such a resurgence of religion was not possible, since, according to our modernization myth, we were to expect a continuous universal trend toward the secularization and privatization of religion. There were several options for the fate of religion in the modern world, but neither a return of religion as a public force nor its ability to shape people according to its own ethos or habitus was among them.

Certainly, very few people expected religion to totally disappear. Most assigned religion to a legitimate space in the private sphere and assumed that religious institutions would undergo a process of internal secularization and would increasingly adapt to the requirements of modern structures while maintaining their religious symbolism. Some imagined that national ideologies or civil religions would functionally replace religious traditions or expected religious values to permeate modern societies leaving behind the traditional forms of religion. But few were prepared for the global resurgence of religions as a public force and powerful shapers of religious subjects.

The attempts of social theorists to cope with their own cognitive dissonance have been nearly as interesting as this surprising return of religion itself. The two most typical reactions were denial and instant conversion. Some authors have simply insisted that their expectations of modernization and secularization are basically sound. Focusing on the resurgence of religion outside the modern West allowed them to pretend that these revivals of religion are still part of a modernizing process. And, not surprisingly, many have taken pains to detect a "Puritan spirit" or an "inner-worldly asceticism" in such movements, revealing their misreading of Weber's "Protestant Ethic" (1993) thesis as a general theory of modernization.

Other authors have chosen the opposite route of instant conversion by denying any general trend toward secularization in the West and elsewhere. Rational choice theorists and their allies in particular have argued that secularization is just an effect of European-style religious monopolies. Wherever religious pluralism and competition have predominated, such as in the United States, secularization has not taken place. Here religion is—and has always been—alive and well.

Against these two positions I claim that neither a denial of the secularizing tendencies of Western modernity nor a blind belief in an irreversible universal trend toward secularization will do. On the one hand, the resurgence of religious movements and personal piety on a global scale has shed serious doubt on the secularization thesis. On the other hand, it would be ludicrous to deny that secularization in terms of processes of institutional differentiation has actually taken place. Modern states, including the United States, are widely secular. Neither capitalism and bureaucracy, nor modern science and modern culture are based on or even compatible with religious principles. And since much of the religious resurgence is directed against modern secularism, one would actually misunderstand these movements unless one acknowledges secularization as a fact.

Therefore, instead of explaining away the apparent contradiction between processes of secularization and of religious resurgence, we should attempt to understand why these processes occur simultaneously and how they might be interrelated. Since conventional theories of religion have failed to provide us with a convincing explanation, this might be a good occasion to revisit them critically and to attempt to formulate a theory which makes better sense of religion in the modern world.

CAN ONE THEORIZE ABOUT RELIGION?

But, is such a general theory of religion actually possible? The very concept of religion has been criticized recently. Some have argued that religions exhibit such a great diversity of beliefs, practices, and symbols that one cannot capture them in one definition, or have emphasized that "religion" is a Western invention, the meaning of which is differently socially constituted at different times in history and across traditions. Moreover, such general definitions of religion have usually expressed ethnocentric Western views and normative claims in the disguise of universal truths.

Admittedly, many theories have been based on rather Eurocentric rationalist and normative models of cognitive progress and on expectations of secularization and privatization of religion as well as on a modern Western notion of the "self." Certainly, occidental parochialism is implicit in much of sociological and anthropological theorizing. However, this is not a necessary consequence of any general concept and theory of religion but rather the result of specific definitions and theoretical perspectives. Moreover, the widespread use of the term *religion*, even by authors who claim to reject it, suggests that a general concept like religion seems to be logically required whenever people are aware of a plurality of religious faiths and practices and make comparisons. Also the objection that religion is discursively constituted and therefore historically and culturally related is not very convincing since this applies not just to religion but to any concept, like gender, class, ethnicity, genealogy, medieval Christianity, or Islam.

Since the usefulness of a general concept and theory of religion cannot be decided a priori, I will very briefly outline some basic elements of such a theory that is capable of explaining religious phenomena on a global scale despite obvious differences between religious traditions, great diversity within traditions, and historical transformations of traditions, bracketing for the moment the problematic notion of tradition itself. This requires as a first step the clarification of what is meant here by religion and by theory.

I suspect that objections against attempts at conceptualizing and theorizing religion are often based on erroneous assumptions about the epistemological status of such an enterprise. Of course, religion is an analytical category that only exists as an intellectual construct. No one can believe in or practice "religion as such," and we only can observe culturally, socially, and historically definite religious practices. Moreover, a social scientific concept of religion is different from a theological or a legal one. Therefore, a sociological concept and theory of religion neither intends to capture any essence of religion nor to distinguish good from bad religion, or legitimate from illegitimate religion. It rather offers a systematization and explanation of phenomena defined as religious from a consciously chosen one-sided perspective based on a cross-culturally comparative analysis of processes of social action and interaction. The justification of this perspective should be based on historical relevance, theoretical consistency, and empirical validity. Obviously, the possibility exists that more than one theoretical perspective fulfills these requirements.

Moreover, it is equally legitimate to subsume phenomena defined by one approach as religious under conceptual and theoretical frames other than religion, like ideology, knowledge, or discourse. For example, instead of theorizing religion universally, one could theorize the discourses through which different concepts of religion (or comparable terms) are produced. Such alternative theorizing has to meet the same criteria of relevance, consistency, and empirical validity. My own approach affirms the usefulness of the concept of religion, but draws the following conclusions from the shortcomings of other theories.

First, a theory of religion should avoid any implicit or explicit value-judgment about religious beliefs and practices. It should not rank them according to evolutionist or developmental schemes, higher or lower forms, good or bad religions. The problem of evolutionary perspectives is their obvious ideological design. They usually claim implicitly or explicitly either that Protestantism is the highest form of religion, or that science is the highest form of knowledge. I have not met an evolutionist yet who constructed a scheme where he or she ended up in the middle or at the bottom.

Second, religion should be analyzed in terms of a relatively autonomous system of meaningful actions and interactions which is interconnected with other systems of practices but not their reflection. I will explain this concept later in more detail.

Third, a theory of religion should attempt to account for the subjective as well as the objective side of religion, the perspective from the individual social actor as well as from the institutional order.

Fourth, a theory of religion should account for the emotional as well as the cognitive aspects of religion. In their intentions and effects, religious practices like other practices, are neither exclusively rational and instrumental nor exclusively irrational.

And finally, a theory of religion should pay attention to the content of religious beliefs and practices, but avoid homogenizing them into closed systems of traditions writ large. Any such essentialization of religious traditions implicitly favors orthodoxy and orthopraxy and often overlooks the internal pluralism and historical transformation of traditions. "Tradition" in its scientific use is an ideal-type and has as such only a heuristic value. It is not meant to interpret and explain the empirical evidence but only provides us with a hypothetical model.

The Methodological Priority of Practices

In order to formulate such a theoretical frame I propose to focus on religious practices. Unlike religious beliefs and experiences, religious practices lend themselves to empirical observation. Instead of first systematizing religious beliefs of a culture, tradition, or society and then interpreting religious practices as enactments of such beliefs, I propose an ideal-typical description of beliefs which are implied in practices. What is the difference?

The first approach puts the emphasis on a rich construction of worldviews, cosmologies, and complex symbol systems. This necessarily directs attention to those who have the broadest knowledge of religious beliefs and are able to articulate and systematize them: religious intellectuals and specialists or scholars who substitute for them. A deductive interpretation of practices as enacted beliefs, hence, becomes theological in its basic outlook. It reinforces distinctions between high and popular religion, sees ordinary practitioners as lacking the knowledge of the real meanings of their actions, and emphasizes particularistic features of religious traditions.

Starting from a model of religious practices and their implicit logic shifts our perspective. The actual practices of different groups and categories of people are seen as culturally and socially embedded meaningful actions. But these meanings are not assumed simply to be deficient versions or unconscious enactments of the "theologically correct" or the culturally most complex ones.

A model that constructs a logic of religious practices underlying their concrete culturally and socially shaped forms shifts the focus from intellectual metadiscourses to practitioners, from a theological to a pragmatic perspective. Such an approach overcomes the value judgments implicit in distinctions between higher and lower forms of religion (e.g., popular or folk religion) or good and bad religion (e.g., magic, superstition, or cult). It treats the practitioners as competent actors and provides a theoretical frame which allows for generalizing as well as particularizing comparisons. This approach does not deny, however, that the reconstruction of complex worldviews has a heuristic value and that institutionalized meanings can shape the explicit and implicit motivations of religious practitioners, but treats it as an empirical question.

The Logic of Religious Practices

Religious practices can be distinguished from other kinds of social actions on the basis of three logically implied core assumptions: (1) there exist superhuman, extraordinary, amazing, and in modern Western terms generally supernatural personal or impersonal powers; (2) these powers control dimensions of human/social life which normal social actors cannot control directly by their own power: and (3) social actors are able to gain access to these powers. Depending on how these powers are imagined social actors can influence or manipulate them, can communicate, exchange gifts and services with them. Or, they can empower themselves beyond the ordinary through the internalization or internal activation, or through fusion with such powers.

These basic assumptions come to bear in the distinction between three types of religious practices: interventive, discursive, and derivative. *Interventive practices* engage in attempts at getting access to superhuman powers, communicating and exchanging gifts and services with them, manipulating them, or empowering oneself. Examples of such practices are sacrifices, prayers, spells, divinations, ascetic and mystical disciplines.

Discursive practices engage in linguistic exchanges among social actors about the nature of superhuman powers, appropriate ways of interacting with them, manipulating them, or acquiring them. Such practices pass on, reinforce, interpret, and revise religious knowledge and in conjunction with interventive practices shape the ethos or habitus of social actors. Discursive practices are by no means restricted to intellectuals, like theologians, but are common to all kinds of religious actors.

The concept of *derivative practices* refers to the religious shaping of social action where social actors expand their notions of religious significance and make their nonreligious practices conform to religious rules by committing acts which are believed to please the powers or produce blessings or by avoiding acts that are believed to anger the powers or effect misfortune.

All three types of practices are often only analytically separable and even the same practice in the same context could be classified differently. For example, the reading of a sacred text could take on the meaning of a discursive practice but also that of an interventive practice. These different types of practices often occur simultaneously, mutually reinforce each other, and are equally involved in religious socialization, in the creation of "moods and motivations" as well as "conceptions of a general order of existence" as Clifford Geertz (1973) has aptly put it.

Whereas much attention has been paid in classical social theories to derivative practices, and in recent theories to discursive practices, this theory focuses on interventive practices. From the perspective employed by this proposed theory, discursive practices primarily serve as facilitators of interventive practices while derivative practices are their effects. Accordingly, interventive practices represent the analytical core, and I will focus on them by turning to the question of why they are performed.

I argue that a common theme in interventive practices across traditions lies in their attempt to prevent crises or misfortune from happening or to manage them when they have occured. The crises (or dangers, risks) addressed in such practices are primarily found in domains which could be classified in Western terms as nature, the human body, and social relations. With regard to nature, interventive practices refer primarily to phenomena which are beyond the routine technical control of a given society but are believed to pose a major threat. With regard to the human body, they refer mostly to its reproductive capabilities and mortality (e.g., fertility and birth, illness and death). With regard to society, interventive practices center on the precariousness of social relations, especially inequality, authority, conflict, changes in status, or crises of solidarity and identity.

Within interventive practices I distinguish among three types: routine, occasional, and virtuoso. *Routine practices* cultivate and affirm the exchange relationship between superhuman powers and social actors on a regular basis. They follow, for example, a daily, weekly, monthly, or yearly cycle. The more frequent ones tend to primarily maintain good relations, while the others may commemorate significant past events when the powers intervened in people's lives in order to help or punish them. Accordingly, routine practices honor the powers or express gratitude, hope, grief, or joy.

Occasional practices are linked to events which are not defined by the calendar but rather follow the individual or the family life-cycle. They are performed at the occasions of births, initiations, weddings, and deaths. They also take place in response to actual crises, like illnesses, catastrophes, or war.

Virtuoso practices seem to be different in motivation from routine as well as occasional practices. But I think they can be interpreted as often attempting to overcome the conditions for the possibility of crises, dangers, risks, and suffering in principle, for example, through contemplative or ascetic disciplines. The self-empowerment through such practices often has the consequence of elevating virtuosi to the status of superhuman powers or mediators who then become themselves objects of interventive practices.

CULTURE: PROFANE AND RELIGIOUS

Obviously, the response to the challenges of crises does not have to be religious since such experiences do not necessarily lead to the assumption of the existence of superhuman powers which control what we do not. As one could formulate with reference to Freud, other illusions are available. However, the universality of religious practices suggests that the conditions for the possibility of religion lie in shared features of the human species. As Peter Berger and others have argued, in the process of human evolution, instinctual regulation of social behavior has been increasingly replaced by ratiocination, communication, and interpretation. The lack of directedness through instincts has made it not only possible but necessary for the human species to interact creatively with its natural environment and "invent" regulatory systems for social interaction. Humans are by biological necessity cultural beings who through social interaction and communication order their social relations cognitively, morally, and emotionally. Part of this process of culturalization of the human species is the development of religion. Without exactly mirroring these evolutionary processes, the development of children shows certain parallels.

I propose to distinguish between religious and profane dimensions of culture in terms of an ideal-typical opposition between practices which contain a reference to superhuman powers and practices which lack such a reference. If culture in general refers to the cognitive, moral, and emotional repertoire of a given society through which practices are regulated, then the religious culture primarily refers to practices which are based on interactions with superhuman powers, and to discourses and symbolizations which reflect on the character and will of such powers, our relationship to them, and the appropriate methods of approaching or manipulating them. In contrast to profane culture, the religious repertoire contains, preserves, and cultivates the resources to cope with those dimensions of human life which are beyond routine social control and therefore are believed to require the intervention of superhuman powers.

Since human beings cannot but interpret their external and internal relationships, there is a special need for interpretation and explanation when confronted with one's own powerlessness, with lack of control, crises, or high risks. The cognitive need to understand and the emotional one to cope with these situations can be seen as two related modes of reassurance. Since the distinction between profane and religious culture is an ideal-typical one, its boundaries can be rather fluid. Moreover, those distinctions are not static. Profane practices can become sacralized, religious practices profanized.

THE LOGIC OF RELIGIOUS INSTITUTIONS

So far I have abstracted from institutional contexts to which I am turning now. What is the nature of religious institutions, and how are they interconnected with other social fields? Given the approach to religious practices I have taken, religious institutions can be defined as rules and norms which regulate the interaction between human beings and superhuman powers; the discourse about these powers; their nature, significance, and interventions into our lives; as well as the religious penetration of everyday life. Religious institutions tend to exhibit at least a rudimentary division of labor which ascribes to different categories of people certain in-born or acquired qualifications in terms of knowledge and skills for the performance of practices or the acquisition of religious knowledge, but the degree of this differentiation can vary immensely across history and traditions.

With increasing division of religious labor, religious institutions become more systematized, rationalized, and centralized and are transformed into religious organizations. Through these processes a permanent and stable system of religious inequality and authority is created which often attempts to monopolize the means of salvation by controlling religious know-how, symbols, objects, and spaces as well as the training and licensing of religious specialists. This enables religious organizations to expand their control over people and to accumulate wealth and power far beyond their mediating religious functions.

Nevertheless, it is important to analytically distinguish the authority of superhuman powers from the authority of religious institutions or organizations because the latter is derived from the acceptance of the former. To fuse these two dimensions means to buy into the ideology of religious organizations. The claim of religious organizations to legitimately, efficaciously, and often exclusively mediate between humans and superhuman powers may be rejected while the authority of the superhuman powers themselves is not doubted and alternative mediators may gain legitimacy. We deal here with two systems of authority which can be merged but also separated again.

Religious institutions are obviously interlinked with the profane culture, social structure, and institutional order. Already the definition and framing of a crisis tend to be informed by the degree to which a given society understands and controls its natural environment. And the imagination of superhuman powers is often shaped by social structures of authority. Moreover, religious organizations permanently interact with other systems of power and authority which are derived from the control of force and warfare as well as the control of wealth which may or may not be institutionally differentiated from each other. Here, again, I propose to not simply fuse these different dimensions into one block of power, authority, and wealth, but to distinguish them analytically and determine their interrelatedness under concrete historical circumstances.

I propose to understand religion as a "relatively autonomous" social field. This implies, that, on the one hand, religious practices and institutions cannot be adequately understood outside of their concrete social, historical, political, and economic context. But, on the other hand, they are not simply a reflection or symbolization of political or economic orders. Religions can have a rather ambiguous relation vis-à-vis political, economic, and even religious organizations. Since religions offer complex repertoires of beliefs and practices they can be selectively instrumentalized not only for the legitimation of authority and privilege but also for their delegitimation and sometimes transformation. Moreover, religions also constitute—from the actors' point of view—a relatively autonomous field of communication and exchange with superhuman powers. Although these exchanges are related to the anticipation, experience, or management of crises which may originate in the social, political, or economic sphere, they also create their own internal logic and dynamics that may well be in competition or in conflict with political and economic interests as well as with the mediation offered by dominant religious organizations.

As this approach is suggesting, crises are the seed-bed of religious work. This does not mean that people are or become religious only in moments when they experience crises. To the contrary, most religious practices are fully embedded in everyday social relations and are part of daily, weekly, and monthly routines. However, crises tend to add a dynamic dimension to religion. Religious beliefs and practices are invented, abolished, revitalized and reinterpreted as reaction to perceived crises, and may thereby confirm, reform, or even revolutionize social structures, institutional orders, and religious traditions. As long as traditional structures and practices of crisis prevention and management are seen as successful and beyond doubt, they are reaffirmed. Otherwise, new practices and cognitive orders may be created which revise how superhuman powers are imagined and how one can gain access to them. New modalities of interaction between human and superhuman beings may be institutionalized. New groups and categories of people may now qualify to access them directly or serve as mediators. And finally, the pragmatic effects of the communication between social actors and superhuman powers may be drastically revised. For example, religious specialists may be replaced by lay people, priests by prophetic preachers, or sacrifices by ascetic or ethical practices.

The universality of religious beliefs, practices, and institutions suggests that humans have a limited ability to cope with extreme uncertainty. Historically, it has been mostly through religions that the chaotic potential of crises has been culturally transformed into the semblance of cosmos. Religions have created the trust in the ability of social groups to prevent crises from happening or cope with them if they do happen. Religion as a resource of cultural crisis prevention and management, hence, equally serves collective and individual needs.

SECULARIZATION AND THE GLOBAL RESURGENCE OF RELIGION

What, now, are the advantages and consequences of this approach? First of all, the theory allows for a relatively clear distinction between religious and other kinds of practices. Unlike approaches that define religion in terms of a supposed function, phenomena like rock concerts, football games, or shopping in a supermarket are not regarded as religious here. At the same time, religion is also not defined in terms of an "experience" that usually is neither empirically accessible nor universal. Such an emphasis on individual sensibilities excludes the rational, pragmatic, and institutional sides of religion. Instead, religion is defined as a specific type of meaningful social action and interaction which can be equally theorized from the perspective of actors as from that of institutional orders.

Second, the approach directs our attention to religious practices on different levels of social aggregation—from society to intermediary groups to the individual—as well as to religious practices of different classes and categories of people. The emphasis shifts from seeing religion primarily from an orthodox and intellectualist perspective as a unified cognitive, moral, and practical system to seeing it as a field in which people of different class, gender, ethnicity, or age deal with their specific risks, crises, and experiences of powerlessness. This emphasis urges us not to be content with the fiction of a given culture or society as a whole, but to theorize, study, and explain the specificity of religious practices of men and women, of people in different stages of their life-cycle, of dominant and subordinate classes, status groups, and ethnic groups who make creative use of religious repertoires and attribute meanings to their practices with reference to shared institutions, symbols, and beliefs.

Finally, this approach allows us to make better sense of religion in the modern world. Initially, I have claimed that processes of secularization and of global resurgence of religion have not only taken place to various degrees but are interrelated. From the perspective of this theory, secularization has occurred as a consequence of increasing human control and "world-mastery" and its institutionalization in separate social spheres. The massive growth of scientific knowledge and its practical application, most importantly in medicine, has vastly expanded human control over spheres of high risk and threat. The development of a welfare state has neutralized some of the major existential risks for the middle and lower classes. The replacement of monarchical and aristocratic systems of authority by democratic ones has disenchanted politics. Religious narratives of salvation history have in part been replaced by or fused with historical narratives of the nation. Bureaucratic principles of organization and the institutionalization of "efficiency" have widely removed religious ethics from the economy and politics. These processes have objectively weakened the relevance of religion in many respects and have widely restricted it to a separate sphere, primarily serving individual and private needs.

However, in part simultaneously, in part with some time lag, new dimensions of uncertainty, risk, and powerlessness have opened up. Science and technology have not only extended our control over nature but have also created new risks, like the threat of environmental catastrophes. Democratization has not only profaned politics, it has also re-enchanted politics by enabling "charismatic" leaders to mobilize mass support. Capitalism has not only freed certain social groups and women from patriarchal bonds and given them new opportunities but has also enforced on them a mobility of nearly unprecedented scope. As a consequence, kinship relations have been dissolved, family structures destabilized, and people have been exposed to the uncertainties and irrationalities of the market.

Capitalism is a revolutionary force which permanently transforms social structures and promotes upward and downward social mobility as well as geographical mobility. In particular, its recent global spread has simultaneously created wealth and poverty of immense proportions dramatically undermining not only the economic standings of masses of people but also their social identities. To the degree that Western modernism could convincingly instill the belief in its ever-increasing ability to control nature, the human body, and society, religion receded. But the destabilizing effects of Western modernization have undercut such beliefs and paved the way for a resurgence of religious modes of crisis prevention and management. Seen from this theoretical perspective, secularization and the global resurgence of religion do not represent a contradiction but rather two sides of the same coin.

Max Weber once suggested with respect to the ancient Near East and Greece that "epochs of strong prophetic propaganda" in all its different forms are related to "the reconstitution of the great world empires in Asia, and the resumption and intensification of international commerce" (1993: 48). These processes in the ancient world may exhibit some interesting parallels to what we presently like to call globalization. Certainly, many of the contemporary revival movements, in particular fundamentalist ones, react to crises which can be characterized as effects of such dramatic economic and political transformation processes.

However, their reactions, like the ancient ones, are nevertheless specifically religious. Contemporary fundamentalist movements do not articulate a socioeconomic agenda nor organize as class movements, but rather represent *cultural milieus* in the sense that their group identity and the perception of a common fate are primarily defined by shared ideals of a religiously grounded sociomoral order. These movements do not represent religious traditionalists but appropriate and reinterpret their traditions quite selectively and innovatively in the light of specifically modern experiences. Despite many differences between religious traditions, fundamentalist movements across traditions react to comparable social experiences and as a result develop similar countervisions of a better society. They all tend to unanimously demand the restoration of patriarchal principles of authority and morality claiming that only such a return can solve the problems and crises of modernity.

Since secularism and religious revivalism constitute each other socially and ideologically, religious revivals neither represent the realization of the religious essence of any civilization, nor are they momentary aberrations from a predestined path toward secularism, but they are and will remain a recurring historical phenomenon, even in the modern world.

BIBLIOGRAPHY

Asad, Talal. 1993. *Genealogies of Religion*. Baltimore: Johns Hopkins University Press.

Bellah, Robert. 1970. *Beyond Belief*. New York: Harper and Row.

Berger, Peter L. 1967. *The Sacred Canopy*. Garden City: Anchor Books.

Casanova, Jose. 1994. *Public Religions in the Modern World*. Chicago: University of Chicago Press.

Durkheim, Émile. 1995. *The Elementary Forms of the Religious Life*. Translated by Karen E. Fields. New York: Free Press.

Freud, Sigmund. 1961. *The Future of an Illusion*. Translated by James Strachey. New York: W.W. Norton.

Geertz, Clifford. 1973. *The Interpretation of Cultures*. New York: Basic Books.

Juergensmeyer, Mark. 2000. *Terror in the Mind of God: The Global Rise of Religious Violence*. Berkeley: University of California Press.

Luckmann, Thomas. 1967. *The Invisible Religion*. New York: Macmillan.

Martin, David. 1978. *A General Theory of Secularization*. New York: Harper and Row.

Parsons, Talcott. 1963. "Christianity and Modern Industrial Society." In *Sociological Theory, Values and Sociocultural Change*. Ed. E. A. Tiryakian, 33–70. New York: Free Press.

Riesebrodt, Martin. 1993. *Pious Passion: The Emergence of Modern Fundamentalism in the United States and Iran*. Trans. Don Reneau. Berkeley: University of California Press.

Riesebrodt, Martin, and Mary Ellen Konieczny. Forthcoming. "Sociology of Religion." In *Penguin Companion to the Study of Religion*. Ed. John Hinnells. New York: Penguin.

Smith, Jonathan Z. 1982. *Imagining Religion*. Chicago: University of Chicago Press.

Spiro, Melford E. 1994. *Culture and Human Nature*. New Brunswick, N.J.: Transaction.

Weber, Max. 1993. *Sociology of Religion*. Trans. Talcott Parsons. Boston: Beacon Press.

Young, Lawrence A., ed. 1997. *Rational Choice Theory and Religion*. New York: Routledge Press.

CHAPTER 59

ANTI-GLOBAL RELIGION?

ROLAND ROBERTSON

THE events in Seattle surrounding—or more accurately, opposing—the meeting of the World Trade Organization in the fall of 1999 have been widely regarded as a turning point. They constituted a symbolic beginning of the targeting of the global. Seattle 1999 amplified a strong switch away from the adage, "think globally, act locally." While such a turn from the half-local to the totally global was easy to recognize among long-standing students of what has come to be called globalization, in reality the adage "think globally, act locally" has had a life of its own until it was more or less exploded by not merely the events in Seattle but also those subsequently in Washington, D.C.; Windsor, Canada (where protests were mounted against the Organization of American States); London and some other cities on May Day, 2000; Davos, Switzerland, in connection with meetings of the World Economic Forum; the fall 2000 demonstrations in Prague against the World Bank and the International Monetary Fund; and the agitation against the European Union summit in Nice in December 2000. Other protests against globalization and capitalism took place, inter alia, in 2000 in Biarritz and Seoul, and elsewhere in 2001 and in subsequent years. Nearly, if not all, of these have involved mixtures of nationalities and of motives, a collage of peoples and intentions.

One might also mention the protests against McDonald's that rapidly developed in 2000 in France, following the "McLibel Trial" in London in the mid-1990s. Although French intellectuals are particularly well known for blaming the "Anglo-Saxons" (whoever might be meant by this term) for most of the world's problems, the United States is taken to be the primary locus of globalization and thus McDonald's and a number of other supposedly U.S.-based corporations, such as Starbucks, Gap, and Blockbuster, are portrayed as prominent and highly effective agents of globalization. I say supposedly because many corporations that are widely thought of as American are not in fact anywhere near as all-American, at least as far as their ownership is concerned, as they are often thought to be.

Of course McDonald's is often taken as the strongest symbol of global capitalism (cf. Ritzer 2000). But regardless of its actual, practical impact around the world, a crucial aspect of the academic attention to McDonald's is that it does, indeed, have an enormous symbolic significance. McDonald's represents the USA in a way that is only rivaled by Coca Cola and, in more recent years, Nike, Starbucks, and so on. Yet McDonald's claims to be highly respectful of local traditions and of cultural variety generally. And this is, to a degree, validated by Watson's edited book on McDonald's in East Asian capitals (Watson 1997), in which a number of anthropologists illustrate the argument that McDonald's facilitates *localization*. This phenomenon is part of the larger argument that much that is taken to be hegemonically homogenizing is, on closer inspection, actually the basis upon which locality becomes more evident. This is, to put it all too simply, one of the ways in which the global produces the local.

Much of this overall activity concerns the forgiveness of Third World debt, in which religious participation has been strong. Particularly active in this process has been the organization called Jubilee 2000 that closed down at the end of 2000, to be replaced by Drop the Debt. But when the G7/8 met in Genoa, Italy, in 2001 it took place in a country where agitation for forgiveness of Third World debt is considerable and has papal backing. In fact the role of the Roman Catholic Church in opposing economic globalization has been considerable in recent years. For, to the Catholic hierarchy and many lay Catholics, globalization represents the high point of capitalism, against which the church throughout the twentieth century expressed much opposition. The present pope (John Paul was the pope when this chapter was written) has, in fact, spoken vividly against globalization in recent years—but the present author's impression is that even though the ostensible target of papal complaint has been against global capitalism, there is considerable concern in the Vatican about the ways in which what is commonly called globalization (in the broad sense) is challenging the worldwide presence of Catholicism as the most powerful and influential of the "world religions." Or, to put this differently, (Roman) Catholicism has for many centuries had global aspirations, but the present form of globalization constitutes a profound challenge to the hegemonic ambitions of the church.

The idea that Seattle 1999 constituted a real turning point certainly cannot be fully investigated here, not least because not enough time has elapsed since then to estimate with any confidence that Seattle did, so to say, alter in a very significant way our orientations toward, to use the term yet again, globalization. (The present chapter was, it should be noted, written in 2001.) The more important point is, however, that Seattle 1999 does constitute a *symbolic* representation of a major turn in the general and diffuse conceptions of globalization and globality. Suffice it to say that among many of those who might loosely be described as global activists, as opposed to relatively detached analysts (although there can be no clear distinction between the two), Seattle has become symbolic of fundamental changes with respect to the relationships between the local and the global, as well as the particular and the universal. Since Seattle the rallying cry appears to be *global* action is required to confront perceived exploiters of the deprived, the poor, the oppressed, and so on; or that "localization" can only be achieved globally (Hines 2000). And this is precisely one point where religion becomes particularly salient.

Religion and Economic Globalization

Frequently, but not exclusively in the relatively short history of the explicit discourse of globalization (c. 1980 onward), religion has been treated in terms of "local" religious traditions being swept by a wave of secular and homogenizing, consumerist forces. Indeed it is common for some analysts and activists to equate globalization with the homogenization of culture and social practice (see, for instance, the truly egregious comments of Halliday 2000). In contrast there are those who have joined me in resisting this tendency, by conceptualizing globalization as a complex mixture of homogeneity and heterogeneity—more specifically as involving the universalization of particularity and difference (as well as the particularization of universality and sameness). The latter is, I argue, an evident feature of religion in our time. So my emphasis upon what I call difference-within-sameness—or, perhaps, we could say, sameness-within-difference—has both theoretical and empirical features.

It should be added that there are many in the field, broadly conceived, of religious studies who have focused on such issues as "the spiritual meaning" of globalization itself (in its most comprehensive sense), the role of ecumenicism in the globalization process, the viability of a religiously grounded global ethic, and so on. Moreover, some academic writers (e.g., Robertson 1992; Beyer 1994) have emphatically resisted limiting the focus on religion in relation to globalization to the prospects for survival of established religious traditions, large or small, old or new. Rather they have embraced globalization as an empirical development that is the occasion for the elaboration of new ideas about religion and the world, as well as new developments in the field of religion itself.

Nonetheless, globalization has, for many speaking from within religious organizations and movements, now become something like the Antichrist, at least in areas where Christianity prevails. Parallel views are to be found in areas where other major religions are dominant, such as in Muslim regions. The pope has made, as I have already emphasized, numerous pronouncements against globalization, and attacks on the inequities and injustices allegedly produced by globalization (as a primarily economic phenomenon) are very common among Catholics deeply concerned about injustice in the contemporary world as a whole. In this regard it is indeed strange that academic Catholics have seemingly ignored the intellectual debate about globalization and rushed into the arms of Catholic resistance to (allegedly) economic definitions of globalization. But such orientations toward what is in popular discourse called globalization are not by any means confined to Catholics among adherents to Christianity. They are also to be found among a number of relatively leftist Protestants. Protestants of the ideological right have, on the other hand, by and large welcomed globalization—in the narrow, fashionable sense of the shift to global capitalism as well as the somewhat broader sense of providing more space for evangelical work, notably in ostensibly post-Communist areas in Eastern Europe and Asia, not to speak of Latin America and Africa. In spite of this, however, the ideology of "anti-globalism" or the pejorative use of terms like "one-worldism" are strong themes on the right-wing of fundamental evangelicalism, notably in the United States (e.g., Bowen 1984). There has been much debate as to whether the extension of capitalism and the global expansion of evangelistic Protestantism, with more than a fundamentalist tinge, especially in Latin America, constitute a definite alliance or whether, on the other hand, the relationship between the two trends is more subtle than this.

What, then, is most significant about the "Seattle Turn" is that anti-globalization activists and groups have in recent years become global—or, at least, transnational actors—themselves. This had become a very significant phenomenon among movements of indigenous peoples' movements well before Seattle, but the latter was more dramatic and attracted much more attention; although indigenous movements were certainly not absent from the carnival-like events in that city. To use the world "carnival" in this context is not at all a cynical move. For there is undoubtedly a fusion of what we (older) moderns have got used to thinking about as entirely separate forms of practice. One of the most interesting things about demonstrations since 1968 has been their ritualistic-carnivalistic character, combining aspects of "orgiastic" liminality with extremely "serious" purposes, this distinction running parallel to Juergensmeyer's two-fold image of religious terrorism as consisting in varying degrees of "strategic" and "symbolic" violence (Juergensmeyer 2000:123). This was certainly a feature of Seattle 1999 as well as of some subsequent "demo-festivals." Lest, however, we forget the "more serious" side of Seattle et al., it must be remarked that anti-global events of the recent past have brought into sharp relief a new internationalism in the labor movement.

Anti-global movements have inexorably become part of the globalization process itself. This is so because the two primary aspects of globalization considered in its comprehensive, as opposed to its economistic, sense are rapidly increasing global connectivity, on the one hand, and fast expanding and intensifying reflexive global consciousness, on the other. The reflexivity of contemporary global consciousness is to be witnessed precisely in the fact that ostensibly anti-global movements represent a crucial enhancement of such reflexivity. This, I think, is something that movements previously claiming to be anti-global now increasingly recognize. For they are becoming self-consciously global participants in a massive, although obviously contested, reflection upon what it means to live in the world as a whole and the manifold ways in which questions previously thought to have only a national or regional significance now clearly have a global import. This largely accounts for the not inconsiderable talk recently about "globalization from below" (e.g., Falk 1999). In other words, influential participants in what were thought of initially as anti-global movements began to realize, with assistance from Internet culture, that in order to act anti-globally, one has also to act globally.

Inevitably, when we begin to consider the very closely connected circumstances in the global arena of our time in the light cast by this reflexive consciousness, spiritual issues come to the fore. For it is difficult to envisage such a form of collective consciousness as not involving what we have conventionally thought of as religious matters, quite apart from the carnivalistic and ritualistic themes I have invoked. This is most easily to be seen, perhaps, in controversies of an environmental nature that have been addressed by the German sociologist Ulrich Beck (1999) within the framework of "world risk society." But it is also to be seen more obliquely in the less easily specifiable enhancement of interest in matters religious, as well as theological themes, among social and cultural theorists who would, only a few years ago, have proclaimed themselves to be, and to have heretofore been, considered as secularists uninterested in religion.

It is, therefore, not easy—I would suggest not really worthwhile—attempting to separate sharply the religious from the nonreligious within the frame of the present discussion. Writing about six weeks before the Seattle events, Barry Coates (director of the World Development Movement) wrote that the massive protests which he forecast were about to take place in the Pacific Northwest would involve "trade unions, consumer groups, farmers, indigenous peoples, anti-poverty campaigners, aid agencies, academics, churches, environmentalists, animal rights activists and women's groups" (Coates 1999: 29). Coates turned out to be more or less correct in his predictions, save for the attention that was, during and after the Seattle events, paid to the revival of anarchism, particularly of the Northwest

U.S. variety. Moreover, in the actual reporting of what occurred in Seattle toward the end of 1999, little attention was, in fact, paid to "the protest's religious dimension" (Killen 2000: 13).

Killen remarks on the "interfaith ecumenicism among religious traditions" in the Seattle protests and makes the interesting comment that "in the cultural quasi-anarchy of the Pacific Northwest, what made the protest possible was the fluidity of social boundaries—between rich and poor, young and old, union and non-union, religious and non-religious" (14). But, in spite of Killen's not unpersuasive stress on the particularly heterogeneous culture of the Pacific Northwest, one should not overlook the claim of MacKinnon (2000: 70) that big battles against the WTO "could happen in anytown, USA," pointing to the fact that cities such as Austin, Boulder, and Indianapolis have passed "precautionary declarations" on globalization in an effort to create what has been called "an immune system against the WTO at a local level" (quoted by MacKinnon 2000). MacKinnon nonetheless both draws, inadvertently, attention to the United States as a center of anti-globality and overlooks, on the other hand, the extent to which anti-globality is itself a globalized phenomenon. The former is particularly ironic in view of the fact that the United States is frequently, as I have already remarked, identified—particularly on the left—as the repository and promoter of institutionalized global*ism* and the vehicle of the "the new imperialism" (Biel 2000).

THE CRUSHING OF "LOCAL" RELIGION?

Over the past ten or more years one frequently hears concerns raised regarding the future of local or indigenous religious traditions in the face of the sweep of globalizing tendencies. In recent years this worry has been compounded by Huntington's (1996) controversial argument about "the clash of civilizations." Yet there are several factors that counter the notion that local religions are particularly vulnerable at the present time: (1) there is a strongly willfully nostalgic component involved in much of this argument, and (2) in this age of the reflexive *invention or manipulation of tradition*, the prospects for many traditions—"authentic" or not—is particularly bright; not least because of their commodification in the name of "the heritage industry," in which process many representatives of traditions are certainly not unreluctant participants. It should be observed, however, that in debates to date about what are called "cultural goods" in international trade agreements, such as those in the WTO, NAFTA, and the Organization for Economic Co-operation and Development (OECD), religion per se is not often treated as a cultural good or a component of the "culture industry" (Arizpe and Alonso 1999).

In these days of "faith tourism" it seems strange that religion has not, by now, been fully regarded as a cultural good. This is *not*, however, to say that religion *should* be so identified. Nonetheless it would appear to be inevitable that in countries, such as Turkey and Israel, that are so rich in sites of great significance in the history of Abrahamic religions, religion is rapidly becoming, or is already, a cultural commodity. This is not without irony in the case of Turkey where successive regimes since the Turkish Republic was founded in 1923 have been militantly insistent in claiming that Turkey is a secular society. Thus ensures the ironic touristic message: come to Turkey for religious experience, even though you will be in a thoroughly secular—indeed, anti-religious—society.

Space precludes much discussion of the highly problematic issue of authenticity. However it can be mentioned here that there is an interesting parallel between what is usually called world music and the traditional cultures and religions of the world. In the quickly burgeoning, and very profitable, field of world music the paramount intellectual controversy concerns the matter as to whether local traditions are being patronized and critically evaluated in terms of their authenticity. Specifically, many local musicians have been criticized for being too international and/or commercial and insufficiently authentic. Their very global popularity is thus sometimes taken as a sign of their inauthenticity. Thus in the case of religion we find an almost globewide hybridization of indigenous religious beliefs and practices, on the one hand, and employment of modern, Western popular music and forms of representation and ritual, on the other. This phenomenon is particularly evident in some of the newer religious movements in Japan.

Another parallel is provided by the native Indians—or members of First Nations—of Canada and the United States. To quote from a newspaper commentary on a recent BBC TV program: "(W)hile Indian children were forcibly sent to boarding schools and made to lose their culture, white American boys were donning Indian headdress and whooping around camp fires." The commentator, Mary Novakovich (2000: 24), goes on to say that this contradiction includes "environmentalists' attitudes: lobbyists . . . crudely use Indians as a symbol of people at one with nature, but only if Indian ways [conform] with their own."

A very different facet of this issue of local traditions is described by Juergensmeyer in his discussion of religious nationalism, when he claimed that "religious nationalists are more than just religious fanatics: they are political activists seriously attempting to reformulate the modern language of politics and provide a new basis for the nation-state" (Juergensmeyer 1993: xiii). Here again we find a disinclination to make a clear distinction between the religious and the nonreligious. But the more important point is Juergensmeyer's views of "religious nationalism" as an attempt to reconstitute the *discourse* of contemporary politics. As is by now well established, control of discourse is a vital part of the so-called

knowledge-power relationship, this having been a central motif in the later writings of Michel Foucault. Or, to put the issue in very different terms, religion is,
as Saint-Simon observed, the major political institution, an argument that was
strongly echoed in the work of Tocqueville—and not infrequently invoked by
American intellectuals and politicians, particularly those on the right-wing of the
ideological spectrum, as a feature of the modern United States.

So the problematic as to whether local religion is in danger from the spread
of an allegedly homogenizing, mainly secular, culture (of Western origin) is exceedingly more complex than it is often made out to be. Full exploration of this
would include much discussion of the increasingly significant, but thorny, question of religion and human rights, not to speak of the insecurities arising, as I
have intimated, from virtually all religious traditions from ongoing processes of
relativization. These processes have been responsible for the recent and widespread
interest in so-called fundamentalism. As has been cogently stated, "when religion
manifests itself politically in the contemporary world, it is conceptualized as *fundamentalism*" (van der Veer and Lehmann 1999:3). In other words fundamentalism
is, or is perceived to be, a consequence of relativization.

Certainly processes of relativization of religious beliefs and practices have been
occurring throughout the history of humanity, but these have become increasingly
evident as the world as a whole is being so rapidly globalized. Original fundamentalism grew, of course, in the United States in the late nineteenth century
and first quarter of the twentieth century. American fundamentalism was in a
number of respects a reaction against the perceived threat of relativization of
American Protestantism by other religio-cultural doctrinal tendencies, such as
German theology, Judaism and nascent Zionism, and Catholicism—not to speak
of the growing challenge of European, notably Russian, socialism or Communism.

The reaction against the growing Jewish presence, particularly in the state of
New York, was a defensive one—i.e., "back to the Christian fundamentals, pivoted
on the norm of Biblical inerrancy"—not least because Jews began to constitute a
significant electoral presence in New York and adjacent states. It is fruitful to fast
forward by about fifty years in order to highlight the links that began to develop
in the 1970s between American fundamentalism and Zionistic fundamentalism.
While not, in a clear-cut way, an example of *anti*-global religiosity, the alliance
that grew between American fundamentalists (previously thought to be anti-
Semitic) and Jewish Zionists is a classic, recent example of the ways in which
matters religious (or, better, politico-religious) have become transnationalized and
globalized.

In fact, fundamentalism provides some fertile ground for the exploration of
anti-global religious movements and trends. I have serious reservations about the
loose use of this term, but movements usually classified as fundamentalist have
certainly been primary examples of "rage against the global machine" of globalization. Micklethwait and Wooldridge, in their brief but insightful comment on

"the backlash against globalization" (2000: 275), consider this theme, as I have been doing, primarily in a post-Seattle perspective and, in this regard, draw attention to the Christian Identity movement in the United States, a member of which may have been involved in the bomb planting at the Olympics in Atlanta in 1996 on the grounds that the Olympic Games represent the apotheosis of race-mixing and one-worldism. The line between what is and what is not religious becomes particularly hard to discern in this connection and, in fact, illustrates the futility of striving to establish a boundary. Micklethwait and Wooldridge (2000: 275) say that the anti-global movement's war cry is that "every day, God-fearing Americans are being turned into slaves in a worldwide plantation economy . . . and the only way to avoid enslavement is to take up guns and fight."

Beyond the United States, anti-global movements are related to their American counterparts in the sense that they apparently feel, or exploit the feeling, that massive forces are overwhelming them. In contrast, however, they see the United States as "not the slave but the enslaver" (Micklethwait and Wooldridge 2000: 275) and provide three major examples of anti-globalism: the Aum Shinrikyo movement based in Japan; the Zapatistas in Chiapas, Mexico; and what they describe as "the most powerful anti-globalist group [of] militant Islam" (2000: 276–78).

"Militant Islam" is, however, a somewhat problematic example of an anti-global movement or tendency. Indeed, Micklethwait and Wooldridge admit as much when they subsequently contend that what they call militant Islam "may be an exercise in globalization in its own right" (2000: 276). The thesis that I would propose is that Islam generally, but "militant Islam" in particular, is certainly opposed to the present form of globalization, but that far from being doctrinally and ideologically opposed to globalization per se that, like much of Catholicism, evangelical Protestantism, Communism, even Buddhism—not to speak of certain imperialisms (often combining religious with political and economic ambitions)—"militant Islam" has a definitely pro-global stance. In fact, one could go further than this and propose that the general orientation in Islam throughout much, if not all, of its history has been in the direction of *world-encompassment*. And its tendencies in this respect are well exemplified in the history of the Ottoman Empire.

In the history of the (Muslim) Ottoman Empire, extending at one stage from Southeastern—indeed Central—Europe round the Eastern Mediterranean across North Africa into Iberia, perhaps its most central feature was its calibrated acceptance of religio-cultural variety and heterogeneity. This was institutionalized as the millet system, an imperial-organizational arrangement that allowed different religio-cultural "domains" a high degree of autonomy within their respective spaces. My main point in raising this feature of the Ottoman Empire is to suggest that in a number of ways Islam, at least in its Ottoman version, provided a template as to how the world-as-a-whole might be institutionally patterned.

As Pasha and Samature (1997:191) maintain, "while elements of Westernization and capitalism are both important to globality, the notion critical [to us] is an appreciation of globality as the product of an intercivilizational encounter and dialogue." They specifically address Islam, but their claim is differentially generalizable to the history of the entire world and is also very close to my own conception of what we should mean when we speak of globalization (Robertson 1992). Indeed, to conceive of globalization as being centered empirically, over a very long period of history, on intercivilizational encounters, in which religion has pivotally figured, is a particularly effective and cogent procedure.

CONCLUSION

In spite of the fact that capitalistic, economic globalization has become such a conspicuous theme of the late twentieth and early twenty-first centuries and a focus of much religious concern, indeed discontent, should not trap us into admission that this phenomenon of recent times is or has been the key feature of globalization. How we define the latter is a matter for well-informed dialogue between and among serious—as opposed to dogmatic and/or flippant—intellectuals. And yet, on the other hand, we cannot override the empirical reality of quotidian discourses and rhetorical exchanges concerning globalization.

In concluding, I should summarize the thrust of my argument: To me, and to quite a considerable number of social scientists and people working in departments of religious studies, schools of divinity and the like, as well as other intellectual domains, the concept of globalization refers in a comprehensive form—mainly cultural (including religious), political, economic, and social-communicative dimensions—to global change in recorded history (a not unproblematic phrase) that has led to our now living in what I call "a single place." In spite of this embracive conception of globalization—to which I continue, vigorously, to adhere—I have concentrated mainly in the present deliberation mainly, but not exclusively, on the ways in which there has arisen in various parts of the world discontent with a truncated, economistic version of globalization, a discontent that has significant religious elements.

Thus there has been, in effect, a detachment of the economic from the other dimensions of globalization. And even though much of the early elaboration of the concept of globalization was undertaken by sociologists of religion and people working in the fields of religious studies, comparative religion, and theology in the late 1970s and early 1980s and was enlarged by practitioners in cultural studies, anthropology, and other disciplinary adherents, globalization is overwhelmingly now seen as a primarily economic phenomenon. But, as I have said, we cannot nor should we attempt to obliterate what has now appeared as a target of partly religious opposition—namely globalization. The term is for some a significant theological one; while for others it is an evil manifestation of the anti-religious, secular world in which we inevitably live.

BIBLIOGRAPHY

Alston, P. 1999. "International Governance in the Normative Areas." In *Globalization with a Human Face*. Background Papers Vol. I. Human Development Report Office, 1–36. New York: United Nations Development Programme.

Arizpe, L., and G. Alonso. 1999. "Culture, Globalization and International Trade." In *Globalization with a Human Face*. Background Papers Vol. I. Human Development Report Office, 37–56. New York: United Nations Development Programme.

Beck, U. 1999. *World Risk Society*. Cambridge, U.K.: Polity Press.

Beyer, P. 1994. *Globalization and Religion*. London: Sage.

Biel, R. 2000. *The New Imperialism: Crisis and Contradictions in North/South Relations*. London: Zed Books.

Bowen, W. M. 1984. *Globalism: America's Demise*. Shreveport, La.: Huntington House.

Browning, D. S. 1986. "Globalization and the Task of Theological Education in North America." *Theological Education* 23, no. 1: 43–59.

Campbell, G. V. 1999. *The Relativization of Tradition: A Study of the Evangelical Post-Conservative Contrivers in Contemporary American Evangelical Protestantism*. Ph.D. diss., Department of Religious Studies, University of Pittsburgh.

Coates, B. 1999. "Why Free Trade Is a Myth," *The Independent on Sunday* (U.K.), 10 October, 29.

Falk, R. 1999. *Predatory Globalization: A Critique*. Cambridge, U.K.: Polity Press.

Frith, S. 1991. "Critical Response." In *Music at the Margins: Popular Music and Global Cultural Diversit*. Eds. D. C. Robinson, E. B. Buck, and M. Cuthbert, 280–287. London: Sage.

Gustafson, C., and P. Juviler, eds. 1999. *Religion and Human Rights*. Armonk, N.Y.: M. E. Sharpe.

Halliday, F. 2000. *The World at 2000: Perils and Promises*. New York: Palgrave.

Hines, C. 2000. *Localization: A Global Manifesto*. London: Earthscan.

Hirst, P., and G. Thompson. 1996. *Globalization in Question*. Cambridge, U.K.: Polity Press.

Hobsbawm, E., and T. Ranger, eds. 1983. *The Invention of Tradition*. Cambridge, U.K.: Cambridge University Press.

Holton, R. J. 1998. *Globalization and the Nation-State*. New York: St. Martin's Press.

Huntington, S. 1996. *The Clash of Civilizations and the Remaking of World Order*. New York: Simon and Schuster.

Juergensmeyer, M. 1993. *The New Cold War? Religious Nationalism Confronts the Secular State*. Berkeley: University of California Press.

————. 2000. *Terror in the Mind of God: The Global Rise of Religious Violence*. Berkeley: University of California Press.

Killen, P. O'C. 2000. "Faithless in Seattle? The WTO Protests." *Religion in the News* 3, no. 1: 12–14.

Klein, N. 2000. *No Logo*. London: Flamingo.

Lash, S., and J. Urry. 1987. *The End of Organized Capitalism*. Cambridge, U.K: Polity Press.

Lawrence, B. B. 1998. "From Fundamentalism to Fundamentalisms: A Religious Ideology in Multiple Forms." In *Religion, Modernity and Postmodernity*. Ed. P. Heelas, 88–101. Oxford: Blackwell.

MacKinnon, J. 2000. "When the Global Goes Loco: The Next Big Battle Against the WTO Could Happen in Anytown, USA." *Adbusters*, June/July: 70–71.

Majur, J. 2000. "Labor's New Internationalism." *Foreign Affairs* 79, no. 1: 79–93.

Marsden, G. M. 1980. *Fundamentalism and American Culture*. New York: Oxford University Press.

Micklethwait, J., and A. Wooldridge. 2000. *A Future Perfect: The Challenge and Hidden Promise of Globalization*. London: William Heinemann.

Nairn, T. 1988. *The Enchanted Glass: Britain and its Monarchy*. London: Hutchinson Radius.

Novakovich, M. 2000. "Today's TV." *The Guardian*, G2 (U.K.) A, Thursday, September 14: 24.

Nussbaum, M. C. 1996. "Patriotism and Cosmopolitanism." In *For Love of Country: Debating the Limits of Patriotism*. Edited by J. Cohen, 2–17. Boston: Beacon Press.

Pasha, M. K., and A. I. Samatar. 1997. "The Resurgence of Islam." In *Globalization: Critical Reflections*. Edited by J. H. Mittelman, 187–201. Boulder, Colo.: Rienne.

Ritzer, G. 2000. *The McDonaldization of Society*. London: Sage.

Robertson, R. 1985. "The Development and Implications of the Classical Sociological Perspective on Religion and Revolution." In *Religion, Rebellion, Revolution*. Ed. B. Lincoln, 236–265. London: Macmillan.

————. 1988. "Christian Zionism and Jewish Zionism: Points of Contact." In *The Politics of Religion and Social Change*. Eds. A. Shupe and J. K. Hadden, 239–258. New York: Paragon House.

————. 1989. "Globalization, Politics, and Religion." In *The Changing Face of Religion*. Edited by J. A. Beckford and T. Luckmann, 10–23. London: Sage.

————. 1992. *Globalization: Social Theory and Global Culture*. London: Sage.

————. 1994. "Religion and the Global Field." *Social Compass* 41, no. 1: 121–135.

————. 1995a. "Glocalization: Time-Space and Homogeneity-Heterogeneity." In *Global Modernities*. Eds. M. Featherstone, S. Lash, and R. Robertson, 25–44. London: Sage.

————. 1995b. "The Search for Fundamentals in Global Perspective." In *The Search for Fundamentals and Modernization*. Eds. L. van V. Tijsson, J. Berting, and F. Lechner, 213–31. Berlin: W de Gruyter.

————. 2000a. "Globalization Theory 2000+: Major Problematics." In *Handbook of Social Theory*. Edited by G. Ritzer and B. Smart, 458–70. London: Sage.

————. 2000b. "Globalization and the Future of 'Traditional Religion.' " In *God and Globalization: Theological Ethics and the Spheres of Life*, vol. 1. Ed. M. L. Stackhouse with P. J. Paris, 53–68. Harrisburg, Pa.: Trinity Press International.

————. 2001. "Opposition and Resistance to Globalization." In *Globalization and the Margins*. Eds. by J. R. Short and R. Grant. London: Palgrave.

Robertson, R., and H. H. Khondker. 1998. "Discourses of Globalization: Preliminary Considerations." *International Sociology* 13, no. 1: 25–40.

Robertson, R., and R. Mouly. 1983. "Zionism in American Premillenarian Fundamentalism." *American Journal of Theology and Philosophy* 4, no. 3: 97–109.

Scholte, J. A. 2000. *Globalization: A Critical Introduction*. London: Macmillan.

Sklair, L. 2000. *The Transnational Capitalist Class*. Oxford: Blackwell.

Stackhouse, M. L., with P. J. Paris, eds.. 2000. *God and Globalization: Theological Ethics and the Spheres of Life*, vol. 1. Harrisburg, Pa.: Trinity Press.

Tomlinson, J. 1999. *Globalization and Culture*. Chicago: University of Chicago Press.

van der Veer, P., and H. Lehmann. 1999. "Introduction." In *Nation and Religion: Perspectives on Europe and Asia*. Eds. Peter van der Veer and Hartmut Lehmann, 3–14. Princeton, N.J.: Princeton University Press.

Watson, J., ed. 1997. *Golden Arches East: McDonald's in East Asia*. Stanford, Calif.: Stanford University Press.

CHAPTER 60

THE GLOBAL FUTURE OF RELIGION

NINIAN SMART

THE present state of the world—one of intense globalization—has its effect on religion. In a time when travel is almost instantaneous, and communications wholly so, and trade is conducted everywhere, all aspects of life are affected. In addition to the fast physical togetherness of the globalized world there are close ties of communication via radio, television, and now the Internet. Papua-New Guinea is connected to London, Moscow to Cape Town, Hong Kong to Santiago, Tonga to Kazakhstan. This amazing interconnectedness has, of course, had its influence on how people live and think.

As any acquaintance with the history of religions will show, especially in the last four hundred years, faiths alter. There are evolutionary changes in their rituals, their societal emplacement, their doctrines, and perhaps especially their ethics and laws. One of the great myths is that religion is always the same: that an evangelical from Missouri has the same values as the Apostle Paul, for example. People dearly believe that they believe exactly as did their forefathers. They may of course get the heart of their faith essentially right—they may conform to the basic values of the great leaders and creeds of their traditions. But this does not mean that the religions have not changed. In a global world they are probably doing so more than ever.

One of the first aspects of globalization to develop in the modern era was in sea travel, which bore almost inevitably the tides of European colonialism. The Chinese, admittedly, had been great navigators, traveling as far as the African continent. But it was a series of European seamen who virtually conquered the world: Columbus, Magellan, Drake, Captain Cook. In their wake came gunboats and eventually battleships. Colonial conquest ensued. After World War II the colonies of seaborne Europe faded and were quietly extinguished. Oddly, it was the land empires that lived on: the Soviet Empire survived until the closing years of the twentieth century. The Chinese one is still with us: but it will also in due course crumble. The collapse of empires resulted in roughly sovereign countries, based on linguistic and other criteria of nationhood. Yet as the colonial empires faded so did the sovereign states.

Though the seaborne, mostly colonial, connections remain the antecedents of our global world, it is the great land-based empires that have had the most immediate impact. The Soviet Union was a reformed version of the Russian Empire. After it collapsed it fragmented into disparate states—such as Kazakhstan and Ukraine. But the Russian Federation, the USSR's residue, still remained an empire—as rebellious regions such as Chechnya discovered. The other great enduring empire is China. About half of it is the region populated by the Han Chinese: the rest by Tibet, the Uighurs, Inner Mongolia, and other areas. We have been accustomed to thinking that imperialism involved overseas adventures. It was thought that the land expansion of the Soviets was not imperialist, nor that of the Chinese. It came to many people as a bit of a shock when former President Ronald Reagan spoke of the USSR as an "evil empire." He was not, however, entirely wrong—it, like China, was an empire. But both of these empires badly needed development, and eventually the Soviet one came apart. In the Chinese sphere, eventually Tibet and the others will also become sovereign states. Empires cannot be sustained in a global world, and China will eventually break up. The inexorable demands of sovereignty by those defining themselves as a "people" will be realized (even though many aspects of nationalism are now fading through global interaction).

The great empires of the modern world needed ideologies to justify their existences. The Soviet and the Chinese employed varying forms of Marxism. The British had an ideological version of Christian civilization. But when the varied empires from Europe faded and dwindled after World War II they retained a residue of thinking that is still with us in the global world. The non-Marxist colonial ideologies had been built on three central ideas: an expansive nationalism, democracy (at least up to a point), and capitalism. In a postcolonial era, expansive nationalism was wiped away (though a bit of superiority remained) and older ideologies resumed their places of prominence: Hindu, Muslim, and Buddhist values re-entered the public sphere. The European ideal of a global Christendom retreated as various forms of Asian values permeated Christianity, African varieties of Christianity emerged in the form of new religious movements, and everywhere indigenous themes were incorporated into Christian beliefs.

This cultural interaction increased due to demographic shifts. Globalization and its preceding colonialism led to the proliferation of diasporas. The slave trade

created a large African culture in South, Central, and North America. The subsequent suppression of slavery by the British navy led to a substitute: indentured
labor. This labor traffic led to new outposts of Asian culture. Sizable Indian settlements were established in South Africa, East Africa, Guyana, Trinidad, Fiji, and
other regions of the empire. Major subcolonies of Chinese were located in what
is now called Malaysia, Indonesia, Singapore, and the Americas. Japanese migrated
to the United States and South America.

Mobility has been greatly enhanced by the advent of the airplane and during
World War II the astonishing development of the jet. By 1970 jets had become
jumbo jets, such as the 747. These developments meant that now everywhere was
connected to everywhere. Of course on the whole it is people from richer societies
who are able to travel hither and thither. But freight planes also ply the globe, so
virtually every capital of the world receives goods from one another. An easy
mobility has enhanced the spread of populations and the emergence of diasporic
cultures around the globe.

After World War II a heavy flow of migration from India and Pakistan entered
into Britain; Turks came into Germany; North Africans (notably Algerians) settled
France; and later Vietnamese arrived in Australia and the United States. This
demographic pattern—a northward pressure into Europe, coupled with a westward influx following the collapse of the Soviet Union, and a northward flow into
the United States from Latin America—will likely increase over the years. To these
population shifts one must add the migrations fomented by wars. The displacement of populations has multiplied as small but bitter conflicts have broken out
in the latter part of the twentieth century in Cyprus, Indonesia, Sri Lanka, Kashmir, Afghanistan, Iraq, Iran, the Congo, West Africa, and numerous other places.
Displacements have also resulted from rivalries between old neighbors: Palestinian
Muslims and Israeli Jews, Orthodox Christians and Muslims in former Yugoslavia,
Muslims and Christians in the Moluccas, and Christians and Hindus in Fiji.

In this global pluralism, suspicions abound. Religions have reinforced nationalism and ethnic divisions (and in some cases replaced them) as a reason for
hating or suspecting "otherness." Religion is sometimes perceived as the reason
for ethnic and national division, and it often gives ideological bases for the conflicts. Despite religion's ability to impart positive values about life, it can be a
basis for the negative. As the pope has learned in Northern Ireland, it is not
enough to say, "love they neighbor as thyself"—the admonition often falls on
deaf ears. It is difficult for most religious persons to fathom how much hypocrisy
and hatred are associated with religion in contentious areas of the world; it is
easy to assume that religion's moral high ground will be realized.

Ideologies, whether religious or otherwise, allow people to do frightful things
in their names with a feeling of justification. Not all the inquisitors, I am sure,
were cruel men; nor were the colonizers in Britain who organized the empire;
nor were the Chinese leaders who ordered troops into Tienanmen Square. It is

good to remember that even some Nazis were squeamish about what they were doing and did not want to confront the consequences of their ideology. Palestinians who want Jews to be driven into the sea do not want children to be treated in that way, and perhaps they do not really want their rhetoric to be turned into ugly reality. Alas, however, firmly held convictions, though praised by many, often lead to unimaginable cruelties.

On the positive side of global cultural encounters is the promise of dialogue. The living religions of the world usually have some elements within them—often the elites—who are willing to reach out and explore the similarities and differences among the faiths. Their aim is to provide mutual education. These gestures occur even in the midst of the most bitter divergences between peoples. In Israel, for instance, there is the Peace Now movement. Britain has the World Congress of Faiths. Such organizations devoted to harmony abound. And in ordinary lives of common folk in pluralistic societies often such goodwill abounds as well, though of course there is always a darker side that needs to be reckoned with.

Another positive development is mutual interaction. In addition to harmony and dialogue, religions and ideologies sometimes affect one another; there are crossovers. Liberation Theology in the 1980s and 90s, for example, provided an interesting mingling of Marxism and Catholic Christianity. In South India, Dharmaram College was the center of a strong and flourishing movement to blend Christian and Hindu thought. In parts of the Americas we find various ways of merging Catholic Christianity with African religions in mixtures such as Haitian Vodou. One of the most significant blending of ideas is that between traditional religion and Enlightenment values, leading to the modernist point of view that is found in most faiths today. The modernist strand opens up religions to scientific and scholarly ideas and practices. It opens up religions to change. It is these various forms of blending of ideas from religions and ideologies that offer hints at the possibility of a global ideology drawn from various sources—an idea to which I will soon return.

Yet the same time that religions have been more open to one another, there has also been a significant tendency in the other direction, toward consolidation of traditional values. Ironically, the same global communications that makes possible increased interaction provides the resources for more intense consolidation as well. This is true of conservative religion, but it is also true of humanism. Humanism is an important worldview, one often neglected in discussions of religions. Yet it is the dominant faith among many modernists, especially scholars and philosophers in the West. If one adds humanism to the list of major world religions, and also adds those smaller religions which still survive in what is moving toward a global federalism of religions, the incompatibilities among worldviews are considerable. The likelihood is that in the future these differences will continue.

This is not necessarily a bad thing. Mutual criticism among worldviews has its merits. It prevents any single worldview from dogmatism and exclusivity. The awareness of the pluralism of worldviews has the advantage of allowing each religion to adapt to the complexities of a global world. The ideology of modernism may still attempt to exert its superiority and unnerve those who otherwise would be able to feel at home in their traditions in the contemporary world. Egoism is a powerful force, but it often comes from its social milieu; and both other cultures and other faiths can threaten it.

In such a context, what possibilities exist for a common ideology for the new global world? One value that might be a part of this common ideology is the commitment to seek nonviolent solutions in situations of conflict. A remarkable aspect of our times is the way that, in part because of religious and humanistic values, great tyrannies have collapsed with scarcely any bloodshed. Consider Czechoslovakia's Velvet Revolution and most other Eastern European rejections of the Soviet's grip; the Philippine's ouster of Marcos; Indonesia's overthrow of Suharto; Nigeria's return to democracy; South Africa's rebuke of Apartheid; Peru's rejection of Fujimori; the ending of Chile's dictatorship; and the gradual democratization of Cambodia (following, however, a ghastly genocide). The peaceful aspects of these transitions are encouraging signs. They indicate an awareness that bloodshed is not the only way and that it can have dangerous repercussions in an interconnected world. It can be countered that sometimes violence is necessary in the face of great evil—a Hitler, for example, or Stalin. Yet there are hopeful signs that the world has changed: the great totalitarian empires are dead, every dictatorship is under the bright light of global journalism, citizens everywhere have e-mail and other forms of electronic communications, and the best that any tyrannical control over information can achieve is a partial concealment. This openness is one of the great merits of globalization.

Another widely accepted value in a global world is democracy. Democracy as it is usually understood and accepted is the best nonviolent means of changing regimes. It allows people their say. It gives the majority of folk the opportunity to express their values and their grievances. It is not, however, without its defects: the majority, for example, can in the name of democracy oppress minorities. Moreover, the global world is not composed solely of sovereign states, democratic or not: it also consists of hundreds if not thousands of transnational corporations, some of which have larger economies and are more politically important than many sovereign states. The world also consists of great religions and their organizations: Christianity—or more correctly its three main branches; Islam in two or more forms; Judaism in its various shades; Buddhism in three major branches; Hinduism and Sikhism; Chinese values; African values; and many other traditions and groups. These three worldwide entities interact with each other—states, corporations, and worldviews. Each has exercised its powers in the recent world. Consider, for example, how the pope and the Dalai Lama have influenced the course of international affairs. Already the conference of Islamic states is being taken seriously in the world; Judaism has its political clout both through U.S. policy and the state of Israel; Hinduism is beginning to flex its muscles through political parties in the Republic of India; and in South Africa the various Christian groups have considerable influence.

This, then is a portent of the future: two seemingly opposite trends. On the one hand, the great religious traditions—including, as I have said, humanism—are part of the global world and because of their size and ambivalent relationship to political authority they are vital actors in it. Yet they disagree with each other over much, including the nature of ultimate reality. Some are theistic, others are not; they have divergent gods. As I have mentioned before, however, this is not necessarily a bad thing, since their very differences enable them to keep each other in check. But in order to do so it is vital that they respect one another. They should seek to understand one another so that their divergences of ethical and other messages are kept in play.

This means that in addition to a congeries of different religions in the world it will be essential for there to be some overarching sense of order and respect. The worldview that is emerging for the global world, therefore, is in essence a kind of higher order. That is, it does not lay down who is right or wrong but rather determines how peacefully the differing groups and beliefs can live together. It provides the civility, the common rules, so that one particular worldview cannot use force to establish itself over others.

Yet even if this higher order comes about, it would not necessarily guarantee the end of discord. The globe always has had and will continue to have people who for religious or other ideological reasons feel called upon to blow up citizens of other countries, countries that they deem as oppressive. There might also be the use of weapons of mass destruction for religious purposes to destroy a New York or a Congo-Braazavile. Perhaps such an atrocity would bring the world to its senses, much as the bombs at Hiroshima and Nagasaki frightened the world so much that thus far these events have never been repeated. The hope is that even if there were such a religious disaster—the first major crime of the twenty-first century—its sheer terror would insure that it would never be repeated. A disaster felt here is a disaster felt everywhere, in an integrated world.

All of this is speculative, about a higher order that will become the global worldview. Yet the necessities of global interaction may force it upon us. The threat of globalization is that it tries to get everyone doing the same thing and thinking alike. In some ways the world is becoming too compact. The idea of a global higher order has the advantage of not imposing a single ethic or ethos on the rest of the world, except for the higher order pattern of civility. It may be the coming global civilization.

INDEX

....